WORD
BIBLICAL
COMMENTARY

General Editors
David A. Hubbard
Glenn W. Barker †

Old Testament Editor
John D. W. Watts

New Testament Editor
Ralph P. Martin

WORD
BIBLICAL
COMMENTARY

VOLUME 48

James

RALPH P. MARTIN

WORD BOOKS, PUBLISHER • WACO, TEXAS

Word Biblical Commentary
JAMES
Copyright © 1988 by Word, Incorporated

Library of Congress Cataloging-in-Publication Data
Main entry under title:

Word biblical commentary.

  Includes bibliographies.
  1. Bible—Commentaries   Collected Works.
BS491.2.W67   220.7′7   81–71768
ISBN 0–8499–0247–9 (vol. 48)   AACR2

Printed in the United States of America

The author's own translation of the Scripture text appears in italic type under the heading *Translation*.

    1239   AGF   98765432

Contents

Editorial Preface

The launching of the *Word Biblical Commentary* brings to fulfillment an enterprise of several years' planning. The publishers and the members of the editorial board met in 1977 to explore the possibility of a new commentary on the books of the Bible that would incorporate several distinctive features. Prospective readers of these volumes are entitled to know what such features were intended to be; whether the aims of the commentary have been fully achieved time alone will tell.

First, we have tried to cast a wide net to include as contributors a number of scholars from around the world who not only share our aims, but are in the main engaged in the ministry of teaching in university, college, and seminary. They represent a rich diversity of denominational allegiance. The broad stance of our contributors can rightly be called evangelical, and this term is to be understood in its positive, historic sense of a commitment to Scripture as divine revelation, and to the truth and power of the Christian gospel.

Then, the commentaries in our series are all commissioned and written for the purpose of inclusion in the *Word Biblical Commentary*. Unlike several of our distinguished counterparts in the field of commentary writing, there are no translated works, originally written in a non-English language. Also, our commentators were asked to prepare their own rendering of the original biblical text and to use those languages as the basis of their own comments and exegesis. What may be claimed as distinctive with this series is that it is based on the biblical languages, yet it seeks to make the technical and scholarly approach to a theological understanding of Scripture understandable by—and useful to—the fledgling student, the working minister, and colleagues in the guild of professional scholars and teachers as well.

Finally, a word must be said about the format of the series. The layout, in clearly defined sections, has been consciously devised to assist readers at different levels. Those wishing to learn about the textual witnesses on which the translation is offered are invited to consult the section headed *Notes*. If the readers' concern is with the state of modern scholarship on any given portion of Scripture, they should turn to the sections on *Bibliography* and *Form/Structure/Setting*. For a clear exposition of the passage's meaning and its relevance to the ongoing biblical revelation, the *Comment* and concluding *Explanation* are designed expressly to meet that need. There is therefore something for everyone who may pick up and use these volumes.

If these aims come anywhere near realization, the intention of the editors will have been met, and the labor of our team of contributors rewarded.

General Editors: *David A. Hubbard*
Glenn W. Barker †
Old Testament: *John D. W. Watts*
New Testament: *Ralph P. Martin*

Author's Preface

Years ago—in 1924 to be exact—F. C. Burkitt wrote of the letter of James in the New Testament:

> The problems presented by this work are in many ways unlike that of the other canonical and deutero-canonical writings. . . . The ordinary English reader of the Epistle of James is troubled by few doubts as to its authenticity. There is an air of rugged freedom about it, of interest in practical ethics and the poorer classes, that recalls the Synoptic Gospels rather than the other New Testament Epistles. . . . If the document be a forgery, we feel, why was it ever accepted? What stage of second-century thinking can it be supposed to represent? Why should it have been written? and why should it have been accepted as canonical? (*Christian Beginnings,* 65–66)

Many issues are raised in this one short paragraph; and the following pages of *Introduction* and *Commentary* will attempt to address them. By any reckoning this letter of James stands alone among the New Testament books. It has about it an appeal that is timeless, and we are hard pressed to place it in a historical time-frame. Ethical challenges leap out from the page at every turn, and they are concerned about such practical matters as wealth and poverty, trials and temptations, social crimes of fighting and war, along with graphic depictions of wealthy magnates living in uncaring luxury and a downtrodden, victimized labor force. The writer's sympathies are expressed in no uncertain way; he is the champion of the poor and persecuted.

When he seeks to offer a basis for his moral outcry and his earnest hope that the cause of the needy will be vindicated, his appeal is to strictly Old Testament-Judaic ideas and principles. He has a marvelously wide range of images—from the worlds of nature and human nature—at his command; and he uses metaphors and models to telling effect. The language of "law" is very near the surface of his ethical admonition both as a way of obedience and as an instrument of condemnation. But of new life in Christ and the power of the Holy Spirit he is more or less silent.

Yet side by side with nomistic idioms, suitably qualified by such terms as "royal" and "perfect" and related to the command to "love your neighbor" as their epitome, there is the vocabulary of grace: key terms like faith, prayer, and the word are in rich profusion. This is surely the paradox of the epistle, and sets the puzzle we must try to solve. Even more than its lack of positive christological teaching and reference, the strange blend of "works" (but not "works of law" in the sense used by Paul of his "Judaizing" opponents) and "faith" (but not "faith in Christ" as Paul handles the expression) presents us with a conundrum. It also invites us to consider again some suggestions for a historical setting of this document, and the possibility that there were two distinct stages in its composition, as recent studies are suggesting.

The quest of the historical James is a topic we cannot evade, though many modern interpreters disavow its relevance as a clue to the meaning of the letter. The attempt to locate the ethical matters presented in the letter in some defined time-span (e.g., in Palestinian social and economic conditions in the early 60s) gives point to some of the material. As G. H. Rendall put it: "ethical values depend upon the surroundings which bring them into play" (*The Epistle of St. James and Judaic Christianity*, 110).

The pages that follow will be the place to justify the positions taken regarding such controverted matters as the setting of the letter, both in its traditional and redacted form, and its relevance to proposed situations. The *Introduction* will seek to consider the data regarding the role played by the historical James in the New Testament and later church circles along with other matters of historical and literary criticism. The section headed *Form/Structure/Setting* is concerned with tracing a literary and contextual pattern through the document, and offers some reason why the view that James is only a mélange of loosely connected moral maxims ought to be resisted. The *Comment* section is no more than routine commentary on individual words and phrases, and draws on modern exegetical books for comparison. The author has used the *Explanation* pages to offer timely help in applying the letter to some prevalent situations, using the historical investigations of what may be known of Palestinian political and economic stresses in the first century of the common era. Readers who wish for a synopsis of what this letter has to say, in both its original setting and in its appeal to the church in the world today, should turn to the *Explanation* first.

It is time to cast up one's debtors and express appreciation, mainly to three pieces of writing that have been a catalyst for this book. I have mentioned Rendall's *The Epistle of St. James and Judaic Christianity*, a work which—appearing in 1927—anticipated many of the trends in more recent studies. The treatment of the epistle is amazingly suggestive and seminal. It has been neglected by recent commentators, I believe, to everyone's loss. Then, B. H. Streeter's *The Primitive Church* (1929) is another older study which the present author first read in student days and found to be both stimulating and a model of lucid reasoning. Ahead of Walter Bauer and others he accurately discerned the influence of geographical locations in the development and diversity of early Christianity. His chapter on the apostles and the churches still makes interesting reading for reflection.

Passing by—but not without gratitude—recent commentators from Dibelius to Laws, Davids, Moo, and Vouga by way of Windisch, Adamson, Mussner, and Mitton, I must indicate appreciatively my principal creditor, Martin I. Webber, for parts of the *Introduction*. His unpublished dissertation "ΙΑΚΩΒΟΣ Ὁ ΔΙΚΑΙΟΣ: Origins, Literary Expression and Development of Traditions about the Brother of the Lord in Early Christianity" was prepared when he was my *promovendus* and it was accepted for a Ph.D. award in 1985. While his work is not strictly that of a commentator, his grasp of historical development and his knowledge of the trajectory that runs from the pre-Pauline traditions about James to gnostic literature and the patristic writers have greatly helped me, and I gladly pay tribute to his efforts. His hypothesis of a line of development from the James of New Testament times to the varied ways later groups (Jewish Christian, Catholic, and gnostic) formed a picture of James according to their interests and desires has been strikingly confirmed by the full study of Wilhelm Pratscher, *Der Herrenbruder Jakobus und die Jakobus-tradition* (1987), whose concluding paragraph I have just summarized and whose work, regrettably, reached me only when this commentary was in its final stage. I regret also that Wiard Popkes' useful survey of Jacobean problems, *Adressaten, Situation und Form des Jakobusbriefes*, SBS 125/126 (Stuttgart: Verlag Katholisches Bibelwerk, 1986) arrived too late to be consulted.

With Dr. Webber's permission I have been able to give some of his work visibility in what follows, and the section entitled "The Role of James in Ecclesiastical Circles" is almost wholly his contribution. As with an earlier volume in this series, Richard E. Menninger has assisted me with some excellent drafting of parts of the commentary, and with proofreading. In the latter task Lynn A. Losie has also ably contributed to make the sense clearer. Tertullian's words may be adapted to justify this procedure: "it is allowable that that which pupils publish should be regarded as their masters' work" (*Adv. Marc.* 4.5).

A final acknowledgment is made to the staff of the Word Processing Department, including Janet M. Gathright, David Sielaff, Sandy Underwood Bennett, and Carey Jo Wallace, for much valued and uncomplaining work in preparing the text for publication. No faculty member has been better served—and saved many hours of tedious revising and alteration which go into a commentary like this. At a time of transition from the United States to Britain, I have been especially grateful for their cooperative effort.

Christmas 1987   RALPH P. MARTIN
Fuller Theological Seminary/
Department of Biblical Studies,
The University of Sheffield, England

Abbreviations

A. General Abbreviations

A	Codex Alexandrinus	in loc.	*in loco,* in the place cited
ad	comment on	Jos.	Josephus
Akkad.	Akkadian	Lat.	Latin
א	Codex Sinaiticus	LL	Late Latin
Ap. Lit.	Apocalyptic Literature	loc. cit.	the place cited
Apoc.	Apocrypha	LXX	Septuagint
Aq.	Aquila's Greek Translation of the Old Testament	M	Mishna
		masc.	masculine
		mg.	margin
Arab.	Arabic	MS(S)	manuscript(s)
Aram.	Aramaic	MT	Masoretic text
B	Codex Vaticanus	n.	note
C	Codex Ephraemi Syri	n.d.	no date
c.	*circa,* about	Nestle	Nestle (ed.) *Novum Testamentum Graece* revised by K. and B. Aland
cf.	*confer,* compare		
chap., chaps.	chapter, chapters		
cod., codd.	codex, codices		
contra	in contrast to	no.	number
CUP	Cambridge University Press	NS	New Series
		NT	New Testament
D	Codex Bezae	obs.	obsolete
DSS	Dead Sea Scrolls (see **F.**)	OL	Old Latin
ed.	edited, edition, editor; editions	OS	Old Syriac
		OT	Old Testament
e.g.	*exempli gratia,* for example	p., pp.	page, pages
Egyp.	Egyptian	*pace*	with due respect to, but differing from
et al.	*et alii,* and others		
et passim	and elsewhere	par.	paragraph, parallel(s)
ET	English translation	Pers.	Persian
EV	English Versions of the Bible	Pesh.	Peshitta
		Phoen.	Phoenician
f., ff.	following (verse or verses, pages, etc.)	pl.	plural
		Pseudep.	Pseudepigrapha
fem.	feminine	Q	Quelle ("Sayings" source in the Gospels)
FS	Festschrift		
ft.	foot, feet	q.v.	*quod vide,* which see
gen.	genitive	rev.	revised, reviser, revision
Gr.	Greek	Rom.	Roman
Heb.	Hebrew	RVm	Revised Version margin
Hitt.	Hittite	Samar.	Samaritan recension
ibid.	*ibidem,* in the same place	sc.	*scilicet,* that is to say
id.	*idem,* the same	Sem.	Semitic
i.e.	*id est,* that is	sing.	singular
impf.	imperfect	Sumer.	Sumerian
infra	below	s.v.	*sub verbo,* under the word

syr	Syriac	u.s.	*ut supra,* as above
Symm.	Symmachus	viz.	*videlicet,* namely
Targ.	Targum	vol.	volume
Theod.	Theodotion	v, vv	verse, verses
TR	Textus Receptus	vs.	versus
tr.	translation, translator,	vg	Vulgate
	translated	WH	Westcott and Hort, *The*
UBS	The United Bible		*New Testament in Greek*
	Societies Greek Text	x	number of times words
Ugar.	Ugaritic		occur
UP	University Press	§	section

B. Abbreviations for Translations and Paraphrases

AmT	Smith and Goodspeed, *The*	TLB	The Living Bible
	Complete Bible, An American	Moffatt	J. Moffatt, *A New Translation*
	Translation		*of the Bible*
ASV	American Standard Version,	NAB	The New American Bible
	American Revised Version	NASB	New American Standard
	(1901)		Bible
AV	Authorized Version	NEB	The New English Bible
Beck	Beck, *The New Testament in the*	NIV	The New International
	Language of Today		Version
BV	Berkeley Version (The	Ph	J. B. Phillips, *The New*
	Modern Language Bible)		*Testament in Modern English*
GNB	*Good News Bible*	RSV	Revised Standard Version
JB	The Jerusalem Bible	RV	Revised Version—1881–1885
JPS	*Jewish Publication Society*	TEV	Today's English Version
	Version of the Old Testament	Wey	R. F. Weymouth, *The New*
KJV	King James Version		*Testament in Modern Speech*
Knox	R. A. Knox, *The Holy Bible: A*	Wms	C. B. Williams, *The New*
	Translation from the Latin		*Testament: A Translation in*
	Vulgate in the Light of the		*the Language of the People*
	Hebrew and Greek Original		

C. Abbreviations of Commonly Used Periodicals, Reference Works, and Serials

AAS	*Acta apostolicae sedis*	AGSU	Arbeiten zur Geschichte des
AASOR	Annual of the American		Spätjudentums und
	Schools of Oriental		Urchristentums
	Research	AH	F. Rosenthal, *An Aramaic*
AB	Anchor Bible		*Handbook*
ABR	*Australian Biblical Review*	AHR	*American Historical Review*
AbrN	*Abr-Nahrain*	AHW	W. von Soden, *Akkadisches*
ACNT	Augsburg Commentary on		*Handwörterbuch*
	the New Testament	AION	*Annali dell'istituto orientali di*
AcOr	*Acta orientalia*		*Napoli*
ACW	Ancient Christian Writers	AJA	*American Journal of Archae-*
ADAJ	Annual of the Department		*ology*
	of Antiquities of Jordan	AJAS	*American Journal of Arabic*
AER	*American Ecclesiastical Review*		*Studies*
AFER	*African Ecclesiastical Review*	AJBA	*Australian Journal of Biblical*
AfO	*Archiv für Orientforschung*		*Archaeology*
AGJU	Arbeiten zur Geschichte des		
	antiken Judentums und des		
	Urchristentums		

AJSL	*American Journal of Semitic Languages and Literature*	ATANT	Abhandlungen zur Theologie des Alten und Neuen Testaments (AThANT)
AJT	*American Journal of Theology*	ATD	Das Alte Testament Deutsch
ALBO	Analecta lovaniensia biblica et orientalia	*ATR*	*Anglican Theological Review*
ALGHJ	Arbeiten zur Literatur und Geschichte des hellenistischen Judentums	*AUSS*	*Andrews University Seminary Studies*
ALUOS	Annual of Leeds University Oriental Society		
AnBib	Analecta biblica	*BA*	*Biblical Archaeologist*
AnBoll	Analecta Bollandiana	BAC	Biblioteca de autores cristianos
ANEP	J. B. Pritchard (ed.), *Ancient Near East in Pictures*	*BAR*	*Biblical Archaeology Review*
ANESTP	J. B. Pritchard (ed.), *Ancient Near East Supplementary Texts and Pictures*	BASOR	Bulletin of the American Schools of Oriental Research
ANET	J. B. Pritchard (ed.), *Ancient Near Eastern Texts*	*BASP*	*Bulletin of the American Society of Papyrologists*
ANF	The Ante-Nicene Fathers	BBB	Bonner biblische Beiträge
Ang	*Angelicum*	*BCSR*	*Bulletin of the Council on the Study of Religion*
AnOr	Analecta orientalia		
ANQ	*Andover Newton Quarterly*	BDB	E. Brown, S. R. Driver, and C. A. Briggs, *Hebrew and English Lexicon of the Old Testament*
ANRW	*Aufstieg und Niedergang der römischen Welt*, ed H. Temporini and W. Haase, Berlin		
		BDF	F. Blass, A. Debrunner, and R. W. Funk, *A Greek Grammar of the NT*
Anton	*Antonianum*		
AOAT	Alter Orient und Altes Testament	BDR	F. Blass, A. Debrunner, and F. Rehkopf, *Grammatik des neutestamentlichen Griechisch*
AOS	American Oriental Series		
AP	J. Marouzeau (ed.), *L'année philologique*	*BeO*	*Bibbia e oriente*
APOT	R. H. Charles (ed.), *Apocrypha and Pseudepigrapha of the Old Testament*	BETL	Bibliotheca ephemeridum theologicarum lovaniensium
ARG	*Archiv für Reformationsgeschichte*	BEvT	Beiträge zur evangelischen Theologie (BEvTh)
ARM	Archives royales de Mari	BFCT	Beiträge zur Förderung christlicher Theologie (BFCTh)
ArOr	*Archiv orientální*		
ARSHLL	Acta Reg. Societatis Humaniorum Litterarum Lundensis	BGBE	Beiträge zur Geschichte der biblischen Exegese
ARW	*Archiv für Religionswissenschaft*	BGD	W. Bauer, F. W. Gingrich, and F. Danker, *Greek-English Lexicon of the NT*
ASNU	Acta seminarii neotestamentici upsaliensis		
ASS	*Acta sanctae sedis*	*BHH*	B. Reicke and L. Rost (eds.), *Biblisch-Historisches Handwörterbuch*
AsSeign	*Assemblées du Seigneur*		
ASSR	*Archives des sciences sociales des religions*		
ASTI	*Annual of the Swedish Theological Institute*	*BHK*	R. Kittel, *Biblia hebraica*
		BHS	*Biblia hebraica stuttgartensia*
ATAbh	Alttestamentliche Abhandlungen	BHT	Beiträge zur historischen Theologie (BHTh)

Bib	*Biblica*	CAT	Commentaire de l'Ancien Testament
BibB	Biblische Beiträge		
BibLeb	*Bibel und Leben*	*CB*	*Cultura bíblica*
BibOr	Biblica et orientalia	*CBQ*	*Catholic Biblical Quarterly*
BibS(F)	Biblische Studien (Freiburg, 1895–) (BSt)	CBQMS	Catholic Biblical Quarterly—Monograph Series
BibS(N)	Biblische Studien (Neukirchen, 1951–) (BibSt)	CCath	Corpus Catholicorum
BibZ	*Biblische Zeitschrift*	CChr	Corpus Christianorum
BiTod	*Bible Today*	*CH*	*Church History*
BIES	Bulletin of the Israel Exploration Society (= Yediot)	*CHR*	*Catholic Historical Review*
		CIG	*Corpus inscriptionum graecarum*
BIFAO	*Bulletin de l'institut français d'archéologie orientale*	*CH*	*Corpus inscriptionum iudaicarum*
BJRL	*Bulletin of the John Rylands University Library of Manchester*	*CIL*	*Corpus inscriptionum latinarum*
BK	*Bibel und Kirche*	*CIS*	*Corpus inscriptionum semiticarum*
BKAT	Biblischer Kommentar: Altes Testament	*CJT*	*Canadian Journal of Theology*
BL	*Book List*	*ClerRev*	*Clergy Review*
BLE	*Bulletin de littérature ecclésiastique*	CNT	Commentaire du Nouveau Testament
BLit	*Bibel und Liturgie*	ConB	Coniectanea biblica
BNTC	Black's New Testament Commentaries (=HNTC)	*ConNT*	*Coniectanea neotestamentica*
BO	*Bibliotheca orientalis*	*Corp Herm.*	Corpus Hermeticum
BR	*Biblical Research*	*CQ*	*Church Quarterly*
BS	*Biblische Studien*, Freiburg	*CQR*	*Church Quarterly Review*
BSac	*Bibliotheca Sacra*	*CRAIBL*	*Comptes rendus de l'Académie des inscriptions et belles-lettres*
BSO(A)S	*Bulletin of the School of Oriental (and African) Studies*	*CrQ*	*Crozier Quarterly*
		CSCO	Corpus scriptorum christianorum orientalium
BT	*The Bible Translator*		
BTB	*Biblical Theology Bulletin*	CSEL	Corpus scriptorum ecclesiasticorum latinorum
BTS	*Bible et terre sainte*		
BU	Biblische Untersuchungen	*CTA*	A. Herdner, *Corpus des tablettes en cunéiformes alphabétiques*
BVC	*Bible et vie chrétienne*		
BWANT	Beiträge zur Wissenschaft vom Alten und Neuen Testament	*CTJ*	*Calvin Theological Journal*
		CTM	*Concordia Theological Monthly*
BZ	*Biblische Zeitschrift*		
BZAW	Beihefte zur *ZAW*	*CurTM*	*Currents in Theology and Mission*
BZET	Beihefte z. Evangelische Theologie		
BZNW	Beihefte zur *ZNW*	*DACL*	*Dictionnaire d'archéologie chrétienne et de liturgie*
BZRGG	Beihefte zur *ZRGG*		
		DBSup	*Dictionnaire de la Bible, Supplément*
CAD	*The Assyrian Dictionary of the Oriental Institute of the University of Chicago*	*DISO*	C.-F. Jean and J. Hoftijzer, *Dictionnaire des inscriptions sémitiques de l'ouest*
CAH	*Cambridge Ancient History*		

DJD	Discoveries in the Judean Desert	GKC	*Gesenius' Hebrew Grammar,* ed. E. Kautzsch, tr. A. E. Cowley
DOTT	D. W. Thomas (ed.), *Documents from Old Testament Times*	GNT	Grundrisse zum Neuen Testament
DS	Denzinger-Schönmetzer, *Enchiridion symbolorum*	GOTR	*Greek Orthodox Theological Review*
DTC	*Dictionnaire de théologie catholique (DTHC)*	GRBS	*Greek, Roman, and Byzantine Studies*
DTT	*Dansk teologisk tidsskrift*	Greg	*Gregorianum*
DunRev	Dunwoodie Review	GThT	*Geformelet Theologisch Tijdschrift*
EBib	Etudes bibliques (EtBib)	GuL	*Geist und Leben*
EBT	*Encyclopedia of Biblical Theology*		
EDB	L. F. Hartman (ed.), *Encyclopedic Dictionary of the Bible*	HALAT	W. Baumgartner et al., *Hebräisches und aramäisches Lexikon zum Alten Testament*
EHAT	Exegetisches Handbuch zum Alten Testament	HAT	Handbuch zum Alten Testament
EKKNT	Evangelisch-katholischer Kommentar zum Neuen Testament	HDR	Harvard Dissertations in Religion
EKL	*Evangelisches Kirchenlexikon*	HE	*Church History* (Eusebius)
EncJud	*Encyclopaedia judaica* (1971)	HeyJ	*Heythrop Journal*
EnchBib	*Enchiridion biblicum*	HibJ	*Hibbert Journal*
ErJb	*Eranos Jahrbuch*	HKAT	Handkommentar zum Alten Testament
EstBib	*Estudios biblicos*		
ETL	*Ephemerides theologicae lovanienses (EThl.)*	HKNT	Handkommentar zum Neuen Testament
ETR	*Etudes théologiques et religieuses (EThR)*	HNT	Handbuch zum Neuen Testament
EvK	*Evangelische Kommentar*	HNTC	Harper's NT Commentaries
EvQ	*The Evangelical Quarterly*	HR	*History of Religions*
EvT	*Evangelische Theologie (EvTh)*	HSM	Harvard Semitic Monographs
EW	*Exegetisches Wörterbuch zum Neuen Testament*	HTKNT	Herders theologischer Kommentar zum Neuen Testament (HThKNT)
Exp	*The Expositor*		
ExpTim	*The Expository Times*	HTR	*Harvard Theological Review*
FBBS	Facet Books, Biblical Series	HTS	Harvard Theological Studies
FC	Fathers of the Church		
FRLANT	Forschungen zur Religion und Literatur des Alten und Neuen Testaments	HUCA	*Hebrew Union College Annual*
		HUTh	*Hermeneutische Untersuchungen zur Theologie*
FTS	Frankfurter Theologischen Studien		
FzB	Forschungen zur Bibel	IB	*Interpreter's Bible*
GAG	W. von Soden, *Grundriss der akkadischen Grammatik*	IBD	*Illustrated Bible Dictionary,* ed. J. D. Douglas and N. Hillyer
GCS	Griechische christliche Schriftsteller	ICC	International Critical Commentary
GeistLeb	*Geist und Leben*	IDB	G. A. Buttrick (ed.), *Interpreter's Dictionary of the Bible*
GKB	Gesenius-Kautzsch-Bergsträsser, *Hebräische Grammatik*		

IDBSup	Supplementary volume to IDB	JPSV	Jewish Publication Society Version
IEJ	Israel Exploration Journal	JQR	Jewish Quarterly Review
Int	Interpretation	JQRMS	Jewish Quarterly Review Monograph Series
ISBE	International Standard Bible Encyclopedia, ed. G. W. Bromiley	JR	Journal of Religion
		JRAS	Journal of the Royal Asiatic Society
ITQ	Irish Theological Quarterly	JRE	Journal of Religious Ethics
		JRelS	Journal of Religious Studies
JA	Journal asiatique	JRH	Journal of Religious History
JAAR	Journal of the American Academy of Religion	JRS	Journal of Roman Studies
		JRT	Journal of Religious Thought
JAC	Jahrbuch für Antike und Christentum	JSJ	Journal for the Study of Judaism in the Persian, Hellenistic and Roman Period
JAMA	Journal of the American Medical Association	JSNT	Journal for the Study of the New Testament
JANESCU	Journal of the Ancient Near Eastern Society of Columbia University	JSOT	Journal for the Study of the Old Testament
JAOS	Journal of the American Oriental Society	JSS	Journal of Semitic Studies
		JSSR	Journal of the Scientific Study of Religion
JAS	Journal of Asian Studies	JTC	Journal for Theology and the Church
JB	A. Jones (ed.), Jerusalem Bible		
JBC	R. E. Brown et al. (eds.), The Jerome Biblical Commentary	JTS	Journal of Theological Studies
		Judaica	Judaica: Beiträge zum Verständnis . . .
JBL	Journal of Biblical Literature		
JBR	Journal of Bible and Religion		
JCS	Journal of Cuneiform Studies	KAI	H. Donner and W. Röllig, Kanaanäische und aramäische Inschriften
JDS	Judean Desert Studies		
JEA	Journal of Egyptian Archaeology		
		KAT	E. Sellin (ed.), Kommentar zum A. T.
JEH	Journal of Ecclesiastical History	KB	L. Koehler and W. Baumgartner, Lexicon in Veteris Testamenti libros
JEOL	Jaarbericht . . . ex oriente lux		
JES	Journal of Ecumenical Studies	KD	Kerygma und Dogma
		KEK	Kritisch-Exegetischer Kommentar
JETS	Journal of the Evangelical Theological Society	KIT	Kleine Texte
JHS	Journal of Hellenic Studies		
JIBS	Journal of Indian and Buddhist Studies	LCC	Library of Christian Classics
JIPh	Journal of Indian Philosophy	LCL	Loeb Classical Library
JJS	Journal of Jewish Studies	LD	Lectio divina
JMES	Journal of Middle Eastern Studies	Leš	Lešonénu
		LLAVT	E. Vogt, Lexicon linguae aramaicae Veteris Testamenti
JMS	Journal of Mithraic Studies		
JNES	Journal of Near Eastern Studies	LPGL	G. W. H. Lampe, Patristic Greek Lexicon
JPOS	Journal of the Palestine Oriental Society	LQ	Lutheran Quarterly
		LR	Lutherische Rundschau

LSJ	Liddell-Scott-Jones, *Greek-English Lexicon*	*NIDNTT*	C. Brown (ed.), *The New International Dictionary of New Testament Theology*
LTK	*Lexikon für Theologie und Kirche (LThK)*	NIGNTC	New International Greek New Testament Commentary
LUÅ	Lunds universitets årsskrift		
LW	*Lutheran World*		
		NKZ	*Neue kirchliche Zeitschrift*
McCQ	*McCormick Quarterly*	*NorTT*	*Norsk Teologisk Tidsskrift (NTT)*
MDOG	Mitteilungen der deutschen Orient-Gesellschaft		
		NovT	*Novum Testamentum*
MeyerK	H. A. W. Meyer, Kritischexegetischer Kommentar über das Neue Testament	NovTSup	Novum Testamentum, Supplement
		New Docs	*New Documents Illustrating Early Christianity*, A Review of Greek Inscriptions etc. ed. G. H. R. Horsley. North Ryde, NSW, Australia
MGWJ	*Monatsschrift für Geschichte und Wissenschaft des Judentums*		
MM	J. H. Moulton and G. Milligan, *The Vocabulary of the Greek Testament*	NPNF	Nicene and Post-Nicene Fathers
		NRT	*La nouvelle revue théologique (NRTh)*
MNTC	Moffatt NT Commentary		
MPAIBL	*Mémoires présenté à l'Académie des inscriptions et belles-lettres*	*NTA*	*New Testament Abstracts*
		NTAbh	Neutestamentliche Abhandlungen
MPG	*Patrologia Graeca*, ed. J. P. Migne, 1844 ff.	NTD	Das Neue Testament Deutsch
MScRel	*Mélanges de science religieuse*		
MTZ	*Münchener theologische Zeitschrift (MThZ)*	NTF	Neutestamentliche Forschungen
MUSJ	*Mélanges de l'université Saint-Joseph*	*NTS*	*New Testament Studies*
		NTSR	The New Testament for Spiritual Reading
MVAG	Mitteilungen der vorderasiatisch-ägyptischen Gesellschaft	NTTS	New Testament Tools and Studies
		Numen	*Numen: International Review for the History of Religious*
NAG	*Nachrichten von der Akademie der Wissenschaften in Göttingen*		
		OCD	*Oxford Classical Dictionary*
		OIP	Oriental Institute Publications
NCB	New Century Bible (new edit.)		
		OLP	Orientalia lovaniensia periodica
NCCHS	R. C. Fuller et al. (eds.), *New Catholic Commentary on Holy Scripture*		
		OLZ	*Orientalische Literaturzeitung*
NCE	M. R. P. McGuire et al. (eds.), *New Catholic Encyclopedia*	*Or*	*Orientalia* (Rome)
		OrAnt	*Oriens antiquus*
		OrChr	*Oriens christianus*
NClB	New Clarendon Bible	*OrSyr*	*L'orient syrien*
NedTTs	*Nederlands theologisch tijdschrift (NedThTs)*	ÖTKNT	Ökumenische Taschenbuch-Kommentar zum NT
Neot	*Neotestamentica*	OTM	Oxford Theological Monographs
NFT	New Frontiers in Theology		
NHS	Nag Hammadi Studies	OTS	Oudtestamentische Studiën
NICNT	New International Commentary on the New Testament	PAAJR	Proceedings of the American Academy of Jewish Research

PC	Proclamation Commentaries	RestQ	*Restoration Quarterly*
PCB	M. Black and H. H. Rowley (eds.), *Peake's Commentary on the Bible*	RevExp	*Review and Expositor*
		RevistB	*Revista biblica*
		RevScRel	*Revue des sciences religieuses*
PEFQS	*Palestine Exploration Fund, Quarterly Statement*	RevSém	*Revue sémitique*
		RevThom	*Revue thomiste*
PEQ	*Palestine Exploration Quarterly*	RGG	*Religion in Geschichte und Gegenwart*
PG	*Patrologia graeca,* ed. J. P. Migne		
		RHE	*Revue d'histoire ecclésiastique*
PGM	K. Preisendanz (ed.), *Papyri graecae magicae*		
		RHPR	*Revue d'histoire et de philosophie religieuses (RHPhR)*
PhEW	*Philosophy East and West*		
PhRev	*Philosophical Review*		
PJ	*Palästina-Jahrbuch*	RHR	Revue de l'histoire des religions
PL	*Patrologia Latina,* J. P. Migne		
		RivB	*Rivista biblica*
PNTC	Pelican New Testament Commentaries	RNT	Regensburger Neues Testament
PO	Patrologia orientalis	RQ	*Revue de Qumrân*
PRU	*Le Palais royal d'Ugarit*	RR	*Review of Religion*
PSTJ	*Perkins (School of Theology) Journal*	RSO	*Rivista degli studi orientali*
		RSPT	*Revue des sciences philosophiques et théologiques (RSPhTh)*
PVTG	Pseudepigrapha Veteris Testamenti graece		
PW	Pauly-Wissowa, *Real-Encyklopädie der klassischen Altertums-wissenschaft*	RSR	*Recherches de science religieuse (RechSR)*
		RscPhTh	*Revue des Sciences Philosophiques et Théologiques*
PWSup	Supplement to PW		
		RTL	*Revue théologique de Louvain (RThL)*
QDAP	*Quarterly of the Department of Antiquities in Palestine*		
		RTP	*Revue de théologie et de philosophie (RThPh)*
		RTR	*The Reformed Theological Review*
RA	*Revue d'assyriologie et d'archéologie orientale*		
		RUO	*Revue de l'université Ottawa*
RAC	*Reallexikon für Antike und Christentum*		
RArch	*Revue archéologique*		
RB	*Revue biblique*	SacPag	*Sacra Pagina*
RBén	*Revue bénédictine*	SAH	*Sitzungsberichte der Heidelberger Akademie der Wissenschaften (phil.-hist. Klasse),* 1910 ff.
RCB	*Revista de cultura biblica*		
RE	*Realencyklopädie für protestantische Theologie und Kirche*		
		SANT	Studien zum Alten und Neuen Testament
RechBib	Recherches bibliques		
REg	*Revue d'égyptologie*	SAQ	Sammlung ausgewählter kirchen- und dogmen-geschichtlicher Quellen-schriften
REJ	*Revue des études juives*		
RelArts	Religion and the Arts		
RelS	*Religious Studies*		
RelSoc	Religion and Society	SB	Sources bibliques
RelSRev	*Religious Studies Review*	SBFLA	*Studii biblici franciscani liber annuus*
RES	*Répertoire d'épigraphie sémitique*		
		SBJ	*La sainte bible de Jérusalem*

SBLASP	Society of Biblical Literature Abstracts and Seminar Papers		SPAW	Sitzungsberichte der preussischen Akademie der Wissenschaften
SBLDS	SBL Dissertation Series		SPB	Studia postbiblica
SBLMasS	SBL Masoretic Studies		SR	*Studies in Religion/Sciences religieuses*
SBLMS	SBL Monograph Series			
SBLSBS	SBL Sources for Biblical Study		SSS	Semitic Study Series
			ST	*Studia theologica (StTh)*
SBLSCS	SBL Septuagint and Cognate Studies		STÅ	*Svensk teologisk årsskrift*
			StBibT	*Studia Biblica et Theologica*
SBLTT	SBL Texts and Translations		STDJ	Studies on the Texts of the Desert of Judah
SBM	Stuttgarter biblische Monographien		STK	*Svensk teologisk kvartalskrift*
SBS	Stuttgarter Bibelstudien		Str-B	[H. Strack and] P. Billerbeck, *Kommentar zum Neuen Testament*
SBT	Studies in Biblical Theology			
SC	Sources chrétiennes			
ScEs	*Science et esprit*		StudNeot	Studia neotestamentica, Studia
SCR	*Studies in Comparative Religion*		StudOr	Studia orientalia
			SUNT	Studien zur Umwelt des Neuen Testaments
Scr	*Scripture*			
ScrB	*Scripture Bulletin*		SVTP	Studia in Veteris Testamenti pseudepigrapha
SD	Studies and Documents			
SE	Studia Evangelica I, II, III (= TU 73 [1959], 87 [1964], 88 [1964], etc.) (*StEv*)		*SWJT*	*Southwestern Journal of Theology*
			SymBU	Symbolae biblicae upsalienses (SyBU)
SEÅ	*Svensk exegetisk årsbok*			
Sef	*Sefarad*			
SeinSend	*Sein Sendung*		*TAPA*	*Transactions of the American Philological Association*
Sem	*Semitica*			
SHAW	Sitzungsberichte heidelbergen Akademie der Wissenschaften		TBC	Torch Bible Commentaries
			TBI	*Theologische Blätter (ThBl)*
			TBü	Theologische Bücherei (ThBü)
SHT	Studies in Historical Theology			
			TBT	*The Bible Today*
SHVL	Skrifter Utgivna Av Kungl. Humanistika Vetenskapssamfundet i Lund		*TD*	*Theology Digest*
			TDNT	G. Kittel and G. Friedrich (eds.), *Theological Dictionary of the New Testament*
SJLA	Studies in Judaism in Late Antiquity		TextsS	Texts and Studies
SJT	*Scottish Journal of Theology*		*TF*	*Theologische Forschung (ThF)*
SMSR	*Studi e materiali di storia delle religioni*		*TGI*	*Theologie und Glaube (ThGI)*
SNT	Studien zum Neuen Testament (StNT)		*Th*	*Theology*
			ThA	*Theologische Arbeiten*
SNTSMS	Society for New Testament Studies Monograph Series		*ThBer*	*Theologische Berichte*
			THKNT	Theologischer Handkommentar zum Neuen Testament (ThHKNT)
SO	Symbolae osloenses			
SOTSMS	Society for Old Testament Study Monograph Series		*TLZ*	*Theologische Literaturzeitung (ThLZ)*
SPap	*Studia papyrologica*			

TNTC	Tyndale New Testament Commentary	VoxEv	Vox Evangelica
		VS	Verbum salutis
TP	Theologie und Philosophie (ThPh)	VSpir	Vie spirituelle
		VT	Vetus Testamentum
TPQ	Theologisch-Praktische Quartalschrift	VTSup	Vetus Testamentum, Supplements
TQ	Theologische Quartalschrift (ThQ)		
TRev	Theologische Revue	WA	M. Luther, Kritische Gesamtausgabe
TRu	Theologische Rundschau (ThR)		
TS	Theological Studies		(= "Weimar" edition)
TSK	Theologische Studien und Kritiken (ThStK)	WBC	Word Biblical Commentary
		WC	Westminster Commentary
TT	Teologisk Tidsskrift	WDB	Westminster Dictionary of the Bible
TTKi	Tidsskrift for Teologi og Kirke		
TToday	Theology Today	WHAB	Westminster Historical Atlas of the Bible
TTS	Trierer Theologische Studien		
		WMANT	Wissenschaftliche Monographien zum Alten und Neuen Testament
TTZ	Trierer theologische Zeitschrift (TThZ)		
TU	Texte und Untersuchungen	WO	Die Welt des Orients
TynB	Tyndale Bulletin	WTJ	Westminster Theological Journal
TWAT	G. J. Botterweck and H. Ringgren (eds.), Theologisches Wörterbuch zum Alten Testament (ThWAT)		
		WUNT	Wissenschaftliche Untersuchungen zum Neuen Testament
TWNT	G. Kittel and G. Friedrich (eds.), Theologisches Wörterbuch zum Neuen Testament (ThWNT)	WZKM	Wiener Zeitschrift für die Kunde des Morgenlandes
		WZKSO	Wiener Zeitschrift für die Kunde Süd- und Ostasiens
TZ	Theologische Zeitschrift (ThZ)		
		ZA	Zeitschrift für Assyriologie
UBSGNT	United Bible Societies Greek New Testament	ZAW	Zeitschrift für die alttestamentliche Wissenschaft
UF	Ugaritische Forschungen	ZDMG	Zeitschrift der deutschen morgenländischen Gesellschaft
UNT	Untersuchungen zum Neuen Testament		
US	Una Sancta	ZDPV	Zeitschrift des deutschen Palästina-Vereins
USQR	Union Seminary Quarterly Review		
		ZEE	Zeitschrift für evangelische Ethik
UT	C. H. Gordon, Ugaritic Textbook		
		ZHT	Zeitschrift für historische Theologie (ZHTh)
UUÅ	Uppsala universitetsårsskrift		
		ZKG	Zeitschrift für Kirchengeschichte
VC	Vigiliae christianae	ZKNT	Zahn's Kommentar zum NT
VCaro	Verbum caro	ZKT	Zeitschrift für katholische Theologie (ZKTh)
VD	Verbum domini		
VF	Verkündigung und Forschung	ZMR	Zeitschrift für Missions-kunde und Religions-wissenschaft
VKGNT	K. Aland (ed.), Vollständige Konkordanz zum griechischen Neuen Testament		
		ZNW	Zeitschrift für die neutestamentliche Wissenschaft

ZRGG	*Zeitschrift für Religions-und Geistesgeschichte*	ZTK	*Zeitschrift für Theologie und Kirche (ZThK)*
ZST	*Zeitschrift für systematische Theologie (ZSTh)*	ZWT	*Zeitschrift für wissenschaftliche Theologie (ZWTh)*

D. Abbreviations for Books of the Bible, the Apocrypha, and the Pseudepigrapha

OLD TESTAMENT

Gen	2 Chr	Dan
Exod	Ezra	Hos
Lev	Neh	Joel
Num	Esth	Amos
Deut	Job	Obad
Josh	Ps(Pss)	Jonah
Judg	Prov	Mic
Ruth	Eccl	Nah
1 Sam	Cant	Hab
2 Sam	Isa	Zeph
1 Kgs	Jer	Hag
2 Kgs	Lam	Zech
1 Chr	Ezek	Mal

NEW TESTAMENT

Matt	1 Tim
Mark	2 Tim
Luke	Titus
John	Philem
Acts	Heb
Rom	James
1 Cor	1 Peter
2 Cor	2 Peter
Gal	1 John
Eph	2 John
Phil	3 John
Col	Jude
1 Thess	Rev
2 Thess	

APOCRYPHA

1 Esd	1 Esdras	Ep Jer	Epistle of Jeremy
2 Esd	2 Esdras	S Th Ch	Song of the Three Children
Tob	Tobit		(or Young Men)
Jud	Judith	Sus	Susanna
Add Esth	Additions to Esther	Bel	Bel and the Dragon
Wisd Sol	Wisdom of Solomon	Pr Man	Prayer of Manasseh
Sir	Ecclesiasticus (Wisdom of Jesus the Son of Sirach)	1 Macc	1 Maccabees
		2 Macc	2 Maccabees
Bar	Baruch		

E. Abbreviations of the Names of Pseudepigraphical and Early Patristic Books

Adam and Eve	Books of Adam and Eve	*T. 12 Patr.*	Testaments of the Twelve Patriarchs
2–3 Apoc. Bar.	Syriac, Greek Apocalypse of Baruch	*T. Benj.*	Testament of Benjamin, etc.
Apoc. Abr.	Apocalypse of Abraham		
Apoc. Mos.	Apocalypse of Moses	*T. Levi*	Testament of Levi, etc.
Asc. Isa.	Ascension of Isaiah	*Acts Pil.*	Acts of Pilate
As. Mos.	Assumption of Moses	*Apoc. Pet.*	Apocalypse of Peter
Bib. Ant.	Ps.-Philo, Biblical Antiquities	*Gos. Eb.*	Gospel of the Ebionites
		Gos. Eg.	Gospel of the Egyptians
1–2–3 Enoch	Ethiopic, Slavonic, Hebrew Enoch	*Gos. Heb.*	Gospel of the Hebrews
		Gos. Naass.	Gospel of the Naassenes
Ep. Arist.	Epistle of Aristeas	*Gos. Pet.*	Gospel of Peter
Ep. Diognetus	Epistle to Diognetus	*Gos. Thom.*	Gospel of Thomas
Jub.	Jubilees	*Prot. Jas.*	Protevangelium of James
Mart. Isa.	Martyrdom of Isaiah		
Odes Sol.	Odes of Solomon	*Barn.*	Barnabas
Pss. Sol.	Psalms of Solomon	*1–2 Clem.*	1–2 Clement
Sib. Or.	Sibylline Oracles	*Did.*	Didache
T. Abr.	Testament of Abraham	*Diogn.*	Diognetus

Herm. Man.	Hermas, Mandates	*Smyrn.*	Ignatius, Letter to the
Sim.	Similitudes		Smyrnaeans
Vis.	Visions	*Trall.*	Ignatius, Letter to the
Ign. *Eph.*	Ignatius, Letter to the		Trallians
	Ephesians	*Mart Pol.*	Martyrdom of Polycarp
Magn.	Ignatius, Letter to the	Pol. *Phil.*	Polycarp to the
	Magnesians		Philippians
Phld.	Ignatius, Letter to the	*Adv. Haer.*	Irenaeus, Against All
	Philadelphians		Heresies
Pol.	Ignatius, Letter to	*De Praesc.*	
	Polycarp	*Haer.*	Tertullian, On the
Rom.	Ignatius, Letter to the		Proscribing of Heretics
	Romans		

F. Abbreviations of Names of Dead Sea Scrolls and Related Texts

CD	Cairo (Genizah text of	1QM	*Milhāmāh* (*War Scroll*)
	the) Damascus	1QS	*Serek hayyaḥad* (*Rule of the*
	(Document)		*Community, Manual of*
Hev	Nahal Hever texts		*Discipline*)
Mas	Masada texts	1QSa	Appendix A (*Rule of the*
Mird	Khirbet Mird texts		*Congregation*) to 1QS
Mur	Wadi Murabbaʿat texts	1QSb	Appendix B (*Blessings*) to
p	Pesher (commentary)		1QS
Q	Qumran	3Q*15*	Copper Scroll from
1Q, 2Q,			Qumran Cave 3
3Q, etc.	Numbered caves of	4QFlor	*Florilegium* (or
	Qumran, yielding		*Eschatological Midrashim*)
	written material;		from Qumran Cave 4
	followed by abbreviation	4QMess ar	Aramaic "Messianic" text
	of biblical or apocryphal		from Qumran Cave 4
	book	4QPrNab	Prayer of Nabonidus
QL	Qumran literature		from Qumran Cave 4
1QapGen	*Genesis Apocryphon* of	4QTestim	*Testimonia* text from
	Qumran Cave 1		Qumran Cave 4
1QH	*Hôdāyôt* (*Thanksgiving*	4QTLevi	*Testament of Levi* from
	Hymns) from Qumran		Qumran Cave 4
	Cave 1	4QPhyl	Phylacteries from
1QIsa*a,b*	First or second copy of		Qumran Cave 4
	Isaiah from Qumran	11QMelch	*Melchizedek* text from
	Cave 1		Qumran Cave 11
1QpHab	*Pesher on Habakkuk* from	11QtgJob	*Targum of Job* from
	Qumran Cave 1		Qumran Cave 11

G. Abbreviations of Targumic Material

Tg. Onq.	*Targum Onqelos*	*Tg. Ps.-J.*	*Targum Pseudo-Jonathan*
Tg. Neb.	*Targum of the Prophets*	*Tg. Yer. 1*	*Targum Yerušalmi I* [*]
Tg. Ket.	*Targum of the Writings*	*Tg. Yer. 11*	*Targum Yerušalmi II* [*]
Frg. Tg.	*Fragmentary Targum*	*Yem. Tg.*	*Yemenite Targum*
Sam. Tg.	*Samaritan Targum*	*Tg. Esth I,*	*First or Second Targum of*
Tg. Isa.	*Targum of Isaiah*	*II*	*Esther*
Pal. Tgs.	*Palestinian Targums*		
Tg. Neof.	*Targum Neofiti I*	[*] optional title	

H. Abbreviations of Other Rabbinic Works

ʾAbot	ʾAbot de Rabbi Nathan	Pesiq. Rab Kah.	Pesiqta de Rab Kahana
ʾAg. Ber.	ʾAggadat Berešit	Pirqe R. El.	Pirqe Rabbi Eliezer
Bab.	Babylonian	Rab.	Rabbah (following
Bar.	Baraita		abbreviation for biblical
Der. Er. Rab.	Derek Ereṣ Rabba		book: Gen. Rab. [with
Der. Er. Zuṭ.	Derek Ereṣ Zuṭa		periods] = Genesis
Gem.	Gemara		Rabbah)
Kalla	Kalla	Sem.	Semaḥot
Mek.	Mekilta	Sipra	Sipra
Midr.	Midraš; cited with usual	Sipre	Sipre
	abbreviation for biblical	Sop.	Soperim
	book; but Midr. Qoh. =	S. ʿOlam Rab.	Seder ʿOlam Rabbah
	Midraš Qohelet	Talm.	Talmud
Pal.	Palestinian	Yal.	Yalquṭ
Pesiq. R.	Pesiqta Rabbati		

I. Abbreviations of Orders and Tractates in Mishnaic and Related Literature

ʾAbot	ʾAbot	Nazir	Nazir
ʿArak.	ʿArakin	Ned.	Nedarim
ʿAbod. Zar.	ʿAboda Zara	Neg.	Negaʿim
B. Bat.	Baba Batra	Nez.	Neziqin
Bek.	Bekorot	Nid.	Niddah
Ber.	Berakot	Ohol.	Oholot
Beṣa	Beṣa (= Yom Tob)	ʿOr.	ʿOrla
Bik.	Bikkurim	Para	Para
B. Meṣ.	Baba Meṣiʿa	Peʾa	Peʾa
B. Qam.	Baba Qamma	Pesaḥ.	Pesaḥim
Dem.	Demai	Qinnim	Qinnim
ʿEd.	ʿEduyyot	Qidd.	Qiddušin
ʿErub.	ʿErubin	Qod.	Qodašin
Giṭ.	Giṭṭin	Roš. Haš.	Roš Haššana
Ḥag.	Ḥagiga	Sanh.	Sanhedrin
Ḥal.	Ḥalla	Šabb.	Šabbat
Hor.	Horayot	Šeb.	Šebiʿit
Ḥul.	Ḥullin	Šebu.	Šebuʿot
Kelim	Kelim	Šeqal.	Šeqalim
Ker.	Keritot	Soṭa	Soṭa
Ketub.	Ketubot	Sukk.	Sukka
Kil.	Kilʾayim	Taʿan.	Taʿanit
Maʿaś.	Maʿaśerot	Tamid	Tamid
Mak.	Makkot	Tem.	Temura
Makš.	Makširin (= Mašqin)	Ter.	Terumot
Meg.	Megilla	Ṭohar.	Ṭoharot
Meʿil.	Meʿila	T. Yom	Tebul Yom
Menaḥ.	Menaḥot	ʿUq.	ʿUqṣin
Mid.	Middot	Yad.	Yadayim
Miqw.	Miqwaʾot	Yebam.	Yebamot
Moʿed	Moʿed	Yoma	Yoma (= Kippurim)
Moʿed Qat.	Moʿed Qaṭan	Zabim	Zabim
Maʿas. S.	Maʿaśer Šeni	Zebaḥ	Zebaḥim
Našim	Našim	Zer.	Zeraʿim

J. Abbreviations of Nag Hammadi Tractates

Acts Pet. 12		Melch.	Melchizedek
Apost.	Acts of Peter and the Twelve Apostles	Norea	Thought of Norea
Allogenes	Allogenes	On Bap. A	On Baptism A
Ap. Jas.	Apocryphon of James	On Bap. B	On Baptism B
Ap. John	Apocryphon of John	On Bap. C	On Baptism C
Apoc. Adam	Apocalypse of Adam	On Euch. A	On the Eucharist A
1 Apoc. Jas.	First Apocalypse of James	On Euch. B	On the Eucharist B
2 Apoc. Jas.	Second Apocalypse of James	Orig. World	On the Origin of the World
Apoc. Paul	Apocalypse of Paul	Paraph. Shem	Paraphrase of Shem
Apoc. Pet.	Apocalypse of Peter	Pr. Paul	Prayer of the Apostle Paul
Asclepius	Asclepius 21–29	Pr. Thanks	Prayer of Thanksgiving
Auth. Teach.	Authoritative Teaching	Prot. Jas.	Protevangelium of James
Dial. Sav.	Dialogue of the Savior	Sent. Sextus	Sentences of Sextus
Disc. 8–9	Discourse on the Eighth and Ninth	Soph. Jes. Chr.	Sophia of Jesus Christ
		Steles Seth	Three Steles of Seth
Ep. Pet. Phil.	Letter of Peter to Philip	Teach. Silv.	Teachings of Silvanus
Eugnostos	Eugnostos the Blessed	Testim. Truth	Testimony of Truth
Exeg. Soul	Exegesis on the Soul	Thom. Cont.	Book of Thomas the Contender
Gos. Eg.	Gospel of the Egyptians	Thund.	Thunder, Perfect Mind
Gos. Phil.	Gospel of Philip	Treat. Res.	Treatise on Resurrection
Gos. Thom.	Gospel of Thomas	Treat. Seth	Second Treatise of the Great Seth
Gos. Truth	Gospel of Truth		
Great Pow.	Concept of our Great Power	Tri. Trac.	Triparite Tractate
Hyp. Arch.	Hypostasis of the Archons	Trim. Prot.	Trimorphic Protennoia
Hypsiph.	Hypsiphrone	Val. Exp.	A Valentinian Exposition
Interp. Know.	Interpretation of Knowledge	Zost.	Zostrianos
Marsanes	Marsanes		

Note: The textual notes and numbers used to indicate individual manuscripts are those found in the apparatus criticus of *Novum Testamentum Graece*, ed. E. Nestle and K. Aland et al. (Stuttgart: Deutsche Bibelgesellschaft, 1979[26]). This edition of the Greek New Testament is the basis for the *Translation* sections.

General Bibliography

Barker, G. W., Lane, W. L., and **Michaels, J. R.** *The New Testament Speaks.* New York: Harper & Row, 1969. **Bengel, J. A.** *Gnomon of the New Testament.* Ed. A. R. Fausset. 2 vols. New York: Sheldon, 1862. **Beyer, K.** *Semitische Syntax im Neuen Testament.* Göttingen: Vandenhoeck und Ruprecht, 1962. **Bornkamm, G.** *The New Testament: A Guide to Its Writings.* Tr. R. H. Fuller and I. Fuller. Philadelphia: Fortress, 1973. ———. *Paul.* Tr. K. Grobel. New York: Harper & Row, 1971. **Bruce, F. F.** *New Testament History.* London: Nelson, 1969. **Bultmann, R.** *Theology of the New Testament.* 2 vols. New York: Scribner's, 1951–55. **Burkitt, F. C.** *Christian Beginnings.* London: University of London Press, 1924. **Cullmann, O.** *The New Testament: An Introduction.* Tr. D. Pardee. Philadelphia: Westminster, 1968. **Dalman, G. H.** *Words of Jesus.* Tr. D. M. Kay. Edinburgh: T. & T. Clark, 1902. **Dibelius, M.** *A Fresh Approach to the New Testament and Early Christian Literature.* New York: Scribner's, 1936. **Ellis, E. E.** *Paul's Use of the Old Testament.* Edinburgh: Oliver & Boyd, 1957. **Enslin, M. S.** *Christian Beginnings: The Literature of the Christian Movement.* New York: Harper, 1956. **Feine, P., Behm, J.,** and **Kümmel, W. G.** *Introduction to the New Testament.* Tr. A. J. Mattill, Jr. Nashville: Abingdon, 1966; 1st ed. in ET. See Kümmel. **Fuller, R. H.** *A Critical Introduction to the New Testament.* London: Duckworth, 1966. **Grant, R. M.** *A Historical Introduction to the New Testament.* New York: Harper & Row, 1963. **Guthrie, D.** *New Testament Introduction.* Chicago: Inter-Varsity Press; London: Tyndale Press, 1963 (2d ed.), 1970 (3d ed.). **Harrison, E. F.** *Introduction to the New Testament.* Grand Rapids: Eerdmans, 1964. **Hoppe, R.** *Der theologische Hintergrund des Jakobsbriefes.* FzB 28. Würzburg: Katholisches Bibelwerk, 1977. **Hunter, A. M.** *Introducing the New Testament.* 2d ed. Philadelphia: Westminster, 1957. **Johnson, L. T.** *The Writings of the New Testament: An Interpretation.* Philadelphia: Fortress, 1986. **Koester, H.** *Introduction to the New Testament.* Vol. 2, *History and Literature of Early Christians.* Philadelphia: Fortress, 1982. **Kümmel, W. G.** *Introduction to the New Testament.* Rev. ed. Tr. H. C. Kee. Nashville: Abingdon, 1975. **Martin, R. P.** *New Testament Foundations.* Vol. 2. Grand Rapids: Eerdmans; Exeter: Paternoster Press, 1978 (1st ed.), 1987 (rev. ed.). **Marxsen, W.** *Introduction to the New Testament.* Tr. G. Buswell. Philadelphia: Fortress, 1968. **Maynard-Reid, P. U.** *Poverty and Wealth in James.* Maryknoll, NY: Orbis, 1987. **McNeile, A. H.** *Introduction to the New Testament.* Rev. ed. C. S. C. Williams. Oxford: Clarendon, 1953. **Metzger, B.** *A Textual Commentary on the Greek New Testament.* London: United Bible Societies, 1971. **Michaelis, W.** *Einleitung in das Neue Testament.* 2d ed. Bern: Berchthold HallerVerlag, 1954. **Moffatt, J.** *An Introduction to the Literature of the New Testament.* 3d ed. New York: Scribner's; Edinburgh: T. & T. Clark, 1918. **Moule, C. F. D.** *An Idiom Book of New Testament Greek.* 2d ed. Cambridge: Cambridge UP, 1959. **Moulton, J. H., Howard, W. F.,** and **Turner, N.** *A Grammar of New Testament Greek.* 4 vols. Edinburgh: T. & T. Clark, 1908–76. **Perrin, N.** *The New Testament: An Introduction.* New York: Harcourt Brace Jovanovich, 1974; rev. D. C. Duling, 1982. **Price, J. L.** *Interpreting the New Testament.* New York: Holt, Rinehart & Winston, 1961. **Richardson, A.,** ed. *Theological Word Book of the Bible.* New York: Macmillan, 1951. **Riddle, D. W.,** and **Hutson, H. H.** *New Testament Life and Literature.* Chicago: University of Chicago Press, 1946. **Robert, A.,** and **Feuillet, A.** *Introduction to the New Testament.* Tr. P. W. Skehan. New York: Desclée, 1965. **Roberts, C. H.** *Manuscript, Society, and Belief in Early Christian Egypt.* London/New York: Oxford UP, 1979. **Robertson, A. T.** *A Grammar of the Greek New Testament in the Light of Historical Research.* 4th ed. Nashville: Broadman, 1934. **Schenke, H.-M.,** and **Fischer, K. M.** *Einleitung in die*

Schriften des Neuen Testament. Berlin: Evangelische Verlagsanstalt, 1978. **Spittler, R. P.** "Testament of Job." In *The Old Testament Pseudepigrapha*, ed. J. H. Charlesworth. 2 vols. Garden City, NY: Doubleday, 1983–84. 1:829–68. **Thayer, J. H.** *A Greek-English Lexicon of the New Testament*. 4th ed. Edinburgh: T. & T. Clark, 1901. **Trench, R. C.** *Synonyms of the New Testament*. Grand Rapids: Eerdmans, 1947. **Vielhauer, P.** *Geschichte der urchristlichen Literatur*. Berlin: de Gruyter, 1975. **Wikenhauser, A.** *New Testament Introduction*. Tr. J. Cunningham. New York: Herder & Herder, 1958. **Zahn, T.** *Introduction to the New Testament*. Tr. J. M. Trout et al. Edinburgh: T. & T. Clark, 1909. **Zerwick, M.** *Biblical Greek*. Rome: Pontifical Biblical Institute, 1963. ——— and **Grosvenor, M.** *A Grammatical Analysis of the Greek New Testament*. Rome: Biblical Institute, 1974.

Commentary Bibliography

Adamson, J. B. *The Epistle of James.* NICNT. Grand Rapids: Eerdmans, 1976. **Barclay, W.** *The Letters of James and Peter.* The Daily Study Bible. 2d ed. Philadelphia: Westminster, 1960. **Blackman, E. C.** *The Epistle of James.* TBC. London: SCM, 1947. **Burdick, D. W.** *James.* Expositor's Bible Commentary. Vol. 12. Ed. F. E. Gaebelein. Grand Rapids: Zondervan, 1981. **Cantinat, J.** *Les épîtres de s. Jacques et de s. Jude.* SBib. Paris: Gabalda, 1973. **Carpenter, W. B.** *The Wisdom of James the Just.* London: Isbister, 1903. **Chaine, J.** *L'épître de s. Jacques.* EBib. Paris: Gabalda, 1927. **Davids, P. H.** *Commentary on James.* NIGNTC. Grand Rapids: Eerdmans, 1982. **Dibelius, M.** *James: A Commentary on the Epistle of James.* Hermeneia. Reissued by H. Greeven. Tr. M. A. Williams. Philadelphia: Fortress, 1976, ET of *Der Brief des Jakobus.* MeyerK 15. Göttingen: Vandenhoeck und Ruprecht, 1964. **Easton, B. S.,** and **Poteat, G.** *The Epistle of James.* IB. Ed. G. A. Buttrick et al. Vol. 12. New York/Nashville: Abingdon, 1957. **Hauck, F.** *Die Briefe des Jakobus, Petrus, Juda und Jakobus.* NTD 10. Göttingen: Vandenhoeck und Ruprecht, 1937. **Hiebert, D. E.** *The Epistle of James: Tests of a Living Faith.* Chicago: Moody, 1979. **Hort, F. J. A.** *The Epistle of St. James: The Greek Text with Introduction, Commentary as far as Chapter IV Verse 7, and Additional Notes.* London: Macmillan, 1909. **Hubbard, D. A.** *The Book of James: Wisdom That Works.* Waco, TX: Word, 1980. **Kistemaker, S. J.** *The New Testament Commentary: Exposition of the Epistle of James and the Epistles of John.* Grand Rapids: Baker, 1986. **Knowling, R. J.** *The Epistle of St. James.* WC. London: Methuen, 1904. **Kugelman, R.** *James and Jude.* New Testament Message. Vol. 19. Wilmington: Glazier; Dublin: Veritas, 1980. **Laws, S.** *A Commentary on the Epistle of James.* HNTC. London: A. & C. Black; San Francisco: Harper & Row, 1980. **Martin, R. A.** *James.* Augsburg Commentary on the New Testament. Minneapolis: Augsburg, 1982. **Marty, J.** *L'épître de Jacques.* EBib. Paris: Alcan, 1935. **Mayor, J. B.** *The Epistle of St. James. The Greek Text with Introduction, Notes and Comments.* 1897. Reprint. Grand Rapids: Zondervan, 1954. **Mitton, C. L.** *The Epistle of James.* Grand Rapids: Eerdmans; London: Marshall, Morgan & Scott, 1966. **Moffatt, J.** *The General Epistles of James, Peter, and Jude.* MNTC. London: Hodder & Stoughton, 1928. **Moo, D.** *James.* TNTC rev. Grand Rapids: Eerdmans, 1987. **Motyer, J. A.** *The Message of James.* The Bible Speaks Today. Leicester/Downers Grove, IL: Inter-Varsity Press, 1985. **Mussner, F.** *Der Jakobusbrief.* HTKNT Vol. 13/1. Freiburg: Herder, 1964. **Oesterley, W. E.** *The General Epistle of James.* Expositor's Greek Testament. Vol. 4. Ed. W. Robertson Nicoll. London: Hodder & Stoughton, 1910. **Plummer, A.** *The General Epistles of St. James and St. Jude.* New York: A. C. Armstrong, 1903. **Reicke, B.** *The Epistles of James, Peter, and Jude.* AB. Vol. 37. Ed. W. F. Albright and D. N. Freedman. Garden City, NY: Doubleday, 1964. **Ropes, J. H.** *A Critical and Exegetical Commentary on the Epistle of St. James.* ICC. Ed. C. A. Briggs, S. R. Driver, and A. Plummer. Edinburgh: T. & T. Clark, 1916. **Ross, A.** *The Epistles of James and John.* NICNT. Grand Rapids: Eerdmans, 1954. **Ruckstuhl, E.** *Jakobusbrief, 1.-3. Johannesbrief.* Neue Echter Bibel. Würzburg: Echter Verlag, 1985. **Scaer, D. P.** *James, the Apostle of Faith: A Primary Christological Document for the Persecuted Church.* St. Louis: Concordia, 1983. **Schlatter, A.** *Der Brief des Jakobus.* Stuttgart: Calwer, 1956. **Schrage, W.,** and **Balz, H.** *Die katholischen Briefe.* NTD 10. Göttingen: Vandenhoeck und Ruprecht, 1973. **Sidebottom, E. M.** *James, Jude, and 2 Peter.* NCB. London: Nelson, 1967. **Spitta, F.** *Der Brief des Jakobus untersucht.* Göttingen: Vandenhoeck und Ruprecht (in *Zur Geschichte und Litteratur des Urchristentums*, 2:1–239), 1896. **Stevenson, H. F.** *James Speaks for Today.* London: Marshall, Morgan & Scott, 1966. **Tasker, R. V. G.** *The General*

Epistle of James. TNTC. Grand Rapids: Eerdmans; London: Tyndale Press, 1957. **Vouga, F.** *L'épître de s. Jacques.* CNT. Vol. 13a. Geneva: Labor et Fides, 1984. **Wessel, W. W.** "James, Epistle of." *ISBE* (1982) 2:959–66. **Williams, R. R.** *The Letters of John and James.* The Cambridge Bible Commentary. Cambridge: Cambridge UP, 1965. **Windisch, H.** *Die katholischen Briefe.* Ed. H. Preisker. HNT 15. Tübingen: Mohr, 1951.

Introduction

1. JAMES IN THE NEW TESTAMENT

Blinzler, J. *Die Brüder und Schwestern Jesu.* SBS 21. Stuttgart: Katholisches Bibelwerk, 1967. **Brown, R. E., Donfried, K. P., Fitzmyer, J. A.,** and **Reumann, J.** *Mary in the New Testament.* Philadelphia: Fortress; New York: Paulist Press, 1978. **Bruce, F. F.** *Peter, Stephen, James, and John: Studies in Early Non-Pauline Christianity.* Grand Rapids: Eerdmans, 1979 (British title: *Men and Movements in the Primitive Church.* Exeter: Paternoster, 1980). **Crossan, J. D.** "Mark and the Relatives of Jesus." *NovT* 15 (1973) 81–113. **Gunther, J. J.** "The Family of Jesus." *EvQ* 46 (1974) 25–41. **Günther, W.** "Brother." *NIDNTT* 1:254–58. **Lambrecht, J.** "The Relatives of Jesus in Mark." *NovT* 16 (1974) 241–58. **Lightfoot, J. B.** "The Brethren of the Lord." In *St. Paul's Epistle to the Galatians.* 20th ed. London: Macmillan, 1896. 252–91. **McHugh, J.** *The Mother of Jesus in the New Testament.* London: Darton, Longman & Todd, 1975. 200–254. **Meyer, A.,** and **Bauer, W.** "The Relatives of Jesus." In *New Testament Apocrypha,* ed. E. Hennecke and W. Schneemelcher, tr. R. McL. Wilson et al. London: Lutterworth, 1963. 1:418–32. **Patrick, W.** *James the Lord's Brother.* Edinburgh: T. & T. Clark, 1906. **Schmithals, W.** *Paul and James.* SBT 46. Tr. D. M. Barton. London: SCM, 1965. **Scott, J. J.** "James the Relative of Jesus and the Expectation of an Eschatological High Priest." *JETS* 25 (1982) 323–31. **Ward, R. B.** "James of Jerusalem." *RestQ* 16 (1973) 174–90.

A. INTRODUCTION

No fewer than six or seven persons known to the New Testament writers carry the name of James. In Mark 3:16–19 two members of the apostolic band whom Jesus called were known as James: the son of Zebedee and brother of John, and James the son of Alphaeus. Among the persons associated with the Gospel story there was "James the younger" (ὁ μικρός) in Mark 15:40, whose mother named Mary evidently reappears in Mark 16:1 as "mother of James" (= Matt 27:56; Luke 24:10). Other characters also surnamed Ἰάκωβος are not so well known: there is James the father of Judas (Luke 6:16; Acts 1:13), possibly otherwise identified with Thaddaeus or Lebbaeus, to distinguish him from Judas Iscariot (Mark 3:18; Matt 10:3), and there is James the brother of Judas (= Jude) by whom the letter of Jude claims to have been written (v 1).

Outside this circle there is James the brother of Jesus, who may or may not be the same as the author of the letter known as *James* (1:1).

For our purposes attention may be directed to three persons in the above list.

(1) About *James son of Alphaeus* all that is known for certain is his place in the lists of the Twelve (Matt 10:3; Mark 3:18; Luke 6:15; Acts 1:13), where he is named as "one of the Twelve." If he is the same person as "James the little one" referred to in Mark 15:40 and other texts along with Mary his

mother, it seems that Joses was his brother's name (Mark 15:47). This link uniting James and Joses encouraged Jerome to suggest that the Mary in question is the one referred to in Mark 6:3, thereby coalescing in one person no fewer than the three Jameses identified as "the small one," "the son of Alphaeus," and "the Lord's brother." He made Mary's children (James, Joses, Judas, Simon, some sisters) cousins of Jesus by a different mother, also called Mary. The two women were each called Mary, and one of them had as her husband Alphaeus, also known as Clopas (in John 19:25). These identifications have remained fairly standard in the Catholic tradition, but are to be questioned (see Ropes, 59–62). We must remain content with the little we do know about "son of Alphaeus."

(2) *James the son of Zebedee* (and evidently of Salome, Matt 20:20; based on Mark 15:40 = Matt 27:56) is a more prominent figure in the Gospel tradition. His family connections (Mark 1:19–20) and the role he played in Jesus' ministry (Mark 5:37; 9:2; 13:3; 14:32–33) suggest a person of some importance. The stories in Luke 9:28, 54–56; Mark 10:35–41 involve James as coupled with his brother John, and are illustrative of the designation Boanerges (mentioned in Mark 3:17 and interpreted there as "sons of thunder"). His early martyrdom, according to Acts 12:2, virtually excludes him from consideration when the question of his continuing role in early Christianity is asked. There is no reason to link him with the letter written by "James."

(3) We are left with *James "the Lord's brother"* as a final candidate, though it is possible that the James of 1:1 in the letter may be an unknown, either with or without ties to connect him with James of the holy family.

The hoary debate over the precise relationship of this James to Jesus need not be rehearsed here (see for full coverage McHugh, *The Mother of Jesus,* chaps. 6–9; Blinzler, *Die Brüder,* 55–63, 119–29), for there is no fresh evidence to report, though the documents in the Nag Hammadi library named after James throw some indirect light on the matter (see later, pp. xliii, xlvi, lx–lxi). The view associated with Epiphanius (A.D. 315–403) that the brothers including James were sons of Joseph by a former marriage and all older than Jesus has been accepted as the Eastern tradition in Greek Orthodox circles; it is stated and defended by Lightfoot, "The Brethren," 258–59. The evidence is mainly based on John 19:27, where Mary, Jesus' mother, is entrusted to "John," not to Joseph's sons, who were opposed to Jesus throughout his ministry (Mark 3:21, 31–34; John 7:2–9). But such data also show a connection between Mary and the brothers and sisters during the ministry; and there is a naturalness about Paul's allusion to the "Lord's brothers" (1 Cor 9:5) which suggests no such indirect or foster relationship.

Jerome's attempt to establish a relationship between Jesus, son of Mary, and "the brothers" as children of Clopas and Mary, sister of the mother of Jesus, runs into a lot of problems, e.g., in equating Clopas with Alphaeus and the absence of any term for "cousin" (ἀνεψιός). Jerome was seeking to refute Helvidius (fourth century) who maintained that the brothers of the Lord were sons of Joseph and Mary, all born subsequent to the birth of Jesus. Mayor (chap. 1) has said all that needs to be remarked in defense of this Helvidian position on the strength of the plain sense of Matt 1:24–25; Luke 2:7 (πρωτότοκος, "firstborn" as opposed to μονογενής, "sole child" in

Luke 7:12; 8:42); and Mark 6:3 (though McHugh, *Mother*, 246, proposes that "brother" here means "foster-brother," not necessarily blood-brother; it can denote, he remarks, a first cousin known as a brother. The argument is impressive but fails to convince, since dogmatic considerations seem to have entered into McHugh's reckoning, 20–22, 254. The evidence of Mark 15:40; Luke 24:10 which McHugh [205] invokes does not seem so germane because it is uncertain, as the discussion in Brown, *Mary*, 68–72, shows). Church fathers such as Tertullian and Origen add important evidence (Ropes, 54; but see McHugh, *Mother*, 205–7, 217, 448–50). It is justifiable, then, to continue to speak of "James the Lord's brother," as Paul does (Gal 1:19), though later tradition knows him also as "James the Just," and in gnostic circles as "James the Revealer."

B. James the Lord's Brother

Bibliography

Aune, D. E. *Prophecy in Early Christianity and the Ancient Mediterranean World.* Grand Rapids: Eerdmans, 1983. **Bagatti, B.** *The Church from the Circumcision.* Tr. E. Hoade. Jerusalem: Franciscan Press, 1971. **Baur, F. C.** *Paul, The Apostle of Jesus Christ: His Life and Works, His Epistles and His Doctrine.* Tr. E. Zeller. 2 vols. 2d ed. London/Edinburgh: Williams & Norgate, 1876. **Boring, M. E.** *Sayings of the Risen Jesus.* SNTSMS 46. Cambridge: Cambridge UP, 1982. **Brown, R. E.** and **Meier, J. P.** *Antioch and Rome: New Testament Cradles of Catholic Christianity.* New York: Paulist Press, 1983. **Brown, R. E. et al.** *Mary in the New Testament.* Philadelphia: Fortress; New York: Paulist Press, 1978. **Dunn, J. D. G.** "The Incident at Antioch." *JSNT* 18 (1982) 3–57. ———. *Unity and Diversity in the New Testament.* Philadelphia: Westminster, 1977. **Elliott-Binns, L. E.** *Galilean Christianity.* SBT 16. London: SCM, 1956. **Ellis, E. E.** "Traditions in 1 Corinthians." *NTS* 32 (1986) 481–502. **Haenchen, E.** *The Acts of the Apostles.* Tr. B. Noble and G. Shinn. Ed. R. McL. Wilson. Philadelphia: Westminster, 1970. **Hengel, M.** "Between Jesus and Paul." In *Between Jesus and Paul.* Tr. J. Bowden. London: SCM, 1983. 1–29. ———. *Acts and the History of Early Christianity.* Tr. J. Bowden. London: SCM, 1979. **Jeremias, J.** *Jesus' Promise to the Nations.* SBT 24. Tr. S. H. Hooke. London: SCM Press, 1958. **Kearney, P.** "'He Appeared to 500 Brothers' (1 Cor xv,6)." *NovT* 22 (1980) 264–84. **Lang, Fr.** *Die Briefe an die Korinther.* NTD. Göttingen: Vandenhoeck und Ruprecht, 1986. **Lührmann, D.** *Die Redaktion der Logienquelle.* WMANT 33. Neukirchen-Vluyn: Neukirchener Verlag, 1969. **Martin, R. P.** "The Setting of 2 Corinthians." *TynB* 37 (1986) 3–19. ———. "The Opponents of Paul in 2 Corinthians." In *Tradition and Interpretation in the New Testament,* FS E. Earle Ellis, ed. G. F. Hawthorne and O. Betz. Grand Rapids: Eerdmans, 1987. 279–89. **Murphy-O'Connor, J.** "Tradition and Redaction in 1 Cor 15:3–7." *CBQ* 43 (1981) 582–89. **Schmithals, W.** *The Office of an Apostle.* Tr. J. E. Steely. Nashville: Abingdon, 1969. **Theissen, G.** *Sociology of Early Palestinian Christianity.* Tr. J. Bowden. Philadelphia: Fortress, 1978. **Trocmé, E.** *The Formation of the Gospel according to Mark.* Tr. P. Gaughan. Philadelphia: Westminster Press, 1975.

It is convenient to group the material to do with James under several headings, corresponding to the type of literature in which the data are set.

(a) *Pre-Pauline Traditions.* Two sections of 1 Corinthians contain data concerning James. In 15:7 Paul mentions James as one of those who saw the risen Lord, in a section that carries all the marks of a traditional formulation on which Paul draws (see Ellis, "Traditions"). There is some uncertainty over the issue of whether Paul himself composed the remark about James to balance and offset the confessional inclusion about Peter (Cephas) and the Twelve (so P. Kearney, "'He Appeared to 500 Brothers' (1 Cor. xv,6)," 264–84) or drew directly from a preformed tradition that already included the reference to James (so J. Murphy-O'Connor, "Tradition and Redaction in 1 Cor 15:3–7," 582–89). The latter's argument, based on stylistic criteria, leads to the more likely conclusion that it seems more probable that *Iakōbō eita tois apostolois*, "[he appeared] to James and then to the apostles," came to Paul as a fixed formula. The origin of the formulation is also much canvassed, with options that it arose in an Aramaic-speaking community in Jerusalem or that, in view of some Jewish-hellenistic linguistic features, it stemmed from a bilingual setting in Antioch. There is some substance in the argument that James is more usually attached to Jerusalem in the tradition of Acts and Paul than to Antioch. But a recent proposal, which has some bearing on the locale of the Letter of James, wishes to trace the resurrection-appearances formula to those Jewish Christians of Stephen's school who migrated from Jerusalem to Antioch and presumably brought the tradition with them (M. Hengel, "Between Jesus and Paul," 4–12, where he links some of the Hellenists to the "five hundred brothers" of the Pauline text; see too J. P. Meier's discussion in Brown and Meier, *Antioch and Rome*, 32–36).

From this datum it may be deduced that James is known to have had standing among early Christians both in the holy city and in Antioch, even though he is not identified with the Twelve and his rank as an apostle is not clear.

In 1 Cor 9 Paul has two comments on the early Jewish Christian mission: in v 14 the introductory phrase "the Lord has commanded" leads on to a logion of Jesus (Matt 10:10 = Luke 10:7, Q) regarding the support of "missionaries." In this context, while Paul applies the saying to the apostolic ministry at Corinth, its primary reference has been taken to be to early Jewish Christian emissaries who derived their claim to congregational support from such an authorization (see G. Theissen, *Sociology of Early Palestinian Christianity*, 8–16, who calls them "wandering charismatics"; for a classification of these prophets see Aune, *Prophecy*, 213–17). These men are conceivably linked with Paul's opponents in 2 Cor 10–13 (Martin, "Setting"); and on another view (cf. Martin, "Opponents"), they are to be identified as the certain men who came "from James" (Gal 2:12) to Antioch, where, as we shall see, James' influence was a factor strong enough to carry weight and to affect the conduct of Cephas and through him Barnabas and others (Gal 2:13).

At 1 Cor 9:5 there is a less problematic allusion to "the Lord's brothers," among whom James is certainly to be numbered. Paul is speaking of the maintenance to be claimed by those who engage in mission and who take along their wives. Here again there is evidence that James was known presumably at Corinth to have sponsored missionary activity, though there is no way of telling how far that missionary travel took him. Perhaps he went no further than Antioch. But it seems clear that Paul is appealing to some attested traditions, and so drawing on a report of missionary service involving "the Lord's brother."

(b) *The Early Jewish Mission.* The text in 1 Cor 9:14 speaking of the preroga-
tives of an apostle probably is our first recorded evidence of the existence
of a Jewish Christian mission. Other sources of information may be inferen-
tially appealed to, stemming from Matt 10:6; 15:24, which restrict the mission
to Jews (see Jeremias, *Jesus' Promise to the Nations,* 19–39; Brown, in Brown
and Meier, *Antioch and Rome,* 53–54). It is less certain that we can trace behind
Mark's accounts of the call (1:16–20; 2:13–14) and mission charge (6:7–13)
the program for Jewish Christian missionaries, as E. Trocmé (*The Formation
of the Gospel according to Mark*; on this see R. P. Martin, "The Theology of
Mark's Gospel," *SWJT* 21 [1978] 23–36, esp. 29–32) has attempted to do.
The strongest piece of evidence in Mark is in 10:28–31 with its teaching on
denying family ties and the corresponding rewards for such heroisms. Care
of traveling missionaries was certainly a theme in Mark's church, and while
he may have included an encouragement to those workers who forsook family
and home, it is clear that the mother and brothers of Jesus stayed together
after Pentecost (Acts 1:14; cf. John 19:25–27) and did not take this mission
call to apply to themselves.

The Q-mission of Matt 10 = Luke 10 reflects, we may surmise, the interests
of the early community that assembled the Jesus-traditions found in the two
Gospels. Although some scholars (e.g., D. Lührmann) posit a hellenistic provenance of Q, most are persuaded that this teaching reflects a community of
Palestinian and Jewish Christians (see Martin, "Q," in *ISBE* 4:1–4, for an
overview of recent discussion on Q as a common source behind Matthew
and Luke). Three features in Q's teaching on mission mark advances on the
pre-Markan portrayal outlined above (see M. E. Boring, *Sayings of the Risen
Jesus,* 147–49). Let us review first the emphases of Q. (1) The sayings concen-
trate on the suffering and persecution that are the lot of "prophets and
teachers"; (2) miracle-working by prophets in Q shows how they act as God's
agents of his kingdom and mission; and (3) prophetic oracles appealed to
the Old Testament to highlight the eschatological hour in which the Q-
community lived and by which it interpreted charismatically its existence. On
these bases the Q command of confession and witness shows a heightened
sense of the cost to the disciples, even involving death (Luke 12:2–9 = Matt
10:26–33); and this threat takes the teaching a step beyond pre-Markan evidence. Then, for Q its mission preachers may have had a settled base, which
Boring connects with Antioch (cf. Acts 13:1–3). A third difference is seen in
the greater urgency for the mission in Q, betraying an intensified eschatological consciousness (see Luke 10:2 = Matt 9:37–38, in contrast to Mark 6:8–
12). It is an interesting suggestion (made by Webber, "ΙΑΚΩΒΟΣ," 105–6)
that these three themes in Q (persecution and even martyrdom; prophets
and teachers in a settled ministry; eschatological urgency) may have points
of contact with the letter of James, and correspond to the way James was
perceived in some Jewish Christian communities as a suffering, righteous
prophetic figure. Early Palestinian communities evidently cherished stories
about the holy family (Mark 6:3) and remembered that the mother of Jesus
and his brothers were involved in certain episodes (e.g., Mark 3:21, 31–35;
John 2:1–10; 7:3–9). Some of these recalled stories are set in Galilee; unfortunately, our knowledge relating to a Jewish Christian presence there is limited

(cf. L. E. Elliott-Binns, *Galilean Christianity*; B. Bagatti, *The Church from the Circumcision*, 19–24, 122–32, who discusses the archeological evidence of a Christian presence in Galilee from the fourth century). Indirectly the witness of Matt 11:23 = Luke 10:15 (Q) may signify resistance to the Jewish Christian mission in Capernaum. The holy family's presence and influence, especially that of James, is more positively attested from Acts 1:14; 15:13; 21:18–20 and Paul (Gal 1:18–19; 2:9), to which we now turn.

(c) *Paul's Attitudes.* In Gal 1:15–2:12 Paul adverts to the role of James in such a way as to suggest his growing awareness of the latter's importance. At Gal 1:19 it seems that the contact between Paul and James was more or less casual, or at least informal. "I saw none of the other apostles—only James, the Lord's brother" (NIV). Evidently Paul's chief interest in his visit to Jerusalem at this time was to make contact with Peter (Gal 1:18) with whom he stayed for a fortnight. His time with James meant only that he spoke with him—and nothing more (W. Michaelis, *TDNT* 5:341 n.138). At Gal 2:7–9 the roles are reversed and it is the pillar-apostles (οἱ στῦλοι), including James, who observe the validity of Paul's gentile ministry. There is a note of cordiality, moreover, in v 9, suggesting that James concurred with the arrangement for Paul's mission to be approved.

At Corinth, however, there were groups that formed themselves in opposition to Paul's ministry (1 Cor 1:10–12; 3:3–4:21). No "party of James" is mentioned, it is true. But the allusions to James in 1 Cor 9:5 (and possibly in 9:14, as we saw) as well as in 15:7, which records a resurrection appearance to James, may indicate the need, on Paul's part, to react defensively to those who championed the claims of the recognized leader of the Jerusalem church. If we knew more about the opponents in 2 Corinthians (especially in the "polemical letter," chaps. 10–13), we might be in a stronger position to link these intruders on the Corinthian scene with a pro-James faction in early Christianity. As it is, the veiled allusions to a rival mission at Corinth, at odds with the Pauline founding ministry (in 10:12–18; 11:4–5, 13–15), suggest a Palestinian-Judaic origin of these preachers—but they are not precisely the "Judaizers" of Galatians and Philippians since the debate over circumcision and the issue of Torah-righteousness are not urgent in 2 Corinthians. One suggestion is that these persons came from a locale in the Dispersion (Antioch is favored by the latest commentator on the Corinthian epistles, Fr. Lang, *Die Briefe*, 357–59) where Peter's authority was dominant and was being claimed by these emissaries. On the other hand, the one piece of evidence that does trace opposition to Paul and his gospel to Antioch—in Gal 2:11–14—attributes such opposition to "certain men from James" who arrived in Antioch in Syria from the mother church, determined to undermine Paul's stand on a universal gospel without ceremonial requirements.

The reasons for their motivation have been variously assessed, but it seems clear that Paul's mission, once—at least tacitly—accepted by Jewish Christians, was giving cause for concern in those areas outside of Jerusalem where his work was beginning to show fruit. Hence some emissaries "from James"— with or without James' actual encouragement, since ἀπὸ Ἰακώβου is slightly ambiguous—reached Antioch to exert pressure on Peter and Barnabas, and were in a measure successful (Gal 2:13). As Paul moved away from this base in Antioch, having suffered a defeat there (see J. D. G. Dunn, "The Incident," 3–57) and established himself at Corinth as a power base, so his opponents dogged his steps to that place and were accorded a ready hospitality at Corinth (see 2 Cor 11:4, 16–21). Whether James or Peter actually condoned this rival mission, we cannot say. But all the inferential evidence points to Antioch as the seat of the anti-Pauline missionaries; and the way in which they were able to move out into Paul's mission territories suggests further that they represented a powerful countermovement to Paul's gospel. Otherwise it becomes difficult to explain the serious tones of the apocalyptic-dualistic language of God versus Satan he resorts to in 2 Cor 11:13–15. And the measure of Paul's passionate defense of his apostolic office in that letter tends to endorse the hypothesis that the names of leading apostolic figures were being claimed as legitimating sanction for this rival mission, especially as at the heart of 2 Corinthians is Paul's deep concern not to lose Corinth as a base from which he can carry the collection to Jerusalem and thence travel forward to Rome (see Martin, "Setting of 2 Cor"; "Opponents").

Underlying much of this dark period of apostolic history when our sources of information and the reasons for actions and reactions are less than clear is the growing suspicion on the part of the Jerusalem church about Paul's ministry. For his part, Paul severed connections with a notable representative of Judean Christianity, Barnabas (Acts 15:39–40, where Luke seeks to varnish over the incident by introducing the case of John Mark and appealing to personal matters as justification for Paul's harsh decision made on pragmatic grounds). Paul's gentile mission now gets a fresh lease on life in company with gentile-oriented leaders such as Silas (Acts 15:22, 32: see Hengel, *Acts and the History,* 122–23), and Paul's later colleagues include only a few Jewish Christians (Col 4:11). Yet Paul never willingly abandoned his concern for the mother church. The important place given in the texts to the Jerusalem collection (1 Cor 16:1; 2 Cor 8–9; Rom 15:25–27) shows that he was loath to sever relations with Jerusalem completely. Indeed, the visit to Jerusalem to present the money gifts paradoxically both offered Paul the most telling way to demonstrate his love for his Jewish compatriots in their material need and became the signal occasion on which his ministry was decisively rejected by James and the Jerusalem leadership. The data are in Rom 15:30–31; Acts 21:17–26; 24:17 (Dunn, *Unity and Diversity,* 255–57); and (it has been suggested by Webber, 117–19) 2 Tim 4:16–18.

The first reference (in Rom 15:31) hints that Paul was expecting trouble in Jerusalem from unbelievers in Judea, and expresses the hope that his "service" (i.e., the collection) may be acceptable to the saints there. One does not normally anticipate giving aid to those in need in such a cautionary way, and it suggests that Paul contemplated with some realism the eventuality that the Jerusalem church and people would turn against him. The record in Acts 21 displays a disturbing coolness to Paul on his arrival, and James' speech with its rehearsal of rumor and innuendo that Paul was anti-Jewish and opposed to Torah obedience, coupled with a program to allay these suspicions, only confirms what an earlier statement (Acts 15:22) had suggested—that, in Luke's presentation of the Jewish church, there was mounting hostility. In any event it turned out that way. For when Paul fell into Roman hands, ostensibly for protective custody, and later his life was threatened by Jewish extremists (Acts 23:12–22), there is no record that the Jerusalem church came to the aid of Paul—even though his presence in Jerusalem was precisely intended to bring them needed help and to pledge gentile Christian devotion (2 Cor 9:12–15).

If 2 Tim 4:16–18 is conceivably to be related to this period in Paul's lifetime and the "defense" (ἀπολογία) of 2 Tim 4:16 is the same as that of Acts 22:1, it would be one additional reason to conclude that Paul was left in the lurch, with James' inaction a telltale indication that relations between the apostle to the Gentiles and the *paterfamilias* of the Judaic congregation were severely strained. But this datum from the Pastoral epistles is not too compelling; there is no certainty as to the life-setting of 2 Tim 4:16–18. The strongest point in favor of this reconstruction is the common occurrence of the term ἀπολογία here and in Acts 22:1; 25:16 where the word is found and not elsewhere in Acts.

To sum up, Paul's relations with James underwent a marked change, according to his own developing understanding of his mission and how it was accepted in the eyes of Jewish Christian groups. He recognized James as a leader who was prominent in the mother church. He appealed to James' authority as a witness of the resurrection, and claimed himself to be a member of that company. He was reluctant to state plainly that James was, in Paul's own estimation, an apostle—according to what is perhaps the best conclusion we can reach on the ambiguous wording of 1 Cor 15:7. As regards Gal 1:19, we may quote the considered judgment of W. Schmithals (*The Office,* 65):

> We can only conclude that this lack of clarity was intentional with Paul . . . [he] says: Besides Peter, I saw none other of the apostles, except James. εἰ μή, then, is to be translated in the usual sense: "if not" or "except." Paul limits the assertion that he has seen no apostle besides Peter by leaving room for the possibility that one could, if need be, count James among the apostles—something he was not himself accustomed to doing—whom he had also seen.

This statement acknowledges the studied ambiguity of Paul's text, and perhaps marks a growing distance between Paul and the Jerusalem leadership which James increasingly dominated ever since Peter's departure for "another place" (Acts 12:17). The role of Paul at the so-called Apostolic Council (Acts 15) is problematic, with subsequent events regarding the decree suggesting either that he was not present when the formulation of Acts 15:19–20 was drawn up or that he looked on the promulgation in the gentile churches with a certain coolness and disfavor. Thus he never appealed to it at Corinth. In support of the first alternative it may be noted that the transmission of the Council's findings is left to "leading men among the brothers" (Acts 15:22, 30–33) and Paul was evidently passed over. This turn of events may explain how it came about that in Acts 21:18–25 James announced the decree as "something new and apparently unknown to him" (Hengel, *Acts,* 117).

Paul's separation from Antioch as a mission base drove him further from the Jerusalem community, whose attitude may well be reflected in the hostile intentions of the Jewish Christian missionaries whom Paul denounced in 2 Cor 11:4, 13–15. Yet he was evidently determined to repair the breach with the Jerusalem saints by raising and taking the collection, though he was markedly unsure whether it would be accepted. James received him with some suspicion and aloofness—two features which tempered his visit to James' court (Acts 21:18). In the event such suspicions (as we observed) were only too well confirmed by the failure of the Jerusalem church to come to his side when he was arrested and his life threatened. The distance between the two leaders is evident from the fact that there is no certain proof that the gift Paul brought was actually accepted by the Jerusalem leaders (Dunn, *Unity and Diversity,* 257, based on Rom 15:30–31) or was only received after Paul had proved his sympathy with those leaders (Bruce, *Peter, Stephen, James, and John,* 105–8). The encounter between James and Paul and the subsequent acceptance by Paul of support of four Nazirites has several unresolved difficulties, even if we concur with Schmithals (*Paul and James,* 91) in his conclusion that Luke is working with a reliable source:

> We could then see the connexion between the contributions collected for the Jerusalem poor and the financial help to the poor Nazirites and could let this connexion supply the reason for Paul's being required to show proof in this manner that he on no account forbade Jews to keep the Law.

Yet James' position as titular head of the Jerusalem community needs to be borne in mind. Tensions in Palestine at the time of Paul's collection visit were such that a leader like James would be caught in a delicate position. Acts 21:38 is not the only piece of evidence for the threat to Roman law and order posed by various "terrorist" groups (Josephus, *Ant.* 20.164–66) in the name of Jewish nationalism. We may postulate that James sought to act as a mediating influence, and it would be wrong to see James and Paul as engaged in bitter antagonism to each other, as the early Tübingen school of F. C. Baur (see his *Paul, The Apostle of Jesus Christ* 1:113–16) concluded. We have noted the constraints of Paul to repair the breach by practical demonstrations of concern and aid, based on his theological position that never disowned Israel (Rom 9–11; 1 Cor 9:20; 2 Cor 11:22) and championed the cause of the one people of God (Gal 3:28; 1 Cor 12:13; cf. Eph 2:11–22) and which was displayed in the collection (2 Cor 8:20; 9:12–15). On James' part we may credit him (if the record of Acts 21:18–26 is to be taken at face value: cf. Haenchen, *Acts,* 608) with a desire to maintain peace and harmony within Jewish factions by appealing to ancestral beliefs and customs, and by an endeavor to effect a *modus vivendi* at a time of strained relationships within the Jewish community itself. Whether the epistle that bears his name reflects this situation is a question to be addressed shortly.

(d) *Summing Up.* From the evidence within the traditions of the New Testament documents it may be safely concluded that James was a well-known person in early Christian circles, "a very considerable figure in the tradition of early Christianity" (Laws, 42), perhaps larger than the modern Bible reader gives credit for. He is known, in the earliest strata of evidence, as a witness to the risen Lord, and possibly as one involved in mission in company with his family. In the traditions that lie behind our canonical Gospels he is named first as one of the siblings of the Lord. Although not a believer in the days of Jesus' earthly ministry, he became a part of the infant community, presumably after seeing his brother as the risen Lord. In that context Paul cites his example as a witness to the resurrection.

Paul also acknowledges his place at the head of the Jerusalem church, though he does not clearly classify him with the Twelve as apostles—a role he claims for himself. Yet James' standing is sufficiently secure in Paul's opinion for him to be ranked as first among the "pillars" (Gal 2:9). James' role became more apparent when Peter left the scene in Jerusalem, and the extent of his influence is illustrated by his contribution as chief figure at the Apostolic Conference (Acts 15:19). His position is described in Acts 21:18 where he is surrounded by a collegium of Jewish Christian elders and is able to prescribe a course of action for Paul to take (Acts 21:23: "Do therefore what we tell you"). More ominously still, James in some way is indirectly if not explicitly behind a delegation that arrived in Antioch (Gal 2:12) to challenge Peter, to influence Barnabas, to gain a following among Jewish Christians, and to evoke the vigorous response of Paul that their pressure on Peter led to a betrayal of the gospel he proclaimed (Gal 2:14).

This negative attitude to James and his party recalls that some sectors of early Christianity developed an antipathy to James. At one extreme there is the Gospel of Mark, which most likely places the family of Jesus in a poor light (3:21, 31–35; 6:1–6; 15:40, 47; 16:1: these pericopes are examined by Crossan, "Mark and the Relatives of Jesus," to show how there was, in Mark's community, a polemic against the Jerusalem mother-church based on hostility between Jesus and his relatives. Lambrecht's rejoinder, "The Relatives," is less than convincing) because Mark's Jewish Christian opponents appealed to them for support in their claims for maintenance by the congregations— a tradition that may lie behind the anti-Pauline missionaries of 2 Cor 10–13 (cf. 1 Cor 9:5). By contrast, the Matthean picture of the holy family is decidedly ambivalent, by tempering the strictures in Mark (e.g., Matthew in 13:57 omits the reference to the family's rejection in Mark 6:4) and showing a decidedly favorable attitude to Jerusalem (Matt 5:35) and the Davidic origins of Jesus (Matt 1–2). Not least the prominent place given to Mary, always referred to in Matthew's birth-infancy narratives as "his mother" (1:18; 2:11, 13–14, 20–21) and the favorable attitudes given in the redaction of Matt 12:46–50 indicate a moderating of Mark's negative tone (6:1–6) in the interests of Matthew's theological and ecclesiological position regarding the Jewish Christian community at Jerusalem and its later influence at Antioch.

With Luke-Acts we see how the full stature of James in early Christianity was presented and supported. The writer openly associates the family of Jesus with potential discipleship. This is clear by contrasting Mark 3:31–36 and Luke 8:19–21. Here Luke has inserted four changes in the tradition: (a) Instead of demanding an audience with Jesus (Mark 3:21, which supplies the motive in mentioning an attempt to restrain his madness) the family simply wishes to see him, as in the case of Zaccheus (19:3). (b) The Markan adverb ἔξω, [those] "outside" (3:31), which carries the theological weight of "unbelieving" (4:11), is omitted by Luke, who changes the phrase to τοῖς λοιποῖς, "to others," in 8:10. (c) In Mark the people who receive Jesus' words are those seated around him who are identified with "the crowd" (3:32) and differentiated from the family of Jesus (v 31). In Luke Jesus' message to those who hear and do the word is directed vaguely to "them" (v 21), which could conceivably include the family, especially his mother, who is described as possessing this obedience in Luke 1:38; 2:19, 51. Mark's ἴδε ("here," RSV) is elided in Luke's version, which apparently joins the family and the crowd together and points to what constitutes the true relationship; but the family are not excluded as they are in Mark 3:33–34. (d) The placement of the crowd in Luke takes the reader back to 8:4, where the crowd receive the parable of the word and are encouraged, in the interpretation which the disciples are given, to be like "the good soil" that receives the word, "hearing [it], hold it fast in an honest and good heart, and bring forth fruit with endurance" (8:15). The inference is that Jesus' family—both spiritual and natural—are in Luke's sights here; and the Nazareth family are "examples of the seed that has fallen on good soil" (R. E. Brown, *Mary*, 170), to be brought to fruition in the scene after the resurrection in Acts 1:14, and after Pentecost.

From the data in the third Gospel and the scattered references in Acts (1:14; 12:17; 15:13; 21:18) it is possible to deduce that, for Luke, James stood in a privileged position. Luke never links James directly with the holy family as a brother of Jesus, but there is a warmth and a potential for discipleship in the family lacking in Mark. When he is named, James is seen as the central figure in Jerusalem Christianity, though Luke does not stop to explain how he rose to this prominence. We can only speculate that, unlike the traditions in the Johannine community which portray the holy family as uncomprehending or unbelieving (John 2:1–12; 7:1–10, though Mary is held in some esteem, 19:26–27), Lukan interests worked in a harmonistic, irenical fashion to picture James as a commanding and reputable leader, a true member of Jesus' family of faith, and a sign of that coexistence between Jewish and gentile Christianity that Luke strove to achieve (Dunn, *Unity and Diversity*, 356).

From Paul's perspective, however, this idyllic picture is not so secure. In James' defense we have observed the pressure that mounted in days of nationalist unrest, and we may sympathize with (if not excuse) his noncommittal attitude to Paul, whose relations with him deteriorated at the last.

2. JAMES IN JEWISH CHRISTIANITY

Bibliography

Barrett, C. K. "Paul's Opponents in II Corinthians." *NTS* 17 (1970–71) 233–54 (= *Essays on Paul*. London: SPCK, 1982. Chap. 4). **Bauer, W.** *Orthodoxy and Heresy in Earliest Christianity*. Tr. and ed. R. A. Kraft and G. Krodel. London: SCM, 1971. **Baur, F. C.** *Paul, the Apostle of Jesus Christ. His Life and Works, His Epistles and His Doctrine.* Tr. E. Zeller. 2d ed. 2 vols. London/Edinburgh: Williams & Norgate, 1876. **Brandon, S. G. F.** *The Fall of Jerusalem and the Christian Church*. London: SPCK, 1951. **Braun, H.** *Qumran und das Neue Testament*. 2 vols. Tübingen: Mohr, 1966. **Brown, Kent S.** "James: A Religio-Historical Study of the Relations between Jewish, Gnostic, and Catholic Christianity in the Early Period." Ph.D. diss., Brown University, 1972. **Bruce, F. F.** *New Testament History*. London: Nelson, 1969. **Cullmann, O.** *Le problème* *littéraire et historique du Roman Pseudo-Clémentin.* Paris: Librarie Félix Alcan, 1930. **Dan-iélou, J.** *The Theology of Jewish Christianity.* Tr. and ed. J. A. Baker. London: Darton, Longman & Todd, 1964. **Gärtner, B.** *The Theology of the Gospel of Thomas.* Tr. E. J. Sharpe. London: Collins, 1961. **Goppelt, L.** *Jesus, Paul, and Judaism.* Tr. E. Schroeder. New York: Nelson, 1964. **Hengel, M.** *Judaism and Hellenism.* Tr. J. Bowden. 2 vols. London: SCM, 1983. **Hennecke, E.,** and **Schneemelcher, W.,** eds. *New Testament Apoc-rypha.* Ed. R. McL. Wilson. 2 vols. London: Lutterworth, 1963. **Hort, F. J. A.** *Judaistic Christianity.* London/New York: Macmillan, 1904. **Klijn, A. F. J.** "The Study of Jewish Christianity." *NTS* 20 (1973–74) 419–31. **Koester, H.** "Gnomai Diaphorai: The Origin and Nature of Diversification in the History of the Early Church." *HTR* 58 (1965) 279–318. **Lietzmann, H.** *A History of the Early Church.* Tr. B. Lee Wolf. Vol. 1. London: Lutterworth, 1949. **Longenecker, R. N.** *The Christology of Early Jewish Christianity.* SBT 2d ser./17. London: SCM, 1970. **Lüdemann, G.** "The Successors of pre-70 Jerusalem Christianity." In *Jewish and Christian Self-Definition,* ed. E. P. Sanders. Vol. 1. Philadel-phia: Fortress, 1980. 161–73. **Marshall, I. H.** "Palestinian and Hellenistic Christianity." *NTS* 19 (1972–73) 271–89. **Murray, R.** "Defining Judaeo-Christianity." *HeyJ* 15 (1974) 303–10. **Riegel, S. K.** "Jewish Christianity: Definitions and Terminology." *NTS* 24 (1977–78) 410–15. **Schoeps, H.-J.** "Jacobus Ὁ ΔΙΚΑΙΟΣ ΚΑΙ ΩΒΛΙΑΣ." *Bib* 24 (1943) 398–403. ———. *Theologie und Geschichte des Judenchristentums.* Tübingen: Mohr, 1949. **Strecker, G.** *Das Judenchristentum in dem Pseudoklementinen.* 2d ed. Berlin: Akademie-Verlag, 1981. ———. "On the Problem of Jewish Christianity." In *Orthodoxy,* by W. Bauer. 241–85. **Thiering, B. E.** "*Mebaqqer* and *Episkopos* in the Light of the Temple Scroll." *JBL* 100 (1981) 59–74. **Vielhauer, P.** "Jewish-Christian Gospels." In *New Testa-ment Apocrypha,* ed. E. Hennecke and W. Schneemelcher, tr. R. McL. Wilson et al. London: Lutterworth, 1963. 1:117–65.

The first issue here is to define what is meant by "Jewish Christianity," a theme of considerable debate in scientific scholarship. As in several other ways the starting point is the work and continuing influence of F. C. Baur. In 1830 he took as his basic criterion by which to delimit and define Jewish Christianity its essentially negative attitude to Paul. Beginning with the New Testament documents he linked the Jewish anti-Pauline party of 1–2 Corinthi-ans with a Petrine group (see Klijn, "The Study," 419–20) based on a clear antagonism to Paul in the Clementine literature (e.g., *Clem. Hom.* 17.13). In a trend picked up later by F. J. A. Hort (*Judaistic Christianity*) Baur offered an important assessment of what constituted Jewish Christianity, namely the principle that Jewish Christians are defined by their lack of difference from Judaism (Riegel, "Jewish Christianity," 411). Baur's appeal to the Clementine documents was resisted by H. Lietzmann (*History*, 1) but supported by later researchers, notably H. J. Schoeps, *Theologie*, and O. Cullmann, *Le problème littéraire et historique.* Both writers enlarged our understanding of later Jewish Christianity by showing how multiform and complex was the emerging pattern of the movement. The picture was made even more complicated by sugges-tions that the inclusion of Zealots (Brandon, *The Fall of Jerusalem*) and Essenes (Braun, *Qumran und das Neue Testament*) contributed a number of factors of a decisive influence felt on early Christian groups, while syncretistic and gnos-tic characteristics also gathered around such groups according to Goppelt (*Jesus, Paul, and Judaism*).

A full study of Jewish Christianity was made by J. Daniélou (*Theology,* 7–11), who proceeded to outline three criteria for designating Jewish Christianity: (1) a denial of Jesus' divine status as the unique Son of God; (2) a promoting of the original members of the Jerusalem church under the caliphate of James as the holy father (355–56); (3) influences drawn from apocalyptic culture (13). The third criterion is an elusive one, since many religious groups in the Syrian Levant and Near East lands in these centuries cherished visions of an apocalyptic nature. Geographical variations were stressed by W. Bauer (*Orthodoxy*), and the increasingly evident nature (thanks to recent discoveries) of the complexities inherent in the term "Jewish Christianity" was highlighted by Strecker's supplementary essay to Bauer's basic book ("On the Problem of Jewish Christianity," 241–85). Both Daniélou and Strecker concur in noting how Jewish Christianity both in Palestine and the Dispersion was subject to various influences; and the measure of cross-fertilization between the Jewish and Greek cultures makes a rigid separation of "Jewish characteristics" all the more problematical—a cautionary trend to be explored by Hengel's *Judaism and Hellenism* (cf. Marshall, "Palestinian and Hellenistic Christianity"). The most recent finds at Nag Hammadi have spurred scholars such as H. Koester ("Gnomai Diaphorai," 279–80) to call for a "re-evaluation of early Christian history" and for a dismissal of the term "Jewish Christian" as though it meant "heretical." With his dictum "everyone in the first generation of Christianity was a Jewish Christian"—only partly true, if the record of the canonical Acts of the Apostles is to be believed—we have reached a point where Baur's original thesis of a separation of Jewish and gentile into separate compartments is seen to be too neat, and a mutual antagonism between rival factions drawn along these lines is too improbable for belief.

More progress has recently been reported along newer lines of inquiry. We may isolate three. C. K. Barrett ("Paul's Opponents") centers attention on the Jewish emissaries who opposed Paul at Corinth, and remarks that "the kinds of Christianity they represent may be characterized by the ways in which their new faith led them to treat their original Jewish religion" (253 = *Essays*, 82). Riegel ("Jewish Christianity," 415) agrees and opts to apply the term "to Christians who were Jews and *expressed themselves* in the thought-forms of the Semitic world from which they came" (his emphasis). R. N. Longenecker (*Christology*, 1–3) has two categories of Jewish self-consciousness: Jewish beliefs including cultic observances and Christology, and images drawn from their ancestral faith. The chief quarry for this material is the New Testament itself, a point made by R. Murray, "Defining Judaeo-Christianity," 308. A. F. J. Klijn, "The Study," offers a third component, which consciously draws upon extracanonical sources (431):

> We are dealing with isolated phenomena and can, therefore, only speak of the Jewish Christianity of a particular writing or of a particular group of Christians. In these cases we mean that in a writing or a group we can detect ideas having a Jewish background and which were not accepted by the established Church.

With these submissions as to the identity and features of Jewish Christianity we turn to two documents where James is mentioned in the setting of that milieu.

A. THE GOSPEL ACCORDING TO THE HEBREWS

Only one fragment of the *Gospel according to the Hebrews,* an early second-century document, deals with James. The pericope runs:

> And when the Lord had given the linen cloth to the servant of the priest, he went to James and appeared to him. For James had sworn that he would not eat bread from that hour in which he had drunk of the cup of the Lord until he should see him risen from among those that sleep. And shortly thereafter the Lord said: Bring a table and bread! And immediately it is added: he took bread, blessed it and broke it and gave it to James the Just and said to him: My brother, eat your bread, for the Son of Man is risen from among those that sleep. (Translation adapted from Hennecke and Schneemelcher, *New Testament Apocrypha,* 1:165.)

The report has some notable features. First, it describes an appearance to James which, according to Jerome's report of the matter, follows on an account of the appearance of Jesus to a third party to whom as "servant of the priest" he gives a "shroud," which is possibly linked with purificatory rites (Lev 13:47–59). Then, the account implies that James shared in the last supper ("from that hour in which he had drunk the cup of the Lord"). Third, there is a mention made of James' fast. Finally, James is called "the Just" and addressed as "my brother" by the risen Jesus.

Each of these elements in the portrait of James seems to draw from the New Testament traditions. These are: the appearance of the risen Christ (1 Cor 15:7); "the cup of the Lord" (1 Cor 10:21; 11:23–26) while the command to "eat your bread" follows the eucharistic tradition in Matt 26:26, with parallels in the post-resurrection epiphanies and meals (Luke 24:30, 35; John 21:13); the fast has parallels taken from Jewish practice where it was known to be a pious act of a righteous man (*T. Jos.* 3.4–5 of Joseph in Egypt but also based on Dan 1:8–16); the title "Just" is offered without explanation, and this suggests an indebtedness to the gnostic *Gospel of Thomas,* logion 12:

> The disciples said to Jesus: We know that you will leave us. Who is he who will be great over us? Jesus said to them: In the place to which you come, you will go to James the Just, for whose sake heaven and earth were made.

Here James' role as leader is linked with the departure of Jesus to heaven; and James' character, known to be one of piety, suggests the reason why he is chosen to be leader in the absence of his earthly brother (but cf. logion 15: "when you see him who was not born of woman . . ."). The idea of exaltation seems to be the factor that unites these elements in James' designation as the "Just." Although the *Gospel of Thomas* has an anti-Jewish flavor, its portrayal of James as exalted leader "for whose sake heaven and earth were made" has links with the Jewish tradition that the world was created for the righteous Israelites (*2 Apoc. Bar.* 21:24; cf. 15:7) or for Israel (4 Ezra 6:55). The conclusion seems to be that, although there are some conflicting elements within the *Gospel according to the Hebrews* regarding its attitude to Judaism (positive in regarding the Holy Spirit as female, "my mother"; yet negative because of its gnostic elements), the concern of the document is to promote James as a model of piety and to offer him as an example for hortatory purposes. The link between the *Gospel according to the Hebrews* and the *Gospel of Thomas* in their respective characterizations of James—the latter giving him both preeminence among the disciples and a caliphate-like status (see Gärtner, *The Theology of the Gospel of Thomas*, 56–57)—suggests that there is evidence of the way in which Jewish Christian ideas became fitted into a gnostic system. The suggestion is reasonable, therefore, that this was done to strengthen the Jewish Christian readers by such an appeal to a leader for whom exalted status was being claimed.

B. THE CLEMENTINE LITERATURE

The main source of information regarding James under the rubric of the Clementine literature is *Recognitions* 1.43–72. The characterization given to James is both full and interesting. We may accept the modern consensus (in Strecker, *Das Judenchristentum*, 197, and Lüdemann, "The Successors," 172) that the *Recognitions* originated in the Jewish Christian community at Pella in Transjordan, where in the second century a veneration of James was maintained as part of their distinctive belief and ethos. Kent Brown, "James: A Religio-Historical Study," itemizes five elements in the portrayal of the leader in this community. (i) He is referred to as "James the bishop" (68:2) and as president of the Jerusalem church (62:2; 70:3). (ii) He is given authority as one ordained by the Lord (contrast Eusebius, *HE* 7.19) to require a report from both the Twelve (44:1) and Peter (72:1). Thus (iii) he is given some measure of responsibility for the early Christian mission. (iv) He is known as an apologist to the Jews in seeking their conversion to Christianity (69, 70). But (v) he is opposed in this venture by Saul of Tarsus, who throws him from the steps of the temple, and the disciples flee to Jericho (70–71).

What is of interest here is the posthumous status conferred on James and read back into his lifetime. That status is summed up in the title of "bishop," which is met with here in reference to James for the first time but developed later. It is possible that the attribution of an "episcopal" rank to James was made by way of adopting the Essene axiom that the priesthood consisted of "overseers" (*mᵉbaqqērîm*), a link suggested by the evidence of 11Q Temple, according to B. E. Thiering, "*Mebaqqer*," 69–72. But it may not be necessary to go to this source, and James' rank may be a fair deduction from the data known to the New Testament writers that James presided at Jerusalem (in Acts 15) and was described (in Acts 21) as surrounded by a collegium of elders in whose name he spoke. His priestly office—which is met within the later ecclesiastical developments of the trajectory that runs in characterization of James (see Eusebius, *HE* 2.1.2; 3.5.2; 7.9.1 and later, pp. lii–liv)—may be derived from the parallel sought between Jesus as a "prophet like Moses" and his brother James as a "priest like Aaron" (so Bruce, *New Testament History*, 352). Also, we hear of James as a suffering figure, while the other allusions to him as connected with the Twelve and as one involved in a Jewish mission are details picked up from the New Testament.

Other points of contact between the picture of James in *Recognitions* and that in the NT, specifically in the Letter of James, have been noted by Webber, "ΙΑΚΩΒΟΣ": (1) James makes appeal to Scripture, especially the law (68–69); (2) an insistence on monotheism (in his speech in chap. 69) and an indirect mention of baptism connect with James 2:19 and 2:7; (3) the introduction of Saul of Tarsus as James' arch-opponent and his violent actions against the Jewish leader recall the fate of the Jacobean community (James 2:7, 11; 3:10; 4:2, 11) and its venerated leader (5:6); (4) both the note of nonresistance and the rejection of violence are parallel to what the epistle teaches (e.g., 1:20; 3:18; 5:6b). To this we may add (5) James' role reflected in both documents, canonical and later, as conciliator. At a time when Jewish Christians were enduring persecution in the second century (Eusebius, *HE* 4.8.4–5) and were needing to offer a rationale for their religion after the final destruction of the Jerusalem Temple, this tract uses the idealized memory of James, known to be a martyr persona and a pious leader, who at the same time rejected retaliatory violence and sought to persuade his compatriots to embrace the messianic faith.

Both Jewish Christian documents under review move forward the trajectory of James in several decisive ways. We have observed the varied New Testament traditions that see him as a member of the holy family, with both positive (Matthew, Luke-Acts) and negative (Mark) connotations, and as an embodiment of a Jewish Christian, or specifically a Jerusalem, mentality to be equally respected and treated with caution (Paul at different times). In the Fourth Gospel James is a "type" of the world in its hostility to Johannine Asia Minor Christianity.

The embellishment of James' character is carried onward into the second century with an increasing respect for James as an authoritative leader to whom the risen Christ appeared and gave a high encomium (*Gos. Thom.* 12) or who is granted an appointment to the revered office of "bishop" over the Jerusalem church. There are associations that connect him with the Jewish cult, whether he is linked with a priestly figure (in *Gospel of the Hebrews* with its enigmatic allusion to the priest's servant and the linen cloth/shroud: Vielhauer ["Jewish-Christian Gospels," 117–65] refers the action to a proof of Jesus' resurrection for apologetic purposes) or given an intercessory role (in *Clem. Recogn.*). He has a blameless character as "the Just," and becomes the prototype of suffering at the hands of violent persons—a situation mirrored in the persecutions of Jewish Christians in the second century. He is set forth as an idealized person, somewhat larger than life, and a patron for communities that looked to him as their inspiration and pattern. More important for future development of the trajectory, however, was the notion that James was the recipient of special revelation, a fact that was picked up and exploited in the later gnostic treatments of James. The Nag Hammadi documents *Gospel of Thomas, First Apocalypse of James,* and *Second Apocalypse of James* give to James a role of revelator of secret mysteries (*1 Apoc. Jas.* 24.11; *2 Apoc. Jas.* 49.9) and he is accorded an exalted place as a gnostic redeemer figure in *1 Apoc. Jas.* 24.13, 18; *2 Apoc. Jas.* 55.15–56.14; 58.2–25. The exemplary character of James as a "righteous one" (*Gos. Thom.* 12) becomes much more than that of moral virtue. Rather he is hailed as the patron of gnostic believers who endured persecution by the Great Church by drawing on the analogy that James' piety was a rebuke to the Twelve (*1 Apoc. Jas.* 42.20–24; cf. Clement of Alexandria in Eusebius, *HE* 2.1.4).

3. THE ROLE OF JAMES IN ECCLESIASTICAL CIRCLES

Bibliography

Baltzer, K., and **Koester, H.** "Die Bezeichnung des Jakobus als ŌBLIAS." *ZNW* 46 (1955) 141–42. **Bouquet, A. C.** "The References to Josephus in the Bibliotheca of Photius." *JTS* 36 (1935) 289–93. **Brandon, S. G. F.** "The Death of James: A New Interpretation." In *Studies in Mysticism and Religion Presented to Gershom G. Scholem*, ed. E. E. Urbach, R. J. Zwi Werblowsky, and Ch. Wirszubski. Jerusalem: Magnes, 1967. 57–69. **Brown, S. K.** "Jewish and Gnostic Elements in the Second Apocalypse of James (CG v,4)." *NovT* 17 (1975) 225–37. **Carroll, K. L.** "The Place of James in the Early Church." *BJRL* 44 (1961) 49–67. **Ehrhardt, A. A. T.** *The Apostolic Succession in the First Two Centuries.* London: Lutterworth, 1953. **Hyldahl, N.** "Hegesipps Hypomnemata." *ST* 14 (1960) 70–113. **Jeremias, J.** *Jerusalem in the Time of Jesus.* Tr. F. H. and C. H. Cave. London: SCM, 1969. **Kelly, J. N. D.** *Jerome: His Life, Writings, and Correspondence.* London: Duckworth, 1975. **Koester, H.** *Introduction to the New Testament.* 2 vols. Philadephia: Fortress, 1982. **Robinson, J. M.**, ed. *The Nag Hammadi Library in English.* New York: Harper Row, 1977. **Schoeps, H. J.** *Theologie und Geschichte des Judenchristentums.* Tübingen: Mohr, 1949. **Scott, J. J.** "James the Relative." *JETS* 25 (1982) 323–31. **Telfer, W.** "Was Hegesippus a Jew?" *HTR* 53 (1960) 143–53. **Ward, R. B.** "James of Jerusalem." *RestQ* 16 (1973) 174–90. **Webber, M. I.** ΙΑΚΩΒΟΣ 'Ο ΔΙΚΑΙΟΣ. Ph.D. diss. Pasadena, CA: Fuller Theological Seminary, 1985. This piece of work has a more complete documentation for this chapter. **Zuchschwerdt, E.** "Das Naziräat des Herrenbruders Jakobus nach Hegesipp (Euseb, h.e. II 23, 5–6)." *ZNW* 68 (1977) 276–87.

The trajectory along which the character and role of James (representing types of Christianity in the first four centuries) travels makes fascinating reading. Our purpose is to plot the nodal points on that line of development, which stretches from the early second century to the late fourth century. Epiphanius and Jerome serve as terminal points for this study. The Council of Nicea (A.D. 325) allows a natural break in the line; and Eusebius of Caesarea's *HE* is reckoned to be complete by this date. Epiphanius (c. A.D. 315–403) shows an expansion of the traditions in the church, as well as the explicit appeal by certain heretical groups (particularly the Ebionites) to James as an authoritative figure. His one extended description of James reflects an awareness of Eusebius (*Haer.* 3.2), alongside continued concern that physical brotherhood would impinge upon the perpetual virginity of Mary, a problem which first appears in Origen. Epiphanius includes other details about James that can be explained only in connection with the canonical epistle (following Eusebius) or else in reaction to its use by heretics. Reference to the "leaf" on the head of James (*Haer.* 3.2.14) appears to indicate his role as martyr and bishop in the church. Reference to the effective prayer of James for rain recalls the Epistle of James (5:17–18). As a member of the holy family, James remained celibate throughout his life. Epiphanius uses Mark 14:51 to support the Hegesippian claim that James wore pure linen (*Haer.* 3.2.13). Perhaps because it made no sense to him, Epiphanius changes the protesting

Rechabite in Hegesippus (*HE* 2.23.17) to Simon/Simeon the son of Clopas. He also does not refer to the siege of Vespasian.

Jerome's work *De Viris Illustribus* was published somewhat later—say A.D. 392–93—than the "Antidote" of Epiphanius against heresies (Kelly, *Jerome*, 174). Since, however, neither work indicates any acquaintance with the other, together they provide a suitable joint *terminus ad quem* for this study. Jerome explicitly acknowledges his source in his account of James: Eusebius (preface to *Vir. Ill.*). He also appears to use Clement of Alexandria for confirmation of the sending of Albinus; Eusebius contains no such reference from Clement. Jerome conflates the two separate accounts from Hegesippus and Josephus contained in Eusebius. Like Epiphanius, Jerome shows that non-orthodox traditions about James were circulating. But instead of quoting the claims of the heretics, he cites an otherwise unknown source: *The Gospel according to the Hebrews* (*Evangelium quoque quod appellatur secundum Hebraeos*). This source (cf. 1 Cor 15:7) describes the appearance of James in eucharistic language, as we noted (earlier, p. xliv).

One other feature of the tradition about James according to Jerome requires mention. While Eusebius doubts both the authenticity of the Epistle of James and the claims that James the Just was its author, Jerome asserts James wrote a single epistle (*unam tantum scripsit epistolam*) and that some claim it was published (*edita*) by another under his name. This testimony suggests that the epistle had gained authority. Consolidation of traditions about James along with the ascendancy of the epistle point to the time between the second and fourth centuries as the formative period for these traditions. This review of their development focuses on the evidence presented by four ecclesiastical writers: Hegesippus, Clement of Alexandria, Origen, and Eusebius of Caesarea. We shall mention the context of each writer, the content of the traditions, their relation to earlier traditions about James, and possible functions of the tradition in each writer's presentation.

A. HEGESIPPUS

The *Memoranda* of Hegesippus are preserved in such fragmentary form by Eusebius that we cannot be sure of their precise contents or even the date of their composition. Eusebius knew five divisions of this work (*HE* 2.23.3; 4.32.1) and uses material from it for establishing episcopal and apostolic succession (3.11.12), for determining early heresies (2.23.9; 3.32.7, 8), and for relating early martyrdoms in the church—besides James, there are Simon (3.32.6) and those under Bar Kokhba (4.8.4).

When Eusebius first cites Hegesippus (on James, *HE* 2.23), he puts him "in the first generation after the apostles." But this conflicts with two other references to the writings of Hegesippus. He mentions the building of Antinoopolis, which probably occurred after Hadrian's later travels, after A.D. 134 (4.8.2). Hegesippus also claims to have been in Rome until the episcopate of Eleutherus, according to an indirect citation by Eusebius. Eusebius correlates this visit with the prominence of Justin, who wrote to Antoninus Pius (4.12.1), thus between A.D. 138 and 161. Finally the *Paschal Chronicon* (C.E. VII) places the death of Hegesippus in the reign of Commodus, which lasted until A.D. 192.

The wide spectrum in dating the life and work of Hegesippus—spanning almost the entire second century A.D.—permits a rough estimate of the writing of his *Memoranda* between 150 and 180 or in the third quarter of that century. The expression "in the first generation after the apostles" thus refers to the account of Hegesippus and not to his life. He wrote about the immediate post-apostolic era but, as other evidence shows, probably lived later.

While this interpretation of the comment by Eusebius puts some distance between Hegesippus and the traditions he records, it raises questions about another more direct statement by Eusebius. Drawing upon what he calls quotations of the *Gospel according to the Hebrews* in Syriac or Hebrew, Eusebius infers that Hegesippus was a Jewish Christian (a "believer from the Hebrews," *HE* 4.22.8). Besides this inference, two other points may support this claim. First, as independent references of Jerome confirm, some *Gospel according to the Hebrews* was found among syncretistic Jewish Christians. Second, as has long ago been observed (Ehrhardt, *Apostolic Succession,* 81–82, 107–9), episcopal succession in the church was modeled on high-priestly succession in Judaism.

Despite this evidence, however, two aspects of the Hegesippian material cast doubt upon the inferences of Eusebius. Both aspects occur in traditional material about James. First, much of what Hegesippus records is contrary to Jewish custom and practice of the early centuries—whether in Scripture or in developing interpretations. Whereas in the Torah and later tradition only the high priest is permitted to enter the "holy of holies," James has this privilege in the *Memoranda*. As a Jew, Hegesippus would know this was not permitted for sons of David, but only those of Levi. Similarly, in the light of the New Testament witness of Jewish opposition to the early Jewish Christians, it is unlikely that James alone would have been favored by Jews (*HE* 2.23.11, 12). To this we can add the apparent ignorance by Hegesippus of Jewish regulations regarding capital punishment (see *b. Sanh.* 6).

A second, and decisive, objection to the view that Hegesippus was a convert from Judaism is his citation of the Scriptures. Eusebius says that Hegesippus called Proverbs all-virtuous wisdom (4.22.9). Yet, based on his citations, he apparently did not know the Scriptures as a Jew. He says that opposition to James fulfilled a citation from Isaiah (3:10), then proceeds to quote a conflation of that text and the Wisdom of Solomon (2:12). Then he claims that Jeremiah bore witness to the Rechabite priesthood, but no extant text of Jeremiah comes close to making such a statement (cf. Jer 42 [35]:19 LXX). A third reference to Scripture (2.23.7, 8) claims that the prophets declared about James that he was "Just and Oblias" (see Baltzer and Koester, "Die Bezeichnung," 141–42), the second title (*Oblias*) being interpreted as "Bulwark of the People." *Oblias* is evidently a corrupt form of a Semitic designation given to James, as though it were ʿopel ʿam. See F. F. Bruce, *New Testament History,* 370 n.9.

How can conflicting evidence about the background and context of Hegesippus be reconciled if he was not a Jew? Apparently he, like the writers who followed him (see below), had some protracted contact with Jewish Christian groups which supplied the traditions he later incorporated into his writings. Further, we may infer that these Jewish Christians, perhaps because of their relation to the holy family, were not considered heretical by Hegesippus. Since a certain *Gospel according to the Hebrews* (*Vir. Ill.* 2) contained a reference to the appearance of Jesus to James, a similar document also may be the source of Hegesippus' traditions about James which are preserved in Eusebius.

Content of Traditions

Some references have already been made to the content of traditions about James in Hegesippus (see pp. xlvii, xlix). These can now be brought together under four headings. Hegesippus passes on information about the piety, title and office, relation with Jews, and circumstances surrounding the death of James.

Piety. Various elements in the picture of the pious James have led some (e.g., Carroll, "The Place of James," 60; contra Ward, "James," 179–80) to the too hastily reached conclusion that he was a "Christian Pharisee." The piety of James is cast primarily in priestly terms (cf. Lev 10:9; 21:10–12; Ezek 44:17). But certain features of this piety are inconsistent with Jewish models. These features include vegetarianism, avoidance of oil and baths, and the wearing of linen. Furthermore, camel-like knees do not occur as a sign of piety elsewhere in early Jewish tradition. More consistent with other early data about Christianity is the perceived relationship between the early church and various Jewish groups (*HE* 2.23.8). As a Jewish Christian, James could have facilitated these kinds of contacts, but we find no evidence of them in earlier traditions about him. We cannot now know how substantial a role James played in this regard.

Title. Among ecclesiastical writers, Hegesippus is the first to call James "the Just." He claims that everyone from the "Lord's time" used this title of the Lord's brother, yet none of the NT writers refers to James in this way, nor is the piety of James emphasized so as to anticipate association of "the Just" with the brother of the Lord (with the possible exception of James 5:6). Although Eusebius never quotes Hegesippus to the effect that James was called "bishop," he implies that James held that office. As the story goes, Simon/Simeon was chosen to take the throne of James (*HE* 3.11.12). Hegesippus also calls this an appointment to the office of bishop (4.22.4). But Eusebius may depend upon Clement of Alexandria here (cf. 2.1.3, where Clement calls James the Just "bishop of Jerusalem").

Family. In traditions preserved by Hegesippus, members of the holy family have a status equal to the apostles. So James, called the brother of the Lord, is "spoken of as" a child of Joseph (2.1.2). He was κατὰ σάρκα of the family of the Lord (3.11; cf. Rom 1:3–4). According to Hegesippus, James and Simeon are both ἀνεψιοί (kinsfolk) of the Lord (4.12.4), a designation indicating only near-relationship. Apparently Hegesippus furnished the material for the report of Eusebius that the apostles and members of the holy family, along with the disciples, made Simeon their choice for bishop after James was martyred (3.11).

Death. The account of the death of James in Hegesippus consists of a dialogue, a confession, the execution of the Just, and its consequences. Because of his contacts with Jews, many are converted (2.23.9–10). Therefore the religious leaders try to get James to stem the tide of conversions to the messianic faith (2.23.10–11). Instead James responds to their request by confessing the apocalyptic Son of Man (2.23.12–13) and more people are converted. Then the Jewish leaders "throw down" the Just and begin stoning him (2.22.15–16). A Rechabite priest protests concerning the action, since James is praying for his persecutors. One of the laundrymen clubs James on the head and he dies a martyr's death (2.23.17–18). Consequently Vespasian begins his siege against Jerusalem (2.23.18). Numerous biblical motifs in this account suggest to the modern reader that the death of James is made to resemble the death of the Lord (4.22.4) and other early martyrological accounts, e.g., Stephen's (Acts 7).

Relation to Earlier Traditions

These resemblances provide a suitable starting point for suggesting possible antecedents to Jewish Christian traditions preserved by Hegesippus. His account of the death of James contains elements from early Christian literature. His description of the piety of James reflects Jewish traditions, but with inconsistencies that in all likelihood have gnostic connections. His use of the title "the Just" for James may be based on earlier Jewish Christian traditions. This material about James does not stem from Josephus or NT data about the brother of the Lord, however. Quotations from the Old Testament and later Jewish literature indicate how these earlier contexts influenced the account of James' death. The prophet Isaiah (3:10 ff.) pronounces judgment upon the leaders of the people for their evil counsel against the righteous (3:9). Hegesippus holds the "scribes and Pharisees" responsible for the death of James and interprets Vespasian's conquest as a judgment on Jerusalem. In the Wisdom of Solomon, the righteous man is killed because he opposes the works of the ungodly (2:12; cf. 1:16). (See later, pp. xcvi–xcvii.) Following the wisdom tradition, James opposes the scribes and Pharisees and is condemned to a shameful death (Wisd Sol 2:20). As the truly righteous man, James himself becomes an offering to God (Wisd Sol 3:5–6; cf. 4:7–16).

The death of James also resembles those of Jesus and Stephen in the early church to such an extent that some have posited a common martyr tradition behind all three accounts. The strongest link between the accounts is provided by the final intercessory prayer of James (*HE* 2.23.16). Various manuscript traditions and ecclesiastical writers include a similar prayer by Jesus in Luke (23:24). Stephen, on his knees as he is stoned (cf. *HE* 2.23.16), asks that his persecutors may be forgiven (Acts 7:60).

Less closely linked are confessions made by Jesus, Stephen, and James about an apocalyptic Son of Man. Jesus predicts what Stephen and James experience. They see the Son of Man seated/standing at the right hand of God/the (great) power [here the link with the confession of Stephen ends] and coming on the clouds of heaven (Matt 26:64; Mark 14:62; Acts 7:55; *HE* 2.23.13). However, unlike its counterparts in the NT, the confession by James elicits a positive response (2.23.14; cf. Matt 21:9, 15). The context of each confession identifies Jesus with the Son of Man (Mark 14:63–64 = Matt 26:65–66; Acts 7:55; *HE* 2.23.12, 14).

Multiple attempts at killing James (a fall, stoning, being beaten over the head) suggest that this is a legendary combination of motifs. This is probably true of the presence of the Rechabite priest in the story. As yet no one has explained why James came to have been thrown from the pinnacle and beaten over the head (2.23.12). The stoning corresponds in part to Jewish practice and traditional (i.e., Stephen from the narrative in Acts) precedent. How might the clubbing have become part of the tradition about the death of James?

A partial answer to this question may be contained in the evidence of the Mishnah and Talmud. The tractate *Sanhedrin* (81b) contains the following statement: "If a priest performed the temple service whilst unclean, his brother priests do not charge him therewith at *beth din,* but the young priests take him out of the temple court and split his skull with clubs" (cf. *m. San.* 9:6). The gemara following this statement deals at length with what constitutes uncleanness and what kind of uncleanness deserves death in this manner. Either as a non-Levite or non-priest, James by his piety may have violated (or was thought to have violated) limitations of temple observance (cf. *b. Sanh.* 83b: "A *zar* who performed the [temple] service: for it is written, And the stranger that cometh nigh shall be put to death [Num 18:7]." The main baraitha (83a) describes uncleanness in ways that would fit what the pious traditions about James say. Impurity that deserves death has to do with improper diet (*tebel, terumah*), performance of duty on the same day as ritual washings, improper garments, the drinking of wine, and uncut hair. James appears to be described as one who surpassed the piety of priests in service to the temple, but by someone who did not understand Jewish standards of ceremonial piety.

Three different resolutions have been proposed for the improbabilities in this pious picture of James. Recently Ernst Zuchschwerdt has suggested that the description of the Nazirite James was interpolated into the text of Hegesippus before it reached Eusebius, perhaps by a Jewish Christian group in the third century ("Das Naziräat," *ZNW* 68 [1977] 276–87). He appeals to a quotation from Epiphanius (*Haer.* 29.4) which shows that Hegesippus did not know the Nazirite tradition about James. In view of the confused nature of the description, it is more likely that the passage would have been omitted than added. Furthermore, Nazirite and priestly piety are connected in Talmudic tradition.

Another way of dealing with the confusions of Hegesippus is to dismiss them as legendary accretions around a core of historical knowledge of early holy men or martyrs in the church. This has been the approach taken by most recent critics of the traditions about James. Yet it begs the question of how these particular pious motifs came to be associated with James.

Consideration of the purpose of the *Memoranda* may shed some light upon both the use and the origin of this picture of James. If, as has been argued (Telfer, "Was Hegesippus," 144; Hyldahl, "Hegesipps Hypomnemata," 86–94, 113), Hegesippus wrote to attack specific gnostic theological claims and to condemn unbelieving Jewish sects, he could be presenting the piety and death of James in an apologetic context. This is a submission worth exploring.

An apologetic intention and connection with heretical sects might explain some of the inconsistencies of Hegesippus' account. Against Jews he would be likely to stress the superiority of Christian leaders. To them also he would want to direct his comments about judgment upon Jerusalem from Rome.

References by Irenaeus and Clement of Alexandria to the practices of heterodox Christian groups might also account for certain elements in the pious description of James: his diet, prayer habits, and dress. Although Judaism knows no strict vegetarianism in this period, James the Jewish Christian avoids animal food (*HE* 2.23.5). But Irenaeus, writing around the same period as Hegesippus, cites this avoidance as superficial piety of the disciples of Saturninus (*Adv. Haer.* 1.24.2). These he later calls Encratites, who have introduced abstinence from animal food (1.28.1). Epiphanius associates Ebionites with this practice (*Haer.* 30.15).

James' ministry in the temple included constant prayers seeking forgiveness for the people (*HE* 2.23.6), a fitting response to heretical sects in the days of Hegesippus. Irenaeus describes one Marcus who purportedly mediated grace to his wayward followers through cups (*Adv. Haer.* 1.13.1–2) among various other questionable modes of redemption (1.21.1–5). In contrast to these heretics, James was in constant prayer to God for forgiveness (cf. James 5:16).

A third feature of the piety of James, that he wore only linen (based on Lev 16:4–28), may also reflect apologetic concerns of Hegesippus. In the *Stromateis,* Clement of Alexandria offers an allegorical interpretation of cultic elements in Hebrew religion as part of an extended polemic against gnostic heresies. Since this work appeared around the end of the second or beginning of the third century, it provides evidence of heresies contemporaneous with Hegesippus. For comparison with James we may consider the robe of the high priest (*Strom.* 5.6). The consecrated robe of the priest represents the material world. When the priest sets that aside for the "holy-of-holies" tunic, he symbolizes the Gnostic and the Levite, and distinguishes himself as completely pure. For Clement, this exchange of robes signifies the pure faith of leaders.

> He who through Him has believed puts off and puts on, as the apostle intimated, the consecrated stole. Thence, after the image of the Lord, the worthiest were chosen from the sacred tribes to be high priests, and those elected to the kingly office and to prophecy were anointed.

Julius Scott ("James," 328–30) recently has shown the plausibility of a high-priestly view of James in the early church. James "by his background, nature, life and sympathy for the more Jewish elements in Christianity was the most likely candidate for the legendary position of priestly accompaniment of the Messiah."

Further evidence that this picture of James was prevalent in gnostic Jewish Christian circles comes from the *Gospel of Thomas*. This collection of wisdom sayings originated in Syria/Palestine sometime late in the first century. Logion 12 of the Gospel contains the earliest reference to James as the Just. Standing as it does next to logion 13 (a reference to Thomas), the mention of James indicates a tension between the authority of both figures among the esoteric readers of the *Gospel of Thomas*. Scott ("James," 328 n.23) gives parallels to the accolade "for whose sake heaven and earth came into existence" which prove its Jewish provenance.

Function of Traditions

Little additional information is needed to determine how Hegesippus used traditions about James. The above similarities lead us to infer that Hegesippus knew that James was a significant leader in the early church. At the same time, Hegesippus sought to show how his church stood in a line of succession traceable to James. Resemblances between traditions in Hegesippus and those from various groups in the second century indicate why this may have become necessary. These various groups also may have claimed the authority of James as their own.

B. CLEMENT OF ALEXANDRIA

What appears implicitly in Hegesippus becomes explicit in Clement of Alexandria when he considers James. Writing in the early years of the third century, Clement defended Christianity against a flourishing Gnostic Christian movement in Alexandria. His counterattack upon the gnostic threat was unique in that Clement used the terminology of his opponents but injected it with a different content. This difficult apologetic tack may account for the relatively infrequent mention of Clement by later writers.

We ought to take care in determining the central concerns of Clement, especially when the work quoted has not been independently preserved, as is the case with the *Hypotyposes*. From later quotations of this text we can infer it contained a sort of running commentary on the Scriptures.

Content of Traditions

The two references to James by Clement suggest continuing concern with matters recorded by Hegesippus. At the same time Clement takes the traditions in a different direction. He shows little contact with Jewish Christian features of the accounts. Yet he, like Hegesippus, gives information about the piety of James, his position in the Jerusalem church, and his death (*HE* 2.1.2–5).

With others of the "inner circle" James received knowledge from the resurrected Lord (*HE* 2.1.4). Clement apparently understood this gnosis both as the true doctrine of the church and as elevated spiritual contemplation. It comes only to those worthy of receiving it. As "the Just," James certainly would have qualified for the possession of either kind of knowledge.

James is first called "bishop" (ἐπίσκοπος) by Clement. The way he is appointed differs from the Hegesippian mode of succession. Instead of the apostles and relatives of Jesus choosing James (cf. *HE* 2.11 on Simeon), only Peter, James, and John choose him as the bishop of Jerusalem. This interpretation may be an anti-gnostic reaction, when one recalls the *Gos. Thom.* logia 12 and 13 (probably earlier than Clement noted above). Whereas in the *Gospel of Thomas* disciples are told to go to James because of his exalted status (12), Clement reports that they defer to James because they were previously honored by the Savior. Since Clement does not explain the title "the Just" for James, he probably used it only as a title.

Although Eusebius notes agreement between Clement and Hegesippus in their reports about the death of James (2.23.19), some differences exist between the two. As far as Clement knew, James the Just was thrown from the pinnacle of the temple and beaten to death. But according to Hegesippus, all this occurred "while they were stoning him" (2.23.17). The description of the beating also differs from Hegesippus. Hegesippus portrays it as a single blow "brought down on the head of the Just." Clement leaves the reader with the impression of a prolonged beating "beaten to *death* with a laundryman's club" (emphasis added).

Relation to Earlier Traditions

Clement probably does not draw upon Hegesippus. Nevertheless, similarities between them suggest that they had access to a common tradition. Because Clement attributes the giving of γνῶσις to a resurrection appearance, he may have information like that in the *Gospel according to the Hebrews* about the appearance to James. On the other hand, he does not add to information from 1 Cor 15:7, and elsewhere he reveals his knowledge of that epistle. Since he does not reveal any knowledge of the stoning of James, Clement is evidently unaware of Josephus' account. What Clement did not infer from the NT, he probably borrowed from his gnostic opponents.

Function of Traditions

Less is known about the contents of Clement's *Hypotyposes* than about the *Hypomnemata* of Hegesippus. Reaction to the work varied greatly from the glowing comments of Origen's successors to the misguided critique of Photius. The latter misunderstood Clement's appropriation of gnostic terminology and remonstrated with the Alexandrian teacher for writing things unworthy of piety and orthodoxy.

Comparison with gnostic (*Gos. Thom.*) and other orthodox (Hegesippus) traditions about James highlights some of Clement's concerns with James the Just. He used him as a representative bearer of the true gnosis. He also resisted efforts of gnostic Christians to exalt James unduly above the Twelve, and he identified the leader as an early Christian martyr.

C. ORIGEN

Two major references to James occur in Origen's works from the later period of his life, while he was in Caesarea (c. A.D. 244–249). One work (*Contra Celsum*) purports to be an apologetic against Jewish objections to the Christian faith. The work itself confirms recent studies: Origen had extensive contact with and sympathy for the Jewish community. The other work in which Origen refers to James is his commentary on Matthew (*Comm. Matt.*).

Since the two documents come from the same period in Origen's life we might expect them to resemble each other. They may also be directed to similar audiences—Christians who needed encouragement, nurture, and a resource to make a ready response to their Jewish critics. If Eusebius' comments are to be taken seriously (*HE* 6.25–32), *Contra Celsum* probably followed the *Commentary on Matthew* by a few years.

Content of Traditions

In his brief remarks about James, Origen presents data that agree with earlier patristic references, as well as data that differ from them. Against Celsus, Origen does not describe the manner of James' death. Further he expands upon the consequences of that death for the Jews beyond what Hegesippus had recorded (1.47; cf. 2.13). He is the first ecclesiastical writer to explain the relationship between Jesus and James as "brothers." He names Josephus as his source for this information.

Concern to explain the relationship among members of the holy family also is evident in Origen's commentary on Matthew (13:54–58). Here he offers another explanation for the term "brothers." He also repeats his claim (from Josephus) that the killing of James caused the destruction of the temple in Jerusalem. As did writers before him, Origen associates righteousness with James. Yet only in *Contra Celsum* does he call him "the Just" (1.47).

Alleged dependence upon Josephus for the claim that Jerusalem fell because of the treatment accorded James is only one of a number of new elements in Origen about the just brother of the Lord. Origen (*Contra Celsum* 1.47) appeals to Paul (Gal 1:19) for the explanation that brotherhood means discipleship (cf. Matt 12:46–50, a comment that is not extant in Origen's commentary). James was called brother of the Lord because of his words and deeds. In the *Commentary on Matthew*, while Origen again quotes Paul, he puts the "problem" of relation to Jesus in a different light, that of the perpetual virginity of Mary. As with Eusebius after him (*HE* 2.1.2), Origen notes that James and the others appeared to be sons of Joseph and Mary. But he observes with approval that a "Gospel of Peter" or a "Book of James" (probably the *Protevangelium* of James) take these to be children of a previous marriage of Joseph. Origen also is first to link this James with Jude (Jude 1).

Relation to Earlier Traditions

Origen claims to draw upon two sources for his knowledge of James: Josephus (*Ant.*) and some extracanonical Jewish Christian writing. Origen's relationship to Clement and other evidence of the influence of Clement on Origen lead us to conclude that the former furnished the latter with the title "the Just" for James. Origen was also familiar with the NT picture of James (Gal 1:19).

Unfortunately the basis of Origen's dependence on Josephus is extremely weak. No known copy of Josephus' *Antiquities* contains any passage linking the destruction of Jerusalem to the death of James. The nearest parallel is a brief indication that behavior contrary to the ancient laws made the Jews liable to punishment (20.218). It was pointed out by Bouquet, "References to Josephus," that the text of Josephus probably did not have such a passage, at least by the mid-ninth century. How is this discrepancy between Origen and Josephus to be resolved?

An easy reply to this question credits Origen with confusion, whether between Hegesippus and Josephus or between the martyrdoms of John the Baptist and James (both in Josephus). Five parallels with Hegesippus may support the former alternative. Like Hegesippus, Origen recognizes the righteousness of James, calls him the Just, may imply that he died by conspiracy (*Contra Celsum* 1.47: "despite his righteousness"), calls his death a witness (*Comm. Matt.* 10.17), and views Vespasian as the instrument of retribution upon the Jews (*Contra Celsum* 2.13).

Against this notion of a confusion are its improbabilities. Given the early association between James and righteousness (see on *Gos. Thom.* above) and Origen's knowledge of both the NT and Clement, it seems more likely that these traditions provided Origen with the title, which Origen applies infrequently, unlike Hegesippus. Secondly, given Origen's attitude toward the Jews (particularly in *Contra Celsum*) and his own inclination toward asceticism, why would he omit references to the plot against James or his piety? Further, the term $\mu\acute{\alpha}\rho\tau\upsilon\varsigma$, already in the NT (Stephen in Acts 7; Revelation), may connote one faithful unto death. Finally, Origen writes that it was Titus, not Vespasian, who destroyed Jerusalem. Vespasian is mentioned only as governor.

Citing another misquotation of Josephus by Origen, we may argue, on the other hand, that Origen mixes up the deaths of James and John the Baptist. Josephus states explicitly that John did not baptize for the forgiveness of sins (*Ant.* 18.117). But Origen quotes Josephus to the opposite effect, equating purification and forgiveness (*Contra Celsum* 1.47). The similarities between the accounts of James and John the Baptist in Josephus could lead to other confusions: both exhibit righteousness; divine retribution follows the death of each; in both cases the Jews recognize the act of providence; and both are martyred by those in authority. These parallels have, in fact, led some to argue that Origen quotes a more original text of Josephus which was altered by later Jewish hands (so Brandon, "Death of James," 65–67).

A third explanation of the differences between Origen and Josephus would make hypotheses of a confused Origen or an amended Josephus unnecessary. We suggest that the statement by Origen about the cause of the fall of Jerusalem is Origen's interpretation of Josephus (e.g., *Ant.* 18.117). He takes Josephus to mean (perhaps unknowingly) that the death of James is connected to the fall of the temple.

A similar approach occurs elsewhere in Origen. First, as was noted above, Origen may present his view as purporting to come from a source before accepting it as his own (*Comm. Matt.* 10.17 on the "family" of Jesus). Origen also conjectures on the basis of Matt 21:23 that the Jews had secret traditions (*Comm. Matt.* 17.2). Or he appropriates, then moves beyond, the *Martyrdom of Isaiah* (*Hom. Isa.* 1.5). Additionally, divine retribution was an integral element of Origen's eschatology. Punishment is necessary for correction (*Hom.*

Ex. 12; cf. *Comm. Matt.* 15.11) and need not imply hostility since it serves a good purpose.

Function of Traditions

Initial comments about Origen's apologetic use of James now require qualification. This is true of references in *Contra Celsum*, where Origen uses James as the penultimate example of Jewish injustice, thus reinforcing the connection between James and Jesus.

Comm. Matt. served a different purpose in a homiletic context. Seen in this light, Origen's references to James are the earliest preserved example of an effort to explain Scripture about James (two NT references) by using extra-scriptural traditions about him. Origen's wide-ranging use of traditions suggests that James continued to be held in high esteem by Christians. Parallels with non-orthodox texts suggest that many kinds of Christians retained an exalted attitude toward the brother of the Lord.

D. EUSEBIUS

Eusebius of Caesarea left the earliest comprehensive account of events and persons "from our Savior's time to our own" (*HE* 1.1.1), completed c. A.D. 325. Generally he repeats and connects various testimonies that preceded his own. Not surprisingly, he also echoes issues raised by these earlier writers. Despite this dependence, however, his writings manifest a development of traditions about James which reflects his own concerns.

Although he does not hesitate to draw historical inferences from his data (e.g., the claim that Hegesippus was a Jewish Christian; see above), later students of history may be grateful for the historian's lack of originality. No doubt conscious of heretical threats to the church (false introducers of gnosis, *HE* 1.1.1–2), he tries to distinguish carefully between forged and authentic sources. At every turn he also displays a strong tendency to follow Origen, both in themes and in theology of history. This may account for his attraction to the "providential" connection between the death of James and the fall of Jerusalem, which he found in Origen and Hegesippus. This interest in providence in turn may explain why Eusebius changes his account of the martyrdom of James from his earlier *Chronicle* to his later *Church History* (*HE*).

Content of Traditions

To determine these developments in Eusebius' account of James, we begin by removing explicit citations of earlier writers. These can then be compared with Eusebius' own comments to evaluate their influence upon him. Such a limitation further confirms the observation above about Eusebius' lack of originality.

The *Chronicorum*, 2, of Eusebius has two new pieces of information about James. Eusebius calls him ἀδελφόθεος ("brother of God"), a startling indication of his exalted status. He also is the earliest to name James as *first* bishop of Jerusalem.

New information in his church history consists mainly of inferences from his source. Eusebius takes the reference from Clement, *Hypotyposes,* book 6, to mean that James had pride of place as bishop of Jerusalem (*HE* 2.1.2–3). He summarizes both Hegesippus and Josephus (*HE* 2.23.1–3) before repeating their accounts.

Two aspects in Eusebius' account differ from the evidence of his earlier sources. According to Eusebius, James was known as a child of Joseph and called the brother of the Lord (*HE* 1.1.2). Later, after describing the death of James, Eusebius connects James the Just to the Epistle of James. Like his relation to Joseph, the epistle "is said" to come from this James. But Eusebius does not render a clear verdict on its authenticity (*HE* 2.23.24–25). This ambiguity diminished considerably by the time Jerome wrote *De Viris Illustribus.*

Relation to Earlier Traditions

Comparison with Josephus indicates that Eusebius had a copy of the *Antiquities* before him. Beyond that, as Eusebius admits, he draws from the writings of Clement and Hegesippus. Since these references have been evaluated already in the present study, they need not be reiterated here. Instead we need to identify his unnamed source.

That unnamed source appears to be Origen. The discussion of the virginal conception in relation to the family of Jesus (*Comm. Matt.* 10.17) is echoed in Eusebius (*HE* 2.1.2). Since Eusebius does not quote Galatians elsewhere, he probably took his reference to 1:19 from Origen. Origen appears to be the source of Eusebius' claim that Josephus (the "wise among the Jews," *HE* 2.23.19) blamed the fall of Jerusalem upon the mistreatment of James (see also *Chronicorum,* 2).

Eusebius (*Chronicorum,* 2) remarks that James was called "the Just" by everyone. He offers several reasons for that ascription to James. The first is the moral character of James—his virtue (*HE* 2.1.2). A third is given by Hegesippus (2.23.4–7), namely an appeal to Scripture (see p. xlviii). The second, however, appears odd. The righteousness of James meant (according to Eusebius) that he had attained a height of philosophy and religion (2.23.2). Because φιλοσοφία occurs rarely in Christian writers of the time (in both apologists and gnostics), it may point to another apologetic use of traditions about James.

Function of Traditions

Two different sets of evidence support an apologetic purpose for Eusebius. From the introduction to the *Historia Ecclesiastica* we can see how traditions about James suited Eusebius' stated purposes. James was part of the apostolic succession. According to tradition (Hegesippus and Clement), he distinguished himself as an early leader. His death sealed the fate of the Jews. Himself a victim of their hostility, he became a martyr (this a result of a comparison between *HE* 1.1.1–5 and references to James). James is included by Eusebius because of his distinguished role in church history.

Existence of various non-orthodox documents possibly contemporaneous with Eusebius may provide additional evidence of his apologetic intent relative to James. Documents attributed to James among the Nag Hammadi books probably circulated during the second and third centuries (see translations in *The Nag Hammadi Library*, ed. J. M. Robinson). The *Second Apocalypse of James* draws from a source similar to that used by Hegesippus (K. S. Brown, "Jewish and Gnostic Elements," 225–37) with common material such as the mention of "the door," and "the height" (i.e., "pinnacle of the Temple"[?]; see *Library*, ed. Robinson, 251–54). The *Second Apocalypse of James* contains indications of the spiritual brotherhood of James and Jesus. The *Apocryphon of James* (NH I, 2, 15, 6–23: ed. Robinson, 30) has James and Peter take a celestial journey like the one of the gnostic priest referred to by Clement (see above), but this reference may be to James, son of Zebedee. Each of these documents attributes distinctive authority to James as one worthy to receive special revelation, typical of the Nag Hammadi literature. The *First Apocalypse of James* highlights James' role as example, and the *Second Apocalypse of James* turns the figure of James into a heavenly guide destined to lead men into the heavenly realm as a gnostic redeemer: "You are an illuminator and a redeemer of those who [are] mine" (*2 Apoc. Jas.* 44, 55; ed. Robinson, 252). By contrast, Eusebius places James with the apostles as a conserver of the true traditions.

As we have seen, the Pseudo-Clementine literature exalts James beyond his position in the orthodox traditions (earlier, pp. xlv–xlvi). *Epistula Petri* calls James "the lord and bishop of the holy church" (1.1). Peter warns James against careless transmission of Peter's preaching but commends instruction for the seventy (1.2.1) Jewish Christian (circumcised) believers. Clement's "letter" to James calls the latter "bishop of bishops." Reference has been made above to the disputant role James assumes in the *Recognitions*. Even in this context James is made to speak against the gnostics (*Recogn.* 1.69). Eusebius called the Epistle of James first of the Catholic letters (*HE* 2.23.25) to distinguish it from other epistles of James such as the one named by Origen (*Comm. Matt.* 10.17).

That James was appropriated in this manner is witnessed by both Victorinus and Epiphanius. The former writer says the Symmachians have made James to be an apostle (in *Ep. ad Gal.* 1.15). The latter charges the Ebionites with fabricating writings from James, Matthew, and others (*Haer.* 30.23.1). This tactic probably did not originate in the latter half of the fourth century. Circumstantial evidence and clues from Eusebius himself, therefore, lead us to conclude that he—like others before him—sought to claim James for the tradition of the Great Church, for the "orthodox" wing of Christianity.

CONCLUSION

Most studies are limited by the amount of new material and new methods for evaluating that material. The preceding investigation is no exception. Comparatively recent discoveries from Nag Hammadi have shed new light upon traditions about James in the early church and have filled in gaps left by ecclesiastical writers, confirming some conceptions about heresies in the church and correcting others.

These discoveries indicate that in the early post-apostolic period of the church, James remained at the center of theological controversy. Often traditions about him appear to develop in the context of this conflict between the "orthodox" and the "heretics." The gnostics claim that James held supreme ecclesiastical authority (*Gos. Thom.* 12). Hegesippus counters with a picture of the elevated piety of James which nevertheless subordinates him to the apostles. The gnostics claim that James received the secret tradition from the Lord. Clement counters that it was passed on to others, and that James bore the true Christian gnosis. Uneasiness about the physical relationship between James and Jesus (and Mary) may even reflect gnostic thought about the holy family (*1 Apoc. Jas.*). Finally Eusebius seeks to establish an unbroken line of apostolic tradition and succession, including James, to safeguard the church against the gnostic threat.

This differs from the perspective of Jewish Christians who may have appealed to James as patron of their ethos and beliefs. Traditions preserved by Hegesippus about the piety of James and later comments by Epiphanius imply that these views of James persisted.

Attempts by non-orthodox believers to claim James as patron account for the difficulty that the Epistle of James had being accepted in the canon (see later pp. lxxii, cv). We cannot trace the developments very clearly from Eusebius to Jerome. The church in the East apparently consolidated itself after the Council of Nicea and so rested upon a firmer doctrinal consensus than it had earlier. From this base, church leaders were able to evaluate the ancient writings more consistently and eventually the epistle "gained authority."

The fading of its competitors did nothing to hurt acceptance of the epistle by the church. Gradually, aberrant Jewish Christian sects disappeared in Christianity, taking with them suspicions about the doctrinal propriety of James. Since little mention is made of noncanonical writings by James from the fifth century onward, these other documents probably disappeared as well.

Acceptance of both the brother of the Lord and the Epistle of James by the church bore witness to his continuing value for it. In a different time and setting, he became regarded—for the Great Church—as a bearer of authoritative tradition and a faithful martyr for Christ.

4. JAMES AND HIS EPISTLE

Bibliography

Argyle, A. W. "Greek among the Jews of Palestine in New Testament Times." *NTS* 20 (1973–74) 87–89. **Barnett, P. W.** "The Jewish Sign Prophets, A.D. 40–70—Their Intentions and Origins." *NTS* 27 (1980–81) 679–97. **Brandon, S. G. F.** "The Death of James the Just: A New Interpretation." In *Studies in Mysticism and Religion Presented to Gershom G. Scholem*, ed. E. E. Urbach et al. Jerusalem: Magnes, 1967, 57–69. ———. *Jesus and the Zealots*. Manchester: University Press, 1967. **Bruce, F. F.** *New Testament History*. London: Nelson, 1969. **Cabaniss, A.** "The Epistle of Saint James." *JBR* 22 (1954) 27–29. ———. "A Note on Jacob's Homily." *EvQ* 47 (1975) 219–22.

Conzelmann, H. *History of Primitive Christianity.* Tr. J. E. Steely. Nashville: Abingdon, 1973. **Cullmann, O.** *Peter: Disciple, Apostle, Martyr²*. Tr. F. V. Filson. London: SCM, 1962. **Eichholz, G.** *Glaube und Werke bei Paulus und Jakobus.* Theol. Existenz heute, NF 88. Munich: Kaiser, 1961. **Findlay, J. A.** *The Way, the Truth and the Life.* London: Hodder Stoughton, 1940. **Geyser, A. S.** "The Letter of James and the Social Conditions of the Addressees." In *Proceedings of the Eleventh Meeting of the New Testament Society of South Africa, Pretoria, S.A.: April 29–May 1, 1975.* 25–33. **Goppelt, L.** *Theology of the New Testament.* 2 vols. Tr. J. E. Alsup. Grand Rapids: Eerdmans, 1981, 1982. **Hadas-Lebel, M.** "L'image de Rome auprès des Juifs 164–70." *ANRW* II 20.2. 1987. 717–856. **Hengel, M.** "Der Jakobusbrief als antipaulinische Polemik." In *Tradition and Interpretation in the New Testament.* FS E. Earle Ellis. Ed. G. F. Hawthorne and O. Betz. Grand Rapids: Eerdmans, 1987, 248–78. **Horsley, R. A.,** and **Hanson, J. S.** *Bandits, Prophets, and Messiahs.* Minneapolis: Winston, 1985. **Jeremias, J.** "Paul and James." *ExpTim* 66 (1954–55) 368–71. **Kirk, K. E.** *The Vision of God.* London: Longmans, 1931. **Kümmel, W. G.** *Introduction to the New Testament.* Tr. H. C. Kee. Nashville: Abingdon, 1975. **Marxsen, W.** *Introduction to the New Testament.* Tr. G. Buswell. Oxford: Blackwell, 1968. ———. *Mark the Evangelist.* Tr. J. Boyce et al. Nashville: Abingdon, 1969. **Reicke, B.** *The New Testament Era.* Tr. D. E. Green. London: A. & C. Black, 1968. **Rendall, G. H.** *The Epistle of James and Judaic Christianity.* Cambridge: CUP, 1927. **Robinson, J. A. T.** *Redating the New Testament.* London: SCM, 1976. **Schürer, E.** *The History of the Jewish People in the Age of Jesus Christ.* Vol. 1, rev. G. Vermes and F. Millar. Edinburgh: T. & T. Clark, 1973. **Sevenster, J. N.** *Do You Know Greek?* NovTSup 19. Leiden: Brill, 1968. **Shepherd, M. H.** "The Epistle of James and the Gospel of Matthew." *JBL* 75 (1956) 40–51. **Smallwood, E. M.** "High Priests and Politics in Roman Palestine." *JTS* ns 13 (1962) 14–34. ———. *The Jews under Roman Rule: From Pompey to Diocletian. A Study in Political Relations.* 2d ed. Leiden: Brill, 1981. **Sparks, H. F. D.** *The Formation of the New Testament.* London: SCM, 1952. **Thyen, H.** *Der Stil der jüdisch-hellenistischen Homilie.* FRLANT 65. Göttingen: Vandenhoeck und Ruprecht, 1955. **Townsend, M. J.** "Christ, Community and Salvation in the Epistle of James." *EvQ* 53 (1981) 115–23. ———. "James 4:1–4: A Warning against Zealotry?". *ExpTim* 87 (1976) 211–13. **Turner, N.** "The Style of the Epistle of James." In *A Grammar of New Testament Greek,* ed. J. H. Moulton and W. F. Howard. Edinburgh: T. & T. Clark, 1976. 4:114–20. **Ward, R. B.** "James of Jerusalem." *RestQ* 16 (1973) 174–90. **Wikenhauser, A.** *New Testament Introduction.* Tr. J. Cunningham. Dublin: Herder, 1967. **Zimmermann, A. F.** *Die urchristlichen Lehrer.* WUNT 2.12. Tübingen: Mohr, 1984.

We are now in a position to assess the relation between James and the letter that traditionally goes under his name (1:1 and the churchly evidence). The procedure will be to begin with the historical data relating to James' fate as reported by the pieces of evidence in Josephus. Then, the role of James in its Jerusalem setting will be considered. Third, the witness of what the letter of James has to say about its author's situation will be discussed. Finally, a section will be devoted to themes in the letter in the light of these matters.

A. JAMES AND ANANUS II: HISTORICAL QUESTIONS

The starting point will be reports from Josephus that contain information about James' fate. There are three parts to the data.

1. The clearest and most historically reliable report is in *Ant.* 20.197–203, on which H. Conzelmann commented: "This is one of the rare cases in which

the writing of the church's history can lean for support on non-Christian sources" (*History*, 111). In the three- or four-month interval between the decease of the procurator of Judea, Porcius Festus, in A.D. 62 and the arrival of his successor L. Lucceius Albinus in the office, signs of the reawakening power of the patriotic party in Jerusalem were seen in the actions of the high priest Ananus II. He took the opportunity of a hiatus in Roman administrative presence to rid the province of a number of popular leaders who were suspected of not supporting the patriotic front. One of those leaders was "James the brother of Jesus," who was arraigned and put to death, along with certain other men. A formal Sanhedrin trial was called and an indictment brought against James and others for offenses against the law. "He accused them of having broken the law" (παρανομησάντων, *Ant.* 20.200). At first glance the text looks to be a reference to some alleged transgression of Torah, but this can hardly be so (*pace* Smallwood, *The Jews under Roman Rule*, 279), since after the execution of James, "the citizens who were reputed to be most fair-minded and devoted to the law" (i.e., the Pharisees) openly expressed their regret for James' death and secretly petitioned Herod Agrippa II, who had appointed Ananus, to have him deposed. Others went in private delegation to meet Albinus on his journey from Alexandria to Caesarea and emphasized that the high priest had convoked the Sanhedrin without Roman consent and had acted *ultra vires*. This too suggests that James was not indicted on a specific religious charge, though his death by stoning does support this idea. At least it indicates that Ananus was invoking the Sadducean penal code.

There is tantalizing obscurity as to the real nature of the charges brought against him. It is possible that the text refers to a violation of Roman law, but then it is difficult to account for the way this could have been done and not have provoked the Roman authorities to reprisals. Just possibly it reflects on the situation in the previous decade when Paul had allegedly introduced Trophimus and others into the temple area (Acts 21:27–29)—in violation of both Roman and Jewish law. It may be that the memory of James' failure to rebuke Paul openly and publicly to dissociate him and his fellow Jewish believers in Jerusalem from the apostle to the Gentiles still rankled. Such an act of disloyalty to the patriotism for which Ananus stood would be sufficient grounds to bring a capital charge against James. But Ananus at this time (A.D. 62) was pro-Roman in his attitude (which subsequently changed), so there is less than certainty as to why he took action against James if we confine our attention to exclusively political issues.

In the later hagiography of church writers the role of James and the opposition of the Jewish leaders are set within a theological framework. The memoirs of Hegesippus (in Eusebius, *HE* 2.23.4–18) and Clement of Alexandria's acceptance of the tradition (in his *Hypotyposes* 7, cited in Eusebius, *HE* 2.1.4) fill in the details of a public debate between the leaders and James. As part of the *mise en scène* James was hurled from the temple pinnacle and clubbed to death for his audacity in proclaiming, "Why are you asking me about the Son of Man? He is seated in heaven at the right hand of great power, and will come again on the clouds of heaven." This allusion to the exalted Son of Man who is to come is doubly interesting: it is clearly influenced by the martyrdom of Stephen (Acts 7:56) and seeks to put in a bid for James' reputation as a true martyr for the faith; and then with a reference to the Parousia, it may refer to the occasion of the debate in *HE* 2.23.10: "There was an uproar among the Jews, the scribes, and the Pharisees, who said that the whole people was in danger of looking for Jesus as the Messiah." But the latter is also clearly a theologoumenon to explain how the Jewish James may be claimed for the orthodox church.

2. When we turn to the second account of the events in A.D. 62 in Josephus, *J.W.* 4.314–25, the narrator's sympathy for Ananus and the Sadducean aristocracy is plain to see (see Smallwood, "High Priests," 13–34 [especially 25–30] and *The Jews under Roman Rule,* 272–84, 314). There is an illuminating cross-reference to the actions of Ananus II as he put down popular leaders such as James in the Palestinian politics of that era. What recent historians, e.g., Horsley and Hanson, *Bandits, Prophets, and Messiahs,* have concluded as a series of factors in first century Jewish-Palestinian society includes the presence of a disadvantaged and disgruntled peasant population contrasted with "the illegitimate character, the compromised position, and the exploitative behavior of the Jewish ruling class" (Horsley and Hanson, 61). The social and political consequence of this tension was the appearance of popular prophets and social bandits who sought to redress the grievances of the masses by playing the role of Jewish Robin Hoods. Jewish brigands and the peasant masses did share a common cause, namely, to raid "the wealthy landowners and the representatives of foreign domination" (ibid., 72), usually the Romans, whose presence in Israel ever since Pompey's invasion in 63 B.C. was a sore spot on the body of Israel's theocratic life. Apocalyptic hopes may have spurred on this turbulence in anticipation of the day when, just prior to the outbreak of the war with Rome in A.D. 66, those hopes were fanned into a burning flame (cf. Barnett, "Jewish Sign Prophets," 687–88).

When Ananus took decisive action against popular figures like James, the best guess is that he was motivated by an animus against prophetic movements in general, which had racked Palestinian life for several decades. Josephus for obvious reasons can speak of these outbreaks only with undisguised contempt:

> Impostors and demagogues, under the guise of divine inspiration, provoked revolutionary actions and impelled the masses to act like madmen (*J.W.* 2.259).

Such leaders offered an array of accrediting signs to promise liberation—or social justice, as they would have claimed, "For they said that they would display unmistakable signs and wonders done according to God's plan" (*Ant.* 20.168). Clearly these men were notable figures: the Samaritan who led a group of followers to Mount Gerizim (*Ant.* 18.85–87); Theudas (*Ant.* 20.97–98; Acts 5:36), who seems to have capitalized on popular ill-will over Herod's extravagant building plans and gifts to hellenistic cities (*Ant.* 19.299 ff.) and professed to be a second Moses leading the people to a new land of freedom; and the Jewish prophet, mistakenly linked with Paul in Acts 21:38, who, in a later decade than Theudas, portrayed his mission as that of a second Joshua (*Ant.* 20.169–71) and prophesied the collapse of Jerusalem's city walls and the onset of a new age located at Mount Olivet in fulfillment of the eschatological hopes of Zech 14.

In the esteem of the people, the charismatic quality and personal magnetism of these prophets would have commanded a widespread following linked with the eschatological overtone that a deliverance from Roman occupation was imminent. The group within Judaism that would view such a prospect with fear and dismay was the Sadducees. They would see such a disruption of the social order in the early 60s as a direct challenge to their power held at the behest of Rome. And if this state of affairs accurately depicts what were the tension points between Ananus II and Jewish Christian leadership in this period then we can understand why the Sadducean high priest would feel his position threatened by James' popular image.

Josephus (*J.W.* 4.305–17) adds some detail to this reconstruction, for, when he records that Ananus was put to death during the events of A.D. 68–69 when the Zealots desecrated the temple, he alleges that the former's shameful exposure at the hands of the Jewish fanatics was an unmitigated disaster for his nation. This was because it took away "the captain of their salvation" and led to the train of events that soon climaxed in the catastrophe of A.D. 70 in the fall of the temple (see Smallwood, *The Jews under Roman Rule,* 314 n.90, on the shift in Josephus' attitude to Ananus; the change is accounted for by the high priest's anti-Roman stance, which became more obvious by A.D. 66). This link of cause and effect—"the capture of the city began with the death of Ananus"—is found in Christian circles. Hegesippus (in Eusebius, *HE* 2.23.18) notes that immediately (εὐθύς) following the death of James, the siege of Jerusalem was begun under Vespasian. Historically speaking this is a telescoping of events separated by several years (from A.D. 62 to 67–68). The chronology may be askew, but the interpretation of events may not be wide of the mark (cf. *Sib. Or.* 4.115–18).

The bias of Josephus is well known. One of his clearest motives in writing is to explain how the Jewish war came about and how the collapse of the Jewish state was directly attributable to "gangs of brigands" (*J.W.* 4.84) who fomented the great rebellion (*J.W.* 4.318–25). It is only to be expected that he would cast Ananus finally in a good light which implies that Jerusalem's fall was a punishment for impiety and desecrating acts of murder in front of the sanctuary and indicates that the sacerdotal aristocrats, represented by the group around the high priest, were anxious to distance themselves from the revolutionaries and bolster their relations with Rome. The question which presents itself at this point is: was that the real reason why Ananus moved against James? Was it that James had got himself involved in revolutionary politics (as Brandon argued in "The Death of James," using the pragmatic principle of a cover-up in Christian literature that was embarrassed by too close a link with the later Zealots to account for the strange silence he perceives in conceding James' involvement)? And did Ananus feel little compunction about his action in calling a *synedrion* on his own authority in defiance of Roman custom because he believed that he could justify the putting down of a populist movement championed by the Jerusalem Christian leader to his Roman overlords?

3. The third place, one in which Josephus writes of relations within the Jerusalem temple personnel, may give yet another aspect to the situation in A.D. 62. In *Ant.* 20.180–81 we are informed that from A.D. 59 on, there was

internecine strife between the different strata of the temple clergy. The priests were in contention with the aristocratic high-priesthood. The latter retaliated by acts of violence and by instructing their servants to expropriate the priests' tithes and so deprive them of their sole source of income, thereby starving them into submission (Smallwood, *The Jews under Roman Rule*, 281; she goes on to discuss further social and economic problems to disturb the peace in Jerusalem in Albinus' procuratorship). Josephus sums up: "Enmity and class war flared up between the high priests on one side, and the priests and leaders of the Jerusalem masses on the other" (*Ant.* 20.180). Part of the tension may be due to the perennial use of legitimacy as Horsley and Hanson, *Bandits*, 62, observe. The high-priestly families who owed their tenure in office to Herod were not Palestinian Jews but powerful families imported from the Diaspora who looked to Rome to maintain them in office and were ill-famed for their exploitation of the poor generally and the lower priests in particular. The result is that here was a situation in which religious questions (are the high priests legitimate or non-Zadokite usurpers?) and socioeconomic issues met and mingled (Brandon, "Death of James," 66). The aristocratic hierarchy was wealthy—by inheritance and business acumen (Josephus refers to the way the Sadducean high priests were both landowners and entrepreneurs in the world of commerce, trade, and agriculture)—and, out of concern for the status quo that brought them prosperity, preferred Roman rule. By contrast, the priests and Levites, who had no such preference, were open to the cause of the poor, with whom they were often identified since they themselves were sometimes employed as day laborers. They would be supportive of the nationalist movements that aimed to overthrow the current regime and took what opportunity they could to strike a blow against Rome. In fact it was the issue of tribute, withheld by the people, and the withdrawal by the lower priestly orders of the daily sacrifice for the emperor's well-being that, in A.D. 66, Rome construed as overt rebellion. The insurrection that occurred a few weeks later was directed as much against the priestly aristocracy as against the Romans (so Horsley and Hanson, 62). There were other issues as well, to be sure, which account for the great rebellion. Josephus (*Ant.* 20.184) mentions the conflict over equal civil rights (*isopoliteia*) at Caesarea. But in fact the ground was prepared over the period in the second procuratorship from A.D. 44 with Cuspius Fadus to A.D. 66 and Gessius Florus' continued economic pressure and increased exactions (*J.W.* 2.277–83) for the outbreak of revolution (see Reicke, *New Testament Era*, 202–210; Schürer, *History*, 1:455–70; Smallwood, *The Jews under Roman Rule*, 284–92; M. Hadas-Lebel, "L'image de Rome," 803–9).

It is not possible to draw any closer lines between the historical James and the political-religious movements that swirled around him and the Jerusalem *Urgemeinde* in those tumultuous years. But certain assumptions and educated guesses may be offered. James' sympathies would certainly have lain with the peasant people and the lower priests. There is some evidence in Acts 6:7; 21:20, which, if taken at face value, would suggest that among the messianic pietists that gathered around James in the Jerusalem church a number of priests were to be included. We may not place too much credence on the tradition in Hegesippus (in Eusebius, *HE* 2.23.5, 6) that turns James into a Nazirite and a member of the priesthood who was "permitted to enter the sanctuary." Many motives seem to run together here, such as a bid to establish a succession-list, with primacy accorded to James, on the analogy of the succession-list of the Jewish high priests after the exile. It may be too that many of these idealized pronouncements and descriptions of James' authority and priestly status stem from a desire to claim him as a second Aaron, in tandem relationship with Jesus, "the prophet like unto Moses" (F. F. Bruce, *New Testament History*, 352). There may equally be, as the previous chapter has suggested, a response to heretical groups that were claiming James' authority for their own ends.

The most we may want to affirm is that both early Christian history and later ecclesiastical development in reaction to other movements on the fringes of the Great Church make James a person of commanding stature and leadership. It is not difficult to conceive of him as playing a significant role in opposing injustice and defending the poor. He could hardly have remained aloof from the social disturbances and political pressures of events that occurred around him. And if one reason above all for the animosity of Ananus II that led to James' hurried trial and violent death is to be offered, it may well be sought in James' desire to cast in his lot with the needy priests and people, whether Jewish or messianic. This action may well have been construed as a support for the revolutionaries, who were guilty, in Ananus' eyes, of subversion and rebellion.

B. James' Role in a Jerusalem Setting

From our résumé of the historical events (however problematical some of them may be and capable of diverse interpretation) we turn to what the letter of James suggests. The spirit of the document, which in some ways has a timeless quality, shines through the chief theme of its pages; it professes a deep concern for and sympathy with the poor and persecuted (2:1–9; 5:1–6). No NT document—not even Luke-Acts (Hengel, "Der Jakobusbrief," 263)—has such a socially sensitized conscience and so explicitly champions the cause of the economically disadvantaged, the victims of oppression or unjust wage agreements, and the poor who are seen in the widows and orphans who have no legal defender to speak up for their rights (1:27). The rich merchants (4:13–17) and luxury-loving agricultural magnates (5:1–6) are held up to withering and scornful reproach. Not only are their practices condemned as part of their profane attitude that forgets God and boasts in proud achievement. Their treatment of the workers and the needy is just as forthrightly exposed. And, to cap it all, James directs his shafts not simply at their amassing of wealth, nor even at the wealth itself—represented in the grain and the gold and the garments that were their trademark (5:2–3)—which is doomed to be blighted. The rich people themselves will share the fate of their possessions (1:11). This indictment marks one of the Bible's most thoroughgoing judgments on wealth and its possessors. We are invited to consider whether there may be some specific historical cause for this extreme verdict; by so doing we are departing from the position of such commentators as Dibelius (40–41) for whom the stereotypical nature of the parenetic material makes identifying the historical allusions difficult if not impossible.

On the other side, the tract deplores violence, anger, and killing, and counsels against impatience and taking action in a precipitate way (1:20–21; 2:11–13; 3:13–18; 4:1–4). Each of these pericopes poses its own exegetical conundrums, and we may refer to the *Commentary* for details. Some telltale signs in the language of these sections, however, may be noted. Human anger is set in antithesis to the divine righteousness, and it is implied that the way to attaining God's kingdom is not along a road of an angry display of self-will. Committing murder is branded as a social crime, we hear, and moreover it is a transgression of the divine law. These prohibitions are given in a context that suggests that James needed to remind his readers of the moral issues when they were in danger of forgetting them or bending the ethical imperatives to their own desires (4:3). The most praiseworthy quality of wisdom—which is God's gift from above (1:17; 3:17) to be given to all who ask (1:5–7) in sincere faith and with altruistic motives (4:2–3)—is that it is peacemaking. Yet his readers were in a situation where "fighting and quarrels" led to such social dislocation that they needed to be warned against the taking of human life in a way that suggests that when they did so they believed they were fulfilling the divine purpose. The better way, says our author, is to seek God's help by prayer (4:1–3) and to turn from friendship with the world (4:4). God will bring in his kingly rule at his own time and in his own way (1:20; 2:13; 5:7–9).

We may thus picture James as a Jewish Christian pietist and leader caught in a delicate position. His ambition, given the two strands of teaching in the letter, was evidently to reconcile opposing factions and effect a *modus vivendi*. He was in declared sympathy with the oppressed poor, whether people or priests, and championed their cause. Our study of 4:13–5:6 will seek to bring to light specific details of their plight in the context of economic and social conditions that prevailed in Palestine-Syria in the mid-sixties of the first century. On the other hand, James opposed the revolutionary manifesto, later to be taken up by the Zealots prior to the A.D. 66 war with Rome, of violent lawbreaking, murder, and class hatred. He has learned from both the Jewish piety of his fathers and the Christian elements in his tradition (to be codified in the Great Sermon of Matt 5–7 and the Q-digest in particular) the need to be tolerant and restrained, which are the virtues commended in 3:17. The call he issued was an appeal for his audience to live with others in mutual respect and without recrimination (3:8–10; 4:11; 5:9; the divisive name-calling condemned by these verses could run parallel with a feature in Jerusalem society to which Josephus, *Ant.* 20.180, makes reference). At the same time, he knew the hollowness of mere religious profession without practical application (1:26; 2:14–16). In a day when economic and social wrongs cried out for redress James directed attention to ways in which the poor and victimized could be helped (1:27) as a sign of a living faith, and equally he was caustic in his judgment of the rich Sadducean priests and their associates who despised and exploited the poor (1:10–11; 5:1–6).

This double-fronted interest on behalf of the poor and against the powerful is in keeping with the two key phrases that characterize the letter. The writer sets his face against the favoritism (προσωπολημψία—2:1) that supports and approves of the rich and refuses to give a fair hearing to the complaints of the oppressed (2:6–9; 5:4). He is just as adamant by his use of δίψυχος, "double-minded" (1:8; 4:8), and the series of contrasts that punctuate his letter that those who sought to gain their rightful aims by violent means stand self-condemned. They lack the quality of single-mindedness that sets its hope on God and awaits his intervention. James issues an overt call to have done with revolutionary method as a way of accomplishing the divine purpose. His counsel is to be "slow to speak, slow to get angry, for human anger does not promote divine righteousness" (1:20); and the warnings against hasty speech and the uncontrolled tongue (3:2–8) are paving the way for a refusal to condone oath-taking (a feature of later Zealot practice: cf. Acts 23:12–15 for an example of an oath undertaken by Jewish extremists) in 5:12. The better path is that of patient waiting for God to act (5:7–11) with the paradigm of Job, who in the end by his perseverance was brought through his trials. This inaction may entail an acceptance of prevailing injustice and hardship (1:2–4). But the promise of eventual vindication is given, based on the Jewish Christian pietist maxim of "the humble will be exalted" (4:6; cf. 4:10) and drawn from the model of the "righteous sufferer."

Yet James is not to be classed as quietist and fatalist. His eschatological hope is pinned on the coming Judge who will soon arise to vindicate the afflicted (5:7, 9). Then the proud will be humbled (4:6) and the Judge will execute his righteous sentence (4:12). Already the process is underway and its outworking is as inevitable as the rising sun (1:10–11) or the harvest home (5:7, 18), even if it takes the unsuspecting by surprise. The Judge has already taken up his position at the door (5:9). The pious are encouraged to hold on until the end comes, with renewed calls to patience and prayer in time of national crisis. Elijah's example should be an incentive (5:17–18).

James is under no illusion that this path is easy or without risk. The prophets met adversity (5:10); Job was sorely tried; Elijah had his enemies both inside and outside the covenant community (5:17: he was a "fellow-sufferer-with-us," ὁμοιοπαθὴς ἡμῖν). And there is the case of the "righteous man," ὁ δίκαιος (5:6), which akin to the fate of the "righteous man" in Wisd Sol 2:12–13 (see later pp. xciii–xcviii), we submit, mirrored the historical James. The latter was renowned for his impartiality (Hegesippus in Eusebius, *HE* 2.23, 10 reports the Jewish leaders as saying, "You respect no man's person": Brandon, *Zealots,* 125 n.1). He also prayed for God to avenge the cause of the poor and judge the oppressor. And he paid the price. Ananus II reacted violently to James' eschatological denunciations of the rich and influential, perhaps more so than to James' messianic pietism and lack of patriotism; and he had him killed. James exemplified in his martyrdom the same spirit he had lived by; now his "testament"—snatches of his didactic legacy—is brought together, woven into epistolary shape, and published in a new *Sitz im Leben* by those who venerated him as "James the Just" and exemplary martyr.

C. The Letter of James

But what of the "letter" that traditionally bears the name of James? There are several reasons why modern scholarship has queried the direct association of the letter with the historical James. Among the more impressive arguments and the responses they have called forth are:

(i) The Greek style, mirroring the higher *koinē* language, is consciously literary (see Turner, "Style," 115, for a cautious estimate of James' so-called classical flair, against Mayor, ccxliv). Its fluent and elegant style would appeal to readers living in the Greek world. The author makes several allusions (e.g., 3:6) which would seemingly only be understood in the world of Hellenism and hellenistic Judaism (Kümmel, *Introduction*, 411). Doubts have also been raised as to whether a Galilean Jew could have composed in this ornate way; but this suspicion has been countered by the argument that such literary composition would not have been beyond the bounds of possibility for a first-century Palestinian Jew (Sevenster, *Do You Know Greek?*, 3–21; Argyle, "Greek," 87–89; Robinson, *Redating*, 132–35; Hengel, "Der Jakobusbrief," 251, on the evidence for a bilingual ethos in Jerusalem). We may point to examples that lead Rendall (*The Epistle of St. James*, 39) to conclude:

> It is time surely to discard the figment of Galilean illiteracy. . . . Philodemus the philosopher, Meleager the epigrammatist and anthologist, Theodorus the rhetorician, and one may almost add Josephus the historian, were all of Galilee.

Rendall's conclusion is that the epistle has its candidate for authorship in a Palestinian Jew, at home in all parts of the hellenistic Scriptures—a conclusion that may stand, while permitting us to doubt whether that author is James in the traditional sense. We have still to account for the conscious literary style modeled on the Septuagint, which is the author's main court of appeal, and the presence of rare terms with some 65 *hapax legomena*, of which 45 are drawn from the LXX. Colloquial turns of phrase and interrogations; a dramatic form of address betraying the spoken word; adages and maxims, replete with paronomasia and rhetorical forms and devices—all these features make this a puzzling document simply because it conforms to no set pattern. As commentators have observed, it would be difficult to categorize it. For some, it uses a type of *parenesis* (exhortation); for others, it is an example of a rhetorical style with its frequent appeals to diatribe, an artificial debating style called into play by hellenistic moral philosophers like Epictetus to enforce a point; yet again homiletic-sapiential literature, parallel with the Jewish synagogue sermons (cf. Thyen, *Der Stil der jüdisch-hellenistischen Homilie*), has been seen as the nearest comparison (Turner, "Style," 116–20, gives the evidence of James' Semitic models). It looks as if there are specimens and *exempla* of all these literary forms and traits.

Aside from the issue of direct authorship, the most secure conclusion is that this document—whether in epistolary form or not—betrays a debt to the literary conventions and idioms of hellenistic Judaism (see J. A. Findlay, *The Way, the Truth, and the Life*, 158). It may have some connection with James in Jerusalem; but its final author, whether as redactor or amanuensis, was well versed in the bilingual vocabulary and writing techniques of the Roman provinces.

(ii) The characterization of the "perfect law of freedom" (1:25) does not seem to square with James' attitudes recorded in Acts and Galatians, which suggest a more legalistic frame of mind. The opponents who challenged Paul were men who "came from James" (Gal 2:12), but we cannot say if they were sent with his approval or as representing his position. They may simply have assumed it, akin to the emissaries' actions in visiting Corinth in 2 Cor 11 and probably claiming to speak for "the 'highest-ranking' apostles." If the traditions that have gathered around James' death have substance, they may indicate that James was not put to death for any infraction of Torah, and that he had close connection with the Pharisees. But the evidence from Josephus (*Ant.* 20.200), as we saw, is ambiguous. Paul, to be sure, may have had little sympathy for James' proposal (in the so-called decree of Acts 15) and may have felt abandoned by James when he was arrested and his life threatened. But we cannot turn James into a Judaizer and so an inveterate opponent of Paul (as the later Clementine literature did) nor regard his references to "law" (in 1:25; 2:8–13) as the sign of a nomism that transformed the gospel into a *lex nova*, a step taken in (say) *1 Clement* (Kirk, *The Vision of God*, 136–38; Ward, "James of Jerusalem," 179–80). More probably the "perfect law" and the "royal law" relate to love for one's neighbor in Lev 19:18, cited in 2:8; and if so, that is very much Paul's understanding of *nomos* in Gal 5:14, "The entire law is summed up in a single command: 'Love your neighbor as yourself' "; and in Rom 13:8–10, "He who loves his fellow has fulfilled the law. The commandments 'Do not commit adultery,' 'Do not murder,' 'Do not steal,' 'Do not covet,' and whatever other commandments there may be, are summed up in this one rule: 'Love your neighbor as yourself.' Love does no harm to its neighbor. Therefore love is the fulfillment of the law." For all James' reputation as a teacher of the law in popular reconstruction, he never once uses the Pauline polemical expression "works of the law" to be set opposite to the faith that justifies (*pace* Hengel, "Der Jakobusbrief," who seeks to show an anti-Pauline polemic directed against Paul's theology [254] and conduct [255–58, 265]).

(iii) Turning to the disputed passage (2:14–26) we observe how it is a common assumption that the telltale presence of the phrase "alone" (μόνον) in 2:24 (a person is shown to be righteous by deeds, not by faith alone) points to a post-Pauline period. W. Marxsen (*Introduction to the New Testament,* 226–31) makes much of this argument. He maintains that the insistence on the formulation "by faith alone" can only make sense against the background of a situation where Paul's attitude expressed in Rom 3:28 is being opposed by Judaic teachers.

For Paul, faith is trust and obedience, showing itself in love (Gal 5:6). But in James a perversion of the Pauline position has appeared which understands faith in terms of intellectual assent and acknowledgment of doctrine (2:19); this aberration James writes against polemically to controvert and correct. Marxsen believes that James only made matters worse, for instead of appealing to the Pauline statement, James so exalts "works" as to end up with "an isolated ethics, a pure nominalism" (*Nominismus*, better translated as nomism; 230).

But this ingenious argument for dating the epistle, while correct in placing the discussion in a setting where Paul's teaching had been distorted, is weak. It overlooks the way in which the debate over justification was already current in Jewish circles (Jeremias, "Paul and James," 368–71). It ignores the fact that James' polemic is not directed in favor of "works of the law" (as in Paul). His opponent is not indicative of a Judaizing trend but of a false creedalism or outward profession that failed to express itself in practical action. Both writers agree on the primacy of faith; Paul sets his face against any attempt to subvert God's gracious initiative by making "works" meritorious (e.g., Rom 4:3–5; Gal 3:6–9; Phil 3:9); James argues that living faith will complement itself by what it does (2:17, 22). Yet the same appeal to Gen 15:6 with a varying deduction drawn from the case of Abraham suggests that there is some tension. The most likely resolution (see *Commentary*) is that James is polemicizing against an ultra-Pauline emphasis that turned faith into a slogan, a badge of profession, and thereby led to a position close to an antinomian disregard for all moral claims. Paul himself disavowed this false step in his lifetime (Rom 3:7–8; 6:1–14, 15; Gal 5:13); now the argument in James 2:14–26 re-engages the extremists who sought to claim that "faith by itself" was all one needed, irrespective of the empirical outworking (see Goppelt, *Theology* 2:208–11, for this term).

(iv) One historical difficulty is less easily disposed of: the slow recognition of the letter and its only eventual acceptance into the church's canon (see Ruckstuhl [8]: how does it come about that the letter was not widely known before the end of the second century if the author was the Lord's brother?). In fact the attestation of the document is unknown until the time of Origen, later than A.D. 200. Origen (*Comm. John* 19.6) calls it Scripture and draws on its content. Yet he is aware that it was not universally accepted, though he occasionally refers to James as the author. Eusebius (*HE* 3.25, c. A.D. 325) placed James among the NT books that are challenged (*antilegomena*) yet he admits that the letter is "well known and approved by many" (cf. 2.23); in 6.14 he implies that Clement of Alexandria accepted James as the author, though no precise exhortation from the letter has been found in the patristic writer's works (Wikenhauser, *Introduction*, 474). Earlier than A.D. 367 when Athanasius' Festal Letter listed "seven Catholic epistles," including James, there is a singular omission of any reference to or extract from this document. The writings of Tertullian, Irenaeus, Cyprian, and Hippolytus are all lacking in allusion to James. It is absent from the Canon Muratori, usually dated around A.D. 180.

Its passage into the canon was slow and halting. Doubted in the East, though the letter is found in the Peshitta version (early fifth century), it gained acceptance in the West under the influence of Hilary (315–68), Jerome (354–419), and Augustine (354–430), yet the witness is not unequivocal. Jerome (*Vir. Ill.* 2) has the most interesting comment: "James wrote a single epistle [*unam tantam scripsit epistolam*] and some claim that it was published [*edita*] by another under his name."

For what it is worth, the evidence of 2 *Apoc. Jas.* 44.13–17 (NH 5) from Nag Hammadi also has this notion of a double authorship, though in a less precise way: "This is [the] discourse that James [the] Just spoke in Jerusalem, [which] Mareim, one [of] the priests wrote."

The puzzle this body of data presents to us is that of explaining why there was such tardy acceptance of the document as authoritative if it was known to have come from James, the relative of Jesus, as Ruckstuhl (see above) observed. Some explanations are decidedly tame. For example it is said that apostolic figures such as the Twelve were accorded more authority than teachers (see 3:1) in the early church, and that this letter had only a limited circulation and appeal (Tasker, 19); or that as a Jewish Christian document it suffered under a liability, whoever wrote it, in the eyes of gentile Christians, while its practical emphasis would have made it of little consequence (Sparks, *Formation of the New Testament,* 129; Mitton, 227–28); or that matters of citation and attestation in patristic sources are largely accidental (Robinson, *Redating,* 132); or that addressed to a specific church (but cf. 1:1!), its message was less applicable than the general letters (Hiebert, 14–15).

The array of objections seems formidable, and on the several grounds of the letter's style, its Jewishness in tone and content, its post-Pauline ambience, and the suspicions it engendered among the church fathers and canon makers, it seems hardly to have been written *as it stands* by James of Jerusalem. Not all the arguments against Jacobean authorship are of equal weight and force, as we observed, but taken together they do pose a serious threat to the traditional view.

On the other side, there is no denying some contrary—and positive—observations. The Palestinian milieu of much of the illustrative matter is undoubted, with allusions to the natural elements of sun, wind, and rain, and the horticultural context. The verbal links between this letter and the speeches of James in Acts are not easily dismissed (e.g., 1:27 // Acts 15:14 ἐπισκέπτεσθαι; 5:19–20 // Acts 15:19 ἐπιστρέφειν; 1:16, 19; 2:5 // Acts 15:25 ἀγαπητός), though the data are still meager in quantity and conviction even when we add in 1:1 // Acts 15:23 χαίρειν; 2:5 // Acts 15:13 "men and brothers, listen"; 2:7 // Acts 15:17 "the . . . name called upon/over you." Robinson (*Redating,* 121) almost certainly overstates a good case when he concludes that "there is nothing in James that goes outside what is described in the first half of Acts"; but there is still some substance in his argument for the setting of much of the letter in a Palestinian context and as redolent of a rural, unsophisticated Christianity for which the burning issues of the Pauline mission were not in view. The Christology is rudimentary (1:1; 2:1); the soteriological questions found in Paul, 1 Peter, Hebrews, and the Johannine literature are passed over; the delay of the Parousia is not a concern to provoke discussion (5:7–11 stands in the parenetic tradition, as Mussner [203] remarks, but the pericope does not grapple with the problem of why the end has not arrived; the verses are simply written to encourage Christians to be loyal in the interim between the now and the then of the endtime).

Yet in one matter Robinson's full coverage of the antiquity of James' provenance may be questioned. And this criticism will bring us directly to a proposal regarding the setting of the letter in its edited and final form. The matter in question relates to ministry and church leadership (Robinson, *Redating,* 124). Granted that there are no references to orders of liturgy and church hierarchy, there is still concern to press the claims of two functional ministries: elders and teachers. The writer identifies himself as both servant (1:1) and teacher (3:1). The elders are recognized as a group within the congregation (5:14) but hardly does the "bishop" appear in 1:27 as Cabaniss, "The Epistle," 29, claims, along with a door-keeper (*ostiarius*) in 2:2, 3. There is some special dignity accorded to the "righteous one" (5:16), which may be connected to the fate meted out to that one—or one like him—in 5:6. Yet there are problems and frictions within the assembly (2:2–12; 4:19; 5:9); and the tendency to defect (5:19–20) is one which has reared its head and needs to be addressed. In all, the main stress falls on the office of teacher, and the entire third chapter is devoted to the use and misuse of the tongue with specific application made to the teacher. The "wise and understanding" teacher (3:13) must reflect in his conduct and his instruction the ways and words of wisdom. The warning signals are listed as "bitter envy and selfish ambition" (3:14), which false teachings have promoted within the community (3:16). The inevitable consequence is "disorder" (3:16; and in 3:8), a term that recalls the congregational problems at Corinth (1 Cor 14). "Selfish ambition" (ἐριθεία) is reminiscent of (but not directed against: so Hengel, "Der Jakobusbrief," 259, by inference) the congregational discord at Philippi (Phil 2:3; cf. 1:17) and Galatia (Gal 5:20) as at Corinth (2 Cor 12:20)—all texts where problems of leadership were involved (cf. *1 Clem.* 5, which has its key term in ζῆλος as in James 3:16: see Cullmann, *Peter*, 104–6). Robinson's remark (loc. cit.) that there is no suggestion of "crisis of authority or need to resort to credentials" may be an unwarranted denial, once we take seriously the emphatic use of the σῶμα-motif in chap. 3 where the teacher's power—by using the tongue—to steer the congregation into right channels as the body is brought under control evidently has some social and theological disturbance in mind. There are good teachers who keep the tongue in check; and there are—by parity of reasoning—false leaders who promote distress by their wrongheaded ideas, their recriminations and boastful ways, and their resort to scheming ambition. The latter are bringing the church to the edge of disaster. The editor's counsel is directed to a regaining of some who have succumbed to their erroneous ideas; they must be brought back (5:19–20; Hengel, ibid., 262, asks if a particular "sinner" [Paul?] is in view, which is most improbable) in a way similar to the pastoral vade mecum of Matt 18:14–20. He encourages them to rejoin the company under obedience to the wise teachers in whose name he has put out this compendium of Jacobean teaching.

It is the Matthean church tradition that he resorts to; with great precision we may find his authority in the pre-canonical stage of that *didache*, as Ropes (39) notes: "James was in religious ideas nearer to the men who collected the sayings of Jesus than to the authors of the Gospels." In fact, the editor's use and adaptation of the Matthean logia tradition (with twenty-three allusions drawn from Matthew in the letter) places his work alongside the document that closely parallels James' epistle in its defense of genuine teachers, namely, the *Didache*, especially chaps. 11–13; 15:2. Both Matthew and the *Didache* share a common viewpoint in some key matters, e.g., the call to perfection (Matt 5:48; 19:21; *Did.* 6.1–2), the place of the law, in particular the Decalogue (Matt 19:16–20; *Did.* 2.1–7), and the honor to be given to the true teacher (Matt 13:52; *Did.* 13.2; 15.2) with due warning that no one should aspire to the office too hastily (Matt 23). There is a noteworthy correspondence in James with these and other ideas. "Perfection" is a key term (see later, pp.

lxxix–lxxxii). The royal law of love to one's neighbor is exalted (James 2:10–12; Matt 22:36–40). The warning in 3:2 is closely similar to what the other documents say, and all three have in their sights the presence and influence of false teachers who would lead the people astray whether as misguided charismatics or false prophets or those who say and do not support their teaching by genuine behavior (see Matt 7:21–27; 23:3; *Did.* 11.4–12; 12:3–5; James 1:22–26; 2:14–26). Sometimes the link is as close as the common use of rare idioms, e.g., James 2:9 (ἁμαρτίαν ἐργάζεσθαι) // Matt 7:23 (ἀνομίαν ἐργάζεσθαι).

Common links between Matthew and James may be observed:

Rejoice in trials (Matt 5:12)
Count it a joy when you are tried (James 1:2)

Ask and it will be given you; seek, and you will find (Matt 7:7)
Let such a person ask from God . . . and he will give it (James 1:5)

Be therefore perfect (τέλειοι) as your heavenly Father is perfect (Matt 5:48)
Let endurance yield its complete (τέλειον) work that you may be perfect (τέλειοι) and complete (James 1:4)

Blessed are the meek . . . peacemakers (Matt 5:5, 9)
Wisdom is both meek . . . peacemaking (James 3:17–18)

He that endures to the end will be saved (Matt 24:13)
The person who endures testing . . . will receive a crown of life (James 1:12)

Don't judge, lest you be judged (Matt 5:7; 6:14–15; 7:1)
The one who shows no mercy will be judged (James 2:13)

Prohibition of oaths (Matt 5:33–37)
Prohibition of oaths (James 5:12)

In praise of meekness (Matt 5:3)
In praise of meekness (James 3:13; contrast 4:6, 16)

Against hoarding (Matt 6:19)
Against hoarding (James 5:2–3)

Against anger (Matt 5:22)
Against anger (James 1:20)

Against lip service (Matt 7:21–3)
Against lip service (James 2:14–16)

Against divided loyalty (Matt 6:24)
Against divided loyalty (James 4:4)

Against slander (Matt 5:22; 7:1–2)
Against slander (James 4:11)

Blessing of the poor (Matt 5:3 // Luke 6:20)
Blessing of the poor (James 2:5)

Warning against the rich (Matt 19:23–24)
Warning against the rich (James 2:6–7)

Help to the poor (Matt 25:35)
Help to the poor (James 2:16)

Example of the prophets (Matt 5:12)
Example of the prophets (James 5:10)

Eschatological imminence (Matt 24:33)
Eschatological imminence (James 5:9)

Comparing the *Didache* with James, we observe that the cardinal sins to be watched for are the double mind or the double tongue (*Did.* 2:4: διγνώμων . . . δίγλωσσος: 4:4 οὐ διψυχήσεις) and the unfeeling indifference that bypasses a fellow-Christian in need (*Did.* 5:2). Impartiality in dispensing justice is advocated (*Did.* 4:3). The name invoked in baptism is the triune Godhead (*Did.* 7:1–3), which James may allude to *simpliciter* as the "worthy name" called over you (James 2:7). Problems to do with exposure to temptations and deliverance from evil are common; in *Did.* 8:2–3 it is a matter of praying the Lord's Prayer, while James 1:13–16 raises it as a pastoral issue. Forgiveness of sin and united confession are major items of pastoralia to be reckoned with (*Did.* 11:7; 14:2; James 5:9, 16). And the eschatological overtones are heard in view of the imminence of the Lord (*Did.* 10:6; chap. 16; James 5:9).

The three documents we have looked at do not belong to the same literary category. Matthew shares in the genre "gospel"—or more especially βίβλος (from Matt 1:1: Marxsen, *Mark the Evangelist,* 50). The *Didache* is a church order-cum-"manual of discipline," incorporating earlier and common traditions such as the Two Ways (*Did.* 1–6; *Barn.* 18–20; Kirk, *The Vision of God,* 111–24; Streeter, *The Primitive Church,* 281–83). James has its own pristine form (*Gattung*) as a parenetic miscellany (Dibelius, 3), but it has been editorially completed to conform to the genre "epistle" with both superscription (1:1) and closing section (5:12–20) designed to give the impression of a letter format (see later, pp. xcviii–c, and *Commentary,* with reference to Francis). Yet all three compositions do possess common elements (cf. Shepherd, "The Epistle of James"), and may each be justifiably located in the same geographical region, namely, Antioch in Syria (see Streeter, *The Primitive Church,* chap. 5).

The deposit of James' teaching, according to our understanding, was carried there—to Antioch on the Orontes—by his disciples; and in this bilingual setting the "testament of James" was edited and adapted to meet the pastoral needs of some community in the Syrian province. Two discussions may be noted. Geyser, "The Letter of James," proposes an Antiochene locale, seen as the place to which Jewish refugees or displaced persons (*niddachim*) fled. But he identifies this migration with the one referred to in Acts 11:19–30 as the sequel to Stephen's death in Acts 7 and (improbably) puts the letter before A.D. 48 and the Jerusalem Council. More plausible is Zimmermann's set of five arguments in favor of an Antiochene provenance of the document: (1) the importance given to teachers (3:1); (2) the witness of the letter in the later church in Syria (cf. Kümmel, *Introduction*, 414); (3) the literary connections between this treatise and Matthew, Ignatius' letters, and the *Didache*; (4) the climatic allusion in 5:7 corresponding to weather conditions in Syria-Palestine; and (5) the evidence of James' presence and influence at Antioch, according to Gal 2:12, or in Syria, according to Acts 15:13–21, with a resultant debate over pseudo-Paulinism in James 2:14–26. On the other hand, Zimmermann's denial of all connection with James the Lord's brother is unwarranted. See *Die urchristlichen Lehrer*, 194–96.

In our view, assuming a two-layered stage in the production of the letter, the presence of hellenistic idioms and the polishing of the material ascribed to James the Jerusalem martyr with stylistic traits and literary flourishes such as the diatribe and the repartee would be the work of an enterprising editor. He published his master's work in epistolary form as a plan to gain for it credibility as an apostolic letter. And in doing so, he aimed to address a situation of critical pastoral significance in his region. The nub of the problem was a challenge to the authority of teachers in a congregation whose listeners' roots went back to the early days when "prophets and teachers" were the chief leaders (Acts 13:1). Drawing on James' testamentary legacy and more on his role as preeminent teacher, the editor has put in a plea for unity within the ranks of a congregation that was sufficiently socially stratified to have poor and rich together. His voice was raised on behalf of the underprivileged and the disadvantaged, as he used what James had left on record in indictment of the Sadducean hierarchy and in defense of the Jerusalem "pious poor" at an earlier time.

Whether the editor succeeded we cannot tell. But what may be affirmed with some confidence is that in publishing this letter under the aegis of James the Lord's brother he set in motion a train of events that led to a veneration of the master as both model teacher and heroic martyr. In gnostic circles James became the leading apostolic figure as both ascetic and revelator; in the Catholic tradition of the Great Church he took his place as a venerable member of the holy family, an episcopal figurehead, and the preeminent "just one." On both wings he became idealized; and perhaps the first step in the process of that exaltation of James came when his followers collected his scattered sayings, put them into an epistolary framework, and hailed him as the "righteous man."

D. THEMES IN JAMES

Bibliography

Davids, P. H. "Theological Perspectives on the Epistle of James." *JETS* 23 (1980) 97–103. **Dix, G.** *Jew and Greek: A Study in the Primitive Church.* London: A. & C. Black, 1953. **Elliott, J. H.** "Peter, Silvanus, and Mark." In *Wort in der Zeit*, FS K. H. Rengstorf, ed. W. Haubeck and M. Bachmann. Leiden: Brill, 1980. 250–67. **Malina, B. J.** "Wealth and Poverty in the New Testament." *Int* 41 (1987) 354–67. **Mánek, J.** "Mit wem identifiziert sich Jesus? Eine exegetische Rekonstruction ad Matt. 25:31–46." In *Christ and Spirit*, FS C. F. D. Moule, ed. B. Lindars and S. S. Smalley. Cambridge: Cambridge UP, 1973. 15–25. **Manson, T. W.** *The Sayings of Jesus*. London: SCM, 1949. **Maynard-Reid, P. U.** *Poverty and Wealth in James*. Maryknoll, NY: Orbis, 1987. **Mussner, Fr.** "Der Begriff des 'Nächsten' in der Verkündigung Jesu." *TTZ* 64 (1955) 91–99. **Schnackenburg, R.** *The Moral Teaching of the New Testament*. Tr. J. Holland-Smith and W. J. O'Hara. London: Burns and Oates, 1965. **Streeter, B. H.** *The Primitive Church*. London: Macmillan, 1929. **Zmijewski, J.** "Christliche 'Vollkommenheit': Erwägungen zur Theologie des Jakobusbriefes." In *Studien zum Neuen Testament und seiner Umwelt* 5, ed. A. Fuchs. Linz, 1980. 50–78.

Irrespective of the precise setting of the letter—or its settings, if we are correct in our attempt to suggest two *Sitze im Leben*: one in Jerusalem in the early 60s and a second some decades later in Antioch in the Syrian province, about which G. Dix (*Jew and Greek*, 33) wrote, "[it was] a bastion of Hellenism in the Syriac lands . . . the inevitable meeting point of the two worlds"— there are several outstanding features of James' teaching. But the exact flavor of that teaching will naturally depend on the background. The first collection of utterances attributed to the historical James, we submit, was made in Jerusalem. It arose directly out of his involvement in the Jewish Christian contretemps centered upon the opposing factions of the poor and the messianic priests on the one side, and the Sadducean aristocracy on the other. The third member of a triangle of influences is represented by the forerunners of the Zealots, whose bitter hatred of the rich made them an attractive choice for the poor. James, planted firmly in the welter of this situation, sought to exercise a moderating and mediating role. What he advocated may be seen in the elements of the teaching that champion the cause of the poor and persecuted, and at the same time that discountenance resort to violence and class enmity. His martyrdom sealed this witness, which was later handed on to his followers who escaped to settle in urban communities along the Syrian coastline.

It is to these hellenistic disciples of James that we owe the codification of the master's teaching that venerated his martyrdom and memory, and edited his words in order to make them available in new situations that arose in later decades. In the Jewish Christian synagogues and communities there were manifold problems of social snobbery; of legal disputes; of wealth and privilege and the care of the needy; of theological disputations that turned on the place of "good works" against a background of extreme fideism that raised the Pauline cry "by faith alone" in an exaggerated way; and above all of a challenge to leaders and teachers on the part of those who promoted personal ambition and fanaticism and led others astray (5:19–20; these verses form the basis of Davids' argument that "some are not standing firm," "Theological Perspectives," 98). These, we may affirm, were the conditions that called forth the edited publication of James' testamentary document, and in this way what is known as the letter of James the Just saw the light of day. In its final form it received its superscription (1:1), which claimed Jacobean authority for it, and it was thought to be a timely document to transmit to a wider audience in a way akin to the distribution of the letter of 1 Peter.

Streeter's understanding of how 1 Peter—originally a sermon and a letter—was subsequently edited and circulated by the addition of 1:1–2 and 5:12–14 is suggestive (*The Primitive Church*, 128–30) and may be seriously entertained without his further speculation that the actual author was Aristion of Smyrna and that the additions were made in Pliny's time. Indeed, recent studies in 1 Peter support the idea of a Petrine collegium that sought to preserve the testament of the apostle and make his influence more widely known than in Rome (J. H. Elliott, "Peter, Silvanus, and Mark") or the Asian province (Streeter). The fact that both superscriptions (1 Pet 1:1; James 1:1) use the same term, διασπορά, *diaspora*, for their addressees may be significant as indicating that in this way both documents were given a more-than-local appeal, with the common element the conviction that believers, whether Jewish Christian (James) or gentile (1 Peter), formed a new Israel (cf. F. F. Bruce, *New Testament History*, 353 n.7). But we should also include the character of the new Israel as a suffering community, which is typical of the verb διασπείρω in the LXX (where it is found twelve times).

Leading themes in James may now be considered.

1. Perfection

The use of τέλειος has been surveyed by J. Zmijewski ("Christliche 'Vollkommenheit,'" 52–55), who finds it to be a key word in the epistle. Of the nineteen times it occurs in the NT, five are in this document (1:4a, b; 1:17; 1:25; 3:2), with other occurrences of the same root in 2:8 (τελεῖν) and 2:22 (τελειοῦν). Corresponding terms are also to be reckoned: ὅλος ("whole," "entire") in 2:10; 3:2, 3, 6 and ὁλόκληρος (1:4). The opposite term δίψυχος, found in 1:8; 4:8, is unique to James and "denotes the divided man as opposed to the 'simple' [e.g., singlehearted]" person (Schweizer, *TDNT* 9:665). Also as a counterpoint to τέλειος there is ἀκατάστατος (1:8; 3:8) and the noun ἀκαταστασία ("disorder") in 3:16.

A lexical point worth noting is the way τελ- is used with important nouns in the letter: with ἔργον (1:4; 2:22), σοφία (cf. 1:5, 17); πίστις (2:22; cf. 1:6) and νόμος (1:25; 2:8, 10). This is no accident, since "the perfect person" (τέλειος ἀνήρ) in 3:2 is one for whom there is no disparity between word and act, faith and works. Also James' notion of "completeness" is not a human achievement but a divine gift (1:17). Yet it requires application to situations in order to ward off the double-dealing of which the readers were in peril. The letter was written, Zmijewski argues (78), to prevent the danger of a separation (*diastasis*) between faith and works, and τελ- plays the part of uniting the two. It is this coherence of faith and deeds that gives a unifying theme to the entire document and makes it a genuinely Christian writing (75–76).

Clearly the intention behind the letter's exordium (1:2–4) is that the reader should attain to the goal of a "perfect work" (ἔργον τέλειον), a phrase capable of being taken in several ways, whether it means that their endurance will be carried through completely (Mayor, 36) or their character will be achieved in its completeness as endurance "does its work of perfecting" (so Dibelius, 74). Evidently completeness is related to the quality of "heroic endurance" implied in ὑπομονή, and the result is that they will become τέλειοι καὶ ὁλόκληροι—almost synonyms—"perfect and complete," with no part lacking. The background here is the Old Testament idea of *tām*/*tāmîm* or *šālēm* which, when the terms are used in a noncultic context (Vouga, 40; cf. Delling, *TDNT* 8:72–87; Hoppe, *Theologische Hintergrund*, 26–32), suggests the integrity of obedience to the divine commands rather than the rabbinic idea of "free from defect." The term has an eschatological promise of life in the new age (Mussner, 67) and is part of James' advocacy of the new creation (1:18) rather than a bid to claim ethical "perfection" (Schrage, 15, who notes how "completeness" is achieved only by testing).

Several references to the root τελ- illustrate what is meant: 1:17, God's bounty is τέλειον, as is the "law that makes free" (1:25) when the believers render obedience that translates into positive action. At 3:2 the person who is able to keep the tongue in firm check is pronounced τέλειος ἀνήρ, and this self-control is elaborated by what follows in terms of the ability to use the power of speech to guide the church aright and to offer worthy praise of God with wisdom-words, the chief trademark of the kind of teacher whom James approves of. In fact, the road to perfection for the author is that of a practical and peace-loving wisdom (3:17–18) which joins together the three ideas associated with the profession of true religion (1:26–27). The first of these is obedience to the law which in 2:8–10 is defined as supreme among all the commandments, i.e., love for one's neighbor, and so the law that sets its adherents and practitioners free (2:12) from the imprisoning circle of egocentrism and enables them to "fulfill the law" (perhaps in the sense of Matt 5:17 and Rom 13:8).

The second element of Jacobean perfection is faith, spoken of in 2:22. The way by which Abraham's faith-obedience to God was "completed"/"perfected" (ἐτελειώθη) was by his deeds, and James' insistence on this close nexus of faith issuing in works and works energized by faith (2:22) allows no room for any misconceptions regarding what he deems perfection to be (Eichholz, *Glaube und Werke*, 44, on the unity of faith and works in James). It is not mere profession of a sentiment (2:15–16; 1:27) nor a statement of creedal assent (2:19).

There is the active element in faith which aspires to the goal. So, third, the emphasis on ἔργα, "deeds," must be included in any assessment of James' description of the path to perfection. "Works" are evidently for this writer similar to the Jewish teaching on "acts of kindness" (גמילות חסדים, *gᵉmîllûṭ ḥᵃsādîm*, lit., "handing out of kindnesses": cf. *'Abot* 1:2; and Matt 5:16, τὰ καλὰ ἔργα). By such demonstrations of practical concern and tangible support pious Jews could show their interest in and help for the poor; the fact that in rabbinic Judaism such charitable acts were treated as meritorious should not, however, lead us to the same conclusion regarding James' requirement. Rather he views ἔργα as the necessary counterpart to and complement of πίστις. When the two characteristics of the moral life are conjoined, they point the road to τελείωσις.

But faith is a broader concept than initial belief even when that expresses itself in positive endeavor. Trials have come to the readers to subject their faith to testing (1:3), and there is need for dogged persistence (ὑπομονή) to keep on believing to the end that will surely come as deliverance is promised

(5:11). Perfection, then, is not easily secured, and the addressees must expect to share the afflictions of Israel's loyal pietists, such as the prophets, Job, and Elijah (5:10–11, 17). Faith is seen in social relationships; those who believe "in the glorious Lord Jesus Christ" (2:1) should not imagine that they can combine that faith with respect of persons in their splendid clothes and advertised self-importance. Faith refuses to be swayed by these appearances and casts in its lot with the poor who are "rich in faith" (2:5) even if they are despised and victimized by the world's court of opinion. For James this identity with the pious poor and a disavowal of the influential rich is what is meant by "religion," which is more than a profession in name only (1:26) but shows itself in open sympathy with the socially depressed and helpless (1:27). This grounding of faith in a this-worldly situation where there is an existential call to take sides and a corresponding refusal to be content (and so self-deceived, 1:26) with verbal platitudes (even if expressed as "pious prayers," 2:16) and stately creed (2:19) comes to dramatic expression in 2:14–26. In thirteen verses, πίστις occurs eleven times, with varying nuances ranging from a futile expression (2:15: can this kind of faith save?) to an ineffective belief (2:20), with James' own clear preference for a faith which is not "by itself" (καθ' ἑαυτήν, 2:17) but rather is expressed by deeds of compassion and so brought to perfection (2:22). That perfection is then called the blessedness of being justified by God, as Abraham was (Gen 15:6), and believers like the patriarch share the privilege of friendship with God (2:23; cf. 4:4). Rahab illustrates how faith is shown to be justifying when the sign of her inclusion in the covenant community is conveyed by what she did, i.e., she assisted the spies and helped them on their way. The association of practical assistance betokening faith is similar to Matt 25:31–46 where the service of missionaries in their various distresses is said to be rendered to the Lord of the mission himself and the givers are rewarded with bliss (see T. W. Manson, *The Sayings of Jesus*, 251; J. Mánek, "Mit wem identifiziert sich Jesus?" 15–25).

Finally we should note how faith is the driving force behind prayer. In time of serious need—such as experiences of persecution and living under duress (5:13: see *Comment*)—James advocates the primacy of "the prayer of faith" (5:15), which is effectual, at least in securing God's will to be done (5:16). Here and at 1:6 this type of praying needs both a firm conviction (not having doubt) and an undivided allegiance that resists distraction. Both features go back to James' indictment of the "two-souled individual" (δίψυχος, 1:8; 4:8), a puzzling term that suggests on its Old Testament-Judaic background an attempt to live with competing allegiances (cf. 1 Kgs 18:21). Professing devotion to God, the "divided person" also seeks a compromise with "the world" (4:4) or makes a secret agreement with the devil (4:7). There may be a historical context in which these warnings were fashioned, namely, a time of tension within the Jewish Christian community in Syro-Palestine under the Romans which led to the polarities of high-priestly rapprochement and Zealot activism. James is counseling a *via media* that puts its whole trust in God and his eschatological vindication without human aid or enterprise. So in 1:5–8 the invitation is to ask for heavenly wisdom to guide the nation's destiny and the church's future. But a caveat is entered (1:6): do not try to compromise by seeking entanglements whether political or military (a scene akin to Isa 7:1–17: Ahaz's real trust was not in Yahweh but in the Syro-Ephraimite coalition), and don't think that prayer designed for selfish ends will ever prosper (4:2–3). Such an attitude is branded "immoral" (4:4), using the prophetic language against Israel's apostasy as a harlot from her true Husband, Yahweh.

2. Wisdom

Outstanding among the gifts that proceed from God is wisdom (1:17; cf. 1:5: for wisdom in the background of this letter see the following chapter). The character of God, according to James, is such that all his giving is good and is meant to reassure the congregation that their lives are not at the mercy of fate or subject to the vagaries of astral religion (see the *Comment* on 1:17–18, where it is argued that the reminder of God's control of the stars and his initiative in bringing about the "new birth" of his children is intended to meet this kind of objection). He is the Father in realms of both nature and grace, and it is his delight to give what is wholesome as gifts "from above." When we set this adverb alongside its recurrence in 3:17 the link with wisdom will be seen:

All good gifts are from above (ἄνωθεν) coming down (καταβαῖνον) from God: 1:17. The wisdom from above (ἄνωθεν) is true, set over against the false wisdom which does not come down from above (οὐκ . . . ἄνωθεν κατερχομένη): 3:15, 17.

The heavenly wisdom must be sought and asked for by mortals (1:5), but they may do so with the assurance that God's giving is generous and gracious—twin qualities that mark out divine giving from much human benevolence and benefaction, however well-intentioned.

The path of the two wisdoms suggests a context in which some were claiming that their commitments to violence and hatred were sanctioned by God. To this James retorts with a firm denial (1:20), and proceeds to berate their recourse to wars, fightings, and murder as a way to achieve the divine purpose in history (4:1–4). His outlook is very similar to *Diogn.* 7:4: "Coercion is not God's method of working." The better way is that of a wisdom marked by peace-loving and tolerant policies; only thus will the ends of righteousness be secured (3:17–18).

James, however, is under no illusion that the "way of wisdom" is an easy road or that his counsel promises success and acceptance. The historical James met bitter hostility and was hastened to death where he received a martyr's crown. Now the legacy of his testimony warns that since wisdom is a virtue of the righteous sufferer in Israel, those who follow his line must expect to join the ranks of the noble army of martyrs. Teachers, in particular, in the school of James are encouraged to show by their good conduct that they are committed to wisdom supported by meekness (3:13). When they are called on to suffer, they should not find it a cause for alarm or querulous anxiety. On the contrary the call "reckon it pure joy, my brothers, when you become involved in testings of many kinds" (1:2) is the opening gambit placed as the frontispiece of the final draft of the letter. It requires wisdom—the Hebrew tradition of wisdom as ability to make sense of life's perplexities when there is no apparent reason for the righteous to suffer is pressed into service here (see below, pp. lxxxvii–lxxxix)—to handle these attacks. So the just person will pray in faith and with wholehearted allegiance to God's cause for the very gift (1:5); and in the confidence that "it will be given to him."

The temptation to be filled with doubt and distraction must have been strong; otherwise it is difficult to explain why the writer should return to the theme in the second member of the letter's "double opening" (1:12 paired with 1:2). There is a subtle shift of nuance, however. Testings of external persecution (1:2) lead to temptations (1:12–16) to cast aspersion on God's character. So James offers an extended theodicy (Mussner, 86, 92) seeking to justify the ways of a strange providence that permits suffering and trial. Thereby he is meeting the objection that these outward persecutions are a sign of divine displeasure and disfavor. He replies: God tempts no one (1:13); rather the temptation to turn testings into occasions of stumbling is a wrong step for which his people are held personally accountable (1:14). There follows the record of a sad chain reaction whereby desire entices and impregnates with an evil seed only to produce the offspring of sin, which in turn develops into the full-grown monster, death. Jewish rabbinical ideas of the "evil desire" (*yēṣer hā-rāʿ*) are clearly in mind, with the same intent—namely, to fasten responsibility for evil not on God or the devil (otherwise to be resisted, 4:7), but to lay its accountable weight on the individual. This is developed in 4:3, where failures to gain answers to prayer are traced to the same evil desires when the readers intend to "use God" (in Luther's phrase) for their own ends.

Another mark of wisdom is to recall how frail our life is (4:14), and to have regard to the contingent element that should run through all our plans and proposals. The famous "Jacobean condition" (4:15) reminding the reader that the phrase "if the Lord wills" should rightly preface all human decisions and determinations underlines the same point. The immediate background is the case of the godless merchants (*pace* Hengel, "Der Jakobusbrief," 255, 258, who sees a tirade against Paul in these verses. But this suggestion is not supported by the commercial terms used, in spite of 1 Cor 9:19–22; 2 Cor 2:17) whose business enterprises and desire to get wealth are an invitation to divine retribution—not because wealth is evil per se or because they are possessed of entrepreneurial skill and good business foresight but because they "glory" in their pretended independence and self-sufficiency (4:16–17), which James treats as the essence of sin.

Patient waiting for God to act is the obverse of this mood of self-congratulatory ambition and unthinking indifference to the poor (5:1–6), qualities that are the hallmarks of "folly" in the sapiential literature (Sirach, Wisdom of Solomon, *1 Enoch* in particular: see *Comment*). The note of joy-in-suffering sounded in chap. 1 is now justified. Afflicted believers may be glad in their low estate because their exaltation is at hand (1:9–10), just as the godless rich have only a prospect of humiliation and judgment (paradoxically) to console them. That "eschatological reversal" is imminent (5:8–9), and forms the backcloth of much of the wisdom instruction in chap. 5. The hortatory call, however, is new as the virtue of heroic endurance, first stated in 1:4, is amplified and illustrated by the Old Testament-Judaic traditional models. Eminent wise men like Job and practical leaders such as Elijah have set the pattern for the readers to follow.

3. The Piety of the Poor

This handy phrase, used by the Germans (as *Armenfrömmigkeit* leading to *Armenethik*), sums up several leading motifs throughout this letter. It is seen in 1:9–11; 2:3–7 (15–16); 5:1–6, 7–11. The counterpoint (in the majority of these texts) is the present godless and uncaring attitude of the wealthy whose riches have dulled their sensibilities, led them into an unthinking confidence that the future is at their disposal (4:13–17), and above all, have closed their hearts and pockets against the poor in their distress and brought rank injustice to the harvest field. As we noted earlier (pp. lxii–lxix) James' scathing indictment of the godless merchants and unjust agriculturalists may well be set against a historical background of Palestinian economics and social order prior to the leader's death in A.D. 62.

It is helpful to make a distinction that the letter as we have it seems to imply between the various classes of "poor" and correspondingly of the "rich." In 1:27 the set pictures of need are drawn from the OT stereotypes of the two classes most vulnerable to oppression and neglect: widows and orphans. Pure religion is concerned to help such cases. The question is an open one whether there were actual widows and orphans in James' congregation (cf. Acts 6:1) and he is using their plight in a concrete, rather than a merely illustrative, way. The term for their "distress" (θλῖψις) has an eschatological overtone, which suggests that they belong to the group whom God will vindicate at the last day, pointing on to chap. 5. Clearly in 5:1–6 there are day laborers and harvesters who are being cheated out of their due (daily) wages, and this is causing hardship which James seeks to rectify. The spirit of "complaining" (5:9) may be part of the picture, though it may also refer to the internecine strife of 4:11. A mood of dissatisfaction within James' (or his editor's) community is to be detected; and it looks as if false teachers are partly to blame along with the obviously unjust estate owners who have withheld wages and caused hardship.

In 2:3 the poor person who enters the meeting is called ὁ πτωχός (strictly speaking, this refers to economic state: so it means the beggar who has only filthy clothes to cover him). The complementary term is ὁ ταπεινός, "the humble," in 1:9, and he is clearly a member of the community as ὁ ἀδελφός, "the brother"; whereas the visitor to the synagogue may be an interested inquirer, perhaps a person casually seeking help in his impoverishment or redress in his grievance. Perhaps at 2:15–16 we are meant to see the beggar who has made some sign of attachment to the community (the man and woman are called respectively "brother," "sister": ἀδελφός, ἀδελφή) but their need is most obvious from their wretched appearance in dress and demeanor. The piety referred to in 4:6b is not disputed. The promise of exaltation is given to the humble, representing a group who await God's deliverance. They are the "afflicted of the Lord," the ʿanawim, who wait for vindication at the last day. If they meet trouble in the interim they are encouraged to pray and seek the elders' ministrations (5:13–15) and the fellowship's mutual support (5:16). Thus there were several classes of "poor" known to James' community: those who were disadvantaged and neglected through no fault of their own, widows and fatherless; those who were economically victimized, workers whose sad state was due to their employers' greed and indifference; and those who were reduced to dire straits of poverty and wretchedness, perhaps because they had no legal rights. In some way not quite clearly defined these groups represented people who trusted in God for help, and so their poverty was equally a "poverty in spirit" in the sense of Matt 5:3; 11:5 (cf. Luke 4:18), and their religious outlook was similar to that of the pious ones in the Lukan nativity stories (Luke 1–2).

In both sets of teaching (James; the Synoptic writers' accounts of Jesus' mission and message) the poor are promised the gift of the kingdom (Luke 12:32; James 2:5). Other points of connection unite the two strands of teaching: both show how the rich attack the poor; both warn against the greed and avarice of the rich; both have the encouragement and consolation set in the framework of the humiliation-exaltation of the poor; and both insist on tangible help for the needy neighbor whose "definition" is that he or she is any person in distress, without qualification, as in Luke 10:25–37 (see Mussner, *Der Jakobsbrief*, 83–84, and his essay, "Der Begriff des 'Nächsten'").

Yet there is one distinction to be noted. Whereas the oppression of the poor by the rich is mainly depicted in parabolic form in Jesus' teaching (e.g., Mark 12:1–12; Luke 16:19–31; 18:1–8), in James the antipathy to the rich is more forthright and couched in the style of diatribe by the use of what Mussner (84) calls "drastic examples," notably in 2:1–7; 5:1–6, where "concrete experiences" (Mussner, 80) are set forth in such a way as to lead Dibelius to conclude that "being a poor person and being a Christian are one and the same" (adapted from *James* [ET], 44). The converse of this statement, which concludes that the "rich" are treated as either non-Christian or "people whom [James] considers no longer to be included in a proper sense with[in] Christendom" (Dibelius, 87–88), is not accurate, as Maynard-Reid, *Poverty and Wealth*, 43–44, shows. James' community evidently had not fully identified with the poor, and the author hopes to steer them to a deeper identity with the oppressed (so Bammel, *TDNT* 6:911; Schnackenburg, *Moral Teaching*, 362–64) by exposing the follies and excesses of professed believers. He does this by giving to the social connotation of πτωχός (brought out by Malina, "Wealth and Poverty," who seeks to show that the rich in the culture of Mediterranean society in NT times were by definition regarded as avaricious, while the poor were those who had lost their social status and power) a religious quality inherent in the term ταπεινός. He does not exalt poverty for its own sake (contra Davids, 27: implied in his heading to 2:1–26; see later). Rather he interprets poverty as desirable only insofar as it offsets the world's verdict (2:5a πτωχοὶ τῷ κόσμῳ: cf. 2:6) and contrary to outward appearance is a sign that God has chosen the poor and endowed them with a status that includes them in his kingdom (2:5–6), and so paradoxically they are πλουσίους ἐν πίστει, "rich in faith," a description that paves the way for the disquisition on "true faith" in 2:14–26.

Attempts to evade responsibility to assist the needy are contemptuously dismissed in several places: 1:22–25 ("doing the work" looks on to the practice of 1:27), while in 1:26 it is the essence of self-deception to make a loud protestation of sympathy for the poor and do nothing more. The latter is a species of "vain religion," which is then illustrated in the scenario of 2:2–4 (the treatment of the beggar) and that of 2:15–16, where false faith merely expresses platitudes but "does nothing about . . . physical needs" (v 16, NIV).

The poor—whether as impoverished or as victims—are portrayed as helpless to aid themselves. Yet they have the ear of God (5:4), who will swiftly come to their rescue. So James not only holds out the pledge of inheritance in God's future kingdom (2:5); he promises divine action here and now in the vindication of the cause of the ill-treated and offers divine solace and healing in their affliction (5:7–8, 13–16).

5. BACKGROUNDS TO JAMES

Bibliography

Baasland, E. "Der Jakobusbrief als neutestamentliche Weisheitsschrift." *ST* 36 (1982) 119–39. **Bergant, D.** *What Are They Saying about Wisdom Literature?* New York: Paulist Press, 1984. **Bonnard, P.-E.** "De la Sagesse personnifée dans l'ancien Testament à la Sagesse en personne dans le nouveau Testament." In *La Sagesse de l'Ancien Testament*, ed. M. Gilbert. BETL 51. Leuven: Leuven UP, 1979. 117–49. **Clarke, E. G.** *The Wisdom of Solomon.* Cambridge: Cambridge UP, 1973. **Collins, J. J.** "Cosmos and Salvation: Jewish Wisdom and Apocalyptic in the Hellenistic Age." *HR* 17 (1977) 124–42. **Crenshaw, J. L.** *Old Testament Wisdom: An Introduction.* Atlanta: Knox, 1981. ———. *Studies in Ancient Israelite Wisdom.* New York: KTAV, 1976. **Davis, J. A.** *Wisdom and Spirit: An Investigation of 1 Corinthians 1:18–3:20 against the Background of Jewish Sapiential Traditions in the Greco-Roman Period.* Lanham, NY/London: University Press of America, 1984. **Gammie, J. G.**, et al. *Israelite Wisdom: Theological and Literary Essays in Honor of Samuel Terrien.* Missoula: Scholars Press, 1978. **Halson, B. R.** "The Epistle of James: Christian Wisdom?" *SE* 4 (1968) 308–14. **Hengel, M.** *Judaism and Hellenism.* Tr. J. Bowden. 2d ed. 2 vols. London: SCM, 1983. **Hermisson, H.-J.** "Observations on the Creation Theology in Wisdom." In *Israelite Wisdom*, ed. J. G. Gammie et al. 43–57. **Hubbard, D. A.** "Wisdom." In *The Illustrated Bible Dictionary*, ed. J. D. Douglas. Leicester: Inter-Varsity Press, 1980. Pt. 3, 1650–51. ———. "The Book of Proverbs." *ISBE* 3:1015–20. **Jacob, E.** "Wisdom and Religion in Sirach." In *Israelite Wisdom*, ed. J. G. Gammie et al. 247–60. **Kirk, J. A.** "The Meaning of Wisdom in James: Examination of a Hypothesis." *NTS* 16 (1969) 24–38. **Kleinknecht, K. T.** *Der leidende Gerechtfertige.* WUNT 2,13. Tübingen: Mohr, 1984. **Küchler, M.** *Frühjüdische Weisheitraditionen.* Freiburg and Göttingen: Universitätsverlag, 1979. **Mack, B. L.** *Wisdom and the Hebrew Epic.* Chicago: University of Chicago Press, 1985. **Morgan, D. F.** *Wisdom in the Old Testament Tradition.* Atlanta: Knox, 1981. **Rad, G. von** "'Gerechtigkeit' und 'Leben' in der Kultsprache der Psalmen." *Gesammelte Studien zum Alten Testament.* ThB 8. 4th ed. Munich: Kaiser, 1971. 225–47. ———. *Wisdom in Israel.* Tr. J. D. Martin. Nashville/ New York: Abingdon, 1972. **Ruppert, L.** *Der leidende Gerechte.* Forschungen zur Bibel 5. Würzburg and Stuttgart: Katholisches Bibelwerk, 1972. **Schnabel, E. J.** *Law and Wisdom from Ben Sira to Paul.* WUNT 2,16. Tübingen: Mohr, 1985. **Schoedel, W. R.** "Jewish Wisdom and the Formation of the Christian Ascetic." In Wilken, R. L., ed., *Aspects of Wisdom in Judaism and Early Christianity.* Notre Dame: University Press, 1975.

169–99. **Schweizer, E.** *Lordship and Discipleship.* SBT 28. London: SCM, 1960. **Scott, R. B. Y.** "Solomon and the Beginnings of Wisdom in Israel." In *Wisdom in Israel,* ed. M. Noth and D. W. Thomas. VTSup 3. Leiden: Brill, 1955. 262–79. ⸻. *The Way of Wisdom.* New York: Macmillan, 1971. ⸻. "Wisdom in Creation: The ʾAmôn of Proverbs viii.30." *VT* 10 (1960) 213–23. ⸻. "Wisdom: Wisdom Literature." *EncJud.* Jerusalem: Keter; New York: Macmillan, 1971. 16:558–63. **Skehan, P. W.** *Studies in Israelite Poetry and Wisdom.* Washington, D.C.: Catholic Biblical Association of America, 1971. **Welten, P.** "Leiden und Leidenserfahrung im Buch Jeremia." *ZTK* 74 (1977) 123–50. **Whybray, R. N.** *Wisdom in Proverbs.* Naperville: Allenson, 1965. ⸻. *The Intellectual Tradition in the Old Testament.* Berlin: de Gruyter, 1974. **Wolff, H.-W.** *Jesaja 53 im Urchristentum.* 3d ed. Berlin: Evangelische Verlagsanstalt, 1953. **Wood, J.** *Wisdom Literature.* London: Duckworth, 1967. **Zimmerli, W.** "Concerning the Structure of Old Testament Wisdom." In *Studies in Ancient Israelite Wisdom,* ed. J. L. Crenshaw; tr. B. W. Kovacs. (= "Zur Struktur der alttestamentlichen Weisheit." *ZAW* 51 [1933] 177–204). ⸻ and **J. Jeremias.** *The Servant of God.* SBT 20. Tr. H. Knight et al. London: SCM, 1957.

By common consent among modern interpreters of this epistle (see in particular the works of Halson and Kirk) there are two major motifs in the background of the writer and his document: the idea of wisdom and the picture of the righteous sufferer in the Jewish community. We shall devote some space to these as a way of elucidating the kind of situation this letter is addressing.

A. WISDOM

The term "wisdom" stands for two aspects of Jewish culture and religious ethos. On the one hand, it may refer to a body of texts that extol the virtue of wisdom as part of the pious person's way of belief or practice in society. The other side is covered by an understanding of wisdom as a religious stance undertaken by godly persons in Israel. In this context wisdom represents their world-view and response to situations usually of a problematic kind, e.g., those occasioned by the presence of evil, the prosperity of godless people, and the trials that come to all. Wisdom is that outlook which when embodied in practical endeavor enables the pious believer in Yahweh to face life, to make sense of its enigmas, and to surmount its problems. "Wisdom takes insights gleaned from the knowledge of God's ways and applies them in the daily walk" (Hubbard, "Wisdom," 1650). Part of the meaning of wisdom is knowledge or understanding, a facet which is classically stated in Sir 39:1–11, a text written in praise of the scholar-sage (Mack, *Wisdom,* 92–104) and which is emphasized by von Rad (*Wisdom in Israel,* 78):

> The good man is the one who knows about the constructive quality of good and the destructive quality of evil and who submits to this pattern which can be discerned in the world.

Yet this is not, for von Rad, the whole story. The wisdom that is sought lies within the world order but it is beyond human grasp. Speaking of wisdom in Job 28, he remarks:

> It is also . . . something separate from the works of creation. This "wisdom," this "understanding" must, therefore, signify something like the "meaning" implanted by God in creation, the divine mystery of creation (ibid., 148).

The component of "mystery" as a necessary adjunct to the experiential or cognitive side (brought out by Whybray, *Intellectual Tradition*, who treats wisdom as "shrewdness," part of an intellectual tradition addressed to the problems of ordinary individual citizens in Israel, alongside the attitudinal aspects, 8, 69–70) emphasizes how human beings are driven to seek wisdom as a divine gift, while at the same time acknowledging that there are unexplained dimensions in the world and existence. These we may call surd evil, before which no rational account of theodicy is possible (see on Job, von Rad, *Wisdom*, 221). The world of "contingency and ambiguity" (in Bergant's phrase, *What Are They Saying*, 18) poses problems in the human attempts to "cope with reality" (von Rad's chapter title, *Wisdom*, chap. 7).

If von Rad highlights the element of surrender to life's patterns of good and evil and the disposition of being content to live within them, Zimmerli (in *Studies in Ancient Israelite Wisdom*, 198) is more positive. He argues that wisdom permits the righteous not only to know life's secrets, pleasurable and painful, but to gain mastery over them:

> Wisdom seeks to be a human art of life in the sense of mastering life in the framework of a given order of life.

Crenshaw (*Old Testament Wisdom*, 24) adds in the dimension of a search for wisdom, which is obvious from some of the best-known OT texts (Job 28:12–28; Prov 1:5; 2:1–15; 4:1; 6:6–11). Wisdom is

> the reasoned search for specific ways to assure well-being and the implementation of those discoveries in daily existence.

This search is a leading theme in the later sapiential tradition. There, in Sir 14:20–27, it assumes the character more of an obsession or a master passion as wisdom becomes the object of committed inquiry. It has turned into a quest for survival (Crenshaw, *Old Testament Wisdom*, 173) when both Yahwism and the wisdom legacy itself were at stake (E. Jacob, "Wisdom and Religion in Sirach," 257–58).

Yet another aspect of wisdom falls to be noticed. It is the theology of creation in Israel's wisdom writings. Zimmerli writes: "The wisdom of the Old Testament stays quite determinedly within the horizon of creation. Its theology is creation theology" (cited according to H.-J. Hermisson, "Observations," 43). Divine wisdom is seen in the act of creation (Prov 3:19–20) and its maintenance (Prov 8:22–31), so that the Lord of creation is the fit subject of praise (Sir 24), who by wisdom ordered all things (Ps 104:13–15). The epitome of wisdom as the artificer (Prov 8:30: on *'āmôn* = "craftsman," see Whybray, *Wisdom in Proverbs*, 101–3) of Yahweh and as the agent that ensures that creation is both a work of art and full of meaning is in Eccl 3:11: "He has made everything beautiful in its time" (see Crenshaw, *Studies*, 34: "creation . . . assures . . . that the universe is comprehensible"). At the heart of this Hebrew-Jewish understanding of God's creation is that of an ordered universe—with its corollary of the essential rightness of things—to which evil poses a challenge, and demands a justification of God.

To this definition of wisdom's function we should reiterate the qualification that wisdom itself is a divine gift (hence it is associated with Torah in Sirach as in Proverbs; see Davis, *Wisdom and Spirit,* 16–23, on interrelated ideas represented by σοφία, νόμος, and πνεῦμα). The single human response that brings wisdom within the reach of attainment is *obedience.* It is those who hearken to Yahweh's law and seek to apply it to the multifarious ways of life who will gain wisdom and know how to walk before Yahweh with humility and devotion, especially in time of testing.

One final feature needs also to be added in: wisdom increasingly took on an international, transcultural flavor appropriate to the way the wisdom movement was part of a much wider religious and intellectual ferment within the ancient Near Eastern world. The result is that among Israel's sages cultic issues tended to drop into lesser prominence, and wisdom became, in the hands of those wise teachers, a perfectly suited instrument for emphasizing how Israel's faith was a world religion capable of appealing to a wide variety of cultural and social needs. So R. B. Y. Scott ("Wisdom," *EncJud* [1971] 16:558) writes:

> It was a way of thinking and an attitude to life that emphasized experience, reasoning, morality, and the careers of man as man rather than Israelite. Its interest was in the individual and his social relationship rather than in the distinctive national religion and its cult.

It remains. to be seen how far these descriptions of the role of wisdom illumine James' thought. At face value there are several pointers in the direction of a conclusion that makes James a teacher of wisdom in the Israelite-Jewish tradition, in spite of Dibelius' disclaimer (4, 27, 35–37) that it is only accidental or coincidental that James' idioms are parallel with what we have in the wisdom corpus. Halson ("The Epistle of James," 308–10) appeals to the way that James self-consciously reflects the wisdom traditions; and we may note with Webber, "ΙΑΚΩΒΟΣ," 14–22, such features as the use of a common language to describe how rich people *drag* (ἕλκουσιν) the poor into court (2:6; Job 20:15 LXX: "an angel will *drag* [ἐξελκύσει] riches out of his house"); the *withering* of riches with the verb common to James 1:10–11 and Job 15:30 LXX: "a wind will *wither* (μαράναι) his bud, but his flower will fall"; and the call to constancy (ὑπομένειν) in James chaps. 1, 5 evoking memories of Job 15:31 LXX: "Let him not believe that he will *remain* (ὑπομενεῖ)." But these are examples that hardly suggest conscious indebtedness.

More interesting is the use of a common set of pictures and metaphors (see Scott, *The Way of Wisdom,* 75–85), vividly told to suggest some dramatic turn of events like the brevity and frailty of life, e.g., the fading flower (James 1:11; cf. 4:13–15) which is seen in Prov 27:1; Eccl 12:6; Job 13:28; Sir 11:20. Or, the movement of the heavenly bodies in James 1:16–18, recalling Job 38:33 LXX, which runs literally: "Do you understand the turning (τροπάς) of the heavens / or the happenings under the heaven in harmony?" See too Wisd Sol 7:18, 19 (Vouga, 57).

The most obvious figure of speech, leading to personification in Jewish ideology, is that of wisdom herself (Heb. חכמה, *ḥokmāh,* sometimes *ḥokmōṯ;*

Greek σοφία). The evolution of this personification begins with Prov 8:22–
31 where wisdom shares in the divine creation as God's *'āmôn* (a troublesome
word, capable of several meanings, e.g., "master-workman" or "child" [NEB
"darling"] or "guardian" or even "living link/vital bond" uniting Yahweh
and his world; for the last meaning see Scott, "Wisdom in Creation," 213–
23) and so praiseworthy as an "ideal feminine" in Prov 7:4, 8:30–33 as well
as in contrast to "Dame Folly" in 9:13–18. She thereafter picks up several
laudable epithets which make her the object of devotion, loyalty, and acclama-
tion. For example, she is hailed as the tree of life (Prov 3:18; Sir 1:6, 25;
14:26–27; 24:12–14, 16–22); the source of living water (Sir 15:3; 24:23–31);
a divine perfume (Sir 24:15); the light of God (Wisd Sol 6:12; 7:10, 26, 30;
cf. Eccl 2:13). Above all, she is associated with Torah as a divine gift to
Israel (K. Hruby, "La Torah identifée à la Sagesse et l'activité du sage dans
la tradition rabbinique," *Bible et vie chrétienne* 76 [1967] 65–78). See P.-E.
Bonnard, "De la Sagesse personnifée," 126. The Book of Wisdom develops
in a direction that betrays a strong hellenistic-stoic influence and moves beyond earlier models in its grounding of moral exhortation in ontological
ideas (see Schoedel, "Jewish Wisdom," 180–83, in Wilken, *Aspects of Wisdom*).
It draws on the traditions that emerge with Job 28; Prov 8; Sir 24. It gives
to wisdom a quasi-independent, ethereal concept as God's breath (7:25): see
Wisd Sol 17:26:

> She is a reflection of the eternal light, an untarnished mirror of God's creative
> power, and an image of his goodness.

Wisdom, while not personified in this remarkable way in our epistle, is
extolled as a divine gift and a superlative virtue, and is possessed of some
personal characteristics that form a wisdom aretalogy, i.e., a poem in which
the virtues of wisdom are listed (as in Wisd Sol 7:22–24) and praised (see
Scott, *The Way of Wisdom,* 219; cf. James 1:5; 3:13–18). There is also the
notion of wisdom in motion in Wisd Sol 9:10–18 in a way that could be
compared to the verbs of descent in James 3:13–18, though it is going beyond
the evidence to suggest the idea of *katabasis* in Wisd Sol 9 as Bonnard, "De
la Sagesse," 144 n.54, does.

Less obvious examples are seen in the use made of such images as the
ship (Prov 30:19; Sir 33:2 LXX; 4 Macc 7:1–3), and the horse, which is a
symbol of untrammeled freedom of movement (Wisd Sol 19:9) and head-
strong power (Ps 31 [32]:9 LXX; Sir 30:8; Prov 26:3; cf. Prov 21:31) as in
James 3:3–5. (The two illustrations of the ship and the horse are brought
together in a specimen of hellenized wisdom instruction known as *The Teachings of Silvanus* in the Nag Hammadi library, 7.4.90: he who lacks the mind
is like a ship without a helmsman and is tossed about, and a man without
reason is like a horse that has no rider.) In that context too fire is a pictorial
term for an evil that spreads (Sir 11:32; 28:11–12), thereby bringing down
divine wrath (Prov 17:5; Sir 28:22–23), and this is connected with the ill
effects of the tongue (Sir 28:14, 18–21; *Pss. Sol.* 12.2–3).
   We turn now to a larger issue, namely, that of themes which conceivably

show the way in which this epistle is heir to the Jewish wisdom tradition. We may isolate three examples:

(a) *Figures who embody wisdom.* The most celebrated person to be intimately linked with wisdom in the Hebrew-Israelite religion is Solomon, traditionally associated with various collections of wise sayings in the canonical book of Proverbs (1:1; 10:1; 25:1), and known as the one who prayed for the divine gift of wisdom (1 Kgs 3:5–12; 4:29–34; 10:1–10, 23–24; cf. Wisd Sol 7:5–7; Sir 47:12–18; see Scott, "Solomon and the Beginnings," 262–79).

In the Book of Wisdom other OT personalities are praised, though often indirectly: Noah (10:4), Jacob or Joseph (10:9–14); and in the list of heroes in the *Laus Patrum* of Sir 44:4, 15 wisdom is mentioned as one of the attributes for which they were renowned (ἔνδοξοι, 44:1) and are now lauded. Philo picks out Abraham as a wise one (*Migr. Abr.* 122, 149) and Moses as "all-wise" (*Migr. Abr.* 76) along with the nation that is blessed by being wise (*Migr. Abr.* 25; cf. *2 Apoc. Bar. 3.9–4.7*). Enoch (in *1 Enoch* 92.1) is lauded for his wisdom, as is Hezekiah, who is also known as righteous and who received answers to his prayers (*2 Apoc. Bar.* 63.5; cf. Prov 25:1).

Interestingly in our letter the stress falls on Abraham, Job, and Elijah as persons of practical faith and prayer, probably because Enoch and Hezekiah were less well-regarded Old Testament worthies.

(b) *Prayer and wisdom.* These are intimately conjoined in many of the characters referred to above. In an extended prayer (Wisd Sol 7–9) Solomon prayed for "the spirit of wisdom" (Wisd Sol 7:7), which exceeded all wealth (v 8). The links to this passage with the teaching on prayer in James are several (9:4, 6 to be compared with James 1:5 referring to a lack of wisdom; 9:6–13 to be paired with James 1:5 by common terms "perfect," "wisdom that comes from" God; with James 2:1 by the term "glory"; with James 4:15 by an appeal to "what the Lord wills").

Job was a prayerful person (Job 42:8–10) whose intercessions were effective as he remained constant in faith (James 5:11). That same note of availing prayer is the hallmark of the righteous man (Prov 15:8, 29; *2 Apoc. Bar.* 63.5) as in our epistle (5:16). If prayer is unanswered, the cause is a person's disobedience to Torah (Prov 28:9) and a failure to practice his religion consistently in matters of social justice (Sir 34:23–26)—both marks of the wisdom tradition in James. This trait of consistency is lacking in divided (1:6–8) and disobedient (4:3) persons who do not put their faith into action (1:22–27; 2:16–17).

(c) *Wisdom and peace.* The close link in James between wisdom as God's gift to be sought (1:5) in prayer (4:2) and the blessing of "peace" (3:17–18) invites a comparison with the way a similar connection is drawn in Jewish sources. Sirach is a rich deposit of this teaching (Schnabel, *Law and Wisdom*, 25–26). Wisdom bestows her first gift with the offer of peace: Sir 1:18: "The fear of Yahweh is the crown of wisdom, making peace (εἰρήνην: שָׁלוֹם, šālôm) and perfect health to flourish." Cf. James 1:12. The teaching goes back to Prov 3:2, 17 (cf. 12:20), and to Deut 4:40; 5:33; 6:2; 11:8–9, 18–21 where both peace and longevity are a consequence of faithfulness to God's commands.

"Goodwill" (Heb. רָצוֹן, rāṣôn; in Sir 1:27 God's delight—εὐδοκία—is associated with wisdom when practiced with faithfulness [πίστις] and meekness [πραότης]) is another fruit of wisdom. It is seen in obedience to God's law (Sir 2:16; 15:1) and the pursuit of forgiveness (Sir 35:5). These are both evident virtues in our letter (1:25; 2:8; 5:16). Peace brings joy (Sir 4:12 LXX; 6:28) and is a prophylactic against sin (24:22). Again these are concerns of James' pastoral counsel.

It is in Sir 24:13–17 that wisdom like a tree produces both peace and prosperity in a nature study that James, in his own way, exploits: see 1:11; 3:11–12; and especially 3:18: "Peacemakers who sow in peace produce a crop of righteousness."

(d) *Eschatological motifs.* The nexus between a pragmatic and this-worldly religion and the yearning for divine intervention into cosmic history is one that at first glance is hard to justify. Yet in the later wisdom books (e.g., Wisd Sol) the link is there, probably because of a common concern to trace all activity, divine and human alike, to the creator. At the center of the Hebrew faith is the belief in a creator-God who places all things "in order" (Gen 1; Job 28; Ps 104: on the connection with the Egyptian concept of *maat* [order] see Whybray, *Wisdom in Proverbs,* 61–63). Evil, which connotes disorder and disharmony with the will of the creator, is a challenge to that divine purpose. But in the end order—on a cosmic scale as well as in human society and individual lives—will be restored. Hence the sages anticipate a near end (cf. Job 19), later transformed into a threat of retribution on the godless but implying the salvation of the righteous (see Collins, "Cosmos and Salvation," 121–42).

James carries forward this teaching with his stress on the divine creation (1:18) and the call for order to reverse the destructive and disintegrating effects of evil (3:6). His main interest, however, lies elsewhere, namely, in the social inequalities and injustices that cry out for divine visitation and rectification (2:5–7; 4:11–12; 5:1–9). In the meantime, as an "interim ethic," the readers are counseled to patience and quiet waiting for God to act (5:10, 16), in the spirit of the wisdom teachers who took Job as their model.

Conclusion

Among the several lines of investigation that give evidence of Jewish influences and point to the conclusion that James' letter is built on ideas found in Jewish antecedents is the use made of a *wisdom ideology.* The way in which the author cites his material suggests that he is drawing from a common stock or fund of tradition, and he uses the concept of wisdom in a thoroughly Jewish manner, i.e., in a way that is primarily practical and hortatory (his frequent "brothers" replacing the familiar "son" [υἱέ] in Proverbs; this usage of ἀδελφοί appears to be unique in the OT wisdom school, Webber claims, 22. We may note, with Schoedel ["Jewish Wisdom," 174–76, in Wilken, *Aspects of Wisdom*], how *The Teachings of Silvanus* in the Nag Hammadi library builds on classical Jewish wisdom forms like "my son" and emphasizes "discipline" [*paideia*] while going beyond Jewish teaching in many ways). Wisdom for our writer is intensely active; hence verbs of implied motion may be ascribed to it, in 3:15, 17. It is at work in God's creation (1:18) and is itself a divine gift (1:5; 3:17). It centers on moral aspects of life, both restraining evil and promoting the good and the right course of endeavor. Wisdom's rationale is that life is transitory (1:9–11, 15; 4:13–16) and the end is near (4:12; 5:9). In that setting wisdom calls for social justice in the community and a straightening out of inequalities that displease the Almighty (5:1–10). Yet two outstanding differences between Jewish sages (who tended to reflect upper-class values: Hubbard, *ISBE* 3:1018) and James may be noted. First, James has a much more forthright condemnation of the rich members in his target audience than we meet in the Jewish literature (see 1:11; 5:1–6), yet he does not praise poverty as a virtue *in se*. The nearest he comes to the latter is 1:9, but he still draws back from extolling poverty and equating it *simpliciter* with piety. See the qualification in 2:5.

Second, his linkage of suffering and wisdom shares the outlook of the Judaism of the Dispersion (in 4 Macc) more than the Palestinian wisdom tradition, and he is less concerned to connect wisdom with Torah obedience than was customary in the OT-Judaic tradition in books such as Proverbs, Sirach, and *Second* [or *Syriac*] *Apocalypse of Baruch*. True, he employs the terminology of "law" (νόμος) but sets it in contrast with any legalistic obedience by stressing the relationship of νόμος to faith, love, and its practical outworking (see 1:6; 2:5; 2:23; 5:15).

We may conclude by remarking on the general impression of James' recourse to wisdom teaching. He is content to stay within the framework set by Jewish teachers with their emphasis on religious practicality and propagation. The summons is to obedience to God's will made known in his "royal law" and actualized in a living, loving response to human need (a response that Baasland, "Jakobusbrief," 119–20, has classified as *hortatio*). Yet in troubled times the righteous who seek to live by this standard will meet opposition and persecution (Wisd Sol 2–5). Hence the call is to patient endurance in expectation of God's imminent vindication.

B. The Righteous Sufferer

The character in Old Testament-Judaic religion who may be called "the righteous sufferer" has a long history. (The development of this persona has been chronicled by K. T. Kleinknecht, *Der leidende Gerechtfertige,* and we have largely followed his lead.) The two sides of the designation belong together, with a third term that joins together the twin ideas of (i) those who strive to be humble and devoted to Yahweh and his way, and (ii) the vocation of suffering that is laid on such persons. The third term is a connecting one that suggests that the one who is humble will be rejected by the world and despised, yet he will look to God for his ultimate vindication and reward. That destiny is usually described in terms of exaltation and final glory for the righteous in Israel. At issue in this type of literature is the realization that since God's character is just and faithful he may be relied on to bring the afflicted righteous out of distress into ultimate triumph. Inasmuch as the "poor in spirit" tended also to be socially disadvantaged without human resource and economically weak in the face of strong enemies, it was natural that they should look solely to God to vindicate them. Their present sufferings were uniformly regarded as praiseworthy and meritorious; and from this last idea there developed the notion of suffering as having atoning power (see Zimmerli and Jeremias, *The Servant of God*, 50–78).

With this broad survey we may look at selected examples of the ways in which the "righteous sufferer" was viewed, noting in advance that the picture is by no means a homogeneous one. Rather, the idea goes through a long process of development and adaptation to changing conditions and beliefs.

(a) The origins of "the righteous" in Israel are probably to be traced to a cultic setting, as in Pss 15 and 24. The righteous here is known for his devotion to Yahweh expressed in the liturgy of the Torah and the worship of the sanctuary. Moral qualities of personal and communal integrity are seen to be equally important (Pss 15:2–5; 24:4), and there is the promise given of blessing from Yahweh and vindication (צְדָקָה, *ṣᵉdāqāh*) from the God of salvation.

Such a character, almost inevitably, will meet opposition and become the target of abuse and attack. So the righteous person has to contend with "enemies," both personal and as a group. This is the awareness to which the Psalms give expression, e.g., Ps 35:24–27. Vindication and redress are described in the prayer that is offered both *against* the opposing forces ("Let them be put to shame and confusion altogether who rejoice at my calamity!") and *on behalf of* the group whom the speaker represents ("Let those who desire my vindication [צֶדֶק] shout for joy and be glad, and say evermore, 'Great is Yahweh, who delights in the welfare of his servant!'"). The psalmist's enemy is personalized in Ps 35:10 as the one who is "too strong" for "the weak" and "needy"; here we meet the theme that runs like a thread through this literature: the oppressing rich and the victimized poor, with a hint expressed in Ps 7:14–16 (cf. Prov 11:8) that when God intervenes (Ps 7:6, 8) to deliver the righteous the roles will be reversed as the wicked rich are brought low.

(b) Israel's prophets encountered the social problems caused by economic oppression. Amos 2:6b–7 is typical and sets the pattern for future development: "because they sell the righteous (צַדִּיק, LXX δίκαιος) for silver, and the needy (אֶבְיוֹן, LXX πένης) for a pair of shoes; that trample the head of the poor (דַּלִּים, LXX πτωχοί) into the dust of the earth, and turn aside the way of the afflicted (עֲנָוִים, LXX ταπεινοί)."

The merging together of synonymous terms such as "righteous" and "poor"/"afflicted" is an important factor, alongside the indictment of the luxury and selfishness of the rich in Israel (Amos 6:1, 4–6) abetted by the corrupt priests (7:10–17) and the popular expectation of "the day of Yahweh," which Amos challenged (5:18–20; 8:1–14). In current parlance the day of Yahweh was anticipated as an occasion for nationalist pride and prosperity. Amos defused such a hope by standing popular ideas on their head. When Yahweh intervened, the rich would be punished by going into exile (7:17) and the nation destroyed (5:27; 8:1; 9:1), save for the righteous remnant (9:8b, 11–15).

The model of an afflicted minority comes to poignant expression in a succession of individual pictures: the individual laments of the Psalms that reflect the invasion and fall of Judah and the Davidic kingdom (e.g., Ps 137);

the prophet Jeremiah who "in his message (e.g., 8:18–22) is the first prophet to make use of the category of individual lament" (so P. Welten, "Leiden," *ZTK* 74 [1977] 123–50, esp. 148); and after the exilic experience has run its course, the suffering servant of Isa 40–55, which in chap. 53 reaches its high point with its characterization of "the righteous one, my servant" (צַדִּיק עַבְדִּי). He is the epitome of affliction (Isa 53:3–4) and suffering that is borne vicariously (53:5–6); yet in the end Yahweh vindicates and exalts him (53:11–12).

(c) One feature of the postexilic psalms contained important seeds for the future, namely, the interrelation of suffering and wisdom. The connection may be seen in Lam 3, but it is vividly expressed in such psalms as Ps 34, which is a thanksgiving eulogy of God conveying the experience of the afflicted pietist who lives by the fear of Yahweh (34:7, 9, 11) and gives voice to that experience in language that became typical of Israel's wisdom tradition (34:13–18). "The afflictions of the righteous" (34:19; cf. 34:2 for the writer as a member of the circle of the "afflicted" [עֲנָוִים]) sums up the writer's lot; but Yahweh's delivering power is the main theme. Suffering, as Kleinknecht notes (*Der leidende Gerechtfertige*, 60), is here taken to be, not an exception, but a normal part (*Normalfall*) of the righteous pietist's experience; and this observation is foundational for the later wisdom schools. The wicked are a real threat, but their fate is sealed by Yahweh's judgment shortly to be executed (Ps 37:10–13, 17). Divine chastisement may be visited on the righteous but God's rebuke (as in Ps 39:11) is intended to lead to a deeper awareness of his covenant faithfulness that will not fail his people (Ps 94:14–15), even when the righteous are not spared the bitterness of death (Pss 49:15; 73:24). The wisdom motif in the Psalms (e.g., 90:12–15) is joined with the expectation that God will ultimately vindicate the pious and abase the wicked (Ps 147:6). In the meantime—while divine intervention is delayed—the psalmist receives consolation in the belief that suffering is Yahweh's will, however inscrutable (Pss 44:22; 69:7, 33), and that in the end all will be well (the Book of Job is an extended commentary on this theme).

(d) Three documents of early Judaism contribute much to the progressive understanding of suffering endured by the righteous: Sirach, Wisdom of Solomon, and the *Psalms of Solomon*. Each of them offers material that illumines the topic as a background to the Epistle of James.

We look briefly at the Wisdom of ben Sirach. (i) Sir 2:1–11 announces, as its leading theme, the prospect that those who serve Yahweh must expect trial (πειρασμός, 2:1). The experience of affliction, to be borne with steadfastness (v 2), is likened to the refining process of gold when it is tested (δοκιμάζεται) in the fire; approved persons will be subjected to a "furnace of humiliation" (ἐν καμίνῳ ταπεινώσεως, v 5), as in Prov 17:3. Such a trial introduces the righteous to "a time of affliction" (ἐν καιρῷ θλίψεως, v 11); but deliverance is at hand since "Yahweh is compassionate and merciful" (οἰκτίρμων καὶ ἐλεήμων). If the sufferer shows perseverance (ἐνέμεινεν, v 10) he will attain to eventual joy (εὐφροσύνη, v 9).

The synthesis here of the sapiential teaching on purification through trial and a submission to Yahweh is a marked feature, coupled with the promise of a reward (2:8). The believer in time of testing must not fail through allowing his tongue to lead him astray (22:27, echoing Ps 141:3). The "discipline of wisdom" (παιδεία σοφίας, 23:2) is his security and restraint. The outcome will be a happy one, if he follows Yahweh's law (51:1–12, which is a hymn of praise for deliverance and answered prayer).

(ii) The conjoining of Torah and wisdom is already a part of the psalmist's idiom (Pss 37:31; 40:9; 94:12). In Sir 24 it is especially important because thereby the link with "the righteous" is established. The section is a wisdom aretalogy, that is, wisdom sings her own praise (24:1) and seeks a dwelling place in Israel (24:8–12); in fact, she is incarnated in Torah (24:23), which is designed for the instruction of Israel's leaders and people (24:34: see von Rad, *Wisdom in Israel*, 245–47, 254, who downplays Torah's role in Sirach's thought in favor of placing wisdom at the center; Bergant, *What Are They Saying*, 69, puts the point epigrammatically: "The question [for Sirach] is not 'How can wisdom be Torah?' but rather 'How can Torah be wisdom?'" But the issue is raised afresh in Schnabel, *Law and Wisdom*, who argues the case for treating ben Sirach's contribution as that of identifying Torah and wisdom, united by "the concept of the fear of the Lord which is the goal of both wisdom and law" [88–89] and going back to Deuteronomic theology and the OT wisdom psalms). This feature marks out the righteous who contend for "the truth" (4:28: LXX; MT צדק) and gain instruction (παιδεία, 32:14).

The document called the Wisdom of Solomon is celebrated for its portrayal of the *passio iusti*, the suffering of the righteous man, with which the book opens (chaps. 2–5). Kleinknecht has happily used the term "diptych," a two-paneled scenario, to show how this literary device offsets the theme. In 2:12–20 "the righteous poor man" is depicted as maltreated and condemned to a shameful death. His moral character was evidently a protest against the indolence and pride of the godless (2:12, 15). His claim to be a "child of God" (παῖς θεοῦ, 2:13) was the crowning indictment, and he is harried to his painful and ignominious end (2:20; 3:10). There was none to help, not even God (2:18). But the oppressors were self-deceived (2:21–22).

At 5:1–7 the righteous man returns, in a dramatic *peripeteia* or sudden reversal of fortune. His forthrightness (παρρησία) causes amazement, and it leads to repentance on the part of the onlookers in a way akin to Isa 52:13–53:12 or Ps 94 (93 LXX) or Dan 12 (see Kleinknecht, *Der leidende*, 105–6, for the options, citing Ruppert and Wolff). If the last-named reference is the closest parallel, it is tempting to relate the text to strife within Jewish sectarian movements (Sadducees vs. Pharisees in the reign of Alexander Jannaeus, 103–76 B.C.; or Qumran vs. the Jerusalem establishment, with the "Teacher of Righteousness" being cast in the role of the persecuted servant of God). What is perhaps more important is the way these contrasting pericopes of the fate and rehabilitation of the righteous set the stage for the apocalyptists' more developed antithesis between good and evil. The language of God's servant who is victimized and killed only to be restored and exalted to join the saints (5:5) is part of the religious vocabulary of Jewish sages in time of testing, though portrayed in a highly dramatic way.

The writer's enemies, described in 1:16–2:11, represent the powerful and unbelieving (2:11 with a play on the term δικαιοσύνη, "Let our might be our law of *righteousness*, for what is weak shows itself to be useless"). Faced with such formidable opposition there is little the righteous minority can do in self-defense. Their attitude, however, is one of compliance and acceptance that yields to God's testing so that "like gold in the furnace he tried them and found them worthy of himself" (3:6). In the end they will come through to glory, while the ungodly will be judged (3:10); the secret of their victory is that they stand firm with him in love (οἱ πιστοὶ ἐν ἀγάπῃ προσμενοῦσιν αὐτῷ, 3:9).

The *Psalms of Solomon* is written from the standpoint of those who are variously designated "those who fear Yahweh" (2:33), the pious (2:36), the servants of God (2:37). The disciplinary aspect of suffering is set forth in a common term, παιδεία, e.g., *Pss. Sol.* 13:7–12, with a central text: "For he will admonish the righteous as a beloved son and his discipline (παιδεία) is as for a firstborn" (13:9; cf. 18:4). Such a bitter experience is a mark of divine favor (13:12; 17:42), and there is the promise of eternal life (13:11: "the life of the righteous is forever," εἰς τὸν αἰῶνα) contrasted to the fate of the wicked who is to be removed to destruction (cf. 3:12, which is an assurance of resurrection that builds on the hope in 2 Macc 7 promising that the martyrs will be raised [cf. Dan 12:2; Job 33:29–30]).

The present-time affliction is to be understood as a divine supervision (ἐπισκοπή, 10:4) by which sins are cleansed away (3:8). The call is for the righteous to endure (ὑπομένειν) what comes their way, assured that they will receive the Lord's mercy (16:15), if they are faithful to the end.

A feature of this document, with its summons to obey Torah and remain steadfast in evil days when Sadducean princes held sway (17:5–6, 23, "the arrogance of sinners") and the Romans under Pompey in the mid-first century B.C. had invaded the holy land (17:11–18, 22, "the unrighteous rulers . . . the Gentiles trample [Jerusalem] to destruction"), is the presenting of a theodicy. By this attempt to "explain" in a rational way the cause of recent events and to point to a divine purpose overruling them, the psalmist is offering encouragement to accept suffering willingly. He also is a messenger of consolation, pointing forward to the messianic days when Yahweh will be acknowledged as supreme when Jerusalem is elevated to the place of supremacy (17:30–31).

(e) These selected examples have exposed the two-beat rhythm that runs through much of the literature of early Judaism: trial is followed by vindication. The implicit teaching and exhortation is that the righteous (usually a poor, law-abiding, Torah-keeping minority) must expect to suffer in this world at the hands of overlords and oppressors, characterized as sinners, unjust, godless, etc. The prevailing disposition is to be one of patient endurance and fortitude with the hope that in the end Yahweh will redress their lot and rescue them. There will be a reversal of roles in that day, as the ungodly are judged and punished, while the righteous are established and promoted.

Such a statement passed into rabbinic and later Judaism as a *sententia recepta*, "so obvious that we do not need proof" (Schweizer, *Lordship*, 23). Examples, however, of this principle embodying the twin correlates of humiliation/expectation—which are central to James' thought—may be culled from 1 Sam 2:7–8; Ps 113:7–8; Prov 29:23; Sir 3:18 as background to rabbinic teaching,

though with a blunting of the eschatological edge found in the earlier literature.

> My humiliation is my exaltation, my exaltation is my humiliation (Hillel, c. 20
> B.C.).
> If you make a fool of yourself for the sake of Torah, Torah will exalt you in the
> end (Ben Azai, c. A.D. 100).
> If I exalt myself they will lower my seat . . . and if I humble myself they will
> raise my seat (Rabbi Tanhumah ben Abba, c. A.D. 380).

See more illustrations in Str-B 1.192–94, 249–50, 774, 921.

The axiomatic form of these dicta suggests that here was an idea that
had passed into Jewish mentality; and the place of this connection between
humiliation and exaltation is well attested in the literature of the NT (Matt
23:12 par.; 2 Cor chaps. 11–12; Phil 2:6–11; 4:12; 1 Pet 5:6; James 4:10).

6. STRUCTURE AND OUTLINE OF THE LETTER

Bibliography

Amphoux, C.-B. "Systèmes anciens de division de l'épître de Jacques et composition
littéraire." *Bib* 62 (1981) 390–400. **Burge, G. M.** "'And Threw Them Thus on Paper':
Rediscovering the Poetic Form of James 2:14–26." *SBT* 7 (1977) 31–45. **Davids,
P. H.** *Commentary on James.* 29. **Doty, W.** *Letters in Primitive Christianity.* Philadelphia:
Fortress Press, 1973. **Forbes, P. B. R.** "The Structure of James." *EvQ* 44 (1972) 147–
53. **Francis, F. O.** "The Form and Function of the Opening and Closing Paragraphs
of James and 1 John." *ZNW* 61 (1970) 110–26. **Motyer, J. A.** *The Message of James.*
12–13. **Vouga, F.** *L'épître de s. Jacques.* 18–23.

Accepting (if provisionally) the conclusion that this composition is an example of a genuine letter modeled on a hellenistic letter-writing pattern (Francis,
125–26) we have yet to determine, if possible, what is the flow of the letter's
contents. Obviously this is an unusual type of letter, lacking personal greetings
and an epistolary conclusion. The author's person (aside from 1:1 and 3:1)
is hidden behind his words, and the readers' identity is left very much to be
teased out of what is said concerning their dangers, problems, needs, and
hopes.

Chaps. 2 and 3 each form a unity and are devoted to distinct themes.
Chap. 4 is more of a miscellany with a collection of themes that extend to
5:6. At 5:7 we catch the notes of a closing admonition, which (following
Francis) is best understood as an eschatological instruction, followed by a
reprise of James' salient themes (5:7–11). 5:12–20 are to be viewed as pastoral
injunctions and encouragements, to round off the treatise.

The most problematical section to fit in any proposal for the letter's plan
is chap. 1, which after the opening (1:1) engages the twin themes of "Joy in
Suffering" (1:2–11) and "Blessing through Endurance" (1:12–25). 1:27
(joined with and commenting on 1:26) is a recapitulatory verse acting as a
hinge to connect what has gone before (unruly tongue, self-deception, vain
religion) with what will be expanded later (pure religion, faith translated

into deeds). This is Francis' chief argument for the letter's unity, i.e., it is not an assortment of diverse subjects loosely joined but a unified whole. In fact, the section 1:1–27 with its double opening at 1:2 and 1:12 lays down themes that are subsequently developed in the body of the letter.

Within chap. 1 are two subsections that set the pattern for what follows at greater length:

1:9–11	—poor and rich	—elaborated in 2:1–7;
1:22–25	—hearing and doing	—elaborated in 2:14–26.

What is said of faith in chap. 2 is applied to wisdom in chap. 3; but the common theme is testing and a response thereto. Abraham is the model in chap. 2; Job is the background of 3:1–5:11; the last verse couples the terms μακάριος/ὑπομένειν with a retrospective look at 1:12, just as the final verse with the theme of wandering (πλανᾶν, 5:19–20) recalls 1:16.

There have been several notable attempts to offer a structural analysis of this letter. From these suggestions we have selected the following for comment.

1. Francis

F. O. Francis divides the epistle into four large sections, based on certain presuppositions (which he proceeds to argue for): one is that the letter has a double opening in 1:2–11 and 1:12–25 corresponding to the twin themes of joy and blessedness. These preambles also state the three leading ideas, namely, testing leading to steadfastness (1:2–4 → 12–18), wisdom-words-reproaching (1:5–8 → 19–21), and rich-poor-doers of the word (1:9–11 → 22–25).

A second presupposition is that 1:26–27 is "a kind of literary hinge, both recapitulating the preceding introduction of the two main sections and turning the readers to the initial argumentative sections of the body of the epistle" (Francis, "Form and Function," 118).

Third, the two main sections referred to are 2:1–26 and 3:1–5:6. The theme of the first section is one of testing, ending on the "violent" note that Abraham sought to kill Isaac, who did not resist him (which looks forward to 5:6). The second chief part of 3:1–5:6 is unified by several themes, namely, judgment, the law, the rich, and works, which (he maintains) flow together in an orderly sequence of paragraphs (opposing Dibelius, who treated the document as a type of parenesis, "a text which strings together admonitions of general ethical content," 3, and Doty, *Letters,* 70, who regards it as "a collection of moral maxims and exhortations").

Fourth, 5:7–8 gives a restatement of the themes, with 5:12–20 marking an epistolary closing section in which there is a "thematic reprise" as well as statements that are found to be parallel in hellenistic epistolography, such as oath formulas, wishes for health, and prayer. The conclusion is established that James has to be "understood as an epistle from start to finish" (126). Its content may be set down, following and amplifying Francis' discussion:

1. 1:2–27   A lengthy proem falling into parallel panels:

1:2–11   Joy in suffering (2–4); endurance in prayer (5–8); rich and poor and their roles reversed (9–11);

1:12–25   12–18 matches 2–4;
19–21 matches 5–8;
22–25 matches 9–11.

(1:26–27: the epistolary fulcrum)

2. 2:1–26   Faith and partiality.

This section divides into blocks: 1–7; 8, 9–13; 14–17; 18–25 which is subdivided into 18–20/21–24/25/recapitulated in 26, as a closing "punch line."

3. 3:1–5:6   The section is made up of several units:

3:1–12   Words bad and good;

3:13–18   Two wisdoms;

4:1–12   Conflict situations;

4:13–5:6   Arrogance and injustice in practice picking up early themes, e.g. 3:13–16.

4. 5:7–20   Final exhortations, again to be seen in sub-units with recall of previous parts of the letter.

5:7–11   Patience in criticism (cf. 4:11), blessedness (cf. 1:12);

5:12   Against oaths (cf. misuse of the tongue, 3:6, 9, 10);

5:13–20   Prayer (cf. 1:5; 4:2) and recovery of the lapsed (cf. 1:16: "don't be deceived, dear brothers").

2. Amphoux

C.-B. Amphoux offers a more straightforward analysis ("Systèmes anciens," 390–400):

1. 1:1–27   Testing and hope
1:2–12   Testing—a source of joy
1:13–27   Response to temptation

2. 2:1–26   At the synagogue
2:1–13   Giving heed to appearances
2:14–26   Acts reveal faith

3. 3:1–4:10   Daily life
3:1–18   Words and wisdom
4:1–10   Pleasures and humility

4. 4:11–5:20   Judgment and salvation
4:11–5:12   Danger of judgment
5:13–20   Hope of salvation

The attractiveness of this proposal lies in its simplicity and neat arrangement into pairs, both complementary and contrasting. Its weakness is that it overlooks many of the subtle allusions in the final form of the document which crisscross to make it more consciously a literary whole.

3. Davids

P. H. Davids regards 2:1–5:6 as the body of the letter, as do most writers who depart from the position taken by Dibelius (and most recently Ruckstuhl, who detects what he calls the author's inclination to write in a "staccato" style with unattached sentences put together by catchwords and picking up what was said earlier, 5). This letter-body develops three themes announced in the double letter-opening of 1:2–27 and expanded in what follows:

1. 1:9–11, 22–25 on the theme of the rich and the poor is elaborated in 2:1–26.
2. 1:5–8, 19–21 relating to the use of the tongue is developed in 3:1–4:12.
3. 1:2–4, 12–18 to do with trials is picked up in 4:13–5:6.
4. 5:7–11 rehearses these three themes and begins the conclusion in 5:7–20.

This way of seeing the letter as a whole has much to commend it, with the comment that the second theme (3:1–4:12) has a number of subthemes (e.g., in 4:6) that should be brought out and not subsumed under a general heading of the "Demand for Pure Speech." Also the designation of 2:1–26 as "The Excellency of Poverty and Generosity" is unfortunate, since poverty is hardly a virtue in itself as generosity is.

4. Motyer

A similar arrangement of verses is found in Motyer's popular treatment (*The Message of James*), but with a quite different orientation of James' thought suggested. It is noted how 1:26 on the control of the tongue is amplified in 3:12; and 1:27a on the care of the needy is illustrated in 2:1–26, thus forming a chiastic arrangement (literary device of a crisscross arrangement to be seen in 2:14–26: Dibelius, 156, and especially Burge, "'And threw them thus on Paper,'" 35–37). But it is difficult to accept other parts of this literary analysis: (i) The ruling themes of birth (1:13–19c), growth (19b–25), and development (1:26–5:6) are too general to be helpful. (ii) To be sure the topic of 1:27b is purity but to use the same description of the entire section of 3:13–5:6 is to put together a large number of disparate themes under one umbrella. (iii) The "preaching style" of James may be noted, but in its written form this document is far more artistically arranged than Motyer gives credit for. The letter is indeed "about relationships" (Motyer, 25) but there is more social dimension to what James is setting down than Motyer's analysis and descriptions will allow when he refers the idioms of birth-growth-development to the individual (73).

5. Vouga

Under this name we address a suggestion that the letter is a collection of illustrations mounted on a surface in decorative arrangement (a découpage). The leading motifs and designs are listed:

1. 1:2–19a Enduring Trials
   The main theme: testing of faith (1:2–4)
   a. Opposition to distraction (1:5–8)
   b. Opposition to riches (1:9–11)
   c. Blessing on those who endure (1:12)
   d. Opposition to fatalism (1:13–19a)
2. 1:19b–3:18 Applying the Word and Opposing Reliance on Force
   The main theme: obedience of faith
   a. Opposition to partiality (2:1–13)
   b. Ventures of faith (2:14–26)
   c. Watch your language (3:1–13)
   d. Service and control of wisdom (3:14–18)
3. 4:1–5:20 Witnessing to Divine Providence before the World
   The main theme in 4:1–10: faithfulness of faith
   a. Words and mutual respect (4:11–12)
   b. Words to "men of the world" (4:13–17)
      words to the rich (5:1–6)
      words to believers (5:7–11)
   c. Live in truthfulness (5:12)
   d. Illness and healing of sinners (5:13–18)
   e. Restoring the wanderers (5:19–20)

Much of this analysis is clear, granted Vouga's desire to give an "existential" application to James' admonitions. Any idea of the immediate context (so far as it may be recovered) of James' teaching and the readers' situation tends to get lost; and it will be observed that 4:1–10 is left obscured under the simple rubric of the "faithfulness of faith." Vouga's threefold categorization of faith in the letter—its testing, obedience, and fidelity—is to be applauded; but some more detail may surely be wished for.

6. Some Conclusions and a Suggested Plan of the Letter.

In a later section of his work, Vouga returns to the themes of the letter in a bid to see the progression and coherence of the writer's thought (21–23). Here his analysis is far more profound and suggestive, and has links with Francis. We may borrow his divisions and use his work as a basis for our summary.

Chap. 1 holds the key to the letter's structure and sets out the basic issue to be faced: how is human existence to fulfill its goal and find its dignity? The setting of this question is the encounter with trials, announced in 1:2–4. There are two main causes of trials: on the one side there are misgivings (1:5–8) related to the merchant adventurers of 4:13–17; on the other side, the problem of wealth (1:9–11) leading to oppression by the wealthy (5:1–6). Human life is at risk on both counts. Blessedness is promised to those who win through (1:12 // 5:7–11). Another answer to paralyzing fear is the affirmation that God is Lord of the cosmic and astral powers (1:13–18 // 5:12–20); this should be a ground for encouragement to enable believers to live out their calling.

The second main section expounds Christian existence in a two-part way:

a practicing of the word and a call to resistance (1:19–3:18). The key idea is located in 1:20: human anger (with a resort to violent means and hatred) does not promote the divine righteousness. Five topics (1:19–27) are introduced as an overture to themes which then recur throughout the letter:

(a) True religion (i.e., right relationship that binds [Latin *religare*] us to God) is announced (1:27a), and its practical outworking is dramatized in 2:1–13 in the keeping of the royal law of love to one's neighbor and the call of freedom to obey.

(b) At the heart of James' understanding of religion is "the word," which is to be observed as well as heard (1:22–24), since it is planted within believers as a seed intended to grow into evident fruit (1:18). The emphasis on root-fruit comes to the fore in 2:14–26.

(c) The hook-device of the term "word" connects with a disquisition on the human "words" (1:18–20, 26), which is elaborated in 3:1–13, a set piece on the power of words for good or ill and inserted against a background of the role of church teachers (3:1–2).

(d) Wrong use of words (1:19) especially by teachers leads on to a diptych, a two-paneled contrast, between Dame Folly and Dame Wisdom (heavily indebted to Israel's wisdom school in, e.g., Prov 8–9) in 3:15–18; it is prefaced by the connecting allusion to teachers who are placed in that sapiential tradition (3:13).

(e) Christians have a duty to live "in the world" (a theme first announced in 1:27b). The major segment of 4:1–5:11 occupies the rest of the letter, with 5:12–20 forming a letter closing and rehearsing many of the previous themes as a postlude and recapitulation.

The vocation of believer in 4:1–5:11 is to remain constant in the face of evil powers arrayed against them. "To be stainless and unpolluted by the world's contagion" (1:27b) is a statement of an abstinence motif (common in the Pauline and later house-codes); this is applied in 4:1–10 in an invective directed against the warmongering spirit and the sad driving force of jealousy that motivates it. Further items in the parenetic code are included: submit to God, resist the devil (4:7).

What appear to be separate panels round off this long section:

(i) Against mutual recrimination in the community (4:11–12)
(ii) Against arrogance, exemplified by the godless merchants (4:13–17) in an urban milieu
(iii) Against the wealthy and oppressing farmers in a rural setting (5:1–6)
(iv) Against impatience that will not wait for God to intervene (5:7–11); and a replay of the wrong use of words (5:12)
(v) Reprise with special reference to daily life for the individual and the community, with a final encouragement to prayer and a salutary warning to the erring church member (5:13–20).

Arranged in sections, the entire letter falls into the following pattern:

I. Address and Greeting (1:1)

II. Enduring Trials (1:2–19a)
   1. Trials, Wisdom, Faith (1:2–8)

7. CANONICAL STATUS OF THE LETTER

Bibliography

Baur, F. C. *Das Christentum und die christliche Kirche der ersten drei Jahrhunderte.* 2d ed. Tübingen: Siebeck, 1860. **Childs, B. S.** *The New Testament as Canon.* Philadelphia: Fortress Press, 1985. **Cranfield, C. E. B.** "The Message of James." *SJT* 18 (1965) 182–93, 338–45. **Dunn, J. D. G.** *Unity and Diversity in the New Testament.* London: SCM, 1977. **Kittel, G.** "Der geschichtliche Ort des Jakobusbriefes." *ZNW* 41 (1942) 71–105. **Kümmel, W. G.** *The New Testament: The History of the Investigation of Its Problems.* Tr. S. McL. Gilmour and H. C. Kee. Nashville: Abingdon, 1972. **Lake, K.,** and **Lake, S.** *An Introduction to the New Testament.* London: Christophers, 1937. **Martin, R. P.** "St. Matthew's Gospel in Recent Study." *ExpTim* 80 (1968–69) 132–36. **Massebieau, L.** "L'épître de Jacques, est-elle l'oeuvre d'un chrétien?" *RHR* 16 tome 32 (1895) 249–83. **Meyer, A.** *Das Rätsel des Jakobusbriefes.* BZNW 10. Giessen: Töpelmann, 1930. **Mussner, Fr.** "'Direkte' und 'indirekte' Christologie im Jakobusbrief." *Catholica* 24 (1970) 111–17. **Robinson, J. A. T.** *Redating the New Testament.* Philadelphia: Westminster, 1976. **Scaer, D. P.** *James, The Apostle of Faith: A Primary Christological Epistle for the Persecuted Church.* St. Louis: Concordia, 1983. **Schoeps, H. J.** *Theologie und Geschichte des Judenchristentums.* Tübingen: Mohr, 1949. **Sigal, P.** "The Halakhah of James." In *Intergerini Parietis Septum (Eph. 2:14),* FS Markus Barth, ed. D. Y. Hadidian. Philadelphia: Pickwick Press, 1981. 337–53. **Spitta, F.** *Zur Geschichte und Litteratur des Urchristentums II.* Göttingen: Vandenhoeck und Ruprecht, 1896. 382–91. **Zmijewski, J.** "Christliche 'Vollkommenheit': Erwagungen zur Theologie des Jakobusbriefes." In *Studien zum Neuen Testament und seiner Umwelt* 5, ed. A. Fuchs. Linz, 1980. 50–78.

We drew attention earlier to the slow reception of this document into the church's list of books held to be "sacred literature." Councils of Rome (A.D. 382) and of Carthage (A.D. 397, 419) eventually placed the letter within the boundaries of the canon, thereby endorsing the decision that lay behind the inclusion of James in Athanasius' Thirty-ninth Easter Letter (A.D. 367). In the East acceptance was more problematic, but it is true that the presence of James in the West provoked no controversy such as surrounded the reception of Hebrews and the Apocalypse.

At the Reformation, however, doubts were again raised but with a different set of agenda. Early in its history the Epistle of James was one of the neglected books of the NT. Its content is first explicitly referred to by Origen (d. A.D. 253/4) and then in the West by Hilary (c. A.D. 357), and it is a puzzling fact that "no one directly cites the book for one hundred to one hundred twenty-five years after it was completed" (Davids, 8, assuming a mid-first century dating for the first stage of its composition). Luther, however, turned his critical attention to this book when in his September Testament of 1522 he gave it a lower place. He did so on several grounds: (i) It "contains nothing evangelical (*keyn Evangelisch art an yhr hat*)," defined as calculated to proclaim the gospel, and (ii) it was not of apostolic authorship (*keyns Apostelschrift*). (iii) On the contrary, James was held to introduce and teach matters considered erroneous, such as justification by works; there was no allusion to the passion or resurrection of Jesus; the name of Christ was found only twice (1:1; 2:1), but "it teaches nothing about him"; and it opposes Paul and the rest of the NT to such an extent that "he does violence to Scripture." Other comment from the Reformer follows this line: James "mixes up law and works," and in 2:14–26 he has set the interpreter of Paul's gospel an impossible task. Many have tried to reconcile James and Paul, sweating hard at it, he jibes; but anyone who can harmonize these sayings (faith justifies/does not justify) "I'll put my doctor's cap on him and let him call me a fool!" (For these allusions see Kümmel, *The New Testament*, 24–26.)

Yet alongside such a negative assessment there is still another aspect to Luther's evaluation. "I praise it and hold it a good book, because it sets up no doctrine of men and lays great stress on God's law" (Kümmel, ibid.). About James 4:11–17 Luther was candid enough to admit that it contains "many a good saying" (Kümmel, 25). Yet it is his excessively pejorative remark that has gone into the history books and emerged as a popular verdict on this letter in comparison with the other NT books that do "urge to Christ" (*Christum treiben*): "it is no apostolic letter" but rather "a right epistle of straw" (*das die Epistel Jacobi keyn rechte Apostolisch Epistel ist . . . sanct Jacobs Epistel eyn rechte stroern Epistel gegen sie*). See Mussner, 42–47.

Modern criticism of this NT document has produced a variety of interpretations that bear upon the question of its status within the NT canon. At one extreme is the eccentric hypothesis put out by A. Meyer in 1930 that the solution to the "riddle of James' letter" was to be found in seeing in it a fundamentally *Jewish document*. In this proposal Meyer was building on the earlier works of Massebieau and Spitta (see *Bibliography*) but adding a novel idea regarding the composition of James' letter. It was said to be written pseudonymously to the twelve tribes by an author who used the name of patriarch Jacob representing the tribes as an onomastikon to supply an allegorical interpretation based on their names in Gen 49. For instance, 1:18 depends on the wording of the ascription to Reuben (Gen 49:3) as the firstborn (Meyer, 268–69). The names of Jesus Christ in 1:1; 2:1 are held to be interpolations by a later hand (Meyer, 118–20). While few have followed Meyer in turning the epistle into a Jewish writing (though Windisch shows some interest in this idea on formal grounds, and Sigal, "The Halakhah of James," views the letter as standing entirely in the Jewish tradition, albeit as a Palestinian Christian document), his work was influential in establishing a trend. He denied the epistolary form of James as original, regarding 1:1 as "a simple covering and a fiction" (as Schrage, 6, calls it, marking a consensus that has prevailed in European circles. See the list in Zmijewski, "Christliche 'Vollkommenheit,' " 50 n.4). The classification of James as "moral exhortation," put together as a potpourri of loosely connected sections of teaching and instruction, rhythmically formed (Schlatter, 85), has remained a firm conclusion, especially through Dibelius' commentary. With this form-critical axiom taken for granted, it is difficult to give the letter—which is how it stands in the present NT—much weight as possessing canonical rank.

The opposite extreme is adopted by a few commentators who treat the letter as a *dogmatic Christian treatise*. A recent example is seen in D. P. Scaer, who gives this subtitle to his exposition of the document: *A Primary Christological Epistle for the Persecuted Church*. He proceeds to extract the maximum christological value from unlikely sources, e.g., by relating 1:9–10 to a statement of Christology based on the wordplay (ταπεινός, "humble") with Matt 11:29; Phil 2:8; 2 Cor 8:9. "Understanding James' terminology as being Christologically freighted thus rescues this epistle from the common opinion which consigns it to a type of moralistic, rabbinic literature" (49). But this example of comparative word-study and a type of *sensus plenior* exegesis hardly commends itself, as when 1:17–18 is seen as a latent reference to the Incarnation because of the verbal form describing a gift "coming down from above" (cf. John 3:13, 31).

We are not driven to either extreme. James is neither an exercise in rabbinic moralism nor a cryptic christological treatise. It is best viewed as "a genuine Christian writing" (Zmijewski, 75), yet with strong Jewish flavor that permeates the whole. Its canonical status has to be sought elsewhere than where Luther proposed. A first principle of interpretation must be that the document deserves to be understood *on its own terms*, before comparisons and contrasts are drawn with Jewish wisdom literature or rabbinic tracts or writings of Christian moralism (e.g., the *Didache*) as representing a reaction to Paul and gentile Christianity. Granted that there are several points of contact in language, concepts, and ethos on both sides of what these proposals offer, it still remains true that James stands in a class apart. Its present form is epistolary; its stress is on the practice of true religion; and its idioms (with some notable exceptions especially in 3:6, often taken to be a fragment of Orphic teaching; and less probably 5:20, regarded by Schoeps, *Theologie*, 345, as a warning against a gnostic errorist) and paradigms are drawn from Israelite wisdom literature and behind that the Old Testament world. Yet it does purport to have a muted christological voice (1:1; 2:1) and it draws so heavily

on the sayings of Jesus (see especially Mussner, 48–50; Davids, 47–48) that
G. Kittel, "Der geschichtliche Ort," 84, can justly remark: "No writing in
the New Testament outside the Gospels is so interlaced with reminiscences
of the words of the Lord as this one" (cited in Mussner, 47). Its use of terms
normally associated with a moralistic setting (ἔργα, νόμος, τέλειος) is offset by
a counterbalancing array of fideistic-evangelical idioms (δώρημα, πίστις, λόγος).
Unless James is consciously using the latter vocabulary to polemicize and
is employing opponents' terms for his own ends, it is natural to conclude
that he is building on the evangelical foundation as his own conviction. The
superstructure, however, which emphasizes the necessity of "deeds of mercy,"
help for the needy, a resolute turning from evil ways, and a following of
the course of peace and integrity, is put in place to show how the two parts
of his Christianity fit together.

The "canonical function" (Childs, *The New Testament as Canon*, 438) of
the document is similar to at least one other part of the NT. We refer to
Matthew's Gospel, which according to our understanding (not Childs's, which
is somewhat different) adapted and angled the gospel of Christ to meet a
situation in the post-Pauline period when two dangers loomed large (see
Martin, "St. Matthew's Gospel," 132–36). On the one side, for Matthew's
Jewish Christian congregation in Syria there was the problem of a Christian
nomism that sought to rejudaize the message as it aligned itself with the
Jewish heritage and paved the way to Ebionism. At the other extreme, the
threat of antinomian trends leading to a relaxed morality was beginning to
assert itself, and Matthew warned against the gentile-oriented universalism
of his church when it was producing a moral indifference. Perhaps Paul's
teaching of free grace and "by faith" as the sole condition of salvation was
misunderstood and misapplied. So Matthew endeavored to reestablish obedience to the law—seen to be binding on Christians—as an expression of the
new life that grace had brought them in the fulfilled age of Messiah's coming.

We submit that James' thought in this letter moves in this world of tension.
It may be conceded that the situation is not precisely the same in the case
of James as with Matthew, as Robinson (*Redating*, 120) notes. There is no
overt polemic against Judaism, at least against Pharisaism. The enemies in
view are more the Sadducean aristocracy and plutocracy, but the references
in 2:2–3, 6–7; 5:1–6 are sufficiently imprecise to make absolute identification
impossible. (James, moreover, is equally implacable when the Zealot option
at the other end of the political spectrum to the Sadducees was advocated,
as in 1:20; 3:15–18; 4:1–5.) If the historical James had a clear picture of
the landowning high-priestly family in his sights, the present text is not that
explicit, though the language would fit the case of the Sadducees. Relations
with the Jewish religion reflected in the letter are not bitter to the point of
a breach with the synagogue, as parts of Matthew's Gospel might suggest.
But that conclusion regarding Matthew is open, and the controversy could
well be an ongoing one, a debate *intra muros*, as Matthew's church and the
Jewish community are yet in dialogue.

The common ground with Matthew should be sought in other places.
James asserts the validity and relevance of the Old Testament teaching on
"the perfect law" (1:25), "the law of liberty" (1:25; 2:12), and "the royal

law" (2:8)—summed up in Lev 19:18—and he opposes any false reliance on "simple faith" when it is used as a slogan and an excuse for evading moral obligations. It is Paul's teaching taken out of context (as Dunn, *Unity and Diversity*, 252, calls it) that James wants to correct. Whether his failing to root moral teaching in a soteriological-christological soil eventually led to a new understanding of the gospel as *lex nova* and finally issued in Ebionism (as Dunn claims, 257) is possible, but not provable. That movement was indeed the direct consequence of the way the anti-Pauline polemic often seen in this epistle was understood in Jewish Christianity. The Clementine literature shows how such an opposition to Paul did happen (see Schoeps, *Theologie*, 261–62, 343–49; but Schoeps argues convincingly that the author of James' letter was not Ebionite as Baur, *Das Christentum*, 123, had maintained. Rather, he avers, the Epistle of James is a postapostolic, catholic document conserving some customs and the generally accepted Jewish Christian features of early times). But whatever the resolution of the historical problem regarding the way the letter was interpreted in the later centuries, its eventual place in the NT canon poses the issue of how it speaks to the church in times when the twin dangers of legalism and moral laxity threaten. Then this epistle points the way to the basis of Christian moral practice interpreted as love to one's neighbor and committing the church to a tangible expression of help to the needy and socially disadvantaged. To that extent Paul and James stand in the NT as side-by-side witnesses. B. S. Childs (*New Testament as Canon*, 443) remarks:

> At times in the life of the church the message of Paul will sound the primary note of the gospel, bearing witness to salvation by faith alone. At other times, the word of James will faithfully testify that faith and works are indissolubly joined in a faithful response to God. The role of the Christian canon is to assure that both witnesses are heard as part of the one divine revelation of truth.

The postulated earlier version of the document embodying the witness of the historical James made these points even clearer. In a suggested time-frame of Palestinian economic and political stress it embodied the testament of James set against a particular historical background. This, however, is a minority opinion (though one we have preferred). Most commentators are content to admit that "the epistle of James is one of those apparently timeless documents that could be dated almost anywhere" (Robinson, *Redating*, 118; K. Lake and S. Lake, *Introduction*, 164, offer a span from the second century B.C. to the eighteenth century A.D.; but this is not to be taken as a serious judgment. More credibly Sigal, "Halakhah of James," 337, observes that the period of A.D. 40–150 marks the range of possibility for dating James). The emphasis on social justice and a resolute turning from violence and class animosity was made by the Jerusalem leader. His life and martyrdom gave added emphasis, since his legacy lived on not only in his teaching as codified in this letter but in his memory. In both Catholic and gnostic circles he was revered as a righteous teacher and model of piety. That aura was retained in the letter that bears his name. Such distinction recalls to us the line of continuity the church has with Israel as a community of those who respect social righteousness (Deut 16:20) and are prepared for suffering obedience. This historical continuity points us not only to James but to James' human brother κατὰ σάρκα.

The ultimate test of canonicity is christological. By that standard for many this document falls lamentably short. But to conclude thus would be an intemperate judgment. The explicit statements of Christology are indeed minimal (1:1; 2:1), but the spirit of Jesus and his teaching of the Great Sermon shine through almost every line. So in that way we may accept the startling contention of E. Thurneysen that "James preaches Jesus Christ, His cross and resurrection, the power of forgiveness and the obedience of faith, and nothing else; but he preaches this in his own peculiar way" (quoted in Cranfield, "The Message in James," *SJT* 18 [1965], 184–85).

It is that preaching with a distinctive Jacobean accent that ultimately justifies the inclusion of the letter in the church's canon, as one face of the multifaceted witness to Jesus Christ that the NT contains.

James

I. Address and Greeting (1:1)

Bibliography

Brandon, S. G. F. "The Death of James the Just: A New Interpretation." In *Studies in Mysticism and Religion Presented to Gershom G. Scholem.* Jerusalem: Magnes, 1967. 57–69. **Francis, F. O.** "The Form and Function of the Opening and Closing Paragraphs of James and I John." *ZNW* 61 (1970) 110–26. **Howard, G.** "Was James an Apostle?" *NovT* 19 (1977) 63–69. **Kirk, J. A.** "Apostleship since Rengstorf: Towards a Synthesis." *NTS* 21 (1975) 249–64. **Kramer, W.** *Christ, Lord, Son of God.* Tr. B. Hardy. SBT 50. London: SCM, 1966. **Lieu, J. M.** " 'Grace to You and Peace': The Apostolic Greeting." *BJRL* 68 (1985) 161–78. **Murphy-O'Connor, J.** "Tradition and Redaction in 1 Cor 15:3–7." *CBQ* 43 (1981) 582–89. **Niederwimmer, K.** "Ἰάκωβος," *EW* 2, cols. 411–15. **Pratscher, W.** *Der Herrenbruder Jakobus und die Jakobustradition.* FRLANT 139. Göttingen: Vandenhoeck & Ruprecht, 1987. **Sass, G.** "Zur Bedeutung von δοῦλος bei Paulus." *ZNW* 40 (1941) 24–32. **Scaer, D. P.** *James, Apostle of Faith: A Primary Christological Epistle for the Persecuted Church.* St. Louis: Concordia, 1983. **Schmithals, W.** *The Office of Apostle in the Early Church.* Tr. J. Steely. Nashville: Abingdon, 1969. **Trudinger, L. P.** *"Heteron de tōn apostolōn ouk eidon, ei mē Iakōbon:* A Note on Galatians 1.19." *NovT* 17 (1975) 200–202.

Translation

1:1 *[From] James, a servant of God and of the Lord Jesus Christ,[a] to the twelve tribes of the Dispersion, greeting.*

Notes

[a] Motyer (27), Scaer (27), and Vouga (31, 36) want to link θεοῦ and κυρίου, both referring to Ἰησοῦ Χριστοῦ, thus producing the translation "a servant of Jesus Christ who is God and Lord." 2 Peter 1:2; Jude 4; Titus 2:13 look to be parallel, but in each case these verses have the definite article with θεοῦ, which James 1:1 lacks.

Form / Structure / Setting

The homiletical form of the "letter" is clear from the introductory greeting. The writer's name is given in the nominative case, a usage that is unusual in English. This explains the attempt in our translation to indicate that James is the sender. It was traditional for authors to include their personal names in the superscription, a feature found also in the Pauline corpus. What is problematical is why the author here chose to describe himself in these precise terms as "servant of God and of the Lord Jesus Christ." The absence of any apostolic rank is noteworthy and poses a question to those who see the document as pseudonymous (Kugelman, 12). If the author of James wished to place his writing under the aegis of the Lord's brother, why does he not say so clearly? Failing to identify himself as "the brother of the Lord Jesus Christ," the writer seems to be using the name of James as a convenient source, without necessarily claiming to reproduce explicitly the teaching of James the Lord's brother. But this line of reasoning makes too much of what the text does not say. It is sufficient for the author to appeal to the leader in the Jerusalem church as an authority.

This is the only place in the NT where the exact title "servant of God and of the Lord Jesus Christ" is found. "Servant," δοῦλος (Heb. עֶבֶד, *ʿebed*) is a designation of privilege and honor, used of Israel's great leaders of the people such as Moses (Deut 34:5; 1 Kgs 8:53, 56; Dan 9:11; Mal 4:4; Josephus, *Ant.* 5.39) and David (2 Sam 7:5; 1 Kgs 8:66; Jer 33:21; Ezek 37:25) as well as the prophets (Jer 7:25; 44:4; Amos 3:7). The note of authority is also implicit in such a title, and this factor may well have determined the choice of the designation here, as in Paul (Rom 1:1; Gal 1:10; Phil 1:1). Thus δοῦλος does not signify "slave" in the sociological sense nor simply "a believer," which is a usage in some texts (1 Cor 7:22; Eph 6:6; 1 Pet 2:16), where it is a general designation; nor is it a title for the writer, as it is in the Pauline texts. The writer is not associating himself with his readers (so Cantinat) but distinguishing himself from them as a figure of authority (Vouga, 37 n.6) or even as an office holder (which is less likely, though Sass's term *Amtsbegriff* argues for it: "Zur Bedeutung," 32).

The addressees are named as "the twelve tribes of [lit., in] the Dispersion." This again is an unusual description of a letter's recipients, parallel in the NT to 1 Peter 1:1, though the sociological flavor of the term there (see L. Goppelt, *Der erste Petrusbrief* [KEK, Göttingen: Vandenhoeck und Ruprecht, 1978] 78) is not so evident in this letter. See *Comment.*

The salutation χαίρειν, "greeting," is best understood as an imperatival infinitive (Moulton, *Grammar* 1:179). But J. M. Lieu, " 'Grace to You,' " traces the infinitive to the content of an oral message delivered by a third party; when the oral element receded, the verb of saying was dropped and the infinitive retained (163). This usage, common in hellenistic Judaism's literature (Ropes, 128), is often paralleled with Acts 15:23 (in a letter of James, the Lord's brother) and Acts 23:26 (a letter from the tribune Claudius Lysias to the procurator Felix). Mayor (31) sees here an argument for a pre-Pauline date for the entire letter, since the full Pauline formula of "Grace and peace" is lacking. But this is doubtful. The most we may conclude is that the opening greeting speaks of James' double background in the OT-Judaism and the world of hellenistic-popular Greek. Cf. Add Esth 16:1; 1 Macc 10:25; 12:6; 2 Macc 1:1, 10; 3 Macc 7:1; *Ep. Arist.* 41. On the later Christian usage of χαίρειν see C. H. Roberts, *Manuscript, Society, and Belief in Early Christian Egypt* (London: OUP, 1979) 15–16.

Comment

1 Ἰάκωβος θεοῦ καὶ κυρίου Ἰησοῦ Χριστοῦ δοῦλος, "[From] James, a servant of God and of the Lord Jesus Christ." The identity of the author as James is much disputed. See *Introduction*, pp. xxxi–xxxiii. Of the various persons in early Christianity who carried this name the three most likely candidates for the authority behind this letter are as follows: (1) James, son of Zebedee was one of the Twelve (Mark 3:16–18 // Matt 10:2 // Luke 6:14 // Acts 1:13). According to Acts 12:2 he was beheaded by Herod Agrippa I around the year A.D. 44, and no further allusion to him is made in the NT. (2) Another James is referred to in the list of the Twelve (Mark 3:18 // Luke 6:15 // Acts

1:13), identified by Matthew 10:3 as "James son of Alphaeus." He is a largely unknown figure in the early church. (3) By contrast, James the Lord's brother (on the precise meaning to be given to ἀδελφός, see Mayor, vi–lv, concluding that James the Lord's brother was the natural son of Joseph and Mary) played a significant role in early Christianity. G. H. Rendall hardly exaggerates when he comments:

> Apart from Paul and Peter, no figure in the church of the first days plays a more substantial part upon the historic and legendary stage than James, first Bishop of Jerusalem (*The Epistle of St. James and Judaic Christianity,* 11–12).

Surnamed by Paul as one of the "pillars" (στῦλοι) of the church, along with Peter and John (Gal 2:9) James enjoyed contact with other leaders (Acts 15:13). His entry into the story of the narrative in Acts (12:17) is unheralded— a fact that has led to some speculation as to Luke's embarrassment over what James came to stand for (see S. G. F. Brandon, "The Death of James the Just: A New Interpretation," 60).

Later in Acts (15:13–21) he assumed a commanding position at the Council, which suggests that by that time he was a recognized figure of authority in early Judaic Christianity. The encounter with Paul, according to Acts 21:18, has to be noted here, with more detailed discussion relegated to another section (see *Introduction,* p. xli). In the Pauline letters there is mention of James in 1 Cor 15:5–7 (possibly belonging to a pre-Pauline stratum), where his name appears in a fixed formulation (J. Murphy-O'Connor, "Tradition and Redaction in 1 Cor. 15:3–7," 587), and it has been proposed that 1 Cor 9:14 with its allusion to those who "preach the gospel" and who "should get their living by the gospel" relates to Jewish Christian missionaries who had reached Corinth as envoys from James. Whether they are the same persons as the "false apostles" of 2 Cor 10–13 is another issue, but it is possible that the latter individuals, whom Paul sternly denounced in 2 Cor 11:13–15, were claiming to have some authorization from "the highest-ranking apostles" (2 Cor 11:5, 12), among whom James is almost certainly to be reckoned. The Paul of the epistles evidently held James in high regard. He acknowledges making his acquaintance (Gal 1:19; 2:2, 6, 9; 1 Cor 9:5; 15:7), and he seeks to place his own ministry in a context of cordial relations with the leader of the Jerusalem community (Gal 2:1–10), even if those relations were strained at a later time (Gal 2:12–21; cf. Acts 21:18–26 for one version of James' latent hostility to Paul, albeit based on what the narrator regarded as unfounded rumor, 21:21).

If we confine our interest here to the canonical record—and church tradition, both catholic and sectarian, adds a rich quota of additional material— it is a firm conclusion based on the data already cited that James, the Lord's brother, was a person of considerable stature in early Jewish Christianity (Niederwimmer, "Ἰάκωβος," 412–14) and a leader whose authority Paul and Peter were unable to ignore. Not least among his credentials is his claim made in the preamble to the letter to be "a servant of God and of the Lord Jesus Christ."

Ἰάκωβος, "James," is the OT name "Jacob" (Gen 27:36; Isa 41:8; 43:22;

Jer 26:27 [30:10] LXX; Ezek 28:25). The self-designation of δοῦλος is based on the OT, as we have observed, and is used of Israel's leaders as persons of dignity in Yahweh's service. Here aspects of the writer's authority—or, more precisely, of the authority claimed for James in whose name the letter is sent out—are registered. Whether the historical James was ever regarded as an "apostle" (based on 1 Cor 15:7) is a vexed question (see Kirk, "Apostleship," 257, for a positive attitude to James' apostleship; a negative assessment is given by Trudinger, "Heteron," 200–202). An earlier discussion (see p. xxxviii) has concluded that Paul did not unequivocally give the designation to James, or if he did, it was not his normal practice, whatever claim was being registered by a James-party (on 1 Cor 15:7 as witness to a "formula of rivalry" [Rivalitätsformel], see Pratscher, Der Herrenbruder, 32–46). The cautious assessment of a modern writer may be cited, as noted earlier.

> Paul limits the assertion that he has seen no apostle besides Peter by leaving room for the possibility that one could, if need be, count James among the apostles—something he was not himself accustomed to doing—whom he had also seen (W. Schmithals, The Office, 65).

κύριος refers to Jesus as in 2:1; 5:7–8, 10. Vouga's argument (31, 36) in support of taking θεοῦ and κυρίου together is doubly based: (1) other divine titles are linked in 1:27; 3:9 to provide a model for this parallelism; and (2) patristic interpretation of Pseudo-Andrew of Crete (ca. A.D. 740) supports this link. Motyer (27) similarly argues for the rendering and cites parallels from the later NT literature. But Mitton criticizes the translation "servant of Jesus Christ, who is God and Lord," while granting the linguistic possibility, on the score that such an explicit ascription of deity to Jesus is rare in the NT and is unlikely in this letter, which he takes to be a primitive document. He does concede, however, that "even if Jesus is not here identified with God, He and the Father are clearly associated together in what is in effect a unity. One who becomes a servant of Christ thereby becomes a servant of God" (14).

But what are we to make of the words θεοῦ καὶ κυρίου Ἰησοῦ Χριστοῦ δοῦλος when taken together? At first glance one is tempted to correlate δοῦλος with the predication of God as κύριος, the LXX equivalent of Yahweh (so Dibelius, 65). This correlation, however, overlooks the primary member in the double expression: θεοῦ. The present case thus bears a partial resemblance to the probable LXX practice of rendering עבד יהוה, ʿebed Yahweh, as δοῦλος κυρίου (Josh 14:7 [A]; 24:30[29]; Judg 2:8; 1 Kgs 8:66; 2 Kgs 10:23; 18:12; Pss 33:23[34:22]; 35[36] tit.; 77 [78]:70; 115:7 [116:16]; 133 [134]:1; 134 [135]:1; Jonah 1:9; Isa 48:20; Dan 3:84–85 LXX). The oldest LXX fragments retain the tetragrammaton (H. Bietenhard, NIDNTT 2:512) but correspond more closely to the expression δοῦλοι τοῦ θεοῦ (which is the pluralized rendering of עבדי יהוה in Isa 42:19 LXX). By contrast, for Philo the phrase is "a dubious term which does not really describe the relationship of the righteous to God as it is in practice" (K. Rengstorf, TDNT 2:269). This presents us with a divergence from Josephus, who uses δοῦλος of a worshiper but without the corresponding genitive (Ant. 5.39 where the inference is made of Moses as "your servant," τοῦ σοῦ δούλου). The New Testament usage reflects a similar reserve with regard to the phrase (Rev 1:1; 2:20; 7:3; 10:7; 15:3; 19:2; 22:3, 6; Acts 4:29; 16:17; 1 Pet 2:26) and for the sub-apostolic writers it equals "Christian" (2 *Clem* 20.1; *Herm. Man.* 5.2.1; 6.24; 8.10, etc.).

Consideration of the above evidence along with the relative infrequence of the phrase δοῦλος θεοῦ in early Christian letters (otherwise only at Titus 1:1) leads us to conclude that the author uses the term in one of two senses: either as a representative of the pious in Israel or else as one who stood in line with Israel's famous servants of old—Joshua, Moses, David, the prophets, and Jacob. Since, however, he does not apply the servant terminology to his readers (as equivalent to Israel; cf. 1 Pet 2), it probably has no significant eschatological overtones. Later writers connect James with Obadiah as a righteous prophet (see *Introduction* and Eusebius, *HE* 2.23.7). The author blends an old covenant confession of relationship with one under the new, that Jesus Christ is the κύριος (cf. 2:1 and, e.g., Acts 2:36; 1 Cor 12:3; Rom 10:9; Phil 2:11).

κυρίου Ἰησοῦ Χριστοῦ. That the full title used by the author for Jesus occurs frequently in the introductory section of Pauline correspondence (Rom 1:7; 1 Cor 1:3; 2 Cor 1:2; Gal 1:3; Phil 1:2; Col 1:3; 1 Thess 1:1; 2 Thess 1:2; Philem 3) suggests either a common Christian prescript (cf. also 1 Pet 1:3; 2 Pet 1:2; H. Bietenhard traces the parallel benediction to pre-Pauline observance of the Lord's Supper, *NIDNTT* 2:516) or a distinctive title for Jesus. In support of the latter meaning we may draw attention to the other occurrence of the title in James (2:1) where ἡμῶν and τῆς δόξης are added. Furthermore, other examples in the NT suggest that it became a fixed title early in the church. In Acts it appears on the lips of Peter (11:17), as part of the "decree" of Jerusalem (15:26) and as a summary of Paul's message at Rome (28:31).

Two examples from Paul may explain the origin and significance of the title. In 1 Cor 8:6 Paul presents the confession of a unique lord over against the plurality of κύριοι. Recent studies have shown the probable pre-Pauline background of elements in the text (R. Kerst, "1 Kor. 8.6—ein vorpaulinisches Taufbekenntnis?" *ZNW* 66 [1975] 130–39; R. A. Horsley, "The Background of the Confessional Formula in I Kor. 8.6," *ZNW* 69 [1978] 130–35; J. Murphy-O'Connor, "I Cor. VIII.6: Cosmology or Soteriology?" *RB* 85 [1978] 253–59). Among these elements we should include the expression κύριος Ἰησοῦς Χριστός, since it parallels other early confessions (Rom 10:9; 1 Cor 12:3; Eph 4:5). The other text in Paul that depends upon earlier statements is Phil 2:11. Here the pre-Pauline origin of this part of the confession is generally accepted (see the preface to Martin, *Carmen Christi: Philippians 2:5-11 in Recent Interpretation* [Grand Rapids: Eerdmans, 1983] xxv–xxxii) even if the debate continues over its Jewish Christian or hellenistic provenance (ibid., 306–311). The eschatological and confessional import of the original hymn and of the use Paul makes of the material is unmistakable. This exclusive confession of Jesus as Lord recognizes his exalted status and his present, ultimate demand upon human beings who are accountable to him for their actions (see W. Kramer, *Christ, Lord, Son of God,* 169–71, 47).

Since, however, the author of James gives little information to supplement his use of the full title, we can determine its meaning only from a limited context. The occurrence of κυρίος with θεός parallels 1 Cor 8:6 and points to a confession of the early church which persisted (Titus 1:1). The use of δοῦλος here reminds us of a theme of the Philippian hymn and, when linked with James 2:1, suggests an interest in the exaltation of both God and Christ (note the goal of glory in Phil 2:11 and the phrase τῆς δόξης in James 2:1).

The addressees are described in the phrase ταῖς δώδεκα φυλαῖς ταῖς ἐν τῇ διασπορᾷ, "to the twelve tribes of the Dispersion." Two views of the background are possible: (1) in the racial or geographical sense (Mayor, Hort, Chaine) the term Dispersion referred to Jewish people seen as emigres from Palestine and distributed among the hellenistic kingdoms and later throughout the Roman Empire, especially after the destruction of the Jerusalem Temple in A.D. 70 (see John 7:35 for this sense). (2) The term came also to stand for the remnant of Israel, the true Israel of eschatological salvation (cf. Jer 31:8; Ezek 37:19, 25; 1QS 8.1; 2 Apoc. Bar. 78.5–7; Laws, 48) and in that sense it was appropriated by Christians who laid claim to their status as the "Israel of God" (Gal 6:16; cf. Rom 9:24–26; Heb 3:6; 4:9; 1 Pet 2:9–10).

It is possible to bring these two options together and to view (tentatively) James' address as directed to the worldwide community of believing Jews of the messianic faith. F. F. Bruce thus states this conclusion (New Testament History, 353 n.7): the term speaks of "the sum-total of Jewish believers in Jesus, considered as the new Israel." See 1:18 where "kind of first fruits of his creatures" has the same connotation, with ἀπαρχή as the term of election used of historic Israel and the new Israel (1 Cor 16:15; Rom 11:16; 16:5; Rev 14:4).

But more is to be said about this phrase δώδεκα φυλαῖς. Some commentators have taken this term to symbolize "new Israel," corresponding to other ideal associations uniting the church and Israel (Rom 9:24–26; Gal 6:16; 1 Pet 2:9; so most recently, Laws, 48). Certainly strong evidence exists for the use of the term in a representative sense, particularly in 2 Baruch: "Behold how many are left from the twelve tribes of Israel" (77:2); "Are we not all, the twelve tribes, bound by one captivity as we descend also from one father?" (78:4, in letter to the nine and a half tribes).

Although these examples reflect a symbolic use of the "twelve tribes," both 2 Apoc. Bar. and the Qumran War Scroll (1QM) do not eliminate ethnic usage from the term. The author of 2 Apoc. Bar. consistently distinguishes ethnic Israel from other nations (42.5; 48.20, 23; 77.5). Despite the dispersion of God's people after the destruction of the Temple (1:4), God will gather faithful Jews (78.7 contra 41.3; 42.4) to experience the resurrection and a new earthly life (30.1–2). Similarly 1QM describes the eschatological battle of the faithful community against non-Israelite nations (1QM 12 ff., esp. 15.1: "to war against all the nations"). To this evidence we can add the fact that Josephus rarely alludes to twelve tribes without meaning "Israel" (Ant. 1.221, referring to the sons of Ishmael, cf. Gen 12:12–18). The only twelve tribes in the LXX are those of Israel (Exod 24:4; Josh 12:5; Ezek 47:3).

The situation is the same in the NT. (1) Some references to the twelve tribes have in view physical or ethnic Israel. The Q-saying (Matt 19:28 // Luke 22:30) probably contained the phrase "the twelve tribes of Israel" for the following reasons: (a) Neither Matthew nor Luke shows much interest in "tribes" per se (see, e.g., Acts 2:5 where Luke refers to the Jews as part of a wider company drawn from all nations, ἔθνη; and the general reference in Matt 24:30, "all the tribes of the earth," is probably a Matthean addition. Mention of the ancestry of Anna, in Luke 2:36, stands out in the context as pre-Lukan); (b) Matthew knows the Twelve as a title (Matt 11:1; 20:17; 26:14, 47; cf. 1 Cor 15:5) but in this context apparently has Jesus address a larger group of disciples (Matt 19:23, 25). To add δώδεκα here might confuse the Matthean reader as to the focus of Jesus' statement; (c) therefore a contrast in both settings between the disciples and Israel must be intended. The contrast cannot be between Gentiles and ethnic Israel; the pronoun ὑμεῖς necessarily includes those of Jewish origin.

References to the "twelve tribes" in Revelation can be interpreted less certainly of physical Israel, since the book contains highly symbolic language and imagery throughout. Rev 21:12 clearly has historical Israel in view. (a) A direct contrast is drawn between the twelve apostles and the twelve tribes (21:12–14); (b) the only other reference to Israel in the book of Revelation is to historical Israel (Rev 2:14; cf. Num 31:16) in a story well known in apocalyptic Jewish Christian circles (Jude 11; 2 Pet 2:15). Rev 7:4 is more difficult to interpret. Two aspects of that context suggest that these 144,000 represent Christians in general: (i) elsewhere the seal of God indicates only that one is a follower of God (Rev 9:4); (ii) the term (note the similarity to the expression above) need not refer only to Jews in the Apocalypse (1:1; 2:20; 6:15; 19:5; 22:3, 6). Nevertheless, two other pieces of evidence favor a more literal interpretation here: (i) in this context these tribes are distinguished from others (7:9), referring to those of "every . . . tribe." These two are elect because they wear the garments of the righteous martyr (cf. 6:11 and a similar scene in 5:9); (ii) the other context (21:12) also distinguishes between subgroups of the elect.

(2) A second reason for taking James 1:1 to refer to historical Israel is the qualified use of the term φυλή. Only when the word is modified by πᾶς or τῆς γῆς, etc., does it have a non-Jewish reference. Some examples of φυλή indicate its occurrence as an identifying or legitimizing mark. This usage would be meaningless if the term were purely symbolic (Luke 2:36; Acts 13:21; Rom 11:1; Phil 3:5).

The above evidence thus indicates that the author saw his readers as "true Israel," those who had expressed faith in Jesus as Messiah, who anticipated the great ingathering foreseen, e.g., in the *Psalms of Solomon* (17:28). That they had not yet experienced that unity is suggested by the phrase that qualifies the expression δώδεκα φυλαῖς. Since, however, we have no evidence of the phrase being used of non-Jews (except *Ant.* 1.221, which quotes Gen 12:16) and since the setting contains no indication of a mixed (Jew-Gentile) congregation (see *Introduction*) we cannot take this term to refer to the church as an entity distinct from historical Israel. More likely, the audience of James is seen as the "true Israel" because the people in mind are Jews of the messianic faith.

ἐν τῇ διασπορᾷ. This qualifying phrase suggests, first of all, that part of the twelve tribes may not have been scattered and thus confirms the above conclusion on syntactical grounds. If the meaning of διασπορά could be established it might clarify the meaning of the larger title. The author here expresses solidarity with the suffering of his readers while recalling the historical situation of many Jews.

Solidarity in suffering has precedents in the LXX. The twelve occurrences of the word διασπορά (Deut 28:25; 30:4; Neh 1:9; Ps 146 [147]:2; Isa 49:6; Jer 13:14 [א]; 15:7; 41 [34]:17; Dan 12:2; 2 Macc 1:27; Jud 5:19; and the LXX [A] title of Ps 138 [139]; the verb occurs sixteen times in Josephus but the noun never occurs) translate various Hebrew equivalents for terms meaning "outcast," "terror," "destruction," and "preserved." Association between suffering and dispersion in these LXX contexts focuses on the condition of those described rather than the place where they have been scattered (cf. Sir 44:23; 45:11; 2 Esd 6:7; 1QM 2.2; 3.14; 3.23–9.17; 1QSa 1.15). A similar interpretation of the term fits with a primary theme of the epistle, namely, the testing of faith.

The noun διασπορά occurs only three times in the NT (James 1:1; 1 Pet 1:1; John 7:35). Twice it has the article (James and John) and once is further qualified (John).

The author of 1 Peter probably intends διασπορά to apply to all believers, whether Jew or Greek. Other terms in his salutation are applied in the body of the epistle to Christians (2:4, 5, 9, 11). This application is clearest in the author's use of passages previously applied to Israel but now meant for the new Israel (2:6, 9). The character of that epistle as reflecting an appeal to the (Christian) dispersion appears from enumeration of specific geographical locations outside of Palestine.

The similar reference in the Fourth Gospel connotes Jews living in the Mediterranean world, a conclusion drawn from its extra term: τῶν Ἑλλήνων (7:35). Yet this identification is not as clear-cut as it first appears. The author of the Gospel uses the title Ἕλληνες only once more (12:20) but otherwise is silent on the subject of the Dispersion. (J. A. T. Robinson, "The Destination and Purpose of St. John's Gospel," NTS 6 [1959–60] 120–21, sees these people as Greek-speaking Jews [12:20] because of their purpose in coming to Jerusalem—to worship at the feasts—and their approach to Jesus through Philip, who had a Greek name. But the reference is ambiguous. It could mean (i) people of the Greek-speaking Diaspora, hence non-Palestinian Jews, or (ii) Greek inhabitants living among Diaspora Jews. R. E. Brown, *The Gospel According to John I–XII* [Garden City, NY: Doubleday, 1966] 314, argues that they are non-Jews. Both see the geographical reference to places outside of Palestine where Jews lived. See also C. F. D. Moule, "Once More, Who Were the Hellenists?" *ExpTim* 70 [1958–59] 100, and M. Hengel, *Acts and the History of Earliest Christianity*, 71–80.)

References to διασπείρειν in Luke-Acts (Acts 8:1, 4; 11:19) furnish the basis for Christian associations with the concept of dispersion. Each of the three examples describes the situation in Jerusalem after the martyrdom of Stephen and thus relates it to a specific context of persecution. Since διασπορά in Christian literature is applied in a different way (1 Pet 1:1), its meaning cannot be limited to this event. Close occurrence of εὐαγγελίζεσθαι/λαλεῖν (Acts 8:4; 11:19) in context may reflect Luke's attempt at transforming a negative historical situation into a positive one according to his pattern of salvation history. It may also draw upon an earlier mention of the dispersion in an eschatological and missionary context (Isa 49:6). The association of διασπείρειν with θλῖψις (Acts 11:19) resembles the difficult situation reflected in James (Acts 14:22 and James 1:27). See *Introduction*, pp. lxix–lxxvii.

Explanation

In an opening salutation James directs his writing to his compatriots of the messianic faith whom he regards also as one in kinship with ethnic Israel in the international arena. This use of a conventional "greeting" is meant to pave the way for the call which follows, with the link-word of "joy" (*chara*) producing a word association with greeting (*chairein*). His authority as God's servant is placed in a prominent position; he chooses to pass over his natural kinship with his brother Jesus since now Jesus is the exalted Lord, known by faith and crowned with "glory" (2:1). Alternatively, the opening greeting has been set in place by the letter's final editor, with James' role as teacher and mentor becoming more prominent by the ascription to him of a full title as "servant of God and of the Lord Jesus Christ."

II. Enduring Trials (1:2–19a)

1. Trials, Wisdom, Faith (1:2–8)

Bibliography

Amphoux, C.-B. "Une relecture du chapître 1 de l'épître de Jacques." *Bib* 59 (1978) 554–61. **Flew, R. N.** *The Idea of Perfection in Christian Theology.* Oxford: Oxford UP, 1934. **Kirk, J. A.** "The Meaning of Wisdom in James: Examination of a Hypothesis." *NTS* 16 (1969) 24–38. **Kuhn, K. G.** "New Light on Temptation, Sin, and Flesh in the New Testament." In *The Scrolls and the New Testament*, ed. K. Stendahl. London: SCM, 1958. 94–113. **Marshall, S. S.** "Δίψυχος, A Local Term?" *SE* 6 (1973) 348–51. **Plessis, P. J. du.** ΤΕΛΕΙΟΣ: *The Idea of Perfection in the New Testament.* Kampen: Kok, 1959. **Preisker, H.** *Das Ethos des Urchristentums.* Gütersloh: Bertelsmann, 1949. **Seitz, O. J. F.** "Afterthoughts on the Term 'Dipsychos,'" *NTS* 4 (1958) 327–34. ———. "Antecedents and Signification of the Term δίψυχος." *JBL* 66 (1947) 211–19. ———. "The Relationship of the Shepherd of Hermas to the Epistle of James." *JBL* 63 (1944) 131–40. **Spicq, C.** "La vertu des simplicités dans l'Ancien et le Nouveau Testament." *RSR* 22 (1933) 1–26. **Thomas, J.** "Anfechtung und Vorfreude, eine biblisches Thema nach Jak 1,2–18 im Zusammenhang mit Ps 126, Röm 5,3–5 und 1 Petr 1,5–7." *KD* 14 (1968) 183–206. **Turner, N.** *Christian Words.* Edinburgh: T. & T. Clark, 1980. **Wibbing, S.** *Die Tugend- und Lasterkataloge im NT.* BZNW 25. Berlin: Töpelmann, 1959. **Wichmann, W.** *Die Leidenstheologie: eine Form der Leidensdeutung im Spätjudentum.* BWANT 53. Stuttgart: Kohlhammer, 1930. **Wolverton, W. I.** "The Double-minded Man in the Light of Essene Psychology." *ATR* 38 (1956) 166–75.

Translation

[2] *Treat it as altogether* [a] *an occasion for joy, my brothers, when you meet trials of various kinds* [3] *in the knowledge that the testing* [b] *of your faith* [c] *produces patient endurance.* [4] *Let endurance yield its complete work so that you may be complete and blameless with no deficiency at all.* [5] *But if there is one among you who does lack wisdom, let such a person ask from God who gives to all without hesitation or recrimination, and he will give it.* [6] *Let the asking, however, be accompanied with faith, and no doubting: for the doubter is like the billowing sea driven by the wind and tossed about.* [7] *Such a person must not think that he will gain anything from the Lord.* [8] *He is a double-minded person, distracted in all his conduct.* [d]

Notes

[a] Assuming with Ropes (129–30) that the point of πᾶσαν, "all," is to heighten the effect of the noun χαράν, and that its usage is adverbial. NIV takes πᾶσαν as adjectival: "pure joy." See BDF § 275.3.

[b] δοκίμιον is to be read rather than δόκιμον attested in a few MSS and possibly P[74]. The influence of the text in 1 Pet 1:7 has been suspected. Metzger, *Textual Commentary*, 679, notes how the two words were run together in meaning in the papyri so that δοκίμιον ("means of testing") could be regarded as the neuter of the adjective δόκιμον.

ᶜτῆς πίστεως is omitted in B² ff syrʰᶜˡ presumably on the ground that the words are derived from 1 Pet 1:7. See later for the parallels in 1 Pet 1:6–7 (Mussner, 65 n.5).

ᵈThe punctuation of vv 7–8 is disputed, the decision depending on what is the subject of λήμψεται in v 7. Either ἀνὴρ δίψυχος is the subject, thus producing in v 8 a general statement (so Hort on the ground that ἐκεῖνος in v 7 refers to the person who lacks wisdom in v 5; but this is unlikely since the description in v 8 can hardly be limited in this way) or ἀνὴρ δίψυχος stands in apposition to the foregoing on the analogy of 3:2, 8; 4:12 (so Dibelius, Ropes, Vouga). The latter is the reading behind B and the Peshitta, and is to be preferred.

Form / Structure / Setting

The limits of this pericope are chosen to express certain exegetical and literary convictions. One is that the form of the passage is parenetic, expressing forceful exhortation and based on the sapiential axiom, illustrated in the Wisdom literature of Judaism, that "affliction teaches endurance" (Dibelius, 72). Then secondly, the definition given to πειρασμός, "trial" (v 2), marks the term out as conveying the readers' condition as a persecuted community, facing specific dangers (2:6; 5:1–6, against Ropes, Laws, and others who see here only general trials). The testing of 1:12 is therefore not the same problem, and the two sections should not be quickly run together. They are only loosely connected with a distinction to be seen in the meaning of πειρασμός (see on 1:12). On the other hand, Dibelius's contention that 1:2–4 stands without logical connection to what follows in v 5 is not persuasive, since it is more than a coincidence or a literary device that the catchwords "lacking—lack wisdom" (λειπόμενοι—λείπεσθαι σοφίας) stand in close proximity in vv 4–5. The parallel of vv 1–2 is too close to be ignored.

Thirdly, the presence of these link-terms to form a concatenation is a noteworthy literary feature of the hortatory style. We may point to vv 1–2 where χαίρειν-χαράν are clearly part of the author's reminiscence and the wordplay (Mussner, 62). The repetition of ὑπομονή in vv 3–4 (with the theme further developed in v 6), and of the root αἰτ- ("ask") in vv 5–6 with the recurrence of τέλειον-τέλειοι in v 4 as of διακρινόμενος (twice in v 6) are further evidence of an artistically crafted piece, in which the author's mind moves from one exhortation to another and purposefully carries the readers along with him.

The subject matter of "reaction to trials" is the first admonition of the letter, but the theme will be picked up later, notably in chap 5. There the example of Job, a favorite character of the Wisdom school, will be appealed to in support of the thesis that "affliction produces endurance" (5:11). Here the teaching is set in a generalized context, but drawing on several parallels, mainly in Sirach (2:1–6; 4:17–18: wisdom comes to the aid of the godly in Israel who are exposed to trials and tested in the ways of righteousness where they have chosen to walk) and 4 Maccabees, in which the theme is one of the constancy of the martyrs when persecuted (see 4 Macc 1:11; 9:30; 17:12; cf. Job 19:8; *T. Jos.* 2:7: all illustrating ὑπομονή as an example of the staying power shown by those who suffer for their faith). "You must endure (ὑπομένειν) all evil for God's cause" (4 Macc 16:19) is a typical sentiment which James echoes.

The verbal links with Rom 5:3–5 and 1 Pet 1:6–7 are studied by several commentators (cf. Dibelius, Davids, with the theological aspects noted by Thomas, "Anfechtung," especially 197–99). It is now conceded that, although there are a number of common terms, notably the need for ὑπομονή, the test(ing) of faith, and the call to rejoicing, there are also significant differences. Therefore there is little reason to suppose that any of the three NT writers is drawing directly on the work of the others. Among the points of distinction are the assumption in 1 Peter that the believers who suffer are blameless and so the suffering is undeserved (1 Pet 2:20; 3:17) and the strongly worded eschatological note in Rom 5, which is not so pronounced in our author. The indebtedness of all NT writers to both the Wisdom tradition and the parenetic genre explains both the similarities and the differences (Dibelius, 76). The most notable of the literary forms to which the NT authors are indebted is the use of a chain-argument (*Gedankenkette*, as Windisch, 6, describes it), denoted by the technical rhetorical term *sorites* (see W. G. Kümmel [with O. Kaiser], *Exegetical Method: A Student's Handbook*, rev. ed., tr. E. V. N. Goetchius [New York: Seabury Press, 1981] 61). This literary feature describes the way one term is piled upon another to form a stairway of ideas, with each building on its predecessor to produce a memorable and forceful series of moral exhortations.

Comment

2 πᾶσαν χαρὰν ἡγήσασθε, ἀδελφοί μου, ὅταν πειρασμοῖς περιπέσητε ποικίλοις, "Treat it as altogether an occasion for joy, my brothers, when you meet trials of various kinds."

With verbal links to the prescript, which ends with χαίρειν, James' opening section invites the readers to wrestle with the paradox of "rejoicing in affliction" (cf. Jud 8:25: "let us give thanks to the Lord our God, who is putting us to the test [πειράζει ἡμᾶς] as he did our forefathers"; Wisd Sol 3:4–9; 4 Macc 7:22: "It is a blessed thing to endure all hardness for the sake of virtue"; 9:29–30; 11:22; Josephus, *J.W.* 1.653; 2 *Apoc. Bar.* 52.5–6: "and as for the righteous, what will they do now? Rejoice in the suffering which you now suffer"). The NT writers also engage this theme: see Matt 5:4, 10–12; Luke 6:20–25; Rom 5:3–5; 1 Pet 1:6–7. The Wisdom tradition traces human joy to a love of wisdom (Sir 40:20), and warns that the path of wisdom will often lead to discipline and testing (Sir 4:17; *Pss Sol* 10:1–3; Thomas, "Anfechtung," 187–90, who compares Heb 10, 12).

The relationship of the author to the readers is a warm one, as the frequent title "(my) brothers" (2:1, 14; 3:1, 10, 12; 5:12, 19 which include the pronoun "my"; also 4:11; 5:7, 9–10 have simply "brothers," while a more endearing "beloved brothers" is found in 1:16, 19; 2:5) shows. This feature could be a rhetorical ploy (Vouga, 38); but it is also a sign of affection and esteem, calculated to enforce the hortatory and homiletic appeal (Mussner, 63). That appeal is marked by the use in v 3 of the participle γινώσκοντες, lit., "knowing," which is used as an imperative, a style derived from rabbinic parenesis (W. D. Davies, *Paul and Rabbinic Judaism*, 2d ed. [London: SPCK, 1955] 329).

The addressees are already facing threats to their faith, expressed by their having to encounter (lit., "fall into," περιπέσητε: cf. Luke 10:30 for the verb;

and for exposure to unwelcome misfortunes such as sickness, see Prov 11:5; 2 Macc 6:12–13) adversities of various kinds (lit., "multicolored"; ποικίλος, which suggests an intensity and variety added for emphasis, as in 1 Tim 3:6; Titus 3:3; Heb 13:9; but the closest parallel is 1 Pet 1:6). The verb makes it plain that these trials are not such as the brothers would have chosen nor are they simply the ills the human lot is heir to. They are met with because of the believers' loyalty to God, who permits such experiences to occur to test his people (a common OT idea: Gen 22:1; Exod 15:25; 16:4; Deut 8:2, 16; 2 Chr 32:31; Job 1–2; cf. Jud 8:25–27; Wisd Sol 3:4–6).

The latter point is clarified by the use of πειρασμός, which has two distinct meanings: (1) incitements to evil thoughts and wrongdoing, usually known under the name of "temptation" (see 1:12–15 for the customary way of understanding this meaning of πειρασμός and cf. the title ὁ πειράζων, "the tempter," of Satan as the one who seduces people to evil ways: Kuhn, "New Light," 95–96, 111) and (2) trials which human beings have to endure as part of life's adversities and hardships. It is possible to give the present verse a broad definition (so Ropes; Laws, 3) of the sufferings which believers face as economically and socially disadvantaged people (2:7; 4:7–10; 5:1–6). But these references say more about the readers' bitter experiences. They are better understood as signs of oppression and persecution endured for one's religious convictions. Hence we should interpret our present verse as a reference to the tension in which persons who were faced with the task of reconciling the will of God and dominating evil powers would and did find themselves. So Vouga, 39. Support for this latter sense comes in the following line.

3 γινώσκοντες ὅτι τὸ δοκίμιον ὑμῶν τῆς πίστεως κατεργάζεται ὑπομονήν, "in the knowledge that the testing of your faith produces patient endurance."

Appeal is made to both the readers' faith and the occasion of trial in which that faith (sc. in God) is being put to the test (τὸ δοκίμιον). The latter term, which could be construed in the sense of "act of proving," is better to be understood as "means of testing" (see Dibelius, 72–73). The thought is that the trials pose a threat to faith. When the trials are borne in the right way they serve to test the quality of faith by producing the result of ὑπομονή ("patient endurance"). The endurance thus becomes "[the] new facet of the believer's character that could not exist without testing" (Davids, 68), when trials are viewed not as necessarily welcome and certainly not to be sought after in a foolhardy or masochistic way (cf. Ign. *Rom.* 4:1–2). Rather, trials serve as a feature of the life of trust that refines and shapes believers' knowledge of divine providence and God's holy purpose. Hence suffering of this kind is rightly viewed "from the perspective of *Heilsgeschichte*," as God's saving plan is worked out in the crucible of trials endured for the faith (see 4 Macc 17:2–4; *Jub.* 17:17; 19:8; and *T. Jos.* 2:4–7, which has several verbal links with πειρασμός, δοκίμιον/δόκιμον, ὑπομονή: "in ten trials [πειρασμοῖς] he [God] showed that I was approved [δόκιμον] . . . and endurance [ὑπομονή] yielded many good things").

ὑπομονή is more than patience, though it does contain that element of passive staying power (from the verb ὑπο—μένειν: cf. Sir 2:14; 17:24; 41:2) and constancy (Sir 16:13), with Abraham as the prime model in Jewish thought (especially in 4 Maccabees, which stresses the active elements in trust). There is also the idea of "hope," "expectancy," drawn from the LXX where ὑπομονή renders מִקְוֶה, *miqweh* (Jer 14:8; 17:13; 1 Chr 29:15; note too Ps 70 [71]:5 where ὑπομονή and ἐλπίς stand in parallelism in LXX). But the word has more to its meaning than a quietistic acceptance and wistful longing for better things (better represented by תִּקְוָה, *tiqwah* in Pss 9:19 [18]; 61:6 [62:5]; 70 [71]:5; Job 14:19—in LXX also ὑπομονή). The component of steadfastness under trial and a persistent determination to win through to the end is marked as believers yield their lives to God (Vouga, 39) and remain faithful in anticipation of their reward (as in 4 Macc 1:11; 9:30; 17:12: "on that day virtue was the umpire and the test to which they were put was a test of endurance. The prize for victory was incorruption in long-lasting life").

See Turner, *Christian Words*, 318–19, for the various NT nuances of ὑπομονή. He prefers "patient endurance" as a most adequate rendering of the Greek, with a component that suggests also "an unruffled expectancy of God's salvation" to be fulfilled at the Parousia (cf. 5:7, 11, which stress more than in 4 Maccabees the divine intervention).

4 ἡ δὲ ὑπομονὴ ἔργον τέλειον ἐχέτω, ἵνα ἦτε τέλειοι καὶ ὁλόκληροι ἐν μηδενὶ λειπόμενοι, "Let endurance yield its complete work so that you may be complete and blameless with no deficiency at all."

The constancy and perseverance of James' readers are designed to promote a laudable goal. If we give emphasis to δέ as adversative ("but," which however need be no more than a simple connective with a transitional use [BGD 171.2] and so unnecessary in translation), then James may be warning that endurance, however dogged and determined, should not lead to obstinacy or fanatical stubbornness (so Vouga, 40); rather it has in view a "complete work," ἔργον τέλειον, which on face value implies a completeness of character, producing the choice fruits of Christian disposition and expressed in good works (so 2:14–26; cf. Matt 7:15–20; so too Ropes, citing Gal 5:6; Rom 6:22). But more than "good deeds" are intended, for James' use of τέλειος reflects the Hebraic tradition of the righteous person (see 5:6) such as Noah, who was "blameless (תָּמִים, *tāmîm*) in his generation," as he walked with God (see Gen 6:9; Sir 44:17; *Jub.* 23:10).

Obedience to God's laws and the stress on a character free from defect are traits implicit in תָּם/*tām* (otherwise expressed as תָּמִים or שָׁלֵם, *šlm*; see du Plessis, ΤΕΛΕΙΟΣ, 33–34, 94–103) as used in the OT, whether of human beings or sacrificial animals (Exod 12:5; Lev 1:10; 3:6). It is natural, therefore, that the writer's use of τέλειος should include the apparently synonymous term ὁλόκληρος (a rare word: only here and 1 Thess 5:23), meaning a growth in perfection and a reaching of full maturity. It also is found with the sense of being morally blameless, intact (see H. Preisker, *Das Ethos*, 130; but it is also a religious term, 134), complete (see of Abraham's character in Philo, *De Abr.* 34, 47, 117). We may refer also to 3:2, a text leading Windisch to conclude that "James is a perfectionist." (See also Wisd Sol 9:6.)

But in what sense is the call to perfection to be understood? Rightly Windisch cites Matt 5:48 where the motif of *imitatio Dei* sets the pattern for the disciples' aspiration to be "perfect" (Flew, *Idea*, 4–5). What is at the heart of James' admonition is seen in 2:22 where the call of τελειοῦν, "to perfect" one's faith, comes in a discussion of vital faith as evidenced by "works." But behind both aspects is the Christian's character. So *"you* are that perfect work" (Dibelius, Davids). See du Plessis, ΤΕΛΕΙΟΣ, 235, 240, for the conclusion that by "perfect" James means the "complete character" of the believer, expressed by the coherence of faith and works, i.e., in conduct.

To sum up, τέλειος is obviously a key term for James (see *Introduction,* pp. lxxix–lxxxii), with five occurrences (1:4, twice; 1:17; 1:25; 3:2). "No NT book uses it as much as this epistle" (Davids, 69), i.e., in proportion to its length, since Paul has seven references. Three ideas are to be seen in the use of τέλειος in our verse: (1) it is primarily a statement about a person's character, not simply a record of his or her overt acts, though ἔργον looks forward to the disquisition on faith and works in 2:14–26; (2) the achieving of a "perfect work" of moral character is not simply human endeavor writ large as in the Stoic ideal (Mussner, 67, citing Wibbing, *Tugend- und Lasterkataloge,* 127, who notes the fact of continuing "trial" [πειρασμός] needed to attain "perfection") but is modeled on the divine pattern which sets the standard and inspires the believer, as the subsequent verses will illustrate (1:5, 17–18); (3) "the 'perfection' of James is eschatological" (Mussner, 67), that is, it looks ahead to its fullest maturity at the end time when God's purposes will have been achieved. Until then, the believer has to endure trials en route to the goal and to strive to attain the fulfillment of God's plan, not excusing himself or permitting any failure to block the way thereto (ἐν μηδενὶ λειπόμενοι is a negative reinforcement to the positive declarations of τέλειοι καὶ ὁλόκληροι and a prelude to what will be the writer's next subsection).

5 Εἰ δέ τις ὑμῶν λείπεται σοφίας, αἰτείτω παρὰ τοῦ διδόντος θεοῦ πᾶσιν ἁπλῶς καὶ μὴ ὀνειδίζοντος, καὶ δοθήσεται αὐτῷ, "But if there is one among you who does lack wisdom, let such a person ask from God who gives to all without hesitation or recrimination, and he will give it."

The catchword is the verb "to lack," picked up from the preceding verse. The situation of the readers who are facing trial is such that they need to know how to cope with these experiences. Hence there is the need of "wisdom" (σοφία). The conditional clause opening with εἰ δέ does not imply doubt or suggest a contingency. Rather it presupposes "a standing fact" (Hiebert, 79). The readers are facing some real problems arising from persecution, and it is the gift and application of wisdom to see these trials in their proper light and respond accordingly.

Wisdom, as noted earlier (*Introduction,* pp. lxxxii–lxxxiv), is one of the great terms of practical religion. The question "Where shall wisdom be found?" (Job 28:12) is answered by the sages of Israel in Prov 1:7: "The fear of the Lord is the beginning of knowledge," implying a devotion to Yahweh and a resolve to walk in the ways of his law. For the Jewish mind wisdom meant practical righteousness in everyday living. And it is God's gift, not a native human disposition. Hence the verbs here, "let such a person (τις) ask (αἰτείτω) from God . . . and he will give it," lit., "it will be given" (δοθήσεται αὐτῷ), are part of the grammatical construction of the divine passive, i.e., the use of the passive voice to denote the hidden agency of God (see J. Jeremias, *New Testament Theology,* tr. J. Bowden [London: SCM, 1971] 9-14, for this important clue to interpretation).

The gift of wisdom in James is linked with the trials his readers were

enduring. The connection is made in Sir 4:17 where the children of wisdom
(4:11) are trained by her discipline (παιδεία) and tested by her ordinances.
There may be some such connection in James (Mussner, 68). But there is a
more definite link between wisdom and perfection, which is the goal set in
v 4. Wisd Sol 9:6 offers a clear statement parallel to James' thought: "for
even if one is perfect (τέλειος) among the sons of men, yet without the wisdom
that comes from thee he will be regarded as nothing" (though Dibelius questions the relevance of this text on the ground that v 4 and v 5 are not to be
joined by an appeal to Wisd Sol 9:6. But the link uniting "test," "perfect,"
and "wisdom" is too strong to pass over). The theme of testing as linked
with wisdom is a common feature in the Wisdom tradition. In time of trial
(Wisd Sol 5:1–14) the righteous person will seek help from God (see Wisd
Sol 7:7: "I prayed, and understanding was given me; I called upon God,
and the spirit of wisdom came to me"; 8:21: "I perceived that I would not
possess wisdom unless God gave her to me . . . so I appealed to the Lord
and besought him with all my heart"). These expressions underscore the
teaching that wisdom is a divine gift. "Yahweh gives wisdom" (Prov 2:6).
James is very much in this tradition.

The actions of God are characterized as a giving that is ἁπλῶς καὶ μὴ
ὀνειδίζοντος highlighting two divine attributes of generosity and graciousness.
The adverb ἁπλῶς (*hapax* in the NT) has in classical Greek the sense of
"simply," "plainly," "straightforwardly," or "foolishly." Here it stands in contrast to δίψυχος (in v 8), "double-minded," and reassures us that God is not
in two minds about his giving. This assurance may be expressed in the idea
of being generous, but the rendering "without hesitation" stresses that there
are no conditions to his giving, no *arrière-pensées* (Vouga, 43), an understanding
of God's nature and of Christian virtue that is found too in the Pauline
epistles (Rom 12:8; 2 Cor 11:3; Eph 6:5; Col 3:22). See Spicq, "La vertu,"
RSR 22 (1933) 1–26.

The other attribute is contained in the participle μὴ ὀνειδίζοντες from a
verb meaning "to insult, to hurl an invective, to harm." It is frequent in
Sirach to express the need for generosity and a kind word to accompany
giving to the poor (see Sir 18:15–18; cf. 41:22). But the closest parallel is
Sir 20:14–15 because of the connection with the thought of ἁπλῶς:

> A fool's gift will profit for nothing for he has many eyes instead of one. He gives
> little and upbraids (ὀνειδίσει) much; he opens his mouth like a herald . . . such a
> one is a hateful man.

God's nature, on the contrary, is not to be questioned, and his giving is
marked by a spirit of spontaneity and graciousness. The theme of James is
that of the "prodigality of God" (Vouga). God's willingness to hear and respond
to his children's call in their need is well attested in the teaching of Jesus
(Matt 7:7 par.; 18:19 [M]; 21:22 par.; cf. John 14:13–14; 15:7; 16:23). Jer
29:12–13 (LXX 36:11–12) is one of the main OT anticipations of this assurance
believers have that God is ready to hear. James' teaching on the need to
supplicate God is continued in the next verse.

6 αἰτείτω δὲ ἐν πίστει μηδὲν διακρινόμενος· ὁ γὰρ διακρινόμενος ἔοικεν κλύδωνι θαλάσσης ἀνεμιζομένῳ καὶ ῥιπιζομένῳ, "Let the asking, however, be accompanied with faith, and no doubting: for the doubter is like the billowing sea driven by the wind and tossed about."

The link-verb is αἰτεῖν, borrowed from the preceding verse, where it functions as a technical term for prayer viewed as asking. James has painted in some bold strokes the scope of such praying: it is universal (God gives to all who petition him), it is beneficent, it is without regard to merit, and it is a response with no equivocations. Now it is opportune to underline the human side to prayer. Marked by a contrast (δέ), it is not simple prayer that succeeds, but prayer with confidence (Hubbard, 20–22; Mussner, 69). So the praying that receives answers from God is marked by faith (πίστις) and the absence of doubt (μηδὲν διακρινόμενος). Already mentioned in v 3, "faith" has for James the ideas of full conviction and certitude, especially when associated with prayer (see 5:15, 16). The other references to faith as a noun or a verb are in 2:1, 5. The word also occurs eleven times in 2:15–26 where it is set in contrast to "works," and has a more specialized meaning, ranging from a confessional statement (2:19) to the spurious declaration of mock sympathy (2:17, see Turner, *Christian Words*, 157, for this and other kinds of faith in chap. 2) with the true meaning implied in the phrase "faith and actions working together" (2:22).

The present verse recalls Mark 11:24; Matt 21:22 and illustrates the definition of faith as "a painstaking and concentrated effort to obtain blessing for oneself or for others, material or spiritual, inspired by a confident belief that God in Jesus can supply all human need" (J. A. Findlay, *Jesus As They Saw Him* [London: Epworth, 1934] 107).

In the light of an insistence on faith as strong conviction, διακρίνεσθαι has a meaning that can only imply "doubt," though other meanings are "to separate, distinguish, decide, judge" (see 2:4, 9 for other contexts). The disposition of doubt places the character of God in question (as in Matt 21:21; Rom 4:20) and blocks our access to his bounty. James' illustration is a dramatic one as he turns to describe the waves of the sea driven by the wind (ἀνεμιζομένῳ) and tossed about (ῥιπιζομένῳ). The participles are alliterative and rhythmical, suggesting to Rendall (*Epistle of St. James*, 37–38) an impressionistic description of a squall on Lake Galilee: "the light spray whisked (ῥιπιζόμενος) from the curling wave," offered as a picture of human instability. This may be so, but it is doubtful if James is consciously referring to Peter's experience (in Matt 14:28–32) and is thereby rebuking Peter's lack of confidence in the setting of early Judaic Christianity, as Scaer (43–44) surmises.

The point to be enforced is that the doubter is as insecure and unsteady as a boat rocked in turbulent seas. The allusion draws on a familiar theme in Jewish literature, denoting the wicked or heretical or hypocritical people as those who are at the mercy of the unruly ocean (Isa 57:20; Sir 33:2: "he who is hypocritical about Torah is like a boat in a storm"; cf. Eph 4:14; Jude 13: cf. Virgil, *Aen.* 12.487, for a classical allusion to Aeneas' conflict).

The line is artistically formed as a tag. ἔοικεν, "is like," is perfect tense with a present force (Thayer, 175, 276, cited by Hiebert, 86, for the grammatical conclusion that the verb implies "a subjective judgment which has feeling rather than thought for its ground").

7–8 μὴ γὰρ οἰέσθω ὁ ἄνθρωπος ἐκεῖνος ὅτι λήμψεταί τι παρὰ τοῦ κυρίου, ἀνὴρ δίψυχος, ἀκατάστατος ἐν πάσαις ταῖς ὁδοῖς αὐτοῦ, "Such a person must not think that he will gain anything from the Lord. He is double-minded person, distracted in all his conduct."

Now the person afflicted by doubt is more fully described. Plagued by such indecision—which for James is the hallmark of unbelief—such a person is characterized by one of the most expressive words in the letter: he is δίψυχος, "double-minded"; here it means "wavering," "lacking in faith," especially in time of persecution when constancy and resolution in faith are called for (Turner, *Christian Words*, 116–18).

The Greek word is evidently modeled on δίγλωσσος, "double-tongued," in Sir 5:9, "a double-tongued sinner"; cf. διπρόσωπος, "double-faced," (colloq., "two-faced") in *T. Asher* 2:5. The expression recalls the Hebrew בלב ולב, which the LXX renders as ἐν καρδίᾳ καὶ ἐν καρδίᾳ (in Ps 11:3 [12:2], "each one speaks vain things to his neighbor, and with flattering lips and a double heart they speak") and ἐν καρδίᾳ δισσῇ (in 1 Chr 12:34 [33] L) as well as Sir 1:28 ("Do not disobey the fear of the Lord; do not approach [him] with a divided mind" [ἐν καρδίᾳ δισσῇ]: cf. 2:12–14, which may be also compared to the expression). The word speaks of a person marked by irresolution where moral choices are concerned, hence the indictment of that person's character as one controlled by the moods of doubting, hesitating to act decisively; the person is consequently likely to wander from the right path (as in 5:19–20, πλανᾶν). See *1 Clem* 11.2, where the adjective is used about Lot, who typifies those who doubt God's power, incur judgment, and are a warning to all generations. There is an appeal to an apocryphal source found in *1 Clem* 23:3, 4; *2 Clem* 11:2, 3, which Lightfoot claimed to be the *Book of Eldad and Modad*, though Clement cites "Wretched are the double-minded" as "this scripture"; and *2 Clem* has "For the prophetic word also says, Miserable are the double-minded." (Cf. *Herm. Vis.* 3.4.2; 4.2.6; see Seitz, "The Relationship," 131–40.)

The background of δίψυχος has been variously assessed, with suggestions ranging from parallels drawn from Qumran or Essene anthropology (Wolverton, "The Double-Minded Man"; Mussner, who cites the witness of 1QH 4.14; cf. Seitz, "Afterthoughts," 327–34) to hellenistic-gnostic dualism that viewed man as a compound of body and soul thought to be in conflict (see Laws, 59, for references). The precise expression ἀνὴρ δίψυχος is, however, without parallel here and at 4:8, and Laws' suggestion that most likely the phrase derives from an idiom current in Greek-speaking Judaism commends itself, even if her submission (Marshall, "δίψυχος") of a Roman provenance may be doubted. If a canonical source is to be suggested, the most obvious reference is to warnings against divided loyalty to Yahweh (seen in, e.g., Deut 6:5; 13:3; 18:13; Pss 18:24; 101:2, 4, 6; 1 Chr 12:38; 2 Chr 31:21; cf. Sir 1:28 cited above). The rabbinic comment (in *Taᶜan.* 23b) on Deut 26:16 makes the same point as James with a similar setting: "When you make your prayer to God, do not have two hearts, one for God and one for something else" (Str-B, 3:751).

The final verdict on ἀνὴρ δίψυχος (not ἄνθρωπος perhaps to avoid a repetition from v 7) is a further reminder of instability: such a person is ἀκατάστατος, lit., "unsettled, not at rest." If there is an allusion taken from Isa 54:11, the maritime analogy from v 6 is continued, since LXX has ἀκατάστατος as a rendering of סֹעֲרָה, *sōⁿrāh*, "storm-tossed." The adjective is found in the NT only here and 3:8. "In all his conduct," lit., "ways," is an OT turn of phrase (Pss 91:11; 145:17; Prov 3:6; Jer 16:17) for a person's daily life in its affairs and business.

Explanation

In a section that is full of powerful and suggestive images James concentrates on the importance of prayer as the believer's line of access to the fountain of help in time of need. To a community under obvious duress and facing the perennial issues of a theodicy, i.e., how to understand present experience in the light of divine sovereignty and human exigency, he addresses the answer culled from Israel's wisdom teachers; it is the appeal to God's gift of wisdom based on faith in God's overruling providence and grace.

Hence it is appropriate to stress the character of God. There are three reasons supplied to encourage the approach in prayer: God is good to all who call on him; he gives with an open hand and without reservation; and his giving is not intended to demean the recipient with feelings that God is reproachful or reluctant to give what is for our good. The parable in Luke 11:5–8 (L: the Friend at Midnight) illuminates Jesus' teaching in Matt 7:7–12 // Luke 11:9–13, and picks up the same general themes to do with prayer. Prayer arises from a sense of need (Luke 11:5, 6) and God's answers often exceed what we ask for (11:8). By contrast God is not like the reluctant householder who is compelled to act only by the friend's persistence (11:8) or shameless behavior (J. Jeremias, *The Parables of Jesus*, rev. ed., tr. S. H. Hooke [New York: Scribner's, 1963] 157–60).

Having stated the clear character of a beneficent and bountiful giver James moves on to stress how appropriate also is the human response in a faith that is wholehearted and loyal. Building on the (mainly) Deuteronomic teaching on Israel's calling to be devoted to Yahweh with a single heart, he exposes the folly of a person with divided affections, likening that person's predicament to that of a storm-tossed boat. That same imagery supplies the punch line of the pericope: the double allegiance that people cherish, hoping to serve God and Mammon (Matt 6:24), leaves them in no better shape than a frail vessel on angry seas; they are tossed about in all their ways.

It is difficult to suggest a life-setting for this instruction. Obviously James is concerned to offer a theodicy, as we noted. There may also be in the background the idea of caution against those in the community who had despaired of praying for God's help because they had resolved to trust their own devices and were confident that human resources would avail to bring about their deliverance from trial. James enters a warning plea that, contrary to their premature abandoning of faith, God's goodness is to be relied on. But only if their faith is centered in him alone. They must therefore resolutely turn to him and so turn away from the ways of folly and self-trust, to be outlined in 1:20; 3:13–18; 4:1–6, in reliance on God's gift of heavenly wisdom. Wisdom and folly are clearly opposites, and as obviously mutually exclusive as faith and skeptical unbelief.

2. The Reversal of Fortunes (1:9–11)

Bibliography

Bammel, E. "πτωχός," *TDNT* 6:910–11. **Bultmann, R.** "καυχάομαι," *TDNT* 3:646–54. **Furfey, P. H.** "*Plousios* and Cognates in the New Testament," *CBQ* 5 (1943) 243–63. **Keck, L. E.** "The Poor among the Saints in the New Testament," *ZNW* 56 (1965) 100–29. **Maynard-Reid, P. U.** *Poverty and Wealth in James.* Maryknoll, NY: Orbis, 1987. Chap 3. **Moldenke, H. N.,** and **Moldenke, A. L.** *Plants of the Bible.* New York: Dover Publ. Inc., 1952 = 1986 ed. **Osiek, C.** *Rich and Poor in the Shepherd of Hermas.* CBQMS 15. Washington: Catholic Biblical Association, 1983. 32–37. **Williams, R. L.** "Piety and Poverty in James." *Wesleyan Theological Journal* 22, 2 (1987) forthcoming.

Translation

⁹ *The (Christian) brother who is lowly should boast when he is exalted,* ¹⁰ *but the rich man when he is brought down, for as the flower of grass he will disappear.* ¹¹ *The sun rises with a scorching hot wind; it dries up the grass; its flower falls and its attractive beauty is gone. In this way the rich person will also fade away in the midst of his enterprises.*

Form / Structure / Setting

For the first time in the letter the theme of the poor and the rich in James' community makes its appearance. The same topic will be picked up in 2:2–4, 5–12, 15–16; 4:13–17; 5:1–6. If we follow the view that these opening sections of the letter announce themes to be expanded later, this will account for the fairly sudden switch to vv 9–11 following the earlier consideration of testing-prayer-faith. We are left, however, with the question of why James moves at this point to contrast the poor and the rich. Several answers are possible, listed by Vouga, 45–46: (1) If the humble and rich are matched with the persons who exemplify respectively faith and double-mindedness this may explain the transition. (2) Or else the present section is a reprise of the teaching in vv 2–4 on the need for perseverance. But it is difficult to see how the latter section develops out of the earlier one, except by taking the position that the rich people have brought on the persecution that afflicts the poor; then 2:6–8 may be quoted in support (see Ropes). In favor of this is the identity of the rich in both passages where it is most probable that non-Christians are in view. (3) Perhaps James is introducing the topic of wealth as a test of true faith and warning those who amass wealth of the perils they face. In support of this view we should observe how the judgment brought in v 11 is directed not against wealth in itself but against the rich people who (apparently) trust in wealth, a distinction also found in 5:1–6. (4) Finally, the section may be an independent one and may be seen as a separate word of encouragement to the poor and a warning directed to the rich.

It is not easy to fasten on one option as the best, but if we take our cue from the identification of the rich as those outside the congregation and interpret their possession of wealth as a sign of a boastful spirit (implied in the verb καυχᾶσθαι, used at least by extension and paradoxically of their attitude), then the idea behind (3) has most to commend it. James is making his point primarily to encourage and support the humble (as in 4:6, 10) who trust in God as their hope. Note that James distinguishes between the social status of his readers, for whom he uses the term ταπεινός and that, on the other hand, of the economically poor, for whom he uses πτωχός (2:2–3, 5–6). The people James wishes to help are those who, by reason of their religious affirmation and affiliation as "the Lord's poor," feel themselves socially disadvantaged and slighted. Their trust is in God, and it is James' counsel that in due time God will exalt them. In the meantime let them "boast" (καυχᾶσθαι, which is closely allied to "trust" in the OT: see Bultmann, *TDNT* 3:646–54) in their ταπείνωσις ("lowliness," "shame")—a sentiment drawn from the idiom of the pious poor who are typified by Hannah (1 Sam 2:1–10) and Mary (Luke 1:52). There is an eschatological flavor to this admonition (cf. 1 Pet 5:5), since the expectation is that God's intervention in their lot will reverse their fortunes—but not necessarily with a consequence that is economically or materially to their advantage. It is in terms of their relationship to God's favor that they are actually to be elevated to share his kingdom (2:5).

By contrast the rich person (ὁ πλούσιος), who is not explicitly called a "brother" as is the ταπεινός, is addressed in an invective. His ταπείνωσις is impending at the time of eschatological intervention. Drawing on a succession of biblical images, mainly from Isa 40:6–8, James graphically paints the picture of the fate of the godless rich. "The flower of grass" (also in Ezek 28:1; Pss 90:5–6; 103:15–16; Job 14:2) will soon wither when the hot sun and the scorching sirocco wind devastate the fields in which anemones grow (for the species *Anemone coronaria* in the Bible, see Moldenke, *Plants*, 28; cf. Job 15:30–33).

Clearly Isa 40 is the main source of James' imagery, commencing with a reminder of the people's ταπείνωσις in 40:2 LXX, a term used of Israel's disgrace in exile. The "mountains" on the road of their return to the land are to be brought low (ταπεινωθήσεται) to prepare the way of Yahweh (see James 1:11 for πορεία which is virtually identical with Hebrew דֶּרֶךְ, *derek*, "way"; cf. v 8, ἐν πάσαις τοῖς ὁδοῖς αὐτοῦ). The prophet's hope is couched in the eschatological language of a divine interposition into human affairs and destinies.

But, with Vouga, we should observe the point of distinction as James has modified or supplemented Second Isaiah's text: (1) The sentence ἀνέτειλεν γὰρ ὁ ἥλιος has no counterpart in the OT text but seems drawn from the parable in Mark 4:6, where it is interpreted in terms of "trials" (Mark 4:17); (2) in Isaiah the desolation of nature is a picture of the ephemeral character of human life in general; in James the pointed reference is to the rich who are destined to "pass away" (παρελεύσεται). (3) James adds the allusion to the "attractive beauty" (εὐπρέπεια) of nature's "appearance" (πρόσωπον), using the strong eschatological verb ἀπόλλεσθαι, "to destroy." (4) Paradoxically, where Isaiah attributes these events to Yahweh's direct action (Isa 40:7 MT) James is content to stress how natural processes—the hot sun, the sirocco wind, the dried-up grass—effectively ruin the scene. (5) Whereas Isaiah ends on a note of hope (40:6–8: "The word of the Lord endures forever"; cf. 1 Pet 1:25), our text moves to a judgmental punch line that reinforces the fate of the impious rich whose hope lies in his wealth. As he is still immersed in his enterprises the end comes swiftly and without warning. "The rich man perishes while he is still *on the move* before he has attained the state of restful enjoyment which is always expected and never arrives. Without some such hint of prematurity the parallel with the grass is lost" (Hort). The link is 4:13.

Comment

9 Καυχάσθω δὲ ὁ ἀδελφὸς ὁ ταπεινὸς ἐν τῷ ὕψει αὐτοῦ, "The [Christian] brother who is lowly should boast when he is exalted." These words open a new section which introduces for the first time in James the issue of the rich and the poor. Earlier (see p. 22) it was discussed how the topic of 1:9–11 appears to be unconnected to the material preceding it. However, a denial of the link between vv 9–11 and the foregoing is unnecessary, once it is conceded that the document has several themes that run through it like a thread.

The connective δέ of v 9 may function simply as a transitional particle, thus joining vv 9–11 to vv 2–8 (hence the absence of "but" in our translation; contra Dibelius, 83–84, n.72). Also, the idea of testing, found in 1:2–4, may be continued into 1:9–11. The writer or editor may be thinking that poverty provides an arena for the testing of one's faith in God. This is especially true if the ungodly rich are the ones who oppress and oppose the poor (2:1–13), while all the time seeming to flourish despite their evil ways. James will speak again about the fate of the rich and in doing so he will implore the poor to remain faithful to God (5:1–11). The pressures of poverty will lead persons to humble themselves before God and to place their total dependence in him, not only for survival on earth but also for vindication in the world to come (2:5). We should beware of spiritualizing the condition of "the poor," as Maynard-Reid, *Poverty,* 40, and Williams, "Piety and Poverty," show by insisting on the real economic need felt by James' readers. Attempts to relate "the humble" exclusively to the ʿănāwîm, i.e., the spiritually poor, are not successful (Keck, "The Poor," 116–17), though this epistle has no hard and fast division between the categories of the poor who trust God and the poor who are victims of social inequality and injustice (cf. Dibelius, 85), and Maynard-Reid (ibid.) unnecessarily downplays the motif of the "piety of the poor."

The readers' faith is tested in poverty, and if they remain faithful, they will become the mature Christians that God desires (1:2–4). Not only that, they will be wise and will avoid becoming "double-minded" persons (1:5–8). It is because of these thoughts that we classify 1:9–11 as a continuation of the thought of 1:2–8. The later verses isolate and illustrate a specific test of 1:2.

ὁ ἀδελφός ὁ ταπεινός ("the humble brother") shows that the use of ἀδελφός identifies this person as a Christian and a member of James' community. It appears that this Christian is poor in the double sense of the term. By itself ταπεινός does not necessarily mean "poor person," for the term usually means "humble" or "low" ("of no account," BGD, 804). But the context here clearly suggests that the "humble one" is socially and economically poor. Note that ὁ ταπεινός is contrasted with the rich person (ὁ πλούσιος, v 10). Since poverty is such an important theme of James (2:2–4, 5–12, 15–16; 4:13–17; 5:1–6), there is no reason to doubt that the humble brother of 1:9 is "poor," in the social sense, combining the stress of poverty with a reliance on God.

Yet, James exhorts this brother to boast in his exaltation (τὸ ὕψος; lit., "the high position"). The use of καυχᾶσθαι here is exceptional because normally the verb and related nouns are used in the NT in a negative sense, as in pride or boasting in oneself or one's righteousness (cf. 4:16; Rom 2:17, 23; 3:27; 1 Cor 1:29; 4:7; 5:6; 2 Cor 5:12; 11:18; Gal 6:13; Eph 2:9). However, in 1:9 James urges his readers to consider their status as God's chosen ones (2:5). Our author is looking at the situation with the thought that eschatological blessings await (and are presently the possession of) God's humble servants. The readers of James can enjoy their present "exalted" status (cf. Luke 6:20) as well as anticipate their future glorious inheritance. James is writing as one who understands the kingdom of God to have been inaugurated (but not yet consummated) at the coming of Jesus. The tension of "already" but "not yet," i.e., the kingdom is both present and yet its final form is expected, is present in James' thinking (Moo, 67).

10 ὁ δὲ πλούσιος ἐν τῇ ταπεινώσει αὐτοῦ, ὅτι ὡς ἄνθος χόρτου παρελεύσεται, "But the rich man when he is brought down, for as the flower of grass he will disappear."

Scholars are divided over the issue of whether or not the "rich man" in v 10 is to be regarded as a Christian. It is said that the rich man could be a Christian because grammatically ὁ ἀδελφός in v 9 can be taken to govern ὁ πλούσιος. Furthermore, the verb in v 9 (καυχάσθω) governs v 10a, thus leaving the continued thought: "but the rich man must boast in his lowly state" (see Adamson, 61–62; Cantinat, 78; Mayor, 45–46; Mussner, 74; Ropes, 145–46; cf. NEB). This understanding implies that the wealthy Christian is instructed by James to take no pride in his possessions, to humble himself before God and (possibly by extension) to identify with the lowly state (cf. Phil 2:8) of Jesus (Moo, 68–69). A natural result of this action would be that the rich Christian is quick to extend help to the poor Christian; but see 2:14–17, where no such help is forthcoming from professed church members. In this way his "humiliation" is his reason for "boasting" because he has complied with James' instructions.

Other scholars, however, maintain that the rich man is to be taken as a nonbeliever. That is, vv 9–10a should not be taken as directed at both rich Christians and poor Christians on equal terms. This position (1) does not conclude that "brother" governs both "poor" and "rich," holding rather that "brother" is only modified by "poor," and (2) takes the verb "to boast" to be ironic: "The rich man has had his day; all he can expect from the future is humiliation [at the judgment]; that is the only thing left for him to 'boast about'" (Dibelius, 85; cf. Blackman, 51). This understanding complements James' teaching (based on Jewish tradition; see *Introduction*, pp. lxxiv–lxxxvi) that though the rich oppress the poor the latter eventually will be vindicated by God while the former will be destroyed.

An inspection of James' use of πλούσιος (cf. Furfey, *"Plousios"*; H. Merklein, *EW* 3, cols. 277–78) reveals that there is one undisputed instance where the term does clearly designate an unbeliever. In 2:7 we read that the rich slander the name of Jesus (see *Comment* below). Although James is not as explicit in other uses of πλούσιος in his letter, the setting of 2:7 may be enough to tip the scales in favor of the view that the rich man in 1:10 is a nonbeliever. Thus, we concur with Davids, who understands James' use of "rich man" in 1:10 to be polemical and sees a rich nonbeliever set in contrast over against a poor Christian (77: "This rich person is called with a sharp ironic twist to understand the humiliation in which he lives, existing like the rich fool [Luke 12:13–21] in luxury in this age only to discover the true system of values in the coming age").

Maynard-Reid, *Poverty*, 41–44, has reopened the question of the identity of the "rich person" here. He notes how the call to "rejoice" may be taken as *either* a heroic summons (to the Christian plutocrat to display fortitude when his possessions disappear, presumably by reminding him that he has enduring [spiritual] wealth: so Ropes, 145–46; Mayor, 43–44; Mitton, 36–37) *or* an ironic comment that the non-Christian rich person is destined to lose all his confidence in the coming judgment day: cf. BGD, 805. But Maynard-Reid observes that both alternatives set out in Dibelius, 84–85, have a presuppositional fault, namely they assume that the epistle has wealthy Christians in its sights, whereas for James all wealth poses a threat whether owned by Christians or non-Christians. Yet this denial cannot make sense of 4:13–16, and our decision here will await the later treatment. A third option, namely that the verb καυχᾶσθαι is used with an eschatological overtone to sound a warning of impending judgment (so Mussner, 73, citing Ps 49:6 [LXX 48:7], καὶ ἐπὶ τῷ πλήθει τοῦ πλούτου αὐτῶν καυχώμενοι: "even those that boast in their abundant wealth": cf. Jer 9:23; Sir 11:18–19: ʾAbot 4:4) is to be preferred.

Regardless of whether the rich man is a Christian or not, the meaning of vv 10b–11 is fairly clear: riches are worthless in the face of death and judgment. The teaching that the "fortunes" of the rich and the poor will one day be reversed is drawn from tradition both Jewish and early Christian (Luke 1:52–53). The source of the proverb of vv 10b–11 is Isa 40:6–8, though some also see an allusion in James to Ps 103:15, 16 (Davids, 77). While the poor are destined for eternal joy in the great reversal, the rich are doomed to pass away (παρελεύσεται). This carries with it an eschatological flavor to be repeated in 5:5. As the "flower of grass" (ἄνθος χόρτου; a mistranslation of Isa 40:6–8; so Laws, 64, who renders the phrase "meadow flower," in particular, anemones) disappears, so do the ungodly rich. The future is "prophetic," and announces a certain—if tragic—fate in store (Mussner, 75).

11 ἀνέτειλεν γὰρ ὁ ἥλιος σὺν τῷ καύσωνι καὶ ἐξήρανεν τὸν χόρτον καὶ τὸ ἄνθος αὐτοῦ ἐξέπεσεν καὶ ἡ εὐπρέπεια τοῦ προσώπου αὐτοῦ ἀπώλετο· οὕτως καὶ ὁ πλούσιος ἐν ταῖς πορείαις αὐτοῦ μαρανθήσεται, "The sun rises with a scorching hot wind; it dries up the grass; its flower falls and its attractive beauty is gone. In this way the rich person will also fade away in the midst of his enterprises."

James continues discussing the topic of life's transitoriness in v 11. The phenomena described in the verse were familiar to James' readers. All four verbs of v 11a are in the aorist tense which may be gnomic (cf. Mussner, 75) or proleptic (so M. Zerwick and M. Grosvenor, *A Grammatical Analysis of the Greek NT* [Rome: Biblical Institute Press, 1979], 2:692) or representative of the Hebrew perfect, thereby emphasizing "the suddenness and completeness of the withering" (so Moule, *Idiom Book*, 12). The verbs are best translated by the English present tense: so the grass withers (ἐξήρανεν), the flower falls (ἐξέπεσεν), and its attractive beauty (ἡ εὐπρέπεια τοῦ προσώπου αὐτοῦ, which is a Semitism; πρόσωπον being equivalent to פָּנִים, *pānîm*, lit., "face" or "outward appearance"; εὐπρέπεια, "goodly appearance" [Ropes, 149], is a *hapax legomenon*) fades away (ἀπώλετο, aorist of ἀπόλλεσθαι, "to suffer destruction").

The flower is doomed because of the heat that accompanies the rising of the sun. καύσων can mean either "searing heat" (so in essence KJV/AV; RSV; NEB; cf. Gen 31:40; Dan 3:67; Isa 25:6; Luke 12:55; Matt 20:12) or "scorching wind" (NASB; cf. Job 27:21; Hos 13:15; Jonah 4:8; Ezek 17:10; 19:21) called the sirocco. Those who offer the former translation argue that strictly speaking the rising of the sun brings the "scorching heat"—not the "simoom" wind—with (σύν) it (BGD, 425; Davids, 78). However, there is no compelling reason to reject the latter translation (Schneider, *TDNT* 3:644), especially since James' letter at least in its first draft was probably written against a Palestinian background. The words of E. F. F. Bishop (*Apostles of Palestine* [London: Lutterworth Press, 1958] 184) capture vividly the power of the sirocco:

> . . . no one who has lived in Palestine ever forgets as it [i.e., the sirocco] blows continuously night and day once it has started. The temperature hardly seems to vary. Flowers and herbage wilt and fade, lasting as long as "morning glory." Anemones and cyclamen, carpeting the hillsides of Galilee in spring, have a loveliness that belongs only to the past when the hot wind comes. Drooping flowers make fuel. The field of lupins are here today and gone tomorrow.

Two points are to be noted as enforcing James' salutary reminder: (1) the complete and swift destructiveness of the wind; and (2) the inevitability of its coming.

James uses these two observations about the sirocco to make the teaching of his "botanical comparison" clear (Moo, 70): "as goes the flower, so goes the rich man." οὕτως links the two ideas ("just this quickly," Dibelius, 85). Like the flower of the field, the rich man fades away in the midst of life. ἐν ταῖς πορείαις αὐτοῦ is a Semitism, a common expression for "way of life" (so Davids, 78; but against Moo, 70, who understands this Greek phrase to mean a "journey," like the scene described in 4:13–17). The verb μαρανθήσεται (future passive of μαραίνειν) connotes the withering of flowers and the death of persons (BGD, 491). James relentlessly connects the fate of the flower to the fate of the rich person. Both can be flourishing one day and gone the next. The eschatological judgment of God will cause the rich to perish. Dibelius points out that the transitory nature of humanity is often described with the aid of the image of grass and vegetation (85). It was noted earlier (pp. 23–24) that James adapted Isa 40:6–8 specifically to suit the topic of the contrast between the rich and the poor. Thus, the rich man's "humiliation" is the judgment he suffers (v 10). On the other hand, the 'poor man should exult, for his vindication draws near (5:1–11).

Explanation

This letter has as its background a community that was socially stratified. The author must therefore address the issue of how the poor members would react to the presence of wealthy and influential forces, whether inside or exerted from the outside on that community. The pericope of 1:9–11 is designed to offer a measure of consolation and support to James' readers, who, as among the Lord's poor, were faced by the prospect of living in an unequal society. Whether the rich person of 1:10 was a fellow believer or (more likely) a representative of an economic and social power whose hostility to the church may be seen in a later part of the letter (2:6–7) is hard to determine precisely. But since the writer's sympathies are on the side of the poor in this paragraph the choice is not all-important. The point made is that the "brother who is lowly" has reason not to be envious or sour-spirited, since the doom and downfall of the godless rich is on the imminent horizon.

Yet James is here no cynic, gloating over the fate in store for the rich. A more ironical note is struck at 5:1–6; in this short passage he is content to act as reporter, with illustrations drawn from the world of nature and human nature. The poor believer is bidden to reflect that all life is transitory and temporal, yet God is concerned with its ultimate meaning. So the promise of "exaltation" is intended to beckon to eternal values, to be elaborated at 2:5. The rich person is reminded forcefully that the secret in life does not lie in the abundance of one's possessions (Luke 12:15). Indeed, a person's claim to material gains is tenuous at best, as the rich farmer discovered in the parable (Luke 12:16–21). The forces of nature on which, in a Palestinian agrarian culture, farmers depended for livelihood and in good years for prosperity are fickle. The sun that opens the grain can also blister the growing shoots and turn the flower-filled field into a wilderness in a short time. The emphasis falls on the uncertainty of riches and the swiftness of ruin once the natural phenomena turn hostile. The counsel in the different world of the Pastoral Epistles (1 Tim 6:9–10, 17–19) is to the same effect.

As in the case of the enterprising and affluent farmer of whom Jesus spoke, human resources are swept away in a moment, and the real self is laid bare. The perils of those in every age who on the upwardly mobile path of success and fortune never stop to "lay up treasure in heaven" (contrast James 5:3) and take thought for life's true meaning are tellingly exposed.

3. Testing: Its Source and Mischief—and Rationale   (1:12–19a)

Bibliography

Albertz, M. "Die 'Erstlinge' in der Botschaft des NT." *EvT* 12 (1952–53) 151–55. **Amphoux, C.-B.** "Une relecture du chapître 1 de l'épître de Jacques." *Bib* 59 (1978)

554–61. ———. "À propos de Jacques 1,17." *RHPR* 50 (1970) 127–36. ———. "L'emploi du coordonnant dans l'épître de Jacques." *Bib* 63 (1982) 90–101. **Bouttier, M.,** and **Amphoux, C.-B.** "La prédication de Jacques le Juste." *ETR* 54 (1979). **Davids, P. H.** "The Meaning of ἀπείραστος in James 1.13." *NTS* 24 (1978) 386–92. **Davies, W. D.** *Paul and Rabbinic Judaism.* 2d ed. London: SPCK, 1955. **Dupont, J.** *Les Béatitudes II*². EBib. Paris: Gabalda, 1969. 320–50. **Edsman, C.-M.** "Schöpferwille und Geburt. Jac 1,18: Eine Studie zur altchristlichen Kosmologie." *ZNW* 38 (1939) 11–44. ———. "Schöpfung und Wiedergeburt: Nochmals Jak 1.18." In *Spiritus et Veritas,* FS Karl Kundsin. Eutin: Ozolin, 1953. 43–55. **Elliott-Binns, L. E.** "James 1.18: Creation or Redemption?" *NTS* 3 (1956) 148–61. **Francis, F. O.** "The Form and Function of the Opening and Closing Paragraphs of James and I John." *ZNW* 61 (1970) 110–26. **Gantoy R.** "Accueil et mise en pratique de la Parole, Jc 1,17–18." *AsSeign* 53 (1970) 39–49. ———. "L'épître du quatrième Dimanche après Pâques (Jc 1,17–21). Une catéchèse apostolique pour notre temps." *AsSeign* 47 (1963) 15–27. **Gerhardsson, B.** *The Testing of God's Son.* ConBNT 2. Lund: Gleerup, 1966. 28–31. **Greeven, H.** "Jede Gabe ist gut (Jak. 1,17)." *TZ* 14 (1958) 1–13. **Jeremias, J.** *The Prayers of Jesus.* SBT 2/6. Tr. J. Bowden, C. Burchard, and J. Reumann. London: SCM, 1967. 104–7. **Jewett, R.** *Paul's Anthropological Terms: A Study of Their Use in Conflict Settings.* AGJV 10. Leiden: Brill, 1971. **Marcus, J.** "The Evil Inclination in the Epistle of James." *CBQ* 44 (1982) 606–621. **Martin, R. P.** *Reconciliation: A Study of Paul's Theology.* London: Marshall, Morgan & Scott; Atlanta: Knox, 1981. **Palmer, F. H.** "James 1.18 and the Offering of First-fruits." *TynB* 3 (1957) 1–2. **Porter, F. C.** "The Yeçer Hara: A Study in the Jewish Doctrine of Sin." In *Yale Biblical and Semitic Studies.* Yale Bicentennial Publications. New York: Scribner's, 1901. 91–158. **Zeller, E.** "Über Jak. 1,12." *ZWTh* 6 (1863) 93–96.

Translation

12 *Blessed is the man who endures in time of testing because when he has stood the test he will receive the crown that offers the life [God] has promised to those who love him.*

13 *In time of trial no one should remark, God is tempting me. For God cannot be tempted by evil—indeed he tempts no one.* 14 *Rather each person is tempted by his own evil desire by which he is dragged off and enticed.* 15 *Then after desire has conceived, it produces sin; and sin, when it is fully grown, gives birth to death.* 16 *Don't be led astray, my dear brothers.*

17 *All good giving and every perfect bounty* a *is from above, coming down from the Father who made the lights of heaven; with him there is neither wavering nor shadow cast by an eclipse.* b 18 *He willed to give us birth by the word of truth, that we might be a kind* c *of first fruits of what he created.* 19 a *Note this, my dear brothers.*

Notes

a BDF § 487 tentatively classifies this part-verse as a poetic fragment consisting of a hexameter with a tribrach in the second foot of the scansion: πᾶσᾰ δὄ/σις ᾽ᾰγᾰ/θή καὶ πᾶν δῶ/ ρημᾱ τέ/λειον. Two points suggest that this is a quotation: (1) the preceding μὴ πλανᾶσθε: see H. Braun, *TDNT* 6:245; (2) the use of virtual synonyms, δόσις and δώρημα, the latter being a rare and unusual word. See too Greeven, *TZ* 14 (1958) 3–7.

b The generally accepted reading (offered by Nestle-Aland²⁶ and UBS³ text) is παραλλαγὴ ἢ τροπῆς ἀποσκίασμα (in ℵ² A C P TR vg syr). But the inherent difficulty with this reading (though Metzger pronounces it "the least unsatisfactory," *Textual Commentary,* 680) has produced a crop of variations.

ℵ*B have παραλλαγὴ ἢ τροπῆς ἀποσκιάσματος, "variation which is of [=consists in] the turning of a shadow." Taking ἡ as the definite article requires changing τροπῆς to τροπή (in 614 and some minuscules) or ῥοπή (in some versions). But this leads to difficulty. Only the ℵ² A C TR reading makes sense as it stands, though its meaning, "neither variation nor shadow cast by turning," is in doubt. For that reason Ropes (162–64) prefers to go with ℵ*B and to retain ἡ as the definite article on which τροπῆς depends, though he acknowledges that the accumulation of long words makes it turgid, whereas ἤ, "or," breaks up the sentence.

Emendations listed in Davids, 87, and Amphoux, "À propos de Jacques 1,17," 133–36—and none very impressive—have been submitted. Nor are the glosses added by several minuscules (see Metzger, 680) nor the simplification offered by the Sahidic, making the nouns separate as though the text read ἀποσκίασμα καὶ παραλλαγὴ ἤ τροπῆς, helpful in elucidating the sense. See *Comment* for what these three *termini technici* in astronomical language may mean.

    ᶜτίς is often used to qualify a metaphorical expression, as in spoken English, "a kind of": see BDF § 301.1.

Form / Structure / Setting

The theme of "patience in time of suffering" reverts to 1:2–4, where James had sought to ameliorate his readers' problems. There he sought to show how testing leads to endurance which in turn must be practiced with both fortitude and a refusal to give in. Now he continues to extol the virtue of ὑπομονή by using the same vocabulary: testing, standing in time of trial, being approved (δόκιμος) and endurance to the end. But there is a shift in setting, as most commentators recognize.

At 1:2–4 the occasion is the suffering encountered in the face of persecution (*pace* Laws, who thinks of general discomforts). At 1:12 James seems to probe deeper and penetrate beneath the surface of outward distresses and injuries. He sees that persecutions raise questions of faith in God's providence and care for his own—a typical Jewish concern in both the canonical (e.g., Habakkuk; Job) and deutero-canonical (*1 Enoch; Jubilees; Martyrdom of Isaiah*) literature. Hence the πειρασμός of v 12 is more "moral temptation" than testing per se; but with the link to v 2 so direct it is wiser to retain the translation "time of testing" and see the transition to the moral issue of divine governance and control, when believers are challenged by such episodes, as present and developed only at v 13. There it is the Christian who is "tempted" to wonder aloud why these experiences have come about; and James offers a theodicy by his exposition of the origin of evil (specifically the evil of persecution) that follows in vv 13–16.

The lessons the author draws are dependent on the Jewish-rabbinic discussion of the "evil impulse" (יֵצֶר הָרַע, *yēṣer hā-rāʿ*: see Str-B, 4:466–83; Porter, *Biblical and Semitic Studies*, 91–158; Davies, *Paul and Rabbinic Judaism*, 17–35; Marcus, "Evil Inclination") which is represented in James' Greek as ἐπιθυμία, lit., "desire," but usually found in the NT in a bad sense; so the translation here is "evil desire," "lust." The general application of the train of the writer's thought in vv 14–16, suggesting that sin is what yielding to temptation leads to (cf. 2:8–11; 4:17 for other formal definitions of ἁμαρτία), should not blind us, however, to the possibility of a more specific setting of this teaching. James' point appears to be a single one: evil in human experience is that for which human beings are directly responsible. No mention of evil powers, such as Satan in his role as tempter (found in Paul and the NT Apocalypse as in the Jewish apocalypses, e.g., *1 Enoch* 69:4–15), is given. Moreover God is expressly said not to be the author of moral evil (v 13) since he is untouched by evil (ἀπείραστος: Davids, "The Meaning," 386–92) and he is not the direct cause of testing. The latter was a question much debated in early Judaism (see Sir 15:11–20; *Jub.* 17–18 for two important places where the discussion turns on the same question James confronts; a similar issue with a different slant is found in the Nag Hammadi documents representing hellenized wisdom, namely, *The Teaching of Silvanus* VII.4.115–16: "For God does not need to put any man to the test. He knows all things before they happen, and he knows the hidden things of the heart").

Our author locates the source of the trouble in the seat of the human psyche, specifically in the arrogant desire to achieve its ambition independently of God. What is implied will be discussed in 1:20, i.e., the readers' attempt to bring about God's righteousness by resorting to means that James cannot condone since they are the product of human wrath and involve (as we look ahead to 3:13–4:3) violent measures. We may trace here the influence of Zealot policy that sought to introduce God's rule by "worldly" ways and armed revolt. We submit that James is facing the same issue here at 1:13–16 with his explanation that if Christians have to suffer it is part of God's purpose. But if they deliberately yield to the "evil desire" that draws them away from that purpose and incur suffering thereby, they must not turn around and accuse God of neglect or of inflicting punishment. They have only themselves to blame if a Zealot uprising leads to national disaster—and so it turned out to be at the close of the A.D. 66–72 war against Rome.

This attempt to vindicate the divine character in vv 13–16 then moves on to consider a second way in which the readers were doubting God. The call "Don't be deceived" (v 16) is the bridge to vv 17–18. In his theodicy James knows that yet another reason for Christian suffering is being pleaded. Because the text is less than clear we cannot be certain of the full background with its possible allusion to astronomical phenomena (seen in the references to God as the maker of the stars, and in the affirmation that with him there is no "succession" [παραλλαγή, a term perhaps connoting here the movement of the heavenly bodies: cf. Epictetus, *Diss.* 1.14.4, who uses the term of the change of the seasons] nor shadow caused by an eclipse). These statements are usually seen as pointing to an attribute of God's creatorship and unchangeability as part of the overall assertion that all his giving is good (v 17).

But while the link to v 18 does stress the theme of God as creator, it is probably correct with Vouga (57–58) to propose a polemical setting. James, according to this view, is being controversial. The idea he seeks to rebut is that mortals experience human testing because they are at the mercy of fate, and so the troubles that have accrued to the readers are such that they have no control over them. They believe that they are under the power of astral forces and fatalism; hence they doubt the goodness of God's character and regard him as no better than a finite being caught up in the changes that have occurred. The writer, by his use of some technical expressions (vv 17–18), argues that, to the contrary, all divine gifts are true to God's nature (harking back to Gen 1:18, 31). God is the creator of the luminaries (Philo, *De Spec. Leg.* 1.96; *De Ebr.* 81; *T. Abr.* 7:6, texts that develop the basic OT conviction of Ps 135 [136]:7; Jer 4:23) whose power to influence mortal life is thereby denied; and the divine character is uninfluenced by the ceaseless changes that take place in the world of nature (cf. Job 38:33 for this point). The movements of the stars leave their creator and upholder untouched. So determinism that gave a false importance to the stars, as in current hellenistic thought, must not be allowed to lead James' audience astray. When they are tempted, neither God nor other people nor any fatalism is to be held accountable. Moral responsibility derives from God's goodness in making man to be his creature, and if the verb of v 18, ἀποκύειν is linked directly to λόγῳ ἀληθείας, the secondary reference would be to the readers as God's children in grace, brought into his family by the Christian message, "the word of truth," to form the new elect Israel (as in 1:1).

The section is rich in metaphors and word pictures. The two obvious examples are (1) the way sin is personified and its course described. Sin goes through a fearful process of conception, incubation, gestation, and reproduction (1:13–15). Yet the purpose is intensely practical and consonant with James' intent to trace back all evil to human "desire" at a time when his readers were evidently disposed to shift the blame or to give up any rational explanation in the interest of pursuing their own ends. (2) A second piece of powerful descriptive writing is adduced to support a theodicy. God is the heavenly king and sovereign creator whose nature is essentially good. As James has vividly rehearsed the "birth-leading-to-death" motif of sin (v 15), he matches this with a panel of teaching that portrays God as the Father whose progeny represent his chosen family, created to reflect his glory by becoming "children of light." Perhaps, with Ropes (158), we should see James' thought as governed by the related idea of "perfect." Then there is a memorable, pungent paradox. God's perfect work (1:4) when it is complete (τέλειον) yields the end result of holiness, now defined as sharing in the goodness of creation as God's new Israel ("first-fruits"; cf. Palmer, "James 1.18," 1–2) and his eschatological people (1:18; so Vouga, 59). The counterpart is sin's progress which too comes to fruition (v 15: ἀποτελεσθεῖσα) in the course of three generations: its conception is "desire," its progeny is "sin," and its outcome is "death." The last-named is the sign of fallen creation in its rebellion and hostility to the divine purpose.

Comment

12 Μακάριος ἀνὴρ ὃς ὑπομένει πειρασμόν, ὅτι δόκιμος γενόμενος λήμψεται τὸν στέφανον τῆς ζωῆς ὃν ἐπηγγείλατο τοῖς ἀγαπῶσιν αὐτόν, "Blessed is the man who endures in time of testing because when he has stood the test he will receive the crown that offers the life [God] has promised to those who love him."

With Francis ("Form and Function," 118) we should detect at this verse a second member of the double letter opening, corresponding to v 2. Most commentators observe that v 12 prepares the ground for the discussion on "temptation" in vv 13–18. The common term πειρασμός, which earlier denoted "trial," "testing," now takes on the allied meaning of "temptation"—a dominant theme as may be seen from the frequent use of the verb πειράζειν (three times) and the adjective ἀπείραστος (once) in v 13. Correspondingly, ὑπομονή, which is found in both sections, may need to be nuanced differently in each paragraph. In 1:2–8 testings are to be endured with fortitude; in 1:12–15 the temptations are to be resisted with a steadfast resolution (Ropes, 150).

The pronouncing of blessedness on faithful Jews who walk in Yahweh's way and turn aside from evil is common in the Wisdom literature, e.g., Pss 1:1; 31 [32]:1; 33:9b [34:8b]; Prov 8:32, 34; cf. Isa 56:2; Job 5:17; Sir 14:1, 20; 26:1; and Dan 12:12, which in Theodotion's rendering has the interesting reading μακάριος ὁ ὑπομένων as a close parallel with James' view of a test (see also the macarism in *Herm. Vis.* 2.2.7. The same encomium is carried forward from the OT into the teaching of Jesus: Matt 5:3–11 // Luke 6:20–26). The theme of eschatological blessedness, i.e., joy that is pronounced to those who wait for God's salvation to deliver them from their tribulations, is one which binds together Jewish Wisdom teaching and apocalyptic hope (Vouga, 50).

The "crown that offers life" is also an eschatological promise of reward (Prov 1:9; 4:9; 12:4; 16:31; 17:6, where the promise is joined with the bestowal of wisdom). The theme is continued in Wisd Sol 5:15–23, which combines many of the ideas in our pericope. In a document written to assure the faithful who suffer for their religion that God will recompense their sufferings, the idioms are virtually identical with James:

> But the righteous live for ever, and their reward is with the Lord; the Most High takes care of them. Therefore they will receive a glorious crown, and a beautiful diadem from the hand of the Lord. (Wisd Sol 5:15–16a)

στέφανος, "crown," is equally a common term for this reward, expressing the ideas of favor for the king (Ps 20:4–5 [21:3–4]), the victor's garland (1 Cor 9:25; cf. Phil 4:1; 2 Thess 2:19) and the reward of faithful service (2 Tim 4:8; 1 Pet 5:4; Rev 2:10). The subject matter here is "life" (i.e., living in the eschatological joy of the new age that God will bring in) "that [God] promised to those who love him." After στέφανος the genitive τῆς ζωῆς is best taken as genitive of content; "life" belongs to the world of victory enjoyed by those who win through in their battle with temptation (πειρασμός) to emerge as victors. Yet James notes that it is their love for God that motivates such as gain the triumph. As devoted to him, they inherit his kingdom (2:5) by the grace of election. They emulate Abraham, who is called God's friend (2:23), and turn away from all lesser loyalties (4:4). In fact, "those who love God" stands as the diametrical opposite of the ἀνὴρ δίψυχος, the person whose allegiance is divided (v 8; 4:8) and whose faith is unsteady. We noted the possible allusion to Matt 14:28–32 in the earlier descriptions of a storm at sea and Peter's wavering faith. That link may be just possible; it is certainly a fantastic suggestion made by Scaer (53) to play off a contrast between Peter and Stephen—"James weaves into the fabric the duplicity of a wavering Peter and the constancy of a steadfast Stephen"—on the slender basis that στέφανος is also Stephen's name!

13 μηδεὶς πειραζόμενος λεγέτω ὅτι Ἀπὸ θεοῦ πειράζομαι· ὁ γὰρ θεὸς ἀπείραστός ἐστιν κακῶν, πειράζει δὲ αὐτὸς οὐδένα, "In time of trial no one should remark, God is tempting me. For God cannot be tempted by evil—indeed he tempts no one."

There is a persistent tradition in religious literature that attributes evil to the gods or to God or demonic forces. Examples may be culled from Homer (*Od.* 1.32–34; Zeus enters this complaint, "What wretchedness! Hear what men charge against the gods! . . . when it is their own evils that bring them suffering greater than any which Fate apportions them") and the book of Genesis (3:12–13). Especially when misfortune or calamity strikes, the tendency is to look for someone to blame and thereby to evade personal responsibility. Further illustrations are seen in Prov 19:3: "When a man's folly brings his way to ruin, his heart rages against the Lord" and Sir 15:11–20 which forms a close parallel to James' reprobation of this point of view:

> Do not say, Because of the Lord I left the way. . . . Do not say, It was he who led me astray (ἐπλάνησεν). . . . Before a man are life and death, and whichever he chooses will be given to him. . . . He has not commanded anyone to be ungodly, and he has not given anyone permission to sin.

The links with our text (and with 5:20) are notable as Vouga (53) observes.

James continues his analysis with a denial that God leads human beings into evil. He denies outright that God places temptation in men's way, and he is offering "a kind of theodicy" (Mussner, 86) in addressing these issues. The tone is practical, but in the light of 1:17 it is sustained on a theological base (contra Davids, 81). This topic of God's involvement in human trials was actively discussed in biblical religion. Evidence may be cited from 1 Chr 21:1, which "corrects" 2 Sam 24:1 and which avoids the conclusion that Yahweh tempted David to institute the census by ascribing the action to Satan. In a similar manner the testing of Abraham in Gen 22 is said to be Yahweh's work; but in *Jub.* 17:16 the initiative is attributed to "Prince Mastema" (a name for Satan in this document, acting in the role of the prosecutor as in the drama of Job): "He came and said before God, 'Behold Abraham loves Isaac, his son. . . . Tell him to offer him [as] a burnt offering upon the altar. And you will see whether he will do this thing. And you will know whether he is faithful in everything in which you test him.'" True, Yahweh is said to test Abraham (17:17–18), but it is significant that in this greatest test the action is traced to Mastema, who is finally put to shame (18:12) as the sequel unfolds. Other comparative material is in Exod 15:25; Deut 6:16; 13:3; 33:8; Matt 6:13 // Luke 11:4; and 1 Cor 10:13, where Paul has a slightly different perspective on the theme of human testing. (Cf. Philo, *Quod Det.* 112.)

The interlocutor makes his position clear. In direct speech the text places in his mouth the words "I am being tempted by God" (Ἀπὸ θεοῦ πειράζομαι), which is the literal rendering. Other examples of *oratio recta*, which is a device in James' homiletical or debating style, are 2:3, 16, 18; 4:13. The response comes in an adjectival statement about God: he is ἀπείραστος (a verbal adjective, BDF § 117.1; BGD, 83, describes the passive sense "who cannot be tempted"). Since the active "who does not tempt" is introduced in the next line of the verse the passive sense is to be preferred here, otherwise there would be a tautology (see too Davids, "Meaning"). There are several possibilities of translation: (i) God is inexperienced in evil, that is, has no contact with evil (Hort);

(ii) God cannot be solicited to evil, and so he is not tempted by it (Laws, 71, who grants that, on this reading, the logic is not immediately obvious. The basic idea is that God is impervious to evil and so cannot be thought of as desiring that it should be part of human experience; Mussner, 87, translates the Greek as *unversuchbar*); (iii) God ought not to be tempted by evil persons (Spitta, *Commentary*, 34; a meaning championed by Davids, 83, who relates the occasion to the OT scene of Deut 6:16: "When James hears the person start to accuse God, his mind flashes back to Israel in the wilderness and out comes the indignant rebuke, 'God ought not to be tested by evil people' ").

The decision about v 13a cannot be separated from the way the rest of the verse runs: "he himself (αὐτός) tempts no one." The function of this statement—which is not a repetition of what was said earlier but carries forward the author's thought—is to assert that God is not directly responsible for the sending of temptation. Perhaps James is making allowance for the origin of evil to be demonic (as in 3:15; 4:7), but there is no explicit reference to any other source than within the person tempted (so v 14). What then is the point of arguing that God does not test? It is not the corollary that "you test yourself," as Davids, 83, proposes, for that is denied in the wording of 1:2, where the brothers have fallen into (περιπέσητε) many kinds of trials. Rather, the force of the assertion must be: God does not bring about situations like those the readers were experiencing and were interpreting as a sign of evil, e.g., when they alleged that God had forgotten them in those evil experiences. They could not avoid being caught in the midst of evil days; they are reminded that how they handle their problems ought not deny God's providence, since he did not engineer their misery nor does he abandon them in it. Hort's proposal has more to recommend it, therefore, provided we interpret κακῶν to mean the following: God has no contact with the evils that have befallen you, and so [second argument] he cannot be said to entice you to further evil by leading you to deny him in those experiences. This view takes κακά to imply not moral evil or "evil" as a metaphysical idea, but the evil conditions that arose from 1:2 and were threatening to induce the readers to react negatively to what had overtaken them. The support for this reading rests on the attested usage of ἀπείραστος and on the flow of the argument into vv 14–15, where it traces temptation to the person's own ἐπιθυμία. The discussion should be seen in the light of 4:2, which represents a person's determination to have his own way. When he is caught in the throes of evil forces, he turns his back on God as the one he tries to blame.

ἀπείραστος, on any reckoning, is a difficult word. It is *hapax legomenon* in the LXX and NT. Moffatt (18) thinks it is James' own coinage, since it speaks of God in a way not paralleled in the Bible (cf. Seesemann, *TDNT* 6:29).

14–16 ἕκαστος δὲ πειράζεται ὑπὸ τῆς ἰδίας ἐπιθυμίας ἐξελκόμενος καὶ δελεαζόμενος· εἶτα ἡ ἐπιθυμία συλλαβοῦσα τίκτει ἁμαρτίαν, ἡ δὲ ἁμαρτία ἀποτελεσθεῖσα ἀποκύει θάνατον· Μὴ πλανᾶσθε, ἀδελφοί μου ἀγαπητοί, "Rather each person is tempted by his own evil desire by which he is dragged off and enticed. ¹⁵Then, after desire has conceived it produces sin; and sin, when it is fully grown gives birth to death. ¹⁶Don't be led astray, my dear brothers."

James identifies now the real origin of the πειρασμοί (Mussner, 88) and the κακά of v 13, in our view. The particle δέ marks a contrast, while the "each person" (ἕκαστος) stylistically answers to the "no one" (οὐδένα) in v 13. At the heart of the solicitation to evil (which we may connect with a God-denying stance when the person is set in the midst of trying circumstances) lies the personal (ἰδίας) desire (ἐπιθυμίας) that is bent on self-interest and self-pleasing and so is the catalyst that turns outward trials (1:2) into occasions for moral disaster as "desire" is allowed to have its sway and produce its nemesis.

ἐπιθυμία is an ambivalent term in NT vocabulary. Sometimes it has good connotations (Luke 22:15; Rom 15:23; cf. Phil 1:23; 2 Cor 5:2) but more often it carries a pejorative sense of "evil desire, lust, false ambition" (Rom 7:17–23; Gal 5:16–21; 1 Thess 4:5; Eph 2:3).

The verbs ἐξέλκειν, "to drag off," and δελεάζειν, "to entice," are connected to form a sequence of action. Desire is personified as a force that draws out a victim by luring him, "as fish are lured" (Mayor, 54, citing evidence in Xenophon, *Cyrop.* 8.1.32; *Mem.* 3.11.18) and "baited" (δέλεαρ is bait [cf. 2 Pet 2:14, 18]: so BGD, 174, which regards δελεάζειν as a technical term for fishing). So the sense is: "drawn out and enticed by his own desire." Epictetus, *Frag.* 112, connects this imagery to the moral temptations of pleasure (ἡδονή; cf. 4:1), and similarly in Philo, *Quod Omn. Prob. Lib.* 159: πρὸς ἐπιθυμίας ἐλαύνεται ἢ ὑφ' ἡδονῆς δελεάζεται, "driven by passion or enticed by pleasure." The closest parallel to the power of ἐπιθυμία here is the control exercised by σάρξ (flesh) in the Pauline writings (see Jewett, *Paul's Anthropological Terms,* 114–16, for the two chief dimensions of σάρξ, personal and demonic).

Echoes of the temptation in Gen 3 are to be detected at a subsurface level in this verse. The most likely source of the teaching, however, is the rabbinic doctrine of the "evil impulse" that goads men and women into sin (see earlier). The point of emphasis here is to fasten moral responsibility on the individual. Given the context and James' chief interest, it is less likely that Spitta is correct in proposing that Satan is here regarded as the father of sin (*T. Benj.* 7:1) or the prime mover of the evil spirits that (in *T. Reub.* 3) are said to impregnate the sense; or even that the rabbinic interpretations of Gen 6:2–4 which connect a kingdom of demons with human evil are in view (1 Enoch 15:8–10; 16:1; 19:1; 69:4–6; Jub 4:14–22). James' main purpose is to trace the genealogy of sin no further than to the person tempted by ἐπιθυμία (Mayor, 55). Paul's views are both similar (Rom 7) and distinctive in their details of the demonological setting they draw upon (Martin, *Reconciliation,* 51–59).

The "biographical" scenario of evil's progression is then graphically described in terms of human reproductive processes. The verb συλλαμβάνειν is, strictly, "to conceive," used of the female, and is given added point because ἐπιθυμία is a feminine noun. The "desire" that in v 14 was active in setting a trap for the unwary person now assumes a passive role and once having given consent to the temptation (Chaine) is set on the road to motherhood and childbearing (τίκτει . . . ἀποκύει: these verbs for producing offspring should not be set in contrast as Hiebert does, 108, when he proposes that the second verb suggests a malformed fetus, a monster. ἀποκύειν in 1:18 is used of God's act of parenting and we note the application in 4 Macc 15:17, which is full of Jacobean echoes: ὦ μόνη γύναι τὴν εὐσέβειαν ὁλόκληρον ἀποκυσασα: "O mother who alone [among women] brought perfect piety to birth!").

The immediate progeny of the union of "desire" and the human willingness to be carried off is "sin" (ἁμαρτία, here personified as a conceptual reality; elsewhere in James it represents an act of transgression, in 2:9; 4:17; 5:15–16, 20). The growth of sin is described by the verb ἀποτελεῖν (1 Esd 5:70, v.l. 2 Macc 15:39; Luke 13:32 are the only occurrences in biblical Greek). Plato uses the verb once in the sense of the satisfaction of desire (ἐπιθυμία; BGD, 101); but it is more probable that James wants to link the two kinds of "perfection" in a paradox. Evil finds its final form in sin, which in turn produces death. God, on the other side, has designs which in v 18 entail his fathering a race of people destined for "perfection," i.e., the state of being conformed to his will. The common element in both cases is a fixity of character that has inevitable consequences: it leads either to "death" (the inverse of which is "life," ζωή: as in Gen 3:20 LXX; Vouga, 55) or to holy living, which is a goal set in 1:4.

This parallelism assumes that in both instances the reference is to the human being, whose voice we overhear in v 13, and who is the complement intended in the phrase ἡ ἐπιθυμία συλλαβοῦσα κτλ. The ἕκαστος (each person) is the one destined for either death or life. Vouga (55) offers another possibility. He suggests that it is the trial (πειρασμός) referred to in 1:2–4, 12 and alluded to four times in the verb πειράζειν in vv 13–14 which is really the intended subject. It is believers, whose desire is caught by the perturbations of the difficulties they are in, who need to stand firm in resistance. But when their own desires (emphasizing ἰδίας in v 14) fail to lift them out of their troubles, they lead believers into evil ways; and so the believers in not enduring are seduced. The final call is therefore one of vigilance, expressed in the negative imperative of the verb πλανᾶν, "to lead astray." The verb is used in NT parenesis of warnings against a denial of the faith by moral lapses (1 Cor 6:9; 15:33; Gal 6:7; 1 John 1:8; note too the warning expressed in πλάνη in 2 Pet 2:18; 3:17; 1 John 4:6). The injunction may be taken as a final appeal at the close of the section of 1:12–15 (Windisch), though it could also be a transition to 1:17 (Davids, 86). The negative cast of the verse certainly has a serious situation in mind, akin to 5:19–20. Vouga (56) submits that there is a polemical situation in view. It is raised in vv 13–15 and returned to in vv 17–18, with v 16 acting as a bridge between the two sections (en fait un pont entre les deux). The insight that it is the same error in both short pericopes is a useful one, and that wrongheaded notion may be identified as an aspersion on the divine character, which is denied whether by attributing evil to him or by charging him with being powerless to aid those in distress. The nub of the problem James addresses is that when his readers are caught in the throes of evil conditions it will not do to blame either God or others or to resign all hope in a fatalistic way. Individual accountability is at the root of the matter (vv 13–16); and God's goodness and providence in both creation and the new creation (vv 17–18) are the two emphases our author insists on.

17–19a πᾶσα δόσις ἀγαθὴ καὶ πᾶν δώρημα τέλειον ἄνωθέν ἐστιν καταβαῖνον ἀπὸ τοῦ πατρὸς τῶν φώτων, παρ᾽ ᾧ οὐκ ἔνι παραλλαγὴ ἢ τροπῆς ἀποσκίασμα· βουληθεὶς ἀπεκύησεν ἡμᾶς λόγῳ ἀληθείας, εἰς τὸ εἶναι ἡμᾶς ἀπαρχήν τινα τῶν αὐτοῦ κτισμάτων· Ἴστε, ἀδελφοί μου ἀγαπητοί, "All good giving and every perfect bounty is from above, coming down from the Father who made the lights of heaven; with him there is neither wavering nor shadow cast by an eclipse. [18] He willed to give us birth by the word of truth, that we might be a kind of first fruits of what he created. [19a] Note this, my dear brothers."

To those tempted to doubt the wisdom and strength of God's benefactions, already hinted at in 1:5, James retorts with a memorable statement of the divine character. The parallelism between v 15 (ἀποκύει) and v 18 (ἀπεκύησεν) is the exegetical key to this section while the collocation of the terms used confronts the reader with a moral challenge James often presents. The way of self-interest, when earthly desires (to be elaborated in 3:15–16) prevail, yields a progeny of death, both in the spiritual sense and literally (4:1). Such desires express themselves in an uncontrolled tongue, which is death-dealing (3:8). On the contrary, James advocates the way of heavenly wisdom (ἡ ἄνωθεν σοφία, 3:17). If the two terms are not synonyms, the distinction may be drawn that δόσις is the act of giving, δώρημα is the gift itself. The poetic doubling is for rhetorical effect (Ropes, 158), as is the emphasis produced by the near-synonymous adjectives in this context ἀγαθός/τέλειος. Both words play a distinctive role in the argument: in 3:17 the "good fruits" (καρπῶν ἀγαθῶν) are part of the heavenly wisdom coming down from above (ἄνωθεν), and τέλειος denotes throughout the letter the character that pleases God and is in consonance with his nature.

The links with 3:17–18 bring together two poetic pieces (1:18a and the aretalogy of wisdom in 3:17–18). There are terms common to both passages: in ἄνωθεν, verbs of downward motion, and also in the way the character of the giver and the gift is set forth.

The expression ἀπὸ τοῦ πατρὸς τῶν φώτων unites two Jewish theological traditions. God is known as Lord of created forces (Job 38:28) and the Father of the universe (Philo, De Spec. Leg. 1.96: τῷ τοῦ κόσμου πατρί; De Ebr. 81, πατέρα τῶν ὅλων). At the same time his sovereign power is most particularly seen in his creation and control of the heavenly luminaries (T. Abr. 7:6: πατὴρ τοῦ φωτός; CD 5.17–18: "he is the Prince of Lights"; 1QS 3.20: "all the children of righteousness are ruled by the Prince of Light," Vermes' translation). The idea goes back to Gen 1 and Ps 136 [135]:7; Jer 4:23. The association of God and light is used to praise all God's gifts to men (Philo, De Somn. 1.75; in De Abr. 157ff. light as a gift from above is hailed as the loveliest of all gifts). And from this it is a short step to the conviction that God's sustaining power is seen in his ordering the stars in their courses.

"With him there is neither wavering nor shadow cast by an eclipse." παραλλαγή denotes a change, a succession of events, a movement of objects, and belongs, in one of its meanings, to the revolution of the stars in orbit (Epictetus, Diss. 1.14.4). Likewise τροπή and ἀποσκίασμα could be construed as technical terms, all used of the natural phenomena of the astral world (Mussner, 92). As a consequence the images fit together to yield a picture of the alternation of day and night as light is separated from dark (based on Gen 1), with τροπή denoting the apogee of a heavenly body (cf. Deut 33:14 LXX: ἡλίου τροπῶν; Wisd Sol 7:18: τροπῶν ἀλλαγάς, which the RSV renders "the alternations of the solstices"; but this meaning is treated with caution in regard to James' text in BGD, 827, which prefers a more general meaning of "change," "variation"). The other rare term is ἀποσκίασμα, "shadow" projected by an object. The textual difficulty compounds the problem of interpretation. Two views are possible (Vouga, 57). According to one, the text means that God neutralizes the astral powers and gives to man the freedom to decide his own destiny when faced by trials. The force of παρ᾽ ᾧ is brought out in the interpretation: "compared with" God, there is no disequilibrium or shadow caused by movement. The deduction drawn is that there is no change in God, a set of figurative expressions being used to make this single point without necessarily importing the technical meaning into the words. So Dibelius, Ropes, Davids. In the second view, the sovereignty of God over the stars means that while they are always in motion he never changes whether in himself (hence παρ᾽ ᾧ = in God's nature there is no wavering) or in his dealings with his people (so 1:5). The second is preferable (with Mussner, Reicke, Schrage, Vouga) since the logic required by James' thought seems to be that (i) God's nature is unchangeably good in contrast to the fleeting shadows caused by the traversal of the sun across the sky and (ii) his attribute in giving only what is good is not at the mercy of change. Thus the thrust of this (admittedly) obscure text is that James is offering a theodicy to vindicate the divine character in the face of those who doubted the goodness and reliability of God or who had given up hope in time of testing and imagined it was their "fate." James bars the door to these false ideas.

Divine creation (of the stars in their courses) is matched by the new creation, expressed in a series of heavily weighted theological terms. The participle βουληθείς, "he willed," emphasizes how God acted freely without external constraint in the creation of the universe and of humankind. In sum, the verb denotes the free, sovereign will to create based on his determination (βουλή). See Ps 113:11 LXX [115:3]: πάντα, ὅσα ἠθέλησεν, ἐποίησεν; Sir 21:13: ἡ βουλὴ αὐτοῦ ὡς πηγὴ ζωῆς; Job 23:13: "He is unchangeable . . . and what he wills he does" (αὐτὸς ἠθέλησεν καὶ ἐποίησεν; Philo, De Opif. 16; 44; 77; 138; De Plant. 14; De Conf. Ling. 166; 196). The closer link in thought is with v 15, where "desire" is the mother of sin, which in turn produces the offspring of death. God now takes on a feminine role and is the responsible agent for bringing to birth a race of men and women. Naturally the symmetry is not exact; indeed if we press the analogy too much we are bound to say that it is forced in a way that the Johannine idiom (γεννᾶσθαι ἐκ θεοῦ, "born of God") avoids. But the rhetorical effect is striking, with the double contrast: (i) in place of the sorry chain of consequences whereby desire leads to sin which in turn leads to death, it is said that "God brought us (ἡμᾶς) to birth" by his gift of life; (ii) the present tenses, which are perhaps gnomic in v 15, are replaced by the past ἀπεκύησεν, recalling the decisive moment when God's creative power was put forth in the bestowal of life.

The effective instrument of the divine fiat is said to be λόγος ἀληθείας, "the word of truth." In the OT God's word and truth are frequently joined (Deut 22:20; 2 Sam 7:28; 2 Kgs 10:6; 17:24; Pss 15:2; 118:43; Jer 23:28; Dan 8:26; Zech 8:16; Prov 22:21; Eccl 12:10). In the Pauline corpus the phrase "word of truth" means the proclamation of the gospel or the apostolic mission and ministry (2 Cor 6:7; Eph 1:13; Col 1:5; 2 Tim 2:15), based on some near parallels in T. Gad 3:1; Pss. Sol. 16:10; cf. Odes Sol. 8:8.

The background here, however, is the spoken word which God uttered at creation (Gen 1:3; Ps 33:6; 107:20; 147:15; Isa 55:11; Wisd Sol 18:15; Sir 43:26) and which expressed and executed his divine will. Whether that voice of God was heard in a creative or redemptive sense (where creation would be the new creation) is yet to be decided.

The term ἀπαρχή, "first fruits," carries several senses in the OT. Used of the offerings of Israel (Exod 23:16, 19; 34:16; Lev 27:26; Num 18:18; Deut 14:23; 15:19–23), it is also related to Israel, which as the elect nation is the firstborn of Yahweh (Exod 4:22; cf. Philo, *De Spec. Leg.* 4.180) and the chosen people (Deut 7:6; Jer 2:3). In the NT (see Albertz, "Der 'Erstlinge'") it has a wide range of meanings extending from Rom 16:5 (Epaenetus is the first fruits [NIV "first convert"] of Christ in Asia as Stephanas and family are in Corinth [1 Cor 16:15]) to the 144,000 martyrs in Rev 14:4. Christ is the ἀπαρχή of the holy dead (1 Cor 15:20). Some of these references represent a collective singular, with ἀπαρχή referring to a group, as here.

The conclusion so far is that ἀπαρχή could refer to the old creation but more likely is used in regard to believers as the eschatological creation of God (Mussner, 95) in a way akin to 1 Pet 1:23; Col 1:10; Eph 2:15; 4:21–24; 5:26—all conceivably baptismal texts relating to the parenetic expectations made of those who have been newly won over by the messianic Christian message. If so, λόγος ἀληθείας may be a tribute to the response made at baptism (as in Eph 5:26) when Christ's name was invoked by or over the candidate (James 2:7; cf. Rom 10:13). But against that "the word of truth" emphasizes the divine action rather than the human *responsum,* and in 1:23 the phrase the "hearer of the word" is surely related to the word addressed by God to the congregation.

The purpose of God's generating act is contained in the clause opening εἰς τὸ εἶναι, "that we might be," in the sense of our becoming all that God designed. The destiny is described in such a way as to fit the human creation, reflecting God's image in the beginning (Gen 1:26: Rendall, *The Epistle of St. James,* 64, takes ἀπεκύησεν to refer to the paradise will of God, so that the intention here would be to assert how man as God's vice-regent in the universe is not at the mercy of cosmic powers, such as astrological forces). Or alternatively it is the eschatological order of redeemed humankind which is in mind. In favor of the first, James has little to say whether here or elsewhere touching on the drama of salvation, and it is remarkable that the redeemer's name is absent. A cosmological setting is therefore proposed by Elliott-Binns, "James 1.18" (cf. Hort). On the other hand, Mussner (96) offers an interesting pointer to the second interpretation, favored by Ropes, Dibelius, Blackman, namely that the possessive pronoun in τινα τῶν αὐτοῦ κτισμάτων should receive special stress. The first fruits are his creatures and not children of "desire" and "sin" (v 15). Connections with the preceding discussion suggest that the theme of πειρασμός is being continued here. Whenever men and women yield under πειρασμοί and succumb to the fateful nemesis of the sorry train of desire-sin-death they are doomed. But God's new order breaks the entail, and thanks to his sovereign will to save and by means of his word he offers new life to those who confess him in baptism and so enter the eschatological community where the powers of evil are broken. The value of this reconstruction is that it not only regards the eschatological overtone in such OT terms as "bring to birth," "word of truth" and "first fruits," but it completes the theodicy begun in v 13, and makes vv 13–18 a self-contained unit of discourse, dedicated to a single theme.

κτίσμα, according to this view, carries the same connotation as καινὴ κτίσις (2 Cor 5:17; Gal 6:15; Eph 2:10; 4:24) and is a way of recalling believers to their vocation. This is the point of the appeal, "Note this" (ἴστε, an imperative, with Ropes, Dibelius, Vouga; cf. BDF § 99.2). The interpretation offered will gain further support in 1:23 (see *Comment* there).

Explanation

In a question that may be said to characterize the entire letter James asks: "What is your life?" (4:14). The issues behind that deceptively simple question are several; there is the philosophical conundrum of what it is that constitutes a living being; there is a medical-somatic side to do with the distinctiveness of animate life; but for James the practical concern predominates.

How is life to be viewed and lived in concrete situations? He has already remarked on life's frailty and uncertainty (1:9–11), which is part of the scenario in 4:12–18. The thought now attacks the problem of what it is that sums up genuine life, and it does so in two main ways. Life is viewed as a moral struggle whose victory spells the promise of sound character (1:12–15), and life is to be grasped and enjoyed as a divine gift and opportunity (1:16–18).

1. If there is a distinction to be made between the trials of 1:3–5 and the tests spoken of at v 12, it is still feasible to believe that the two ideas are not unrelated. The readers' experience of persecution (to be elaborated in such later places as 2:5–7; 5:6, 13) would only exacerbate the problem of the age-old difficulty: Why do the righteous suffer? James offers one set of answers, in terms of a theodicy, in 1:5–11, but there it is on the practical level of advocating a recourse to endurance, wisdom, faith, and patience to await the divine intervention. It is the turn of the writer now to address the same problem in the light of some new circumstances. We may infer these from the cautionary word in v 16a: "Don't be led astray, my dear brothers." Unless this is an otiose remark, thrown in as an aside, we should take it seriously and find it to register the presence of some alien teaching the readers were being subjected to and were in danger of embracing. At the heart of that error was an aspersion cast on the divine character. The testing referred to in v 12 lay exactly in the threat of unbelief that was brought to the surface by their hardship and which, in turn, compelled them to raise some tough questions about the sovereign control and lordship of God in the face of the trials they were called on to endure.

The obvious "easy answer" offered to explain their present miseries was evidently that God had lost patience with them and as a mark of disfavor had abandoned them to their fate. Or else the proposal was that he was deliberately testing them with malevolent designs in view. James cannot accept either proposition. He retorts with one of the strongest affirmations in biblical literature to the effect that *moral accountability is both personal and inevitable.* Men and women should not imagine that God is an ogre set on their ruin as though he delighted to find fault or to punish them for some unknown reason or imagined sins. Nor should they call in extraneous reasons to account for their moral dilemmas, such as the power of evil to work against them as though God and the devil formed a dualism of equal force, with helpless believers caught in the middle and so becoming the victims of a cosmic struggle where a finite God had to contend with refractory evil. James is at heart— as befits a pastoral counselor—a pragmatist. Each person is tempted by his own evil desires, which is the root cause. Obviously there is an assumption made here, and we are left with the unexplained issue of where those desires originated. James says no more than that they come "from within," a phenomenological observation akin to the teaching of Jesus (Mark 7:14–23). Yet once desire gains our consent, it sets in motion a fearful train of consequences or—as James puts it in picturesque idiom—it gives birth to a progeny of evil, first sin which in turn produces death. Throughout, while the consequences are inevitable, the prime mover and fatal cause is the human consent to evil. Thereafter sad results follow. As Einstein once remarked, "There are no punishments, only consequences."

2. The second problematic facing these people was another version of the same discussion. To men and women caught in the throes of heavy persecution, one solution open to them was to blame God. A second response is even more devastating for faith. It is to deny that God has the ability to help. He may be willing, but his power is so limited that good intentions are thwarted and his designs are frustrated. The earlier exegetical discussion sought to propose this setting for 1:17–19a. Only as we infer a setting in which cosmic forces were regarded as supreme and in active rivalry to the creator can we make sense of the emphases in this section. There is a notable use of astronomical technical terms (v 17); there is a tribute to God as creator of the heavenly bodies; and there is a strong volitional element in the verbs and the imagery of v 18. All of this adds up to a single conclusion: James is being *challenged to offer a theodicy against a powerful belief that, in the name of astral religion and occult mysteries, looked to the stars as arbiters of human destiny.* He replies by appealing to the OT–Jewish tradition in which God is sole creator of the heavenly lights and the sole progenitor of the race, whether of old Israel or the new community of Israel-after-the-Spirit.

While the Jacobean theology is not so explicit as Paul's, there are unmistakable notes of Christian confidence, addressed to a beleaguered people of God. That theodicy offers the assurance that life is not at the mercy of cosmic forces or subject to a meaningless round of random events.

To the pathetic admission of helplessness voiced in A. E. Housman's couplet "I, a stranger and afraid, / In a world I never made," this pericope comes as a vibrant expression of Christian hope in the goodness and control of the sovereign Lord—a theme more familiar to the NT reader in such places as Rom 8:18–39; Eph 1:3–14; Phil 2:6–11; and Rev 5:1–14; 17:14.

III. Applying the Word   (1:19b–3:18)

1. The Obedience of Faith   (1:19b–27)

Bibliography

Almquist, H. *Plutarch und das Neue Testament.* ASNU 15. Uppsala: Appelbergs Boktr., 1946. **Betz, H. D.** *Lukian von Samosata und das Neue Testament.* TU 74. Berlin: Töpelmann, 1961. **Black, M.** "Critical and Exegetical Notes on Three New Testament Texts. Hebrews xi.11; Jude 5; James i.27." In *Apophoreta,* FS E. Haenchen, ed. W. Eltester and F. H. Kettler. BZNW 30. Berlin: Töpelmann, 1964. 39–45. **Braumann, G.** "Der theologische Hintergrund des Jakobusbriefes." *TZ* 18 (1962) 401–10. **Calmet, A.** "Vraie et fausée Sagesse." *Bible et Vie Chrétienne* 58 (1964) 19–28 (on 1:19–27). **Eckert, K. G.** "Zur Terminologie des Jakobusbriefes." *TLZ* 89 (1964) 521–26. **Gantoy, R.** "L'épître du quatrième Dimanche après Pâques (Jc 1,17–21): Une catéchèse apostolique pour notre temps." *AsSeign* 47 (1963) 15–27. **Goppelt, L.** *Theology of the New Testament.* Vol. 2. Tr. John Alsup. Grand Rapids: Eerdmans, 1982. 199–211 (esp. 202–8). ———. *Christentum und Judentum im ersten und zweiten Jahrhundert.* Gütersloh: Bertelsmann, 1954. Partial tr. E. Schroeder. *Jesus, Paul, and Judaism: An Introduction to NT Theology.* New York: Nelson, 1964. **Jeremias, J.** *New Testament Theology.* Tr. J. Bowden. London: SCM, 1971. ———. *The Parables of Jesus.* 3d ed. Tr. S. H. Hooke. London: SCM Press, 1972. **Jervell, J.** *Imago Dei. Gen 1.26f. im Spätjudentum, in der Gnosis und in den paulinischen Briefen.* FRLANT 76. Göttingen: Vandenhoeck und Ruprecht, 1960. **Johanson, B. C.** "The Definition of 'Pure Religion' in James 1:27 Reconsidered." *ExpTim* 84 (1973) 118–19. **Kertelge, K.** *'Rechtfertigung' bei Paulus.* NA n.f. 3. Münster: Aschendorff, 1967. **Manson, T. W.** "2 Cor 2:14–17: Suggestions towards an Exegesis." In *Studia Paulina,* FS de Zwaan, ed. J. Sevenster and W. C. van Unnik. Haarlem: Bohn, 1953. 158. **Nauck, W.** "Lex inculpta in der Sektenschrift." *ZNW* 46 (1955) 138–40. **Nötscher, F.** "'Gesetz der Freiheit' im NT und in der Mönchsgemeinde am Toten Meer." *Bib* 34 (1953) 193–94. **Obermüller, R.** "Hermeneutische Themen im Jakobusbriefes." *Bib* 53 (1972) 234–44. **Reumann, J.** *Righteousness in the New Testament.* Philadelphia: Fortress, 1982. 149–50. **Roberts, D. J.** "The Definition of 'Pure Religion' in James 1:27." *ExpTim* 83 (1972) 215–16. **Rusche, H.** "Standhaben in Gott. Einführung in die Grundgedanken des Jakobusbriefes (1,1–27)." *BibLeb* 5/4 (1964) 153–63, 236–47. **Schnackenburg, R.** *The Moral Teaching of the New Testament.* Tr. J. Holland-Smith and W. J. O'Hara. New York: Seabury; London: Burns and Oates, 1965. **Smend, R. D.- Luz, U.** *Gesetz.* Stuttgart: Kohlhammer, 1981. 134–35. **Spicq, C.** "La vraie chrétienne." *AsSeign* 48 (1965) 21–38. **Stauffer, E.** "Das 'Gesetz der Freiheit' in der Ordensregel von Jericho." *TLZ* 77 (1952) 527–32. **Stuhlmacher, P.** *Gerechtigkeit Gottes bei Paulus.* FRLANT 87. Göttingen: Vandenhoeck und Ruprecht, 1965. **Taylor, C.** "St. James and Hermas." *ExpTim* 16 (1905) 334. **Townsend, M. J.** "James 4:1–4: A Warning against Zealotry?" *ExpTim* 87 (1976) 211–13. **Ziesler, J. A.** *The Meaning of Righteousness in Paul.* SNTSMS 20. Cambridge: Cambridge UP, 1972.

Translation

> [19b]*Let everyone be quick to listen, slow to speak, slow to get angry,* [20]*for human anger does not promote divine righteousness.* [21]*Therefore, get rid of all [moral]*

filth and every trace of evil, and humbly receive the word that is implanted by which you may be saved.
²² *Show yourselves*[a] *those who do not simply listen to the word—and so deceive themselves—but become those who put the word into practice.* ²³ *Anyone who listens to the word but does not do [what it says] is similar to a person looking at the face that nature gave him in a mirror;* ²⁴ *he looks at himself, and then goes off and immediately forgets what he looks like.* ²⁵ *But he who peers intently into the perfect law that makes free and continues to do this, not forgetting what he has heard, but putting it into practice—this kind of person will be blessed in what he does.*
²⁶ *If any person [of your company*[b]*] regards himself as religious and does not hold his tongue in check, then he is self-deceived and his religion is futile.* ²⁷ *Religion that God the Father regards as pure and untainted is this: to take care of orphans and widows in their distress, and to keep oneself pure from the contamination*[c] *of the world's influence.*

Notes

[a] γίνεσθε, lit., "become." Mayor, 66, prefers our translation; yet cf. Ropes, 174.
[b] ἐν ὑμῖν is only poorly attested in TR, but is included in the Greek-English *Diglot* and may be read *ad sensum*.
[c] ἄσπιλον ἑαυτὸν τηρεῖν is read by most authorities, with P⁷⁴ providing the variant ὑπερασπίζειν αὐτούς, "to protect them," i.e., widows and orphans, from the world (ἀπὸ τοῦ κόσμου). The sense then runs: "Religion pure and undefiled before God and the Father is this: to visit orphans and to *protect* widows in their affliction from the world" (M. Black's preference, "Three NT Texts," 45). Black argues that P⁷⁴ gives a more suitable meaning than that offered by the majority text, though he concedes it is a secondary reading, if "a particularly happy one." The latter reading is accepted by Roberts, "The Definition," because, he avers, it is in line with James' thought. This is true up to a point, but it fails to see the link with 4:4 (cf. Johanson, "The Definition . . . Reconsidered"). ἄσπιλος may indeed have a cultic ring, but here when it is used in conjunction with true θρησκεία that is both καθαρά and ἀμίαντος the tone is moral (Oepke, *TDNT* 1:502). The verb in P⁷⁴ is unattested elsewhere in the NT, though it is found frequently (20x) in LXX, with the closest parallel in Prov 2:7–8a, "to guard the path of the just" (Mussner, 113 n.6).
Some minuscules have the plural forms ἀσπίλους ἑαυτοὺς τηρεῖτε.

Form / Structure / Setting

The link between v 18 and v 19a, commencing ἴστε, ἀδελφοί μου ἀγαπητοί, poses the question whether the call (assuming ἴστε to be imperative, with Ropes, Dibelius, Mussner, Davids, and not indicative, with Reicke, Hiebert) belongs at the close of the section of vv 16–18 (so Vouga, and above) or marks the opening of the next pericope. We have preferred to see the admonition as naturally connected with the exposition of God's goodness; then the imperative mood in ἴστε would be preferable, as a confirmation of what the readers already have been taught. Thus v 19b opens a new tack.

The topic now introduced may be stated under the rubric of "a Christianity of practice" (Mussner, 98), or perhaps better, a faith that practices. James' chief interest lies in setting before his readers the need for obedience to the message that translates itself into practical effect. He is warning against the notion of mere assent or tame acceptance of God's truth when it is viewed as an end in itself, or worse, as a substitute for practical religion. V 26 evidently states the prime need: there were some in James' community for whom the formal profession of religion was just that—namely, an outward form that listened to the word but stopped short of implementing the call to action. There was also a moral problem in that community, as v 21 indicates with its parenetic reminder, common in other NT epistles, to get rid of moral uncleanness (lit., "*lay aside* all filthiness"; ἀποθέμενοι in its participial form corresponds to Selwyn's classification of *Deponentes;* see E. G. Selwyn, *1 Peter* [London: Macmillan, 1947] 367—based on 1 Pet 1:22–2:2 and building on P. Carrington, *The Primitive Christian Catechism* [Oxford: Oxford UP, 1940]). The admonition was part of a baptismal catechesis (Braumann, "Hintergrund," 401–5) that made much of the need to rid oneself of evil; an action symbolizing the putting off of the old life and the start of the new life was the stripping for baptism and clothing in new garments after the rite. See Rom 13:12–14; Col 3:8–11; Eph 4:22–25; 1 Pet 2:1 (see Braumann, "Hintergrund," 409); *1 Clem.* 13:1: "putting aside (ἀποθέμενοι) all arrogance and conceit and folly and wrath." See further J. E. Crouch, *The Origin and Intention of the Colossian Haustafel,* FRLANT 109 (Göttingen: Vandenhoeck und Ruprecht, 1972) 147.

The positive side is the call to embrace the virtue of a true (as opposed to a spurious; μάταιος is, strictly, what is worthless or useless, in v 26) θρησκεία, v 27, which is denoted as "pure and untainted" in the eyes of God. The steps to the practice of this Christian version of the Jewish "cult" (Acts 26:5 has the term θρησκεία in its Jewish setting, while Col 2:18 uses the word of the Colossian "philosophy" and its practice) are listed.

At the heart of James' pragmatic and pastoral concern is the desire to inculcate a following of "the perfect law" (νόμος τέλειος, v 25) which is so desirable that it sets its adherents free. This phrase has occasioned much debate, giving rise to "a major interpretive problem" for any student of the epistle (Davids, 99). In spite of parallels in Philo (*De Vita Mos.* 2.3) and in the Stoics (Vouga, 65) that may be adduced (see *Comment*) it is to Judaism that the interpreter should look for the most promising source of James' idea of the implanted law. Beginning with those canonical Psalms (e.g., 18:8 [19:7]; 119; cf. *Ep. Arist.* 31) that extol the perfection of Torah as God's gift to Israel and the joy to be found in its observance (Pss 1:2; 19:7–11; 40:6–8; 119; cf. Sir 6:23–31; 51:13–22; Bar 4:2–4) the line of development moves by way of Qumran, whose documents may possibly contain the exact phrase "law of freedom" (Stauffer, "Gesetz," on 1QS 10:6, 8, 11; Nötscher, "Gesetz der Freiheit"). The rabbinic praise of Torah extolled it as a life-imparting agent, as a medicine to heal and as a means of setting loyal Jews free to serve God (see 'Abot 3:8; 6:2; and T. W. Manson, "2 Cor 2:14–17," for citations that celebrate Torah as a divine medicine). James takes over the concept to enrich it by relating it to his teaching on the "word," which is the agent in birth and/or new birth (1:18) and the instrument of salvation when it is thought of as implanted in a way akin to that in Jer 31:33 (Goppelt, *Theology,* 2:203, 205). Thus, with Schlatter (*Der Jakobusbrief,* 150), we should not make too much of the terminological distinction between gospel and "law" in James. Both are interchangeable with the divine "word" (Mussner, 107, cf. 109, citing du Plessis, ΤΕΛΕΙΟΣ, 237f., for the idea that νόμος in 1:25 is "an inclusive concept" uniting the faith and works mandated by both law and gospel) and are in some important ways removed from the teaching of the Apostolic fathers (*Barn.* 2:6; *Herm. Man.* 4.3.1f., *Vis.* 3.5.1–4; cf. Taylor, "Hermas") that is based on an understanding of Christianity as lex nova or obedience to a formal system. For this fateful transition from gospel to legalism, see Goppelt, *Christentum,* 216 (on *Barn.*), 242 (on *Herm.*).

If this is the setting of James' allusion to "the law of freedom" (on this expression see Eckert, "Zur Terminologie," 521–26) and its point of reference is the eschatological fulfillment of Jer 31, then the force of the critique lies in an exposing of failure on the readers' part to apply their faith and to respond to the claim of God's grace on their lives. The paradox of God's gift (*Gabe*) laying on its recipients the task (*Aufgabe*) of obedience and practical ethics is found at the heart of this pericope. James' interest throughout is in God's δικαιοσύνη (1:20), whether interpreted as "what he requires" or "desires" (NIV) or to be given a specific content as an attempt to promote his kingdom's goal as the Zealots sought to do (cf. Reicke, who seeks to place "law of freedom" in a political context; the Jacobean "law" is polemical, he avers, in that it criticizes and reverses the Zealot program for national freedom). In a general sense it is the way to live so as to please him. But there is no mistaking the prior action and disposition of "grace" implied in the teaching on "the word" that initiates the process, though believers are not allowed to escape the claims of that righteousness. As they do respond in a working faith, they are promised true "blessedness" (1:25) in a manner akin to Matt 5:6–8 (see Jeremias, *Theology,* 248). Hence the law is "perfect" in that it represents God's perfect will. Yet more than that, it conveys his strength to enable those who observe it to attain its end, and become "perfect and mature" (1:4; cf. 3:2 for a realistic concession that full control of the tongue is hardly possible without reliance on the same divine strength and wisdom, 3:17–18).

The tests of adherence to the "perfect law" are (i) getting and keeping a firm rein on the tongue (v 19: "slow to speak and slow to become angry"), a theme that James will elaborate in chap. 3; and (ii) obedience to what the "word" reveals, illustrated by the analogy of the mirror (vv 23–25) which is "a kind of parable" (Vouga, 64) or even an allegory in which the word is represented by a looking-glass that faithfully portrays a person's God-designed "image" (Ropes, Dibelius, Windisch, Davids), a thought perhaps going back to Gen 1:26–27; 5:1 with its teaching on the *imago Dei* that man carries (so Rendall, *The Epistle of St. James,* 65, who renders the phrase τὸ πρόσωπον τῆς γενέσεως αὐτοῦ, "the face of his origin," in v 23 and accounts thereby for the past tense ἦν in v 24 as a direct borrowing from the Genesis creation account). Or else the mirror-image may be taken to refer to the "new creation," reverting to v 18 (Reicke); and (iii) as the thought looks on to chap. 2, the issue is one of concern for the poor, which is the final thrust in James' advocacy of social religion (1:27). The care James wants to see exercised reaches out to the distressed community members, and he will complete this instruction in 2:8 where "the perfect law" is recast as "the sovereign law" of love to one's neighbor, especially the unfortunate and socially marginalized.

Comment

19b–20 ἔστω δὲ πᾶς ἄνθρωπος ταχὺς εἰς τὸ ἀκοῦσαι, βραδὺς εἰς τὸ λαλῆσαι, βραδὺς εἰς ὀργήν· ὀργὴ γὰρ ἀνδρὸς δικαιοσύνην θεοῦ οὐκ ἐργάζεται, "Let everyone be quick to listen, slow to speak, slow to get angry, [20] for human anger does not promote divine righteousness."

This section (1:19b–27) opens with a survey of five themes in swift succession, all of them due to be expanded in later parts of the letter. The first is the wisdom teaching that places a restraint on a hasty and impetuous desire to promote God's cause, seen here as "divine righteousness." The parallel is in 3:14–18. Two major interests then motivate James' counsel: the advocacy of practical obedience to God's message, which must be not only received with humility (v 21) but also acted upon. Fourth, there is concern for the defenseless members of the community, linked with, fifth, a deliberate turning aside from "the ways of the world" (v 27). This last topic, which is enlarged in 4:1–5:20, is already in the author's mind at vv 19b–20.

"Hearing and doing" God's will, with the corollary that believers should not be quick to follow their own desires and designs, is a common theme in the Wisdom literature: see Prov 10:9; 13:3; 15:1; 29:20; Eccl 7:9; 9:18; Sir 4:29; 5:11; 6:33; 21:15; *T. Dan* 1:6; 1QS 5.25. These texts are all variations on the theme of the control of tongue and temper; they instill a prudential ethic that only a fool will be unguarded in his speech and he will learn to rue the day of intemperate statements. Far better, the wisdom teachers say, to be considerate and to listen first before making rash statements. The good student, according to *'Abot* 5:12, follows this rule: "There are four types of disciples: swift to hear and swift to lose—his gain is cancelled by his loss; slow to hear and slow to lose—his loss is cancelled by his gain; swift to hear and slow to lose—this is a happy lot; slow to hear and swift to lose—this is an evil lot" (cf. *'Abot* 1:15: Shammai said: "Make the [study of the] law a fixed habit; say little and do much, and receive all men with a cheerful countenance").

As a part of general advice for the good life, such restraint brings its own reward. But Eccl 5:1–6 puts a special point on this advice when it relates one's words to what is said in the divine presence and in the house of God. In particular such allusions are to promises and vows that carry a solemnity and imply a binding character. The setting in a service of worship may be reflected in our text, with its call to "receive the implanted word by which you may be saved."

Yet again vv 19b–20 contain much hortatory warning that is both like and unlike other examples in its two parts. (a) There is avoidance of anger (ὀργή)—again a frequent theme in the sapiential literature (Prov 15:1; *'Abot* 2.10), in the NT epistles (Col 3:8; Eph 4:26, 31), in later Christian Two Ways morality (*Did.* 3:2; *Barn.* 19:12) as well as in pagan moral values (cf. the dictum of H. Almquist, "The whole of philosophy in late antiquity berated anger," *Plutarch und das NT,* 130–31, condemning it as an antisocial vice). (b) And, in a remark that is special to James, the assertion that δικαιοσύνη θεοῦ, "divine righteousness," is not effected by human anger.

The phrase "the righteousness of God" here may be taken in several ways (listed in Reumann, *Righteousness,* 149–50): (i) it relates to what "the righteousness of God demands" (Ziesler, *Meaning,* 135), giving emphasis to what is God's standard (Schrenk, *TDNT* 2:200–201) as a norm for human conduct; (ii) it is a state of affairs brought about by the action of human beings (Dibelius, 111) as a watchword for a life that is "righteous" in the true sense (so Kertelge,

Rechtfertigung, 47, who includes the eschatological dimension that at the last judgment such behavior will be acknowledged by God); and (iii) with "righteousness" taken to be synonymous with God's salvation, based on the OT's understanding of Yahweh's "saving deeds" (on this see Stuhlmacher, *Gerechtigkeit Gottes*, 142–54, 192–93), the sense is that of promoting the divine saving rule. It is this last-named interpretation which makes it possible (for Reicke, Townsend, and others, see *Introduction*) to put a fine point on the verse that it is best understood as James' response to those who sought to bring in God's kingdom on earth (a view not found in Reumann's survey). The policy James condemns is one of seeking to promote the cause of freedom by politically motivated and engineered violence (an endeavor to be brought into the discussion at 4:1–3).

The last-named interpretation of a life-setting looks for support to the meaning of ἐργάζεσθαι, as "to promote, effect, bring about," i.e., the same sense as in 1:3 (κατεργάζεται) and 2:9 (ἐργάζεσθε).

21–22   διὸ ἀποθέμενοι πᾶσαν ῥυπαρίαν καὶ περισσείαν κακίας ἐν πραΰτητι, δέξασθε τὸν ἔμφυτον λόγον τὸν δυνάμενον σῶσαι τὰς ψυχὰς ὑμῶν· Γίνεσθε δὲ ποιηταὶ λόγου καὶ μὴ μόνον ἀκροαταὶ παραλογιζόμενοι ἑαυτούς, "Therefore, get rid of all [moral] filth and every trace of evil, and humbly receive the word that is implanted by which you may be saved. ²²Show yourselves those who do not simply listen to the word—and so deceive themselves—but become those who put the word into practice."

A second theme opens with the topic of the role of "the word," which will be developed in later sections when the power of human speech is elaborated (1:26; 3:1–12). James begins with a baptismal reminder (the participle has imperatival force), calling on the readers to get rid of (lit., "strip off as a garment": ἀποτιθέναι; so found in Homer, *Il.* 3.89; Herodotus, 4.78) of all evil. The baptismal idioms belong to the act of the rite itself as candidates were encouraged to exchange their normal clothes for new garments received after the baptism was performed (cf. Hippolytus, *Apostolic Tradition* 21.5, Cuming's ed. 18: "They shall take off their clothes . . . let no one take any alien object [e.g., rings, ornaments: the Jewish idea of חֲצִיצָה, *ḥaṣîṣah*, lit., "separation," required for immersion] down into the water").

James' concern is with a renunciation of all moral evil, expressed by πᾶσαν ῥυπαρίαν, which could refer to soiled and dirty garments (2:2) or could be construed in a specialized sense attested in Artimedorus (second century A.D., BGD, 738) as a medical term (ῥυπός) for earwax that must be washed away to give good hearing. This second sense fits the context nicely. "Every trace of evil" may be rendered "the abundance/excess of wickedness," and is a tautologous expression to sum up the complete moral renovation James is calling for. Laws translates "the great mass of malice," so defining κακία as vulgar and malicious talk. If NEB—"the malice that hurries to excess"—is chosen, it would suggest that James has in mind a warning that would, if unheeded, lead to immoral conduct. But James does not otherwise find an antinomian spirit among his congregation. See too Col 3:8–10; Eph 4:22–26; 1 Pet 2:1 where κακία has the general sense of evils to be renounced in a baptismal profession.

The positive side of the catechetical call is humbly to receive (ἐν πραΰτητι opposed to ὀργή in v 19) the word, i.e., the Christian message (but hardly a

Christological reference as in John 1:1–14, as Scaer suggests). The image of the implanted (ἔμφυτον) word recalls also the baptismal response made when the message was heard and acted on (e.g. Rom 10:9–10) with language that belongs to the initiatory act (Rom 6:5: σύμφυτοι . . . τῷ ὁμοιώματι τοῦ θανάτου αὐτοῦ) and missionary baptismal instruction (1 Cor 3:6). The idiom is also OT-Jewish (4 Ezra 8:6: "give us seed for our heart and cultivation of our understanding so that fruit may be produced"; cf. Deut 30:11–14, cited in Rom 10:8). See too Josephus, *Contra Ap.* 2.169. There is also a Stoic background if the meaning of ἔμφυτος is "inborn," "innate" (Knox, "The Epistle of James," *JTS* 46 [1945] 14–15, cf. Wisd Sol 12:10 used of "inborn evil"). But, as Davids rightly remarks in opposition to seeing a hellenistic sense, "something inborn could have nothing to do with receiving" (95) or obeying, which presupposes a moral response. The "word" then on its Jewish background is a virtual synonym for the "word of truth" (λόγος ἀληθείας) in v 18; and both refer to God's message of new life and salvation (δυνάμενον σῶσαι is common in this epistle for eschatological salvation the readers share, though there is a warning in 5:19–20 that some can wander away from it). Hence the parenetic-catechetical summons is to act responsively and responsibly. Mussner (103) rightly notes that with all James' preoccupation with "works" he does not lose sight of the saving power of the "word" to effect salvation and to lead to daily conduct that is in keeping with a person's profession of faith. There is no magical salvation or automatic result of simply hearing the word. This is a warning that looks on to the discussion in 2:14–26.

The caution that logically follows is not to rest content with a formal acceptance of the message; that path leads to self-deception. Rather, the readers should become (γίνεσθε = ἔστε) "doers of the word" (ποιηταὶ λόγου). This is a favorite Jacobean expression: see 1:25 (ποιητὴς ἔργου); 4:11 (ποιητὴς νόμου). The use of ποιεῖν (= עשׂה, ʿasah) in the ethical sense is typically Semitic, e.g., Exod 24:3 LXX has the rendering πάντας τοὺς λόγους . . . ποιήσομεν and the rabbinic phrase תורה עשׂה, "to practice Torah," is well known (ʾAbot 1.17; cf. 3.9b, 17b; 5.14; 6.4b; Str-B 3:753). See too Rom 2:13, alongside the teaching of Jesus in Matt 5:19; 7:21, 26–27; cf. John 4:34; 7:17; 9:31; 15:14. But the evidence is not all the same, since for a Jew of Mishnaic times Torah observance means one thing, while Jesus redefined the practice of God's will as "love for the neighbor," a theme to be picked up in 1:25 in James' comment on the "perfect law" and in 2:8–11 on "the royal law" (Lev 19:18).

Failing to see the positive application of a religious attitude which is merely professed (v 26) leads only to a person's being self-deceived (παραλογίζεσθαι ἑαυτούς; the force of the reflexive pronoun is that of ὑμᾶς αὐτούς; cf. Acts 15:29, the apostolic edict associated with James). To sum up, what James is defining is the nature of true piety (Mussner, 105, against Dibelius, 114).

23–25 ὅτι εἴ τις ἀκροατὴς λόγου ἐστὶν καὶ οὐ ποιητής, οὗτος ἔοικεν ἀνδρὶ κατανοοῦντι τὸ πρόσωπον τῆς γενέσεως αὐτοῦ ἐν ἐσόπτρῳ· κατενόησεν γὰρ ἑαυτον καὶ ἀπελήλυθεν καὶ εὐθέως ἐπελάθετο ὁποῖος ἦν· ὁ δὲ παρακύψας εἰς νόμον τέλειον τὸν τῆς ἐλευθερίας καὶ παραμείνας, οὐκ ἀκροατὴς ἐπιλησμονῆς γενόμενος ἀλλὰ ποιητὴς ἔργου, οὗτος μακάριος ἐν τῇ ποιήσει αὐτοῦ ἔσται, "Anyone who listens to the word but does not do [what it says] is similar to a person looking at the face that nature gave him in a mirror; 24 he looks at himself, and then goes

off and immediately forgets what he looks like. ²⁵ But he who peers intently
into the perfect law that makes free and continues to do this, not forgetting
what he has heard, but putting it into practice—this kind of person will be
blessed in what he does."

This short paragraph amplifies and illustrates what has been said about
"hearing and doing." At the heart of the section is "a kind of parable" (Vouga,
64), which recalls the style of stories Jesus told in the Synoptic Gospels: the
kingdom of God is like a person who . . . (see, e.g., Matt 13; the point of
both sets of teaching is exactly that in Matt 7:26–27). The form is contained
in ʾAbot 3.17b but the theme is that stressed in ʾAbot 5.14, which characterizes
four "types" who patronize the House of Study. Four sorts of persons are
held up to review: (1) he who goes to the synagogue but after hearing Torah
does not practice; (2) he who practices without going is rewarded for so
doing; (3) he who goes and practices is the pious person; while (4) he who
does neither is an ungodly man. James clearly is using type (1) as a foil to
praise the virtue of type (3).

The point of comparison that may liken this centerpiece to an allegory is
seen in two contrasting reactions to what takes place when a person looks
(κατανοοῦντι: the verb suggests "attentive scrutiny of an object," TDNT 4:975)
at the face that nature gave him (τὸ πρόσωπον τῆς γενέσεως). The Greek is
so rendered by NEB, but we may observe Rendall's suggestion (noted earlier,
p. 46, that the past tense of v 24, "what he looks like" (ὁποῖος ἦν), goes back
to Gen 1:26–27 and should be understood as "the manner of man that he
was (ὁποῖος ἦν) as made in the image of God . . . according to the design of
God in his creation." See too J. Jervell, Imago Dei, 185–89, who points to
the equivalence of image and mirror in Wisd Sol 7:26; Odes Sol. 13:1; cf. 1
Clem. 36:2 (Christ as the heavenly mirror) in the light of the Pauline texts
and Heb 1:3 that go back to Gen 1:26–27. In the Explanation this suggestive
line of interpretation will be pressed into service.

What is seen in a mirror is meant to lead to action, usually regarded as
remedial. The face is seen to be dirty (going back to v 21) or blemished and
needing attention. Instead the thoughtless person "goes off and forgets" (gnomic aorists) what he has seen. By contrast (v 25) the person who "peers
intently" (παρακύψας, a verb denoting "penetrating absorption," TDNT 5:815;
Prov 7:6; Sir 21:23) into the "perfect law that makes free" (εἰς νόμον τέλειον
τὸν τῆς ἐλευθερίας) and continues in it, i.e., does not walk away in forgetfulness,
but rather practices the will of God whose law he examines, receives the
accompaniment of this exercise. The outcome is blessing, as v 25 that closes
with a macarism that takes us back to v 12: μακάριος ἀνὴρ ὅς.

The parallelism drawn is thus an exact one (following but also adapting
Mussner, 106):

Pictorially *vv 23–24*	*Actually* *v 25*
1. The man sees himself (as he really is, or perhaps as he was intended to be, as the *imago Dei*)	1. The man peers

2. in a mirror;
3. antithetically he marches off and promptly forgets.
4. So he is no doer. (οὐ ποιητής)

2. into the perfect law of liberty;
3. he perseveres (παραμείνας; cf. 1:12: ὑπομένει) and does not forget.
4. By contrast (ἀλλὰ) he is a "doer of the work" (ποιητὴς ἔργου) and by inference he takes steps in obedience and practical faith to attain his destiny as God's creature, which is clearly depicted in the mirror.

The centerpiece in this diagram is clearly the analogy of the mirror as illustrating "the perfect law of liberty." The latter turn of phrase has OT roots, e.g., Ps 18:8 [19:7]: "Yahweh's law is perfect (ἄμωμος) converting the soul" (ἐπιστρέφων ψυχάς; cf. v 21, σῶσαι τὰς ψυχᾶς ὑμῶν), and there are many facets to its background (see earlier). In this context "law" is for James a norm of conduct, and he can write of the equivalence of the obedient and faithful ποιητὴς ἔργου and the ποιητὴς λόγου. So νόμος and λόγος seem to be equal terms, and this leads to the conclusion that for our writer "the perfect law" is none other than the "word implanted" in the hearts of responsive believers. The content of that "law" will be made clear in 2:1–13. It is the "law" of love to one's neighbor as well as the law written on the human heart. Both ideas stem from the eschatological fulfillment of the new covenant prophecy of Jer 31:31–34 (Goppelt). That fulfillment is evidently what James means by τῆς ἐλευθερίας. This implies that we are set free from ourselves to serve our neighbors, and the term τέλειον used of the law takes on a salvation-historical character (Mussner, 108–9) as it yields the fruit of a character that has been touched and renewed by God's salvation (v 21). Freedom is not *from* the works of the law (as in Paul; James has no precise phrase ἔργα τοῦ νόμου as in Rom 3:20; Gal 2:16; 3:10), but rather it connotes a release from self-interest and a new capacity to practice God's will in the interests of one's needy neighbor (v 27). In ʾAbot 6.2b on Exod 32:16 the comment is made, "Read not *haruth* (graven) but *heruth* (freedom), for you find no free man except him who occupies himself with the study of Torah." James exploits this meaning of law but gives it a richer content from a Christian perspective by his recourse to the eschatological fulfillment of Jer 31 in the age of God's new creation (v 18).

26–27 Εἴ τις δοκεῖ θρησκὸς εἶναι μὴ χαλιναγωγῶν γλῶσσαν αὐτοῦ ἀλλὰ ἀπατῶν καρδίαν αὐτοῦ, τούτου μάταιος ἡ θρησκεία· θρησκεία καθαρὰ καὶ ἀμίαντος παρὰ τῷ θεῷ καὶ πατρὶ αὕτη ἐστίν, ἐπισκέπτεσθαι ὀρφανοὺς καὶ χήρας ἐν τῇ θλίψει αὐτῶν, ἄσπιλον ἑαυτὸν τηρεῖν ἀπὸ τοῦ κόσμου, "If any person [of your company] regards himself as religious and does not hold his tongue in check, then he is self-deceived and his religion is futile. ²⁷ Religion that God the Father regards as pure and untainted is this: to take care of orphans and widows in their distress, and to keep oneself pure from the contamination of the world's influence."

"With disconcerting ease, our text jumps from one topic to another," comments Vouga (66). Well, not quite. Granted that there is an abrupt transition, without any connective, from the discussion concerning the two types of "hearers of the word" to what constitutes true religion, it is still possible to see how James' mind is working. The link-term is that of self-deception, applicable to both the uncomprehending person in v 24 and the individual who refuses to bridle his tongue and is thereby deceived into imagining that religion of mere profession is good enough. We incline to accord to χαλιναγ-ωγεῖν, lit., "to check or guide an animal by placing an iron bit in its mouth," as in 3:2–3 of horses (cf. *Rhetores Graeci* 1.425.19: with ἵππον)—a word found only in James in the NT vocabulary (BGD, 874) but given a moralizing sense in *Herm. Man.* 12.1.1, cf. Betz, *Lukian,* 193 n. 2—a specific meaning here and in chap. 3. James is holding up to condemnation the picture of the use of the tongue when it utters merely formal religious platitudes that have no substance evidenced by practical deeds. The present verse looks back to v 19 with the caution to be "slow to speak" and more especially it looks on to 2:15, 18 where the objector says that he can demonstrate his type of faith by deeds when all he means is that he bids the needy look after themselves. He is content to repose confidence in a confession of monotheistic belief. These statements are for James' opponent enough to make him "religious" (θρησκός—a rare adjective, attested only here in scripture, but formed evidently from θρησκεία, a term for "religion" found in Wisd Sol 14:18, 27 where it is coupled with idolatry, εἰδώλων θρησκεία; in Josephus, *Ant.* 1.222; 4.74; 5.339; 9.273–74; 12.253, 271, where it is used of Judaism, as also in *1 Clem.* 45.7). The other NT references are in Acts 26:5, which employs it of Jewish worship and practice, and Col 2:18, where it is said to characterize a veneration devoted to or practiced by angels in the Colossian philosophy. The sparsity of NT references, however, stands in contrast to the popularity of the term in later Christian writers, e.g., *1 Clem.* 62.1: "The things that befit our religion"; *Diogn.* 3.2, which compares Jewish and Christian worship; and the frequency of the term in the apologists is evident. θρησκεία on its negative side for James has the sense of worship and belief as expressed in religious observance or profession (*TDNT* 3:155–59) when it fails to measure up to the standards set in v 27. Where religion does not conform to the criteria set in the words θρησκεία καθαρὰ καὶ ἀμίαντος (lit., "religion that is pure and unstained"—both originally OT cultic terms which it is the duty of the priest, according to Ezek 22:26, to foster: Hauck, *TDNT* 3:419, but moralized in this letter), then James pronounces the professed religion as μάταιος, "futile." He will return the same negative verdict in 2:20, 26 regarding a spurious faith that fails to express itself in deeds and so is branded as both "futile" and "dead."

The positive evidence of sound religion is then spelled out. The two ways are (1) to take care (ἐπισκέπτεσθαι as in Matt 25:36, 43; Sir 7:35) of orphans and widows (who are often linked in OT writings, e.g., Exod 22:21; Deut 10:18; 14:28; 16:11, 14; 24:17–21; 26:12–13; 27:19; Ps 68:5; Isa 1:17; Jer 5:28; Ezek 22:7; Zech 7:10); and (2) to maintain (τηρεῖν) a moral purity (ἄσπιλος: another cultic term matching ἀμίαντος in the first part of the verse [cf. 1 Pet 1:19] but given in our text a moral flavor as in 1 Tim 6:14; 2 Pet 3:14 ἀμίαντος carries the same force in 1 Pet 1:4).

Orphans and widows are joined because they represent two social classes open to exploitation and θλῖψις ("affliction") in Israel, as in Isa 1:10–17; 58:6–7; Zech 7:10; Mark 12:40; Luke 18:2–8 (Jeremias, *Parables,* 153). Yahweh is known as the special protector of these needy ones (Deut 10:18; Ps 68:5); and a special blessing is given to their human preservers:

Be like a father to orphans,
and instead of a husband to their mother;
you will then be like a son of the Most High,
and he will love you more than does your mother.

(Sir 4:10)

The "affliction" spoken of in the term θλῖψις may anticipate the eschatological woes preceding the endtime (which is the common NT idea behind the word; Schlier, *TDNT* 3:144); so Laws (89–90), who also notes that James may be using eschatological language to offer guidance amid the current stresses of his readers (as in 1:2, 12; 5:7, 9). His expectation of an imminent Parousia in chap. 5 suggests a type of "realized" eschatology in which he plays down the current search for signs by pointing to more obvious social maladies that cry out for divine intervention and redress. The application of this ethical teaching will be apparent in 2:5–7.

The second feature of a religious profession that is acceptable before God the Father (παρὰ τῷ θεῷ καὶ πατρὶ: the preposition suggests "in the presence of," equivalent to לִפְנֵי, *lipeneēy;* cf. Wisd Sol 2:16; 3 Macc 5:7) is expressed as keeping oneself (ἑαυτὸν τηρεῖν: 1 Tim 5:22; Wisd Sol 10:5: "Wisdom preserved [ἐτήρησεν] the blameless man before God") unsullied by moral evil and so setting a distance between oneself and the world (κόσμος). The latter term has in this letter a range of meanings extending from the social ambience of the readers (2:5: "poor in the eyes of the world" if τῷ κόσμῳ is treated as dat. of [dis]advantage) to the alien sphere (3:6) which believers must steer clear of if they would retain friendship with God (4:4). The term then has a moral connotation throughout the letter, akin to 1 John 2:14–15, cf. John 14–17; Eph 2:2; Titus 2:12; 2 Pet 1:4; 2:20, and similar to Jewish negative attitudes in apocalyptic literature (*1 Enoch* 48.7; 108:8; *T. Iss.* 4:6: so Windisch).

To guard oneself from (ἀπό) worldly influence may seem to be an ethical call to asceticism and the practice of a recluse. But James' stress is very much on life *in* society where he detects corrupting influences at work (4:1–10, 13–17; 5:1–6). His admonition is for the readers to retain and guard their distinctive ethos as practitioners of true piety. The variant reading of ᴘ[74] (ὑπερασπίζειν, "to protect") gives one side of the meaning admirably, though we have rejected it (see *Note* c). The moral tone set by ἄσπιλος should be given a counterbalancing positive weight (Turner, *Christian Words*, 483, who indicates the eschatological dimension of the word).

Above all, the author's pericope is a polemical one. The target in his sights is, however, not a distinction between cultic or ceremonial religion and its opposite, but the control of the tongue (Mussner, 113). The speaker either promotes true "piety of action" on behalf of the needy or his profession leads to self-deception when he says but does not do.

Explanation

The overruling theme in this section is the definition and practice of true religion. "Religion" (1:27) and its adjective form "religious" in v 26 cannot be regarded as popular terms in modern theology, and they were the *bête noire* and target of Karl Barth's attack. *Religion ist die Angelegenheit des gottlosen Menschen*: "Religion is the affair of godless man" sums up his attitude. To him religion savored of humanistic liberalism against which he rebelled. In terms of biblical word-usage Barth has a strong case. The actual term is found only three times in the NT, each with a different—mainly negative— connotation (elsewhere Acts 26:5; Col 2:18). But James uses the word positively and gives it a content in terms of practical Christianity. Perhaps the word may be reclaimed by offering two observations. First, it stands for the outward expression of faith in liturgy and worship (Barclay), and so it reminds us that however inward-looking and individualistic personal trust must be there is also a horizontal plane on which true faith operates. Faith unites us to God in Christ; it also relates us to our fellow men and women. We need a term such as "religion" to assure us that faith has a social context and is never adequately covered by the dictum, "What a man does with his solitariness" (A. N. Whitehead).

Second, much depends on how the word is defined. Richard Holloway offers the following: Religion is "the celebration of God and the discovery of his will for our lives" (*The Way of the Cross* [London: Collins, 1986] 26). This excellent way of accounting for the whole essence of the Christian religion is very much on James' wavelength. It also invites us to consider the various ways in which religion is applied by those who "claim to be religious" (1:26).

Strangely, James goes to the various parts of the human body to express his application. He presents the anatomy of worship by a recourse to body language; thereby his writing carries a universal appeal since all religious exercise, except the most philosophical and ethereal, involves bodily movement. This factor imparts a timeless appeal to what he says in 1:19b–27.

The following anatomical features may be observed: (1) There is the controlled tongue (1:19b), which is a theme to be expanded in 3:1–12 and reintroduced at the close of the letter in 4:22; 5:12. The warning here is directed to one particular kind of wrong speech, namely hasty utterances, spoken without due reflection or consideration of their consequences. It is a commonplace observation, going back to Zeno of Citium, the founder of Stoicism, that human beings have two ears but one mouth that they may hear twice as much as they speak. (2) Obedient ears are therefore needed to listen for the truth and receive it with a willing and unprejudiced disposition (v 21). The author knows that this is not easy since we tend to hear selectively and to filter out unwanted or unpleasant truth. Hence there is the call to "get rid of all evil" that could block the passage and cause our hearing to be less than total or accurate. The quasi-medical terminology in this verse may contribute to this advice. What is clear and beyond dispute is the way James insists on a willingness on the part of his readers to expose themselves to God's word of grace even when it rebukes their follies and foibles (v 20). (3) The little story (*narratiuncula*) of vv 23–25 is telling in its effect and full of pathos and humor. He begins with the recall that it is a privilege to look into God's law, later to be lauded as "royal" (2:8) and promising freedom (1:25; 2:12). But the observant eye must do more than merely "see"; it must see not "with" but "through" the eye, to use William Blake's language; and having penetrated to the real essence of God's truth, the person must be ready to act upon it. The emphasis falls on "doing" as much as on "hearing" and "seeing." And in the parable of the mirror James applies the comparison in pointed fashion.

In a looking glass of polished bronze or an alloy of tin and copper a less-than-perfect image is seen (1 Cor 13:12), but it does at least reveal some defects needing attention. The foolish person takes note, but promptly forgets what is seen. It is the mark of wisdom to attend to what is needed and *then to do it.* The soul of the religion is expressed in the practical value it gives to action and endeavor, not simply contemplation.

A deeper meaning may be here too. The wording of v 23, as was said earlier, recalls Gen 1:26–27 with its picture of man as *imago Dei,* reflecting the divine likeness. James may be consciously calling into play this link between God's design and human destiny. The foolish person catches only a fleeting glance of who he or she really is by a cursory look in a mirror. Preoccupation with lesser things distracts, and nothing further is done. The wise person takes a longer, deeper look and finds what is the character God intended as mirrored in the "law that sets [us] free" from imprisoning, egocentric horizons. That person, catching sight of all that God purposes for life in "the word," both written and incarnate in the glorious Lord (2:1), is bidden to rise to full potential and attain what Paul surnames as one's "high calling in Christ" (Phil 3:14) or later is called "the full measure of perfection found in Christ" (Eph 4:13; cf. 2 Cor 3:18; Gal 4:19).

(4) Yet such a vision needs translating into practical down-to-earth terms; otherwise self-deception, caused either by sheer forgetfulness or a false appreciation of religion as mere ecstasy or emotion, sets in. The employing of a helping hand means that the readers cannot escape the summons to do what lies in their power: to come to the aid of defenseless members of society and reach out actively on their behalf (1:27). Yet living in the world, where James locates the praxis of the religious people, poses a threat which they must be aware of, as 4:1–6 will illustrate.

Kierkegaard made much of this section to drive a firm line between true religion and mock religiosity. More simply, the verses lay on us the mandate to match the word of the gospel with its action.

2. Problems in the Assembly   (2:1–13)

Bibliography

Bousset, W. *Kyrios Christos: A History of the Belief in Christ from the Beginnings of Christianity to Irenaeus.* Tr. J. E. Steely. Nashville: Abingdon, 1970. **Braumann, G.** "Der theologische Hintergrund des Jakobusbriefes." *TZ* 18 (1962) 401–10. **Brinktrine, J.** "Zu Jak 2.1." *Bib* 35 (1954) 40–42. **Burchard, Ch.** "Gemeinde in der strohernen Epistel." In *Kirche,* FS G. Bornkamm, ed. D. Lührmann and G. Strecker. Tübingen: Mohr, 1980. 315–28. ———. "Zu Jakobus 2,14–26." *ZNW* 71 (1980) 27–45. **Dyrness, W.** "Mercy Triumphs over Justice: James 2:13 and the Theology of Faith and Works." *Themelios* 6

(1981) 11–16. **Furfey, P. H.** "*Plousios* and Cognates in the New Testament." *CBQ* 5 (1943) 243–63. **Heitmüller, W.** *Im Namen Jesu*. Göttingen: Vandenhoeck und Ruprecht, 1903. **Hengel, M.** *Property and Riches in the Early Church*. Tr. J. Bowden. London: SCM, 1974. **Johnson, L. T.** *Sharing Possessions*. Philadelphia: Fortress, 1981. ———. "The Use of Leviticus 19 in the Letter of James." *JBL* 101 (1982) 391–401. **Judge, E. A.** *The Social Pattern of the Christian Groups in the First Century*. London: Tyndale Press, 1960. **Keck, L. E.** "The Poor among the Saints in Jewish Christianity and Qumran." *ZNW* 57 (1966) 54–78. ———. "The Poor among the Saints in the New Testament." *ZNW* 56 (1965) 100–129. **Kilpatrick, G. D.** "Übertreter des Gesetzes, Jak 2,11." *TZ* 23 (1967) 433. **Longenecker, R. N.** *The Christology of Early Jewish Christianity*. SBT 17, 2d ser. London: SCM, 1970. **Massebieau, L.** "L'épître de Jacques, est-elle l'oeuvre d'un chrétien?" *RHR* 16 vol. 32 (1895) 249–83. **Maynard-Reid, P. U.** *Poverty and Wealth*, chap. 4. **Meyer, A.** *Das Rätsel des Jakobusbriefes*. BZNW 10. Giessen: Töpelmann, 1930. **Montefiore, H. W.** "Thou Shalt Love Thy Neighbour as Thyself." *NovT* 5 (1902) 157–70. **Rost, L.** "Archäologische Bermerkungen zu einer Stelle des Jakobusbriefs (Jak. 2,2f.)." *PJ* 29 (1933) 53–66. **Trocmé, E.** "Les églises pauliniennes vues du dehors: Jac 2,1 à 3,13." *SE* 2, *TU* 87 (1964) 660–69. **Ward, R. B.** "Partiality in the Assembly." *HTR* 62 (1969) 87–97.

Translation

2:1 *My brothers, you should not try to combine* [a] *the faith of our glorious* [b] *Lord Jesus Christ with [the practice of] favoritism.* 2 *To illustrate: if a man enters your meeting wearing a gold ring and dressed in splendid clothes, and if also a beggar in filthy clothes comes in, and* 3 *you pay attention to the man with the splendid clothes and invite him, "Do sit here, if you will," but to the beggar you say, "You, stand there* [c]—*or sit here at my feet,"* 4 *have you not become divided among yourselves,* [d] *and so become criminally minded judges?*

5 *Hear this, my dear brothers! Did not God choose those who are poor in the eyes of the world* [e] *to become wealthy in faith and sharers in the kingdom promised by him to those who love him?* 6 *Yet you have disgraced the poor person. Is it not the rich people who exploit you? Is it not they who hale you before tribunals?* 7 *Is it not they who bring into disgrace the fine name by which you have been called [and are known]?* 8 *If you truly fulfill the supreme law according to the Scripture "You shall love your neighbor as yourself," you do right.* 9 *But if you show favoritism you commit sin, and you are convicted by the law as transgressors.* 10 *It follows that if a person keeps* [f] *the entire law but stumbles over one item he has become guilty in all points.* 11 *For He who said, "Do not commit adultery," said also, "Do not murder." If you do not commit adultery but do commit murder, you become a transgressor* [g] *of the law.* 12 *Speak and act as those who are to be judged by the law that sets free.* 13 *Judgment is merciless to the one who has shown no mercy; yet mercy triumphs over judgment.*

Notes

[a] Giving to the verb ἔχετε a conative force. Some interpreters, such as Goodspeed, opt for this sense; and Chaine takes the sentence as a question: "Are you holding the faith . . . ?" (but the μή argues against this; see Mussner, 115 n.1).

[b] τῆς δόξης is a difficult phrase. The translation above interprets it as an adjective. See the *Comment* section for other possibilities.

[c]Reading στῆθι (in contrast to the preceding κάθου spoken to the rich person) ἐκεῖ ἢ κάθου (picking up the previous verb). This is the reading of A C*vid Ψ and some minuscules vg syr[h]. The order ἢ κάθου ἐκεῖ in B, though preferred by Ropes, is best explained as due to a scribal misunderstanding (see Metzger, *Textual Commentary,* 680–81).

[d]διεκρίθητε is disputed, not textually but interpretatively (see Ropes, 192, who prefers the sense of "waver" [as in 1:6]). The presence of the phrase ἐν ἑαυτοῖς, "among yourselves," however, argues against this meaning (BGD, 212; Chaine, 44) and in favor of either the sense "discriminate," "make a distinction" (Davids, 110), or "divide." The former meaning is that James is accusing his (Christian) readers of discriminating between social classes, i.e., the sin is that of προσωποληψία in 2:1 (Oesterley, 437); the latter, which the translation above follows, is that the church was divided over how to treat the rich and the poor (so Dibelius, 136; Blackman, 79). But clearly there are several possible nuances.

[e]τῷ κόσμῳ (ℵ B) is *dat. commodi* (Windisch, 15) rather than dative of respect (Moule, *Idiom Book,* 46, 204). The phrase is smoothed over by A² C² K L P with the reading τοῦ κοσμοῦ (Ropes, 194).

[f]On the grammatical usage here—τηρήσῃ as a gnomic aorist but without ἄν—see Davids, 116, citing Moule, *Idiom Book,* 123–24; Moulton-Howard-Turner, *Grammar* 3:106–8. Textually the subjunctive becomes fut. indic. in TR A.

[g]The reading ἀποστάτης in P⁷⁴ influenced by the Latin (reading *praevaricator*) of Rom 2:25–27 is defended by Kilpatrick, "Übertreter," 433, who thinks that παραβάτης is repetitious and derives from v 9. Admittedly there is then a progression in the author's thought, climaxing in the warning against apostasy.

Form / Structure / Setting

This pericope is to be isolated as the third in James' series of themes: a warning against a disparaging of the poor and a preference for the rich in the community (Windisch, 13). Earlier, in 1:9–11, 22–27, the author's contrast between those in humble position and the wealthy has been drawn, with practical illustration. Now the same idea is pictured by the dramatic encounter with the two social types when they enter the assembly.

There are two possibilities of the *mise en scène.* James is either describing the churches gathered for worship, assuming that συναγωγή in v 2 means the meeting place on the (Christian) sabbath, or writing against the background of a church court where the congregation has come together to hear a judicial case (συναγωγή then refers to an aspect of Christian assembly, akin to 1 Cor 6:1–6; cf. Matt 18:15–20, borrowed from the function of the Jewish synagogue as a בֵּית־דִּין, *bēṯ-dîn,* lit., "house of judgment": see W. Schrage, *TDNT* 7:840–41; Rost, "Archäologische Bermerkungen." Ward, "Partiality," 92 n.22, has shown that συναγωγή can be taken to refer to a judicial situation).

In the former case, James' descriptions—even if they are purely theoretical (as Davids, 107, inclines to believe, based on the supposititious phrasing ἐὰν . . . εἰσέλθῃ)—relate to a setting in public worship, and the rich and poor are cast in the role of occasional visitors (Laws, 99–100) or new converts seeking to identify themselves with a local Christian group. That group entails a Jewish Christian community, and their composition is reflected in the use of συναγωγή rather than ἐκκλησία (Adamson, 105). The alternative setting, described by Ward, "Partiality," has, however, much to commend it for two particular reasons: he proposed that the scene in these verses is that of a congregation gathered to dispense justice and found Jewish parallels as evidence of the need for impartiality, which would be called in question by the litigants who dressed themselves in fine clothes to impress the assembly and were given good seats as a mark of respect. The second reason for supposing that this law-court setting is to be preferred lies in the wording of v 6: "the rich people hale you before tribunals," which is James' indictment of a division within the community (v 4). The forensic-social language reads more naturally if the scene is one of a church met to consider some legal problem. Then, the folly of the attitude of favoritism, προσωπολημψία (in v 1), is much in prominence as James rebukes it.

This section, in fact, brings no fewer than three charges against the readers. First, they are guilty of social snobbery and partiality, which runs counter to the character of God (vv 1–5). Second, they are strangely and ironically short-sighted. In siding with the rich—here, at v 5, the scope of the argument broadens to include the general situation of how rich persons treat the poor—the readers are taking the part of those who are their opponents and oppressors (vv 6–7). Finally, the social malaise and the topsy-turvy situation where misguided Christians actually prefer to play up to their persecuting foes, is given by the author the name of sin (vv 8–13) as he turns the debate to side with the poor. For James sin is regarded as an infraction of the "supreme [lit., 'royal'] law," found in Lev 19:18, "You shall love your neighbor as yourself." When favoritism implies that the poor neighbor is treated with disdain and his social rights abridged, then the community commits active transgression (v 9); and the same law that is broken turns upon the offenders and "convicts" them as "lawbreakers" (παραβάται, v 9, repeated in the singular in v 11: *pace* Kilpatrick, "Übertreter"; see *Note* g).

The closing mention of "lawbreaker" in v 11 is the link-term to connect with the short subsection (vv 12–13) that enables the editor to state positively what is the true function of "law," not to condemn but to set free, and to promise God's compassion to those who in turn appreciate it in so far as they also are compassionate. The association with the (Matthean) Gospel tradition of Jesus' teaching is evident (see Matt 5:7; 6:14,15; 7:12; 18:22–35). The effect of this parenetic section, cast in the hortatory imperative mood, is to drive home the central point, illustrated by the base treatment of the poor in vv 2–3. The case of the (obvious) poor person, seen in his ragged clothing and willingness to be set in the servile place, shows how the readers had closed their hearts against the socially deprived and had adopted a hard attitude. This suggests to James that they had no evident need of "mercy" from God and were full of pride. He will take up this point in detail later (4:11–12; 5:9).

The tenor of James' argumentation is one of considerable subtlety and sophistication. He moves from an indictment of the audience's paradoxical preference of the rich (vv 6–7) to a crusade on behalf of the poor. The latter's claim to fair dealing and justice is anchored in traditional Jewish convictions, namely that God has chosen the poor to be his elect ones and inheritors of his kingdom (v 5). It is they who belong to God (implied in v 7). Then, his position is that only as the poor are respected and their rights honored in the community can the "law of God" be fulfilled. In typical Jewish-rabbinic style of reasoning, he claims that Lev 19:18 is the summation of the Torah (see C. G. Montefiore and H. Loewe, *Rabbinic Anthology* [New York: Schocken, 1974 ed.] 199, for other attempts to reduce the Torah to a "single item"—

ἐν ἑνί, v 10—with the converse that the Torah-Decalogue is a seamless fabric that cannot be treated piecemeal). This "love of one's neighbor" (as in Rom 13:8–10; Gal 5:14) is the obverse side of the "piety of the poor" motif that stresses how God favors the underprivileged in Israel who trust in him. The use of Lev 19:18 is interesting, since the appeal to impartiality in 2:1—echoed in 2:9 with the verb προσωπολημπτεῖν—may go back to Lev 19:15: "you shall do no injustice in judgment; you shall not be partial to the poor nor defer to the great, but you are to judge your neighbor fairly."

Comment

1 Ἀδελφοί μου, μὴ ἐν προσωπολημψίαις ἔχετε τὴν πίστιν τοῦ κυρίου ἡμῶν Ἰησοῦ Χριστοῦ τῆς δόξης, "My brothers, you should not try to combine the faith of our glorious Lord Jesus Christ with [the practice of] favoritism." The author's address is frequent in parenetic passages, especially when the style is that of diatribe (1:2; 2:1, 14; 3:1, 10, 12; 5:12, 19). The plain "brothers" occurs in 4:11; 5:7, 9, 10, while the more engaging "my dear brothers" is found in 1:16, 19; 2:5. We may trace here a homiletic style, patterned on Jewish hortatory literature.

The caution against προσωπολημψία, lit., "lifting up the face," Heb. נָשָׂא פָנִים, *nāśā' pānîm*, uses an OT expression that had gone through several stages of development ranging from an attitude of general acceptance to the idea of favoritism and unwonted preference. In the latter sense it characterized the wrongfulness of Israel's leaders who inclined to favor the powerful rich and mighty and were therefore reproved (Ps 82:2; Prov 6:35; 18:5; 24:23; 28:31; Mal 1:8; 2:9; Sir 4:22: for the development of the word in the NT see Acts 10:34; Rom 2:11; Col 3:25; Eph 6:9; 1 Pet 1:17 and beyond in Poly. *Phil.* 6.1; *1 Clem.* 1.3; *Barn.* 4.12. Cf. Turner, *Christian Words*, 366–67).

The situation in James' community evidently entailed preferential treatment given to the wealthy on the occasion of their coming into the church assembly either at worship time or when the congregation had gathered to hear a legal case. The latter occasion is more probable in the light of the forensic terms in vv 4, 6, 9. The folly James excoriates is that of the bid of these influential persons to win favor and be regarded with esteem by the community, which is equally to be condemned for its practice of favoritism. The reference to τὴν πίστιν τοῦ κυρίου ἡμῶν Ἰησοῦ Χριστοῦ, "the faith of [i.e., "in"] our glorious Lord Jesus Christ," marks out the distinctive belief of this Jewish Christian group. If 2:14–26 is closely connected to this section, as Burchard, "Zu Jakobus 2," 27–45 (especially 28–30), thinks, then the mere profession of faith as a creedal confession (see 2:19) was being regarded as sufficient without the necessary complement of good deeds; and in that way the church was erring grievously in offering a too-ready welcome to the rich inquirers, whether viewed as pagans or new converts. See later.

The genitive τῆς δόξης attached to the end of the creedal "our Lord Jesus Christ" which, with 1:1, is the clearest sign of the Christian origin of the letter, is much debated. The troublesome feature is that it is a genitive phrase coming in a series of such grammatical usages; this leads to one extreme conclusion that ἡμῶν Ἰησοῦ Χριστοῦ or τῆς δόξης is a later interpolation to give a Christian flavor to an otherwise Jewish document (so Spitta, Massebieau, Meyer; and Windisch, who speaks of "a clumsy piling up of genitives," 13). Reading the phrase as integral to the textual evidence (though it is missing from minuscules 33, 429), as we should, we are left with a variety of renderings: (1) faith in the glory of our Lord Jesus Christ (so Zahn, *Introduction to the New Testament* 1:151, who can appeal to the way the text is read in min 614, syrᴾ in support; but the position of τῆς δόξης, separated as it is from πίστιν, is against it). (2) With τῆς δόξης taken to modify κυρίου the translation runs "faith in our Lord of glory, Jesus Christ" (KJV/AV/RV; Burchard, "Gemeinde," 322 n.52). 1 Cor 2:8 is then parallel, at least in thought but not in precise wording. (3) τῆς δόξης is regarded by others (Hort, Laws, Mayor) as a genitive of apposition, following Bengel's lead. The result now is that "the Glory" becomes a title, "our Lord Jesus Christ, the Glory." It is possible, according to this view, that early Jewish Christian believers hailed Jesus as the Shekinah or visible manifestation of the divine splendor (*TDNT* 2:237; Maynard-Reid, *Poverty*, 50–52, who discusses the force in the genitive after πίστιν, i.e., whether it is subjective or [more likely] objective), a Hebrew name that is carried over into Greek as ἡ δόξα (*ut ipse Christus dicatur ἡ δόξα*, Bengel). NEB carries this view a step farther by giving the genitive a locative meaning: "our Lord Jesus Christ, who reigns in glory." But these translations are more of a paraphrase. (4) The simplest solution of a difficult set of words is to take τῆς δόξης as adjectival, "faith in our glorious Lord Jesus Christ." There are parallels to this usage in 1:25, ἀκροατὴς ἐπιλησμονῆς, lit., "a hearer of forgetfulness," i.e., a forgetful hearer, and in 2:4; and the word order of these verses is best explained by this view (so Cantinat, Chaine, Ropes, Mussner, Davids, Vouga). The point of the ascription "glorious" will be a paradoxical one: Christian faith centers, for James, in the person of a glorious figure who nonetheless abased himself to identify with the poor and cast in his lot with the despised and oppressed to whom the kingdom is promised (v 5). But this is an extension of meaning James does not explicitly draw out, though Scaer (72) typically does and maximizes the Christological significance.

2 ἐὰν γὰρ εἰσέλθη εἰς συναγωγὴν ὑμῶν ἀνὴρ χρυσοδακτύλιος ἐν ἐσθῆτι λαμπρᾷ, εἰσέλθη δὲ καὶ πτωχὸς ἐν ῥυπαρᾷ ἐσθῆτι, "To illustrate, if a man enters your meeting wearing a gold ring and dressed in splendid clothes, and if also a beggar in filthy clothes comes in." This verse begins a question that extends through v 4 and is shaped so as to expect an affirmative answer (οὐ). The conjunction γάρ is translated here "to illustrate" and shows that James connects the thought of 2:1 with what follows (though it may well be that James also has the contents of 1:27 in mind. The subject of the "poor" in the following verses surely includes the treatment of the orphan and widow). James extends the notion of v 1 with the illustration of vv 2–3. ἐάν, "if," introduces a third class condition and suggests to some (Davids, 107; Moo, 89) an example or hypothetical situation, not an actual happening in the church (see, Dibelius, 129, modified by Trocmé, "Les églises," 661, 668). It is better, however, to understand vv 2–3 as depicting a familiar scene, which is implied by the use of the indicative mood in what follows (especially vv 4, 6, 7) The later situation in vv 6–7—where the rich oppress and insult the poor—surely depicts an actual happening in James' church, and it makes little sense to combine reality (vv 4–7) with a hypothetical example (vv 2–3). Vv 2, 3 are an example of the "iterative case in present time" (BDF § 371.4).

James, then, has the following scene in view: two men, one rich and one poor, enter "the meeting" (συναγωγή). The use of συναγωγή here is unusual, for the more common term ἐκκλησία (used in 5:14) might have been expected. If συναγωγή does stand for the church here, then this is the only use of the term in this manner in the NT. It is not clear whether James means the place of meeting in a building, or the assembly of people (BGD 783). Both ideas may merge into each other (Schrage, *TDNT* 7:837–38), though the latter receives stronger support from the context (Mussner, 117). As the earlier discussion has shown (p. 57), συναγωγή (assuming it means "the meeting") could pertain either to a public worship service or a congregational gathering for the purpose of hearing a judicial case. The former interpretation has some credibility because the term is used in this sense in early Christian literature (see Epiphanius, *Haer.* 30.18; also see Ign. *Pol.* 4.2; *Trall.* 3; *Herm. Man.* 11.9, 13, 14), and such a meaning could have been understood by a Jewish Christian congregation (see Adamson, 105). But the verses that follow suggest that the type of meeting referred to in this instance is one that was called to function along the lines of a church court (see 1 Cor 6:1–16; cf. Matt 18:15–20).

The situation that James describes for his readers is one of extremes expressed in "hyperbole," according to Davids, 107. On the one hand, there enters the rich man, described as having gold rings (a sign of social status: in *m. Kelim* 11.8 worn by women; 12.1 worn by men), and fine clothing. Davids, 108, observes that the conventional word πλούσιος is not used here, thus suggesting a circumlocution for wealthy Christians or pagans, depending on how the identity of the person in v 3 is understood (see Windisch, 14: "very likely" a pagan; Schrage, 25; and Burchard, "Gemeinde," 323, who argues from the data in 2:6–7 and 1 Cor 14:23–24. But how to treat pagans would hardly cause division, and Burchard has to make an appeal to the way [he believes] the discussion views the rich and the poor *sub specie aeternitatis*, which is most improbable. See also 4:13–17). The composite term for "wearing a gold ring" is χρυσοδακτύλιος (lit., "[of] gold" + "worn on the finger"; a *hapax legomenon*). Further, James describes the rich man as wearing clothes (ἐσθής) of splendor (λαμπρός), lit., "brightly shining garments" (see Luke 23:11; Acts 10:30; Rev 18:11). Reicke, 27, thinks that this description fits one who has senatorial rank (a member of the *equites;* Cicero, *In Verrem* 3.76, 176; Suetonius, *Div. Iulius* 33; cf. E. A. Judge, *Social Pattern,* 53) or is seeking political office as a magistrate whose badge of office was *toga candida* (Polyb. 10.5.1). His visit to a congregation for support would not be out of the question, if he had that intention. But the wearing of fine garments and rings was generally a mark of opulence and ostentation (Epictetus, *Diss.* 1.22.18; cf. Seneca, *Nat. Quaest.* 7.31–32: *exornamus anulis digitos in omni articulo gemma disponitur,* "we adorn our fingers with rings; a gem is fitted to every joint").

On the other hand, in stark contrast is the πτωχός, "poor man." He is characterized as dressed in "filthy" clothes (ῥυπαρός, from ῥύπος: see 1:21; cf. 1

Pet 3:21 and Rev 22:11). Thus, James has described for us a setting of contrasts that depicts one in "new glossy clothes and [one in] old shabby clothes" (Hort). No one could fail to see his point.

3 ἐπιβλέψητε δὲ ἐπὶ τὸν φοροῦντα τὴν ἐσθῆτα τὴν λαμπρὰν καὶ εἴπητε, Σὺ κάθου ὧδε καλῶς, καὶ τῷ πτωχῷ εἴπητε, Σὺ στῆθι ἐκεῖ ἢ κάθου ὑπὸ τὸ ὑποπόδιόν μου, "And you pay attention to the man with the splendid clothes and invite him, 'Do sit here, if you will,' but to the beggar you say, 'You, stand there—or sit here at my feet.'" δέ, "and," is a continuation, not an adversative (1:14). The two men who have entered the meeting are probably visitors (Laws, 99–100) or at least new converts, since it appears that they are unfamiliar with the type of convocation in progress; otherwise they would not have needed instructions as to their respective places.

ἐπιβλέψητε (aorist subjunctive, still with the ἐάν construction: cf. v 2), "look at" or "pay attention to," is found only here and in Luke (1:48; 9:38) and is always followed by the preposition ἐπί. The earlier verse in Luke is from the Magnificat where Mary praises God because he has "regarded" the lowly condition of his handmaiden. In Lukan thought, representing some Palestinian community (*ISBE* 3:220–21), God is praised for demonstrating his care for the poor and humble. This attitude is evidently unfortunately absent from the congregation to which James writes. It is not that he openly seeks a bias in favor of the poor, but simply pleads for a recognition of equality on their behalf.

V 3 describes the actions James deplores. The clauses Σὺ κάθου ὧδε καλῶς ("Do sit here, if you will") and Σὺ στῆθι ἐκεῖ ἢ κάθου ὑπὸ τὸ ὑποπόδιόν μου ("You, stand there—or sit here at my feet") betray an unchristian attitude (see Dibelius, 132; Adamson, 106–7) exhibited toward the rich man and poor man respectively (Davids, 109, wonders whether, if the assembly was gathered for a worship service, some would be standing during the entire time). Those who are displaying behavior incompatible with faith in Christ (2:1) exhort the wealthy visitor to sit "here" (ὧδε), probably a direction to take the best seat in the synagogue, namely the seat of honor (see Matt 23:6: seating has to do with status; see Maynard-Reid, *Poverty,* 55). But the poor man is commanded "to stand there" (ἐκεῖ, suggesting a location away from the speaker; see also *Note* c) or "to sit at the feet" of the speaker (implied by μου); this suggests a rank of submission or disgrace (cf. Pss 99:5; 110:1; 132:7; Isa 66:1; Lam 2:1; Matt 5:35). (Note the double use of εἴπητε, still in the aorist subjunctive because of the ἐάν clause and added for emphasis in writing.) Whether he stands away from the speaker or at his feet, the poor man has received the brunt of the social snobbery and discrimination of those Christians in the synagogue. It may be conjectured that those (note εἴπητε is plural) who gave the seating instructions probably held some degree of authority in the congregation, though no office such as "doorkeeper" (*ostiarius,* in the later church) is envisaged. Thus, it is not unfair to say that these speakers set the tone for much, but not all (2:4), of the congregation, which took its cue from those in a role of leadership. It might even be that some of these so-called leaders acted as teachers of the congregation. If so, the unfavorable attitude shown toward those of lower social rank is even more deplorable (3:2). James appears to be talking to a congregation rife with practices of discrimination.

4 οὐ διεκρίθητε ἐν ἑαυτοῖς καὶ ἐγένεσθε κριταὶ διαλογισμῶν πονηρῶν, "Have you not become divided among yourselves, and so become criminally minded judges?" With v 4 we reach the apodosis of the long conditional sentence beginning with v 2, which is expressed in the form of a question (introduced by οὐ) expecting an affirmative answer. Both verbs in this verse are aorist, sometimes understood as gnomic. This would leave us with nothing more than a maxim which says "if you act a certain way (to show partiality), then you are definitely guilty of discrimination." But there is no proof that the use of ἐάν in vv 2–3 constitutes a hypothetical situation. More than likely, James is referring to an oft-repeated scene and the use of ἐάν may be his way of conveying to his readers his hope (or conviction) that such ill-mannered practice will not take place any more (see Robertson, *Grammar*, 1022, for a discussion of the possibility of mixed conditions; cf. 1 Cor 7:28).

οὐ διεκρίθητε ἐν ἑαυτοῖς, "have you not been divided among yourselves?" The verb διακρίνεσθαι can be taken (in the active voice) to mean the practice "of making distinctions [among yourselves]" (so RSV), as in the action of discriminating between the rich and the poor. Yet while discrimination may be implied (see Mitton, 84) the text appears to be emphasizing in v 4 the division in the church over the proper treatment accorded to the rich and poor (see *Note* d). The verb should, then, be taken as passive voice ("being divided"; but see also Dibelius, 136–37).

James has already used διακρίνεσθαι in 1:6 to describe a person who doubts (BGD, 185; Ropes, 192), reflecting the inner conflict of one who lacks firm faith. The instability mentioned suggests a person who is divided in his or her loyalties to God and the world (4:4; cf. Matt 6:24; see Moo, 64). While faith means an unwavering trust in God (which includes the belief that God will give what is asked of him, namely, wisdom), doubt implies that the professed believer trusts in riches for security (4:13—5:6). 1:6 parallels the situation of 2:4, for the latter critique implied in the verb is also related to the question of true and false faith (2:1). The readers are urged not to show partiality as they seek to (*Note* a) hold to the profession of the faith. It may well be that James is tracing the sinful behavior described in vv 2–3 back to its source, namely a divided mind. The double-minded (1:8; 4:8) Christian is the one who fails to love and obey God wholeheartedly. Such a mind is characterized by doubts which are typical of those who lack authentic faith. A divided mind is evidenced by the different treatment meted out to visitors, especially along lines of social class.

The early church in Jerusalem, according to Acts and Paul, faced problems to do with the rich and the poor (Reicke, 28, referring to Gal 2:10; 2 Cor 8–9; Rom 15:22–29; Acts 2:44–5; 5:1–11; 11:29; cf. Keck, "The Poor," *ZNW* 56 [1965] 100–129; Trocmé, "Les églises"; Hengel, *Property*). It is only to be expected that the church members in such a text as purports to reflect early Jewish Christianity would be split over the treatment of the rich and the poor, especially since the actions recorded in vv 2–3 seem to condone (and encourage) the attacks of the rich against the church (6b–7). No doubt members of the church who were poor sympathized with other poor people who, upon visiting the church, were humiliated and embarrassed. In contrast, the rich, despite having the power to harass those weaker than themselves, were accorded recognition with attendant pomp and ceremony. James probably echoes the thought of some in the church when he contends that faith and partiality are mutually exclusive. What he adds is the cautionary reminder that it is inconsistent to enter the assembly, demonstrate one's faith (possibly by recitation of accepted doctrine, 2:19), and then act in accordance with worldly standards (4:4c) by discriminating (a second meaning of the verb) against the poor. Such an action reflects doubt of the truth expressed in v 5 that God has chosen the poor to be honored as rich in faith (see Büchsel, *TDNT* 3:948 and n.12).

καὶ ἐγένεσθε κριταὶ διαλογισμῶν πονηρῶν, "and so have become criminally minded judges?" Some of the audience have become judges (κριταί), usurping the role reserved only for God (Isa 45:23; Rom 14:10–12). They are judges (lit.) "of evil reasonings." This descriptive genitive (or qualitative genitive, so BDF § 165; Reicke, 65 n.14) is an idiom of possible Semitic influence (Moule, *Idiom Book*, 175). διαλογισμός carries with it the idea of "thought" or "opinion" and could also mean "decision," as a technical term in a legal setting (BGD, 186). This forensic language is consistent in the context of a church gathering that is to decide a judicial case. Not only have the writer's opponents become judges; they have rendered evil decisions. The determinations in question consist of choices that lead to discrimination among the visitors. In the expression "criminally minded judges," James appears to be alluding to the partiality (λήμψη πρόσωπον) of being "unjust in judgment" (ἄδικον ἐν κρίσει), condemned in Lev 19:15 (in anticipation of the use of Lev 19:18 in 2:8).

5 Ἀκούσατε, ἀδελφοί μου ἀγαπητοί· οὐχ ὁ θεὸς ἐξελέξατο τοὺς πτωχοὺς τῷ κόσμῳ πλουσίους ἐν πίστει καὶ κληρονόμους τῆς βασιλείας ἧς ἐπηγγείλατο τοῖς ἀγαπῶσιν αὐτόν, "Hear this, my dear brothers! Did not God choose those who are poor in the eyes of the world to become wealthy in faith and sharers in the kingdom promised by him to those who love him?" James commands the attention of his "brothers," i.e., fellow believers, but including "sisters" if the evidence of 2:15 is weighed along with the relevance of Rahab in 2:25 (as Burchard, "Gemeinde," 321, notes)—though James is somewhat removed from the equality stated in Gal 3:28. The use of "dear," "beloved" (ἀγαπητοί) underlines James' affection for his readers. Again, James presents his thoughts in the form of a question; the construction with οὐχ (= *nonne* in Latin) anticipates an affirmative answer. He assumes that his readers already know the veracity of the thoughts to be presented.

οὐχ ὁ θεὸς ἐξελέξατο, "Did not God choose . . . ?" The verb (ἐκλέγεσθαι) is concerned with election (see below and Quell-Schrenk, *TDNT* 4:144–76; see also 1 Cor 1:27). The use of the middle voice here as elsewhere in the NT probably underscores the thought that the action performed is of special significance to the subject (i.e., God). The verb is followed by the object of desire and action: τοὺς πτωχοὺς τῷ κόσμῳ, "those who are poor in the eyes of the world." This phrase is either dative of respect (poor in the things of the world; so Moule, *Idiom Book*, 46) or an ethical dative (poor in the eyes of the world; so adopted here; cf. Acts 7:20; 1 Cor 1:18; 2 Cor 10:4; see also BGD, 728; also *Note* e). No doubt the idea of "poor" as found in 2:2 carries with it the association of one who has few of this world's possessions. But primarily the term πτωχός in v 5 suggests a religious or ethical significance undergirded by the concept of election. The evaluation that the poor are dear to God was firmly rooted in both Jewish and Christian thinking. Many groups fulfilled the role of God's "chosen": Israel (Deut 4:37; 7:7; 14:2), the socially weak in Israel (Deut 16:3; 26:7; this concept is also found in intertestamental and rabbinic literature; see Davids, 111) and the church (Acts 13:17; 15:7; Eph 1:4; 1 Pet 2:9), which is elected in Christ the chosen one (Luke 9:35). By the time of James, πτωχός was a technical term for the class of pious and humble people who put their trust in God for redemption and not in material wealth (see also A. Richardson, ed., *Theological Word Book*, 168–69). That the ethical idea is James' intention is also seen in the remainder of v 5. He uses the definite article with πτωχός, which suggests that he did not mean to imply that God chose all the poor because they were poor but simply that God chose poor people (Bammel, *TDNT* 6:911).

πλουσίους ἐν πίστει, "to become wealthy in faith" (see Cantinat, 126; Dibelius, 136) or "from the perspective of faith," matching τῷ κόσμῳ (Vouga, 74). "To become" reflects the interpretation that here is an ellipsis of the infinitive εἶναι (BGD, 242). The case of πλουσίους is an example of a double, or predicative, accusative, with the second accusative (πλουσίους) serving in apposition to the first (see Robertson, *Grammar*, 480). The poor are depicted as "rich" by James (see 1:9–11) in that, unlike the rich (in the material sense), they have a place in the kingdom of God. This (messianic) kingdom (βασιλεία) is promised (ἐπηγγείλατο) to the poor, the heirs (κληρονόμους) of faith. (Note that the relative ἧς is attracted to the case of its antecedent, βασιλεία; one might have expected ἥν.) The promise motif is clear from the use of the verb ἐπαγγέλλεσθαι, which is also used in 1:12 where it is said that the person who stands firm in trials and temptations will receive the crown of life which God has "promised to those who love him" (τοῖς ἀγαπῶσιν αὐτόν; the plural participle of ἀγαπᾶν is found in both instances, 1:12; 2:5). While the testings and pressures referred to in 1:3, 12 probably entail much more than our present topic, it cannot be denied that James believed that some of the poor of the church might be receiving the same treatment as that associated with the "poor" visitor. (That is, it is possible that the poor of the church—like the poor visitor— were being discriminated against.) If so, the poor of the church ("economically oppressed and spiritually inclined," Moo, 91; see Luke 6:20; Matt 5:3) also received the rebuff of church leaders.

6 ὑμεῖς δὲ ἠτιμάσατε τὸν πτωχόν· οὐχ οἱ πλούσιοι καταδυναστεύουσιν ὑμῶν καὶ αὐτοὶ ἕλκουσιν ὑμᾶς εἰς κριτήρια, "Yet you have disgraced the poor person. Is it not the rich people who exploit you? Is it not they who hale you before tribunals?" The adversative δέ marks a change in the direction of the appeal. The "you" (ὑμεῖς) is the "dear brother" and sister of v 5 and is emphatic in its use here. The members of the church "disgrace," "dishonor" (so Ropes, 195; ἀτιμάζειν also means "to insult"; see RSV; cf. Prov 14:21; 22:22; Sir 10:23) the poor person (τὸν πτωχόν). This reference to the poor person may be used in an anaphoric sense, recalling v 2 (BDF § 263), but may also be generic, i.e., it may refer to the class of poor as a whole (Robertson, *Grammar*, 408; Ropes).

James may be saying that those of the church who discriminate against the poor indict themselves because they betray a way of thinking and acting that dissociates them from the poor. This places the audience of James' epistle on dangerous ground, for they are at risk of excluding themselves from the promise to those who inherit the kingdom (see 2:13). While this indictment does not explicitly threaten that those guilty of discrimination were in danger of losing their eschatological salvation, James' caveat is not to be taken lightly. Moreover, by failing to love the poor (and in a sense, wrongly flattering the rich), those who practice discrimination portray an ungodly attitude on two counts—namely, they are guilty of favoritism and they do not fulfill the spirit of the law, a point that James will discuss immediately (vv 8–13).

He attacks the shortsightedness of his readers by "reminding" them (again in the form of a question) that it is the rich (οἱ πλούσιοι)—not the poor—that oppress them (καταδυναστεύειν, "to exploit"; used here and once only elsewhere, in Acts 10:38, where it refers to the tyrannizing of the devil; note the present tense of the verb, which argues against the idea that the entire scenario is only hypothetical). The rich were known for haling the Christians into court for economic gain (cf. Jer 7:6; 22:3; Amos 4:1; 8:4; Hab 1:4; Mal 3:5; Wisd Sol 2:10; 17:2). The rich are the ones who threaten to bring legal action (ἕλκειν: "to drag" or "to hale"; Acts 16:19; 21:30; cf. 8:3 for the idea of violent treatment; cf. Homer, *Il.* 24.52) against the poor and take them before a tribunal (κριτήριον, Xenophon, *Mem.* 3.6.1; here and 1 Cor 6:2, 4; the latter verses refer to a church court, thus affirming our earlier interpretation of συναγωγή; see v 2). In this regard the actions of the church have reached the nadir of absurdity. Since most, if not all, of the church to which James writes were evidently poor, it would make no sense for them to fawn on the rich (though perhaps their motivation was to escape further harassment).

A historical setting is offered by Reicke, who places the social stratification and its problems in the time of persecution under Domitian (cf. Suetonius, *Dom.* 14–16). This view assumes that Christians were being persecuted for their profession of the faith in the name of Jesus (Dibelius, 140–44; Longe-necker, *Christology of Early Jewish Christianity,* 45); but the verb βλασφημεῖν may not be so precise: it may be tantamount simply to acts of ridicule or scoffing, as in 2 Macc 10:34–35; 12:14. A more convincing suggestion is that James is reacting not to physical oppression but to legal pressures on the poor over such matters as debts, rents, wages, and the prevalence of usury. The verses, according to Furfey, *"Plousios,"* 251–52, are critical of Jewish bankers who were using their Christian profession as an excuse to evade Torah's prohibitions (Deut 23:19–20).

7   οὐκ αὐτοὶ βλασφημοῦσιν τὸ καλὸν ὄνομα τὸ ἐπικληθὲν ἐφ᾽ ὑμᾶς, "Is it not they who bring into disgrace the fine name by which you have been called [and are known]?" James continues his indictment by posing yet another question (to be answered by yes, οὐκ). The redundant use of pronoun αὐτοί (as in v 6) is probably due to Semitic influence (Moule, *Idiom Book,* 176). The rich people are those who "disgrace" (βλασφημεῖν, used of slander directed to men, of blasphemy against God) the fine (καλός, "good"; stronger than ἀγαθός) name (ὄνομα, singular) "by which you have been called." The use of ἐπικαλεῖν refers to the occasion when the name of "someone is called over someone else so as to designate the latter as property of the former" (BGD, 294). In the present case, God is the one whose name is invoked over Christians

(the aorist passive of the verb suggests that this has already happened in an initiatory or declarative way). The Christians are thereby God's possession. The thought that God actually gives his name ("surname"; so M. Zerwick and M. Grosvenor [*Grammatical Analysis*, 694]) to his people is an OT concept (2 Sam 6:2; 1 Kgs 8:43; Jer 7:30; 14:9; 2 Chr 7:14; and especially Amos 9:12; cf. also Acts 15:7). The name blasphemed by the rich is (probably) either Jesus (Bousset, *Kyrios Christos*, ET, 131, 295) or the Christian's own title to faith (so Adamson, 112–13; see Acts 11:26; 13:45; 18:6; 26:11, 28; 1 Cor 12:3; 1 Tim 1:13; 1 Pet 4:14, 16). The thought behind ἐπικαλεῖσθαι may also entail baptism (see Reicke, 29). There is a long line of development (see Heitmüller, *Im Namen Jesu*) from the practice of baptism "in/into the name of Jesus" (Acts 2:38; 10:48) to the receiving of the (new) name in baptism (cf. Rev 3:12; *Herm. Sim.* 9.4.8; 13.7) and the use of the Lord's name invoked over the candidate in the rite (*Herm. Sim.* 8.1.1; 6:4). The newly baptized then became bearers of that name (1 Pet 4:14–16; *Herm. Sim.* 8.10.3; 9.13.2–3; 15.2; 16.3; Ign. *Eph.* 7.1). That name, by transference, became a target for the persecutors' attack (*Herm. Sim.* 8.6.4) and was taken maliciously by the pagans, a feature noted in Rom 2:24, citing Isa 52:5; 1 Tim 1:20; 2 Pet 2:2. See Braumann, "Hintergrund," 409–10.

On wider aspects of the "theology of the name" as a Jewish Christian distinctive, see Longenecker, *Christology of Early Jewish Christianity*, 44–46; C. H. Roberts, *Manuscript, Society and Belief*, 42–48.

8 εἰ μέντοι νόμον τελεῖτε βασιλικὸν κατὰ τὴν γραφήν, ἀγαπήσεις τὸν πλησίον σου ὡς σεαυτόν, καλῶς ποιεῖτε, "If you truly fulfill the supreme law according to the scripture, 'you shall love your neighbor as yourself,' you do right." εἰ ("if") is probably affirmative rather than adversative (see Adamson, 113–14; Laws, 107; Dibelius 141; Mayor, 89; BDF § 450.1) and introduces a condition of first class (indicated by the use of the indicative, τελεῶ, "accomplish," in the protasis). The use of Lev 19:18 (see below; it is cited eight times in the NT; Johnson, "The Use") with the idea of fulfilling (τελεῶ) the supreme law (νόμον βασιλικόν; lit., "royal"—as in *lex regia*—as given by a king [namely, God]; see BGD, 136) recalls the issues raised in Matt 22:34–40. The term "supreme law" is not restricted to the OT law. When James wishes to speak of the OT law (or one of its commandments) he simply uses νόμος (see vv 10–11). However, when he is referring to the Christian understanding of "law" (i.e., a "new law"; BGD, 543) he qualifies νόμος, as in 1:25 and 2:12: "the law of freedom." In our present verse the term "law" is equally qualified. There is nothing in our passage to speak against taking the "law of freedom" to be the "supreme law" (see Gutbrod, *TDNT* 4:1080–82). What James is implying is that obedience to the "love commandment" fulfills the royal law, which refers to the entire will of God, especially as revealed in the teaching of Jesus (which lies in the background here; cf. Vouga, 79 n.20, who suggests a *fons et origo* in Antioch; see *Introduction*, pp. lxxvi–lxxvii). Though James is not limiting his thinking to the OT law with his use of "supreme law," neither is he advocating an abandoning of it. He—like Jesus and Paul (Matt 22:34–40, par.; Rom 13:8–10; Gal 5:14)—insists that the "new law" ("given by the King"; this is denied by Ropes, 199, however) includes, expands, and deepens the demands of the "old" law.

The new law is fulfilled by loving one's neighbor. Jesus is said in Matthean circles to have fulfilled the law in his coming (πληροῦν; Matt 5:17) and taught that loving one's neighbor is tantamount to doing all that the law demands (Matt 22:34–40). See *Introduction*, pp. lxxiv–lxxv. V 8b is from OT scripture (κατὰ τὴν γραφήν), specifically Lev 19:18 (see Matt 22:39; Rom 13:9; Gal 5:14). In the future tense, ἀγαπήσεις carries with it the force of an imperative. To follow James' advice is to do well (καλῶς ποιεῖτε). To avoid the sin of partiality berated in v 1 is the negative aspect of what it means to honor the supreme law. However, to discriminate against (or demean) the poor insults those whom God has chosen and, if we carry James' argument one step farther, makes the Christian guilty of discrimination by placing him on the side of those who blaspheme God's name. They who despise the poor insult their creator, namely, God, an aphorism already in Prov 14:21: the poor person and the neighbor are thus coextensive terms (Mussner, 123). The epitome of Torah as found in "love to neighbor" is in line with Hillel's (albeit negative) teaching (*b. Šabb.* 31a: "what you hate do not do to your neighbor. That is the essence of Torah; the remainder is commentary") and stands in contrast to the tendency in hellenistic Judaism to consider piety (εὐσέβεια) or righteousness (δικαιοσύνη) or philanthropy (φιλανθρωπία) as central. See Mussner, cited earlier, p. lxxxv.

9 εἰ δὲ προσωπολημπτεῖτε ἁμαρτίαν ἐργάζεσθε ἐλεγχόμενοι ὑπὸ τοῦ νόμου ὡς παραβάται, "But if you show favoritism you commit sin, and you are convicted by the law as transgressors." The use of δέ anticipates a reversal of the thought of v 8. προσωπολημπτεῖν, "show partiality," is found only here in the NT, with the corresponding noun in v 1. The verb of 2:9 and the noun of 2:1 (Rom 2:11; Eph 6:9; Col 3:25) along with the adjective προσωπολήμπτης in Acts 10:34 are the only places where the root is found in Christian literature (BGD, 720). Both are based on λαμβάνειν πρόσωπον, the translation of the phrase פָּנִים נָשָׂא, nāśā' panîm) in the LXX, lit., "to lift up the face" in favorable regard.

ἁμαρτίαν ἐργάζεσθε, "You commit sin." For other indications of moral evil in James' community see 4:17; 5:16–17, 20. For James, the action of showing favoritism, while considered inconsequential by some in the church, was a serious matter; he equates it with the act of sinning (Matt 7:23; cf. Ps 6:8; for the verb cf. 1:4, 20). In turn, the Christian is convicted (ἐλεγχόμενοι; cf. John 3:20; 8:46; 1 Cor 14:24, passive, "convicted by all") as a transgressor (παραβάτης; see 2:11; Rom 2:25, 27; Luke 6:5; Gal 2:18). The law in view could be the Mosaic law (Schneider, *TDNT* 5:741 n.5). The sin of partiality, as an act committed against the poor, is condemned in the OT. In Lev 19:15 (in close proximity to Lev 19:18) the Israelite is exhorted to refrain from discriminating against the poor (LXX, λαμβάνειν πρόσωπον) and urged to treat one's neighbor fairly (see also Deut 16:19). But it may be that James also is speaking of the new law of 2:8, since one cannot fulfill the "supreme law" and still discriminate against the poor, as is brought out in the next verse (παραβάτης came later to be associated with an "apostate"; Eusebius, *HE* 5.18, 19).

10 ὅστις γὰρ ὅλον τὸν νόμον τηρήσῃ πταίσῃ δὲ ἐν ἑνί, γέγονεν πάντων ἔνοχος, "It follows that if a person keeps the entire law but stumbles over one item he has become guilty in all points." If some of the church thought that certain parts of the law were of less importance than other parts, James quickly dispels that notion. Note the indefinite ὅστις, "whoever," with subjunctive verb (possibly gnomic) but without ἄν (Zerwick, *Biblical Greek,* 336; see Moule, *Idiom Book,* 123–24, for a discussion of the disappearance of distinction between simple and indefinite pronouns). The verb πταίω, "stumble," is found only here and 3:2; Rom 11:11; 2 Pet 1:10. Even if one were to commit but one sin, he would become (γέγονεν, perfect of γινέσθαι; see BDF § 344) ἔνοχος, "guilty," (liable to the penalty) of breaking all the commandments ("has sinned against all commandments," so BGD, 268). ἔνοχος is a legal term (ibid., 262; see Matt 5:21–22) and keeps the idea of a church court before the interpreter.

The present verse anticipates 2:11, where we find the application made that one is a lawbreaker even though not all commandments are actually transgressed. This has been called a unitary understanding of the law (Davids, 117), so that the readers of James' epistle cannot claim innocence of the charge of transgressing the entire law simply because some commandment(s) remain unbroken (i.e., "do not commit adultery"; see *Comment* on 4:4). A failure to love the poor—a failure demonstrated by showing favoritism toward the rich—undercuts the whole intent of the law and places one under condemnation as a transgressor of the law. In summary, from a particular viewpoint, James is saying that one does not have to break all the commandments of the law to be classed as a lawbreaker; on the other side he is remarking that a person must keep all the commandments to be a "perfect" law-keeper (3:2). Such a deduction may recall Pauline thought (Rom 2:25; Gal 5:3) but seems more in line with Matthean teaching. The person may stumble on the road to perfection by one failure (Matt 19:16–22) and yet may "keep" the law in its entirety by loving one's neighbor (Matt 22:34–40: Montefiore, "Thou shalt love"). Though the *Shema* (Deut 6:4) is not explicitly mentioned here, there can be no doubt that for James love of one's neighbor goes hand in hand with love for God (see 2:14–26). Thus, James delivers a double blow to those who discriminate against the poor and yet claim when under duress that such behavior only breaks a small fraction of the law. The appeal to Lev 19:18 counters that thinking. For one thing, to break this commandment (or any other) is equivalent to breaking the entire law (2:10, based on Deut 27:26; *T. Asher* 2:5–10; 4 Macc 5:20). On another level it is this commandment in particular that transcends all others, and so to break it in essence casts one as intentionally rejecting the heart and soul of God's will, namely the love of one's neighbor (in this case, the poor who visit the "meeting").

11 ὁ γὰρ εἰπών μὴ μοιχεύσῃς, εἶπεν καί, μὴ φονεύσῃς· εἰ δὲ οὐ μοιχεύεις φονεύεις δέ, γέγονας παραβάτης νόμου, "For He who said, 'Do not commit adultery,' said also, 'Do not murder.' If you do not commit adultery but do commit murder, you become a transgressor of the law." The γάρ is causal here and the entire phrase is probably a circumlocution for God, following the Jewish style of not using the name of God (Davids, 117). καί ("also") indicates that the same person utters both commandments and thus the basis is laid for the unity of the law (v 10). These two commandments do not concern outward ritual but penetrate to the core of ethical behavior. The order of the Decalogue (Exod 20:13–14; Deut 5:17–18) cited is noteworthy. In the MT and Codex

A of LXX the prohibitions of murder, then of adultery, are given in that sequence. But in Codex B we have the order found in James. There appears to be no set pattern in the Christian tradition (Luke 18:20; Rom 13:9 favor James' order, while Matt 19:18; Mark 10:19 have the reverse). There is some minor textual variation here (Ropes, 201).

εἰ δὲ οὐ μοιχεύεις φονεύεις δέ, γέγονας παραβάτης νόμου, "If you do not commit adultery but do commit murder, you become a transgressor of the law." The present tense suggests that "murder," if not adultery, is actually taking place in the congregation. But what kind of violence does James have in mind? On the face of it, the verb leads the interpreter to suppose that James is referring to the literal taking of another's life. Yet the present context in itself contains nothing that suggests this latter point (see below), but verses such as 4:2; 5:6 (see *Comment*, ad loc.) do raise the possibility that the actual killing of other people in internecine strife may be in view. This must be considered in the light of the entire *Sitz im Leben* of this letter, at least in its first historical setting of James' involvement in Palestinian politics in the 60s. There is a suggestion that James has thrown in his sympathies with the needy priests—whether Jewish or messianic—because of their allegiance with the Zealots; thus James finds himself acting as liaison between the two groups, attempting to effect a *modus vivendi* (see *Introduction*, pp. lxviii–lxix). Such a milieu would lead to the conclusion that the literal understanding of murder remains a possibility, though the context of our present verse is not directly supportive of such an interpretation and may reflect a later setting in which the burning issue is that of a debate over the "keeping of the command-ments."

Murder is frequently associated with discriminating against the poor, which is a failure to love one's neighbor (Davids, 117). Most commentators believe that James must have spiritualized murder, reflecting on the relationship between hate and murder (Matt 5:21, 22; see Reicke, 29). It is possible accord-ing to this view that James understands the lack of love shown toward the poor as tantamount to hate. With this understanding, adultery and murder can be associated as follows. Those who pride themselves as free from fleshly sins (e.g., adultery) and are swift to condemn such sins in others have "made their condemnation of fleshly sins an excuse for indulgence towards spiritual sins" (Hort). Whatever the exact thought behind v 11, James is driving home the point introduced in v 10: the law is broken in its entirety when only one item of the law is transgressed and thus the culprit is convicted as a transgressor (παραβάτης; here and 2:9; see Schneider, *TDNT* 5:741–42).

12   οὕτως λαλεῖτε καὶ οὕτως ποιεῖτε ὡς διὰ νόμου ἐλευθερίας μέλλοντες κρίνεσθαι, "Speak and act as those who are to be judged by the law that sets free." The double imperative (λαλεῖτε, "speak," and ποιεῖτε, "do, act"; note double use of οὕτως for emphasis) carries forward the idea that the readers must act in a positive way in order to be "doers of the word" (1:22; 2:14–26). The present tense of the imperative suggests a call to make such speaking and doing habitual. The use of μέλλειν, "to intend," as a participle describes future action that is certain (BGD, 501; Davids, 118); hence our translation "who are to be judged." The passive voice of the infinitive κρίνεσθαι implies that judgment will be visited upon the people through the law (διὰ νόμου; in an instrumental sense; see Rom 2:12) that sets free (ἐλευθερίας). The use of the qualifier is James' way of distinguishing the law that he has in view (earlier identified as the supreme law, the law of liberty) from the Mosaic law or at least misunderstanding that can accompany the latter. The Christian is judged by a law that sets one free, that is, by the supreme law, the law of love (2:8). To be so judged certifies that an individual is either a complete law-keeper or a disastrous lawbreaker. To love one's neighbor is the highest form of freedom exercised, and ends in fulfillment of the law. What James is telling his readers is that the Jewish law per se is not the seat of authority (*pace* Dunn, *Unity and Diversity*, 251–52) but rather it is the law, as understood and interpreted in the Christian sense, which is the norm that guides the life of the follower of Jesus the Christ (Matt 7:12, 21, 24–29; 19:17–21; 22:36–40; 28:20). The antitheses of the Sermon in Matthew 5:21–48 make the same point, namely, that the new law of love sets a higher standard than Torah obedience can demand and produce (e.g., Matt 5:20). See R. A. Guelich, *The Sermon on the Mount* (Waco: Word, 1982) 155–74, 255–71. The law of freedom can liberate those who fulfill it but it also serves (as will be seen in 2:13) as a solemn threat of eschatological wrath to those who transgress it. Dibelius, 147, may be correct to suggest that 2:12 appears to be a solemn piece of catechetical pronouncement.

13 ἡ γὰρ κρίσις ἀνέλεος τῷ μὴ ποιήσαντι ἔλεος, "Judgment is merciless to the one who has shown no mercy." The γάρ connects v 12 to v 13 regardless of whether or not v 13 is a proverb (Davids, 118; see Dibelius, 147–48; Mussner, 126). Judgment is threatened for those who show no mercy (note the rare use of ἀνέλεος, a *hapax legomenon;* see BDF § 44.1). The switch from the second person in v 12 to the third person may indicate that v 13 is gnomic. James has taken this timeless truth and applied it to the situation at hand. He is pointing the critical finger at those of the congregation who have not shown mercy to the poor and is predicting that they are liable to have the tables turned on them. The Christian who shows mercy fulfills what the "law of love" (supreme law, the law that sets free) requires (cf. Zech 7:9–10). A merciful attitude provides evidence that a Christian disposition is truly being exemplified. κρίσις, taken in the sense of eternal damnation, gives too stern a threat (unless James is driving home the thought that lack of concern is evidence of unreal faith, thus providing grounds for eschatological punishment). It is doubtful that giving preference to the rich at the expense of the poor is meant to be equal to the sin of apostasy (but see Kilpatrick in *Note* g). κρίσις, as used in 5:12, may not speak of eternal judgment, however serious its tone. So at the other extreme some interpreters argue that James is simply exaggerating his point by taking a piece of wisdom teaching and applying it to a pastoral situation in the church. In this vein, the worst that showing "no mercy" can mean for those who are guilty of discriminating is a loss both of "merciful" acts of kindness of the church and of eschatological rewards at the endtime (1 Cor 3:12–15; 2 Cor 5:10).

But such an opposite conclusion, however unwittingly, does lessen the severity of James' warning. For this moral theologian, works, even acts of charity (2:14–16), provide the evidence that Christian faith is genuine (cf. Johnson, *Sharing*, 102–3). On the other hand, failure to live out the message in its social ramification implies (for James) a dead faith that is useless for salvation (2:14). The severity of this verse must not then be diminished. Those who fail to demonstrate a living and consistent faith are in danger of facing harsh judgment at the end, for they live as though ethical issues were of no consequence. Failure to show mercy to others cuts a person off from a true appreciation of the divine compassion (as emphasized in the dominical parable of the debtor servant and its application, Matt 18:21–35). By the standard of the supreme law, those who fail in love to their neighbor stand condemned. Thus, those who discriminate against the poor are reckoned to be in danger of the same fate as the godless. Such stern warning is reminiscent of Matthew's special sources (e.g., Matt 13:24–30, 41–42, 47–50; 25:31–46; Reicke, 30). The question whether those who practice such discrimination against the poor ever had authentic faith to begin with is not answered in these verses. What is in view is the insistence that "showing mercy is the way that love will express itself in [the] new community. This will involve at the very least a welcome for the poor (as for the rich), and it will lead to an active outgoing compassion to all those in need (see 1:27)" (Dyrness, "Mercy," 14). The examples of Abraham in giving hospitality and of Rahab in her action are illustrative; also germane is "The Ethic of Election in Luke's Great Banquet Parable" (Luke 14:12–24), J. A. Sanders's study in *Essays in Old Testament Ethics,* ed. J. L. Crenshaw and J. T. Willis (New York: KTAV, 1974) 245–71.

In contrast to the threat of v 13a is the hope expressed in v 13b: κατακαυχᾶ-ται ἔλεος κρίσεως, "yet mercy triumphs over judgment." Though there is an absence of the connective particle, the link between vv 13a and b is clear: God's mercy is stronger than the condemnation passed by the law. It is said to triumph; the verb is κατακαυχᾶσθαι (used here and 3:14; Rom 11:18; see Mayor, 95; Mussner, 127; Cantinat, 138; Bultmann, *TDNT* 3:653–54; in the middle voice, lit., "boasts against").

V 13b echoes the eschatological promise of Matt 5:7: "Blessed are the merciful, for they shall receive mercy" (by God). This could be an incentive for those who are in a hesitant mood in the congregation. Moreover, v 13b is a pastoral affirmation to those already committed to showing mercy to the disadvantaged because it highlights the promise that forgiveness at the last judgment goes hand in hand with merciful acts performed in this life (Sir 27:30–28:7; Tob 4:9–11). Moo (98) understands ἔλεος to refer specifically to an individual's showing mercy, as though such mercy triumphs over the spirit of judgment (brought by the accuser). The Christian's mercy toward others acts as defense counsel before God and wins the case. He follows Hort (57) in this line of thought. But the courtroom imagery would explain the situation better if we hold that our defense counsel is the glorious Lord himself (2:1) rather than our showing mercy to others. He is our counselor who submits the evidence (our deeds of mercy) to the coming judge and presents our case based on our identity with the poor, in turn patterned on his identity with them (see *Explanation*). It is only because of God's mercy that our acts of mercy (which are inspired by his) are accepted as evidence of a true life in the new creation (1:18) and thus characteristic of salvation (this linkage becomes apparent in 2:14–26). This emphasis in 13b is on God's mercy (not our mercy) and from this perspective Moo's submission of a courtroom scene needs to be corrected.

Explanation

The section of 2:1–13 is a powerful statement of the social dimension of the Christian life. While there is uncertainty as to the setting, whether in a liturgical synaxis for public worship or a courtroom designed to adjudicate legal disputes between members, the main thrust is clear. On the positive side, the insistence the author makes is that in the divine kingdom a litmus test of character is the way Christians treat one another. Unhappily, the congregation to which these words were sent was marked by social disgraces. It was rent by snobbery and class distinctions of the worst kind. The rich were offered preferential treatment in a most obsequious manner (2:2–3); the poor were treated with disrespect bordering on plain discourtesy and rudeness (2:3). The characters are drawn with exaggerated lines of difference, but the contrast is by no means unthinkable. James is intent on registering his central point: true religion (1:27) is shown for its authentic worth by how Christians fare in their respective attitude to the powerful and the lowly, especially to those who are weaker than themselves and who can neither repay any kindness shown nor retaliate when injustice is practiced.

The marks of differentiation are also boldly drawn. One clear way in which the two differing types of treatment will be seen lies in the seating arrangements in public assembly. The best places are offered to the rich and potent person whose outward, ostentatious dress betokens the rank he holds in society. The tone of voice in addressing him is deferential to the point of fawning. By contrast the beggar is commanded to take the place that veils an insult; he may either stand or be seated in an inferior posture (v 3). But worse is to come. The poor has come (evidently, if the setting is a court hearing) to seek justice, and his chances of gaining a fair trial are dim, given the favoritism that is rife. So the reception of the poor is not simply a case of bad manners; it is a policy of downright evil, as v 4 openly declares. These are, then, serious matters, our author insists, as he proceeds to name the problem.

He does so by identifying the real issue; hence the editorial link with 1:23–25 needs to be established. Here is a case where seeing in the "mirror of the word" should have led to a redress of wrong. But there is no sign that it did. Hence James' lament is bitter and scathing (vv 8–12).

What is at stake is a vain bid to join a professed faith in the Lord of glory (2:1) with a way of life which runs counter to the main tenets of that faith. Two cardinal beliefs are turned on their head in the Jacobean community, one overtly, the other by inference.

First, out of loyalty to the OT-Jewish tradition in which his feet are firmly planted, the author announces his commitment to a *theology of justice*, so basic to the OT revelation (see Deut 16:20) and inherent in Jewish piety. It is enriched by the insights and convictions of the author's Christian heritage. Verses 5–6a are a classic statement that God's concern is for social righteousness in his kingdom, where the foundational principle is that stated in Peter's sermon: "God is no respecter of persons" (Acts 10:34, KJV/AV). God's righteous character demands a righteous people, and Israel's judges preeminently are charged to execute what is right and in accord with fair dealing. Amos's poetic line speaks for Israel's writing prophets:

Let justice roll down like water,
And righteousness like an everflowing stream (Amos 5:24).

In any event Israel's judicial system had all the flaws of any human creation, and the divine rebuke was levied at them (Jer 5:20–31). Now in the new Israel a reenactment that repeats the miscarriage of justice calls forth a similar prophetic protest. The added component, derived also from the prophets, is that the poor have only God to look to as their protector and friend, and so James' sympathies are clearly on the side of the oppressed and socially marginalized because he sees God as on their side as well. The link-term uniting God and his downtrodden people is "the kingdom" (v 5); and it is not too presumptuous to see this single phrase, so prevalent in the synoptic Gospels, as binding the ethics of James to that of the new age which Jesus in the same prophetic lineage came both to inaugurate and to embody.

Second, in order to make it clear that James is both like and unlike the Old Testament prophets of social equality and justice it is needful to take note of the *one unequivocal Christological reference in the letter* (2:1). "The faith of our glorious Lord Jesus Christ" is one of the noblest titles accorded to the church's head in the New Testament. Aside from the ascription of lordship the adjectival "of glory" is to be given full weight. Possibly it means no more than "who reigns in glory" (NEB) or "who is the Shekinah," the outward shining of the inward being of God, as *doxa* implies. Yet one inferential line of development explained in the following verses should not be too quickly dismissed (though the Christological element should not be overpressed, as is sometimes done: see *Introduction*, p. cvi–cvii, cix). "Glory" as a biblical idiom is an effulgence of the divine that is there to be seen, and seen as an impressive display intended both to awaken interest and to impress with a sense of the numinous, to use Otto's term drawn from the phenomenology of religion (*The Idea of the Holy,* tr. J. W. Harvey [London: Oxford UP, 1923]). As a frontispiece to this tale of two visitors to the assembly James builds up an impressive picture of the glorious Lord, which will be reminiscent to the NT readers of John 1:1–18; Phil 2:6–11; Col 1:15–20; 2 Cor 8:9; Heb 1:1–4; Rev 1:13–18. The contrast that follows from the two human *dramatis personae* could hardly be more extreme: in dress, demeanor, deportment—and treatment. Yet it is the man in resplendent attire with all the insignia of honor and power who is *persona grata;* the poor fellow in rags receives only scurvy treatment.

No reader of the Gospel story could fail to see some connection. The Lord of glory once entered on the human scene, and came not as might be expected in all the regalia of might and majesty but in the lowly garments of a beggar, and was refused (Luke 9:58; John 1:10–11). While the point is not made explicitly, James may well be preparing the ground for what is to follow—namely, in refusing to see the divine image in one's neighbor (according to the royal law of 2:8–13), however disguised and overlaid, it may be that one is failing to see the Lord himself who laid his glory aside and chose to identify with the least of "these his brothers" (Matt 25:31–46). Not for the last time will this veiled christological nexus be made.

At least the point will not be lost as the next pericope has at its center the case of those who are ill-clad and hungry (2:15); then the professed faith of 2:1 will be put to the test, with surprising consequences.

3. Faith and Deeds—Together   (2:14–26)

Bibliography

Amphoux, C.-B., and **Bouttier, M.** "Prédication de Jacques le Juste." *EThR* 54 (1979) 9. **Bacon, B. W.** "The Doctrine of Faith in Hebrews, James, and Clement of Rome." *JBL* 19 (1900) 12–21. **Bieder, W.** "Christliche Existenz nach dem Zeugnis des Jakobusbriefes." *TZ* 56 (1949) 93–113. **Böhmer, J.** "Der 'Glaube' im Jakobusbriefe." *NKZ* 9 (1898) 251–56. **Bonhoeffer, D.** *The Cost of Discipleship.* Rev. ed. Tr. R. H. Fuller. New York: Macmillan, 1963. **Bultmann, R.** *Der Stil der paulinischen Predigt und die kynisch-stoische Diatribe.* FRLANT 13. Göttingen: Vandenhoeck und Ruprecht, 1910. **Burchard, Ch.** "Zu Jakobus 2,14–16." *ZNW* 71 (1980) 27–45. **Burge, G. M.** "'And Threw Them Thus on Paper': Recovering the Poetic Form of James 2:14–26." *SBT* 7 (1977) 31–45. **Cantinat, J.** "La foi vivante et salutaires accompagne d'oeuvres." *AsSeign* 55 (1974) 26–30. **Cranfield, C. E. B.** "The Message of James." *SJT* 18 (1965) 186–89, 338–45. **Donker, C. E.** "Der Verfasser des Jak und sein Gegner: Zum Problem des Einwandes in Jak 2,18–19." *ZNW* 72 (1981) 227–40. **Eichholz, G.** *Glaube und Werke bei Paulus und Jakobus.* ThEx n.f. 88. Munich: Kaiser Verlag, 1961. **Goppelt, L.** *Theology of the New Testament.* Vol. 2. Tr. J. E. Alsup. Grand Rapids: Eerdmans, 1982. **Hagner, D. A.** *The Use of the Old and New Testaments in Clement of Rome.* NovTSup 36. Leiden: Brill, 1973. 251–56. **Hamann, H. P.** "Faith and Works: Paul and James." *Lutheran Theological Journal* 9 (1975) 33–41. **Hanson, A. T.** "Rahab the Harlot in Early Christian Theology." *JSNT* 1 (1978) 53–60. **Hodges, Z. C.** "Light on James Two from Textual Criticism." *BS* 120 (1963) 341–50. **Jacobs, I.** "The Midrashic Background for James 2,21–23." *NTS* 22 (1976) 457–64. **Jeremias, J.** "Paul and James." *ExpTim* 66 (1954–55) 368–71. **Johnson, M. D.** *The Purpose of the Biblical Genealogies.* SNTSMS 8. Cambridge: Cambridge UP, 1969. 162–65. **Lodge, J. G.** "James and Paul at Cross-Purposes? James 2,22." *Bib* 62 (1981) 195–213. **Lohse, E.** "Glaube und Werke—Zur Theologie des Jakobusbriefes." In *Die Einheit des Neuen Testaments.* Göttingen: Vandenhoeck und Ruprecht, 1973. 285–306. **Lorenzen, Th.** "Faith without Works Does Not Count before God! James 2:14–26." *ExpTim* 89 (1978) 231–35. **Luck, U.** "Der Jakobusbrief und die Theologie des Paulus." *TGl* 61 (1971) 161–79. **Lührmann, D.** *Glaube im frühen Christentum.* Gütersloh: Mohn, 1976. 78–84. **Nicol, W.** "Faith and Works in the Letter of James." *Neot* 9 (1975) 7–24. **Pratscher, W.** *Der Herrenbruder Jakobus und die Jakobustradition.* FRLANT 139. Göttingen: Vandenhoeck und Ruprecht, 1987. **Reumann, J., Fitzmyer, J. A.**, and **Quinn, J. D.** *Righteousness in the New Testament.* Philadelphia: Fortress; New York: Paulist, 1982. 152–58. **Rönsch, H.** "Abraham der Freund Gottes." *ZWT* 16 (1873) 583–90. **Ropes, J. H.** "Thou Hast Faith and I Have Works' (James II.18)." *Exp* ser. 7, vol. 5 (1908) 547–56. **Sanders, E. P.** *Paul and Palestinian Judaism.* Philadelphia: Fortress, 1977. **Schanz, P.** "Jakobus und Paulus." *TQ* 62 (1880) 3–46. 247–86. **Seitz, O.J. F.** "James and the Law." *SE* 2 (1963) 472–

86. **Snodgrass, K. R.** "Justification by Grace—to the Doers: An Analysis of the Place of Romans 2 in the Theology of Paul." *NTS* 32 (1986) 72–93. **Souček, J. B.** "Zu den Problemen des Jakobusbriefes." *EvT* 18 (1958) 460–68. **Swindell, A. C.** "Abraham and Isaac: An Essay in Biblical Appropriation." *ExpTim* 87 (1975) 50–53. **Travis, A. E.** "James and Paul: A Comparative Study." *SWJT* 12 (1969) 57–70. **Usteri, L.** "Glaube, Werke und Rechtfertigung im Jakobusbrief." *TSK* 62 (1889) 211–56. **Via, D. O.** "The Right Strawy Epistle Reconsidered: A Study in Biblical Ethics and Hermeneutics." *JAAR* 49 (1969) 255. **Walker, R.** "Allein aus Wirken: Zur Auslegung von Jak 2,14–26." *ZTK* 61 (1964) 155–92. **Wall, R. W.** "Interlocutor and James, James 2:18–20 Reconsidered." Unpub. art. ———. "Law and Gospel, Church and Canon." *Wesleyan Theological Journal* 22 (1987) 38–70, esp. 53–55. **Ward, R. B.** "James and Paul: A Critical Review." *RestQ* 7 (1963) 159–64. ———. "The Works of Abraham, James 2,14–16." *HTR* 61 (1968) 283–90. **Wiles, G. P.** *Paul's Intercessory Prayers.* SNTMS 24. Cambridge: Cambridge UP, 1974. **Wiseman, D. J.** "Rahab of Jericho." *TynB* 14 (1964) 8–11. **Young, F. W.** "The Relation of Clement to the Epistle of James." *JBL* 67 (1948) 339–45.

Translation

[14] *My brothers, what good* [a] *will it do if anyone claims he has faith, but has no deeds? Can a faith like this save him?* [15] *To illustrate: if a brother or sister is ill-clad and is lacking in daily sustenance* [16] *and one of you says to them, "Go in peace, get warm, and be filled [with food]," but you do not meet their bodily needs—then, what good is that?* [17] *So even faith, if it does not have deeds [to support it] and is on its own, is dead.* [18] *But someone will say, "You have faith; I have deeds.* [b] *Show me your faith apart from* [c] *your deeds, and I will show you my faith [demonstrated] by my deeds.* [19] *Do you believe that 'God is one'?* [d] *Excellent! Yet the demons believe [this], and they shudder."*

[20] *You empty-headed person, don't you understand that apart from deeds faith is ineffectual?* [e] [21] *And that our father Abraham was proved righteous [as demonstrated] by his deeds, when he attempted to offer Isaac his son on the altar?* [22] *You [should] see that his faith was at work with his deeds, and by his deeds his faith was brought to completion.* [23] *The Scripture was fulfilled which says, "Abraham believed God, and it was reckoned to him for righteousness," and he was called God's friend.* [24] *You [should] be aware that a person is proved righteous by deeds, not by faith alone.* [25] *To give another instance: was not Rahab the prostitute proved righteous by her actions, when she welcomed the messengers* [f] *and sent them out by a different route?* [26] *As the body apart from breath is lifeless, so also faith apart from deeds is dead.*

Notes

[a] Reading τὸ ὄφελος with the best witnesses. The omission of τό (B C* 102) is supported by Ropes, who regards the text of ℵ A as having been brought into conformity with 2:16, which has τὸ ὄφελος: cf. 1 Cor 15:32, where also τό is omitted by D F G. The meaning is unaffected.

[b] The punctuation is in dispute. Specifically, we cannot be sure where the objector's quotation ends. See *Form/Structure/Setting*.

[c] This (reading χωρίς) is the text of Nestle-Aland[26], supported by ℵ A B. There is a weaker yet well-attested alternative in the TR, ἐκ τῶν ἔργων σου; the vg has *sine*, which has produced the AV/KJV translations "without" in spite of the TR's ἐκ. Z. C. Hodges, "Light on James Two," 345, wishes to defend the TR as the majority reading on the ground of its wide distribution and on the principle of *lectio difficilior*. R. W. Wall, "Interlocutor and James," has reopened the

debate, concluding that while the uncial support favors the critical reading, it does not do so decisively, and the issue of a correct reading must be decided on internal grounds, namely, that in order to account for the severity of the rebuke (in v 20: ὦ ἄνθρωπε κενέ) it is necessary to have the objector say more than the simple statement that there are two competing claims to authentic religion: You have faith, I have deeds (v 18a). For Wall, this is followed by an interlocutor's second remark which is not tautological, that there are two beginning points of "true religion" (1:27)—faith and deeds—that are "not only mutually exclusive; they have no logical interplay as well." The upshot of the objector's position is that "believers" may choose to have *either* faith *or* works and still be classed as true to religion. Hence the parallelism ἐκ τῶν ἔργων . . . ἐκ τῶν ἔργων (accepting TR). The interlocutor also is responsible for the affirmation καλῶς ποιεῖς, lit., "You do well," which he borrows from James' earlier remark (2:8, καλῶς ποιεῖτε) about obedience to the royal law. He also cites the monotheistic formula as the epitome of *his* faith, seeking James' concurrence along with what he regards as the essence of faith. According to this reconstruction, based on the text-critical issue, James' reply begins in v 20 with a stinging invective. But it is still possible to claim that the flow of the discussion requires the interlocutor's words to include more than v 18a, but to reject TR's witness, which is weakly attested, as Ropes, 209, has shown.

Among translators the quotation marks usually close with v 18a, but Williams, *The New Testament*, offers an interesting exception. In the 1950 edition the quotation ends with v 18a, but this is changed in the 1986 edition to include the whole of the verse in the speaker's discourse.

Vv 18–19b are a unit arranged in chiastic pattern (Donker, "Der Verfasser . . . sein Gegner," 236; but overlooked by Burge, "And Threw Them Thus"), and should not be split between separate speakers. This opponent's chiasmus is matched by James' recourse to the same device in v 22, as Lodge, "James and Paul," has demonstrated.

[d]εἷς ἐστιν ὁ θεός (so P[74] ℵ A vg syr[P] cop[sa,bo]) is the formula of Jewish orthodox belief in the unity of God, the rabbinic conception of ʾemûnâ (Jeremias, "Paul and James," 370). Some MSS omit ὁ, yielding a statement of simple monotheism: There is one God (so B, εἷς θεός ἐστιν). Other recensions are: εἷς ὁ θεός ἐστιν (C syr[h] etc.); ὁ θεὸς εἷς ἐστιν (TR), which is clearly later. Ropes and Hort champion B's reading, arguing that it is unusual to have θεός without the definite article. The reading accepted in the translation above is defended by Mayor, Dibelius, Davids, Laws, Moo.

[e]ἀργή is attested by B C* it[ff] vg cop[sa] arm and some minuscules: νεκρά, found in a A C[2] K ψ syr[p,h] cop[bo], is rejected by the editors of UBSGNT[3] as an assimilation to 2:17, 26 that also destroys the author's attempt at word-play (ἀργή—ἔργων; Metzger, *Textual Commentary*, 681). κένη (read by P[74] it[ff]) looks to be a slip caused by assimilation to the apostrophe in the earlier part of the verse, ὦ ἄνθρωπε κενέ.

[f]For ἀγγέλους C K[mg] L syr[P] bo have κατασκόπους (Josh 2:4, 6; Heb 11:31).

Form / Structure / Setting

Two contextual matters stand at the center of discussion when the setting of 2:14–26—a pericope that is at the theological heart of the letter (Pratscher, *Der Herrenbruder Jakobus*, 213–16)—is considered. (1) What is the connection, if any, between this paragraph and the foregoing vv 1–13? (2) At v 18 we have an introductory "formula of objection" (*Einwandsformel*, Mussner, 137) that begins a counterproposal to James' own conclusion in v 17, and we need to know where the objection ends.

The issues are several: (a) Who is the subject (τις) of the verb ἐρεῖ: "*someone will say*"? Is he an objector to James' position? In that case ἀλλά must be given the force of an adversative, "but." Is he, secondly, James' ally brought in to support the case as stated? The connective ἀλλά will then be understood as "indeed" or "so," but we have to account for the ally's presence, given that he introduces the same point of view as the writer: is he brought onto the scene out of "modesty" (Mayor) on James' part, or because the writer wished to light up his discussion with "dramatic vividness" (Beyschlag, cited by Mussner)? Is he, thirdly, speaking not for a particular viewpoint but for a position that James brings forward for illustrative purposes only? The last-named is Ropes's argument (now supported by Moo) to the effect that the pronouns σύ and ἐγώ in v 18 ("You have faith; I have deeds") refer not to the writer of the letter and his opponent but to two representatives of different types of religion. This view is reflected in the NEB translation: "But someone may object: 'Here is one who claims to have faith and another who points to his deeds.'"

In spite of Ropes's plea for this last interpretation and its endorsement by scholars such as Cantinat, Mitton, and Laws, it does require a detaching of the discussion in vv 18–20 from its context (going back to 2:1–13) and is not aided by an appeal to 1 Cor 12:4–11; Rom 12:6–8. There it is said (by Paul!) that the Spirit gives gifts to God's people. Included are the gifts of faith (to one Christian) and deeds such as healing (to another). The objector makes capital out of this diversity and takes James to task for insisting that all believers should possess both faith and Christian deeds. The issue turns on whether faith and works are optional, a point of view that the objector holds. James, on the contrary, says that they are inseparable and that both are necessary. Grammatically, however, the third interpretation has to overcome the objection that the way to state contrasting positions is not best represented by the use of the pronouns σύ and ἐγώ, when the pairing of ἄλλος . . . ἄλλος could have done the job without obscurity (see Adamson, 137, with a telling quotation from C. F. D. Moule: "To tell the truth, I cannot think of a *less* likely way to express what J. H. Ropes wants the James passage to mean than what there stands written"). We conclude, then, that the choice is between the first two interpretations mentioned above: the respondent in v 18a is either James' opponent or less likely his ally, with the tacit understanding that there is a genuine debate underway in the background, and that it is not the case of "the device [used by James] of the imaginary objector to further his argument for the inseparability of faith and works" (Moo, 106).

(b) How much of what follows from v 18a is to be included in the statement to which James is making a rejoinder at v 20? In *Note* c the textual and literary question was considered, and it was asked whether the sentence commencing in v 18b is better read as the beginning of James' response to v 18a or as a continuation of the remarks of the opponent or ally. In the latter case vv 18–19 form a complete objection to James' position (Donker, "Der Verfasser . . . und sein Gegner," 240) and James' retort opens at v 20.

We have still to consider how 2:14–26 fits into the preceding section (and the limits of the response which opens with v 18a). The links between the two paragraphs are too strong to be overlooked:

My brothers . . . faith (2:1).	My brothers . . . faith (2:14).
The poor person in filthy clothes (2:2).	A brother or sister ill-clad and lacking in daily sustenance (2:15).

The poor . . . wealthy in faith . . . (who) love God (2:5).	Faith . . . works [two terms in association 10x in 13 vv].
You are right (καλῶς ποιεῖτε) (2:8).	Excellent! (καλῶς ποιεῖς) (2:19).
The fine name by which you have been *called* (2:7).	(Abraham) was *called* God's friend (2:23).

These parallels argue for a smooth and connected flow in the author's writing. Common to both sections, on literary and stylistic grounds, is the use of diatribe and polemical illustration, and the same situation lies in the background of the two units: disdain for the poor, seen both in the community's disgraceful treatment of their rights (2:1–13) and in the case of the individual community member who seeks to justify this attitude by an insistence that "faith alone" (v 17, καθ' ἑαυτήν; v 24, μόνον) is all that counts (Burchard, "Zu Jakobus 2," 28–30). James begins with an exposition of the possession of faith (v 1: ἔχετε τὴν πίστιν), offering two dramatic pictures of how "faith" should be understood. Faith cannot abide the favoritism that panders to the rich and despises the poor; faith attains its true meaning only as it is accompanied by—and expressed in—acts of kindness and mercy, such as clothing and feeding the poor (v 15). It shows its genuine character as it "works along with" deeds of helpfulness (v 22). Such faith is living (v 26), not dead (v 17) or ineffectual (v 20) in leading to salvation (v 14b).

James, therefore, is intent on defining the scope of saving faith, which he sets in direct contrast to (i) mere sentiment that never gets beyond a pious expression (v 16), and (ii) an intellectual conviction (voiced in v 19), which he dismisses scornfully as the mark of a mere dilettante (v 20a: "you empty-headed person"). This discussion takes a step further the condemnation already given in 1:11, 23–27 of those rich people in his community who are vulnerable to the point of self-deception by resting content simply with mental agreement and formal concurrence with "the implanted word that is able to save your lives" (v 21). The unit in 2:14–26 picks up his earlier judgment on the peril of a self-deceiving attitude that leads to a person's becoming no better than a "forgetful hearer," rather than a "doer of work" (ποιητὴς ἔργου, 1:25), and falling prey to mere verbal profession (1:26). The upshot is that such a person's religion is "futile" (μάταιος, 1:26b). Chap. 2 illustrates what these strictures mean in practical terms and points to the better way. The truly faithful person will receive the encomium of 1:25: he will be blessed in his action (ποιήσει αὐτοῦ) in company with Abraham and Rahab (2:21–26).

Comment

14 Τί τὸ ὄφελος, ἀδελφοί μου, "My brothers, what good will it do?" V 14 is composed of two questions, both rhetorical and both constructed to expect answers of no (μή). The phrase τί τὸ ὄφελος signals the beginning of an argumentative style that resembles a diatribe (Vouga, 85; Mussner, 130; see 1 Cor

15:32; Sir 20:30; 41:14; Philo, *De Post. Caini* 86; Epictetus, *Diss.* 1,4.16; 6,33; 3,7.30; 3,24.51 for the dialogue style). James appears to be combating some form of misunderstanding that has developed in the church. The source of this problem may be the teachers (to be introduced in chap. 3) who are setting forth erroneous teaching (Moo, 99). The issue at hand is the nature of genuine faith. Is it merely "right belief" expressed in a confession of doctrine or is it essentially practical, requiring "deeds" to authenticate its genuineness? The close association of faith and "works" has led interpreters going back to Luther to view James as in direct conflict with Paul. But such misunderstanding has developed out of the failure to see that Paul and James use two (perhaps three) words—"faith," "justify" (v 21), and "works"—differently to address various situations (see below; also see Jeremias, "Paul and James," 370). ὄφελος, lit., "advantage," "use," (found here and in 2:16; 1 Cor 15:32), may carry the sense "what does it profit?"—a phrase that is repeated in 2:16 and thus possibly forms an *inclusio.* The thrust of James' argument is that indeed there is no profit (i.e., salvation-bringing efficacy) for anyone exhibiting the type of faith described in vv 15–16a. This is serious for the Christian in the light of what has just been said (v 13). Also, the address ἀδελφοί μου is a link between 2:1–13 and 14–16 (see 2:1, 5). The flow of James' thinking is uninterrupted. Those who are depicted in 2:1–13 as guilty of discriminating against the poor demonstrate that they do not have the faith required for eschatological salvation. Lorenzen, "Faith without works," 231, correctly notes that the complementary phrase is "profit *before* God," i.e., the perspective is soteriological, not merely ethical; but, to be sure, it is a question of "both . . . and" for James, who in any case is not concerned with the question of how little or how much faith a person has to put into practice to be treated as righteous. "James is not interested in man's *habitus*" (= disposition), as Bieder, "Christliche Existenz," 103, puts it, going on to note that the entire address of this epistle is "the life of the eschatological community of the Lord" (108) in which "works" mark out "the way" (*der Weg*) to be taken by the church in its Christian existence (113).

ἐὰν πίστιν λέγῃ τις ἔχειν ἔργα δὲ μὴ ἔχῃ, "if anyone claims that he has faith, but has no deeds?" This third class conditional sentence with the present subjunctive λέγῃ/ἔχῃ suggests a repeated assertion: "if a person keeps on saying he or she has faith but keeps on having no works." As in 2:2–4, the use of the subjunctive need not imply a hypothetical illustration but can indicate a real situation in James' church (Laws, 120–21; Reicke, 32). It is highly unlikely that the Christians to whom James wrote were ignorant of Paul's teaching of "justification by faith [alone]," and it is just as unlikely that Paul would have accepted the bogus faith of 2:14 (Moo, 100). Paul uses "faith" to denote a confidence in God's saving act in Christ, who died for our trespasses and was raised from the dead for our justification (Rom 4:24–25). In a different context, James—whose view of faith (as necessary for salvation) does not differ from Paul or any other NT writer—is attacking an understanding of "faith" that sees it merely as a pious sentiment or an intellectual acceptance of doctrine (i.e., "God is one," 2:19; see Jeremias, "Paul and James," 370).

Moreover, it may be that the term "works" (ἔργα) is better translated "deeds," "acts," with Amphoux and Bouttier, "Prédication," 9, to avoid confusion with Paul's teaching on nomistic religion, i.e., "works of the law." Thus ἔργα is used differently by the two writers (Usteri, "Glaube, Werke, usw," 245). Paul in polemical contexts views "works" as the keeping of the commandments of the Torah while James employs "works" to signify acts of mercy and kindness (2:13; the fulfilling of the royal law, 2:8). Moo (101–2) has questioned whether such a distinction is valid and necessary, since Paul can think of works as doing good (obedience) or bad (as in Rom 9:10–11), whereas, as will be seen, Abraham is depicted by James as doing acts of obedience rather than acts of charity. Thus for both Paul and James the term "works" in contexts that do not address issues of nomism is summed up under the meaning "acts done in obedience to God." But Moo's objection does not alter the fact that Paul and James use "faith" and "works" (as later on both writers will use "justification") to encounter different situations. On the one hand, Paul is attempting to overcome the false teaching that salvation is based on faith supplemented by works, a merging that is unthinkable for the apostle (Gal 2:16, 21; Rom. 4:1–5; 9:32). James, on the other hand, is combating a false picture of faith drawn by a misguided believer who has been "saved by faith" but is led astray. Faith without works is useless, James avers. Faith is not seen by James to be deficient as though it needed something extra (i.e., works), but he contends that true faith must find some expression other than verbalization (Davids, 121) or pious sentiment (vv 15–16). The stances of Paul and James are not "salvation by faith without works" versus "salvation by faith plus works" respectively. Rather, Paul denies the need for "pre-conversion works" and James emphasizes the "absolute necessity of post-conversion works" (Moo, 100; see W. C. van Unnik, "The Teaching of Good Works in I Peter," *NTS* 1 [1954–55] 92–100). See too the *Excursus* "Faith and Deeds in 2:14–26."

μὴ δύναται ἡ πίστις σῶσαι αὐτόν, "Can a faith like this save him?" This is the second question of v 14. Rhetorically framed, it implies that the faith of v 14a is useless for salvation. The point made by the aorist infinitive (σῶσαι) may be climactic thus emphasizing the end result. James is not saying that faith (alone) cannot save (see 1:21; 2:24). The πίστις of 14b refers to the "workless" faith of 14a (the use of the definite article ἡ with πίστις suggests a form of the demonstrative [so translated here] though Moule [*Idiom Book*, 111] wonders if ἡ can mean "his" ["Can his faith save him?"]). Yet, even Moule's proposal does not eliminate the reference to the impotence ("and *ipso facto* without worth," Adamson, 122) of faith as defined in 14a, and thus James' referent is quite clear.

The topic of salvation (in the verb σώζειν) is concerned with its eschatological dimension (Davids, 120; Vouga, 86: "σώζειν is always used in the letter in the soteriological-eschatological sense"). To be sure, there is one instance when σώζειν could be understood to mean physical healing (5:15) but it is quite clear in our present verse that the endtime is in view (Foerster, *TDNT* 7:995; see 1:21; 4:12; 5:20). Thus James is saying that faith without works is insufficient for salvation, which makes sense of 2:13. The threat is that damnation, not salvation, is in store for those who fit the description of vv 14–16, a warning that picks up and enforces the fate of those who show partiality to the rich at the expense of the poor (vv 2–3, 12–13). James is drawing the conclusion that works are not optional for the person who claims to have faith; rather the former is inseparable from the latter, since he is advocating the need for a living faith in which belief and practice belong inextricably together. A faith without works is of no profit on two counts: it has no efficacy for the person claiming this kind of a faith, for such self-delusion (cf. 1:22) can end only in eschatological disaster, and it does nothing to alleviate the suffering of the needy, who are not helped by pious words alone.

Excursus: Note on Faith and Deeds in 2:14–26

This section centers on a matter of debate in a twofold sense: there was obviously a lively discussion underway in James' own community; and in the history of interpretation this passage has raised the issue of the interfacing of James' teaching and Paul's and has called forth a number of proposals. No final resolution of some exegetical matters appears in sight. The most we can hope to do is to state the options and express a preference.

(a) Those who see James and Paul as being in irreconcilable antagonism look to this passage as part of the diversity of New Testament Christianity. Thus the two points of view regarding faith and works classically stated by Luther lie unresolved and unrelated (cf. Blackman, 96; Bultmann, *Theology* 2:163; Bornkamm, *Paul*, 153–54; Souček, "Zu Problemen," 467: "What we meet is not only a tension [between Paul and James] but an antithesis").

(b) At the other extreme, it is said (by Ross, 53) that there is no conflict at all, since James and Paul "are not antagonists facing each other with crossed swords; they stand back to back, confronting different foes of the Gospel" (cf. Mitton, 8).

(c) A mediating position is taken by interpreters such as Barclay at the popular level (*Daily Study Bible*, 72–74) and Jeremias ("Paul and James") with the more academic treatment. These interpretations are at one in the central affirmation that both biblical writers are agreed but they start out from different positions. Paul begins with the Christian life at its very commencement: we are saved by faith (alone), according to Rom 3:28; Gal 2:16 with no reliance on the "works of the law" permitted. In Rom 4:2 (ἐξ ἔργων) and 4:6 (χωρὶς ἔργων) "works" is used by Paul without a modifier, but he really means ἔργα τοῦ νόμου (Fitzmyer, in Reumann, *Righteousness*, 220). James, on the other side, begins his discussion much later in the *ordo salutis* with the case of the professing Christian who has fallen into wrong-headed ways and needs the reminder that genuine faith must issue in "good works," which are not salvific but evidential, i.e., they give proof that saving faith is real. Paul agrees with this understanding of the role of "works" (Gal 5:6; Rom 2:6; 14:12) treating them as both a sign of new life and a standard by which believers will be called to account at the final day (Snodgrass, "Justification by Grace—to the Doers"). James, on the other hand, is not contradicting the necessity of "saving faith": "You believe? Excellent!" (2:19); and in 2:22 he writes of "faith at work with his deeds," a phrase that presupposes that faith is prior and indispensable (Mussner, 142), though it cannot really be dissociated from deeds. "The alternative of faith without works is unthinkable for James" (Mussner, ibid.).

This is a neat way to smooth out the differences, but there are residual problems. Granted that the exact phrase "works of *the law*" is not present in James (but see

Wall, "Law and Gospel," 68 n.48) and that Paul can use ἔργον in a positive way (1 Thess 1:3: τὸ ἔργον τῆς πίστεως is the most striking, just as ἔργα ἀγαθά according to Eph 2:10 in the post-Pauline church stands out in its starkness; see G. P. Wiles, *Paul's Intercessory Prayers,* 177–80, citing for comparison 2 Thess 1:11), it still remains that (i) the two writers do not assign the same emphasis to faith. Paul implies—if he does not actually say—that we are saved by faith *alone* (the emphatic addition to Rom 3:28 was made by Luther when he supplied *allein* and gave the slogan *sola fide* to the world [see the discussion and bibliography in Mussner, 148–50]). James, on the contrary, both denies this (in 2:24, which has οὐκ ἐκ πίστεως μόνον; but James does *not* say οὐκ ἐκ πίστεως μόνης) and asserts the contrary by introducing works as having a part to play in the process of full salvation (v 22). And (ii) the two thinkers have varying estimates of the example of Abraham. Paul sees the patriarch as the paradigm par excellence of a faith that responds to God's call and promise and rejoices in God's acceptance (Rom 4; Gal 4:6–29). He becomes the model believer in whose steps gentile Christians are invited to tread. James sets the patriarch less in the framework of salvation history and views him more as a typically pious man who in obeying God validated the faith he professed (2:22) and received a title that betokened the intimacy of a fellowship with God that rested on obedience and action (2:24). The same biblical character is made to speak to two situations, with a change of emphasis.

(d) A further way in which to interpret James' teaching when set alongside Paul's acknowledges two different historical contexts. This line of interpretation is generally accepted today, and if there is anything like a consensus developing, it is in this direction (Laws, 139; Lohse, "Glaube und Werke," 290–92; Souček, "Zu Problemen"). Two recent treatments of the problem may be given. First, for Goppelt (*Theology of the New Testament* 2:200–211) the thrust of James' advocacy of works is directed against a misuse of Paul's teaching (which has become distorted, perhaps by an unwise use of a slogan such as "by faith alone"). However true this axiom may be as a summary of Paul's insistence on the adequacy of faith to save, it is a travesty of his teaching to turn it into a formula of convenience which so exalts faith that it leads to ethical indifference and license. The outcome is a Christianity that shelters behind Paul's language and loses the tension between "already saved . . . not yet fully saved" (Vouga, 85). Indubitably in Paul's career the first rumblings of that distortion are heard (Rom 6:1–12, 15; Gal 5:13–15) and are met by the apostle's firm rejection of antinomianism and his requirement that new life in Christ should be conducted at the highest levels of moral stringency and integrity. James, on this understanding, is conducting his polemic not against Paul but against a slogan championed and misapplied by Paul's followers whose outlook and practice may well be seen in Matt 7:21; 22:11–14 (Goppelt, 209; cf. Davids, 132: "one need look no farther than the situations envisaged in the Matthew 7 passage to find a suitable *Sitz im Leben*").

Second, Reumann (*Righteousness,* 156–58) builds on this view and adds a significant contribution. He sees James cast not only in the negative role of pulling down a misinterpretation of Pauline doctrine but equally as adopting a positive stance in order to rehabilitate Paul. "James protects the Pauline view at a point where it has seemed vulnerable in application" (158). The wheel has turned a full circle, and we are almost at the point of concluding that Paul and James are in agreement. This would be even more apparent if we ventured the supplementary idea that *both* Paul *and* James are standing in need of defense and rehabilitation. Paul must be rescued from those who enthusiastically perverted his teaching of "salvation by faith" and made it an excuse to discount ethical endeavor. James, who was known historically as a central figure in Jewish Christianity and distinct from Paul and his gentile mission, needed to have his emphasis on practical righteousness set in a framework where faith is given a supreme place (as 2:22 does, even if this appeal to Abraham's ἔργα paved the way for a later teaching on "salvation by works" [cf. *1 Clement*], and the medieval doctrine of *fides formata per caritatem* in Aquinas, which, it is claimed, Luther misunderstood [see A. B. Crabtree, *The Restored Relationship* (London: Carey Kingsgate, 1963) 123, 141]; but this is a debatable conclusion: see the review in *Baptist Quarterly* 20.5 [1964] 235–36). In addition, the works that demonstrate true messianic faith must be shown to be best understood as help to the poor and afflicted and a resolute turning aside from the Zealot mandate of strife and violence. Valid faith also entails a refusal to side with aristocratic oppressions. It may be then that not only is this passage a bid to rehabilitate the authentic evangelical theme, stated by Paul, but also an attempt by the Jacobean editor to set his master in the role of one whose works genuinely—if tragically (5:6)—prove his messianic faith.

15 ἐὰν ἀδελφὸς ἢ ἀδελφὴ ὑπάρχωσιν καὶ λειπόμενοι τῆς ἐφημέρου τροφῆς, "To illustrate: if a brother or sister is ill-clad and is lacking in daily sustenance." Against many commentators (Ropes, 206, who uses the expression of vv 15–16, "a little parable"; Mussner, 131; Dibelius, 152–53; Moo, 103; Adamson, 122) vv 15–16 depict a real situation in the church. The third class condition continues with ἐάν followed by the present subjunctive ὑπάρχωσιν (from ὑπάρχειν, "to exist," lit., "be"; see BDF § 414.1). This word, instead of the usual εἶναι, may be James' attempt to show that poverty is a permanent or at least an enduring state for those mentioned in v 15 (Adamson, 122). ἀδελφή, "sister," would imply a female member of the Christian community and taken with ἀδελφός may mean husband and wife (see Cantinat, 141–42). Whatever the relationship, these two persons are ill-clad. Normally, we might have expected the subject to be taken as singular (followed by γυμνός or γυμνή), but this is not the case (BDF § 135.4). γυμνοί probably is not meant to be construed as meaning a person totally naked but as one lacking proper clothing (Job 22:6; Isa 20:2,3; 58:7; 2 Macc 11:12), possibly without the outer garment (John 21:7; Matt 25:36).

Not only do these poor persons lack sufficient clothing but they are without adequate food supplies as well (λειπόμενοι from λείπειν, "to leave," but in the passive it means "be lacking"; see 1:4). τῆς ἐφημέρου τροφῆς speaks of their deficiency "in daily sustenance" (τροφή, "nourishment," "food," BGD, 827). ἐφήμερος, "daily," is a *hapax legomenon* (but see ἐφημερία, Luke 1:5, 8; cf. Matt 6:11; Luke 11:3 in the Lord's Prayer), and may mean that they lack a "daily supply" (Adamson, 122; Dibelius, 153) of the means to stay alive.

16 εἴπῃ δέ τις αὐτοῖς ἐξ ὑμῶν, "One of you says to them." See 2:18, which continues the report of direct speech (*oratio recta*) but poses the issue of the speaker's identity. The opening phrase of 2:16 is an extension of the condition started in v 15.

ὑπάγετε ἐν εἰρήνῃ, θερμαίνεσθε χορτάζεσθε, "'Go in peace, get warm, and be filled [with food].'" This is the response that some in the church are making to other church members (and possibly to non-church members, if these are in view) who are obviously in need. Each verb is in the imperative, resembling a wish-prayer (Wiles, *Paul's Intercessory Prayers*, passim). ὑπάγετε ἐν εἰρήνῃ, "Go in peace" ("Good luck to you," NEB) is probably based on the idiom לֵךְ

לְשָׁלוֹם (*leḵû lešālōm*; לכו is qal imperative of *hālak*, "to go," "to walk"; Judg 18:6; 1 Sam 1:17; 20:42; 2 Sam 15:9; Mark 5:34; Luke 7:50) and suggests a departure in peace offered as a prayer that God may give *šālōm*, i.e., prosperity (ἐν εἰρήνῃ, which is dative of attendant circumstance; see Moule, *Idiom Book*, 70, 79; the ἐν of our present phrase is used in loose fashion, similar to the accusative; BDF § 206.1).

θερμαίνεσθε means "warm yourself" (in middle voice) as from the heat of a fire (Mark 14:67; John 18:18, 25; see Isa 44:16; Hag 1:6; Job 31:20; see BGD, 359). If taken in the passive voice, then it reads, "be warmed." χορτάζεσθε means "be filled [with food]" (the words in brackets are understood; see 2:15). If taken as middle instead of passive (Mayor, 97–98; Adamson, 123) the verb is "eat one's fill" (see Phil 4:12). Probably the middle is better here for both verbs (Davids, 122) though either voice points to the fact that some professed believers are failing to meet the needs of other church members (Dibelius, 153; Moo, 103). This is then a serious charge (see Matt 25:31–46; 1 John 3:17–18), implying a breakdown in response to a dire human condition. The prayer-speech is thus shown to be hypocritical (contrast 3:17: ἀνυπόκριτος).

μὴ δῶτε δὲ αὐτοῖς τὰ ἐπιτήδεια τοῦ σώματος, τί τὸ ὄφελος, "but you do not meet their bodily needs—then, what good is that?" The adversative δέ signals a change in thought ("and yet"). δῶτε is aorist subjunctive (dependent on ἐάν in v 15). The people spoken of (in αὐτοῖς) are the brother and sister of v 15. ἐπιτήδεια is "necessary," "proper" (found only here and in a variant reading of Acts 24:25). The needs of the body have been ignored (Mayor, 99). Instead of food and clothing the needy receive "cold deeds with warm words," which ring as hollow sentiments (ibid.). τὸ ὄφελος begins the apodosis after the long protasis started in v 15 (see Davids, 122).

17 οὕτως καὶ ἡ πίστις, ἐὰν μὴ ἔχῃ ἔργα, νεκρά ἐστιν καθ᾿ ἑαυτήν, "so even faith, if it does not have deeds [to support it] and is on its own, is dead." James draws his conclusion from the case illustrated. οὕτως, "so even," is James' usual way of applying a metaphor or example (1:11; 2:26; 3:5; see Davids, 123). But none of these verses cited rules out the possibility that the example just given is in fact an actual happening, and thus James' use of οὕτως at the beginning of v 17 in no way prevents us from understanding the verse as related to a real problem in the church. ἡ πίστις harks back to the so-called faith of 2:14. Again we have a third class condition with ἐάν and the present subjunctive of ἔχειν (see v 14). νεκρά describes as "dead" the faith that is without works. Such a faith is dead in the sense of ineffectual (see Rom 7:8; Heb 6:1; 9:14). The phrase καθ᾿ ἑαυτήν, placed at the conclusion of the clause for emphasis, modifies "faith" not "dead" ("faith alone," KJV; "faith by itself," RSV). The phrase καθ᾿ ἑαυτήν, lit., "by itself," "on its own," describes a faith that is "not merely outwardly inoperative but inwardly dead" (Mayor, 99). A faith without works (by itself) is no more a living faith than a corpse without breath is a living person (2:26; Adamson, 124). Works are not to be viewed as an "added extra" any more than breath is to be taken as an "added extra" to a living body (Davids, 122). Faith and works (as life and breath) go together and the former cannot exist without the latter. The professed believer who refrains from helping those in need exhibits the type of behavior that is associated with one whose faith is dead, i.e., ineffectual and a make-believe.

18 Ἀλλ' ἐρεῖ τις· σὺ πίστιν ἔχεις, κἀγὼ ἔργα ἔχω, "But someone will say, 'You have faith; I have deeds.'" The problem here has centered on the identity of the one (τις) purported to have spoken the *oratio recta* of v 18. Three views have been offered to account for the role this speaker plays (see *Form/ Structure/Setting*). (1) Some take the person to be an ally of James (Mayor, 99–100; Adamson, 124–25, 135–37; Mussner, 136–38, who translates v 18: "but it is *rightly* said . . .") who takes up James' argument and proceeds to carry it forward. The strength of this view is that it explains how the pronouns are handled consistently throughout the verse. The "you" (σύ) always refers to the "false believer" of vv 14–17 and the "I" (ἐγώ) always refers to the ally of James. But a difficult obstacle to overcome is how to understand the adversative ἀλλά, "but." To hold that the interlocutor of v 18 is actually a proponent of James' argument requires that ἀλλά be understood as "indeed." This latter use of the connective has some support (cf. John 16:2; 1 Cor 3:2; 2 Cor 7:11; 11:1; Phil 1:18), but the usage seems the exception rather than the rule (BGD, 38; Davids, 124; Moo, 104). Besides, why would James introduce a third person here? He has been talking directly to those mentioned in vv 14–17 and to interject a third party seems unnecessary. Also it is probably too much to expect James' readers to draw the inference that the remark of v 18 is actually from an ally of the writer.

(2) Other interpreters understand the speaker as an opponent of James. This allows for the translation of ἀλλά as "but," which commonly introduces an objection (Zerwick and Grosvenor, *Grammatical Analysis*, 695), and fits neatly with the thought that there is presently an ongoing debate in the church and that James has introduced the words of an objector who stands opposed to his position. But if this is so, where do the words of the objector end and those of James begin? The clauses that follow the words "You have faith; I have deeds" do not oppose James' thoughts but in fact support his position. Furthermore, if the words of the objector are simply σὺ πίστιν ἔχεις, κἀγὼ ἔργα ἔχω, then we are left to explain why the opponent of James would take up this position. James has just finished describing the party of vv 14–17 as one who professes faith but offers no works. The more natural way to express opposition to James would be to say: "You (James) have works; I (the objector) have faith" (so emended in the Latin Codex Corbiensis, a twelfth-century work). To explain this difficulty, some suggest that the objector's words, presupposed in the original, have dropped out of the text (Spitta, 77–79; Windisch, 16–17), thus leaving us with James' reply. But there is no manuscript evidence to support this. If the opening words of 2:18 are from an objector, perhaps the comment is in the form of a question: "Do you (James) have faith?" (so Hort 60–61). James then begins his reply with "I do have works," and this reply continues through the remaining verses of the chapter. But such an interpretation is strained, to say the least, and has not been well received (see Moo; Mayor, 99–100).

(3) A third way of understanding the opening statement is to connect the "You" and "I" not to James and his opponent but rather to representative

positions within the church. That is, an imaginary objector points out that some people have faith and others have works. This may be seen as a reference to Pauline teaching that each Christian has been endowed with particular gifts (1 Cor 12), one of which is faith (1 Cor 12:9; Rom 12:3). Then James' contention that faith and works are inseparable is met by the objection that a person with faith is just as religious as a person with works: both are exercising their gifts. The personal pronouns, however, have to be assigned only a mild function in this interpretation and are little more than demonstratives: "one . . . another" (see Ropes, 208–14; Mitton, 108–9; Dibelius, 155–56; Laws, 123–24; Moo, 105–6). The strength of this interpretation is that one can understand the opening words of v 18 as coming from the mouth of an objector without the questions that were raised by the preceding interpretation. However, a telling argument against this position is that grammatically the construction submitted is very awkward. The normal expression would have been the more straightforward ἄλλος . . . ἄλλος ("one has faith, another has deeds"; see Adamson, 137).

No one interpretation is free from problems, but it seems that the third interpretation is the least likely. Of the first two, the latter fits better with the tone of the argument if a case can be made out for continuing the objector's speech into v 19 (see below). The use of ἀλλά as adversative requires that the following words should be in the form of an objection to what has been said previously. The sudden appearance of an "ally"—since his unheralded appearance is uncalled for—speaks against the first position. Dibelius, 154, wrote that this verse is "one of the most difficult New Testament passages," and this pessimistic assessment may be illustrated by two other exegetical possibilities for v 18.

There is more to confirm the interpretation that the opening words of v 18 are spoken against James. One view is to argue that the remainder of chap. 2, beginning with "Show me," stands in opposition to "You have faith; I have deeds." This confirms the interpretation that the words in v 18a are in support of the person accused of having "no works" in vv 14–17. But it may be that even though the thoughts of v 18a are not of James, he has recast them in his own words. The actual words of the objector are: "I have faith; You [James] have deeds"; but James has echoed that argument from his own standpoint: he has become the "I" of the clause and his opponent has become the "You." Such a position does justice to the use of ἀλλά as adversative, is consistent in its use of the pronouns (σύ, ἐγώ), and keeps the tension between v 18a and vv 18b–26. Moreover, James has not adopted the thought of v 18a. He still holds that the party of vv 14–17 has no works and indeed has a useless faith, but by keeping his words in the forefront he has (for the sake of the discussion) rephrased the argument so that the reader is not saddled with the burden of trying to discover who is saying what. In short, someone has posed an alternate position to James and he has simply restated it for all to hear. The τις of v 18 remains an opponent of James, as suggested by the second interpretation above. Another possibility (which we have followed) is to take the speaker's words as continuing beyond v 18. Then we are hearing a full statement of his position, which James reports only to respond to at v 20. All the advantages mentioned above are retained, and further support is gained from two considerations: (a) the heart of the issue is seen to be the nature of what James regards as "true faith" (i.e., it is inseparable from deeds and is always hyphenated with works) and (b) full force is given to the indictment of the opponent in v 20. See later. But v 18b needs to be scrutinized before a final conclusion on v 18a is reached.

After a consideration of this *crux interpretum* in v 18a, we now turn our attention to one issue as a prelude to an examination of v 18b which turns on the definition of πίστις in the pericope. It is given a negative character in vv 14, 17, i.e., it is a faith that is dead because there are no works to complement and so demonstrate its genuineness. The term "works" (ἔργα) refers to acts of charity, though such a categorizing actually places these acts under the heading of acts of obedience to God (see above), i.e., to the royal law of love to one's neighbor. Thus, regardless of how one interprets the "someone" of v 18a (ἀλλ' ἐρεῖ τις) the meaning of the remaining words of v 18a is clear: some have faith while others have works. Such a conclusion based on faith and works as valid alternatives will be vigorously rebutted. But there are two distinct ways to exegete v 18b.

First, James is seen as adding his retort, δεῖξόν μοι τὴν πίστιν σου χωρὶς τῶν ἔργων, κἀγώ . . . πίστιν, "Show me your faith apart from your deeds, and I will show you my faith [demonstrated] by my deeds." In essence, James replies that works prove that one's faith is alive. The issue is not that some have faith and others have works. Rather, for James, the issue is whether one can prove the existence of a saving faith without works (cf. Heb 11:6). The objector says yes; James answers no. By his response in v 18b, James is thought to lay the foundation of a strong argument that says that simple profession of faith is quite inadequate in God's eyes. James challenges his opponent to demonstrate (δεικνύναι: "to prove, make known"; cf. Epictetus, *Diss.* 1.4, 10; 4.13 for calls to validate virtue) his faith apart from works. This is an impossible challenge to meet; for how can one show faith unless by means of visible and tangible evidence? The opponent might be tempted to fall back on the argument that simple profession is a visible proof of faith sufficient for salvation (such as Abraham's turning from idolatry). But if so, James anticipates such a thought and will soon dismiss that belief with the aid of two examples par excellence (i.e., Abraham and Rahab) of faith-with-works.

The second way of understanding the part verse (v 18b) is to take it as a continuation of the rival's statement. It assumes that when James puts this challenge into his opponent's mouth he is following the well-established principle of dialectical debate, namely, to give the strongest argument to the side with which one has the least sympathy. Then the challenge to show proof of faith and works is directed to James and is intended to embarrass him, since if James concedes that the two concepts can be separated, the objector will then have recourse to his "faith" to validate "works" as separate and distinct items. The objector wants James to isolate the two "sides" of what constitutes vital religion (cf. Cranfield, "Message," 341). Once that fateful concession is made, James' case is lost, and the interlocutor has scored his debating point—although it is James himself that has put the rival position into his mouth in order later to refute him. On balance, we have inclined to the second possibility, but with some hesitation.

The same possibility carries over into v 19 where (according to this view) we are hearing the opponent's voice (in either the first part or the entire verse). James' reply opens at v 20. But most scholars take v 19 to be a statement from James.

19 σὺ πιστεύεις ὅτι εἷς ἐστιν ὁ θεός, καλῶς ποιεῖς· καὶ τὰ δαιμόνια πιστεύουσιν καὶ φρίσσουσιν, "Do you believe that 'God is one'? Excellent! Yet the demons believe [this], and they shudder." "You believe" is usually taken to be James' retort, but may well be addressed to James by the opponent of v 18 (cf. Adamson, 125) and may be in the form of a question, as adopted here (UBSGNT[3]; Westcott and Hort [1881]; Nestle-Aland[25]). The use of πιστεύειν with ὅτι leads to the conclusion that what follows is not a call to personal trust in God (for which we would expect ἐν governing the dative, εἰς, or ἐπί; see Bultmann, *TDNT* 6:210–12) but simply a belief that he exists; more specifically, it is the expression of a creed. In this instance the confession is that "God is one" (see *Notes* for textual problems). The origin of this monotheistic belief is the Jewish *Shema,* a confession used by Jews and Christians alike (Deut 6:4; Mark 12:29; Rom 3:20; Josephus, *Ant.* 3.91; 4.201; 5.112, "to acknowledge God as one is common to all the Hebrews"; *Ep. Arist.* 132; *Sib. Or.* 3.629: "there is only one God and no other one"; Philo, *De Op. Mund.*, 171. On the topic of Jewish monotheism, see Fr. Mussner, *Tractate on the Jews,* tr. L. Swindler [Philadelphia: Fortress Press, 1984] 52–59). This confession is given not to criticize it (see 2:8), but to point out its inadequacy by itself.

The question concerns whether it is James who is challenging his debating partner or vice versa. If it is the former, James is remarking that to believe that God is one is to do well (see 2:8). This may suggest that James approves (at least) of this much. But since he will concede next that even the demons believe in monotheism, the use of καλῶς ποιεῖς may be an attempt at irony on James' part (Moo, 106; "semi-ironic," Davids, 125). To believe that God is one is indeed necessary, but not sufficient, for even the demons believe ("they are quite orthodox," Davids, 125), though no one of James' audience would admit that such faith is able to save them. The demons believe and shudder (φρίσσειν, a NT *hapax legomenon;* Lat. *horreo;* the Hebrew is derived from שָׂעַר, *śāʿar;* see Dibelius, 160; Windisch, 18). The demons express a belief in the divine elsewhere in the NT (Mark 1:24; 3:7; Acts 16:17; 19:15) and exhibit fear before God as they confront Jesus (Mark 1:23, 24; 5:7), usually in the stories of exorcisms (BGD, 866). All this leads the reader to agree that the demons' knowledge of God is not able to save them; it indicates that demons react to the divine numen (*1 Enoch* 13.3; 69.1,14). But even with this admission, there is little that can be said for this type of faith: it is worse than useless (Davids, 126).

It is still an exegetical possibility that the challenge about faith in one God is issued by James' interlocutor, who may be pursuing in v 19 the same tactic as in v 18. He is seeking to isolate faith and conceptualize it as an entity apart from "deeds." To do so he makes play with the idea that belief in one God is a central Jewish and Jewish Christian credo, shared also by the underworld (and it appears in pagan exorcistic formulas; Windisch). His retort to a commonly held belief is that confession of one God is a widespread reality: even the demons hold it, and they obviously have no works to demonstrate whether it is rightly or wrongly held. Again, the objector wants James to admit the distinct possibility of faith existing *in vacuo*. But James is not prepared to make such an admission, voiced in vv 18–19, and is ready with his crushing reply in v 20, "You empty-headed person." With less than final conviction we have championed the second of these two readings in v 19.

20 θέλεις δὲ γνῶναι, ὦ ἄνθρωπε κενέ, ὅτι ἡ πίστις χωρὶς τῶν ἔργων ἀργή ἐστιν, "You empty-headed person, don't you understand that apart from deeds faith is ineffectual?" Now comes James' forthright response to convince his opponent. In a single sentence he maintains that faith without works is of no value, i.e., in the debate the two concepts of faith and works are inseparable. The particle δέ is a sign that James is about to commence his reply or (alternatively) to step up his attack. "Don't you understand?" reflects the tone of Greek moralists, as a use of the interrogative found in diatribe (Adamson, 127). Literally, the phrase conveys the idea "Do you need convincing?" (Mussner, 139; Dibelius, 149). The use of ὦ with the vocative is exceptional in the NT (in contrast to classical usage; Zerwick, *Biblical Greek*, 11–12) and the inclusion of it in our present passage underlies the strong feeling behind what James is saying. But we can also infer that James is speaking with emotion from the context (BDF § 146.1b). The address κενέ, "empty-headed" (κενός is "empty" in the sense of "foolish," "inane": Windisch has *ein Hohlkopf*, "a blockhead"), reflects the style of diatribe, as well as the discourse of Jewish teachers (Davids, 126; cf. 1 Cor 15:36; Matt 23:17; Luke 24:25; Gal 3:1; see also 4:4 for direct address; Bultmann, *Stil*, 14, 60–61). κενός may here denote deficient understanding (Mussner, 140; Cantinat, 148); but the term also suggests moral error (Judg 9:4; 11:3 [B] LXX) as well as even sin (4:17). Windisch, 18, thinks that κενός in a context of moral warning (see also 4:5) is almost equivalent to ῥακά (Matt 5:22), which suggests that James sees in the person in 2:20 the "fool" of the Psalms who denies God (Ps 53:1–3; see Oepke, *TDNT* 3:660). The wisdom background is evident.

For James, the person of 2:20 (note the consistent use of singular address and verb in vv 18, 19) does not regard the error of his way; he does not perceive that faith without works is useless. In v 14 a faith without works is said to be of no profit; in v 17 it is treated as dead; and here it is described as ἀργός ("ineffectual"; derived from ἀ + ἔργος, lit., "without work"; see Matt 20:3, 6 for the sense of unemployed, without work to do). We have a play on words here: "faith that has no works does not work" (Moo, 107; Mussner, 140; Rendall, *The Epistle of St. James and Judaic Christianity*, 75 n.3, citing Titus 1:12). This in a sense sums up the preceding section 2:14–19, and useless and unproductive faith (BGD, 104) will be cast in even darker tones when it is compared with the true faith of Abraham and Rahab.

21 Ἀβραὰμ ὁ πατὴρ ἡμῶν, "Our father Abraham." James, by recalling the example of Abraham, epitomizes "faith-with-works," that is, hyphenated faith, as the only proper lifestyle of a Christian. Abraham, the founding father of the Jewish people, is one of the most revered figures in Israel's history. He is often referred to in support of all kinds of Jewish virtues and graces (see Schlatter for rabbinic examples). It may be that the position represented by the opponent of James (2:18) had typically cited Abraham in defense of "faith apart from works," since in Gen 15:6 God is said to reckon righteousness to Abraham because the latter believed in him (see on 2:23 below). For the Jews Abraham was the hero of faith (Dibelius, 161–63; Str-B, 3:186–201). Philo refers to Abraham's offering of Isaac as his greatest work (Philo, *De Abr.*, 167; cf. 1 Macc 2:52); and this is commonplace in early Judaism (H. J. Schoeps, *Paul*, tr. H. Knight [London: Lutterworth, 1961] 141–49). The qualifier "our" father underscores the Jewish background of James and his readers (Isa 51:2; 4 Macc 16:20; Matt 3:9; John 8:39, 53), though such use of the possessive pronoun is not conclusive proof of Jewish provenance (Rom 4:11, 12, 16; 9:7–8; Gal 2:7; 29; 1 *Clem.* 3.12). The entire verse is an interrogative, expecting an answer yes (οὐκ).

This verse becomes problematic because of the term δικαιοῦν, "to justify, to prove righteous," in the opening, οὐκ ἐξ ἔργων ἐδικαιώθη, "wasn't Abraham proved righteous [as demonstrated] by his deeds?" This usage has been the reason for some to conclude that James stands in contrast to Paul because the latter claims that Abraham was justified by faith and not by works (Rom 4:1–3). But we must clarify what each writer means when he uses the word "justify." Paul clearly uses δικαιοῦν to denote that forensic, eschatological, and kingly act in which God declares sinners rightly related to himself in a new world order (Moo, 108–111; Davids, 127–28; Martin, *Reconciliation*, 32–37). This term also designates the initial transfer of the sinner from death to life; from a nonrelationship into a right relationship with God. Such a change is appropriated by the sinner through faith in Jesus Christ (Rom 3:24–26, which may incorporate and rework a Jewish-Christian formulation; Martin, *Reconciliation*, 81–89). Thus Paul could say that Abraham was justified by faith only and not by works (Rom 4:22; Gal 3:6–9).

If James' use of δικαιοῦν (the Hebrew root צדיק, *ṣaddîq* in the hiphil form *hiṣdîq*) here were the same as that of Paul, then we would be forced to agree that James does indeed contradict Paul on the issue of the means of justification. But such is not the case, for in vv 21–24 Abraham's works (which may recall the thought of testings, πειρασμοί, 1:2, 12; see Davids, 127) are the evidence that God declares Abraham as "righteous," i.e., faithful (1 Macc 2:52). This suggests that a mainly demonstrative sense lies behind δικαιοῦν. Such an understanding stresses that works are the only means of demonstrating one's righteous standing (Moo, 109). This use has lexical support (Gen 44:16; Luke 7:29–35; see Schrenk, *TDNT* 2:213–14). When the comment is made that James is not asking "How can one's righteousness be demonstrated?" but "What kind of faith secures righteousness?" (Moo, 109), it may be that James would not have entertained such a dichotomizing. The nub of his response to the objection in vv 18–19 is that no such tearing apart of faith and works is possible and that the only faith that justifies is faith-united-with-works as a single reality. On a wider front, whereas Paul uses δικαιοῦν to depict the initial gift of righteousness by God to the believer on the basis of faith alone (Rom 4:5 for a classic statement of Pauline *justificatio impiorum*), James uses the term to denote God's eschatological pronouncement on one who is shown to be righteous, i.e., his faith is authentic; it is part of James' "apocalyptic pareneation" (so Wall, "Law and Gospel," 54, but his setting of James *against* Paul may need revision in the light of Snodgrass's study on the role of works in the apocalyptic theology of Pauline justification-teaching: see the latter's "Justification by Grace—to the Doers").

This line of interpretation takes up the Jewish understanding of "justification" because righteousness is there seen as the covenant fidelity or obedience expected of those who are to survive the judgment (Bultmann, *Theology of the New Testament* 1:271–73). God's verdict is given based on one's conduct within the covenant of grace (E. P. Sanders, *Paul and Palestinian Judaism,* 107–25, 198–205). Such an understanding is seen in the OT (Isa 43:9; 45:25; 50:8) and in the NT (Matt 12:37; Rom 2:6–11; 1 Cor 4:4–5; Phil 1:11; on these texts see J. A. Ziesler, *The Meaning of Righteousness in Paul,* SNTSMS 20 [Cambridge: Cambridge UP, 1972], ad loc. and in particular 128–32, and for righteousness as both gift and demand in Matthew and James, 142–43). This is not to imply that righteousness is secured on the basis of works (Ps 143:2) but that a person is declared righteous in the light of works performed as part of "covenantal nomism" (Sanders's term, ibid., 236), not least of which are acts of mercy. Abraham is noted for his deeds of kindness toward the visitors of Gen 18 (cf. *Rabbinic Anthology,* ed. Montefiore and Lowe, no. 1172; see also Ward, "The Works of Abraham," 286–90). Thus James uses δικαιοῦν in terms of the final judgment (as in Matthew's theology, e.g., Matt 25:31–46), which is evident from the context where those who fail to show mercy will not receive mercy at the last judgment (2:13) because of a faith that does not result in works (2:17). James assumes that Abraham had faith, however inchoate it may have been, *before* his trial (2:23). But for James—unlike his adversary—the patriarch's faith could not be so adequately designated unless and until he demonstrated it by what he did in obedience to the God who justified him. Abraham had "faith"—common ground between the opponent and James—but it was a faith that needed to come to expression by his deeds.

ἀνενέγκας Ἰσαὰκ τὸν υἱὸν αὐτοῦ ἐπὶ τὸ θυσιαστήριον, "When he attempted to offer Isaac his son on the altar?" ἀναφέρειν is a technical term for sacrifice (Jeremias, "'Lass allda deine Gabe' (Mt 5:23f.)," *ZNW* 36 [1937] 150–51). The offering of Isaac (which was actually limited to the binding of Isaac; see Gen 22:9, 16–18 in the light of Heb 11:17–19) is a confirmation that Abraham had a faith that saves. Whereas Paul cites the earlier Gen 15:6 (Rom 4:3) to focus on God's initial declaration of Abraham as righteous on the basis of faith alone (a declaration that James would have agreed with but forthwith would have modified), James recalls the same verse in Genesis (v 23) to show God's ultimate declaration of Abraham as righteous because of what he did (Gen 22:16, ἐποίησας) in obedient faith. That is, James understands Genesis 15:6 to be a "'motto,' standing over all of Abraham's life" (Moo, 114). This last point would not be disputed by Paul, while he does carefully avoid an appeal to the 'Aqedah (the binding of Isaac episode in Gen 22: on which see G. Vermes, "Redemption and Genesis xxii" in his *Scripture and Tradition in Judaism,* SPB [Leiden: Brill, 1961] 218–23) because it was commonly believed by Jewish interpreters to show how Abraham's obedience was meritorious (1 Macc 2:52). For James, whose polemic interest is not that of Paul, the faith of Abraham led to his works of obedience, namely (in our present verse), the offering of Isaac, as a sign of his covenant faithfulness.

22 βλέπεις ὅτι ἡ πίστις συνήργει τοῖς ἔργοις αὐτοῦ καὶ ἐκ τῶν ἔργων ἡ πίστις ἐτελειώθη, "You [should] see that his faith was at work with his deeds, and by his deeds his faith was brought to completion." The partnership of faith and works as if to form one entity is emphasized again. "You [should] see" may be an attempt to dissuade James' opponent (note the continued singular "you," 2:18, 19, 20) from relying on a monotheistic faith or perhaps a Pauline *sola fides* as the sufficient requirement of God ("confessing faith and trusting faith are for James not complete faith," Mussner, 142). Yet Jewish tradition (see Dibelius, 163) was well aware of how Abraham had turned from idols to the one God, namely, Yahweh (Philo, *Virt.* 216; *Leg. All.* 3.228; *Gen. Rab.* 38; *Jub.* 11, 12; Josephus, *Ant.* 1.154–57). But v 22 is a quick attempt by James to dispel the thought that faith and works are to be considered as separate. Mussner, 142, sees here a deliberate play on words: Abraham's faith (the first explicit mention of the patriarch's faith, though it was assumed by James in 2:21) "worked" with works to produce a "working faith." The use of the imperfect συνήργει suggests a continuous, ongoing activity: the offering of Isaac was but one (though a great one, to be sure) of the works (ἔργα) that demonstrated Abraham's faith. τελειοῦν carries with it the idea of "completion," "bring to maturity." See *Introduction,* pp. lxxix–lxxxii, for James' call to "perfection" expressed in acts of piety (ἔργον is found twelve times in 2:14–16, out of fifteen times in the letter). Not that works "perfect" a defective faith (Adamson, 130), since such faith would not be sufficient for justification (in either the Pauline or the Jacobean senses), but that such works complete the unfinished state of faith (Davids, 128).

23 καὶ ἐπληρώθη ἡ γραφὴ ἡ λέγουσα, "The scripture was fulfilled which says." The copulative καί connects the thought of v 22 to v 23. What we have here is not a prophecy-fulfillment scheme (Mayor, 104; Ropes, 221) but a use of Gen 15:6 to show that this OT verse (so often connected with Abraham; see *Mek. Bešallaḥ* 4 [35b] on Exod 14:15 and 7 [406] on Exod 14:31; Philo, *De Abr.* 262; *Jub.* 18.6; 1 Macc 2:52) is confirmation of what James has been saying (Davids, 129). The opponent may well have cited Abraham to show that the patriarch was reckoned righteous because he believed in God (a Pauline conviction doubtless pressed into service in the debate). James develops the picture of Abraham so as to depict him with an active faith in contrast to an expression of bare fideism, which is the way that parts of Paul's argument (in Rom 4:16–22) could conceivably be interpreted and used polemically. James displays a midrashic type of thinking here (Jacobs, "Midrashic Background") by including Gen 15:6 (which follows the LXX except for the addition of δέ, as in Rom 4:3; cf. Gal 3:6; *1 Clem.* 10.6; Justin, *Dial.* 91; the passive ἐλογίσθη stands against the MT and the active ויחשבה, *wayyaḥšᵉbehā*) as a secondary text to the primary event (or to a primary scripture, Gen 22:9: the binding of Isaac; Davids, 129). But in doing so James does not consider faith as a ground "for righteousness" independently as did some of the rabbis (*Tg. Ps.-J.* on Gen 15:6) and Philo (see the evidence displayed in Ziesler, *Righteousness,* 109: "Abraham's faith . . . a sort of work, a form of righteousness") nor (in our present case) as the basis for the initial proclamation of God that Abraham was righteous as Paul argued (Dibelius, 161–65). Rather, James' use of Gen 15:6 is to be understood as meaning either that Abraham's faith-work combination is the type of faith that God considers righteous (so Mussner, 144) or that the first clause of Gen 15:6 refers to Abraham's monotheistic faith and the second clause to his deeds that are accounted righteous (Dibelius, 164–65). The latter option sets James apart from strict Jewish exegesis and as distinct from Paul (Ellis, *Paul's Use of the Old Testament*, 93–94), regardless of whether one sees Gen 15:6 as referring to the single work of the binding of Isaac (Ellis, 94) or to several previous deeds of charity (Ward, "Works," 288). In any event, James employs Gen 15:6 to prove that faith and works ran together in Abraham's life (Davids, 130).

Because of this combination, Abraham has been reckoned (ἐλογίσθη, a verb that Dibelius thinks relates to the imagery of heavenly bookkeeping, citing *Jub.* 19.9; 30.19–20; but this is unlikely, cf. Mussner, 144 n.3) as righteous. The passive voice shows that this verdict was initiated by God on Abraham's behalf. Both Paul and James utilize a well-known verse to prove a point (Dibelius, 168–74), they address different situations by the use of the same terms (Lorenzen, "Faith without Works," 234), though the contexts call for different understandings of these terms (see *Comment* on 2:21). Both writers are agreed that "faith" does not function as "a principle of achievement" (Mussner, 137, 146), but each has his own application of how Abraham's faith is paradigmatic for salvation history.

καὶ φίλος θεοῦ ἐκλήθη, "and he was called God's friend." The tribute is not found in the canonical OT, although it is similar to the designation "the one loved by God" (2 Chr 20:7; Isa 41:8; cf. Isa 51:2 and Dan 3:35 LXX), and common to writings outside the OT (*Jub.* 19.9; 30.20; *4 Ezra* 3.14; Philo, *De Abr.* 273; *De Sob.* 56; CD 3:2; cf. *1 Clem* 10.1; see also Cantinat, 154; Jeremias, *TDNT* 1:8; Stählin, *TDNT* 9:168 n.180). James associates the person who has faith-with-works with Abraham, a link which entitles him to be "God's friend," in stark contrast to the one who is later called God's enemy (4:4).

J. G. Lodge, "James and Paul," 208–12, has an interesting proposal regarding the origin of the title "friend of God." He traces it to Wisd Sol 7:27, which in turn is connected with James' discussion of the mirror in 1:23–24 (see Wisd Sol 7:26). The "wise man" practices what he sees in the word; he gets wisdom and obtains the divine friendship (Wisd Sol 7:14)—a series of ideas to be picked up in our letter at 3:13–18. The doer of the word may also be regarded as a son, for all those who come to wisdom may be called "sons" or "friends of God" (so Lodge, 211, drawing on Luck, "Der Jakobusbrief," 167–72, and citing Wisd Sol 2:6–20). So Abraham is an apt exemplar of the wise man, and in his obedience to the point of being willing to sacrifice Isaac he "showed his works in the meekness of wisdom" (3:13) and "reaped the harvest of righteousness" (3:18; cf. Sir 3:17; Prov 3:12 for the trials of the righteous whom Yahweh loves).

Abraham, for James as for Paul, illustrates faith working in a life of love (Gal 5:6; 1 Cor 13:2, 7; summed up in the expression *aus gelebtem Glauben* by Jeremias, "Paul and James," 371). Mussner concludes: "The works of love for James make saving faith a *fides viva!*" (151). What that statement entails is best expressed by Cranfield, "The Message," 340: "Had there been no works, Abraham would not have been justified; but that would have been because the absence of works would have meant that he had no real faith."

24 ὁρᾶτε ὅτι ἐξ ἔργων δικαιοῦται ἄνθρωπος καὶ οὐκ ἐκ πίστεως μόνον, "You [should] be aware that a person is proved righteous by deeds, not by faith alone." On the surface James comes as close to contradicting Paul in 2:24 as in any place in his letter. Rom 3:28 reads, "For we hold that a man is justified by faith apart from the works of the law." Davids, 130, calls 2:24 the *crux interpretum* for NT theology in general. With a switch in person from singular to plural, James has turned his attention from his opponent of 2:18–23 back to the brethren (ἀδελφοί) at large, though it is likely that the church in general was meant to overhear what James told the "someone" of v 18. It appears that the specific example of Abraham has been broadened to include the general principles of Jacobean justification.

Two exegetical questions are posed here in this resumé (Mussner, 145) applicable to all the readers: (1) whether or not James stands against Paul, and (2) whether or not James was dependent directly on Paul. Let us take the issues in reverse order. Regarding the second question, Davids (130–32, against J. T. Sanders, *Ethics in the New Testament* [Philadelphia: Fortress Press, 1975] 115–28) replies that James is not aware of Paul's thinking, especially as contained in Romans (3:20, 28; 4:16). For one thing, vocabulary that might be considered Pauline ("works," "justified," "faith") is not concentrated in a single quotation in James' treatment but dispersed throughout some twenty-five verses (in point of fact this is not quite so, since faith and works are mentioned together ten times in thirteen verses). To this we might add the observation that the vocabulary of righteousness as found in the NT (outside James) is not peculiar to Paul (see Matthew; Ziesler, *Righteousness*, 128–46). Thus, the use of such vocabulary does not prove that James borrowed only from Paul. Another point supporting a negative answer to the second question is that in several critical places James' vocabulary differs from Paul's. For example, James never uses "law" (as in "works of the law," as Paul does in Rom 3:20, 28) to speak of the claim of one who is seeking to be justified by God. It would seem that if James were opposing Paul he would at least be careful to adopt Paul's specific vocabulary. A third point, and probably the most important, is that Paul and James are best understood as addressing quite dissimilar situations (see *Comment* on 2:21, 23). Whereas Paul's audience is in danger of relying on "works" for salvation, James' readers are excusing themselves from good works, thereby showing only a faith that is dead (see Cantinat, 155–57; Mussner, 146–50; Laws, 131–33).

Our conclusion is that James did not depend *directly* on Paul for his argument in 2:24. The adverb μόνον is not in Paul's vocabulary (though it may be inferred from his logic) in such places as Rom 3:28; Gal 2:16. Conceivably, James may have drawn his use of the adverb from a similar point made in Josephus (in *Ant.* 3.91) where Israel's belief in the unity of God and divine worship are categorized under the rubic of μόνον, i.e., Jews are strict monotheists. Having said this, we cannot insist with complete certainty that the historical James was ignorant of Paul. On the contrary, it may be that the former was aware of the latter's mission theology, however garbled the report may have been (see the witness of Acts 15:1–29; 21:18–22; and importantly Gal 2:9). But if this is so, then any conflict with Paul is based on a mistaken understanding by James or more likely by James' later disciples in reaction to an extreme Paulinism adopted by the apostle's followers (cf. Eph 2:1–10). Here we speak to the first exegetical matter. As we have seen above, James could have argued from a more informed position than he did. It is more probable that the editor in the name of a Jacobean "testament of faith" is responding to a "grotesque parody" (Reumann, *Righteousness*, 156, 221) of Paul's theology as expressed by his intemperate followers. We, however, should not be too quick to make James a theologian of Paul's stature. Instead, we "must allow James to speak out of his own background" (Davids, 132).

Yet the writer is on Paul's side in this verse. James is not belittling the importance of faith in 2:24. His use of μόνον shows that faith (the type described in 2:19) *alone* is not enough. As this exact phrase is not found in Paul, it is possible that ἐκ πίστεως μόνον is a pseudo-Paulinist slogan (Mussner, 145 n.7) that James is berating. The inclusion of the adverb (if it has positive value) demonstrates that faith is an essential part of salvation (Moo, 115). James is disturbed at a faith that has no works to demonstrate its reality in the life of a believer. Paul would not accept the understanding espoused by some in James' church situation that faith without works is acceptable to God (Gal 5:6; 1 Cor 13:2; 2 Cor 9:8; cf. Col 3:17; see also Matt 7:15–21). As Paul could forcefully assert his disapproval of the misunderstanding of soteriology (Rom 6:1–15), so could James (see Via, "The Right Strawy Epistle Reconsidered"). And though the two teachers address dissimilar situations, both are known for the fervency with which they champion the truth they express. This summarizing verse thus becomes evidence for the theory that what we have throughout this entire debate is a defense conducted by James' followers in their master's name of teaching that *also* sought to rehabilitate the authentic notes of Pauline *sola gratia sola fide* (Reumann, *Righteousness*, 158, and earlier, pp. 82–84).

25 ὁμοίως δὲ καί, "To give another instance." This carries with it the force of a second example of equal weight to the first. It is as if James feels his argument is still incomplete. Ῥαάβ ἡ πόρνη, "Rahab the prostitute." Despite the less than honorable vocation of Rahab, she became a heroine in the Jewish religion. Rabbinic tradition speaks of her as marrying Joshua and becoming an ancestress of Jeremiah and Ezekiel (*b. Meg.* 14b, 15a; other data in Str-B, 1:20–23; Young, "Relation"). οὐκ ἐξ ἔργων ἐδικαιώθη ὑποδεξαμένη τοὺς ἀγγέλους καὶ ἑτέρᾳ ὁδῷ ἐκβαλοῦσα, "was not Rahab the prostitute proved righteous by her actions, when she welcomed the messengers and sent them out by a different route?" This concludes v 25, which is a rhetorical question shaped to be answered in the affirmative (οὐκ). Her faith is not explicitly mentioned in v 25 (as it is in *m. Ber.* 2:8, Vouga, 90 n.18) but there is no doubt that James is referring to her in support of his faith-works position.

Rahab is singled out because she showed hospitality (ὑποδεξαμένη) to the messengers (here the term is ἄγγελοι, which often refers to heavenly messengers; the OT verses in view are Josh 2:1–21; the LXX follows the MT and employs νεανίσκοι or ἄνδρες; but see Heb 11:31; *1 Clem.* 12 for the more direct κατάσκοποι: see *Note* f) sent from Joshua. She not only protected them from the king (Josh 2:4–7) but sent them out a different way so that they would not be captured (not exactly in Josh 2:15–16 but found in the Christian telling of Rahab's story: see Young, "Relation," 342). As a result she and her household were spared annihilation when the city of Jericho was destroyed

(Josh 6:17, 23). It may be argued that her kind treatment of the messengers was self-serving, but James is probably following his Jewish tradition, which made Rahab a prize example of obedience (Josephus, *Ant.* 5.2). Moreover, she is listed in the Christian tradition, e.g., Matt 1:5; Heb 11:31; *1 Clem.* 12:18, as an example of one who had faith. That Rahab was seen to have done the right thing is also attested in Jewish sources (see Johnson, *Genealogies,* 162–65).

Rahab was evidently a good example to buttress James' argument. But was such a recall purely incidental? Maybe not, because there appears to have been some connection in the background between the figures of Abraham and Rahab. Later, they are seen in *1 Clem.* chaps 10–12 as providing hospitality for others (Hanson, "Rahab," 53–60; Hagner, *The Use,* 251–56). This is obvious for Rahab (in James) but not for Abraham. He is remembered for his offering of Isaac on the altar. The link of "hospitality" between Rahab and Abraham would have been more explicit had James cited Abraham's hospitable acts toward the three messengers in Gen 18, which could have easily been transferred from the discussion associated with the care of the poor (2:14–17) which initiated the argument in 2:1–13 (see Ward, "Works of Abraham," 286–87; and Jacobs, "Midrashic Background," 463, has shown from rabbinic-Jewish writings how Gen 18 and 22 were brought together, especially 18:17–18, the former being given the reading, "Shall I conceal from Abraham *my friend* . . . ?"). If James was thinking of the hospitality of Rahab and Abraham, then we see another point of evidence to argue for the unity of 2:1–26.

Another common element of the lives of Abraham and Rahab may be their background as proselytes. Abraham is known as an original proselyte (Str-B, 3:195) and was called from Ur of the Chaldeans to belief in Yahweh (Gen 11:31; 12:1–5), while Rahab came over from the paganism of Jericho to the camp of Israel (Josh 6:23). Thus we have the father of Israel juxtaposed with the pagan prostitute. The latter was seen as the "archetypical proselyte" (Davids, 132, referring to *Num. Rab.* 3 [139b]; *Midr. Ruth* 2 [126a]: "a kind of saint for later Judaism"; cf. Kittel, *TDNT* 3:1–3). Both were far off and drew near to God. No one could now argue that the principle of "faith-with-works" was not universal: the father of the faithful and the most illustrious convert both exemplify a living, active faith.

Or it may be that Rahab was chosen by James simply because of her works as vindicating her faith (Adamson, 133). That is, the motifs of hospitality and pagan backgrounds are not the principal reasons that the OT figures Abraham and Rahab are linked together. Rather, the connection between the two is the conviction James has that their deeds will lead God to pronounce them righteous at the final judgment (Moo, 117). Indeed, this last point must have figured prominently in James' selection of the two figures, especially Rahab, but this suggestion does not rule out the possibility that the aforementioned motifs also influenced James' choices.

26 ὥσπερ γὰρ τὸ σῶμα χωρὶς πνεύματος νεκρόν ἐστιν, "As the body apart from breath is lifeless." We see James "in his usual circling fashion" (Adamson, 134) bringing his argument to a close with a "concluding verdict" (Windisch). He harks back to 2:17, which also denounces faith without works as dead. That verse in conjunction with the present one forms an *inclusio* (Davids,

133), which follows on the heels of the *inclusio* of 2:14–16 (Lodge, "James and Paul"). James offers yet another comparison (almost a "rhetorical overkill," Davids), as shown by ὥσπερ. The γάρ also ties the present verse to the preceding one and helps to demonstrate that the concluding analogy is meant to explain James' reference to Rahab. This helps to dispel any doubts as to whether James was concerned with Rahab's faith when he recalled her "justification by works."

James compares faith without works to a body without breath. His analogy is as follows: faith is compared to the body and works to the spirit. Such a correspondence has caused concern for some (Spitta) but the details of this analogy should not be unduly pressed (Adamson, 134). It is not clear why James chose this figure unless he has a point in mind leading to his next topic as well (3:2, 3, 6; see *Comment* on these verses). Most likely, we are to understand the body-breath relationship in terms of Jewish Christian anthropology (Davids, 133). That is, the separation of the two does not produce a type of release for the spirit (as in Orphic-philosophical thought which spoke of the body as a tomb or prison, σῶμα-σῆμα) but results in a dead corpse. The Greek dualistic thought would not comport well with what James has been arguing. The source behind James' analogy here may be Gen 2:7 (Moo, 117). πνεῦμα, "spirit," carries with it the OT idea of "life-giving breath" (רוּחַ, *rûaḥ*). A body without breath is dead (cf. Gen 6:17; 7:15; Ps 104:29; John 19:30; Luke 23:46). The principle is clear: a faith (body) that is not supported by works (spirit) is lifeless. As breath enables a body to live, likewise works produce a living faith. The conclusion matches Matt 5:16 in the context of a positive evaluation of "good deeds" as summing up the Golden Rule (Matt 7:12) and "doing the will of God" (Matt 7:21–23; 12:50) expressed in love to one's neighbor, especially in his need (Matt 25:31–46).

Explanation

The previous discussion of 2:14–26 has sought to come to some conclusions regarding the two canvassed exegetical questions. (1) It was proposed that the flow of the author's thought moves with little break at v 14 from the foregoing indictment of the community's failure to show respect to all, both rich and poor, who enter the assembly. The description James gives in the "little parable" of vv 15–16 echoes the treatment of the socially deprived in v 3, and the spoken words of harsh treatment in v 3 are re-echoed in the pious but unavailing sentiments expressed in v 16.

(2) The second link has to do with the major theme of vv 1–13, identified as the nature of authentic faith. Its starting point is in v 1, where the appeal is made to those in the community who profess to be "believers in the glorious Lord Jesus Christ." The literal wording is even more emphatic; they claim to "have the faith of our Lord Jesus Christ, the glory." James proceeds to expose the hollowness of this pretension, since it seeks to coexist alongside the practice of social snobbery and rank favoritism. These latter traits are not merely signs of discourtesy nor even of a confusion of moral values in a topsy-turvy society where the rich are fawned on and the poor are neglected and despised. At its heart this partiality is a clear token that faith, however

loud the protestation, is nongenuine and a misnomer. The law that is summed up in the royal command to love one's neighbor is openly flouted and its authority effectively challenged. It now has turned into a death-dealing agent, pronouncing judgment on those who willfully break it. Showing no mercy to those in need, they can expect none from the lawgiver, and they stand condemned. Their sentence is righteous because they vainly repose their confidence in a faith that is a tissue of self-deceit.

The same exposure of hollow pretense is carried forward into 2:14–26, with its opening question, "Can this kind of faith save?" setting the stage for all that follows. The entire pericope is engaged with the theme of authentic faith set in contrast to its rivals and challengers. The author adopts a debating style and a polemical stance, though it is not easy to pinpoint the exact nature of the opposition. The *Comment* section has tried to erect a background in a situation in which James' followers, accused of works-righteousness, come to his defense against the pseudo-Paulinists who have moved to the other extremity of the spectrum and are mouthing the slogan "by faith alone" as a weapon to wage their war against all kinds of nomism, i.e., respect for law, even the law of Christ (Gal 6:2; cf. 1 Cor 9:21).

If the modern interpreter could be more certain than appears possible at present who the speaker in v 18 is, and how far his words extend, more light would be thrown on an enigmatic text. Assuming that it is a hostile interlocutor who engages James' spokesperson in debate by setting up some antitheses between faith and deeds, and that the opponent's main aim is to drive a wedge between the two recognized, shorthand terms, it becomes feasible to carry his argument down to v 19a (or v 19b). The thrust of his argument is that faith and deeds are separable counters in the dialogue, and for him the issue turns on which is the more valuable and which may claim precedence. For the Jacobean rival, if faith is validated by deeds (anticipating James' own position) then faith can be said to exist *before* its validation. So, he maintains faith is both prior and preeminent, since it may exist without deeds, whereas the reverse is not true. His example borders on the grotesque. Consider the demons in Sheol; they hold faith but have no deeds, otherwise they would be saved—granting James' point. The case of "demons who believe" appears to prove the rival's point, since it offers an extreme illustration that, if conceded by James, makes the argument conclusive.

James, in reply, refuses to grant the possibility that faith and deeds can be torn apart and treated as individual entities. For him the only faith worth the name is the faith that is expressed in deeds, just as deeds take on their meaning as the fruit of the faith that is both salvific and sound. This concept of faith-declared-by-works in the hyphenated construction is alone the true faith; any other "kind of faith" (v 14b) is branded as "dead" and so false, i.e., unable to do what it claims (vv 14–17), and futile, i.e., it is barren and useless, a play on the words *erga* ("works") and *argē* ("workless") (v 20).

Two sad illustrations drive home James' rejoinder. First, he introduces the instance of a "professed" believer whose faith is just that: mere lip profession. The pious sentiments of v 16, couched in the speech of prayer, ring hollow because they are unaccompanied by helping action. The case goes back to 1:26–27 and may be illustrated further from 1 John 3:16–18. Second, faith as a creedal utterance affirms God's existence but produces no result except the negative reaction of fear (v 19). Whether this is the language of the speaker or of James the point is identical: a credo, however true, that gets no further than the spoken word can never produce salvation. No orthodoxy that fails to lead to orthopraxy comes anywhere near authentic Christian faith!

Indeed, James' position may be stated in more trenchant terms, if our understanding is correct. There is only one species of faith, that is faith that relates the human being to God in a genuine bond of religion (taking "religion" to mean what the Latin root implies, namely, *religare,* "to bind"); and that saving faith is faith in action, working by love (Gal 5:6) and fulfilled in deeds (v 22).

In modern theology no one has seen the contribution of this discussion to the debate about the nature of faith more clearly than John Baillie. In his book *Our Knowledge of God* (Oxford: Oxford UP, 1939) he has shown how Christian faith is a seamless garment and cannot be understood except as a whole and as involving the whole person. We are summoned to believe, in his picturesque phrase, with the "bottom of our hearts" as well as from "the top of our minds." This is exactly the point registered by James.

Final examples are brought in to clinch the Jacobean argumentation. Abraham, father of the faithful, is known as a person who "believed God" (v 23); yet faith was more than an easygoing creedalism, a "head belief," as Reumann, *Righteousness* 156, calls it; it was proved by action when he showed the reality of *what* he believed by *how* he responded to the divine summons. His obedience gave evidence of a sincere faith already held. Rahab in similar fashion threw in her lot with the people of God and was considered righteous by a costly expression of her loyalty, arising from her faith. Heb 11:17–19, 31 elaborates the exemplary pattern of this patriarchal and proselyte faith, and *1 Clem.* 10–12 in an early Christian sermon praises the faith and hospitality of both OT worthies. The case of Rahab is particularly instructive, since later typological exegesis turned her into a figure of the church in a bid to reclaim her from her unsavory past and make her a fit symbol of the "pure" church:

> This harlot, dearest brothers, was a figure of the church which before Christ's advent used to commit fornication, with many idols. But when Christ came, he not only delivered her from fornication, he also by a great miracle made her a virgin (2 Cor 11:2).
>
> (Caesarius of Arles, A.D. 470–542)

No such striking exegetical feat is needed to give Abraham and Rahab their true place in salvation history. They both in different circumstances speak of, what our author strove to maintain, namely that authentic faith shines in its true colors when tested and is a risky venture that unites believers with God's suffering people. In both ways it is faith-in-action that counts (see Bonhoeffer, *The Cost of Discipleship,* 69, 74).

Against those who paraded the *sola fide* slogan in a way that was an invitation to antinomian laxity and ethical indifference James raises the protest that no such quietism "works." Against those who misunderstood James as a nomist with little regard for heart faith his loyal disciples enter the warm retort that the deeds that validate true religion spring directly from a living faith. In summary, as the Puritan John Owen phrased the antinomy, faith alone saves—but saving faith is never alone; it "completes" itself in deeds (v 26).

The same reminder comes from Bonhoeffer (ibid., 69, 74):

> We must never forget the indissoluble unity of the two (faith, obedience); we must place the one proposition that only he who believes is obedient alongside the other, that only he who is obedient believes. In the one case faith is the condition of obedience, and in the other obedience is the condition of faith.

> "Only those who believe obey" is what we say to that part of a believer's soul which obeys, and "only those who obey believe" is what we say to that part of the soul of the obedient which believes. If the first half of the proposition stands alone, the believer is exposed to the danger of cheap grace, which is another word for damnation. If the second half stands alone, the believer is exposed to the danger of salvation through works, which is another word for damnation.

4. Warning about Teachers and Tongues (3:1–12)

Bibliography

Bieder, W. "Christliche Existenz nach dem Zeugnis des Jakobusbriefes." *TZ* 5 (1949) 93–113. **Carr, A.** "The Meaning of Ὁ ΚΟΣΜΟΣ in James iii.6." *Exp*, ser. 7, vol. 8 (1909) 318–25. **Casson, L.** *Ships and Seamanship in the Ancient World.* Princeton: Princeton UP, 1971. ———. *Travel in the Ancient World.* Toronto: Hakkert, 1974. Chap. 9. **Chilton, B. R.** *A Galilean Rabbi and His Bible.* Wilmington: Glazier, 1984. **Elliott-Binns, L. E.** "The Meaning of ὕλη in James iii.5." *NTS* 2 (1955) 48–50. **Filson, F. V.** "The Christian Teacher in the First Century." *JBL* 60 (1941) 317–28. **Hadidian, D. Y.** "Palestinian Pictures in the Epistle of James." *ExpTim* 63 (1952) 227–28. **Harnack, A.** *The Mission and Expansion of Christianity.* Tr. J. Moffatt. 2 vols. London: Williams and Norgate, 1908. **Jervell, J.** *Imago Dei. Gen 1.26f. im Spätjudentum, in der Gnosis und in den paulinischen Briefen.* FRLANT 76. Göttingen: Vandenhoeck und Ruprecht, 1960. **Kittel, G.** "τὸν τροχὸν τῆς γενέσεως." *Theologisches Literaturblatt*, Beilege 1. 141ff. **Kosmala, H.** *Hebräer-Essener-Christen.* SPB 1. Leiden: Brill, 1959. **Moldenke, H. N.**, and **Moldenke, A. L.** *Plants of the Bible.* New York: Dover, 1952-1986 ed. **Stiglmayr, P. J.** "Zu Jak 3,6: Rota nativitatis nostrae inflammata." *BZ* 2 (1913) 49–52. **Trocmé, E.** "Les églises pauliniennes vues du dehors: Jac 2,1 à 3,13." *SE* 2, TU 87 (1964) 660–69. **Völter, D.** "Zwei neue Wörter für das Lexicon des griechischen Neuen Testaments?" *ZNW* 10 (1909) 326–29. **Wandel, G.** "Zur Auslegung der Stelle Jak. 3,1–8." *TSK* 66 (1893) 679–707. **Wanke, J.** "Zur urchristlichen Lehrer nach dem Zeugnis des Jakobusbriefes." In *Die Kirche des Anfangs.* FS H. Schürmann, ed. R. Schnackenburg, J. Ernst, and J. Wanke. Leipzig: St. Benno-Verlag, 1977. 489–511. **Zimmermann, A. F.** *Die urchristlichen Lehrer.* WUNT 2.12. Tübingen: Mohr, 1984.

Translation

[1] Let not many of you become teachers, my brothers, because you are aware that we [who are teachers] will receive severer judgment (if we fail). [2] All of us go astray in many ways; if a person does not go astray in what he says, then he is a perfect man, able to hold in restraint the entire body as well. [3] When[a] we put bridles in horses' mouths to make them obey us, we also turn their entire body (to our will). [4] Consider the case of ships, though they are so huge and are driven along by powerful winds, they are nevertheless steered by a very small rudder, which course the pilot's choice decides. [5] In the same way, the tongue is equally a tiny part (of the body), yet it makes great[b] claims for itself. Consider how a small fire[c] sets ablaze a great[c] forest!

[6] Likewise the tongue is a fire; a world of wickedness, it is set among the parts of our body; it corrupts the entire body, and sets on fire the course of human existence, and is itself set on fire by Gehenna.[d]

[7] All[e] species of beasts and birds, of reptiles and sea creatures, are being tamed and have been tamed by humans, [8] but no human being can tame the tongue. Disorderly[f] evil! Replete with lethal poison!

[9] With the tongue we bless the Lord[g] and Father; with it we curse our fellows, who are made in the likeness of God. [10] Out of the same mouth come both blessing

and cursing. My brothers, this should not be the case. [11] *Does a spring from the same source yield both fresh and salt water?* [12] *My brothers, can a fig tree produce olives, or a vine bear figs? Neither* [h] *can a salt-water spring produce fresh water.*

Notes

[a] Reading εἰ δέ on the principle of *lectio difficilior* (attested in some uncials, ff[2] vg boh), over against the widely supported ἴδε, which Ropes prefers (229). ἰδού (TR), however, is clearly to be rejected, since its occurrence here is evidently to be explained as a scribal harmonizing with v 4. So Metzger, *Textual Commentary*, 681–82, referring to Moulton-Howard, *Grammar* 2:76–77. Other options are εἴδε (= ἴδε) γάρ in ℵ*, and εἰδέ (one word) in other uncials. The reading εἰ δέ has the support of recent editors and commentators (listed in Davids, 138), with Ropes' view championed by Mayor, 108–9, and Laws, 146. See too BDF § 22–23 for how vowel changes occur.

[b] Reading μεγάλα αὐχεῖ where ℵ and TR have one word μεγαλαύχει, probably based on Ps 9:39 [10:18].

[c] The same Gr. word (ἡλίκος) can have a dual meaning: "how small" or "how great" (see BGD, 346).

[d] This is a text found difficult by several textual authorities and adjusted in the supposed interests of clarity. See Ropes, 233–39; Davids, 141–44, for illustrations. See *Comment*.

[e] πᾶσα. See BDF § 275.3 for this sense.

[f] Reading ἀκατάστατον with the majority witnesses. The variant ἀκατάσχετον, "unchecked," is read by C 33 Ψ syr[h] Jerome[pt] as well as TR, but must be rejected as an attempt to use a more common term for a word that is obviously a favorite with James (cf. 3:16).

[g] τὸν κύριον (ℵ A B C P and some minuscules, syr[P] cop[bo mss]), whereas the TR has θεόν with K L and most of the minuscules, vg syr[h] cop[sa, bo]. Metzger's defense (682) of κύριον is strong: (i) κύριος is less expected than θεός, and (ii) the external textual evidence is superior.

[h] Before οὔτε ἀλυκόν many texts (including ℵ C[2] K L P it[ff] vg syr cop[bo]) have the adverb οὕτως or οὕτως οὐδεμία πηγή ἀλυκὸν καί (K L P). The reading οὔτε ἀλυκόν is supported by A B C* and found in Nestle[26]. It is argued for by Metzger, *Textual Commentary*, 682, in defense of the UBSGNT[3] text, which has this preferred shorter reading on textual and contextual grounds. Davids (148, 149) concludes that the TR is an attempt to smooth out difficulties by making v 12b repeat v 11, and it is only the shorter text that "carries the thought on toward 3:13–18" (149).

Form / Structure / Setting

The connection of 3:1–12 with the preceding section is not easy to see. The rhetorical proverb in 2:26 seems to round off the discussion on "faith and deeds"; there is a lack of grammatical connective between 2:26 and 3:1, making a transition hard to follow; and teachers have not been in prominence up to this point in the letter, which has been hitherto addressed to the congregation generally. These are the arguments adduced by Zimmermann, *Die urchristlichen Lehrer*, 201–6, to argue for the opening of a new *topos*. His discussion sets out the contrast between 2:14–26 and 3:1–12, but he does not consider the possibility that 3:1–12 may have links with earlier texts that relate to wrongful speaking, and in particular 2:16–18.

At first glance James seems to be embarking on a novel theme, namely the use and power of the tongue as exemplified in the role of the charismatic teacher in the church (Wanke, "Zur urchristlichen Lehrer," 491). The overall theme is that of "sincere speech," as applied to the teaching office of the church. This conclusion is reached as we observe the frequent reference in these verses to the "body" (σῶμα), a term that obviously has first application to the human anatomy of which the tongue forms a small (v 5) yet significant (v 6) part. (But there is a secondary reference to "the body" meaning the church implied in the way the argument proceeds.) Whoever can control his tongue, says our author, if ironically (v 2b), has power over his entire body and may justifiably lay claim to being regarded as a "perfect individual" (τέλειος ἀνήρ). This may be taken in a strictly personal sense, referring to individual believers. And we should take note of the way an earlier theme is picked up by glancing back at 1:19–21, and more particularly at 1:26. According to one analysis of the letter (see *Introduction,* pp. xcviii–xcix), James is elaborating at greater length on the dangers of human speech, which can so easily become a facade for spurious religion. But there are two factors in the setting of this paragraph (which, in our view, finds its natural sequel in 3:13–18) which suggest that there is a more precise background to James' severe attitude in the *topos* of the power of the tongue (following Wanke, ibid., 492; *pace* Zimmermann, ibid., 206). That background fits better into a discussion where (i) "the body" in question is the ecclesial one, not the anatomical one, and (ii) the tongue is used in a setting of the congregation at worship (Mussner, 158).

First, the repeated use of σῶμα indicates the author has in mind the baneful influence of speech in the public assembly. He is less concerned with Christians seen as private persons and more with what is said in a churchly setting. This means that James' condemnation of hasty speaking (1:19) now takes on a more serious cast as he focuses on the way worshiping people can use their tongues to the detriment of the community as evil report and rumor are spread to affect the entire range of their corporate life (ὅλον τὸ σῶμα, v 6). If 3:9–10 are interpreted in a liturgical setting in which "praising God" is the chief component, it becomes feasible to see an even more nuanced application. James is directing his shafts of criticism against the misuse of the tongue in worship—in a manner that indirectly recalls 1 Cor 12–14, especially 12:3; 14:27–39—and is concerned for the "good order" or οἰκοδομή of the church in a way akin to the Pauline maxim of 1 Cor 14:40: "let everything (you do) be done in a seemly manner and in good order" (εὐσχημόνως καὶ κατὰ τάξιν). See Vouga, 95.

Second, the introductory sentence of admonition regarding teachers (v 1) in which James includes himself (the verb glides from the second person to the first person in the verb λημψόμεθα) confirms the fact that the author has the church as a "house of instruction" (*bēt-hammidraš,* to use the Jewish phrase of the synagogue) in his sights. It is primarily the teachers in the community who are causing dissension and division. The writer self-consciously adopts the pose of a person who enjoys the *charisma* of teaching (1 Cor 12:28; Eph 4:11; and such as Prisca should be included [according to Acts 18:26] as well as those in the teaching office in the Pastoral Epistles: 1 Tim 3:2; 4:11–14; 5:17; 2 Tim 2:24; Titus 2:3, even if some teachers are a source of mischief: 1 Tim 2:12; 4:17–18; 2 Tim 4:3: H. Greeven, "Propheten, Lehrer, Vorsteher bei Paulus," ZNW 44 [1952–53] 1–43) with a view to administering an authoritative rebuke. Those in his line of sight are evidently leaders who are summoned to control and guide the course of the church's life and destiny. Hence the twin imagery of the horse's bit (v 3) and the ship's rudder (v 4) is used. Together these represent "the sum total of what men steered in those days"

(Davids, 139). The former picture more exactly would have the reader conclude that the tongue, likened to an iron bar set in the horse's mouth to bring the animal under control, rules the whole body (ὅλον τὸ σῶμα, v 3, which repeats this phrase from v 2). Applied to human activity this analogy is not strictly true, but the comparison is not to be pressed. As a fact of observation, horses are turned by a tug at the bit and bridle, and so kept in check. James evidently wants to enforce the single point: those who use their tongues must learn to hold them under restraint and should not aspire to be false teachers (so Reicke). Rather their teaching role should contribute to the well-being of the "entire body" of the faithful; and this at least implies that their teaching should be wholesome and not deviant (see 5:19, 20 for what such "deviance" has led to). Teachers who permit their tongues to get out of control are well on the way to becoming false leaders. Their "rule" of the church will be baneful.

The latter illustration, the ship and its rudder, is an even clearer sign that the tongue in question is in the mouth of the church leader. By means of a relatively small tongue-shaped rudder a large vessel is steered at the will of its helmsman (v 4: ὁ εὐθύνων may be linked with the κυβερνήτης of Acts 27:11; see L. Casson, *Ships and Seamanship*, 316–18: ancient ships could sometimes be large; there were 276 passengers and crew on the ship referred to in Acts 27:37; see Casson, *Travel*, 158–59, on Lucian's sense of amazement at the size of the *Isis*, capable of holding 1,000 passengers plus cargo, as she berthed at Piraeus, the port of Athens; *Navigium*, 5). The idea of a pilot at the helm (cf. Rev 18:17) is taken over into ecclesial use by Paul (1 Cor 12:28 where κυβέρνησις, "administration," is used in the plural to indicate "proofs of ability to hold a leading position in the church," BGD, 456). Granted that James does not work through this metaphor in any systematic way, and that it was not until the second century that the equation of the church and a ship (as *navis ecclesiae*: see G. Bornkamm and H.-J. Held, in *Tradition and Interpretation in Matthew*, ed. G. Bornkamm et al., tr. P. Scott [London: SCM, 1963] 54, 55, 202) was made, it still is suggestive that the imagery is used in this way in a section that begins with teachers who are called to account (v 1). Their power of speech in instructing and steering the lives of others is the point registered. As Mayor puts it (112): "by controlling speech we acquire the power of controlling action." Even if this reflects a stock maxim in hellenistic literature (as Mayor and Dibelius illustrate), it is yet striking that teachers' speech is invested with even greater authority and force, with either helpful or destructive consequences. The issue is whether the speech is wholesome and edificatory (vv 9–12), and that question in turn depends on the power of the tongue, anatomically a small part of the human body, to set the direction for the entire ecclesial body. Yet another consequence follows where the tongue "makes great claims for itself" (v 5)—an ironical and alliterative joining of μικρὸν μέλος (small member) with μεγάλα αὐχεῖ (boasts great things: Windisch, 23). Here clearly it is the entire person—the appointed teacher—who is speaking and is exceeding the limits of his or her office, leading to calamitous results (v 5b: ἡλίκον . . . ἡλίκην are part of a structured and symmetrical apostrophe: "Consider how a *small* fire sets ablaze a *great* forest").

The next illustration of the effective power of the tongue is that of a

destructive fire (vv 5b–8). Here, as we observed, James repeats the theme of
v 4, namely, that the tongue is small but sets in motion a train of events
disproportionate to its diminutive size. Especially in the terrain of Palestine
and in a climate of long dry weather when the brush becomes tinder-dry
the menace of forest fires is ever-present (see L. E. Elliott-Binns, "The Meaning
of ὕλη"; D. Y. Hadidian, "Palestinian Pictures"). James' allusions, however,
are drawn equally from the language of the OT (Ps 83:13, 14; Isa 9:18),
which speaks of the destructive power of a fire that gets out of hand. The
enigmatic turns of phrase in "the world of wickedness" (ὁ κόσμος τῆς ἀδικίας)
and "sets on fire the course of human existence" (φλογίζουσα τὸν τροχὸν τῆς
γενέσεως: lit., "setting ablaze the wheel of nature") in v 6 betray an indebtedness
to contemporary philosophical-moralistic culture—whether the latter term
stems from the Orphics or popular hellenistic philosophy—where it could
be idiomatic for "the ups and downs of human life" (Windisch, 23).

At v 11 the setting changes to describe the inconsistency and incongruity
of words of blessing and imprecation proceeding from a single mouth. The
analogy draws on an argument of the absurd (cf. Amos 6:12–13). It is unthinkable to contemplate, from the world of nature, a spring yielding at the same
time and from a single opening (ὀπή, lit., "a hole") both fresh and bitter (or
brackish) waters. The closest parallel to this hypothetical situation is 4 Ezra
5:9: "And salt waters shall be found in the sweet," rendering *in dulcibus aquis
salsae invenientur*. The portent, as Ropes (242) notes, citing Spitta (104), describes the events of the endtime, when nature reverses its order as a sign
that all things are to be destroyed. Whether or not James is consciously reflecting this eschatological phenomenon (cf. Davids, 147–48, for a denial of this
but with no satisfactory solution), he uses the argument to telling effect. The
human mouth sends out words that are meant to reflect divine praise;
yet his readers are guilty of issuing (βρύειν is "to gush out, to burst forth,"
as headwaters of a river) abusive and evil language. Either he has the teachers
of v 1 still in mind and is rebuking their untamable speech, or he is looking
on to 4:11–12 which condemns καταλαλιά, evil words used against a fellow
believer. The two target audiences may well overlap.

The final recourse to illustrative material draws on the world of horticulture
(v 12a) before the author returns to the example of the two-source fountain
(v 12b). Once more the argument proceeds from the known to the inconceivable. The monstrous phenomenon contradicting the natural order of the
orchard is one of a hybrid plant that is designated at one and the same
time a fig-bearing tree and an olive bush, or a plant that yields simultaneously
grapes and figs. It is ludicrous to imagine such a case. No more so, says the
text, than to justify the action of the double-tongued person (δίγλωσσος) who
speaks out of a "divided soul" (δίψυχος, in 1:7–8; 4:8).

In all of these *exempla* drawn from a wide range of human activity (horseman-
ship, navigation, the menace of fire, the need for clean water, and horticulture),
James is pressing into service a homiletic style that employs various rhetorical
and stylistic devices. The following are to be noted: (i) Alliteration and asso-
nance are prominent, especially at v 2, where Vouga (97 n.9) observes the
emphasis on words with initial letter π: πολλά, πταίομεν, πταίει; also the μικρὸν—
μέλος—μεγάλα sequence in v 5; γενέσεως . . . γεέννης in v 6; ἀκατάστατον

κακόν in v 8 with a neat coupling and traits of epiphora as well as anaphora; similarly with ἰοῦ θανατηφόρου; and at v 12: ἀλυκὸν γλυκύ, which is a natural pairing. Then (ii) rhetorical questions in vv 11–12 introduced by μήτι and μή, raise a possibility only to hold it up to a scornful denial; (iii) closely associated with such questions is the use of paradox and hyperbole, familiar in the Jewish parenetic literature as well as the hellenistic moralists. The graphic and colorful idioms coupled with an occasional declamatory style (if the verbless v 8b is to be so understood: "Disorderly evil! Replete with lethal poison!") give the impression of a spoken discourse in the tradition of the contemporary popular philosophers (cf. Theophrastus) joined to the wisdom tradition of Israel. The latter influence carries over into the next pericope (3:13–18: contrary to Vouga [102, 103], who wishes to incorporate v 13 into the preceding section and make it a conclusion by relating the call to "the wise and understanding" in v 13 to the teacher [v 1]. The better view, with Ropes, 243; Wanke, "Zur urchristlichen Lehrer," 492, is to see v 13 as continuing the theme of vv 1–12 but marking a new section).

Comment

1 Μὴ πολλοὶ διδάσκαλοι γίνεσθε, ἀδελφοί μου, "Let not many of you become teachers, my brothers." James changes his topic of discussion from "faith and works" to the issue of those aspiring to become teachers. His advice is simple: "Let not many hold to this desire." Much of what follows may have been originally a series of maxims and proverbs that were taken and shaped to fit into the present context by James. But there is no compelling reason to deny unity to 3:1–12 (contra Dibelius, 182). No author, ancient or modern, would deliberately write something that confuses and bewilders his readers.

The negative μή is placed at the beginning of this verse for emphasis (though it is removed somewhat from its imperative partner γίνεσθε; see BDF § 433.1). The imperative is directed at the immediate situation in the church. If one is presently desirous of a teaching position then it is best that such a notion be seriously reconsidered. Or it may be a command for some to step down as teachers. Whatever the case, the Jacobean author is quite serious in his words of advice to "would be" or contemporary teachers in his day. The idea that "many" should not hold the office of teacher underlines the gravity of the situation (πολλοί is not adverbial as though it was equivalent to πολύ; see Mussner, 159 n.3; nor is it to be understood as ἐθελοδιδάσκαλοι, "self-willed teachers" [cf. Col 2:23], so Völter, "Zwei neue Wörter," *ZNW* 10 [1909] 326–29). The words of 3:1 are addressed to ἀδελφοί μου, i.e., James' own fraternity. This could certainly refer to the church at large but in the light of the use of the first person in 3:1b (λημψόμεθα), James or more probably the editor may be directing this admonition specifically to the teachers of the church at Antioch, with whom he associates himself (see *Introduction*, pp. lxxvi–lxxvii, and Zimmermann, *Die urchristlichen Lehrer*, 194–201).

εἰδότες ὅτι μεῖζον κρίμα λημψόμεθα, "because you are aware that we [who are teachers] will receive severer judgment [if we fail]." James quickly supplies the reason why the office of teacher is not to be sought. Those who teach come under greater scrutiny and are liable to the greater (μεῖζων) judgment (κρίμα). The question is, at whose hands does this judgment come? Most likely it is expected from God. Though James does not say categorically that Christian teachers are measured against a higher standard of conduct than that required of other Christians at the judgment day, it appears, with Adamson, 141, that James' words have a solemn emphasis. Elsewhere teachers (1 Cor 12:28; Eph 4:11) are not given the same warning, which suggests at first glance that teachers are not necessarily singled out for a stricter judgment than nonteaching Christians. But such a conclusion misses the point. The context makes it clear that in this epistle teachers had aspired to an office that they were using to lead others astray. Hence the reminder of a stricter accountability, since a false teacher is held responsible for influencing others. So teachers must weigh their words carefully (Matt 12:36–37; cf. ʾAbot 1:11). (This application will become clearer as the sins of the tongue in the following verses are reviewed.) The use of εἰδότες, a common Pauline usage to denote a piece of agreed traditional teaching; cf. Rom 5:3; 6:9; 13:11; 1 Cor 15:58; 2 Cor 4:14; suggests that the heavy responsibility associated with the office of teacher was known to the congregation (Davids, 137). Rather than seeing James as imposing something new on his readers, we probably should understand that the serious nature of assuming teaching responsibilities was a widely known matter (cf. Matt 23:1–33; Luke 20:47), though the authority of the Jacobean tradition needed to be reasserted in a situation where it was evidently under fire and where the teaching office was devalued (Zimmermann, *Die urchristlichen Lehrer,* 207).

In the early church to be a teacher brought high status (Davids, 136; see Acts 13:1; *Did.* 11.1–2; 13.2; 15.2; *Mart. Pol.* 12.2; 16.2; 19.1; *Herm. Vis.* 3.5.1; *Man.* 4.3.1; *Sim.* 9.15.4; 9.16.5; 25.2). Such evidence led Harnack, *Mission,* 333–68, to conclude that "'those who spoke the word of God' (the λαλοῦντες τὸν λόγον τοῦ θεοῦ) occupied the highest position . . . and were honoured as preachers who had been appointed by God and assigned to the church *as a whole*" (341); cf. Filson, "The Christian Teacher." But with this office came serious responsibility and great temptation (cf. *Barn.* 1.8; 4.9). Since the primary vehicle of communication of the teacher at that time was the tongue, James reports that one's words will be evaluated very carefully both by those who are taught and by God. The problem of "unfit" teachers appears to have been acute in the early church (1 John 3:7; 2 Pet 2:1; 1 Tim 6:3; 2 Tim 4:3; Jude; see also Rengstorf, *TDNT* 2:152–59; Kosmala, *Hebräer-Essener-Christen,* 282–90; Laws, 140–43). Persons were putting themselves forward as teachers without having paused to reckon with the high standard of behavior required or having faced the temptation of ulterior motives (such as love of prestige or reward; Moo, 120). The church was evidently plagued by teachers who were insincere and were inflicting false doctrine upon unsuspecting listeners. To call the error "gnosticizing" is probably misleading (Wanke, "Zur urchristlichen Lehrer," 492); they were failing to show the fruit of Christian character in their lives, a trait that most likely did have a theological error at its heart (ibid., 493, citing Matt 7:16 // Luke 6:44) as well as promoting party strife, as 3:13–18 will develop (ibid., 509). At issue was evidently the issue of authority, and 3:1–12 is a tacit plea for a recognition of James' primacy as teacher par excellence.

James is not to be seen as detachedly passing judgment on others, for he places himself in the category of teacher ("we"). His words are caution-sounding: "To many of you I say: Avoid entering the teaching ministry. The standard of righteousness [required of teachers] is one that few can hope to approach, and none can hope to reach" (adapting a quotation of Adamson, 141). Those who spurned James' advice were liable to severe consequences, not least because of the damage caused when others were led astray (5:19–20).

2 πολλὰ γὰρ πταίομεν ἅπαντες, "All of us go astray in many ways." The γάρ would suggest that 3:2 is linked to the thought of 3:1. But though James never explicitly mentions teachers in the present verse it is a fair inference that he has them in mind both here and throughout the chapter. πταίειν means "to stumble" and James admits that "all" (ἅπαντες), including himself, are not blameless. The πολλά may refer to the number of sins ("many," so RSV) or to the "variety" of sins (so NIV; see Mussner, 160, appealing to Prov 10:19; Sir 19:16; 25:8; 'Abot 1:17 for similar comment on the need to keep the tongue in check; see BGD, 688) or to both. The verb is found only here and 2:10; 2 Pet 1:10; Rom 11:11 in the NT. The problem of "spiritual failure" (Moo, 120) is common to all (see 2:10 with the sad verdict that by one slip all are guilty of breaking the entire law).

εἴ τις ἐν λόγῳ οὐ πταίει, "if a person does not go astray in what he says." This clause introduces what appears to be a condition of first class. The οὐ accompanies the indicative mood making the grammatical point that the protasis is assumed true—for the sake of argument—regardless of its real truth or falsity. This may (Davids, 137) or may not (see Moule, *Idiom Book,* 149) be a hypothetical situation from the writer's perspective (one must admit that to avoid sinning with the tongue is an extremely difficult level to attain), but it should be noted that if it is the former then James has switched from using a third class condition to depict a hypothetical case in these verses to a first class. Such an observation undercuts the position of some interpreters that the third class conditions in 2:4, 15, 17 refer only to hypothetical—and not real—situations in the church (see *Comment* on these verses).

Although not all sins laid to the account of one person are necessarily the same as those shared by others, all persons have at least one sin in common, namely, the sin of the tongue. The thought behind ἐν λόγῳ refers both to teachers (Mussner, 160) and to general speech, since the term λόγος ("word/ speech") is a synonym for γλῶσσα (3:5; Davids, 137).

οὗτος τέλειος ἀνήρ δυνατὸς χαλιναγωγῆσαι καὶ ὅλον τὸ σῶμα, "then he is a perfect man, able to hold in restraint the entire body as well." The picture is one of keeping the tongue in check (that is, overcoming the tendency of the mouth "to stay open when it were more profitably closed," Moo, 120) and recalls 1:26, but here with a pointed application. It is specifically directed as a warning to teachers whose words of instruction need to be brought under control. The idea of a perfect man (τέλειος ἀνήρ) reiterates the thought of 1:4, which is that of completeness and maturity, not sinlessness. The problem of an unruly or hasty tongue is one that is addressed in the earlier wisdom tradition (Prov 10:8, 11, 19; 16:27, 28; 18:7, 8; 21:25; Sir 19:16; 20:1–8). But more than intemperate speech seems in view here; it is the unrestrained use of the tongue to lead others away from the truth that is condemned.

The τέλειος ἀνήρ is the teacher whose λόγος (in the double sense of speech and behavior) is sound.

James' analogy (Adamson, 142) of the bridle (χαλιναγωγεῖν is the verb, also implying restraint; it is found only here and in 1:26 in NT) begins a list of illustrations (bit, 3:3; rudder of ships, 3:4; fire, 3:5, 6; spring of water, 3:12; fig tree, 3:12), describing what the tongue and its activity are like. As suggested earlier (*Form/Structure/Setting*) the use of the picture of the body (τὸ σῶμα) strongly indicates that James is speaking of the entire congregation (see Reicke, 37) but with special focus on the leaders. This is consonant with the illustrations that follow, for if a horse (v 3) or a ship (v 4) or a forest (vv 5, 6) is destroyed by one small object that gets out of hand, then more than an individual entity suffers; a wider community is seriously affected. Indeed the illustrations almost mandate an ecclesial setting, which is also the context of the previous paragraphs (at least since 2:1). The small anatomical element, namely, the tongue—whether described as a bit, rudder, or small fire—holds power much beyond its size to control the larger part (horse, ship, forest) to which it belongs. When the tongue itself is out of control it can wreak havoc on that which it was meant to help; and an unrestrained teacher can adversely affect the entire community of faith.

3 εἰ δὲ τῶν ἵππων τοὺς χαλινοὺς εἰς τὰ στόματα βάλλομεν εἰς τὸ πείθεσθαι αὐτοὺς ἡμῖν καὶ ὅλον τὸ σῶμα αὐτῶν μετάγομεν, "when we put bridles in horses' mouths to make them obey us, we also turn their entire body (to our will)." The lack of clarity associated with the beginning of v 3 makes it difficult to decide how James intended to structure the following illustration. ἴδε would go better with the following ἰδού (vv 4, 5) than would εἰ δέ, but ἴδε is not found elsewhere in James and ἰδού is a harmonizing attempt. The verse can begin either with "behold" (ἴδε; so Ropes) or "when" (εἰ δέ; so NIV); the present choice is for the latter (see *Note* a; also Moule, *Idiom Book*, 188).

V 3 begins a series of illustrations depicting the power (and potential danger) of the tongue; none of the illustrations that follow can be said to be unique to James. Such examples were used by other writers as well (Plutarch, *Mor.*, 33; Philo, *Op. Mund.*, 88; *Leg. Alleg.* 2.104, 3.98, 223–24; *Spec. Leg.* 4.79. These citations from Philo are all variants of the general theme that both charioteers and helmsmen need to keep firm control on their charges, and that in the case of horses a small iron bit can restrain them). See also Rendall, *The Epistle of St. James and Judaic Christianity*, 38 n.2. The reference to χαλινός ("bit," "bridle") links this illustration with 3:2 (which has the cognate verb). The analogy is somewhat imprecise (Reicke, 32) because the human tongue is not the agent for controlling the movement of the human body as the bridle controls (lit., "in order to obey"; εἰς τὸ with the passive infinitive of πείθειν) the mouths (στόματα) of horses (ἵππων). But James' intention is to show that the tongue is the means by which a body of great size (Mussner, 161)—namely, the church—is controlled by a separate part of much smaller size, namely, the teachers who are decisively influential out of proportion to their number, as they control ("guide," μετάγειν) the direction of the whole body (ὅλον τὸ σῶμα; see 3:2). The use of the example of the bit in a horse's mouth is reminiscent of Greek writers (Sophocles, *Antig. 477–78*: σμικρῷ χαλινῷ δ' οἶδα τοὺς θυμουμένους // ἵππους καταρτυθέντας ["Now I know that lively horses are broken by the use of a tiny bit"]; Cicero, *De natura deorum* 2.34; Lucretius, *De rerum natura* 4.898–904; and Ps-Aristotle, *Mechanica* 5 [but doubtful; Ropes, 231]). Davids' resistance to the idea of the use of "body" as reference to the whole church is unnecessary since James' use of σῶμα—though not exactly Pauline—is in no way "anti-Pauline" (139). Besides, it does not follow that one must mimic exactly the particular understandings that Paul has concerning the church as a body in order to think of the congregation in this way.

4 ἰδοὺ καὶ τὰ πλοῖα τηλικαῦτα ὄντα καὶ ὑπὸ ἀνέμων σκληρῶν ἐλαυνόμενα, μετάγεται ὑπὸ ἐλαχίστου πηδαλίου ὅπου ἡ ὁρμὴ τοῦ εὐθύνοντος βούλεται, "Consider the case of ships: though they are so huge and driven along by powerful winds, they are nevertheless steered by a very small rudder, which course the pilot's choice decides." The idea of a small object controlling a larger body is reinforced with a second illustration. The choice of a ship and rudder would not have perplexed James' readers, for this mode of marine transportation (along with horses) was the chief means people used to get from one place to another (Davids, 139). Thus, the picture of a ship moving through the water would have been a common one for the ancient world (Casson, *Travel*, chap. 9). It may be that such a literary example was taken from extant sources in the light of the combination of horse and ship in contemporary writers (see Dibelius, 185–90; Davids, 139, for citations of Greek authors; cf. also Mayor, 110; Ropes, 231) and the rare vocabulary that is used (τηλικοῦτος, elsewhere in 2 Cor 1:10; Heb 2:3; Rev 16:18; πηδάλιον, in Acts 27:40; ὁρμή, in Acts 14:5; ὁ εὐθύνων, only here). But even with this evidence one is not forced to conclude that James borrowed this imagery from written sources (where even fire is sometimes associated with the horse and ship; see v 5; cf. Philo, *Leg. Alleg.* 3.223–24). These examples are so commonplace that James may simply have drawn on his personal knowledge and chosen what he thought would be familiar illustrations (cf. Moo, 122; Davids, 140, opts for "oral proverbs"). The point is that James is instructing his readers by way of reminder (εἰδότες in 3:1). The emphasis is on the control that the rudder (or bit) exercises over the ship (or horse) despite the disadvantage of size suffered by the former. The rudder (πηδάλιον) is very small (ἐλάχιστος, elative superlative of μικρός) when compared to the ship (τὸ πλοῖον), which is so big (τηλικοῦτος, classified as a "correlative demonstrative" by W. D. Chamberlain, *An Exegetical Grammar of the Greek New Testament* [New York: Macmillan, 1941], 48).

Taken together, the first two instruments of bit and rudder do not correspond exactly with the tongue and its relationship to the human body. The bit and the rudder control the larger bodies, but the tongue does not control the human body. However, if we assume that the body is the church congregation then we have a point of agreement because all three instruments may be characterized under the rubric of *pars pro toto*, exercising influence over the larger body of which they form a significant part. With respect to the tongue, the text is not saying that the church at large is controlled by the tongue; rather it is saying that if we can control the latter then it will prove much easier to control the former (Adamson, 143); or better, if teachers who use their tongue to influence others are kept in firm check, the health and condition of the congregation will be assured thereby. All three examples are used to show that these small instruments determine the direction (or the destiny; Moo, 122) of the larger body. Just as the charioteer guides the horse with bit and bridle and the helmsman steers (μετάγεται, see 3:3) the ship by means of the rudder, so the teaching corps directs the body through the tongue. However, a tongue that is out of control (see vv 5–12) betokens an undisciplined and uncontrolled body. This is especially pertinent to the author's readers if by the thought of strong winds (ὑπὸ ἀνέμων σκληρῶν: Prov 27:16 LXX) driving (ἐλαυνόμενα: used of demonic pressure in Luke 8:29, thus suggesting possibly an assault on the church; see 2:6–7 for outside hostility; cf. the imagery in Eph 4:14 of false teaching) the ship, the author highlights the need of control during a storm.

A ship buffeted by the high wind of storms has no hope of survival save as the pilot can guide it by the use of the rudder. However, without the rudder to control it, the ship is destined to be at the mercy of heaving seas and destructive winds, or else to break up on the rocks along the shoreline (for a graphic description of a ship caught by a wind, then likened to the evil, irrevocable effects of idle words, see Plutarch, *De Garrul.* 10 [Dibelius, 189]). No doubt the author feared that the congregation to which he wrote might suffer a similar fate unless the tongues of those who teach in the authentic Jacobean tradition were used as a rudder to offer true guidance through difficult times.

5 οὕτως καὶ ἡ γλῶσσα μικρὸν μέλος ἐστὶν καὶ μεγάλα αὐχεῖ, "In the same way, the tongue is equally a tiny part (of the body), yet it makes great claims for itself." James here completes the comparison of the bit and rudder (οὕτως is the link). The first half of this verse simply reiterates the thought that firm control is of the utmost importance (3:2–4). V 5a reports that the tongue (ἡ γλῶσσα) is a small (μικρὸν) member (μέλος) but that it boasts (αὐχεῖ; boasting is often considered a sin in the NT; the reason is that it represents an attitude which is in direct antithesis to trust in God: see Bultmann, *TDNT* 3:645–54) of great things (μεγάλα; see *Note* b concerning an alternative reading). Davids, 140, notes the "nice alliteration" (μικρὸν—μέλος—μεγάλα) in v 5a. Further Davids opines that there is a subtle change in James' tone (contra Dibelius, 190–91) concerning the use of the tongue. The pictures of the bit and rudder show them in a positive light (the bit and bridle are used not only to check the horse in a race but to spur it on) and at worst in a neutral light. However, the tongue is at best seen in only a neutral light and at worst (in anticipation of what is to follow) in a negative light. The tongue is powerful and vainly boasts of its might, a comment that goes back to Ps 73:9: "their tongue struts through the earth," as the godless are held up to condemnation. A ship in the hands of a pilot who is undisciplined is liable to shipwreck. Likewise the congregation that is steered by one who cannot control the tongue is doomed to catastrophe. A more positive note, however, when the tongue is rightly employed, is sounded at v 9a.

Ἰδοὺ ἡλίκον πῦρ ἡλίκην ὕλην ἀνάπτει, "Consider how a small fire sets ablaze a great forest." The second half of v 5 begins a discussion of the potential destructive power of the tongue. This topic will run through to v 12. ἡλίκον . . . ἡλίκην is an interesting use of ἡλίκος (lit., "of what size"). This dual use (see *Note* c) effects a balance and a symmetry (Davids, 140; Philostratus, *Vit. Ap.* 2.11.2). The term is found elsewhere only in Col 2:1 and Gal 6:11 (but only in some MSS, P⁴⁶, B*). In our present verse, the term has two different (and opposite) meanings: "how great" and "how small." The word "expresses magnitude in either direction" (Hort). Such a usage reflects the practice of Greek writers (Antiphanes 166.1; Lucian, *Herm.* 5; Epictetus, *Diss.* 1.12.26). But it could well be that James did not go so far afield for his imagery. Rather, it is probable that this is another example culled from everyday life used to illustrate the writer's thought. In this instance the point is the rapidly destructive power of a small fire (πῦρ) that sets the forest (ὕλη; a *hapax*; lit., "wood," but here includes idea of forest) ablaze (ἀνάπτειν, "set alight"; found elsewhere in the NT only in Luke 12:49). With the setting of a hillside covered with dry brush or wood, such an environment is literally a tinderbox just waiting to explode at the slightest spark. The readers of the letter would have no trouble understanding this imagery and appreciating the risk of such a spark's leading to a rapidly spreading fire that would destroy everything in its path (see Elliott-Binns, "The Meaning," 48–50; Mussner, 162; Dibelius, 192; Cantinat, 172).

Jewish tradition is a wellspring of sayings that warn that the tongue is a flame or a fire (v 6; see Pss 10:7; 39:1–3; 83:14; 120:2–4; Prov 16:27; 26:21; Isa 30:27; Sir 28:13–26 [esp. v 22: "it (the tongue) will not be master over the godly, and they will not be burned in its flame"]; Pss Sol 12:2–3). These parallels lessen the need to believe that James borrowed the tongue/fire imagery from hellenistic writers (as distinct from biblical sources), though we may still prefer to conclude that James took his proverbial illustrations from daily living. Davids notes that fire was often connected with the uncontrollable sway of human passions in other literature (141; see citations there). But James is not comparing passions to the flame; rather he links fire to tongue. Such a description of the tongue enforces the idea that great destruction is but a short distance away when teachers are allowed to sway the congregation and introduce dissension (see on 3:13–18).

6 καὶ ἡ γλῶσσα πῦρ· ὁ κόσμος τῆς ἀδικίας ἡ γλῶσσα καθίσταται ἐν τοῖς μέλεσιν ἡμῶν, ἡ σπιλοῦσα ὅλον τὸ σῶμα, "Likewise the tongue is a fire; a world of wickedness; it is set among the parts of our body; it corrupts the entire body." These words comprise a half-verse that at face value is not hard to understand in terms of its general meaning but is extremely complex and difficult when the detailed parts are examined. To begin with, there are five expressions in the nominative case but only one verb in the indicative (καθίσταται). This makes it a problem to know how to combine these different words and phrases. Moreover, several phrases are enigmatic and any proposed understanding of 3:6a has its difficulties. Some have concluded that the text is corrupt. Dibelius reckons that the words ὁ κόσμος . . . ἡμῶν are a scribal gloss (193–95). Adamson, 158, concurs that the text is corrupt and looks to the Syriac Peshitta for the correct reading: "The tongue is fire, the sinful world [is a] wood" (see also Mayor, 115; Ropes, 234). Such suggestions are not to be taken lightly because there are several variants of this half-verse, thereby endorsing the fact that the scribes and copyists found the text difficult to understand and attempted to smooth it out (e.g., καί at the beginning is omitted from א* and οὕτως and οὕτως καί are added; see Hort). But any attempt at recasting the text to produce the way it was "meant to be written" should be viewed with caution and should be considered only as the final option ("last, desperate, resort," Moo, 124). Before seeking to "correct" (or change) the text, the interpreter should be sure that the text before us—as it is—makes no sense (Davids, 142) and emendation is imperative.

The opening words, "the tongue is a fire," follow on smoothly with what was concluded in v 5, but in trying to depict the potential danger that the tongue poses James has left us with a lexical problem. The meaning of ὁ κόσμος is unclear. Some interpreters take the term to mean the "adornment" (1 Pet 3:3), thus suggesting the sense that the tongue makes unrighteousness attractive (Chaine, 81; Carr, "Meaning"). Another solution is to infer that ὁ κόσμος means the "sum total of evil": Vulgate universitas iniquitatis (BGD, 447; Prov 17:6a LXX ὅλος ὁ κόσμος τῶν χρημάτων; other views akin to this one are given in Mussner, 162 n.5). But neither of these definitions proves satisfactory since the other uses of ὁ κόσμος in the letter (1:27; 2:5; 4:4 [2x]) suggest a meaning that speaks of the "fallen, rebellious state of a sinful world-system" (Moo, 124). The phrase κόσμος τῆς ἀδικίας most simply yields the translation "a world of wickedness," i.e., the wicked world. This parallels Luke 16:9 (μαμωνᾶ τῆς ἀδικίας; cf. Luke 16:11; 18:6; Mark 16:14 [W] ὁ αἰὼν τῆς ἀνομίας; 1 Enoch 48.7, "this world of oppression"), in which the genitive replaces the adjective (Davids, 142). So there is little to be said in defense of Carr's novel translation that gives to ὁ κόσμος the meaning "the ornament of embellishment of unrighteousness" ("Meaning," 323) in spite of the way it does account for the definite article.

The next question concerns structure: how does "a world of wickedness," which immediately follows "the tongue is a fire," relate to the latter clause? Any decision rendered will affect the punctuation of the verse. Many translators understand "the tongue is a fire" to be a complete sentence in itself, followed by a full stop, with the verb ἐστιν being understood. The second occurrence of ἡ γλῶσσα, then, is taken as the subject of καθίσταται, with "a world of wickedness" being interpreted as the predicate complement of the verb (so Hort, 71; Mayor, 113; Mitton, 125–26; Laws, 148–49; Moo, 124; Davids, 142; cf. 1:7, 8; 4:4). This gives the translation: "And the tongue is a fire. The tongue is an unrighteous world among our members" (RSV). Such an understanding has something to commend it and sees the piling up of nominatives as a rhetorical figura (Vouga, 99 n.16). In addition to being widely accepted, this view seems to explain the second use of ἡ γλῶσσα (as not redundant) and the use of ἡ σπιλοῦσα (feminine participle of σπιλοῦν, "to stain," "to pollute") as a modifier of ἡ γλῶσσα (so Moo, 125). But such a position does not carry enough weight to rule out completely the possibility that ὁ κόσμος τῆς ἀδικίας is meant to stand in apposition to ἡ γλῶσσα πῦρ.

The difficulty in deciding on the correct punctuation of 3:6 is aggravated by the textual and scholastic witnesses mentioned in Ropes, 234 (see Nestle-Aland[26]; surprisingly Metzger, Textual Commentary, has nothing to say on this verse). Following one option, we have the rendering: "the tongue also is a fire, a world of wickedness set among the parts of our body" (NIV). This rendering makes good sense (Bengel; see Moo, 125) and leaves open the possibility that James' second use of ἡ γλῶσσα is for emphasis: hence "The tongue is a fire, a world of wickedness, [the tongue is] set among the parts of the body" (cf. Mussner, 163, for the preference of taking "world of wickedness" as a judgment on the tongue *simpliciter*). Furthermore, there is nothing in this translation to argue against including ἡ σπιλοῦσα with the article (see below; cf. BDF § 273.1; contra Davids, 142). Yet there is really no difference in meaning between the two choices. The tongue is a dangerous instrument and as such it represents the world of wickedness among the parts of our body. We translate μέλος as a "part" of the body, which is quite consistent with its use in 3:5 (BGD, 501) and flows naturally with σῶμα in the following words. The "tongue" is set (καθίσταται, construed as passive; if the verb is middle, then, "sets itself") among the parts of the body, i.e., the church, and designates that behavior (i.e., expressed in speech) which is extremely hard to control. Such an observation was made by Jesus (Mark 7:14–23). "There are few sins people commit in which the tongue is not involved" (Burdick, 189, against Carr, "The Meaning," 324, who restricts sins of the tongue to deceit and falsehood).

καὶ φλογίζουσα τὸν τροχὸν τῆς γενέσεως, "and sets on fire the course of human existence." The power of the tongue is such that it can stain (cf. 1:27, ἄσπιλον) the whole (ὅλον) body (τὸ σῶμα). The implication is that by the irresponsible speech of errant teachers the whole church is "stained." This is in line with the thought of 3:2, 3, 4, in which it was stated that the small instruments (bit, rudder) determine the course of the entire body. Up to this point, James has said little that is good regarding the tongue. His main emphasis has been on the bad consequence that comes from its misuse. The same indictment continues with the imagery of fire (Ropes, 235) when it is remarked that the tongue "sets on fire" (φλογίζουσα, feminine participle of φλογίζειν; the noun is φλόξ, flame) "the course of human existence" (τὸν τροχὸν τῆς γενέσεως). The latter expression is again problematic, as can be seen from the excursuses included by some exegetes (Dibelius, 196–98; Adamson, 160–64; Ropes, 235–39). In general terms, James is concerned—as his main point—to indicate the "magnitude of the tongue's destructive potential" (Moo, 125). The tongue affects all of life, from the beginning to the end. Yet his choice of words is still unusual. The idea of the "cycle of nature" is found in the literature of the mystery religion of the Orphics, which speaks of a "circle of becoming" (κύκλος τῆς γενέσεως; see Proclus' commentary on Plato, *In Tim.* 5.330A; cf. Dibelius), a technical expression that denotes existence as simply an unending cycle of attempts by people to gain release from the imprisonment of a succession of bodies resulting from reincarnation (Plato, *Tim.* 79B). By the time of James, however, the expression had probably become popularized and was used in a nontechnical way, e.g., in Virgil, *Aen.* 6:748, "When time's wheel has rolled a thousand years"; Stiglmayr, "Zu Jak 3,6." The phrase may have been no more than a mode of speaking about the "*Auf und Ab des Menschenlebens*" ("the ups and downs of life," so Windisch, 23: cf. *Sib. Or.* 2.87: "All have a common lot, the wheel of life," βιοτὸς τροχός // Ps-Phocylides 27: κοινὰ πάθη πάντων· ὁ βίος τροχός· ἄστατος ὄλβος, "Suffering is common to everyone; life is a wheel; happiness is in flux." The chances and changes of life may have something to do with the alternation of sunrise and sunset, according to W. Bieder, "Christliche Existenz," 109. He thereby accounts for the next phrase). For James, the tongue sets on fire everything that comes into contact with it, namely, the entire human existence.

καὶ φλογιζομένη ὑπὸ τῆς γεέννης, "and is itself set on fire by Gehenna." In the closing words of v 6 the source from which the tongue gets its power is traced. The use of Gehenna refers to the Valley of Hinnom (גֵי הִנֹּם, *gēy hinnôm*, Josh 15:8b; 18:16b; Neh 11:30), a place of evil reputation and the location of Satan (*Apoc. Abr.* 14.6–8: Azazel is thought of as fallen to Gehenna; Laws, 152; but cf. Foerster, *TDNT* 2:80). It was depicted as the scene of final judgment (Jeremias, *TDNT* 1:657–58; as in the teaching of Mark 9:43, 47–48 and parallels, which is connected in the rabbinic and Targumic tradition with Isa 66:23–24. There is a good case made by Chilton, *A Galilean Rabbi*, 101–7, for the origin of "Gehenna" in a logion of Jesus, which seems to relate to warnings about false teachers, as in James). The valley was a ravine south of Jerusalem, but it came to be regarded as the location for punishment in the next life (BGD, 153). It is quite apparent that by the time of the letter cosmic evil was traced to Satan (Davids, 143; cf. Rev 9:1–11; 20:7, 8). Thus, James contends that the devil lies behind the poison that is emitted from the mouth of the teacher who cannot control the tongue (cf. *Apoc. Abr.* 31.5–7, where idolaters are burned by the power of Azazel's tongue). Such a verdict would characterize a church beset by teachers who create strife and speak evil and falsehood (4:11). Here was also a reason to resist the devil (4:7). In short, v 6 pronounces the tongue as evil—quite capable of doing deadly (i.e., Satanic) harm to the body of believers—because it emanates from the evil one; and there may be a link with the Gospel tradition about leading others astray (Mark 9:42–50) as well as living in harmony. But in enunciating this truth, James has joined together several phrases in v 6 in such a way that its exegesis is appreciated more for the impression it conveys than for its clarity of presentation.

7 πᾶσα γὰρ φύσις θηρίων τε καὶ πετεινῶν, ἑρπετῶν τε καὶ ἐναλίων δαμάζεται καὶ δεδάμασται τῇ φύσει τῇ ἀνθρωπίνῃ, "All species of beasts and birds, of reptiles and sea creatures, are being tamed and have been tamed by humans." The γάρ ties v 6 to what follows, namely, vv 7–8, which are one sentence in the Greek. The thought expressed in v 6 has been the uncontrollable nature of the tongue, a thought that is reiterated in v 8: James uses v 7 to set up a vivid—but axiomatic—contrast to the idea in v 8 (πᾶς placed before a noun without the definite article carries the sense "all you care to mention"; BDF § 275.3). The mention of φύσις (species) refers to "kind" (κjv/av), and the fourfold list of James may be based on Gen 1:26; 9:2; cf. *1 Enoch* 7.5; Philo, *De Spec. Leg.* 4.110–16: θηρίον, "beast," probably referring to undomesticated animals (Foerster, *TDNT* 3:133–35); πετεινόν, "bird"; ἑρπετόν, "reptile"; ἐνάλιον, "sea creature" (a *hapax legomenon*, although common in classical Greek writing; cf. Sophocles, *Antig.* 345, where biblical Greek prefers ἰχθύς).

The ancient world took pride in humanity's ability to tame and control the animal kingdom. Ps 8:6–8 conveys the idea of humankind's superiority over animals both in terms of what is hunted and slain for food and what is domesticated for work and pleasure (Adamson, 145). The Greeks believed that human reason overcame the strength and speed of animals (Cicero, *De natura deorum* 2.60.151–58; Sophocles, *Antig.* 342; Philo, *Decal.* 113; *Leg. Alleg.* 2.104; *Op. Mund.* 83–86, 148; see Mayor, 115–16). The use of the perfect and the present of the verb δαμάζειν (to "subdue," to "tame," found only elsewhere in the NT in Mark 5:4) supports the contention that the animal world has been under the control of the human world since the beginning (Moo, 126). τῇ φύσει τῇ ἀνθρωπίνῃ follows the two instances of the verb in the passive voice. This phrase is probably best classed as an instrumental dative (BDF § 191.5). James in no way is contesting the fact (taken in his day to be an accepted opinion) that humankind rules over the animal world. He has included this illustration to set up a contrast to what follows in v 8. The placement of ἀνθρώπινος at the end of the phrase may be for emphasis.

8 τὴν δὲ γλῶσσαν οὐδεὶς δαμάσαι δύναται ἀνθρώπων, "but no human being can tame the tongue." James quickly introduces the contrast of the unruly nature of the tongue with an adversative clause (δέ) that begins with τὴν γλῶσσαν for emphasis. Even though a person can tame the wild beasts, the same individual cannot control the tongue. The change in subject with the pronoun "no one" (οὐδεὶς) highlights the contrast between the list of wild creatures in the genitive case and the human tongue (Schlatter). James makes this pessimistic assertion, no doubt based on the realities of his situation. The use of ἀνθρώπων, after ἀνθρώπινος v 7, appears somewhat redundant, but this repetition may be for added emphasis. Less likely is Augustine's interpretation (*De Natura et Gratia* 15) that οὐδεὶς . . . ἀνθρώπων ("no human being," RSV) is to highlight the need for God's grace and help in bringing the tongue under control. The thought that the tongue is one "animal" that cannot be controlled was quite common in the literature of hellenistic and Jewish ethics (Plutarch, *De Garrul.* 14; *Lev. Rab.* 16 on Lev 14:4; *Deut. Rab.* 5:10 on Deut 17:4; Prov 10:20; 13:3; 12:18; 15:2, 4; 21:3; 31:26; Sir 14:1; 19:6; 25:8). James will bolster such an understanding with two more illustrations.

ἀκατάστατον κακόν, μεστὴ ἰοῦ θανατηφόρου, "Disorderly evil! Replete with lethal poison!" We evidently have a solecism (an impropriety or irregularity in grammar) here (see BDF § 137.3), with ἀκατάστατον κακόν as an ejaculatory nominative. The NIV places a full stop in translation before ἀκατάστατον . . . θανατηφόρου and treats these words as predicates in a sentence with "the tongue" as subject and the verb εἶναι as understood: "It is a restless evil, full of deadly poison." ἀκατάστατος ("restless" [1:8] or "disorderly"; found only here and in 1:8 in NT; see also *Herm. Man.* 2.3: "Slander is evil; it is a restless demon (ἀκατάστατον δαιμόνιον), never at peace"; cf. H. Beck and C. Brown, *NIDNTT* 2:780) is related to the noun ἀκαταστασία of 3:16. The latter describes the pursuit of base wisdom, classified as earthly and not of God (Davids, 145; cf. 1 Cor 14:33; Luke 21:9; 2 Cor 6:5; 12:20; Prov 26:28 LXX). The idea of "disorderly evil" shows that the tongue is always liable to break out into evil (Ph). In the present context it forms the picture of a caged animal pacing back and forth and seeking an opportunity to escape. But whereas it is possible to secure an animal so as to prevent such an escape, this is not so with the tongue. Moreover, "disorderly evil" suggests the instability and the double-mindedness of the tongue (see 1:8; 4:8). The tongue is an instrument of destruction (Davids, 145), though James is not implying that the tongue never speaks good (vv 9–12). He is simply highlighting the somber fact that it speaks evil for much of the time; and doubtless the text has in its sights a baleful situation in the church.

The tongue is designated as "full" (μεστός) of "lethal (θανατηφόρος) poison (ιός)." The admission that the tongue is full of "death-dealing poison" (Davids, 145) was a familiar cry (Job 5:15; Ps 140:3; Rom 3:13; Sir 28:17–23; 10:11; 1QH 5.26–27; T. Gad 5.1; cf. Michel, TDNT 3:334–35). Mayor, 121, sees a reference to the serpent in Eden, but this may be too specific, since such a description of the sinister power of the tongue was quite common. The actual phrase θανατηφόρος ιός is found in Sib. Frag. 3.32–33: in the judgment on idolatry it is said: "There are gods which by deceit are leaders of mindless men, from whose mouths pour deadly poison."

9 ἐν αὐτῇ εὐλογοῦμεν τὸν κύριον καὶ πατέρα, "With the tongue we bless the Lord and Father." James now turns to specific examples of how the tongue is unstable and duplicitous, as in an interlude he abandons the use of metaphors. An evidence of the tongue as δίγλωσσος (see on 1:8) is that it can both praise God and curse humankind. Such "duplicity" (so Davids, 145) was seen in Jewish thought as a common problem to be overcome (Ps 62:4; Lam 3:38; Sir 5:13; 28:12 [a single mouth can produce two effects—to fan a flame, to spit on a fire to extinguish it]; T. Benj. 6.5; Philo, De Decal. 93; 1QH 1.27–31; 10.21–24; Lev. Rab. 33 on Lev 25:1; Str-B 3:757).

The "sublimest function" (Adamson, 146) of the tongue is to bless God. The action of blessing (εὐλογεῖν) God is an OT-Judaic theme (see the verb used in LXX; e.g., Pss 31:21; 103:1–2: on this verb see the comment and bibliography in 2 Corinthians, WBC 40 [Waco: Word, 1986] 7–8). The Jewish Eighteen Benedictions, which contains liturgical formulas to be recited daily, concludes each of its parts with a blessing of God: "Blessed art Thou, O God." The rabbinic use of "the Holy One, blessed is he" is heavily documented (m. Ber. 7.3; 1 Enoch 77.2; see Dalman, Words of Jesus, ET 202). Likewise, the NT tradition of circumlocutions that speak of God as the "Blessed One" (Mark 14:61; Rom 9:5) sometimes contains prayers that refer to God this way (Luke 1:68; 2 Cor 1:3; Eph 1:3; 1 Pet 1:3). The phrase "Lord and Father" does not match exactly the data in Jewish literature (1 Chr 29:10; Isa 63:16; cf. also Sir 23:1; Josephus, Ant. 5.93), which may explain the attempt to change the text to read "God and Father" (see Note g; Laws, 155). The combination of "Lord and Father" is unique to the NT (the nearest parallel is 1 Cor 8:6), though there may be no great significance behind James' use of the titles here. What seems more likely—in the light of the use of a liturgical blessing in vv 9, 10—is that the use (and misuse) of the tongue is related primarily to the worship setting of the church as a body. If this is true, it makes what follows even more blameworthy. From one side of the worshiper's mouth comes praise to God; from the other side of the same mouth come curses aimed at another fellow worshiper.

καὶ ἐν αὐτῇ καταρώμεθα τοὺς ἀνθρώπους τοὺς καθ᾽ ὁμοίωσιν θεοῦ γεγονότας, "with it we curse our fellows, who are made in the likeness of God." Both uses of ἐν are instrumental. The verb καταροῦσθαι (to "curse") is given in the present tense, as is εὐλογεῖν, which suggests that these two activities were currently taking place in the author's church. The opposite of "blessing," namely, the words of the curse (Deut 30:19), is another common theme in the OT (Gen 9:25; 49:7; Judg 5:23; 9:20; Prov 11:26; 24:24; 26:2; Eccl 7:21; Sir 4:5), though there is a certain critical attitude taken to cursing (Davids, 146). The NT writers speak out against cursing (Luke 6:28; Rom 12:14), but Paul sometimes comes close to cursing others (1 Cor 5:5; Rom 3:8; Gal 5:12). There is evidence, moreover, to support Davids' contention (146) that formal cursing (that is, the aiming of anathemas at those to be excluded from the church) was not strictly forbidden in the early communities (1 Cor 16:22; cf. Acts 5:1–11; 8:20; Rev 22:18–19). Thus, the prohibition of cursing was aimed at those who struck out in anger (see Matt 5:21–26) against other Christians, especially when disputes flared up during internal squabbles. Such a practice could easily characterize those who are pictured as double-minded (1:7, 8), who manifest an attitude of partiality (2:4), and who accept the lopsided doctrine of faith without deeds (2:14–26; see Moo, 128; also Dibelius, 203).

A more serious offense of "cursing" the divine image in fellow human beings may be intended if J. Jervell's reasoning (*Imago Dei*, 240, 295–96) is correct. He argues that Gen 1:27 not only lies in the background of James' text but provides a motive for the ethical parenesis. The point is not to associate the divine image with a veiled christological reference to "the new man" (as in Paul), but to establish the "attribute of humanity" as worthy of respect. This has particular regard to the Jewish prohibition of murder (ibid., 95) based on Gen 9:6; and so James' mention of "cursing man" paves the way for what is to come in 4:1–3, just as it looks back to the citation in the commandment, "You shall do no murder" in 2:11.

The idea, then, that the one on whom the curse is spoken was made in God's image (*imago Dei*) makes the insult even more despicable: "it is the demonic 'paradox' of the tongue" (Mussner, 168, who cites Jewish evidence of warning against directing insults against one's fellows, who are God's creation). The phrase καθ᾽ ὁμοίωσιν was common (Gen 9:6; Sir 17:3; Wisd Sol 2:23; 4 Ezra 8:44). The relation is clear: one cannot praise God in worship along with a murderous disposition and then stand before God and the church body as claiming to fulfill the law (2:8, 12). To bless God ("the highest function of speech"; so Hort) and then "curse people" (which is not merely verbal abuse but an expression of enmity) is "moral and logical nonsense" (Davids, 146). It is interesting to note that the pronoun "we" recurs (from 3:1–2). This may be (i) an identification of James with his readers and also a sign that the weakness of double talk goes with being human. It may also imply that teachers are in the author's sights, though they are not the only ones subject to this malady: all church members must guard against this sin (see Dibelius), even if the primary target audience seems to be the church's teachers. Or (ii) the first person plural idiom may be derived from liturgical usage.

10 ἐκ τοῦ αὐτοῦ στόματος ἐξέρχεται εὐλογία καὶ κατάρα· οὐ χρή, ἀδελφοί μου, ταῦτα οὕτως γίνεσθαι, "Out of the same mouth come both blessing and cursing. My brothers, this should not be the case." The dual deceit of the tongue is now recast in the form of a deception emanating from the mouth. This switch from tongue to mouth (στόμα) is noteworthy, but hardly renders the objects of blessing (εὐλογία) and cursing (κατάρα) "irrelevant" (so Davids, 147).

Rather, at issue is the observation that what comes out (ἐξέρχεσθαι; cf. Matt 15:19) of a person is what defiles that person (Matt 15:11, 20). Like Jesus in Matthew's Gospel, James understands a person's speech to be a "barometer" of spirituality (Moo, 129; cf. Matt 12:33–37). It is as though one's speech (whether thought of as communicated through the tongue or mouth) cannot hide but must express what is in one's heart. If an individual is τέλειος ἀνήρ then he both praises God and speaks well of persons. But if he is disposed toward deceit and hypocrisy, this will inevitably come out in speech. This thought is found in *T. Benj.* 6.5, 6: "the good set of mind does not talk from both sides of its mouth: praises and curses, abuse and honor, calm and strife, hypocrisy and truth, poverty and wealth, but it has one disposition, uncontaminated and pure, toward all men. There is no duplicity in its perception or its hearing."

For James double-natured speech is simply "not right" (Adamson, 147). οὐ χρή (from χρᾶν "to give what is needful," BDF § 358.2; cf. Prov 25:27 LXX) is used only here in the NT and is meant to point to the negative effect of cursing, which is then reprobated. James is not discouraging the act of blessing, but he is decrying the abuse of other Christians. Such language is strongly worded and χρή probably approaches δεῖ, "it is necessary" (Lat. *oportet*) in meaning. The rabbis were well aware of the ambivalent nature of the tongue (*Lev. Rab.* 33 on Lev 25:1).

11 μήτι ἡ πηγὴ ἐκ τῆς αὐτῆς ὀπῆς βρύει τὸ γλυκὺ καὶ τὸ πικρόν, "Does a spring from the same source yield both fresh and salt water?" Both v 11 and v 12a are cast in questions that expect a negative answer. In these verses James has returned to the practice of relating the evil of double talk to the use of metaphors, once more drawn from the world of nature. This time he uses three illustrations. The importance of a spring (πηγή: "fountain," KJV/ AV) in a dry Palestinian climate can hardly be overestimated (Hort, 79). A village or small town may well have depended on spring water for survival. ὀπή ("crevice," "opening") is found elsewhere only in Heb 11:38. βρύειν ("to gush with," "to pour out") is a *hapax legomenon* in the NT (but see Justin, *Dial.* 114.4; Clem. Alex. *Paed.* 1.6.45; Ps. Clem. *Hom.* 2.45.2 for later usage). γλύκυς ("sweet") is found only here, in 3:12, and in Rev 10:9, 10; it contrasts with πικρός ("bitter," "brackish," and so "unfit for drinking"). One would have expected ἁλυκός or ἁλυκώδης (see 3:12) for this latter term (see also 3:14) but it may be that James has chosen πικρός in order to describe the cursing that issues from the tongue in a metaphorical sense (so Davids, 148; Moo, 129). Yet the point is not to be missed. The speech that comes from a tongue so intent on defaming God's creation is bitter indeed (Ps 64:3; Prov 5:4; Sir 29:25). Moreover, James' illustration from nature does not completely break down. He is referring to a rare if natural phenomenon. His audience was no doubt aware that a spring can produce only one type of water— whether that type be good or bad, sweet or brackish, fresh or salt. Yet it was not out of the question for different streams to mix together in a confluence to form a pool of water unfit for human consumption. But the point he makes is that one spring does not alternate between producing good and bad water. It is either one or the other, and the "tragedy of the tongue" (Moo, 129) lies, in fact, in this vacillation and consequent contamination.

The spring was made to produce one type of water; likewise the tongue was created to bring forth only one type of speech—namely, a "good" speech (of blessing). Unfortunately, while the spring "stays" within its assigned boundaries (as the wild animal submits to human authority), the tongue continues to go against its nature and, ultimately, against its creator. The power (and poison) of the tongue (3:8) can be seen from the fact that while fresh water added to salt water does not produce fresh water, salt water added to fresh causes the water to be salty. The poison of the tongue is all-pervasive.

12 μὴ δύναται, ἀδελφοί μου, συκῆ ἐλαίας ποιῆσαι ἢ ἄμπελος σῦκα, "My brothers, can a fig tree produce olives, or a vine bear figs?" V 12 has the author resume his charge against the illogical nature of the double-minded tongue. He first refers to a fig tree and vine in the form of a rhetorical question to be answered in the negative (μή) and then reverts to the example of water, as used in v 11. James writes as one who apparently wishes to remain on good terms with his audience. He employs the term ἀδελφοί μου ("my brothers," cf. 3:10) as a sign that he wishes to endear himself to them, if the appellation is not purely rhetorical. His choices of fig tree (συκῆ) and the accompanying olives (ἐλαία), and vine (ἄμπελος) and figs (σῦκον) are yet more examples of how the tongue should conform to its purpose. (The species of figs [*Ficus carica*] and olive [*Olea europaea*] are frequently referred to in Scripture: Moldenke, *Plants of the Bible*, 104–6, 158–60.) The phenomenon that plants produce after their own kind (as in Gen 1:11) was a common metaphor in ancient times (e.g., among the Stoics; see Ropes, 243; Dibelius, 204–6). For instance, Epictetus (*Diss.*, 2.10.18, 19) wrote: "How can a vine be moved to act, not like a vine, but like an olive, or again an olive to act, not like an olive, but like a vine? It is impossible, inconceivable." Another possible source for this imagery of plants producing according to the laws of nature is the Gospel tradition. Jesus employed observations of nature to support his teaching that a good heart produces good fruit, and an evil heart brings forth evil fruit, each having its fruit in like kind (Matt 7:16–20; 12:33–35; Luke 6:43–45). But neither classical literature nor Christian teaching necessarily has to be the only source of James' imagery here. As with other examples drawn from nature, James is probably also indebted to personal experience and common observation (Adamson, 148).

οὔτε ἁλυκὸν γλυκὺ ποιῆσαι ὕδωρ, "neither can a salt-water spring produce fresh water." James closes this section with a reference once more to the contrast of fresh and salty water (v 11). The main problem with this sentence is the existence of textual variants in the Greek text (see *Note* h and BDF § 445.1). James uses ἁλυκός ("salt water," or "salt spring," BGD, 41) rather than πικρός (see 3:11), for stylistic variation. The aorist infinitive ποιῆσαι is awkward here, but may be an attempt on the writer's part to make v 12b run parallel with 12a.

In concluding this section, we must ask just how far we are to press the imagery. It is axiomatic that the human person is not to be directly compared with a tree, just as no one is a pottery vessel (Rom 9:19–24). The animal, the spring, the plant—all must do what they are designed by nature to do, whereas a human being has the capacity to accept or reject the way of the creator. But even though the imagery may not fit exactly, the warning is quite clear. If the inner springs of character needed to produce the ἔργον τέλειον (1:4; cf. 3:2 τέλειος ἀνήρ) have been renewed, then there should come out of the mouth only pure and wholesome speech. While the Jacobean leader is aware that perfection is impossible (3:2), a consistent behavior pattern akin to the outpouring of fresh water is nonetheless expected of the Christian and the Christian teacher in particular. For all the concentration on the latter, it should still be recalled that in the early communities to be "competent to instruct one another" (Rom 15:14; cf. Col 3:16; Heb 5:12–14) was a virtue expected of all church members (Zimmermann, *Die urchristlichen Lehrer*, 209–10).

Explanation

The ageless question "What is Man?" permits many answers, some frivolous (as Dr. Samuel Johnson discovered when he quoted an ancient philosopher's definition as a "two-legged animal without feathers" and his rival had a cock plucked bare), some facetious (like Johnson's own attempt: an animal that cooks its food), some serious. Among the most thoughtful is the description of Man as a speaking animal (*homo loquens*). Among the species, Man stands alone in commanding the power to use words to communicate ideas, to express personality, and to enter into dialogue. The power of the tongue is a distinctive feature of our race and carries with it all manner of effects, good and ill alike.

James has a considerable interest in the use, misuse, and abuse of the tongue and the words that are articulated thereby. In the setting of chap. 3, which opens with the role and influence of the Christian teacher (vv 1–2), he focuses mainly on the destructive power the human tongue exerts. Teachers, in those days, offered their instruction and wisdom chiefly by the spoken word, so it is not unnatural that the writer would want to conjoin the teaching office and the way in which the tongue can be used for wholesome purposes or for detrimental ends.

While the New Testament churches set a standard for church membership that encouraged all to take an active share in a ministry of instruction (Col. 3:16; Rom 15:14; Heb 5:12–14), there were also gifted leaders called to the office of teacher. Priscilla is one such person (Acts 18:26). Paul and Barnabas are also known by this title (Acts 13:1) and among the charismatic gifts are those of teaching words of wisdom and knowledge (1 Cor 12:28; cf. Eph 4:11: see *The Anchor Bible Dictionary*, s.v. "Spiritual Gifts" [New York: Double-day, forthcoming]). The Corinthian situation, as is well known, was fraught with inherent perils. Charismatic endowments could easily get out of hand and be given a false importance when self-serving ends and personal ambitions crept in. As a consequence the concern for the well-being and growth of the entire community was minimized (1 Cor 14:12) or demoted in the interest of an unhealthy individualism (1 Cor 8:1; 14:4a). More than personal prefer-ence for the more exotic or spectacular gifts of the Spirit seems to be in evidence; there was a deep-seated theological reason for the Corinthian malaise, which may be traced to the infiltration of wrongheaded notions and of doctrines at variance with Paul's gospel. Hence there was need in the

Pauline congregations both to ensure healthy teaching and to keep in check erroneous influences. These two duties are laid on the pastor in the later epistles to Timothy and Titus (1 Tim 4:11–16; 6:3–5; Titus 2:1, 15).

This background, conceivably set in Antioch, seems also to account for some unusual features in the present chapter. The use of "body" in several places has a meaning that oscillates between the anatomical human body, of which the tongue forms a small yet powerful member, and the body of the congregation, in which the tongues of teachers exercise a baneful influence. In fact we may detect no fewer than three separate areas where James speaks of the tongue as a multidimensional metaphor.

1. In *personal terms* the tongue is charged with evil speaking (vv 5, 6, 8) and its power to hurt and destroy is vividly presented in a series of telling word pictures (vv 3–8). Moffatt (47) notes the talkativeness, the reckless statements, the frothy rhetoric, the abusive language, and the misleading assertions that all are characteristic of the uncontrolled tongue. James has already warned against impetuous talking (1:19) and will later enter a plea against defamatory speech (4:11–12; 5:9). Here is the most brilliant exposé of the dire consequences of the tongue when it goes unchecked and is allowed to start a brushfire that spreads beyond human control to contain. From the wisdom tradition James knows well that life and death are in the power of the tongue, and the psalmist's prayer, "Set a watch, O Lord, over my mouth /Keep the door of my lips" (Ps 141:3), is the appropriate antidote to an all-too-human failing in which everyone is implicated (v 2).

2. Yet this set of moral truisms is only part of the story. The frequent allusion to the body (*sōma*), often with the full phrase "the whole body" (vv 2, 3, 6), cannot be fortuitous. There is a *churchly setting* for those verses and a reminder that church leaders in their role as teachers affect the entire congregation, often by way of evil influence. "Poisoning the whole body" (vv 6, 8) is a sad verdict passed on the consequences of wrongful teaching in the Jacobean congregations. The mouths of these false prophets, as in the polemic of Titus 1:10–11, must be silenced lest their teaching spread like a gangrene (2 Tim 2:17). To be sure, we cannot identify the substance of the error, unlike that of Hymenaeus and Philetus in the post-Pauline communities, but it is not unlikely to have been a challenge to James' authority as represented in the disciples who cherished his posthumous influence in Syro-Palestine. If these deviant teachers had connections with the pseudo-charismatics whose ministries Matthew's Gospel sought to repel (e.g., Matt 7:22–23) then we should be able to explain the way James' teaching of the supreme law would serve as a corrective to such antinomian influence and the wild excesses in worship that the untrammeled use of the tongue had produced.

3. The *liturgical background* is clear from vv 9–12. While James is mainly negative and condemnatory where the use of the tongue is concerned, he does extol the tongue as a vehicle of praise (v 9). The human voice was designed to be lifted in the worship of God and in honor of God's creation, which includes Man (= humankind) as made in the divine image. Acts of hatred and murder are reprehensible at any level; and never more culpable than where the *imago Dei* (already touched on in 1:23–25) is violated and

destroyed. James will say this explicitly in 4:1–6. Here he simply warns against the inconsistency of the tongue that is upraised in the assembly to praise the Maker of all and soon afterward becomes the instrument of cursing and name-calling (cf. 4:11). Nature has no such flagrant contradiction whether in its mineral springs or its botanical gardens (vv 11–12). Yet humankind is a bundle of inconsistencies, one moment acknowledging God by high-flown speech, the next directing calculated insults and opprobriums against fellow human beings. If the setting is the worship service, we are reminded of 1 Cor 12:1–3, and the later Pauline discussions of the need to praise with both spirit and mind (1 Cor 14:13–19). All liturgical acts are to be done in a seemly manner (1 Cor 14:23, 40) and with no intruding false teaching that would lead others astray or cause dissension (as happened when [women] glossolalics got out of hand [1 Cor 14:33–38]).

The "cursing of men" in our section suggests an extension of this inconsistency, and it may point to the facile way in which James' people saw no disparity between a fervent Maccabean-like shout of praise to be followed quickly by blood-letting hatred not only of the enemy (the Romans) but of their fellow Jews whom they rejected as no better than compromisers and traitors to the holy cause of Israel. Whatever the occasion, "My brothers, this should not be the case" is a stern approach to Jacobean factionalists. It is an appeal to all who in the name of professed religion—whether Jewish, Christian, or Islamic—measure the strength of their zeal for God by the intensity of their hatred of their fellow human beings on the West Bank or in Northern Ireland or in Beirut or in Tehran.

5. Two Types of Wisdom   (3:13–18)

Bibliography

Bieder, W. "Christliche Existenz nach dem Zeugnis des Jakobusbriefes." *TZ* 5 (1949) 93–113. **Calmet, A.** "Vraie et fausse sagesse." *BVC* 58 (1964) 19–28. **Cantinat, J.** "Sagesse, Justice, Plaisirs. Jc 3,16–4,3." *AsSeign* 56 (1974) 36–40. **Hoppe, R.** *Der theologische Hintergrund des Jakobusbriefes.* FzB 28. Würzburg: Katholisches Bibelwerk, 1977. 12–17, 88, 118. **Kamlah, E.** *Die Form der katalogischen Paränese im Neuen Testament.* WUNT 7. Tübingen: Mohr, 1964. **Kirk, J. A.** "The Meaning of Wisdom in James: Examination of a Hypothesis." *NTS* 16 (1969) 24–38. **Kosmala, H.** *Hebräer-Essener-Christen.* SPB 1. Leiden: Brill, 1959. **Perkins, P.** "James 3:16–4:3." *Int* 36 (1982) 283–87. **Reumann, J.**; **Fitzmyer, J. A.**; and **Quinn, J. D.** *Righteousness in the New Testament.* Philadelphia: Fortress; New York: Paulist, 1982. **Wanke, J.** "Zur urchristlichen Lehrer nach dem Zeugnis des Jakobusbriefes." In *Die Kirche des Anfangs*, FS H. Schürmann, ed. R. Schnackenburg, J. Ernst, and J. Wanke. Leipzig: St. Benno-Verlag, 1977. 489–511. **Wibbing, S.** *Die Tugend- und Lasterkataloge im Neuen Testament.* BZNW 25. Berlin: Töpelmann, 1959. **Ziesler, J. A.** *The Meaning of Righteousness in Paul.* SNTSMS 20. Cambridge: Cambridge UP, 1972. **Zimmermann, A. F.** *Die urchristlichen Lehrer.* WUNT 2.12. Tübingen: Mohr, 1984.

Translation

¹³ *Who among you is the wise and understanding person? Let him demonstrate by fine conduct his deeds [done] in the humility that stems from wisdom.* ¹⁴*But if you cherish harsh envy and selfish ambition in your hearts, don't brag about it, and so deny [your claim to be speaking] the truth.*ᵃ ¹⁵*This kind of "wisdom" does not come down from heaven; rather it is earthbound, sensual, demonic.* ¹⁶*For in such cases of envy and selfish ambition, there is disorder and all manner of evil practice.* ¹⁷*In contrast, the wisdom that does come down from heaven is first of all pure; then it is peacemaking, gentle, deferential, full of mercy and good fruit, impartial and sincere.* ¹⁸*For those who make peace the fruit of righteousness is sown in peace.*

Notes

ᵃThe parenthetic addition (cf. *T. Gad* 5: λαλῶν κατὰ τῆς ἀληθείας) tries to make the sense clear (so Ropes, 246; Mayor, 127–28; Mussner, 171, who regards the initial καί before ψεύδεσθε as explicative to spell out the consequences of "boasting." The sense is, if you do boast, then in that way you will be denying your role as teachers; Laws, 160). The text καὶ ψεύδεσθε κατὰ τῆς ἀληθείας is difficult, and an attempt to improve it is seen in 33 syrᴾ which reverse the order: (κατὰ) τῆς ἀληθείας καὶ ψεύδεσθε, i.e., don't boast against the truth and lie. But this is an unnecessary simplification, and James is probably directing his attack against false teachers (possibly those akin to the persons mentioned in 1 John 1:6; 2:4) whom Vouga (105) associates with current charismatics or proto-gnostics who were claiming to be authentic leaders. James faults them for their wrong disposition (ζῆλος πικρός . . . ἐριθεία = harsh zeal, selfish party-spirit), which invalidates their vaunted claims.

Form / Structure / Setting

The section offers a finely drawn set of contrasts between two kinds of wisdom. Form-critically the verse may be arranged in two panels, corresponding to the "double catalogues" of what is earthly-demonic and what is heavenly-spiritual and traced to the concept of Two Spirit-kingdoms at Qumran (1QS). See Kamlah, *Form*, 39–50, 181. The contrasts are clearly arranged in order, suggesting to some interpreters that the style is poetic or hymnic, comparable with that of 1 Cor 13 (Reicke, 108 n.10). Examples of a carefully crafted style are seen in the following: (i) There is an *inclusio* formed by setting the theme of σοφία // σοφός at the beginning (v 13) and ending (v 17). Alternatively, on a smaller scale, Plummer (213) sees the master theme of vv 17, 18 to be peace: "the whole process begins [with εἰρηνική], progresses, and ends in peace [εἰρήνην]." (ii) The first panel of (negative) vices is devoted to deploring the baneful influence of ζῆλος . . . ἐριθεία (envy . . . selfish ambition)—twin terms that are repeated (vv 14, 16). The signs of the two vices are found in their origin and their consequences. (a) They do not proceed "from above," i.e., from God, but they are "earthbound, sensual, demonic." These three adjectives are placed in ascending order of moral reprobation, commencing with a less blameworthy (ἐπίγειος, which can mean little more than "inferior," "human," as implied in 2 Cor 5:1 with its counterpart in "spiritual," πνευματικός) and climaxing in διαμονιώδης, a term conveying a clear indictment of the

demonic origin of social malaise. That source will be identified by the writer
in 4:7 ("resist the devil"). Not speaking the truth (v 14) is the hallmark of
this kind of wisdom. Cf. John 8:46; and see *1 Enoch* 16.3 for one example
of this kind of "demonic" teaching, called "rejected mysteries," known by
the fallen angels in Enoch's vision. (b) The consequence is seen in v 16:
disorder (ἀκαταστασία, a much stronger term than "confusion," RSV; it connotes
a breakdown of order bordering on unruliness, anarchy [Vouga, 106]; cf.
Luke 21:9, where the word means insurrection; 1 Cor 14:33 refers to a collapse
of harmony and good order in worship and the presence of other forms of
social evil). In James the term looks back to 3:8 and on to 4:1.

(iii) The other side of the diptych is in praise of wisdom that is "from
above," i.e., it comes from God. The phrase ἡ σοφία ἄνωθεν is repeated in
the anaphoric style. Stylistically it is set in the form of an aretalogy, that is,
a tribute in celebration of the divinity or an attribute claimed to be divine.
Here it is wisdom that is lauded as superior by being given a set of descriptions
that virtually hypostasize her as in Wisd Sol 7:22–30. Her purity heads the
list of seven attributes.

The first cluster of four epithets is marked by epiphora, each word beginning
with ε-: εἰρηνική, ἐπιεικής, εὐπειθής . . . ἐλέους; then the next group switches
to the initial α-: ἀγαθῶν, ἀδιάκριτος, ἀνυπόκριτος, the last two containing examples of α- negative and homoioteleuton.

(iv) The climax comes in v 18 with a well-measured, hieratic, i.e., solemn-
sounding, and rhythmical style using a correct syllabic length to be appreciated
when the sentence is read aloud: ἐν εἰρήνῃ σπείρεται τοῖς ποιοῦσιν εἰρήνην (Mussner, 175). It also contains the element of paradox seen in that its subject,
fruit (καρπός), is normally thought of as grown, not sown!

The concluding verse serves also to round off the entire chapter as well
as the shorter section of vv 13–17. It is not an isolated saying (as Dibelius
supposes). After a recital of the evil powers associated with the uncontrolled
tongue and the demonically inspired wisdom the disquisition ends on a positive
note: "for those who make peace (a dative of advantage: BDF § 191.4) the
fruit of righteousness (i.e., peaceable conduct as one of the "good fruits" in
v 17 and as the gift of "heavenly wisdom": so Reumann, *Righteousness*, 150)
is sown (by God: a divine passive construction, with God as the real agent)
in peace."

The self-contained nature of the pericope has raised the question whether,
after all, this is a literary unit quite unattached to James' earlier section in
chap. 3. Dibelius (207) writes of "no connection of thought" with the foregoing.
But this is to be rejected, although it is the position taken by Windisch,
Cantinat, Schrage, and evidently Zimmermann, *Die urchristlichen Lehrer*, 206.
It is better understood as part of the diatribe-oratorical style (Blackman, 120).
The question is still to be decided whether James is led into his consideration
of the two wisdoms by reverting to vv 1, 2a (so Easton, 450) or is concerned
to offer a general comment applicable not just to teachers in the church but
to his readers (Mitton, 134). The issue may be posed in a question, Who is
the precise subject of τίς σοφὸς καὶ ἐπιστήμων ἐν ὑμῖν? James may be referring
to the teachers and reverting to the qualifications and credentials belonging
to those whom he regards as the instructors. They must be able to avoid

the snares of false wisdom and cultivate the virtues of the wisdom from above, which is true and wholesome, in the face of tendencies to lead the congregation astray (5:19–20).

Another possibility is that 3:13/14–18 is a reprise of 3:1–12/13 (Vouga, 104), and as such it also introduces chap. 4. The false wisdom belongs to those whose abuse of the tongue has been excoriated in chap. 3 with particular reference to the "cursing of men" in 3:9 and the allusion to bitterness and impure water in 3:12, which sour and poison human relationships. The effect of the tongue's uncontrolled power is seen in words such as ζῆλος, ἐριθεία, and ψεύδεσθαι; and above all as κατακαυχᾶσθαι, i.e., the arrogant spirit that goes back directly to the boasting tongue of 3:5. Note too 3:6 and 3:15 for the demonic origin of the evil for which the untameable tongue is responsible.

A third option is to combine the two aforementioned preferences. We can then see both the warning to teachers and the misuse of the tongue in wrongful teaching as the *topos* of 3:13–18 (Wanke, "Zur urchristlichen Lehrer," 492). The main support for this idea is the earlier suggestion that James has in mind in 3:1–12 teachers who employ their "tongues" to articulate false notions that corrupt the "entire body" (v 6), i.e., the whole ethos of the church. They are not only formalistic in their profession of the faith (v 2, "bridle" goes back to 1:26); their example and influence is positively and potently injurious to the community (v 8). They introduce dangerous and destructive (vv 5, 8) matters, which not only are signs of their self-assumed importance (v 4), but actively lead people astray (5:19–20). The brief vice-list of 3:15 indicates what our author thinks of these teachers' claim to be "wise and understanding," a collocation of terms that (in Deut 1:13–15 LXX) is used of Israel's tribal judges, who were to set a norm for the nation's conduct as "a wise and understanding people" (Deut 4:6; cf. Hos 14:9).

James opposes such persons, denouncing their claim as no better than lies (v 14) and pretensions (v 14). Their jealousy and selfish ambition indicate their motives. They are intent on introducing a fanatical and factional policy that is the antithesis of the "peace" characterized by the heavenly wisdom. Their promotion of disorder—by their teaching—is to be exposed and corrected; it will be set right by a return to what James regards as the better way, since human anger does not produce the divine righteousness (1:20). In this way he prepares the ground for his direct charge against the deviant teachers in 4:1–12.

The corrective is contained in the phrase τὰ ἔργα . . . ἐν πραΰτητι σοφίας: "deeds [done] in the humility of [true] wisdom." The collation of these words emphasizes how James sees wisdom as essentially practical and as a virtue issuing in social concerns that reach out to help the needy in distress (1:27; 2:15, 16). But it is a concern that respects right relationship to God as paramount (hence the call in 4:7) and seeks his will in a manner consonant with the divine interests listed in vv 17–18.

One suggested setting of the troubles (cf. Vouga) to which James alludes could be that of congregational strife (as in a close-knit community; Perkins, "James 3:16–4:3," 283), leading to unruly behavior, disorderly worship, and a challenge to recognized authority, as at Corinth (1 Cor 14:33; 2 Cor 12:20; *1 Clem.* 3:1–4; 14:1—texts that have several words or their equivalents in common with our passage—ζῆλος, ἔρις, ἀκαταστασία, φρόνιμος). According to this view James or his redactor is countering leaders who aspired to mislead the congregation by a too-enthusiastic type of worship and the creating of party rivalry and dissension that threatened James' own leadership as head of the community, or that assailed the community that looked to James as its model. His reply is to appeal to heavenly wisdom as a panacea—and so tacitly to assert his role as an authorized teacher (3:1) and leader, albeit in a different spirit from that which his opponents (apparently) evinced.

A background in the maelstrom of Judeo-Roman politics in the 60s and 70s may also be suggested as a preferable alternative in view of some link terms (ζῆλος, ἐριθεία, ἀκαταστασία, εἰρηνικός, ἐπιεικής, εὐπειθής—all of which could be given a social connotation to depict the Zealot influence and the anti-Zealot reaction to the disequilibrium in Judean history). The same setting is seen in the way James carries forward into this discussion his concern for the peace-making, reconciling activity of those who are influential teachers. He classes himself as one with that number (3:1) and praises, above all, the "meek" spirit that Matthew records as characteristic of Jesus of Nazareth (Matt 11:29). Cf. Sir 3:17–20: "My son, perform your works in meekness (ἐν πραΰτητι τὰ ἔργα σου), then you will be loved by those whom God accepts. The greater you are, the more you must humble yourself. . . . For great is the might of the Lord; he is glorified by the humble (ὑπὸ τῶν ταπεινῶν δοξάζεται)." See too Str-B 2:641–42.

Comment

13 Τίς σοφὸς καὶ ἐπιστήμων ἐν ὑμῖν, "who among you is the wise and understanding person?" The opening τίς ("who": see BDF § 298.4, and for the Semitic usage of מִי, mî, as interrogative, see Beyer, *Semitische Syntax,* 167) does not suggest that what follows is merely an abstract warning (Davids, 150); or that this interrogative (see 5:13, 14) necessarily introduces a new section (Dibelius, 208–9), as though 3:13–18 were no more than a parenthetical thought (see *Form/Structure/Setting*). The τίς may point specifically to the teachers (Adamson, 151), though the church members at large are not totally out of the picture. The problem seems to be that some self-styled chief people, thinking they were endowed with superior wisdom and understanding, had divided the church because of their teaching, which betrayed a misuse of the tongue. Such a scenario was not uncommon in the early church (Rom 16:17–18; 2 Cor 2:17; Gal 1:7–9; Eph 4:14; and the reference to ἑτεροδιδασκαλεῖν in 1 Tim 1:3–7). The term "wise" (σοφός) may relate directly to the teacher (the "wise teacher" is rabbinic: E. Lohse, *TDNT* 6:962–63 for חֲכָם־תַּלְמִיד, *talmîd-ḥākām*) but the term for understanding (ἐπιστήμων; a *hapax legomenon* in the NT) could also refer to anyone who claimed to have expert knowledge and esoteric understanding. The combination of the two terms in 3:13 reflects the influence of the LXX. These terms are close to being synonyms in Deuteronomy (1:13, 15; 4:6; cf. Dan 5:12). In the first two verses cited in Deuteronomy, the combination refers to leaders; the last Deuteronomic reference is to the people at large. Thus, the description of "wise and understanding" is not exclusively applicable to teachers, but may include all in the community. But it should be kept in mind that those who taught were prone to fall victim to the misuse of the tongue and were obliged to demonstrate their faithfulness to their calling. The opening words are thus a challenge to those whose business was with words spoken and intended to be received as authoritative. What James has in mind here is a wisdom that results not so much in what one thinks or says as in what one does ("practical wisdom": see Ropes, 244). James will shortly contrast two types of wisdom, namely the worldly and that which comes from God. But before doing that he will recall an earlier theme—faith without works is dead (2:14–26)—by recasting this thought in terms of wisdom and the good works that confirm it.

δειξάτω ἐκ τῆς καλῆς ἀναστροφῆς τὰ ἔργα αὐτοῦ ἐν πραΰτητι σοφίας, "Let him demonstrate by fine conduct his deeds [done] in the humility that stems from wisdom." V 13 is a challenge to James' readers similar to 2:18 (δεῖξόν μοι, "show me"), where the interlocutor calls on James to demonstrate a faith without works. The verb at the beginning of the sentence (here and in 2:18) is emphatic, and the aorist imperative (δειξάτω), suggesting a once-for-all action, may be employed here to indicate that a sudden change of "manner of living" (*Lebenswandel* is Mussner's expression, 170) is necessary. The urgency of this needed turnaround is seen because the tone of this letter implies that "actual and present evils" (Adamson, 149) prevail in the congregation to which James writes.

Two concepts relating to wisdom—namely, that wisdom produces works and that wisdom is characterized by meekness—appear to be awkwardly combined (Davids, 150; Moo, 132). The first thought is not completely out of place in the sense that James has already expatiated upon the need to back up a word-of-mouth confession by good works. Earlier James expected (and demanded) that a genuine faith should issue in good works (2:14–26; i.e., in deeds of charity). Now, true wisdom (wisdom from above, 3:17) should likewise be demonstrated by "fine conduct" (καλὴ ἀναστροφή; for the terminology see Gal 1:13; 1 Pet 1:15; 2:12; 3:2, 16; Heb 13:7: Bertram, *TDNT* 7:715–17). The idea that a person will exhibit good conduct if led by wisdom-Torah is quite consistent with OT teaching (Moo, 132), and is common in Jewish-rabbinic parenesis (ʾAbot 3:9b, 17b; 4:5a) and in later Christian literature (*1 Clem.* 38.2: see *Explanation*).

Where v 13b becomes a little awkward is in the expression "his deeds [done] in humility." The genitive construction here may be the result of Semitic influence (Hort, 80; Dibelius, 36–37). Yet this does not really obscure the meaning of the words. The Christian is to pattern his or her life after Jesus, who was meek (Matt 11:29) and who urged his followers to adopt this attitude (Matt 5:5). Meekness (πραΰτης) was considered a vice by some noncanonical writers of James' time (see Laws, 160–61), and even today meekness is often looked upon as a sign of weakness, but in the NT this disposition is seen as a fruit of the Spirit (Gal 5:23). The Christian is exhorted to be gentle or humble particularly in situations that have potential for conflict. This advice is especially urgent when it pertains to a church setting that is fraught with danger arising from members' pride and dissension. The life that can be described as both wise and meek is one that is under the control of God, as the Qumran community acknowledged (1QS 4.22, 5.25, 11.1, cited in Mussner, 170, who also refers to Appian, *Civil War* 3.79 [§ 323], for terms that would translate as σοφία and πραΰτης = *in mansuetudine et prudentia*). Such control results in an attitude that surrenders selfish rights and disallows "pride" that destroys good relations with others.

14 εἰ δὲ ζῆλον πικρὸν ἔχετε καὶ ἐριθείαν ἐν τῇ καρδίᾳ ὑμῶν, "But if you cherish harsh envy and selfish ambition in your hearts." What James sets up in v 14 is a contrast (εἰ δέ) between the meek person of v 13b and the one who is bitter and selfish in v 14a. The word for zeal (ζῆλος) is semantically neutral. But often ζῆλος comes to be viewed in a negative sense (Rom 13:13; 2 Cor 12:20; Gal 5:20), sometimes with the sense of a misplaced or misguided enthusiasm for service to God (Rom 10:2; Phil 3:6; cf. Gal 1:14) as well as the display of a contentious spirit, which James refers to here by the addition of πικρόν, "bitter." Ropes' rendering (245), "harsh zeal," captures the sense. We may go one step farther and render ζῆλος as "envy" or "rivalry" (BGD, 337). πικρόν ("bitter") ties v 14 to v 11. The sins of the tongue, which flow from the inner life of one's disposition, leave a bitter taste that results in accusations and falsehoods hurled at other Christians. It is no accident that those who claimed this so-called wisdom (v 13) have been said elsewhere to have become "puffed up" (1 Cor 8:1). In this setting harsh envy has become a feature of many in James' community.

Moreover, a party split has developed within the church. ἐριθεία is a rarely used word. Some interpreters argue that, since ἐριθεία is derived from ἔρις ("strife," "discord"), Paul's reference to both terms is a legitimate source for understanding the context of James' use of the word (1 Cor 3:3; 2 Cor 12:20; Gal 5:20: Büchsel, *TDNT* 2:660–61). But such a derivation is not accepted by others (see BGD, 309). The term is found only in Aristotle before its appearance in the NT, where (in *Polit.* 5, 3 p.1302b, 4; 1303a, 14) ἐριθεία means "a self-seeking pursuit of political office by unfair means" (BGD, 309; cf. Mussner, 171 n.2). James' use of the term here is not limited to aspiring politicians, though such people were evidently not strangers to the community of believers (see *Comment*, 2:3), but we can readily see the force of James' term. Because of the narrow zeal exhibited by James' rivals in 3:13a and because these same persons held authority in the church, probably they had gathered around themselves a support group that offered physical and emotional aid (Davids, 151); the result was the formation of factions. In turn, bitterness pervaded the church community, so that this group probably had seceded from the body at large (Büchsel, *TDNT* 2:660–61) because of its commitment to the "truth." Thus, we have "fanaticism" (harsh envy; Vouga, 103) and "factionalism" (selfish ambition) in James' church (Moo, 132–33), which was also not uncommon in other churches (1 Cor 1:12–13; Phil 1:17; 2:3).

μὴ κατακαυχᾶσθε καὶ ψεύδεσθε κατὰ τῆς ἀληθείας, "Don't brag about it, and so deny [your claim to be speaking] the truth." But James will have nothing to do with this state of affairs. For him, boasting is an example of a work or action that does not characterize a person led by heavenly wisdom. Furthermore, to boast is—in James' mind—to speak against the truth. The negation of this imperative (κατακαυχᾶσθε: a nonclassical term and found in the OT only three times: Jer 27 [50]:11, 38; Zech 10:12; and four times in the NT:

Rom 11:18 [2x]; James 2:13; 3:14) by μή implies that those guilty of the sins listed in v 14a are to stop what they are presently doing, namely, "bragging about it and so denying the truth." The "it" of our sentence may be "wisdom" (so GNB) and not "truth" (see NEB). Thus we have: "don't sin against the truth by boasting of your wisdom" (GNB). The person who boasts of wisdom— or more likely of possessing the truth, but the two ideas run together—yet harbors harsh envy and party spirit, lies against the truth. The truth denied is that wisdom is accompanied by meekness. In other words, those who are boasting of wisdom are not of God because their lives are not characterized by humility. But if the guilty parties will not cease from having things their own way, James urges that they at least refrain from describing their bitter zeal and party spirit as the result of God's wisdom. (See *Note* a; cf. also Dibelius, 210; Cantinat, 189.)

15 οὐκ ἔστιν αὕτη ἡ σοφία ἄνωθεν κατερχομένη ἀλλὰ ἐπίγειος, ψυχική, δαιμονιώδης, "This kind of 'wisdom' does not come down from heaven; rather it is earthbound, sensual, demonic." James continues to keep his opponents on the defensive. He explicitly describes what type of wisdom these sectaries (or "heretics," as Davids, 152, misleadingly calls them) possess. The wisdom of 3:14–15 is not the wisdom that comes down from heaven (3:17; see by contrast 1:17). To have wisdom from above is to have wisdom from God, and such can be obtained by asking for it (1:5; cf. Prov. 2:6) but with the proviso understood from 4:2. But James is concerned to demonstrate that the wisdom exhibited by those in the preceding text has nothing to do with God. The "wisdom" that results in envy and partisanship (fanaticism and factionalism) is of a different origin, namely, the devil. The contrast is set up by the use of the adversative ἀλλά.

James describes the wisdom of 3:14 in a periphrastic construction with εἶναι, by the use of three adjectives arranged in ascending order of strength. ἐπίγειος is "earthbound" (lit., "earthly"). Although this term can have a neutral significance (John 3:12; 1 Cor 15:40; when set in antithesis to αἰώνιος [2 Cor 5:1]; Philo, *Leg. Alleg.* 1.43, who actually writes of ἐπίγειαν σοφίαν in distinction from οὐράνιον σοφίαν), it usually takes on a negative sense. This latter point is seen especially in Phil 3:19, where Paul states that destruction awaits those who set "their minds . . . on earthly things" (NIV). In contrast to the wisdom that comes down (κατέρχεσθαι) from above (ἄνωθεν), the so-called wisdom of the troublemakers is earthbound or "inferior." It truly "bears the stamp of 'the world'" (Adamson, 152), like the wisdom referred to in 1 Cor 1:20; 2:5, 6, because it reflects the attitude of those who stand at enmity with God (4:4). It takes little imagination to see that the problem discussed reflects the scene in 2:1–7, where we have the congregation looking more like the world at large than the people of God. More especially the worldly ways implied in ἐπίγειος will be exposed in 4:1–18.

Moreover, this wisdom is ψυχικός, "sensual" ("unspiritual," RSV). This adjective (from the noun ψυχή) is found here and elsewhere only in 1 Cor 2:14; 15:44, 46; Jude 19 and suggests a condition that is devoid of the Spirit (πνεῦμα). See also B. A. Pearson, *The Pneumatikos-Psychikos Terminology*, SBLDS 12 (Missoula: Scholars Press, 1973), esp. 13–14 on James' putative dependence on Pauline terminology. Dibelius (211–12) believes that James used the term with a gnostic background in a nontechnical manner (see 3:6). There may be an attempt to write in terms of a dualism (Mussner, 171). This is not certain (Adamson, 152) even when Mussner qualifies dualism by remarking that it is not to be understood as metaphysical, but rather as characterizing attitudes, convictions, and moral qualities.

Even worse, the "wisdom" in mind is demonic (δαιμονιώδης, found only here in the NT; cf. Symmachus' translation of Ps 90:6). Some interpreters understand James to mean that the behavior of those described in 3:14 is only "similar" to the behavior of demons (Hort, 84; Cantinat, 190; Laws, 161, 163). In that sense, the misdeeds of those whom James attacks are being compared to demonic activity (2:19). But something more radical is being suggested. The behavior of those in question is thought to be instigated by the demons themselves (so Moo, 134; Davids, 153; Adamson, 152–53). Demonic forces are viewed in the NT as responsible for thoughts and actions in opposition to God (2 Thess 2:9; 1 Tim 4:1; Rev 6:13–14; cf. Foerster, *TDNT* 2:19; see also Ropes, 148–49). The tongue, according to 3:6, is an unruly member that originated from a demonic region. Moo (134) catches the meaning of James' thoughts here when he writes that the wisdom of those in 3:14 is "characterized by 'the world, the flesh, and the devil.'" Mussner (172) notes the connection between δαιμονιώδης and ψεύδεσθαι κατὰ τῆς ἀληθείας in v 14, which runs parallel with John 8:46 (cf. *1 Enoch* 16.4).

16 ὅπου γὰρ ζῆλος καὶ ἐριθεία, ἐκεῖ ἀκαταστασία καὶ πᾶν φαῦλον πρᾶγμα, "For in such cases of envy and selfish ambition, there is disorder and all manner of evil practice." James summarizes the obvious (note the connective added in the translation; but see Dibelius, 212): a spirit of envy and partisanship can only result in "disorder and all manner of evil practice." We propose that there is a close relation of vv 14–15 to v 16. Envy (ζῆλος) and party spirit (ἐριθεία) are mentioned in v 14 as the characteristics of those who claim to have "wisdom." This pseudo-wisdom (Mussner, 172) is then described as nonheavenly, unspiritual, and ungodly in v 15. In our present verse, James shows that the result of such misbehavior does nothing to build up the body of believers. Rather it leads to the opposite result: disorder. The noun (ἀκαταστασία) suggests a state of unrest. The adjectival form of this noun is found in 1:8; 3:8 (ἀκατάστατος), where James speaks of the unstable man and the restless evil of the tongue respectively. This characterization points to persons who are "double-minded" and double-tongued. The result is "anarchy" (Ropes, 248; Adamson, 153). Such disorder plagued some of the churches of Paul's foundation (2 Cor 12:20; *1 Clem.* 14:1; cf. Luke 21:9 used with πόλεμοι, "wars"). In conjunction with this unrest goes "all manner of evil practice." φαῦλος, "worthless," "bad," is used in the sense of κακόν (3:8; cf. John 3:20; 5:29). It is the opposite sense of "good," ἀγαθός (see Cantinat, 191), but here the phrase may imply no more than "and the rest," like our use of "etc." (so Mussner, 172). James is burdened with a desire for communal unity, but unfortunately the inevitable result of unruly tongues, unholy zeal, and unchecked party spirit is chaos and division (see 1 Cor 14:33).

Davids opines that the troublemakers in mind are "self-appointed" teachers (153). No doubt some of the instigators did fit this description (Wanke, "Zur urchristlichen Lehrer," 493, speaks of the crisis in the Jacobean community over *Lehrautorität*, i.e., What is the authorized teaching?). It is quite possible that these troublemakers have gathered around them other persons who felt that being "right" was all that counted. Whatever the exact situation, the description of James as mediator and peacemaker in Acts (15:21) and in later church tradition (see *Introduction*, pp. lxx–lxxi) may well reflect his role in the congregation to which he writes. There are some affinities here with the situation that occasioned Matthew's polemic against Pharisaic Judaic teachers in Matt 23:8 as Rengstorf, *TDNT* 2:157, suggests by noting the rabbinic character of James' practical emphasis on σοφία (cf. Mussner, 173).

17 ἡ δὲ ἄνωθεν σοφία, "In contrast, the wisdom that does come down from heaven." Having described what heavenly wisdom is not in v 15, James now proceeds to explain what it is. Strictly speaking he is proceeding to say what wisdom results in rather than what it is. It might be noted that there is some similarity between 3:17 and Paul's list of the harvest fruits of the Spirit (Gal 5:22–23; see Windisch, 26). Cf. *Herm. Man.* 9.8; 11.5, 8, 9, 21. Though James never mentions the Holy Spirit explicitly in his work (but see 4:5), this datum lends credence to the thought that James sees wisdom associated with Spirit, a linkage found in Jewish literature (see Kirk, "Meaning of Wisdom"). Windisch asks why πνευματική, "spiritual," is missing from the praise of heavenly wisdom. His answer is that σοφία includes πνεῦμα. W. Bieder, "Christliche Existenz," 111–12, agrees and cites the event of Pentecost when the Spirit "came down," like the designation of σοφία here. See too Wilckens, *TDNT* 7:524–25, who sees a direct polemic between James' rivals who personified *pneuma-sophia* as a revelatory idea, akin to gnostic ideas, and James who moralizes *sophia*, as in 3:13.

For James, the wisdom from above (ἄνωθεν) is in contrast to (δέ) and on a plane above the wisdom of this world. What follows in 3:17 is the picture of how the church's aims should be set, and that includes Christians living a life under the wise rule of God. The result is a body that is united and is walking with one accord by aiming at the ideals of peace (cf. v 18). "Peace" is in fact the ruling idea in vv 17–18 and is placed near the beginning and at the end of the virtue-list.

πρῶτον μὲν ἁγνή ἐστιν, ἔπειτα εἰρηνική, ἐπιεικής, εὐπειθής, μεστὴ ἐλέους καὶ καρπῶν ἀγαθῶν, ἀδιάκριτος, ἀνυπόκριτος, "is first of all pure; then it is peacemaking, gentle, deferential, full of mercy and good fruit, impartial and sincere." James sets down the "fruits" of wisdom in a series of seven adjectives. The series is prefaced with μέν, but lacking the accompanying δέ, sometimes also absent from Paul and Luke (see BDF § 447.2, 3). In this list of adjectives James exhibits his considerable skill as a writer, as was observed earlier. The four adjectives following ἀγνή begin with the same letter, ε, in order to produce an alliteration. Also we see that the second pair of these four have the same ending (-ης). The last two of the series (see below) begin with the letter α and exhibit rhythmical endings (-κριτος).

Wisdom is first and foremost a virtue that is marked by purity (ἀγνή; cf. Sir 21:8). It is no accident that James begins his list with this word, for he who is pure has taken on the characteristics of God's word (Ps 12:6; cf. 19:8). Such a person serves God only and is not defiled (1:27) or unrighteous (3:6). The one who is pure is free of the moral and spiritual defects that are the marks of the double-minded (1:7, 8; 4:8: see *Introduction*, p. lxxix). The pres-

ence of such stains produces the inevitable jealousy and strife that are characteristic of some in James' church. The absence of such blemishes produces a
church that is loving, tolerant, and healthy; above all, it is centered in God's
holy will. The idea of purity is expanded in what follows and can rightly be
considered the "key" to all the qualities of wisdom (Adamson, 154). See on
τέλειος earlier, pp. lxxix–lxxx.

Not only is wisdom pure but it is also peaceable (εἰρηνική, lit., "peacemaking";
only here and Heb 12:11 in the NT). Such a quality is quite appropriate to
the situation for which James writes (see v 18). Wisdom produces peace (Prov
3:12), which is seen by Paul as a fruit of the Spirit (Gal 5:22). Here it carries
with it the Hebraic idea of šālôm (Adamson, 155; see Foerster, TDNT 2:418).
The reason why wisdom is peaceable is that it is "gentle" (ἐπιεικής) and "deferential" (εὐπειθής; a hapax legomenon). The former attribute recalls the demeanor
of the Lord (cf. 2 Cor 10:1). As Hort writes, to be gentle is to be unwilling
"to exact strict claims." Such a person assumes a "non-combative" stance (so
Davids, 154; cf. Phil 4:5; Titus 3:2; 1 Tim 3:3), and avoids getting angry
despite some provocation, which is no mean task in the light of the situation in the congregation. The latter attribute suggests one who "yields to
persuasion" (Adamson, 155), not in the sense of gullibility, but as de-
ferring to others when there are no serious moral or theological issues
that threaten (Moo, 136; as F. F. Bruce said of Paul [Paul: Apostle of the
Heart Set Free (Grand Rapids: Eerdmans, 1977) 186], "where the principles of the gospel were not at stake he [Paul] was the most conciliatory of
men").

Wisdom from above is "full of mercy and good fruits." The use of "mercy"
here refers to the practical qualities of mercy (1:8, 22, 27; 2:13, 15, 16). Those
who fail to show such mercy are under the condemnation of God (2:13).
James may very well be connecting those who fail to help the poor with
those who divide the church. For those showing mercy, good fruits will result
(cf. Matt 7:17–18). Once more it is remarked that profession (whether of
faith or of having wisdom) must be demonstrated by works.

James concludes his list with "impartial" (ἀδιάκριτος using the alpha priva-
tive; the adjective is found only here in NT; but see Ign. Magn. 15.2; Trall.
1.1; Eph. 3.2 for a range of meanings) and "sincere" (ἀνυπόκριτος; cf. Wisd
Sol 5:18; 18:15). The former is to be seen as an attempt to counteract the
party spirit in the church (acting as "impartial," so Mussner, 174; cf. NIV,
"unwavering," so Ropes, 250; also NASB, "not given to party spirit," so Windisch,
26; "harmonious," so Dibelius, 214, and Laws, 164). Also, the idea behind
ἀδιάκριτος may suggest "without discrimination" (T. Zeb. 7.2: καὶ ὑμεῖς οὖν
. . . ἀδιακρίτως πάντας σπλαγχνιζόμενοι ἐλεᾶτε). In short, this description of wisdom's fruits is brought to a close by pointing out that wisdom from above does
not result in division and disunity (see 1:6; 2:4, 9). Finally, James remarks that
wisdom from above is a quality characterizing a person "without show or pre-
tence," as in Rom 12:9; 2 Cor 6:6; 1 Tim 1:5; 2 Tim 1:5 (see Mayor, 132; H.
Kosmala, Hebräer-Essener-Christen, 313). This matches well with ἀδιάκριτος. The
"impartial" (single-minded) person is sincere. The absence of "hypocrisy"—a
term no doubt reminiscent of some of the Pharisees (Hort)—would pave the
way for upright and honest relationships between fellow members. No one has

to doubt the intentions of another (see 5:12 on oaths, and the data regarding community life at Qumran in 1QS 2.24–25).

18 καρπὸς δὲ δικαιοσύνης ἐν εἰρήνῃ σπείρεται τοῖς ποιοῦσιν εἰρήνην, "For those who make peace the fruit of righteousness is sown in peace." James finishes this chapter by emphasizing the recurrent note of peace. This should come as no surprise in the light of the divided congregation to which he writes. Thus v 18 functions here as an "emphatic conclusion" (Mussner, 174). It is probably correct, therefore, to see this verse as an independent proverb attached to sum up the preceding thoughts (Dibelius, 214; Mussner, 174, "ein Schlussmotiv"). Also, this proverb appears to provide a transition to what follows (4:1ff.: see Davids, 155).

The meaning of the phrase "fruit of righteousness" is problematic. This is a common expression in the LXX (Isa 32:16–18; Amos 6:12; Prov 11:30) and the NT (2 Cor 9:10; Phil 1:11). Some interpreters think that the genitive is one of definition: "the fruit which is [i.e., consists of] righteousness." This is more likely than the "fruit is wisdom itself" (Laws, 165–66, following Ropes, who suggests an epexegetic Semitism based on Sir 1:16, καρπὸς σοφίας; cf. Gal 5:22; Eph 5:8; Phil 1:22) or "the fruit is peace." By righteousness is meant that conduct which is pleasing to God (Moo, 137; Ziesler, *Righteousness*, 135–36, 151).

A second concern is whether the phrase τοῖς ποιοῦσιν is to be taken as a dative of agency ("by," RSV, NIV, NASB, NEB, GNB) or dative of advantage ("for"; so BDF § 191.4 and in the above translation). The former—as can be seen— is well regarded (Kamlah, *Form,* 176–96 [esp. 181–82]) and suggests that the fruit of righteousness is produced "by" the peacemaker. The latter— employing the *dat. commodi*—speaks as though the fruit of righteousness is a reward (or an advantage) for the peacemaker. Despite the many translations that opt for agency, the dative of advantage is the more natural in the NT (Moo, 137). The reward in view is the blessing made available to the peacemakers. It is no advantage to be part of a community that is fractured and consists of members who are suspicious of one other. But a congregation that is marked by peace—a congregation reflecting the influence of godly wisdom— is one that affirms and edifies its members. In effect, James is exhorting the people to trust one another and this is only possible if peace reigns supreme.

While this interpretation, which is accepted by most commentators, is undoubtedly true, it should be strengthened by the reminder that James is much more than a moralist offering a species of prudential ethics. He is saying more than is contained in the moral maxim that peace is better than strife. If we could be sure of a historical context, it would be feasible to set this proverb in a specific background. Once we attempt this effort, the proposal may be supported if we give due weight to 4:1–4. It will be maintained that the author there is confronting head-on the politically motivated enthusiasm of his constituents who were resorting to violence, strife, and bloodshed in a holy crusade for what they thought to be God's freedom. As a frontispiece, then, to that discussion, and by way of concluding his short disquisition on "heavenly wisdom," he rounds off the pericope with a tag that praises the peacemakers. As "peace" stands at the head of wisdom's aretalogy in v 17, so at its conclusion it is lauded as the reward of those who seek righteousness-in-peace. This promise goes back to 1:20, where it was remarked that God's righteousness is not promoted by human violence; here in a complementary statement the same righteousness in human conduct is achieved by peaceful means—and no other.

Explanation

This short pericope offers a finely drawn set of contrasts between two kinds of wisdom. The contrasting portrayals are clearly arranged in order and can best be displayed in a "table of contents." The setting of this comparison first needs a comment.

It is most likely that, in spite of the arguments of those who wish to see this document as a loosely arranged miscellany of discrete moral teachings, randomly brought together, there is a thread of continuity running through the various sections. Chapter 3 is a case in point. The earlier part was dedicated to the theme of "teachers and the use of tongues"—two themes not to be separated for the obvious reason that ancient pedagogy was chiefly by word of mouth. James' warnings are mainly negative and cautionary. Now it is time to offer some constructive advice in praise of the wise teacher (v 13). An early Christian homily-like writing based on 3:13–18 shows how this message was understood and applied.

> Let the wise person show his wisdom not in words but in good deeds. Let the humble-minded not testify to his own humility, but let him leave it to others to bear witness (*1 Clem.* 38.2).

In language borrowed from the OT and especially the wisdom scholars he sets down the traits of the character of a wisdom that is self-styled but really inauthentic as a foil to extol the virtues of the genuine wisdom. The rubric under which this comparison is made is given in v 13: let the wise teacher demonstrate by fine, i.e., exemplary, conduct his deeds done in the humility that stems from wisdom. To make his point even sharper he contrasts this ideal with the characteristics of his opponents who practice envy and selfish ambition and advertise their claims to be speaking in truth, when their deeds are a standing and blatant denial. Clearly some criteria are needed to test the spirits of those who claim to be authorized teachers in the congregation. James mounts an attack on his rivals by drawing up a diptych of opposites:

FALSE WISDOM

(a) Its *signs* are denoted by "harsh zeal" for what the teachers regard as their point of view, coupled with a selfish bid for leadership (Hort, 82–83) in the community. To achieve their ends they even stoop to breaking the unity of the church, and they are branded as factionalists as well as "fanatics" (giving to "zeal" its pejorative sense).

(b) The reason for such conduct is traced to their adherence to a wisdom that has all the marks of being "not of God." In ascending order of reprehensibility James labels their character as "of this world" (a term akin to that in 1

Cor 1:20; 2:5–6), "sensual," like the person in 1 Cor 2:14, and "demonic," perhaps suggesting that the teachers are doing the devil's work by undermining Christ's.

(c) The sad *outcome* is "disorder," a term already on view in 1:8; 3:8 and leading to all manner of social ills.

TRUE WISDOM

(a) The *signs* of the heavenly wisdom, already promised as the gift of God to all who ask in faith (1:5, 6), are the character traits of "wise meekness" that shows itself in a true life—that is, one whose roots go down to the "truth." The last-named term is James' favorite expression for an understanding of Christian living that is essentially practical and sincere (1:18; 5:19). Then follows the pen portrait of the ideal teacher extolled in the Jacobean congregation.

(b) That teacher's *character* is marked by a cluster of seven attributes arranged in such an artistic way that use of an earlier model may be suspected. In the Wisdom of Solomon (7:22–30) wisdom is praised as the great teacher of all that is noble, holy, beneficent, humane, and—in particular—pure and peaceful. The tribute is a notable one, climaxing in the divine approbation:

For God loves nothing so much as the man who lives with wisdom (7:28).

And since wisdom enters into the lives of holy souls, she makes them "friends of God and prophets" and so invincible against all the inroads of evil (7:27, 30). Abraham (see 2:23) as God's friend and prophets like Elijah (5:17) are role models. The Jacobean editor no doubt also saw a picture of his own master in this virtue-list, and, if our earlier submission of a setting for the role of the historical James is correct, he found in the martyred hero (cf. 5:6) a living and dying embodiment of his teaching.

The character of the wise teacher on whose shoulders the mantle of the hero-leader has fallen is then given, in seven features. They all are the counterpoint to the indictments brought against the false teachers in vv 14–16. Virtues such as "pure," i.e., single-minded in contrast to the double-minded person of 1:8; 4:8, "gentle," i.e., behaving in a kindly fashion, "deferential" to the point of seeking conciliation and amity between those at loggerheads, "impartial," i.e., far from the party-spirit earlier condemned (Windisch, 26) and "sincere" (lit., with no hypocrisy or feigned piety) are all commendable in any social situation. Where there are persons with strong convictions and determined loyalties that make for dissension and discord, these virtues shine in added brilliance. The telltale adjective "peacemaking," however, stands out as offering something of a clue. Given the proneness to anger and strife already hinted at in 1:20 and in anticipation of the social evils depicted in 4:1–6, the emphasis on the spirit that seeks peace suggests a particular problem in the Jacobean community.

The James of history, we know, earned a reputation for his role as mediator and peacemaker amid the factions and frictions in Jerusalem in the seventh decade of our common era (see *Introduction*, pp. lxvii–lxix). The aretalogy

in praise of heaven-sent wisdom is no less an epitaph to his memory than a
salutary word to the community that looked back to him as its role model.

(c) It is fitting that, in its *outcome,* the cultivation of exemplary traits by
Jacobean teachers should promote peace (v 18). The laudable goal for Jewish
pietists of all shades was to see God's kingdom established on earth. Quietists
(like the company described in Luke 1–2) and Zealots who took their lead
from the warlike Phinehas (Num 25:6–18; Ps 106:30) both longed to see
the redemption of Jerusalem and the salvation of Israel. What mattered to
the writer of James, himself no less a patriot and pietist, was the way that
divine rule was to be set up. Only in peace could righteousness be promoted
(1:20), since in God's kingdom the only law that is recognized is that of love
(2:8–13; 4:11–12) and the noblest of goals can effectively be attained by
methods that are consonant with that royal law.

W. Manson (*Jesus the Messiah* [London: Hodder & Stoughton, 1943] 185)
considers how Jesus—like James—confronted the political and religious options of his day, when Zealot militarism and Essene passivity stood at opposite
ends of the spectrum. Like James, Jesus pronounced blessedness on the peacemaker (Matt 5:9), and Horatius Bonar's lines are quoted to illustrate what
the two brothers in a common faith shared:

> The kingdom that I seek
> Is Thine so let the way
> That leads to it be Thine.

IV. Witnessing to Divine Providence (4:1–5:20)

1. Community Malaise and Its Antidote: (i) False Hopes (4:1–10)

Bibliography

Cantinat, J. "Sagesse, Justice, Plaisirs. Jc 3,16–4,3." *AsSeign* 56 (1974) 36–40. **Coppieters, H.** "La signification et la provenance de la citation Jac. iv, 5." *RB* 12 n.s. (1915) 35–58. **Findlay, J. A.** "James iv.5, 6." *ExpTim* 37 (1926) 381–82. **Hengel, M.** *Die Zeloten. Untersuchungen zur jüdischen Freiheitsbewegung in der Zeit von Herodes I. bis 70 N. Chr.* AGSU 1. Leiden: Brill, 1961. **Johnson, L. T.** "Friendship with the World/Friendship with God: A Study of Discipleship in James." In *Discipleship in the New Testament,* ed. F. F. Segovia. Philadelphia: Fortress, 1985. 166–83. ———. "James 3:13–4:10 and the *Topos περὶ φθόνου.*" *NovT* 25 (1983) 327–47. **Kirk, J. A.** "The Meaning of Wisdom in James: Examination of a Hypothesis." *NTS* 16 (1969) 24–38. **Laws, S.** "Does Scripture Speak in Vain? A Reconsideration of James iv.5." *NTS* 20 (1973–74) 210–15. **Meyer, A.** *Das Rätsel des Jakobusbriefes.* BZNW 10. Giessen: Töpelmann, 1930. **Michl, J.** "Der Spruch Jakobusbrief 4.5." In *Neutestamentliche Aufsätze.* FS J. Schmid, ed. J. Blinzler, O. Kuss, F. Mussner. Regensburg: Pustet, 1963. 167–74. **Paret, E.** "Noch ein Wort über Jac. 4,5 nebst 1 Mos. 4,7." *TSK* 36 (1863) 113–18. ———. "Nochmals das Zitat in Jak. 4,5." *TSK* 80 (1907) 234–46. **Perdue, L. G.** "Paraenesis and the Letter of James." *ZNW* 72 (1981) 241–56. **Reicke, B.** *Diakonie, Festfreude, und Zelos, in Verbindung mit der altchristlicher Agapenfeier.* Uppsala: Lundequistskabokhandeln, 1951. **Rusche, H.** "Vom lebendigen Glauben und vom rechten Beten. Einführung in die Grundgedanken des Jakobusbriefes (2,14–26; 4,1–10)." *Bibel und Leben* 6 (1965) 26–37. **Schökel, L. A.** "James 5,2 [*sic*] and 4,6." *Bib* 54 (1973) 73–76. **Seitz, O. J. F.** "Afterthoughts on the Term '*Dipsychos.*'" *NTS* 4 (1957) 327–34. ———. "Antecedents and Signification of the Term ΔΙΨΥΧΟΣ." *JBL* 66 (1947) 211–19. **Spicq, C.** "Ἐπιποθεῖν, Désirer ou Chérir?" *RB* 64 (1957) 184–95. **Townsend, M. J.** "James 4:1–4: A Warning Against Zealotry?" *ExpTim* 87 (1976) 211–13.

Translation

¹*What is the source of wars and conflicts in your midst? Don't they originate from your (sinful) pleasures that wage war among the members (of your body*[a]*)?* ²*You have desires, but you don't get them [fulfilled]. You kill*[b] *out of jealousy, and yet you cannot get what you want. You contend and join in war.*[c] *So you do not gain, because you do not ask (God for it*[d]*).* ³*When you do ask, you do not receive, because you ask in the wrong spirit, to indulge your (sinful) pleasures.*

⁴*You unfaithful people,*[e] *don't you know that friendship with the world spells hatred toward God? Anyone who is determined to be the world's friend sets himself at enmity with God.* ⁵*Or do you really imagine there is no ground in what Scripture*

says: the Spirit God made to dwell[f] in us opposes[g] envy? [6]*But even greater is the grace which he gives. That is why it says:*

> *God opposes the proud.*
> *To the humble he gives grace.*

[7]*Submit yourselves, therefore, to God. As you resist the devil, he will run from you.* [8]*Come near to God, and he will come near to you. Purify your hands, you sinners, and consecrate your hearts, you double-minded.* [9]*Be miserable, mourn and wail. Turn your laughter into mourning, and your rejoicing into dejection.* [10]*Humble yourselves in the Lord's presence, and he will raise you up.*

Notes

[a]$\dot{\epsilon}\nu$ $\tau o \hat{\iota} s$ $\mu \dot{\epsilon} \lambda \epsilon \sigma \iota \nu$ is vague, and $\mu \dot{\epsilon} \lambda o s$ may refer to the parts of the human body (so Ropes, 254: "James thinks of pleasure as primarily pertaining to the body") or conceivably to the corporate life of the community, i.e., church members. Davids, 157, wrongly attributes the latter view to Ropes, and opposes it on the ground that (i) $\mu \dot{\epsilon} \lambda o s$ has already been used twice (in 3:5, 6) for a part of the human body; (ii) $\mu \dot{\epsilon} \lambda o s$ carries this as its normal usage (cf., e.g., 1 Cor 12:14); (iii) the argument shifts here from the external conflict in the community to its internal basis; and (iv) at the heart of this employment of military metaphors is the rabbinic notion of the יצר, *yēṣer*, the (evil) influence thought to goad people into sin.

Each of these objections may be resisted: (i) the use of $\mu \dot{\epsilon} \lambda o s$ in chap. 3 may equally be applied to the corporate problems among the church members (see *Comment* there); (ii) Paul's use is hardly an exact parallel, even if he does illustrate the oscillation between literal and metaphorical usages of $\mu \dot{\epsilon} \lambda o s$. True, he does add $X \rho \iota \sigma \tau o \hat{v}$ to $\sigma \hat{\omega} \mu \alpha$ in 1 Cor 12:27, but $\mu \dot{\epsilon} \lambda o s$ in 12:26 is vague; does it mean parts of the human anatomy or the Corinthian church members? But 1 Cor 12:27: $\dot{v} \mu \epsilon \hat{\iota} s$ $\delta \dot{\epsilon}$ $\dot{\epsilon} \sigma \tau \epsilon$ $\sigma \hat{\omega} \mu \alpha$ $X \rho \iota \sigma \tau o \hat{v}$ $\kappa \alpha \dot{\iota}$ $\mu \dot{\epsilon} \lambda \eta$ $\dot{\epsilon} \kappa$ $\mu \dot{\epsilon} \rho o v s$ is unambiguous in showing a metaphorical use of $\mu \dot{\epsilon} \lambda o s$ (as in 1 Cor 6:15). (iii) The *Comment* section will seek to argue that James does have external conflicts in view in 4:1–3; and (iv) for that reason James is not referring to inner personal desires as though he were harking back to 1:13–15. The fighting, in our interpretation, is not "within the body of the individual Christian," but within the life of James' church relating to societal or political issues.

$\dot{\epsilon}\nu$ $\dot{v} \mu \hat{\iota} \nu$, therefore, is better rendered "in your midst" than "within you." See Reicke, *Diakonie*, 341–44, for a plausible setting.

[b]There is a problem of punctuation here. The joining together of the two verbs $\phi o \nu \epsilon \dot{v} \epsilon \tau \epsilon$ $\kappa \alpha \dot{\iota}$ $\zeta \eta \lambda o \hat{v} \tau \epsilon$, lit., "you kill and you are jealous," has seemed to some interpreters to be "an impossible anticlimax" (Ropes, 254), leading to proposals to have the text emended or given only a metaphorical or spiritualized meaning. In the first category is Erasmus' conjecture that read $\phi \theta o \nu \epsilon \hat{\iota} \tau \epsilon$, "you are envious," for $\phi o \nu \epsilon \dot{v} \epsilon \tau \epsilon$. In defense of this suggestion, which is supported by Dibelius (217–18), Windisch (27), and Adamson (167–68), the collocation of $\phi \theta \acute{o} \nu o s$ and $\zeta \hat{\eta} \lambda o s$ is well attested in extrabiblical writings (1 Macc 8:16; *T. Sim.* 2.7; 4.5; *1 Clem.* 3.2; 4.7, 13; 5.2) as well as Gal 5:21 in the NT. The last reference also demonstrates how a textual corruption could creep in.

Also it is maintained that $\phi o \nu \epsilon \acute{v} \epsilon \iota \nu$ should be retained in its literal sense of "to kill, to murder," unless we are compelled to seek a metaphorical application (a choice preferred by Davids, 156: "The conflicts are metaphorical"; cf. 158–59).

Alternatively it is possible to keep the text intact (as there is no external textual evidence to emend it) and to stay with the literal meaning. In our translation, $\kappa \alpha \dot{\iota}$ $\zeta \eta \lambda o \hat{v} \tau \epsilon$ is explicative of the strong verb $\phi o \nu \epsilon \acute{v} \epsilon \tau \epsilon$: "You kill out of jealousy." Textual difficulties in v 2b compound and complicate the issue. See *Note* c.

[c]A number of interpreters wish to follow a punctuation sequence that alters the flow by which a set of three propositions is stated. The UBS text prints the Gr. to make these statements:

(i) You desire and you do not have,
(ii) You kill and are jealous, and cannot obtain,
(iii) You do battle and make war.

Ropes (254–55) followed by Mayor (136), Laws (169), and Mitton (147–48) oppose this because it seems to make murder (in ii) part of the early stage of frustrated desire that leads to strife, as well as joining murder and jealousy in an uneasy anticlimax (as noted under b) that is still more problematical because (iii) is made to come at the end of the sequence and to diminish the enormity of murder as the taking of human life.

An alternative scheme, which rests partly on an acceptance of a textual reading that omits the καί before οὐκ ἔχετε διά (it is found in ℵ P Ψ vg^{cl} syr bo; TR has this with an additional δέ) is offered by Nestle[26] and translated in rsv, neb; it makes two parallel statements of cause and effect (Laws, 169):

(i) You desire and do not have: (so) you murder;
(ii) And you are jealous and cannot obtain: (so) you battle and make war. You do not have because you do not ask.

The effect of this repunctuation is, according to Laws, that "murder" becomes a consequence of frustrated desire, rather than an element in that experience. In our view this is less likely, since it downplays the horror of the indictment of murder, which is given a figurative meaning. That is, it is regarded as an attitude tantamount to murder but not to actual taking of human life. We argue for the latter connotation in this passage on the ground of a suggested historical context. See *Comment*. Our conclusion on the textual question is to restore καί before οὐκ ἔχετε with the authorities listed above.

[d]The parenthetic completion of the thought implies that what is sought is "wisdom," going back to the two wisdoms of 3:13–18. The readers are charged with a failure to seek from God (1:5–7) the true wisdom as his gift, which is above all "peacemaking" (εἰρηνική).

[e]μοιχαλίς (lit., "adulteress") is a term borrowed from the idiom of the nuptial union between Yahweh and Israel as his (unfaithful) wife. Metzger (683) accounts for the addition to μοιχαλίδες (fem.) of μοιχοί (male adulterers) in ℵ^c K L P syr^{hl} as a scribal misunderstanding due to puzzlement over why only women were mentioned. The chief Alexandrian and Western authorities have the correct shorter reading. The Bible Society's *Diglot* unaccountably retains the longer text (so kjv).

[f]There are numerous attempts to translate this verse. See *Comment*. Our choice presupposes a textual reading of κατῴκισεν (attested in P^{74} a B Ψ) rather than κατῴκησεν (K L P most minuscules and all the versions) which gives the verb in a noncausative sense. There are two separate verbs attested (κατοικίζειν, which has the stronger attestation and is a NT *hapax*; κατοικεῖν, more common in NT), and the choice is a case of "transcriptional probability" (Metzger, 683) by which the harder reading is explained.

[g]Translation of the Gr. has posed its own problems, with the variations listed by Mitton, 155–56. The rendering above makes one choice out of several options, but the same sense would be obtained if the verse were repunctuated by running ὅτι κενῶς ἡ γραφὴ λέγει πρὸς φθόνον together: lit., "that the scripture speaks in vain against envy," making φθόνον the object of the verb. This is, however, dismissed by Ropes, 263, but for no real reason. Otherwise, with most translators, πρὸς φθόνον is to be construed adverbially, i.e., "jealously," "begrudgingly" (Ropes, 262). Both renderings are supported by the lexical fact that φθόνος as a biblical term is always used pejoratively (Vouga, 117).

More difficult is the meaning of ἐπιποθεῖ, lit., "yearns," used in some places of the lover's affection for a desired person or object. See Spicq, "Ἐπιποθεῖν," for the conclusion that the verb expresses an intense desire in close relation to the idea of ἀγάπη (191). The apparent sense is that God is a jealous lover (Ropes, 264; Davids, 164), but since the implicit object is φθόνος, the meaning must be that God's yearning over his people is set over against (πρός + acc.) their "jealousy"; hence our rendering, admittedly more a paraphrase, "oppose."

Form/Structure/Setting

Once again the initial question of setting turns on the issue of whether this pericope is only loosely connected to the foregoing. Dibelius insists on reading the section as part of the entire letter which, for him, consists of a set of only disjointed and disparate sayings. This way of looking at the text is to be resisted if there are patent lines of connection, between 4:1–6 and 3:13–18, on the one hand, and between 4:1–6 and 4:7–10, on the other.

Our position is that the text from 3:13 to 4:10 is indeed a coherent and self-consistent unit, with some telltale markers to indicate the closely woven texture.

For example: (a) The contrast of the two types of wisdom may be reduced to the opposition of the hostile spirit (3:14–15) to its antithesis, the peace-loving disposition (3:13, 17–18). It is then logical that James would want to pick up the consequences of preferring the former attitude over the latter. He does this by posing rhetorical questions to do with the "wars" and "conflicts" facing the community and rebuking the involvement of his readers in social and political squabbles (3:14). These are based on envy and strife, which in turn lead to devastating consequences (3:16: ἀποκαταστασία, "disorder"; 4:2, 3), already branded as δαιμονιώδης (3:15). See 4:7: ἀντίστητε τῷ διαβόλῳ.

In addition we may note the correspondence between 3:13–18 and 4:1–10. The wisdom "not from above" (3:15) reduces the practitioner to the abasement of true humility (4:6, 10) if ever he is to be converted. The pride (ὑπερηφανία) of 4:6 based on "boasting" (3:14, κατακαυχᾶσθαι) must be replaced by its opposite (κατήφεια, "dejection," 4:9), just as the "selfish ambition" (3:14, ἐριθεία) that has its seat in the human "heart" (καρδία) must be expelled by an act of cleansing and renewal (4:8: ἁγνίσατε καρδίας) leading, in turn, to wisdom that is "pure" (ἁγνή, 3:17). The wisdom "from above" in 3:17 is marked by the quality of ἀδιάκριτος, being "impartial," answering the commonest designation of the malady James exposes in the people of his community, 4:8. They are δίψυχοι, "double-minded." See Johnson, "Friendship," 179 n.22.

(b) The link between 4:6 and the following passage (4:7–10) is less easy to see, in spite of the connective οὖν in v 7 (Johnson, "Friendship," 168). Nevertheless it is obvious that we are dealing with a rhetorically defined unit in which the indicative statement of v 6—God gives grace to the humble (ταπεινοῖς)—is succeeded by the series of imperatives. These latter admonitions reach a climax in the call, "Humble yourselves (ταπεινώθητε) in the Lord's presence," thus forming an inclusion in the overall *topos*. 4:6 may well set the "thematic announcement" (Schökel, "James 5,2") which is then enlarged and applied in the following section, at least up to 4:10 (Davids notes that this is as far as the unit extends, 165). The promise of "grace to the humble" is answered by the axiom in v 10.

The catena of imperatival calls and their consequences is set under the rubric of submission (ὑποτάγητε, v 7), as the divine χάρις is received and integrated into human existence and experience. The following couplets are to be classed either as antithetic or complementary:

> Resist the devil
> Come near to God
>
> Purify your hands
> Consecrate your hearts
>
> Be miserable
> (Turn) your rejoicing into dejection

Humble yourselves
He will raise you up.

If we are looking for a *leitmotif* in 4:1–10, a number of choices present themselves. Johnson ("Friendship") opts for the sharp contrast between two kinds of friendship (φιλία), i.e., the disjunction of friendship that is based on living by worldly standards and that which draws inspiration and incentive from God's "measure," as Johnson calls it, patterned on Abraham the friend of God (2:23). For Johnson, in this treatment ("Friendship"), the thematic verse is 4:4, and he is able to subsume the total message of James under the categories of two loyalties. This construction is certainly more convincing than his earlier (1983, "James 3:13–4:10") exercise in which he sought, with elaborate parallels, to relate 3:13–4:10 to the background of hellenistic moral philosophy and *T. 12 Patr.*, and discovered that James was using a *topos* on envy to issue his pastoral-evangelistic call.

An alternative proposal returns to the previously mentioned problem, denoted by δίψυχος, "double-minded" (cf. 1:8). The issue is the tension between God and idols (cf. *T. Asher* 3.2: "Those who are two-faced [διπρόσωπος] are not of God, but they are enslaved to their own evil desires, so that they might be pleasing to Beliar and to persons like themselves"). The chief problem before James' audience is their hesitancy and indecision, as they wavered in their allegiance to God and were tempted to be drawn away to false hopes and into "diabolic" paths led by Zealot factionalists. The choice may be more clearly described. It was the state of affairs by which the divine righteousness (1:20) and the heavenly wisdom (3:17–18) were set before them with a call to choose: either to accept God's gift, freely available (1:5) and generously given to those who truly ask, or to pray for the false substitute (3:13–16), which, if it were accorded, would be used only for personal ends. The upshot would be an even deeper social stratification leading to an experience of internal dissension and strife (4:1–3). James points out, in typically parenetic fashion, the Two Ways to be decided upon, based on the contending kinds of wisdom and resulting in two opposing ways of effecting God's righteous rule (1:20), whether by peaceable means or by violent methods such as the Zealots practiced and condoned (see Reicke; Townsend, "James 4:1–4"; *Introduction*, pp. lxiv–lxv). In effect, as in the well-founded Jewish tradition, it is the choice between God and his enemy, whether called the devil (4:7; cf. 3:15: "demonic" is the source of this "wisdom") or Beliar (as in *T. Asher* 3.2) or the world (4:4). These forces stand implacably opposed to God whose tender desires for his people's integrity are nonetheless set against all forms of "envy" (4:5; cf. 3:14–16) and "strife" (3:14), which is so debased that it entails "waging war" and "murder" to achieve its patriotic and superficially attractive—but really perverted—ends.

In the final analysis then, the double–minded people are professing if woefully misguided believers. So James can address them as "sinners" (4:8; cf. 5:20: hence the conversion idioms of 4:8–10 which are nonetheless adapted to his fraternal audience, *pace* Johnson) who need to return to their covenantal loyalty as "God's poor." Taking the lowly place, they are bidden to look to him to exalt them according to eschatological promise (cf. Vouga, 119, who, writing on v 10, recalls that the exhortation is at the same time a promise based on the "eschatological reversal" [*eschatologische Umwertung*] that at the last God will lift up the humble and cast down the devil and all his works).

Comment

1 Πόθεν πόλεμοι καὶ πόθεν μάχαι ἐν ὑμῖν, "What is the source of wars and conflicts in your midst?" Having closed on a positive note in 3:18—peace is promised to those who promote peace—James returns to the situation at hand. It was one that was anything but peaceful because of the divided congregation to which he writes. V 1 consists of two questions: both are rhetorical; the second is so constructed as to be answered in the affirmative (οὐκ). The intensity with which James writes is reflected in his pleonastic use of πόθεν ("from where") and his duplication of thought in πόλεμοι ("wars") and μάχαι ("fightings"). Moreover, πόθεν (in the first question) taken in combination with the later ἐντεῦθεν ("from here"; see Adamson, 166 n.1) paves the way for James' answer to the second question.

The terms *wars* and *fighting* are often understood to be used by James metaphorically and not as pertaining to actual conflicts between individuals, groups, or nations (Cantinat, 198–99). According to this former view, what James refers to are verbal disputes that are rampant throughout this congregation. Such a picture is possible in the light of what he says concerning the sins of the tongue in 3:1–12. Acrimonious speech, slanderous accusation, unrestrained anger—all depict a jealous and divided community; it speaks of a church governed by wisdom from "below" (see Moo, 138: cf. 4:12; 5:9). To describe such "battles" in this way (metaphorically) is not out of line with the conditions prevailing in James' day (see Davids, 156, and references there). Although James is not clear as to what specific dispute he has in mind (see Dibelius, 216), he has prepared the ground by earlier allusions to "jealousy and selfish ambition" in 3:16. To be sure, the conflict is apparently *intra muros*, i.e., inside the church. But in the final analysis a metaphorical understanding of "wars" and "fightings" does not adequately explain the strong language in the text, especially at v 2. Since James and his community were situated in a Zealot-infested society and since it is quite conceivable that (at least) some of the Jewish Christians were former Zealots (cf. Luke 6:15; Acts 1:13), the taking of another's life is not out of the realm of possibility for the church members as a response to disagreement (in fact such action may have already taken place; see Townsend, 211–13; see also *Introduction,* pp. lxvii–lxviii). While James' community may have not yet experienced and engaged in literal murder on a mass scale, the contingency is a very real one and must be warned against.

The phrase ἐν ὑμῖν ("in your midst") probably refers to the church members themselves and not the individual Christian's body. This reference was discussed earlier (see *Note* a) and makes the best sense of 4:1. In the light of the party spirit decried in 3:13–17, which is preceded by the discourse against the abuse of the tongue on the part of the teachers, it appears that James describes the consequence of these leaders' wrongdoing in 4:1 (Mussner, 176–77). Such division may have been spurred on by certain leaders' involvement in political and societal issues. In a sense then, James is likely to have been caught in the middle of warring factions—namely, those who wanted peace and those who were ready to fight to the death in the interests of national freedom as they viewed it. Also, the issue of the poor versus the rich finds its way into the discussion (*Introduction*, pp. lxv–lxvii). Such a picture supports the idea that ἐν ὑμῖν refers to external hostilities engaging the membership rather than internal conflicts among the individual members.

οὐκ ἐντεῦθεν, ἐκ τῶν ἡδονῶν ὑμῶν τῶν στρατευομένων ἐν τοῖς μέλεσιν ὑμῶν, "Don't they originate from your (sinful) pleasures that wage war among the members (of your body)?" As was stated above, 4:1b is also a question, but one that is rhetorical. The cause of the wars and fightings is discovered in the pleasures (ἡδοναί) that war "among the members (of your body)" (for discussion of corporate idea of members see *Note* a and *Comment* on 4:1a). The text has ἡδονή ("passion," rsv) instead of the expected ἐπιθυμία (see 1:14–15; also ἐπιθυμεῖ of 4:2), but the former runs parallel to the latter. ἡδονή, though neutral in meaning (see Ropes, 253–54), is used here in the negative sense of "sinful passion" (a link between ἡδονή and ἐπιθυμία is provided by Philo, *De Dec.*, 142–43, 152; cf. *Quod Deterius*, 174; *De Ebr.*, 75). The term is found only three other times in the NT (Luke 8:14; Titus 3:3; 2 Pet 2:13), all with a pejorative connotation. This sense is seen also in 4 Macc 1:25–26: "Included under pleasure (ἡδονή) also is the malicious moral temper which expresses itself in the most widely varied ways of all the passions. In the soul it is pretentiousness, covetousness, seeking the limelight, contentiousness, and malice." This use of ἡδονή in 4 Macc may reflect the thought that the term is the seat of the evil impulse ([יֵצֶר הָרָע‎ רע הר רצי], *yēṣēr hārāʿ*; see Stählin, *TDNT* 2:917–18). The least that can be said is that James chose ἡδονή in preference to ἐπιθυμία so as to be sure to make the point that the person who fits the description of 4:1 strives against God (ibid., 909; see 4:4, 6). Other possibilities for James' choice are either that he borrowed 4:1 from a sermon or that he used the former for stylistic reasons (so as to avoid repetition of similar words, ἐπιθυμία and ἐπιθυμεῖ, though repetition of words is not out of character for this writer; see πόθεν in 4:1a).

Whatever the reason for the choice of the word, James traces the battles within the church to the rise and dominance of passions. These passions—lust for power, popularity, authority—had caused the wars and fightings within the ranks of the members of the church. Again, the military imagery (στρατευο-μένων, "warring") can be taken metaphorically, but this weakened sense is not adequate to describe the likely *Sitz im Leben* of the community. In any case the *agōn* motif remains in the forefront of James' thinking. The double-minded person (δίψυχος; 1:8) must decide in favor of God's way (a course advocated by James). To do otherwise paves the way in the community of James for more division, leading even to physical violence.

2 ἐπιθυμεῖτε καὶ οὐκ ἔχετε, "You have desires, but you don't get them [fulfilled]." Detailed discussion of the problems surrounding this verse is offered in the *Notes*. We have adopted the view that the original text had a full stop following ἔχετε (so UBS, TR, rsv^mg, niv; BGD, 494; against Nestle^26, neb, nasb, gnb; see also Hort, 89; Laws, 169; Cantinat, 197–99). As though his readers were not clear as to his intent, James makes his point more emphatic: the result of unrestrained desire (or passion) is tragically catastrophic. The

wars and fighting are a direct outcome of having unsatisfied (evil) desires
(4:1). Cf. 1:14–15.

φονεύετε καὶ ζηλοῦτε καὶ οὐ δύνασθε ἐπιτυχεῖν, "You kill out of jealousy, and
yet you cannot get what you want." Several arguments for downplaying the
horror of "murder" have been offered (see *Notes*) but in the light of the
putative historical context this appears unnecessary. Instead, the literal meaning of "murder" is indicated. To say that all James means here is "hate"
(Matt 5:21–22; 1 John 3:15) overlooks the fact that the letter of James was
most likely written in a period when murder was accepted as a "religious"
way to solve disagreements (for illustration cf. Acts 9:1 [φόνου, murder]; John
16:2). It is quite possible that James had thrown his lot in with the needy
priests of Jerusalem (some of whom had converted to Christianity), who, in
turn, showed sympathy with the Zealot movement. Combine this with the
hatred that Zealots had for the wealthy (F. F. Bruce, *New Testament History*,
100; *Introduction*, p. lxviii) and it may easily be imagined that some of the
Christians may have had need of correction when they attempted to solve
the disagreements within the church. No doubt different positions on the
most viable attitude toward Roman rule prompted heated discussion and
possible physical confrontation. But it may well be that the prohibition of
murder comes in the light of the desire for more material gains (especially
in the light of δαπανᾶν, "to spend," see v 3). And it is germane to note that
those who were in the lower strata of society saw the rich to be in partnership
with the Romans. Thus, the desire to strike out at the hated Roman government
could even have been a cloak to gain material possessions. It is possible that
if some of the Christians James wrote to were former Zealots, they might
not have been willing too quickly to renounce violence as a way of securing religious freedom. Other suggestions—that James is predicting what
might happen in the future (Moo, 141) or that he is only referring to what
generally happens when desire overtakes a person (Ropes, 255)—do not go
far enough. James is exhorting his readers not to kill any more (see 2:11;
5:6; see Rendall, *Epistle of James*, 30–31, 113), i.e., to abandon a way of life—
and death.

"You kill out of jealousy" explains why the horrible crime of murder is to
be construed as literal. Yet despite such killing, the perpetrators of heinous
crimes still do not have what they desire. Might it be that James is seeking
to offer several lessons here, namely, (1) that killing has not freed anyone
from Roman rule and (2) that those so bent on killing are enmeshed in a
vicious cycle, setting up a train of consequences that promotes violence but
never satisfaction ("fighting" and "warring"; see 4:1)? Until God's peace reigns
in the church James' readers will reflect the spirit of the world around them
and will be "earthly, unspiritual, and devilish" (3:15, RSV).

But James takes up a pastoral slant when he suggests that some of his
readers do not have (οὐκ ἔχετε) because they do not ask for it (διὰ τὸ μὴ
αἰτεῖσθαι). This is paradoxical because on the surface it appears to run counter
the promise in 1:5–6 that whatever the readers ask for they will receive. If
this is so, then we are led to consider what change of circumstances is postulated between the two sets of instruction. It is highly doubtful that James'
reference to asking is simply an urging for his readers to ask of others what

is lacking. Rather, James is exhorting his readers to ask (lit., "to pray to") God for their desires, but in the light of 3:13–17 the object is not gain or power, but wisdom (see *Notes*). Peace will not come as a result of fighting and killing, but this fruit of the Spirit is promised to those who ask God for wisdom from above (3:17; 1:5 explicitly adds the qualification). James has already charged his readers to ask God for wisdom (1:5–7); now he reiterates the same invitation but warns that not every request in prayer can be granted. When prayer is connected to the acts of murder and revenge based on ζῆλος (cf. Sir 28:14–26; Jud 9:2–6; *1 Clem.* 3.4–6.3) it both fails and deserves to fail. Schlatter (244) appeals to the scene in Acts 23:21–22 for a type of piety that stoops to this level. For Zealot practice based on "zeal" (one meaning of ζῆλος) see M. Hengel, *Die Zeloten*, 181–88.

3 αἰτεῖτε καὶ οὐ λαμβάνετε διότι κακῶς αἰτεῖσθε, ἵνα ἐν ταῖς ἡδοναῖς ὑμῶν δαπανήσητε, "When you do ask, you do not receive, because you ask in the wrong spirit, to indulge your (sinful) pleasures." The first part of v 3 is an extension of the closing words of v 2. The sense is: "You do not have because you do not ask God for wisdom; you do not receive because even when you ask God for wisdom you ask incorrectly" (κακῶς, "corruptly," so Adamson, 168–69). The opening words of v 3 are not holding up as a contrast a group of Christians different from those of v 2b. That is, there are not some who fail to ask and then others who ask wrongly. Rather, those who sometimes fail to ask God at other times ask him in the wrong spirit.

Much has been made about James' use of the middle and active voices in vv 2b–3 (αἰτεῖσθαι, middle infinitive; αἰτεῖτε, active indicative; αἰτεῖσθε, middle indicative). Mayor, 138, distinguishes between the prayer of the heart (middle) and the prayer of the lips (active) (see Moulton, *Grammar* 1:160). Hort, 89, suggests that the middle denotes the asking for something while the active refers to the asking of a person. Dibelius, 219, is not convinced that the shift has much significance at all, for the variation occurs in other passages without any difference of meaning (Matt 20:20–22; John 16:23–26; 1 John 5:14–16; but see Mark 6:22–25; cf. also Moo, 142; BDF § 316.2). Another explanation is that James has included the active as a conscious reference to Matt 7:7. Davids (160), following Mussner (179), supports this understanding (see also Adamson, 169). Or, as Adamson also conjectures, James may be attempting to balance his use of the middle with the active (λαμβάνετε) on stylistic grounds.

Regardless of the reason for this interchange in the verbs, the point is that the readers of James do not receive what they ask because (ἵνα) they ask in the wrong spirit. James explains what he means by this when he adds that the answer to their prayer is seen simply as a means to "spending wastefully" (or better, indulging their sinful desires, ἡδοναί, 4:1). The arrangement of the text offers a type of *inclusio* (4:1–3; Mussner, 180). The church members war among themselves because passion is the controlling force in their lives. The term δαπανᾶν does not always have a negative sense (BGD, 171), though the idea of spending the gift from God on selfish desires is prominent here (see Luke 15:14 where the same verb is given a sense *in malam partem* in the parable of the prodigal son). The gift sought was not going to be used to help others or to please God. This was true whether vengeance on enemies was the specific object of prayer, or simply the desire for God's wisdom to gain the upper hand in an internecine conflict as a means of helping oneself was intended. Because of this "evil desire" these prayers were not to be answered.

4 μοιχαλίδες, "You unfaithful people." James breaks off from an analysis of the situation and begins preaching a word of rebuke with a call to repentance (Davids, 160) by his use of OT idioms. Verse 4a (a question to be answered with "yes") opens with the feminine vocative μοιχαλίδες, "unfaithful people" (lit., "adulteresses"; the "unfaithful creatures!" of the RSV is somewhat misleading). The feminine is found alone despite attempts to include the masculine ("adulterer"; see *Note* e; KJV/AV). There is nothing in the context to suggest that the literal sin of adultery was a problem in James' church. It is very likely that the text has the OT idea in view that God is married to his people and that this bride has proven unfaithful. The covenant relationship between Israel and Yahweh is frequently portrayed in terms of a marital imagery (Isa 54:1–6; Jer 2:2). The nation's unfaithfulness is condemned by the prophets (Jer 3:7–10, 20; 13:27; Isa 1:21; 50:1; 54:1–6; 57:3; Ezek 16:23–26, 38; 23:45), especially so in Hosea (chaps. 1–3; 9:1). Jesus compared Israel to an "adulterous generation" (Matt 12:39; 16:4; Mark 8:38) and Paul employed the imagery of bride-bridegroom in his pastoral thinking (Rom 7:3–4; 2 Cor 11:1–2; cf. Eph 5:22–23; also see Rev 19:7; 21:9: see R. A. Batey, *New Testament Nuptial Imagery* [Leiden: Brill, 1971]). This sin of "adultery" is tantamount to apostasy.

οὐκ οἴδατε ὅτι ἡ φιλία τοῦ κόσμου ἔχθρα τοῦ θεοῦ ἐστιν; ὃς ἐὰν οὖν βουληθῇ φίλος εἶναι τοῦ κόσμου, ἐχθρὸς τοῦ θεοῦ καθίσταται, "Don't you know that friendship with the world spells hatred toward God? Anyone who is determined to be the world's friend sets himself at enmity with God." James characterizes this adultery as friendship with the world (ἡ φιλία τοῦ κόσμου; this sentence is probably not a precise quotation; see Spitta, 116–17). The dualistic stance is reminiscent of 1 John 1:15–17 and the Qumran texts (Davids, 161), as well as 2 Tim 3:4 (φιλήδονοι μᾶλλον ἢ φιλόθεοι—a close parallel; *1 Enoch* 48.7). No room for compromise is permitted, as James concludes in the final sentence of the verse: "Anyone who is determined to be the world's friend sets himself at enmity (lit., 'as an enemy') with God." The resulting friendship with the world stems from a deliberate (Adamson, 170; an act of "will with premeditation," so too Hort) choice to do so (the verb βουληθῇ implies this). Those who go this way "constitute themselves" (καθίσταται; see 3:6) as opponents of God. Not that they intend to fall away from God; but rather James is pointing out that such worldly behavior borders seriously on apostasy. He is suggesting that some of the readers do not appreciate that their deliberate choice to befriend the world is actually an action that sets them against God. So he has to summon them to repentance. Indirectly, then, and by contrast they are compared to Abraham, the friend of God (2:23). For the latter was justified by his works expressing faith, while the former are condemned because of their evil works (3:14–16). At the final judgment Abraham's life of faith will be pronounced righteous because he demonstrated it through deeds pleasing to God; but at the same judgment those who fail to honor God by their works will find no mercy (cf. 2:13). While James seems to be suggesting that the Christians of 4:4 are not without hope (though woefully misguided), he is quite clear when he says that their present conduct is deplorable and ranks them with the ungodly. This somber verdict accounts for the kerygmatic idiom in the appeals that follow (vv 7–10).

5 ἢ δοκεῖτε ὅτι κενῶς ἡ γραφὴ λέγει, "Or do you really imagine there is no ground in what Scripture says?" As is the case with most NT writers, James cites Scripture to support his didactic point, which here is a summons to decision (Matt 6:24; cf. 1 Kgs 18:21). The "or" (ἢ) joins v 5 to v 4. This connection is clearer in the light of οἴδατε . . . δοκεῖτε, which are linked verbs. But despite this connection, v 5 remains one of the most difficult to understand in all the letter. Not least of the problems is identifying what James is quoting from (for there is no question that he is quoting a source). Moreover, it is not clear whether James cites these words to confirm the statement of vv 1–3 (that humankind is indeed infected with jealous tendencies) or to combat the sins mentioned in vv 4–5 (that God jealously opposes sinful action in those who claim to be his people).

Regarding the source of the quotation, the use of ἡ γραφή suggests at least that James considered this source as Scripture. In every other case where we read ἡ γραφὴ λέγει in the NT this formula introduces a direct scriptural reference or allusion. This evidence rules out the conjecture that what we have is a midrashic-type construction (cf. Dibelius, 221; Cantinat, 203; see Laws, 174–79, and idem, "Does Scripture Speak?") or a rhythmic quotation, such as a proverbial hexameter (so A. Oepke, *TDNT* 3:991; Ropes, 262; Windisch, 27; Reicke, 65, cf. BDF § 487). It may (but not necessarily) also challenge the idea of a loose paraphrase of scripture (such as Exod 20:5, ". . . for I, the Lord your God, am a jealous God . . ."; so Hort, 93; Mayor, 140). Another possibility is that James is quoting from an unknown version of the OT though elsewhere he usually does appeal to the LXX. Meyer, *Rätsel*, 259, proposed that the quotation is a "midrashic paraphrase" of Gen 49:19. Davids, 162, thinks that James may have quoted from some lost apocryphal work (see also Dibelius, 222; Mussner, 183–84), such as *Enoch* (see Jude 14), the *Apocalypse of Moses* 31, or the lost Book of Eldad and Modad (see Adamson, 170–71). He offers this solution since a more acceptable one has not yet appeared. But this is not sufficient to dismiss the proposal that James is referring in some way to "canonical" Scripture. It may well be that the best we can do is to suggest that he is expressing the theme of God's jealousy as contained in the OT (Moo, 146; cf. Exod 34:14; Zech 8:2; Pss 42:1; 84:2; note that ἡ γραφή in John 7:37–39 is only an allusion to an OT scripture). Whatever the case, James challenges his readers that the "Scripture" was not given "in vain" (κενῶς, a *hapax legomenon*, but cf. Isa 55:11) and that it carries full authority as a word from God.

πρὸς φθόνον ἐπιποθεῖ τὸ πνεῦμα ὃ κατῴκισεν ἐν ἡμῖν, "the Spirit God made to dwell in us opposes envy." This rendering is one of many possible translations of the Greek. The rsv reads: "He yearns jealously over the spirit which he made to dwell in us." "The spirit he caused to live in us envies intensely" is found as the rendering of the niv but the margin reads, "God jealously longs for the spirit that he made to live in us"; or "the Spirit he caused to live in us longs jealously"; the Phillips' version has "this Spirit of passionate jealousy is the Spirit he has caused to live in us" (see also kjv/av, neb).

The Greek text poses a myriad of problems (and has produced several needless attempts to repunctuate or emend the text, given in Mussner, 183 n.8; the best effort is that of Findlay, "James iv.5, 6," to read φόνον for φθόνον, referring to v 2 and relating to "the spirit of murder." The scripture in mind is Gen 4:7; cf. Paret, "Noch ein Wort," but this is far from plausible), the most formidable of which is deciding on the subject of ἐπιποθεῖν ("to yearn/long for"). The possibilities are (1) God, (2) the Spirit (i.e., the Holy Spirit), or (3) the human spirit (the spirit by which God energizes humanity, Gen 2:7; 6:17; 7:15; Isa 2:22; Job 27:3; 33:4; 34:14–15; Wisd Sol 12:1) with all its tendencies often toward evil (a view championed by Coppieters, "La signification," who appeals to nine places in Ecclesiastes—1:14, 17; 2:11, 17, 26; 4:4, 6, 16; 6:9—where the LXX uses πνεῦμα of the human spirit [53]. See in particular 4:4, ματαιότης καὶ προαίρεσις πνεύματος). Cf. also the phrase, "spirit of falsehood" in 1QS 3.18–4.26, although there is no reference to envy or jealousy. Support for the third option comes from the argument that φθόνος, when used adverbially ("jealously," i.e., φθονερῶς, so Mayor, 143; BGD, 711), is never said to modify God's behavior (so Mitton, 155–56, and others). True, God can yearn jealously for his own (Exod 20:5; 34:14; Deut 4:24) but this is seen as a positive action. φθόνος, on the other hand, is "incapable of good" (Trench, *Synonyms*, 87). Thus, the term referring to a human disposition is always used in a negative way, which would fit well if the subject of ἐπιποθεῖ is the human spirit: "the spirit which he makes to dwell within us is one of jealousy and envy."

But such a proposal can be countered by arguing that James may be using φθόνος in this case to modify God's action. It is to be noted that the term is parallel with ζῆλος and that φθόνος can be used interchangeably with ζῆλος, for both are often used for the "jealousy" of God (1 Macc 8:16; *T. Sim.* 4.5; *T. Gad.* 7.2; *1 Clem.* 3.2; 4.7; 5.2). πρὸς φθόνος can thus carry the same sense as πρὸς ζῆλον (Mussner, 183). Furthermore, ἐπιποθεῖν can have a positive connotation. The point is that James could have used φθόνος instead of ζῆλος to show that God jealously longs for his people. Though this use of φθόνος is unusual it is not ruled out of the question, especially when we recall that the subject of κατοικίζειν ("to dwell") is clearly God. It would make better sense to hold that James had the same subject for both verbs of this OT allusion, namely, God.

But there is another argument that speaks against construing "the human spirit" as the subject of ἐπιποθεῖ. To take 4:5b as a scriptural confirmation of human jealousy would require that the author has returned to his description of human nature in vv 1–3, but in v 4 James has issued a call to repentance, warning his readers that friendship with the world means enmity with God. Thus, more than likely, v 5 is set down to highlight God's displeasure with the behavior reported in vv 1–4. To conclude, therefore, that the subject of ἐπιποθεῖ is the human spirit is fraught with much difficulty.

If it is the divine Spirit (taking God as the subject of κατῴκισεν, a *hapax legomenon*) which opposes envy, then we have an understanding of v 5 that continues the flow of v 4. Even though many interpreters prefer to take God as the subject of ἐπιποθεῖ (Hort, 93–94; Ropes, 263; Dibelius, 223–24; Mayor, 144–145; Mussner, 142–43), the same thought could be expressed in terms of God at work in the believer through the Holy Spirit, which opposes the jealous or envious tendencies of our "earthly" human nature (see JB). As a result the effect of "godly wisdom" should prevail. God opposes those who fight and war within the church, and he has placed his Spirit within his people to combat that tendency. Therefore, it is God's jealousy that is described in v 5, for he stands waiting for the belligerent to forsake their envy of others and direct their attention back to him.

6 μείζονα δὲ δίδωσιν χάριν· διὸ λέγει, ὁ θεὸς ὑπερηφάνοις ἀντιτάσσεται, ταπεινοῖς δὲ δίδωσιν χάριν, "But even greater is the grace which he gives. That is why it says: God opposes the proud. To the humble he gives grace." The UBS places a stop after the first χάριν; the Nestle-Aland [26] has a semicolon, evidently to mark a question, but this is a highly unlikely sense. The δέ ("but") suggests a contrast. If we understand v 5b as a description of human sinfulness, then the greater (μείζονα) grace (χάρις) of God overcomes the envy of human nature (see Ph). However, there is nothing to prevent v 6 from supporting our interpretation of v 5b, namely, that God has placed in his people his Spirit, which opposes envy. The δέ then allays the fear that God is inadequate to help to fulfill the demands he places on his people as a result of his "jealousy" (Moo, 146). His demands are strict but his grace (χάρις, mentioned only here in the letter) is more than ample to overcome human deficiencies. The grace or gift in question may be either the Holy Spirit or the aid God gives to those seeking to direct their sole loyalty to him. Davids (164) interprets it as the offer of forgiveness. Perhaps the text includes all three ideas—God has given his Spirit to his people to enable them to give their undivided allegiance to him. Should they fall, there is the offer of forgiveness that will provide the way for the restoration of full fellowship both between God and his people and among God's people.

The theme of forgiveness does not stand out, however, as the primary thought of v 6a. The point of v 6a is the adequacy of God's grace to secure an eschatological "exaltation" of the meek (4:10b; cf. 1:9). But we may note how forgiveness dominates the remainder of this paragraph (6b–10). Basing his thoughts on Prov 3:34 LXX, James launches into a series (ten in all) of imperatives in vv 7–10. The thrust of that OT verse is that God opposes (ἀντιτάσσεσθαι) the proud (ὑπερήφανος, lit., "arrogant"; often used of the godless wealthy; 4:6; cf. 1QH 6.36; CD 1.15 for the Hebrew equivalent) but gives grace (note δίδωσιν is present tense in both uses in v 6) to the humble (ταπεινός; here poverty and piety merge as a mark of the godly in Israel). The "humble" may refer either to those who already practice what God desires or those who, when convicted of sin, will humble themselves, repent, and submit to God. More specifically the term refers to the pious poor (1:6) who await God's deliverance from trials (1:12) and will enter his kingdom (2:5) as they are patient to trust him (5:8) to the end. See Maynard-Reid, *Poverty and Wealth in James*, 61–63. However, God is implacably opposed to the proud. The latter are the (rich) people who are caught up with the world and so are at enmity with God. They scoff at God's concern for their single-minded devotion and set themselves up for a terrible fall (Prov 16:18). This illustration is another example of an OT motif used by James in this section (Pss 18:27; 34:18; 51:17; 72:4; 138:6; Isa 61:1; Zeph 3:11–12). The need to forsake pride in order to receive God's grace is a common one in the NT and later churches (see Matt 18:4; 23:12; 1 Pet 5:5; *1 Clem.* 30.2; Ign. *Eph.* 5.3).

7 ὑποτάγητε οὖν τῷ θεῷ, ἀντίστητε δὲ τῷ διαβόλῳ καὶ φεύξεται ἀφ᾽ ὑμῶν, "Submit yourselves, therefore, to God. As you resist the devil, he will run from you." The οὖν ("therefore") alerts the reader that what follows is an "expansion" of Prov 3:34 (Davids, 165; contra Laws, 180–81). ὑποτάγητε (aorist imperative of ὑποτάσσεσθαι, "to submit") is placed at the beginning of this clause for emphasis, perhaps catechetical in origin. James exhorts his readers to submit to God (demonstrated by humbling oneself before God) and desist from aligning with the devil (shown by the pursuit of "demonic" wisdom, 3:15; selfish ambition, 3:16; murder, 4:2; and friendship with the world, 4:4). The idea of submission suggested by ὑποτάσσεσθαι is usually directed to human authority (Luke 2:51; Rom 13:1; Eph 5:22; Titus 2:9; 1 Pet 2:13) and not God (as here and at Heb 12:9; see Adamson, 174). The thought of submitting to God is rounded off in v 10 by the command to become humble before the Lord (an *inclusio?* See Davids, 165). Between these two commands is a series of couplets:

> ἀντίστητε—ἐγγίσατε
> καθαρίσατε—ἁγνίσατε
> ταλαιπωρήσατε—πενθήσατε
> κλαύσατε—μετατραπήτω

All these imperatives are aorist, and this implies the urgency of the message. The theme of vv 7–10 is repentance and forgiveness. The latter is secured through humble acceptance of God—and his will, awaited in eschatological patience (5:8)—and a turning from worldly methods such as political terrorism. James has launched into a staccato burst of rapid commands to help his readers to see the foolishness (and seriousness) of the demonic behavior described above. An anti-Zealot polemic may be inferred throughout these lines.

The text outlines certain steps to be taken. First, resistance (ἀνθιστῆναι) to the devil. That there is a spiritual power that opposes God and so must be resisted is well attested in Christian tradition (Matt 13:39; 25:41; Eph 4:27; 6:11; 1 Tim 3:7; 1 Pet 5:8–9). διάβολος in LXX translates the Heb. הַשָּׂטָן (*haś-śāṭān*; the adversary; slanderer, accuser) and both titles are equated in Christian thought (Rev 20:2). James urges his readers to resist the devil (a stance God takes up to the proud, v 6a, though the verb is different; however, both imperatives in v 7 may go back to ἀντιτάσσεται in 4:6, as Schökel, "James 5,2 [*sic*]," proposed, 74). James may be suggesting that politically engineered resistance to Rome, as with the Zealot cause and its militancy, is the influence of the devil. This is in contrast to 1:14, where sin is the result of a person's own desire. But it may well be that the writer is simply tracing back the folly of violence to its source. The ultimate responsibility of sin lies with the person who makes moral choices (see Matt 8:28–34; Luke 22:31; John 13:2, 27).

James is confident that the devil can be resisted. This is an idea known in Christian (1 Pet 5:8–9; Eph 6:13) and Jewish thought alike (*T. Sim.* 3.5; *T.*

Iss. 7.7; *T. Dan* 5.1; *T. Naph.* 8.4). Failing to resist the devil is to act like the double-minded person (see *T. Ash.* 3.2: "Those who are two-faced are not of God, but they are enslaved to their evil desires, so that they might be pleasing to Beliar and to persons like themselves"). The direct consequence of resistance is that the devil will flee (see Bengel; see also Matt 4:1–11; Luke 4:1–13). This conclusion may be supported grammatically as καί in the middle of a complex sentence with an initial imperative has the effect of turning the second verb into a conditional future: As you do . . . so it *will be.* The grammar is Semitic (e.g., Mal 3:7, ἐπιστρέψατε πρός με καὶ ἐπιστραφήσομαι πρὸς ὑμᾶς, "Return to me, and I will return to you"). See Beyer, *Semitische Syntax,* 253.

8 ἐγγίσατε τῷ θεῷ καὶ ἐγγιεῖ ὑμῖν, "Come near to God and he will come near to you." "Coming near" completes the thought begun with "resist the devil" (v 7); the negative emphasis gives way to the positive, as v 6b has prepared the reader. "James is no simple preacher of judgment" (Mussner, 184). Though ἐγγίσατε is a command it may well be that James assumes that if one resists the devil then *eo ipso* (i.e., inevitably) one comes near to God. Such thinking is consistent with his "either/or" disjunction in vv 4–6. The coming to God (in the present case) is not the experience of initial conversion (as in the making of proselytes), but the act of contrition involving renouncing evil practices referred to in 4:1–4 for those who are already Christians. It is possible that the thought of drawing near to God is reminiscent of the OT idea of a priest or of Moses coming near to Yahweh (Exod 19:22; 24:2; Deut 16:16; cf. Heb 4:16; 7:19; *T. Dan* 6.2 ἐγγίσατε τῷ θεῷ, "Draw near to God," which follows the warning "Be on your guard against Satan and his spirits" [6.1]) and may be an attempt on James' part to bridge the gap between military and cultic metaphors (so Davids, 166). Of great importance is the immediate and gracious response of God to the one who draws near.

καθαρίσατε χεῖρας, ἁμαρτωλοί, καὶ ἁγνίσατε καρδίας, δίψυχοι, "Purify your hands, you sinners, and consecrate your hearts, you double-minded." Two more imperatives form a second couplet. There is a stronger cultic call to purity in v 8b, when compared to v 8a. Verse 8b is balanced, as both its clauses consist of an imperative, an object, and a pejorative address (Moo, 148). Purifying and cleansing depict two aspects of one action (Adamson, 148–49) and recall the actions of the priests in the temple. Both aspects are connected; the former pertains to deeds and the latter to thoughts (cf. Pss 24:4; 73:13; Sir 38:10). The washing of hands, originally a purely external rite (Exod 30:19–21; Meyer, *TDNT* 3:421–22; Hauck, *TDNT* 3:424), soon became associated with the social as well as the internal religious emphasis of the prophets and sages (Isa 1:16; Jer 4:14; Job 22:30; Pss 24:4; 26:6). Thus James connects inward disposition with outward social concern and action. He is calling his readers to a radical repentance-conversion that orients the whole person to God and his ways in this world. Setting aside the affectionate "brethren" (2:1), James underlines the seriousness of the situation by addressing his readers as ἁμαρτωλοί ("sinners"; see 5:20; cf. Pss 31:1–5; 51:15; Cantinat, 209) and δίψυχοι (both terms are taken as vocative). The latter term is of special importance in this letter. δίψυχοι ("double-minded") characterizes those obviously in need of this type of repentance. James had used the term to depict the one who was unstable, who doubted God (1:8). But in our present context the idea is expanded and made more specific, involving the double-nature (or two-world) syndrome (Sir 2:12: "woe to . . . the sinner who leads a double life," NEB). The reader who is double-minded seeks to be friendly with the world and with God (4:4). But such double allegiance is impossible. To befriend the world (i.e., resort to worldly methods to bring in the kingdom) is to oppose God and his way. This is reflected in the inconsistent behavior in the Jacobean church (3:9–12).

9 ταλαιπωρήσατε καὶ πενθήσατε καὶ κλαύσατε, "Be miserable, mourn and wail." The demands to cleanse oneself are followed quickly by the resounding call to an overt and explicit repentance (μετάνοια). ταλαιπωρεῖν ("to be miserable," a *hapax legomenon*) is not an invitation to or a sanction of asceticism (so Mayor, 147). In prophetic language (in contrast to the priestly idiom of v 8), James urges his readers to change their ways. The opening verb (in the sense of "be devastated") is a favorite with Jeremiah (in LXX, e.g., 6:26) corresponding to שדד (*šdd*). The day of the Lord is near (5:8) and God's people must return to him (Joel 2:12). There is no allowance made for Christians to take a casual attitude toward sin (1 Pet 4:17). Mourning (πενθεῖν) and wailing (κλαίειν) are the accompaniments of repentance, not the substitutes for it (see 2 Sam 19:1; Neh 8:9; Matt 5:5; Luke 6:21, 25; Acts 18:11, 15, 19; 2 Cor 7:10). What James is implying is that (while there is still time) genuine repentance is needed or else those who are unrepentant face the eschatological wrath of God (see Dibelius, 227–28). The fate of those who persist in revolutionary policies may be set in a historical framework too. James was prophetically clearsighted to see that the Zealot cause could never succeed. The same verbs recur in 5:1 in regard to his judgment on the oppressing landlords.

ὁ γέλως ὑμῶν εἰς πένθος μετατραπήτω καὶ ἡ χαρὰ εἰς κατήφειαν, "Turn your laughter into mourning, and your rejoicing into dejection." These negative attitudes should not be construed as though the preacher were a kill-joy. What the writer is saying is that the actions of (foolish) laughing and (senseless) rejoicing hold no place for Christians who refuse to turn to God's paths. The idea of laughter (γέλως) may suggest two things. First, the "festive" outlook of these sinners and double-minded people must change because there is no reason to laugh. Such was the reported teaching of Jesus (Luke 6:25; cf. Amos 8:10; Prov 14:13; 1 Macc 9:41; Tob 2:6). Laughter is usually associated with festivities (see Rengstorf, *TDNT* 1:658–61). Second, laughter can reflect the attitude of a fool (Prov 10:23; Eccl 7:6; Sir 21:20; 27:13), who has no "fear of God" which is the mark of wisdom (Prov 1:7). Rather than reckless laughter—perhaps inspired by some military success or sign of the oppressors' discomfiture—they should mourn; if such advice is taken then there is hope for them. The use of μετατρέπειν (to "turn into," a *hapax legomenon*; perhaps here a pun on the idea behind repentance of "turning to God," Heb. שוב, *šûb*) is to be noted for it is just one of several *hapax legomena* in this passage. Seitz ("Relationship of the Shepherd of Hermas to the Epistle of James," *JBL* 63 [1946] 131–40) understands such evidence to suggest that James has used a written source (cf. *1 Clem.* 23.3–4; *2 Clem.* 11.2–3; but see Davids, 168; Laws, 185). Furthermore, James writes that joy (χαρά: contrast 1:2) should be turned to dejection (κατήφεια, lit., "gloom"; another *hapax legomenon*). Such action is the only appropriate response to sin of this kind. The enormity of the godless attitude—once it dawns on the Christian (Davids, 168)—produces a wailing and mourning, a miserable and dejected state. But this reaction is for purposes of restoration. Those who follow such a path will be qualified to laugh and rejoice. Those who come with clean hands and pure hearts will have every reason to "make merry," at the time of eschatological reversal to be announced in the next line, and amplified in 5:7–8.

10 ταπεινώθητε ἐνώπιον κυρίου καὶ ὑψώσει ὑμᾶς, "Humble yourselves in the Lord's presence, and he will raise you up." This verse picks up and completes the thought of 4:8: there are enduring results for those who submit to God. For those "who humble themselves before the Lord" (see 4:6 and its reference to Prov 3:34) the promise is that God will lift them up (ὑψοῦν). Such a reversal is a well-known Jewish-rabbinic teaching (Job 5:11; 22:29; Ps 149:4; Prov 29:25; Ezek 17:24; 21:31; cf. Sir 2:17; 3:18; *T. Jos.* 10.3; 18.1; 1QH 3.20; 15.16) and also reflects early church thought (see Luke 18:14 at the close of the parable of Pharisee and penitent sinner; 2 Cor 11:7; 1 Pet 5:6). See *Introduction*, pp. lxix, lxxxiv–lxxxv. The point is that humility before God is the only way to true joy. Humility—that state of total dependence on God— is foreign to "the world." To seek to be exalted by the world is dangerous, as well as futile (see 1:9–11). But to humble oneself before God is to await his eschatological reversal and to look to him for his intervention (Luke 14:11). Such is the way of the Christian life for the author, who is consciously adopting a stance of the Jewish apocalyptists in their time of trial.

The grammatical construction with καί linking two verbs is Semitic. See on 4:7 (with reference to Beyer, *Semitische Syntax*, 252–53): the idea is "as you humble yourselves, so the Lord will exalt you."

Explanation

The writer is led to the subject matter by his preceding references to "peace" and "peacemaking" in 3:17, 18. There was need for "heavenly wisdom" because the readers were far from peaceable! Warnings about a "divided self" (1:7– 8; illustrated in 3:11–12) were evidently not wasted, as a return to the same charge in 4:8 shows. These addressees were people living out their inner divisions in a society rent by strife and discord. It is a sad comment on human nature when personal conflicts lie unresolved or boil over into distressful conditions; but worse follows when these bitter conflicts spill over into antisocial behavior and troublemaking in community relations.

No fewer than three causes of strife are diagnosed and their problems faced by the moral theologian. The last term, which makes James a theologian, is chosen to underline his interest in setting community problems in the light of divine revelation and judging the readers' behavior as an affront to God. "God opposes the proud" (v 6) is a summary of his essentially theocentric outlook, while the prescription for change, expressed in terms of repentance and self-humiliation, lies in a recovery of the sense of the divine judgment and grace (vv 7–10). The moral exhortations to humility in v 6b and v 10 are the opening and closing of a section of prophetic admonition that is closely parallel to the Old Testament appeal to Israel to return to Yahweh, the covenant God from whom they have strayed. The indictment of a spiritual infidelity (in v 4) leads James to use the Old Testament covenant relationship as the basis for his call to the new Israel in the Dispersion (1:1). Unless the basically theological underpinning of this parenetic summons is appreciated James will be viewed as a moralist governed by expediency. In fact he stands more in the tradition of the Hebrew prophets of the eighth to sixth centuries B.C., informed by the later sages of Israel when their finest writers (e.g., the author of the Wisd Sol) faced the threat and encroachment of idolatry.

Against a putative background of historical and social conditions that prevailed in Palestinian religio-political life in the early 60s of the common era, these verses reflect the extremes of nationalism and civil war. The catalyst was the policy of Rome to keep the lid on Jewish freedom fighters who were determined to see Israel purified from an alien presence. In collaboration with the Roman imperial authority the Sadducean hierarchy and priestly party strove to maintain the status quo. It is not difficult to imagine how the nascent Jewish Christian pietists with James as their titular head would be caught in the maelstrom, with sympathies leaning to the Zealot cause and the freedom of the poor. Taking the explicit references to "wars and conflicts," "killing," and "fighting" in vv 1–2 as literal, our exegesis has sought to discover in the writer a leader who was engaged in acting as mediator by offering a *via media*. He will shortly turn on the oppressing landowners and Sadducean powerbrokers (4:13—5:12). First he must warn against a too facile regard for the Zealot option, which resorted to bloodshed and mayhem in the interests of patriotic ideals. He does so by setting down three sets of contrasts, and thereby he summons the people to face and register moral choices, much as Elijah did in his day (cf. 5:17–18 for James' recourse to this OT worthy).

(i) When policies are based on "passions" and "sinful pleasures" (vv 1–2) they carry with them the seeds of their own destruction. The reason, James contends, is that at heart they emerge from self-interest. Prayer, which had earlier been cited as the way believers gain access to divine wisdom (1:5–8), has to be viewed in its Christian perspective. Far from acting as a talisman for personal ends or a pretentiously "holy" way of sanctifying our selfish desires, prayer works only when human aspirations are sublimated to higher purposes. In short, availing prayer always operates within the ambience of submission to God's holy will and is tacitly prefaced by the clause, "If it is your will" (as Mark 14:36 par. supremely illustrates). Hence to those who were querulously asking why their prayers were in vain (v 3) James can truthfully reply that they have asked in the wrong spirit because their motives were alien to God's desire for peace and justice in his way. Prayer is removed from being treated as a magic incantation (a fact to be borne in mind at 5:14–15) or a patriotic slogan—a warning unheeded by "Christian" armies who launched the Crusades to exterminate the infidels; who sang of wider and wider boundaries of their imperial domain; or who went into battle with "God with us" on their soldiers' belts.

(ii) James sees the conflict to be not one between fellow Jews and Roman overlords, or even between various factions within the Jewish fold, tragic as the latter must be regarded. Of all social unrest and armed conflict the most bitter must be that of civil war (as in the African state of Biafra or the Central American republic of Nicaragua). James views the hostility on a theological background: it is an engagement between God and "the world" (vv 4–5) or between God and "the devil" (v 7). Both are terms of opposition to the divine purpose, and both must be resisted, if in different ways. "The world" is that system of moral values which tempted Jesus in the wilderness (Matt 4:1–11 // Luke 4:1–13) and which he resisted by a clear-sighted recognition that God's kingdom can only be served by a loyalty that puts him first (Matt 6:24, 33) and turns aside from all lesser allegiances, however plausible they seem to be at first glance.

(iii) A third cause of the social malaise that beset the Jacobean community was that of pride. We learn this from the antidote James gives when he issues calls to humility (vv 6, 10). The snare of pride is brought to light in a searing exposé of the people's reaction to the social pressures of their day. With confidence in their own abilities and policies to lead them to their desired goal, they were acting in independence of God and rejoicing in whatever initial and ephemeral success attended their endeavors (v 9). James spares no words to denounce these attitudes by reminding them that the Spirit opposes envy (again playing on the motif of opposition in which the readers are called to take sides) and that God's help is promised to those who, forsaking their native powers, turn back to him in wholehearted allegiance and confidence. The promise is reinforced by the sapiential maxim of v 10 that while God abases the proud, it is his design and delight to exalt "the humble and meek" (Luke 1:52, Prayer Book Version).

To some in James' day this counsel may have seemed unrealistic and over-pietistic. But the history of the decade in which James of Jerusalem lived and died has strangely confirmed its wisdom, not by offering an easy or quick solution but by reminding both Zealot and Sadducee parties that the final word of deliverance would come neither from armed revolt (however much we applaud the brave resisters at Masada) nor from ingratiating compromise (for with A.D. 70 the Sadducees faded from the scene). Future hopes lay with the godly in Israel, with the "religious" (as James understood the term) who are characterized in John Henry Newman's words as those who "have a ruling sense of the presence of God."

2. Community Problems
(ii) Godless Attitudes   (4:11–17)

Bibliography

Blevins, W. L. "A Call to Repent, Love Others, and Remember God." *RevExp* (1986) 419–26. **Casson, L.** *Travel in the Ancient World.* Toronto: Hakkert, 1974. **Furnish, V.**

P. *The Love Command in the New Testament.* Nashville: Abingdon, 1972. **Jeremias, J.** *Jerusalem in the Time of Jesus.* Tr. F. H. Cave and C. H. Cave. London: SCM, 1969. **Johnson, L. T.** "The Use of Leviticus 19 in the Letter of James." *JBL* 101 (1982) 391–401. **Lofthouse, W. F.** "*Poneron* and *Kakon* in Old and New Testaments." *ExpTim* 60 (1948–49) 264–68. **Manson, T. W.** *The Sayings of Jesus.* London: SCM, 1949. **Maynard-Reid, P. U.** *Poverty and Wealth in James.* Chap. 5. **Noack, B.** "Jakobus wider den Reichen." *ST* 18 (1964) 10–25. **Smallwood, E. M.** *The Jews under Roman Rule: From Pompey to Diocletian: A Study in Political Relations.* 2d ed. Leiden: Brill, 1981.

Translation

[11] *Brothers, don't speak disdainfully of one another. Anyone who disdains his brother or judges his brother, disdains the law and judges it. When you judge the law, you are not observing it but judging it.* [12] *Only one is the lawgiver* [a] *and judge—he is the one able to save and also to destroy. But who are you to pass judgment on your neighbor?* [b]

[13] *Attend to this you who say "Today or* [c] *tomorrow we will go to this or that city, and spend a year* [c] *there. We will do business and make money."* [14] *Yet you do not know what will be tomorrow,* [d] *what your life will be like.* [e] *Because you are* [f] *a mist, appearing for a short while, then disappearing.* [15] *Say rather, "If it is the Lord's will, we will live* [g] *and will do this or that."* [16] *As it is, you boast about your pretensions. All such boasting is evil.* [17] *Anyone, therefore, who knows the right thing to do, and doesn't do it—he sins.*

Notes

[a] Whether ὁ is to be added to νομοθέτης is not a vital decision. Nestle [26] has the article in brackets to denote uncertainty and the external evidence is inconclusive. Ropes (275) prefers to omit the article thus making the noun a predicate and more expressive. On the other hand, ὁ νομοθέτης is the more usual type of construction, and so may reflect scribal work.

[b] In place of πλησίον TR and several minuscules have ἕτερον, along with other minor variants, possibly under the influence of Rom 14:4, 10.

[c] Two sets of textual differences are here. (i) The reading ἢ αὔριον, "or tomorrow," is supported by p74 ℵ B vg bo syr pesh in preference to the Byzantine καί (A K L P syr h1).

(ii) For ἐνιαυτόν, "a year," the Byzantine witnesses offer ἕνα to make the time limit more definite ("one year"). Also the Byzantine authorities cast all the verbs in the aorist subjunctive mood, which is less likely than the better attested future indicative. The merchants' "plans are firm and [their] expectations certain in their own eyes" (Davids, 172). The same phenomenon occurs in Byzantine verbs in v 15.

[d] Reading τὸ τῆς αὔριον (ℵ K L vg: Metzger, *Textual Commentary*, 683–84) where A P 33 have τά; or simply with p74 B τῆς αὔριον, "tomorrow's life." Assimilation to Prov 27:1 in A etc. has been suspected, though LXX reads τὰ εἰς αὔριον.

[e] ποία ἡ ζωὴ ὑμῶν, a reading challenged by p74vid A K L P, which have ποία γάρ. Hence the rendering (cf. NIV): "[for] what is your life?" as an independent question. The presence of γάρ is explained by Metzger (684) as a word inserted under the influence of the following clause and added to prevent ambiguity. In ℵ* B syr h cop bo ms arm eth ποία is dependent on the verb ἐπίστασθε, which is the reading we have followed.

[f] Reading ἀτμὶς γάρ ἐστε where there is insufficient evidence (for example, omitting the γάρ; reading ἐστιν or ἔσται; deleting the entire clause in ℵ as an accidental oversight) to challenge it.

[g] ζήσομεν . . . ποιήσομεν is the preferred reading (with ℵ B A P) with the attempted "correction" of the subjunctive offered by the Byzantine recension on the mistaken notion that the verbs were included under the ἐάν-clause (Ropes, 280).

Form / Structure / Setting

The admonitory section of 4:11–17 subdivides into a concatenation of various appeals directed against community situations. The common theme— if there is one—is usually detected in a continuance of James' exposure of the malaise afflicting the congregation to whom he writes. The problems there were evidently manifold. Hence he warns (i) against slander and name-calling (vv 11–12), which in turn results in a breach of the "royal law" of love in Lev 19:18 referred to in 2:8. The specific application is seen and heard in the sin of evil speaking (καταλαλιά), which picks up the earlier treatment of earthly wisdom in 3:13–16. (ii) At v 13 the direct word of invective is aimed at merchants whose voice is reported (οἱ λέγοντες, "you who say"). It is a moot question whether they are Christians (Davids, 171) or non-Christians (Laws, 190); in favor of the latter is the absence of the appellation ἀδελφοί here, whereas it is three times repeated in 4:11. On the other side, the invoking of the "Lord's will" in v 15 suggests that these merchants could be appealed to as professed believers, however godless their attitude may appear to be. There is also a link with 5:1–10 to be considered, especially since 4:13 and 5:1 open with the same apostrophe ἄγε νῦν, "come, now" (BDF § 144; cf. § 364.2 for the idea of this particle as a "frozen imperative"). Davids (174) sees the two pericopes as quite distinct in their scope when he regards 5:1–10 as aimed at pagans who were persecuting the Jacobean community. Our interpretation is based on seeking a historical setting for both sections in the internecine conflicts within the Jewish and Jewish Christian network of relationships at Jerusalem. There could then be a distinction drawn. In 4:11–12 James is confronting his fellow believers, called appropriately ἀδελφοί, and yet reaching out to his compatriots, identified in the word πλησίον, by his advocacy of a policy of peaceful coexistence within the ancestral fold. At 4:13 his invective becomes sharper and more pointed, and is aimed at the mercantile activity of Jewish traders who threaten, on the basis of their acquired wealth (5:1–3) both domestic and foreign (4:13), to exert hostile pressure on the impoverished Jewish Christian fraternity. They also stand behind the murderous activity of the Sadducean leaders that has already brought James, the Lord's brother, to his death (5:6).

(i) In the search for a thematic thread binding these apparently disparate sections (cf. Blevins' chapter title: he considers the issues under two heads, namely, divine sovereignty and human responsibility, with submission to God the major emphasis) there is another suggestion to be made. James has already devoted much of his writing to *the use and abuse of the tongue*. We propose that these pericopes are a continuation and an application of the same topic, with a variation. Throughout, however, what occupies James' moral treatment is an awareness that the tongue is a powerful member of the body, both personal and corporate. It is "the Achilles' heel of the believer" (Trocmé, cited in Vouga, 99). James first rebukes the purely sentimental utterances that have no counterpart in reality (2:16) as a sign of "faith by itself," i.e., faith that is not accompanied by action (2:17). Merely to pass the remark, "I wish you well; keep warm and well fed" (2:16, NIV), touches the depth of hollow religion, branded as "worthless" in 1:26 because it fails to measure up to the standards of "true religion" in 1:27. Second, our author has a scathing indictment of a double usage: words that are invested with characteristics of hastiness and thoughtlessness. Such outbursts, as part of the situation envisaged in 1:19: "slow to speak . . . slow to anger," give evidence of an uncontrolled tongue that people cannot tame (3:7–8) or hold on tight rein (1:26). By condemning these impetuous words that believers utter but—on reflection—regret (as in 3:2) James clearly is writing of those who do not really mean what they say. The third problem arises from another usage: words that are only too obviously intended to hurt and destroy. Already James has noted the incongruity of words spoken to God in praise and out of the same mouth words calculated to defame one's fellows (3:9).

Now he returns to this general theme by commenting on the different areas of social life where the tongue betrays a proud spirit. When his audience indulges in derogatory words and insults directed against the brothers (4:11–12; cf. Ps 50:20, where slander against one's brother is held up to reproof) this evil speaking is seen as an offense against God's law and against God himself. He is the only one who can be rightly regarded as the all-knowing person and so able rightly to judge (4:12). This is one manifestation of the sin of presumption.

(ii) Another area where the arrogance of the tongue shows itself is when plans and proposals for future business transactions, involving travel, sojourn, and prosperity, are entered into (for the ease and safety of travel in the empire, see Casson, *Travel*, 127, chap. 11; and for Syro-Palestine in particular, Maynard-Reid, *Poverty and Wealth*, 72–77). Note that James is not condemning the desire to get rich; rather what concerns him is the hyper-activity and mobility these persons evince—akin to the thought in Sir 38:24–34, which, however, gives a more sympathetic picture of those devoted to their work (cf. the discussion in 1:5–8, 10–11; see Vouga, 121–22, 124)—and the fact that they look to the future without reference to divine providence (4:13–15). It is in their words, cast in *oratio recta* as an index of their godless character, that their true selves stand revealed. The piling up of future tenses in πορευσόμεθα . . . ποιήσομεν . . . ἐμπορευσόμεθα . . . κερδήσομεν has a powerful literary effect (with alliterations in the verbs and the presence of a rhythmical structure including a chiasmus, formed from the verb endings, and homoioteleuton), and well illustrates and enforces the writer's point against the bourgeois "men of affairs" (Vouga, 122) on whom he has trained his sights. Their presumption lies in their pretended control over their future, to which they really have no claim (v 14). Overlooked by them are both the uncertainty and brevity of life (marked by alliterative participles φαινομένη . . . ἀφανιζομένη, "appearing . . . dis-appearing"). They ignore too the providence of God, who holds all human prospects for the future in his hands (see Luke 12:16–21).

The direct statements, inserted within quotation marks, of the merchants' plans are countered by the author's continued reporting, which he now puts into the mouths of his opponents, prefaced by "Say rather." The so-called *conditio Jacobaea*, consisting of "if it is the Lord's will," has no precise parallel in the Old Testament (see Str-B 3.758) but its equivalent, "if the gods are favorable" (cf. Plato, *Alcibiades*, 1.135D: ὅτι ἐὰν ὁ θεὸς ἐθέλῃ. In reply to Alcibiades' question, "Well, what should I say?" Socrates answers: "If it be God's will"), is a commonplace in hellenistic moralists such as Epictetus (*Diss.* 1.1.17: ὡς ἂν ὁ θεὸς θέλῃ; 3.21.12; 22.2; Marty, 172; Mussner, 191; with more examples in Dibelius, and G. Schrenk, *TDNT* 3:47 n.32, and rabbinic materials in Hauck, *ad loc.* The best illustrative document is Seneca, "On the Futility of Planning Ahead," *Ep.* 101, summed up in the apostrophe, *O quanta dementia est spes longas inchoatium!* "What madness it is [to build upon] far-reaching hopes!" 101.4). What is worth noting is the addition by James of a sentiment that is conspicuously missing from the merchants' plans. He insists, by inserting ζήσομεν, "we will live," that even their existence is dependent on God. How much more are the formulating of plans and the execution of business schemes only possible as God wills! This addendum would be a potent reminder that even the continuance of human life is at the mercy of God. The fitting preface, not only to the merchandising activity of these men, with their entrepreneurial skill (which is not explicitly condemned), but to the drawing of everyday breath, is ἐὰν ὁ κύριος θέλῃ (a common Christian expression: 1 Cor 4:19; 16:7; Heb 6:3; Acts 18:21); and the future tense of this pair of verbs, "we will live and will do this or that" matches v 13 (Hauck; Mussner, 191 n.4, who observes that if ζήσομεν is a Semitism, then the sense will run: If it is the Lord's will that we live, we will do this or that). This reconstruction (cf. Beyer, *Semitische Syntax,* 69) would make the emphasis on human frailty and the contingent element of life even more strong.

(iii) A third and final indictment, involving the misuse of the tongue, comes in v 16 and is expressed by the near synonyms ἀλαζονείαι and καύχησις, lit., "arrogance/pretensions" and "boasting." The nouns are evidently a hendiadys; hence our rendering, which could also be turned (but to less effect) into two verbs: "you boast and brag" (NIV). Both ἀλαζονεία and καύχησις are nouns describing the attitude of one who speaks out with loud claims; and in this context such claims are clearly attributed to the godless who devise future plans without reference to faith in God (Mussner, 192). James' label for this activity is "evil," a moral judgment that is completed in the paratactic statement of v 17, recalling 1:21; 2:13; 3:18. This stylistic trait of closing off a discussion by a sententious axiom is typical of James' role as a moralist. Reverting to the singular person, "anyone," lit., "to him who knows to do good . . . ," adds to the forcefulness of the punchline as a striking way to round off a *topos.* V 17 is not then to be treated as "an isolated aphorism . . . with no real relation to what precedes or to what follows" (Easton, 61; Dibelius, 231). Maynard-Reid, *Poverty and Wealth* (79–80), grants that the maxim does not fit in well or logically with the previous section, but he calls attention to the link in οὖν, and deduces that, from James' angle, the commercial schemers knew better than to plan thoughtlessly. So their actions are branded as sinful. Mussner (189–92) makes a more specific point when he seeks to identify what James means by [τὸ] καλὸν ποιεῖν; [τὸ] καλόν, the "right thing," relates to *Lebensentwurf,* "a plan for living," which is formulated under God's providence and sovereign control. The godless merchants had no such plan, and worked out their future independently of God. This disposition James brands as "sin," i.e., a failure to see what is life's true and essential meaning. And

above all, in an important verb in James, there is a failure *to do* (recalling
the indictment in 2:14–26). The exact expression καλὸν ποιεῖ (do good) is
reminiscent of Matt 5:16 (τὰ καλὰ ἔργα) while the turn of phrase ἁμαρτία
αὐτῷ ἐστιν recalls Deut 15:9; 23:21–22; 24:15.

The accumulation of wealth, hinted at in the verbs ἐμπορευσόμεθα (v 13),
"we will do business," and κερδήσομεν, "make money," has raised a question
whether we may say precisely who these people were. Maynard-Reid, *Poverty
and Wealth*, 75–78, has an interesting suggestion that overseas merchandising
(in spite of Josephus, *Against Apion* 1.12: "ours is not a maritime country;
neither commerce nor the intercourse which it promotes with the outside
world has any attraction for us") was carried on at least by a segment of
Jewish aristocrats and merchants. Foremost were the Sadducees who influenced the rich Jews of the first century (Josephus, *Ant.* 13.293–98). A priestly
prayer on the Day of Atonement asks that this may be a year of low prices,
a year of plenty, and a year of business dealings (*j. Yoma* 5:2). Years of
drought produced famine (as in the mid-forties in Palestine; cf. Acts 11:28);
and with the domestic economic suffering, Palestinian merchants were driven
to other provinces to seek their wealth. Otherwise Jerusalem was rich in
trade and commerce (see Jeremias, *Jerusalem*, 25–57); and the high-priestly
families carried on a flourishing trade in the city (Jeremias, 31, 49, citing
Josephus, *Ant.* 20.205, for the description of the high priest Ananias [in
office A.D. 47–55] who was called "a great procurer of money." Ananias used
his wealth for bribery: see Smallwood, *Jews under Roman Rule*, 281–82). So
James' reproof of the godless merchants may well be directed against merchants throughout Syro-Palestine who, with Sadducean support, engaged in
commercial enterprises and were consumed by a search for more wealth
(Noack, "Jakobus," 23–25, however, questions whether the social conditions
in the letter can be fitted into a Galilean setting, and observes that James is
emphatic in his condemnation of all riches). Against such a spirit of greed,
Sirach (11:19) warns as does *1 Enoch* 94.8; 97.10, while in the Gospel tradition
appeal may be made to Luke 12:16–20 and 16:19–31. Both of the latter
stories feature the rich; one man was a farmer whose wealth had secured
for him an early retirement he planned but never lived to enjoy; the other
rich man is depicted with all the marks of Sadducean luxury, ostentation
and unconcern for the poor: see T. W. Manson, *The Sayings of Jesus*, 296,
who writing on Luke 16:19–31 remarks:

> The description of the rich man in v. 19. He is wealthy; and the Sadducean party
> was the party of the wealthy. He wears purple, the colour associated with royal
> or quasi-royal dignity, and fine linen or lawn, the most luxurious fabric of the
> ancient world. The Sadducees were the aristocratic party in Judaism. He lived in
> luxury: so did the Sadducees. Anyone, in the days of Jesus, hearing this description
> would think at once of the priestly aristocrats of Jerusalem.

Comment

11 Μὴ καταλαλεῖτε ἀλλήλων, ἀδελφοί, "Brothers, don't speak disdainfully
of one another." These verses continue the theme that the tongue is a powerful
and often misused agent in the Christian community (see *Form/Structure/*

Setting). Much discussion centers upon whether or not this passage has anything in common with what precedes it. There are many possibilities to consider to establish the link between our present verses and the earlier words of James. Exposing the misuse of the tongue (4:11) clearly has links with the discourse in 3:1–12. Also, a jealous and selfish person (3:13–14) would be a prime candidate to be included among those speaking evil of other church members. Any attitude that shows disdain or contempt for others reflects pride on the part of the one who adopts the scornful attitude. This is characteristic of the double-minded person (4:8), who needs to exercise humility (4:6, 10). In 4:13–17 is drawn another picture of one who is also guilty of haughtiness. Thus it is not difficult to place 4:11–17 in the sequential flow of James' thinking.

καταλαλεῖν literally means "to speak ill of." The command for God's people to cease from speaking evil against (see RSV) others of the congregation has well-established precedents (Lev 19:16; Pss 49 [50]:20; 100 [101]:5; Prov 18:8; 20:13; 26:22; Wisd Sol 1:11; cf. *T. Iss.* 3.4; *T. Gad* 3.3; 5.4; 1QS 4.9, 11; 5.25–26; 6.26; 7.2–9), and evil speech was a problem for the early church (Rom 1:30; 2 Cor 12:20; 1 Pet 2:1; 2 Pet 2:12; 3:16; *1 Clem.* 30.1–3; 35.5; *Herm. Man.* 2.2–3; 8.3; 9.23; *Sim.* 6.5, 5; 7.7, 2; 9.26, 7; *Barn.* 20). It may very well be that the fighting and wars that had taken place in this church were accompanied by accusations hurled in the heat of debate. James' use of "brother" (ἀδελφός) is a sudden switch from the naming of sinners and the double-minded person of 4:8, and perhaps he is exemplifying the care in use of the tongue that has been his admonition to his readers. Serious consequences follow, as the rabbis knew well. Rabbi Asi (quoted in Dibelius, 228 n.101) remarked: "He who slanders another thereby slanders God"; cf. *Mek.* on Exod 14:31: "Whosoever speaks against the true Shepherd is like one who speaks against God" (quoted in Schlatter). See too *T. Gad* 4.1–3 for some close parallels to the thought of this letter.

ὁ καταλαλῶν ἀδελφοῦ ἢ κρίνων τὸν ἀδελφὸν αὐτοῦ καταλαλεῖ νόμου καὶ κρίνει νόμον· εἰ δὲ νόμον κρίνεις, οὐκ εἶ ποιητὴς νόμου ἀλλὰ κριτής, "Anyone who disdains his brother or judges his brother, disdains the law and judges it. When you judge the law, you are not observing it but judging it." The one who speaks disdainfully of a brother or sister is actually guilty of judging (κρίνειν) the brother or sister. The idea associated with judging here is that of criticizing or finding fault with another (BGD, 452). The law (νόμος) may be the Mosaic law but an earlier reference to the law (2:8) suggests that what James means is the epitome of the teaching of Jesus, which is summed up by the exhortation "to love one another as yourself" (cf. Gal 6:2). This understanding of the law as "love to one's neighbor" based on Lev 19:16–18 has not been practiced by the community to which James writes, as the exposition up to this point makes clear (2:14–4:10). The link between speaking against the brethren (4:11, 13–17) and a lack of respect for the law (see below) and God was the point of 4:9, where those James called to repentance seemed to have taken a nonchalant or carefree attitude toward sin and toward God. These people believed that they were "masters of their own destiny" and in the end responsible to no one but themselves. They are indicted for their "love of the world" (4:4; Mussner, 189).

We are bound to ask how this judging of another Christian may be equated with judging the law. That question is partially answered in the closing sentence of the verse. The one who judges the law (i.e., the one who judges other Christians) is not a doer of the law (ποιητὴς νόμου: a phrase akin to that already found in 1:22, 25, based on Exod 24:3: see H. Braun, *TDNT* 6:469–70). For James, there is but one judge (4:12), namely, God. To usurp that authority implicates the offender as a lawbreaker because the law is not being observed. Such a person becomes a judge of the law and sets himself "outside" and "above" the law. Thus, the law is not kept but is "disdained."

12   εἶς ἐστιν [ὁ] νομοθέτης καὶ κριτὴς ὁ δυνάμενος σῶσαι καὶ ἀπολέσαι, "Only one is the lawgiver and judge—he is the one able to save and also to destroy." Christians are implored to refrain from judging others (Matt 7:1–5; Luke 6:37–42; Rom 2:1; 14:4; 1 Cor 4:5; 5:12) because there is but one judge and lawgiver ([ὁ] νομοθέτης, a *hapax legomenon* in NT; see Ps 9:21 [20] LXX), that is, God (Isa 33:22: κριτὴς ἡμῶν κύριος). The use of εἶς ("one") eliminates any ground for pretense or excuse that those mentioned in 4:11 have for judging others; this right is reserved solely for God, because he is the one who can save and destroy (Deut 32:39; 1 Sam 2:6; 2 Kgs 5:7; Matt 10:28; Heb 5:7). These words of James may mean that those who judge others (in a negative way; see below) pronounce judgment on themselves. James is not discounting the need for honest discussion and constructive criticism within the body of believers. It may be that he would applaud a removal from the congregation of those who deliberately lead astray the flock with their destructive tongues. The point is, however, that jealous and contemptible language has no place in the church, as James emphasizes in the closing words of 4:12: σὺ δὲ τίς ε ἴὸ κρίνων τὸν πλησίον; "But who are you to pass judgment on your neighbor?" This rhetorical question, somewhat sarcastic in nature (Adamson, 178), shames those guilty of judging their neighbor (πλησίον), a term that recalls vividly 2:8 (and in turn Lev 19:16–18), and illustrates the use of the royal law as a standard by which to measure conduct (see Johnson, "The Use of Leviticus 19," 393). This may also be an exhortation to consider those who are presently outside the church and who would be adversely influenced by the unseemly conduct of Christians.

A more specific setting of this pericope (4:11–12) may be offered. In the light of the debate over faith and works in 2:14–26, where one of the central issues was the confession of "one God" (2:19), it is possible to see an extension of the same controversy in this text. "One lawgiver and judge" (RSV) suggests a similarity of wording. The issue raised in chap. 2 was whether faith alone, understood as a verbal or creedal confession, is sufficient for salvation. James' trenchant response was that it is not. True faith must be accompanied by works of compassion to validate its authenticity. Perhaps the same point is now reiterated—against pseudo-Paulinist Christians who are here claiming that the law is not binding on them. If so, they are classically representing the antinomian position. James replies to this aberration with the same animation as in 2:14–26, insisting that there is a divine lawgiver and judge who will hold all people accountable—not least those who profess faith yet fail to obey the royal law of love in attitudes to their brothers and sisters. Lev 19:18, already identified as the sovereign command (2:8), is set in a context that is stern in its opposition to slander and name-calling (Lev 19:16).

13 Ἄγε νῦν οἱ λέγοντες, "Attend to this, you who say." The apostrophe ἄγε νῦν is found only here and 5:1 in the NT (but the meaning is not quite the same; Noack, "Jakobus," 11). This term, however, was quite popular in the hellenistic world (Epictetus, *Diss.* 1.2.20, 25; 1.6.37; 3.1.37; Xenophon, *Ap.* 14). The "circumlocution" (Davids, 171) οἱ λέγοντες prevents us from positively identifying with confidence the relationship of "those who say" to the church members. The lack of any reference to "brethren" suggests that these people were outsiders, but the Christians of 4:9 were addressed in terms ("sinner" and "double-minded person") other than brothers and sisters, and the use of the tag the "Lord wills" (4:15) points to professed members of the congregation. A possible situation is that some of the truths of 4:11–12 (viz., evil speech, judging) reflect the attitude of the rank and file, whereas at v 13 the writer turns to confront the merchants or businessmen of the church. James is led to provide specific examples (4:13–17) of the pride that can result from placing oneself over others (4:11–12). Yet such a proposal is not certain and we must be content to allow the question of the relationship of the merchants to the church to be open, as either possibility (Christians or non-Christian merchants) does little to affect our exegesis. Earlier a more specific, if tentative, submission was offered.

σήμερον ἢ αὔριον πορευσόμεθα εἰς τήνδε τὴν πόλιν καὶ ποιήσομεν ἐκεῖ ἐνιαυτὸν καὶ ἐμπορευσόμεθα καὶ κερδήσομεν, "'Today or tomorrow we will go to this or that city, and spend a year there. We will do business and make money.'" These words are regarded as a quotation (RSV, NIV, NEB), suggesting that James is rehearsing a list of plans that he had heard in the mouth of his addressees. What we have here is typical of someone (whether Christian or not) planning a business trip. All four verbs are in the future—πορευσόμεθα ("will go"), ποιήσομεν ("will spend 'time,'" an expression confined to later Greek: cf. Ropes, 276, but the verb in this sense is found in Prov 13:23, δίκαιοι ποιήσουσιν . . . ἔτη πολλά; and ποιεῖν here may be consciously picked up in v 17), ἐμπορευσόμεθα ("will do business"; cf. 2 Pet 2:3 for a metaphorical usage), κερδήσομεν ("will make money"). The phrase εἰς τήνδε τὴν πόλιν, "to such-and-such a town," is another example of vernacular language (BDF § 289). The problem James has with such an attitude does not stem from the fact that these business people are following a "secular" vocation, since he would not refuse approbation to those who work in the everyday world. What galls our author is that such an attitude reflects a proud complacency that suggests a "this-worldly planning" and a blatant desire to become rich. In other words, James was chastising the merchants because their lifestyle and their thinking had become secular. To approach the Christian vocation in this way was to walk in friendship with the world, an association already reprobated (4:4).

14 οἵτινες οὐκ ἐπίστασθε τὸ τῆς αὔριον, "Yet you do not know what will be tomorrow." The relative οἵτινες should be given its meaning as in classical Greek ("you are those who . . .") and goes back to οἱ λέγοντες in 4:13. "Those who say" what they plan to do (4:13) are actually those who do not know what will happen in the future. "Tomorrow" (τὸ τῆς αὔριον) includes all that was planned by the merchants, but such planning is the "height of foolishness" (Moo, 155) because they have overlooked a fundamental factor to be considered, namely, the transitory nature and the brevity of life, much as the rich person in 1:10–11 did (Mussner, 190–91). If οἴτινες is taken adversatively (so Moule, *Idiom Book*, 124) then what James is implying is that anyone who plans for the future without regard to God is wrong because no one knows what tomorrow will yield. The charge of ignorance, however, leveled against the merchants is not the main point. All humanity—the merchants included— is incapable of seeing into the future, and so no one knows what the future holds. Rather the question is, how does one approach life in the light of not knowing the outcome? The incorrect, i.e., foolish, way is to assume that all will transpire as planned. The more sensible attitude—because it alone is safe—is to assume that whatever happens is under the control of God. James is not suggesting that Christians are to go around in fear that disaster will surely take place. What he is requiring his readers to consider is that a trust in God and not a well-thought-out plan for aggrandizement and gain is the only way to face the future. To live in the recognition that God—not the human being—is in control is to choose a Christian life of humility before God; to live as though we ourselves—not God—have the final say is to adopt a proud and haughty attitude.

ἀτμὶς γάρ ἐστε ἡ πρὸς ὀλίγον φαινομένη, ἔπειτα καὶ ἀφανιζομένη, "Because you are a mist, appearing for a short while, then disappearing." The use of ἀτμίς ("vapor," "mist," BGD, 120) expresses the thought that life is short (cf. Eccl 1:2; 12:8; 4 Ezra 4.24; 2 Apoc. Bar. 82.6; 1 Clem. 7.6). The idea of the brevity of life was not the exclusive belief of Christians. Jewish (Job 7:7, 9; Pss 39:5, 6, 12; 49:13; 102:4, 12; 144:4; Prov 27:1; Sir 11:18–19; Wisd Sol 2:1–2, 5; 3:18; Philo, *Leg. All.* 3.226; 1QM 15.10) as well as Hellenic and Roman thinking (Ps-Phocylides, 116: οὐδεὶς γινώσκει τί μεταύριον ἢ τί μεθ' ὥραν; Seneca, *Ep.* 101.4–6: *quam stultum est aetatem disponere ne crastini quidem dominum*, "how foolish it is to arrange one's life, when one is not even a master of tomorrow!" Cf. Dibelius, 233) ran parallel to Christian ideas (see Luke 12:16–20; 1 Clem. 17.6). The verses in Luke 12 have affinity with the present passage, especially in the parable told by Jesus of how a wealthy man was prevented from enjoying his riches. The uncertainty of life is brought home in this parable because the rich man died unexpectedly. As the similar sounding words (used for effect, Davids, 122; Vouga, 123 n.5) φαινομένη ("seen") and ἀφανιζομένη ("disappear") suggest, a person is here today and gone today. The idea of a mist, especially one that rolls in from the sea and then vanishes, would be especially relevant for sea merchants (Adamson, 180). Instead of looking to God, who alone can sustain life, the person trusts in what can be accomplished by his or her own devices and designs.

15 ἀντὶ τοῦ λέγειν ὑμᾶς, "Say rather." In v 13, James mimics the merchants' boastful description (their "practical atheism," Adamson, 180) of what they feel will surely take place. In v 14, however, he has aptly pointed out that (while it may happen as hoped for) the future is out of the hands of mere mortals. James is not setting his face against making plans for the future— business plans or other. He simply reports that the person who expresses his desires as personal plans should preface such remarks by some contingent reminder. ἀντί, "instead," "rather" (lit., "over against," Moule, *Idiom Book*, 71) alerts the reader to a contrast to the thought presented in v 13 (for ἀντί with τοῦ λέγειν, see Moule, *Idiom Book*, 128).

ἐὰν ὁ κύριος θελήσῃ καὶ ζήσομεν καὶ ποιήσομεν τοῦτο ἢ ἐκεῖνο, "'If it is the Lord's will, we will live and will do this or that.'" See *Note* g and the discussion of the confusion over whether the verbs (ζᾶν, ποιεῖν) are to be in the future indicative (so A B P) or subjunctive (so K L 35). Though the καί preceding ζήσομεν can be taken as the Semitic ו (*waw*) to begin the apodosis (of a conditional sentence), this copulative should be taken with the second καί of the sentence to form a pattern of "both . . . and" (see BDF § 442.7; cf. Adamson, 180 n.80). The idea that what takes place in this life is in the hands of divine power is found in pagan (see Dibelius, 233–34, for citations, notably Epictetus, *Diss.* 1.1.17, 3.21, 22; 22.2; also cf. Mayor, 222–23; Schrenk, *TDNT* 3:47) as well as Jewish (1QS 11.10–11; ʾ*Abot* 2:12) and Christian thought (1 Cor 4:19; 16:7; Heb 6:3; Acts 18:21; Rom 1:10; Phil 2:19, 24; Ign. *Eph.* 20.1). The mere verbalization of a catchphrase like "If the Lord wills" is not the intent here. Just as with any Christian teaching, this phrase can become no more than a vain, thoughtless repetition, a kind of fetish. What James is urging here is a conviction (worked out in a congruent lifestyle) that leads one to acknowledge that indeed God is in control of life's decisions. He is also suggesting that if the sole purpose of business ventures is to make as much money as possible (for oneself; see 4:2) then such plans are wrongheaded and open to sudden change (1:10–11; 5:1–6). The use of ὁ κύριος probably refers to the Father but the person of Jesus as Lord (2:1) also cannot be far from the mind of James. The sovereignty of God is never seen more clearly than in 4:14 (see BDF § 291.2 for a note on the unusual use of ἐκεῖνος in contrast to οὗτος).

16 νῦν δὲ καυχᾶσθε ἐν ταῖς ἀλαζονείαις ὑμῶν, "As it is, you boast about your pretensions." James draws his conclusion by identifying the sin of those mentioned in 4:13: they are guilty of boasting. νῦν δέ (lit., "But now") implies "as it is." Rather than saying (and believing) that their plans will be fulfilled only if God so permits, the merchants plan and act as though God did not exist. Such is the epitome of the secular spirit. This is doubly tragic if (as is probable) the merchants in mind are professed Christians.

To claim certainty for the plans already adumbrated is tantamount to boasting (καυχᾶσθε, here in the present tense). Some translations understand ἀλαζονεία (pretension) as modifying the verb "to boast" (NIV, "boast and brag"; RSV, "you boast in your arrogance"). But to take the noun (which in the text is plural) as describing the manner of the boasting is not the only possibility. The preposition ἐν ("about"), when following καυχᾶσθαι (sixteen times in the NT; e.g., Rom 2:17; 2:23) always points to the object of the boast. On the other hand, it can be argued that James' choice of the term "boasting" (in the second part of this verse) supports the idea that the "manner" of the action governs the structure of 4:16a. Adamson (181 n.97) contends that had James desired to emphasize the object or content of the merchants' boasting he would have chosen καύχημα instead of καύχησις. But such a conclusion is not supported by the evidence cited above. The word "pretensions" (for ἀλαζονεία see Delling, *TDNT* 1:227–28; Noack, "Jakobus," 16–18, on the exegetical question whether ἀλαζονεία signifies what a person boasts about [*materies gloriandi*] or when used with καυχᾶσθαι carries a neutral sense, i.e., marks out the person's wealth. In the latter case the word points on to 5:2–3, and the ground of accusation is their forgetfulness of God and their responsibilities) is not to be understood adverbially "pretentiously"; rather it identifies the root of the sin. The essence of ἀλαζονεία is rooted firmly in the worldly mindset (see 1 John 2:16: ἡ ἀλαζονεία τοῦ βίου, "the pride of life"). The final estimate is that the merchants of 4:13–16, though probably acting "piously enough" (Davids, 123) at church, actually brag (to other merchants?) that they—not God—control everything in life. They not only omit God from their plan-making (4:13) but they boast about their presumed independence as well. For James "all such boasting [is] evil" (πᾶσα καύχησις τοιαύτη πονηρά, emanating from ὁ πονηρός, "the devil," in 4:7: see Lofthouse, "Poneron," 267). James, ever the moralist, condemns this arrogant behavior, so common in the world (see Herm. Vis. 2.3.1; Man. 3.3; Sim. 6.3.5). The copulative ἐστιν ends the sentence. This climactic ending suggests that James wants to emphasize that such behavior—presently a part of the scene—is inherently evil. The reason for this negative judgment is that, as with the godless in Wisd Sol 5:7–10, the presence and providence of God have been left out of consideration. The sad verdict stands: "What good has our pride done us? What can we show for all our wealth and arrogance? All those things have passed by like a shadow . . . [and] not a trace to be found" (NEB).

17 εἰδότι οὖν καλὸν ποιεῖν καὶ μὴ ποιοῦντι, ἁμαρτία αὐτῷ ἐστιν, "Anyone, there-fore, who knows the right thing to do and doesn't do it—he sins." Almost all commentators agree that this verse is an independent maxim (as a "senten-tious" saying, Adamson, 181) incorporated into the text because of the sudden switch from second person to third person and because of the somewhat awkward placement of this verse (see below). We have already noted that the author is in the habit of supplying proverbs to clinch his argument (2:13; 3:18). Several conjectures have been offered to account for the source of this moral maxim. Adamson (181, who cites Resch) understands it to be a lost saying of the Lord. Laws (194) thinks that James may be commenting on Prov 3:27–28, a view drawing support from the use of Prov 3:34 in 4:6. Davids (174) wonders if the verse is of Semitic origin, following Beyer, *Semitische Syntax*, 218, and Mussner, 192 n.3, who observes how the paratactic construc-tion with καί leads to a logical conclusion, "When anyone who knows to do good does not do it, then. . . ." Whatever the case, the source of the saying cannot be finally determined. But a more important question is what James means by v 17.

Though the origin of the saying remains a mystery, it does appear that James intended this adage to sum up what has just been said. This is the importance attached to οὖν ("therefore"; a word surprisingly absent from the RSV translation). But what does James mean by this connection? The use of εἰδότι (lit., "to the one who knows") may imply that the sins of omission are not primarily in mind for James (Davids, 174), though such sins are not any less serious (see Matt 25:31–46). And Moo (158) may be correct in suggest-ing that riches (though soon to be a topic for discussion, 5:1–6) are not yet the subject of James' rebuke (contra Davids). Thus James may be simply highlighting what he has just said and giving a theological basis for his condem-nation. The one who knows (εἰδότι is a dative participle) to do right but does not do it (μὴ ποιοῦντι, the latter is also a dative participle)—he sins. (Note how the copulative verb is placed at the end of the sentence for emphasis;

this parallels v 16; see *Comment* above.) For James, the merchants (if they were in fact of the church) now have no excuse. οὐ καλόν stands as a synonym with κακόν (Vouga, 125) and "*κακόν* always carries with it the idea of moral obliquity" (Lofthouse, "*Poneron*," 266). They know that to make plans (identified as selfishly motivated, profit-making plans), as though they could see into the future, is wrong. Moreover, to brag about their godlike independence (as in the case of the foolish people in *1 Clem.* 21.5) is evil, for it shows a disregard for God and a feeling of immunity to his judgment. The words of Jesus drive home this thought forcefully: "And that servant who knew his master's will, but did not make ready or act according to his will, shall receive a severe beating" (Luke 12:47 RSV; cf. Sir 11:10; 31:5: "the pursuit of money leads a man astray" [NEB]). Once a merchant (or any Christian for that matter, see Dibelius; Mussner, 192: "What James in this verse writes to the church in the Dispersion applies to Christians of all generations") knows what is right, the same person is under moral obligation to do it.

Explanation

In a paragraph such as this one Luther's somewhat grudging admission that the letter of James contains "many a good saying" is illustrated. The background, however, is largely unknown to us, though we can offer some guesses. We know that James was involved in disputes between rival parties in the Jewish leadership of the temple just prior to his untimely martyrdom in A.D. 62. In the preceding three years there were quarrels between the lower order of temple clergy, who sided with the people of Jerusalem, and the Sadducean hierarchy over social and economic issues. Josephus tells us that one of the features of that debate was "name-calling" (*Ant.* 20.180: "and when they clashed, they used abusive language and threw stones"). There is also a fairly well documented background about Jewish traveling merchants in the period, among whom the aristocratic Sadducees, who gained part of their wealth by foreign trade and commercial endeavor, are to be named.

But the instruction is really timeless. James returns to one of his chosen topics, namely, the misuse of the tongue. At earlier places in the tract he has rebuked those who said but did not perform (1:26; 2:16, 18). Then, he has an especially vitriolic word for those who used their tongues but did not mean what they implied since they were "double-tongued" (3:6–12). His third attack on the wrongful use of the tongue is directed at those who speak— and mean only too well what they say. They are guilty of various sins that involve the tyranny of the tongue. Their weakness of moral character is seen only too apparently in the words that are the index of that character (as Matt 12:33–37 makes clear). E. Trocmé (cited on p. 159) is correct to call the tongue and its power to ruin the speaker's life and influence "the Achilles' heel" of professed believers.

The different areas of activity where the tongue rules to the detriment of a person's social and religious relationships are demarcated.

(i) The habit of "judging others" by slanderous speech or gossip is first held up to reproof (vv 11–12). The wisdom teachers in Israel called such a practice the use of a "third tongue" (Sir 28:14 RSV, "Slander has shaken

many," a text where the Greek has translated "slander" as "a third tongue").
It is so called because it "kills" three persons: the speaker, the one spoken
to, and the one spoken about. This unholy triangle deserves exposure for
what it is. For James it leads to two terrible consequences: (a) it entails a
breach of the royal law of love, that we should love our neighbor as ourselves
(2:8, referring to Lev 19:18). A slanderer despises his brother or sister (Ps
50:20) and his neighbor (Ps 101:5); and the presumption is that he is better,
since he has appointed himself as a judge over another's motives, which is a
fateful mistake (Matt 7:1–5). (b) In so doing the slanderer usurps the role
that belongs properly to God (v 12). Human knowledge is at best partial
and often prejudiced. Hence the peril of gossipmongers is that they act as
though they were God and apply the strict law as if they stood above and
outside it.

(ii) The merchants' practice of planning for the future (vv 13–15) by presum-
ing to order their own business lives and destinies is a sign to James that
they are not wise. "Boasting of tomorrow" is warned against in Prov 27:1
for the two reasons adduced throughout Scripture. One salutary recall is
that life's certainty hangs by a fragile thread that may snap without warning
or reason. The parable of Luke 12:16–21 powerfully makes the point that a
person's life is not within his or her power to control. The farmer may confi-
dently speak of "many years" for which he has provided retirement income
and security. The monosyllabic "but God said" introduces the second reason
why no one should presume to know the shape of the future. "Tonight
your life is called to account" is a reminder that all live within the providence
of God, who holds our life in his hand, and that life is his momentary gift
to be granted or withdrawn.

James has two telling phrases to sum up the consentient biblical witness
to life's frailty and God's sovereign control. He answers rhetorically the question, "What is your life?" (v 14 RSV) with the sad but undeniable response,
"You are a mist that appears for a little time and then vanishes." He offers
as the only safe course, on making plans, the need to preface what we intend
to do by the famous "Jacobean condition": "Instead you ought to say, if the
Lord wills, we shall live" (v 15). Otherwise we are victims of our own supposed
mastery of the future, which is the height of folly.

(iii) Once again the writer goes to the heart of the issue under review.
His readers were self-deceived by adopting what he sees as a totally mistaken
and misplaced attitude to life (vv 16–17). Two moral qualities betray their
sin. They are filled with pretensions of their own importance and pride, a
word used to describe the itinerant quack medicine-man who offered fake
cures that were worthless; and they are guilty of "boasting," a term that for
Paul epitomizes the essence of sin and is the antithesis of the life of faith
(Rom 3:27; Phil 3:3–11; 2 Cor 10:17–18). Paul is driven to boasting only
under the constraints of his debate at Corinth (2 Cor 12:9). The reason lies
in what he has learned from the gospel of grace that all boasting is vain (1
Cor 1:30–31) and that his sole hope is centered in the cross of Jesus (Gal
6:14).

James, to be sure, gets no further than the moral dictum, "All such boasting
is evil" (v 16), and the conclusion that to fail to do what we know to be

right is sin (v 17). But in a strange way he both confirms Paul's indictment of vain self-trust for salvation and adds a needed corollary, namely, that the valid evidence of genuine religion is what Christians *do* as they practice a "faith made operative by love" (Gal 5:6).

3. Judgment on Rich Farmers   (5:1–6)

Bibliography

Aland, K. "Der Herrnbruder Jakobus und der Jakobusbrief." *TLZ* 69 (1944) cols. 97–104. **Betz, H. D.** *Lukian von Samosata und das Neues Testament.* TU 74. Berlin: Töpelmann, 1961. **Bratcher, R. G.** "Exegetical Themes in James 3–5." *RevExp* 66 (1969) 403–13. **Feuillet, A.** "Le sens du mot Parousie dans l'évangile de Matthieu." In *The Background of the New Testament and Its Eschatology,* FS C. H. Dodd, ed. D. Daube and W. D. Davies. Cambridge: Cambridge UP, 1956. 261–80 (272–80). **Fry, E.** "The Testing of Faith: A Study of the Structure of the Book of James." *BT* 29 (1978) 427–35. **Furfey, P. H.** *"Plousios* and Cognates in the New Testament." *CBQ* 5 (1943) 243–63. **Grant, F. C.** *The Economic Background of the Gospels.* 2d ed. New York: Russell & Russell, 1973. **Grill, S.** "Der Schlachttag Jahwes." *BZ* n.f. 2 (1958) 278–83. **Jeremias, J.** *Jerusalem in the Time of Jesus.* Tr. F. H. and C. H. Cave. London: SCM, 1969. **Keck, L. E.** "The Poor among the Saints in Jewish Christianity and Qumran." *ZNW* 57 (1966) 54–78. ———. "The Poor among the Saints in the New Testament." *ZNW* 56 (1965) 100–129. **Kreissig, H.** "Die landwirtschaftliche Situation im Palästina vor dem judäischen Krieg." *Acta Antiqua* 17 (1969) 241–42. **Longenecker, R. N.** *The Christology of Early Jewish Christianity.* SBT 2d ser./17. London: SCM, 1970. 46–47. **MacMullen, R.** *Roman Social Relations: 50 B.C. to A.D. 284.* New Haven: Yale University Press, 1974. **Noack, B.** "Jakobus wider den Reichen." *ST* 18 (1964) 10–25. **Philonenko, M.** "Le Testament de Job et les Thérapeutes." *Sem* 8 (1958) 41–53. **Plummer, A.** *The General Epistles of St. James and St. Jude.* Expositor's Bible. New York: Doran, 1920. **Riesenfeld, H.** "Von Schätzesammeln und Sorgen." In *Neotestamentica et Patristica,* FS O. Cullmann. NovTSup 6. Leiden: Brill, 1962, 47–58. **Schökel, L. A.** "James 5,2 [sic] and 4,6." *Bib* 54 (1973) 73–76.

Translation

[5:1] *Attend to this, you rich people, weep and howl in view of the miseries that are coming your way.* [2]*Your wealth has become rotten, your clothes moth-eaten,* [3]*your gold and silver tarnished; and their corrosion will be evidence against you, and devour your flesh like fire. You have amassed wealth for the last days.* [4]*See how the wages of the workers who have reaped your fields, which have been kept back*[a] *by you, are shouting aloud. The cries of the harvesters have reached the ears of the Almighty Lord.* [5]*You have lived off the land in luxury and self-indulgence. You have gorged yourselves in*[b] *the day of slaughter.* [6]*You have condemned and killed the just man; he was not resisting you.*[c]

Notes

[a]Reading ἀφυστερημένος, though it is a rare word (attested here in א B*). The other options are ἀπεστερημένος (A B² P Ψ and minuscules), "defraud," which may be a scribal assimilation to

the text of Mal 3:5 (cf. Sir 4:1; 29:6) and ἀποστερημένος a variant of A B² found in K L. Metzger prefers the reading ἀπεστερημένος on the grounds of a wide attestation and the way that the ℵ B* reading could be an Alexandrian refinement (*Textual Commentary*, 685).

ᵇThe addition of ὡς, "as," seen in the KJV/AV translation "as in a day of slaughter" based on ὡς ἐν ἡμέρᾳ σφαγῆς (ℵᶜ K L), is a Byzantine reading that "changes and weakens the sense because of a failure to note the allusion to the Day of Judgment in ἡμέρᾳ σφαγῆς" (Ropes, 291). Even less acceptable is ἐν ἡμέραις in A.

ᶜPunctuation has contributed to exegesis in the understanding of this verse. οὐκ ἀντιτάσσεται, lit., "he does not resist," may be a question (based on the nonresistance of the righteous to the threat of persecution: Isa 53:7; 1 Pet 2:23), but it is an inappropriate and anticlimactic way of concluding the fierce denunciation of the rich oppressors (Ropes, 292, against WH text; Schökel, 74; and Davids, 180). Alternatively the verb may be construed as an impersonal passive: "no opposition is made." But, as Mayor notes (160), the verb is middle, not active, nor is it a strict passive. Assuming the active voice the implied subject could be ὁ θεός with the verb either a direct statement (as in 4:6: God resists the proud) or an interrogative. The latter sounds unnatural, and really unnecessary in view of the plain sense of the indicative, with the antecedent ὁ δίκαιος (an important singular, not a generalizing plural as in NIV, "innocent men, who were not opposing you"—a rendering to be faulted for more than one reason, since it hardly gives the best sense ὁ δίκαιος or to ἀντιτάσσεται, though defended by Chaine). Nor is it required to interpret the sentence as a christological reference (Feuillet, "Le sens," 272–80, who takes the "just one" to be the heavenly Christ who resists the rich in the divine court; cf. Mussner, 201 n.3; Laws, 204–9; Cantinat, 228–29), or to regard it as a gloss (so M. K. Rustler, "Thema und Disposition des Jakobusbriefes" [unpub. diss. Vienna, 1952], in Mussner, 198 n.4).

Form/Structure/Setting

The voice of James, cast in direct speech with ἄγε νῦν, and using an idiomatic mode of address found only here and 4:13, is heard in condemning the rich farmers. A second audience group is evidently envisaged other than traveling merchants spoken of in 4:13 (Maynard-Reid, *Poverty*, chap. 6). The rhetorical style is very close to that of the OT prophets (Isaiah, in particular, with oracles against foreign nations in chaps. 5, 13, 15, 34) and apocalyptists such as the author of *1 Enoch* (see *1 Enoch* 94.7–11). If the OT prophetic utterance provided a model for James, it would follow that his audience would be primarily pagans, not necessarily professed Christian members of the community (Maynard-Reid, *Poverty*, 81). But it would be wrong to make a sharp disjunction between this invective in 5:1–6 and the foregoing sections (1:9–11; 2:2–4, 5–12, 15–16; 4:13–17) where the godlessness and hostility of the rich are held up to reproach, especially as these actions bear adversely upon the poor members of the Jacobean community. (There is some justification for this if the prophetic model is one of oracles directed against the rich and powerful in Israel, e.g., Isa 3:11–4:1; Amos 4:1–3; 6:1–7; Mic 3:1–4.) The author's sympathies clearly are set in favor of the latter, and his vitriolic condemnation of the rich farmers here picks up the earlier judgments of 2:5–7.

The setting of 5:1–6, however, is not so clear as this similarity to chap. 2 may imply. In the earlier chapter it is not certain whether the "rich" are being addressed directly: James is content to warn his readers against siding with the rich who turn out to be the church's enemies. In 5:1–6 the "rich" are personally confronted with direct address, and though James employs phrases and idioms drawn from the OT (e.g., κλαίειν . . . ὀλολύξετε μετὰ κλαυθμοῦ, Isa 15:2, 3; ὀλολύξοντες, Isa 10:10 LXX; 13:6; 14:31; 15:2, 3, 5;

16:7; 23:1, 6, 14; 65:14; Jer 31:20 LXX = 48:20 in Heb) his speech is intended to serve as an encouragement to his Christian brethren (1:1–2) who have suffered at the hands of the rich (5:6). The words of judgment and the warnings of the coming eschatological fate of the rich (in 5:5, patterned on the OT "day of Yahweh" theme, e.g., Amos 5; Zeph 1:11–15; see Grill, "Der Schlachttag") are not calculated to lead the rich to repentance nor to counsel them in the right use of wealth but to describe the misery that is impending as the fate and doom of the godless (so Ropes, Windisch, Dibelius, Davids, Vouga; contra Mussner, Cantinat, Schrage). The link with the OT "dirge motif" (*Klagemotif*) is a strong one. "This onomatopoetic word [ὀλολύζειν] vividly describes the howls of rage and pain of the damned," as in Isaiah's denunciations (Bratcher, "Exegetical Themes," 410 n. 17).

This eschatological setting may be observed in two features: (1) The term ταλαιπωρία, "misery" (v 1), is drawn from the biblical tradition, according to which it denotes the penalties of distress that accrue to the godless as Yahweh visits his judgment on the nations (Mic 2:3–4). The other side is the hope that the miseries endured by the righteous people of God, known as the poor in, e.g., Ps 38:8 (= 37:7 LXX where the Greek reads ἐταλαιπώρησα καὶ κατεκάμφθην ἕως τέλους, "I am distressed and crushed utterly"), will soon come to an end in the eschatological reversal that God will bring about: cf. Ps 12:5 (= 11:6 LXX "'Because of the misery of the poor . . . I will now arise,' says Yahweh"). This vindication of the poor of Yahweh, based on the theme of the "piety of the poor" (*Armenfrömmigkeit*, Mussner, 198), provides the backdrop against which James' fulmination against the impious rich is to be heard.

(2) The precise terms for the idea of the "day of Yahweh" are given in v 3: "for the last days," and v 5: ἐν ἡμέρα σφαγῆς, "for the day of slaughter." The exact meaning of the latter phrase is in dispute (see *Comment*), but the best proposal is to see the term as drawn from Jer 12:3b: "Set them apart for the day of slaughter" (הָרֵגָה יוֹם, *lǝyôm hǎrēgāh*: LXX εἰς ἡμέραν σφαγῆς αὐτῶν; cf. Jer 32 [25]:34 LXX). This prophetic oracle is directed against the wicked in a way similar to Ps 37 (36 LXX) where the "day" of the unrighteous oppressor is seen to be coming and is greeted with anticipation of judgment (37:13 LXX, ὅτι ἥξει ἡ ἡμέρα αὐτοῦ), a common prophetic and apocalyptic theme of *dies irae* (Isa 34:6; Jer 25:34; Ezek 21:15; *1 Enoch* 94.7–9; 97.8–10; 99.15; *Jub.* 36.9–11; cf. P. Volz, *Die Eschatologie der jüdischen Gemeinde im NT Zeitalter* [Mohr: Tübingen, 1934] 163–65).

The literary features of this pericope are richly varied. The author's argument presses into service a number of standard idioms for the pride that calls out to be rebuked and judged (4:6). The chief complaint is that the possessive spirit (linked with—but not identified with—the entrepreneurial ambitions of 4:13–17, it may be) has led to all manner of social injustice and callous behavior.

(a) The hoarding of wealth—as understood in the ancient Mediterranean-Levant world in terms of the items of grain, garments, and gold (Mayor, 149; Laws, 198)—has brought its own inevitable nemesis. Food has gone bad; clothes have become riddled with moth-holes; and the much vaunted treasure of gold has been tarnished and has lost its sheen. James uses a paradoxical verb, "to rust" (κατιοῦν, a NT *hapax legomenon*), for, strictly speaking, gold does not rust or corrode; but the point made is a general one, namely, "even the most permanent earthly treasure has no lasting value" (Ropes, 285). So it is a senseless practice to invest one's hope in objects that are mundane and transient (cf. Matt 6:19–24, as noted by Riesenfeld, "Von Schätzesammeln," 54–55, though there is no exact verbal parallel here). If James' real target is the folly of idolatry (which is one side to covetousness: see 4:4–10; cf. Luke 12:15; Col 3:5), then his stance is that of the prophet in Isa 44:9–20, and he looks forward to the final day of reckoning (v 3b). Mussner (194) has the suggestive point to make that the folly of hoarding is only one item of James' condemnation of the rich. The rusting of the gold testifies to the social injustice the rich have committed. Instead of using their wealth to aid the poor in time of need, the rich agriculturists have amassed their possessions only to see them destroyed. Ropes (285) dismisses this idea as far-fetched, but such dismissal is made needlessly, if at the core of the prophetic denunciation is the warning against covetousness and ostentation, as Luke 16:19–31 may point to (see earlier). It is the social evil of *avaritia*, against which Seneca protested, seen in the desire to add "estate to estate, evicting a neighbor either by buying him out or by wronging him (*vel iniuria*)" (*Ep.* 90.39). What was true in Italy was equally a feature throughout the Empire in the first century, with the result that rural wealth became concentrated in the hands of a few plutocrats who exerted economic pressure against the poor. The peasant poor were victimized and pressed down socially by this rapacity (MacMullen, *Roman Social Relations*, 6–14, 25–27; Grant, *The Economic Background*, 66; Jeremias, *Jerusalem*, 92).

Legal redress in the courts was not possible when the judges themselves were the big landowners who "had a reputation for oppressive and venal verdicts" (MacMullen, *Roman Social Relations*, 39–40). In Syro-Palestine the Sadducees took the major role in land ownership. Around them "a small knot of moneyed owners and rack-renters" gathered (Rendall, *The Epistle of St. James and Judaic Christianity*, 32), and the Sadducees thereby formed a power base at crucial tension with the dispossessed poor (Josephus, *Ant.* 13.296–98, cited by Maynard-Reid, 87: the text reads: "the Sadducees have the confidence of the wealthy but no following among the populace").

There were other economic factors, discussed in Kreissig, "Die landwirtschaftliche Situation," 241–47, that militated against the rural, independent farmer. For instance, (1) as farming and commerce were linked, the landowners could bring their food directly to market and dominate the price structure with volume production; (2) lack of capital prevented the small farmer from expanding his holding and upgrading his equipment; (3) in time of drought and famine, the large landowner had more resources on which to call and could hoard his produce or, when market forces operated to his advantage, sell at inflated prices. By contrast, the small farmer had no reserves and was driven either to sell out to the magnate or to take a loan at high interest rates, and with the threat of expropriation for the default of payment a real one; and (4) the tendency was for the rural independent to be squeezed out of business and to become a wage earner or tenant farmer or worker in the employ of his feudal master. Maynard-Reid (88) argues that "this is the kind of situation to which James is making reference." Absentee landlords and *latifundia* worked by dependent farmhands assumed a significant position, as may be illustrated from the parables of Jesus (e.g., Matt 20:1–16; Mark 12:1–12 par.) and the Zenon papyri.

(b) The flow of the argument leads on to a statement about a more serious social evil. The rich people have become so captivated by their greed that they are blind to honest obligations. Like the prophets of Israel (Isaiah, Micah, Amos) James is bitter in his reproach of the economic injustice that results from a withholding of wages and a denial to workers of the just reward of their labor (see Lev 19:13; Deut 24:14–15; Jer 22:13; Mal 3:5; Sir 29:9–10; 34:21–22; Tob 4:14; *1 Enoch* 96.5; *m. B. Meṣ.* 9:11–12; *b. B. Meṣ.* 111a, cited in Maynard-Reid, *Poverty,* 85, for this indictment of unjust practices of employers and landowners who refuse to provide adequately in daily wages). The laws requiring the prompt and accurate payment of wages in Palestine are illustrated in the Gospels (Matt 20:1–16) and the Jewish sources.

(c) A final attack of James' invective is directed to his addressees' indulgence and reveling in luxury (v 5). Their selfishness and self-pleasing to the point of excess and gluttony are set in implied contrast to the poor who were dependent on a regular wage for daily food and whose piety (2:5) was expressed in a faith in God that could only await his vindication in due time (4:10). Hence the parenetic call to patience which follows and which, at least by inference, returns to the earlier call to single-minded devotion to God. The opposite is the "divided person" (1:7, 8; 4:8), who is basically an idolator (see 4:4–10). By contrast, the person whose life is oriented to God, according to *T. Iss.* 4.2, "does not covet gold, is not jealous of his neighbours, makes no plans for long life, but waits on the will of God alone" (de Jonge's tr. in H. F. D. Sparks's *The Apocryphal Old Testament* [Oxford: Clarendon, 1984]).

Comment

1 Ἄγε νῦν οἱ πλούσιοι, "Attend to this, you rich people." The opening apostrophe of this paragraph recalls 4:13 and reflects the vernacular form of direct address. This stylistic connection between 4:13–17 and 5:1–6, as well as the similar "atmosphere" (Mussner, 193) and feel in both sections, makes it just possible that "those who say" of 4:13 are to be equated the rich of 5:1. But this is not the case. While 4:13–17 contains the exhortation for the (professedly Christian) merchants to realize the place pride holds in their lives (and in essence is a call to repentance), 5:1–6 simply alerts the rich to the fate that awaits them. There is no call for the rich to change their ways so as to escape the judgment of God. Instead, a prophetic tone of condemnation of the wicked is present.

The stern tone introduced by ἄγε νῦν is softened by the NEB, which renders, "Next a word to you." But no such friendly address is implied in what follows (Maynard-Reid, *Poverty,* 70). κλαύσατε ὀλολύζοντες ἐπὶ ταῖς ταλαιπωρίαις ὑμῶν ταῖς ἐπερχομέναις, "Weep and howl in view of the miseries that are coming your way." The use of κλαίειν ("to wail"; "the proper response to disaster," so Davids, 175) and ὀλολύζειν ("to howl"; a word whose sound is associated with its meaning, as in English) is reminiscent of the prophets' idiom and their cry against the heathen nations. James calls on the rich to wail (Lam 1:1–2; Isa 15:2–3, 5; Jer 9:1; 13:17) and howl (twenty-one times in LXX, all in the OT prophets; a *hapax legomenon* in the NT), for they are doomed (see Amos 8:3; Isa 13:6; 14:31; Jer 31:20, 31; Ezek 21:12; Hos 7:14; cf. Heidland, *TDNT* 5:173–74). Some of these prophetic oracles combine the call to repentance with a reminder of the impending "Day of Yahweh," e.g., Isa 13:6: ὀλολύζετε ἐγγὺς γὰρ ἡ ἡμέρα κυρίου; Amos 8:3, 9: καὶ ἔσται ἐν ἐκείνῃ τῇ ἡμέρᾳ λέγει κύριος ὁ θεός . . . .

The reason for their remorse is traced to the misery (ταλαιπωρία, a prophetic term; it is found elsewhere in the NT only in Rom 3:16) that is coming upon them. The condemnation of the rich is yet another prophetic theme (Amos 6:1–9), which is the reverse side of the poverty-piety theme of Jewish (*1 Enoch* chaps. 94–105: see *Introduction*, pp. lxxxiv–lxxxvi) and Christian thought (Luke 6:20–25; cf. Dibelius 39–45; Mussner, 76–84; and Davids, 41–47; Moo, 53–55). While the term "the rich" is sometimes a synonym for "the unrighteous" (Prov 10:15–16; 14:20), James (in contrast to other NT writers) comes near to joining the rich magnates and their wealth and threatening a dire penalty (see 1:9–11). To be sure, the problem is the misuse of the wealth. Jesus cautioned concerning the difficulty of the rich entering the kingdom of God (Matt 19:23) but did not rule out completely the possibility that a rich person could attain eternal life, even if he did warn of the consequences of a trust in riches. The Pauline pastor's admonition is similar (1 Tim 6:9–10, 17–19). Yet James does not indict all the rich of the world, if, in fact, some wealthy persons are part of the church to which he writes (cf. 1:10 and Moo's comments, 67–69). The idea behind ὑμῶν ταῖς ἐπερχομέναις ("coming upon you") is eschatological in nature, although James is not clear here as to whether he understood such punishment of the godless to be a possibility in this life or to be postponed to the day of judgment (see *Form/ Structure/Setting*).

A point of interest is why (if the rich are outsiders) James decided to include the indictment of the rich (5:1–6) in a letter that is to be read only to church members. Adamson (184) relates the structure of vv 1–11 to that of Ps 58, where the unrighteous are condemned (58:1–9), while the righteous are urged to remain confident that God will one day vindicate them (58:10–11). James similarly informs his readers that judgment is soon to fall (5:1–6) upon the rich farmers (5:4) and that in contrast the poor will be rewarded and vindicated (5:7–11). He has taken up the OT theme of the nexus between judgment/vindication and applied it to the situation at hand. He will now proceed to list his charges against the ungodly rich who oppress the poor (see the discussion of this topic in *Form/Structure/Setting*).

2–3a ὁ πλοῦτος ὑμῶν σέσηπεν καὶ τὰ ἱμάτια ὑμῶν σητόβρωτα γέγονεν, ὁ χρυσὸς ὑμῶν καὶ ὁ ἄργυρος κατίωται καὶ ὁ ἰὸς αὐτῶν εἰς μαρτύριον ὑμῖν ἔσται καὶ φάγεται τὰς σάρκας ὑμῶν ὡς πῦρ, "Your wealth has become rotten, your clothes moth-eaten, your gold and silver tarnished; and their corrosion will be evidence against you, and will devour your flesh like fire." James levels the first of four charges (see vv 4, 5, 6) against the rich: their worldly riches are worthless. The use of wealth (πλοῦτος), garments (ἱμάτια), and gold and silver (χρυσὸς καὶ ἄργυρος) suggests the general picture of worldly goods in the ancient world. The first noun (πλοῦτος) may specifically mean food (Adamson, 184), though it may simply refer to the general matter of wealth (v 1), with the reference to clothes and precious metals as an explanation of the wealth in mind. But the main point of James' discussion here is the temporal nature of such goods. (1) The food (or wealth in general) is rotten (σέσηπεν, perfect tense of σήπειν, "to cause to rot," a *hapax legomenon* in the NT; cf. Sir 14:19); (2) the garment is moth-eaten (σητόβρωτα, taken with γέγονεν, perfect tense, is a *hapax legomenon* in the NT; see Job 13:28 LXX and for the roots cf. Sir 42:13: "out of clothes comes the moth," NEB; cf. Isa 50:9; 51:8); (3) the transitory nature of gold and silver is depicted by James' description of their rusting (κατίωται, perfect tense; another *hapax legomenon;* cf. Sir 12:11, LXX; "as sure as metal rusts," 12:10, NEB). This last point is proverbial rather than actual, for these precious metals do not rust. As an example of this manner of speech used of money rusting, see Sir 29:10; Matt 6:20. But all three images—rotting food or riches, moth-eaten garments, rusting gold and silver— depict the temporary and useless nature of worldly goods.

The use of the three verbs in the perfect tense can be interpreted as a "prophetic anticipation" (Adamson, 185) rather than something that has already taken place. To the prophet's eye the reality is as good as though it had already happened (Mussner, 194, citing as illustration Isa 60:1). Ropes points out that the shift to the future tense with ἔσται ("will be") and φάγεται ("will consume") undercuts the position that literal decay had already set in (284–85). Moo (161–62) notes this argument of Ropes and suggests that if we take 5:2–3a figuratively, then the "decay" of worldly goods only emphasizes the "present worthless state" of the wealth of the rich people. But Moo qualifies his own position by suggesting that it could be that at least some food and garments have actually started to decay as a result of disuse. That is, the rich hoard their wealth, and rather than help the needy they allow such goods to rot.

Moo's last point is not without merit in the light of 5:3b (see below). The rust (ἰός) of the precious metals stands as a witness (εἰς μαρτύριον, "as evidence against"; contra Cantinat, 223) in opposition to the rich. The rust will not only tarnish the gold and silver but will consume the flesh of the rich as fire consumes its fuel. This terrible picture conveys the image of the last judgment as (ὡς; a simile; so Adamson, 185) fire (πῦρ) consumes the flesh (σάρξ, i.e., the person; so Davids, 176–77; see Judg 16:17). In short, the wealth of the ungodly rich stands as a witness to accuse them (ὑμῖν is to be classed as *dat. incommodi*, i.e. of disadvantage!). As a result they will receive punishment in the fires of judgment (Matt 25:41; 2 Pet 3:7; Jude 23; Rev 11:5; 20:9), akin to Gehenna (3:6). On the rabbinic teaching of a fiery punishment for the godless, see Str-B, 4:866–67, based on the prophets' warnings (Isa 30:27, ἡ ὀργὴ τοῦ θυμοῦ ὡς πῦρ ἔδεται; 10:16–17; Amos 5:6; Ezek 15:7; cf. Ps 20:10 [21:9]; 1QH 3:29–31).

The nearest parallel, however, is Ezekiel 7:19: "They cast their silver into the streets, and their gold like an unclean thing; their silver and gold are not able to deliver them in the day of the wrath of the Lord; they cannot satisfy their hunger or fill their stomachs with it. For it was the stumbling block of their iniquity."

3b ἐθησαυρίσατε ἐν ἐσχάταις ἡμέραις, "You have amassed wealth for the last days." The point at issue is whether ἐν ("for") means that the last days are already here or that James is referring to a future day of judgment. In line with other NT writers and in the light of his use of ἐν (lit., "in") it appears that James reflects the belief that the last days have already begun to dawn upon the world (Acts 2:17; 2 Tim 3:1; Heb 1:2; 2 Pet 3:3; 1 John 2:18; Jude 18). Thus, the rich are laying up treasure in the last days, which are imminent to the point of arrival. But James may be offering a specimen of irony here (Davids, 127; "semi-irony," Moo, 162). The treasure in mind is not their vaunted riches but the misery that awaits them. While they think that the wealth accumulated is held as a perpetual possession, they are vulnerable to severe judgment because not only is such wealth temporary, but it is the witness whose testimony condemns the rich. Instead of sharing their wealth with the needy (a response already spoken of as a sign of a saving faith in 2:14–16) they hoard it; what makes this doubly tragic is that they do so in the last days and thus underline the folly of their actions. While the last days represent the period before the Parousia of the Lord (5:8) to vindicate his own, this same period highlights the nearness of judgment for those who oppose the Lord and his "poor." James is not saying that he knows the exact day of judgment; rather, he is implying that the day may come at any time. Thus, with such an ominous event on the horizon, the misuse of wealth is taking place as a prelude to the coming of the Lord.

4 ἰδοὺ ὁ μισθὸς τῶν ἐργατῶν τῶν ἀμησάντων τὰς χώρας ὑμῶν ὁ ἀφυστερημένος ἀφ᾽ ὑμῶν κράζει, καὶ αἱ βοαὶ τῶν θερισάντων εἰς τὰ ὦτα κυρίου σαβαὼθ εἰσεληλύθασιν, "See how the wages of the workers who have reaped your fields, which have been kept back by you, are shouting aloud. The cries of the harvesters have reached the ears of the Almighty Lord." In v 4 James levels a more specific charge: wages have been withheld from laborers who put in an honest day's work. What James does in this verse is to identify (at least some of) the rich as farmers and to expand on the reason they have so much wealth in the first place. The latter point is made in the charge that the wealthy farmers have withheld pay due to the laborers. ἰδού, "see how" (lit. "behold") is often employed by James to alert the reader to important images or examples to follow (3:4–5; 5:4, 7, 9, 11; Davids, 177). The example James uses in our present verse is that of laborers (οἱ ἐργάται, lit. "workmen," more particularly farm workers). These workers (who had mowed [ἀμᾶν, "to reap"; a *hapax legomenon*] the fields [χῶραι; possibly suggesting rural as opposed to city or town]) may formerly have been small landowners who had had their farms swallowed up by the elite, represented by a small but powerful class of large landowners (see *Form/Structure/Setting*).

But James is not presenting a situation that is devoid of hope. Though he will wait until v 7 to make plain specifically the vindication of the poor, he anticipates the good news by relating to his readers that their misery has not gone unnoticed. The wages (μισθός) themselves cry out—a verb used for dramatic effect—against the rich farmer and on behalf of the poor laborer. Though there was no legal recourse to avenge the crime committed against the poor (see Lev 19:13; Deut 24:14–15; Job 31:38–40; Jer 22:13; Mal 3:5; Tob 4:14: "pay your workmen their wages the same day; do not make any man wait for his money" [NEB]), there was hope held out to them. The cries (βοαί, a NT *hapax legomenon*) of the penniless workers (in this case harvesters, οἱ θερίσαντες, thus underlining the fact that if the harvest was completed then the rich farmers had ample supply from which to pay the workers) have reached the ears (anthropomorphic picture of God) of the Lord of Hosts. The perfect tense of the last verb, εἰσέρχεσθαι suggests two things: (i) this cry has already been heard by God and (ii) judgment on the rich has already started; one may recall the perfect tenses of vv 2–3.

The two "cries" unmistakably condemn the rich, for the cry of the unpaid wage is a reminder that the wealthy people hoard their goods and so reserve to themselves not only what could be given to the poor but what is actually due the poor. Their gold and silver are beset by corrosion as a condign penalty for their greed and exploitation. Moreover, the cry of the harvesters reflects the suffering inflicted on them by their inhumane employer. This cry may be the combination of the pain related to hunger and the desire that God should act to vindicate his children (Gen 4:10; 18:20; 19:13; Exod 2:23; 1 Sam 9:16; Ps 12:5; Sir 21:5; 34:25–26; 35:21; Luke 18:17; Rev 6:9–10; *1 Enoch* 47.1; 97.5; of special interest is *1 Enoch* 22:5–9, based on Gen 4:1–10). The phrase "Almighty Lord" (κύριος σαβαώθ, lit., "Lord of Hosts," representing the Hebrew יְהוָה צְבָאוֹת, *Yhwh ṣᵉbāʾôt*; cf. LXX παντοκράτωρ) "combines majesty and transcendence" (Adamson, 186; Laws, 202–3) and describes the "Almighty One" as he who hears the pleas of the poor (Isa 5:9: ἠκούσθη γὰρ εἰς τὰ ὦτα κυρίου σαβαώθ ταῦτα) and comes to their rescue (Pss 17:1–6; 18:6; 31:2; Luke 18:17; Rev 6:10; *Herm. Vis.* 3.9.6; see Mitton, 180), especially those oppressed by owners of large estates (Isa 5:7–9; Mark 12:40; Luke 20:47).

James' extensive use of traditional material that sets the rich against the poor and God against the rich has led some to conclude that our author may not actually be depicting a real situation in James' church (Davids, 178). But a feasible historical context seems indicated (see earlier, pp. 174–75) and the poor-pious motif (which includes oppression of the poor at the hands of the rich) is simply too dominant in the entire letter to suggest otherwise than that James is citing actual events (Moo, 104; and especially Maynard-Reid, *Poverty*, passim, who argues trenchantly against any proposal to soften or spiritualize James' invective against the rich).

5 ἐτρυφήσατε ἐπὶ τῆς γῆς καὶ ἐσπαταλήσατε, "You have lived off the land in luxury and self-indulgence." A third accusation comes from James: the rich live in luxury and pleasure. Such ostentatious living in itself is not branded as evil, but the context of 5:5 strongly hints that James' description is meant to convey that such abundance is accompanied by an uncaring attitude for others. ἐτρυφήσατε (from τρυφᾶν, lit., "to break down," "live in luxury"; a NT *hapax legomenon*; cf. Sir 14:4; Isa 47:8; Neh 9:25; cf. H. D. Betz, *Lukian von Samosata und das Neues Testament*, 198 n.4) is qualified by the words "off the land" (ἐπὶ τῆς γῆς, lit., "on the earth"), which implies both the uninterrupted constancy of their present prosperity and the temporality of earthly riches (Mussner, 196, compares the indictment implicit in Luke 16:19, "the rich man enjoyed his good fortune *daily*, καθ' ἡμέραν, without a break in his prosperity and without a thought of the poor around him"). The expression may also

highlight the contrast that awaits the rich, namely, the torment and misery
that are being stored up for them (5:3b). This latter thought also recalls the
parable of Dives and poor Lazarus (Luke 16:19–31). The center of Jesus'
story is v 25, where Abraham tells the rich man: "Son, remember that you
in your lifetime received your good things and Lazarus in like manner evil
things; but now he is comforted here and you are in anguish." In contrast
to those of 4:13–17 who do the wrong thing, the rich of 5:1–6 fail to do
anything at all! This contrast is supported by ἐσπαταλήσατε (from σπαταλᾶν,
"to be self-indulgent"; only here and 1 Tim 5:6 in the NT; cf. Ezek 16:49;
Sir 21:15; 27:13; "their laughter is wantonly [ἐν σπατάλῃ] sinful"; *Herm. Man.*
6.1.6; 6.2.6; *Barn.* 10.3; see Hort, 107–9; Adamson, 187 n.23).

That James sees such wanton living as an affront to God and humanity is
spelled out in v 5b: ἐθρέψατε τὰς καρδίας ὑμῶν ἐν ἡμέρᾳ σφαγῆς, "You have
gorged yourselves in the day of slaughter." The meaning behind "nourishing"
or "gorging your hearts" is that of indulging one's passion or lusts (so Davids,
178; Isa 6:10; Ps 104:15; Mark 7:21; Luke 21:34). The wealth of the rich
becomes like a wasting disease. In a sense, they have "fattened themselves
up," but not for the end they desire. They are fattened for (see below) "the
slaughter," the time when God will enact the Day of Judgment.

The words ἐν ἡμέρᾳ σφαγῆς are problematic because the certain meaning
of the text is unclear (see *Note* b and *Form/Structure/Setting*). Some want to
take the preposition ἐν as equivalent to εἰς (Chaine, 118). This has the effect
of placing "in the days of slaughter" in the future, as though the writer had
the day of reckoning in prospect. This goes against our understanding of
the "last days" (5:3). Others have a setting in the past when the poor die
(Dibelius, 239). But this second interpretation overlooks the eschatological
tension of the context. The phrase never appears exactly in the LXX (but
see the near equivalent in Jer 12:3). The verse in Jeremiah is part of a long
tradition depicting God's judgment day as the time when God takes action
against his "enemies" (see Davids, 178–79, and citations there). Imagery of
the "slaughter" of the rich is found in *1 Enoch* (94.7–9; cf. 96.8; 97.8–10;
99.15) and in the Dead Sea Scrolls (1QH 15.17–18; cf. 1QS 10.19; 1QM
1.9–12; 13.14; CD 19.15, 19). There can be little doubt that the words "the
day of slaughter" are meant to speak of the eschatological day of judgment
(so Mussner, 197–98; Ropes, 290; Laws, 203–4; Cantinat, 228; Davids, 179;
Moo, 165–66). In a sense, then, for James that "day" has already begun to
dawn. The last days were inaugurated with Jesus' coming. His death-resur-
rection was the harbinger of the last times of mercy and judgment. Thus,
the rich are being fattened "for" (or the more exact preposition is "in") the
day of slaughter. Though the actual event of catastrophic judgment is yet
to begin, for this letter the death-knell of the rich has already sounded. The
wealthy indulge themselves and ignore the poor as if the day of slaughter
(that "great judgment day," Mussner, 197) were not only far away but did
not exist at all! (Feuillet's claim ["Le sens"] that the judgment in mind is not
the final event at the end of history but the fall of Jerusalem in A.D. 70 has
not been widely accepted [so Moo, 166 n.l], though this possibility is not to
be totally dismissed and has considerable support, both ancient and modern,

listed in Mussner, 147 n.5, since in the prophetic perspective there are cases of such double vision.)

6 κατεδικάσατε, ἐφονεύσατε τὸν δίκαιον, οὐκ ἀντιτάσσεται ὑμῖν, "You have condemned and killed the just man; he was not resisting you." James levels the fourth and final charge of this section (vv 1–6) at the rich: they condemn and kill the just man. The accusation list here reaches its high point (Mussner, 198). There seems little to support the notion that φονεύειν simply means a symbolic killing of the poor person, as in the withholding of wages. The term καταδικάζειν ("to condemn") is rightly understood as forensic in nature (Schrenk, *TDNT* 3:621–22) and thus we have the picture of the rich (probably abusing the legal system, in contrast to the poor who cannot use the system at all) condemning the poor, who in turn is murdered. This "judicial murder" highlights and accentuates the role of the underdog played by the poor (see Davids, 179, and citations there). The most likely setting is that of the pious poor in Israel who have no defender and are at the mercy of cruel oppressors. Cf. Ps 36 [37]:14, 32, 35a; Wisd Sol 2:20 (θανάτῳ ἀσχήμονι καταδικάσωμεν αὐτόν = τὸν δίκαιον); Prov 1:11; Amos 5:12; Ps 10:8–10 (9:29–31 LXX); *1 Enoch* 96.5; 99.15; 103.15; 1QH 2.21; 5.17. See *Introduction,* lxxxiv–lxxxvi.

The second clause of this verse is called into question because of the uncertainty surrounding the correct punctuation (see *Note* c). Though Ropes (292) considers the indicative an anticlimax, Adamson, 188 (rightly), counters that the indicative (instead of the interrogative) is quite acceptable. The poor do not resist because they *cannot.* They are helpless. If they cannot even hold their own when it comes to securing the wages due to them, then it should come as no surprise that they are victims to the point of having their blood shed. The concluding remarks present the voice of the one killed crying out against the rich (cf. Heb 11:4). His passive demeanor is thus a silent witness similar to the thought of 5:4. True, the novel suggestion of Schökel, "James 5,2," gives another slant to this verse. He calls attention to 4:6 with its reference to "God's opposing [ἀντιτάσσεται] the proud" and makes the point that 4:6 and 5:6 are connected by an *inclusio.* In this way he accounts for the lack of an explicit subject in 5:6, which is meant to have the noun ὁ θεός understood by transference from 4:6. So the line of development runs: God opposes the arrogant, you behave arrogantly, should he not oppose you? ἀντιτάσσεται is thus a rhetorical question looking back to 4:6 and gives a better overall sense to emphasize the positive interest of God in vindicating the oppressed. But, as in the *Notes,* on balance, the traditional way of translating with an indicative seems preferred. See Maynard-Reid, *Poverty,* 94–95.

The exact identity of the "just one" (ὁ δίκαιος) remains uncertain. Some see Jesus as the one referred to in this title (as in Acts 3:14; 7:52; 22:14; 1 Pet 3:18; 1 John 2:1, 29; 3:7; cf. Feuillet, "Le sens") or even James himself (Dibelius, 240 n. 58; see below). But there seems no evidence to suggest that the rich killed Jesus except perhaps in the sense that it was the rich Sadducean hierarchy that implacably opposed him and brought about the death sentence on Good Friday. In another way Jesus embodied in his person the essential characteristics of Israel's "righteous one(s)" and paid the price in terms of a martyr's death for the divine cause in a wicked world (cf. Isa

53:7; Wisd Sol 2:18–20). ὁ δίκαιος could then be seen as a "collective" singular, and is explained as analogous to the way that one person often functions in a representative capacity in Israelite thought. In Ps 36 [37] the singular ὁ δίκαιος and the plural are interchangeably found (e.g., 37:12, 17; cf. Isa 3:10; 57:1; *Pss. Sol.* 3.5–16; 1QH 15.15–17 for other illustrations of this interchange of persons. At Qumran [in 4QpPs 37 2:13 ff.] the righteous one of Ps 37:12 becomes a plural entity in reference to the "doers of the law," as Mussner notes, 198 n.5). See *Introduction,* xciii–xcviii.

Strictly, then, the term in the singular is a collective (generic) term, describing the kind of person killed by the rich (cf. 2:6; BDF § 139; Moo, 166; Adamson, 189; Davids, 180). The poor person, considered righteous or just, is unable to resist the rich oppressors and subsequently is murdered. Thus James brings his fierce invective (5:1–6) "to an end on a note of majestic pathos" (Tasker, 116).

This last-mentioned understanding may with some justification be extended to apply to James as the titular head of a righteous community that was under attack. The principle of "the one representing and embodying the many" may be employed to explain how James' suffering community could well have seen their own futures mirrored in the fate that befell their leader, martyred in A.D. 62. The present tense of ἀντιτάσσεται would be explained as a historic present, designed to bring vividly to mind the death of the saint and emphasize the enormity of the crime committed by his murderers. It cannot be coincidental that ὁ δίκαιος became the standard designation by which James was known to posterity; and we may offer the submission that 5:6 is a tribute paid to the historical James whose martyrdom is recalled by his followers who in turn look on themselves as part of the afflicted and righteous remnant. See further in the *Introduction.*

Explanation

The note that reverberates through this section is one of prophetic denunciation and reproof against a background of divine retribution. The writer has already embarked on his tirade of warning against the people whom he regards as godless and foolish (4:6–17). In setting before his readers the perils to which they are exposed he has his sights trained on the sins of pride (vv 6–10, 16) and the defamation of fellow Christians (vv 11–12). He turns next to confront the merchant classes whose cardinal mistake is that of presumption and pretended mastery over the uncertainties of life (vv 13–17).

At 5:1–6 a new set of persons is addressed. They are the rich agriculturalists whose grievous sin lies not in what they do to themselves but in how their misconduct affects others. This is a distinct change of tack on the author's part, however much the two sections (4:13–17; 5:1–6) may share a common theme of the denunciation of folly. The essence of what he finds at fault with the men of 5:1–6 is their possessive and selfish outlook regarding material goods and gains, the *amor sceleratus habendi,* "the accursed love of getting," noted by Latin moralists. Paul has an analysis of "covetousness" (*pleonexia*) that may well serve as a rubric under which James' indictments are to be placed. *Pleonexia*, best rendered "acquisitiveness," is, Paul remarks, tantamount to idolatry (Col 3:5). It is a disposition that turns our possessions into objects of false worship and believes that wealth is an end in itself, to be sought and treasured as the *summum bonum* of life. A person may be outwardly religious (like the claimant in 1:26; 2:16), yet if the desire for material gain becomes the dominant and driving force in life, all pretensions are shown up as hollow, since the worship of God and the seeking of his kingdom carry an exclusive demand. "You cannot serve God and Money" (Matt 6:24, NEB).

So far James' exposure of the rich farmers' greed falls into line with the teaching of Jesus (Matt 6:19–34; Luke 12:13–34) and the apostle Paul and his school (1 Tim 6:6–10, 17–19). All these teachers warn against placing confidence in one's earthly goods, which are by definition perishable and transient. They expose the hidden danger of the discontented, lustful spirit that is always seeking for more, the *libido inexplebilis* of which Cicero wrote and which dramatists like Shakespeare have used to telling effect:

> The cloyed will—
> That satiate yet unsatisfied desire,
> That tub both full and running.
> (*Cymbeline*, I.6)

But merely to brand the desire for riches as a mark of insatiableness, while serious in all conscience, is for James only the beginning. He is far more concerned with the social effects of this craving and brings out as perhaps no other NT writer the way that the rich hurt not only themselves but other people. He takes his stand with the weak and the poor, and sees the sad train of what possessiveness leads to through their eyes. Moreover, as on other occasions in the letter he places God on the side of the poor. He interprets social crimes as offenses that contravene the divine law and so entail divine retribution. This is the logical outworking of the justice of God, which may be regarded as the leitmotif of the entire epistle. To see the way the writer moves from an exposé of human failing and forgetfulness regarding the transitory character of wealth to an attack on a different level, we should observe the four charges he brings:

1. The *folly of hoarding* goods that are by nature subject to the ravages of decay and dissolution is vividly shown in vv 1–3. Food items such as grain become stale and unusable; garments are attacked by moths; gold is blighted by rust. The point of this descriptive passage is an obvious one: use your possessions or they get wasted. Cf. Matt 25:25–30; Luke 19:20–27 for the same general application.

2. Even more culpable is the *crime of dishonesty* (in v 4). The rich landowners have become so captivated by their wealth that they do not pay their legal and honest obligations. James stirs the social conscience by denouncing the mock piety of those who make a pretense of "calling upon God" in worship, when the only voice that reaches to heaven is the cry of the oppressed workers who have been cheated out of their daily wages.

In Carlos Fuentes's Mexican novel, *The Good Conscience*, a line from Kierkegaard is used to the same effect as the point in James' denunciation of a false religiosity: The Christian speaks with God; the bourgeois speaks of God. And only the first voice is heard.

3. The *snare of indulgence*, stated in v 5, is a powerful reminder that the rich who are bent on selfish greed with no care for the poor do so because their aim in life is self-pleasing to the point of excess and gluttony.

Not surprisingly, the moral theology of the church has identified gluttony as one of the seven deadly sins. Richard Holloway (*Seven to Flee, Seven to Follow* [London: Mowbray, 1986] 33–35) has called attention to this sin as a classic case of a good that has become disordered and misdirected:

> At the root of the misuse of those instincts [which are God-given, i.e., the desire to survive by ingesting food] is what philosophers call the hedonistic fallacy. This comes from the Greek word *hedone,* pleasure. It has been observed that if we pursue pleasure we fail to get it. Pleasure is a by-product of many activities. . . . The problem arises because of the mysterious tendency in our nature: we try to separate the pleasure from the act that gives it and go after it for its own sake. Unfortunately, it does not work for long . . . because the pursuit of pleasure for its own sake is always ultimately unsatisfying . . . and (becomes) addictive.

To this analysis may be added two extra factors. (a) On the road to addiction the pursuit of the pleasure principle brings with it all manner of physical, medical, and psychological problems, as Karl Menninger has shown in his *Whatever Became of Sin?* ([New York: Hawthorn Books, 1978] 164–66) in which he identified obesity, diabetes, and nephritis as the commonest results of the indulgent appetite. The day of (self-)slaughter is a present danger to the overeater.

(b) But, of course, our text uses the imagery of the "day" of reckoning in a different way again. James is looking ahead, in prophetic vein, to the Great Day of divine reckoning, and in the terrifying imagery of a time when God will "devour" his enemies he warns that the indolent rich—because they have turned away from God and used their wealth to selfish and ignoble ends—will be held accountable.

4. To the antisocial disgraces of hoarding, which betrays greed; dishonesty, which violates the elementary principles of a just society in which honest work demands fair pay; and indulgence, which finds the end of pleasure in personal, instinctual gratification, James adds the *crime of murder* (v 6). As part of the diagnosis that finds in some of his audience the "divided person" (1:8; 3:11, 12; 4:8) there is the sad event of resistance to the good when they are challenged by it. Here the good is embodied in "the righteous one" whose witness is not only refused but whose life is taken away by violent means, as 4:2 had anticipated. The enormity of such a display of terror and mayhem is seen in the martyrdom of one whose character was blameless; and we have suggested that James himself is mirrored in this allusion. His death in A.D. 62 at the hands of his compatriots only intensifies the horror of the crime, which is a tragic commentary on the evil endemic to our world, where, in contemporary history, the champions of righteousness, freedom, and peace often meet a violent death (from J. F. Kennedy and Martin Luther King, Jr., to Gandhi and Archbishop Romero of San Salvador).

4. Call to Patience   (5:7–11)

Bibliography

Bischoff, A. "τὸ τέλος κυρίου." *ZNW* 7 (1906) 274–79. **Björck, G.** "Quelques cas du ἐν διὰ δυοῖν dans le Nouveau Testament et ailleurs." *ConNT* 4 (1940) 1–4. **Carr, A.** "The Patience of Job (St James v 11)." *Exp* 8 ser. 6 (1913) 511–17. **Doty, W. G.** *Letters in Primitive Christianity.* Philadelphia: Fortress, 1973. **Feuillet, A.** "Le sens du mot Parousie dans l'évangile de Matthieu." In *The Background of the New Testament and Its Eschatology,* FS C. H. Dodd, ed. D. Daube and W. D. Davies. Cambridge: Cambridge UP, 1956. 261–80. **Fine, H. A.** "The Tradition of a Patient Job." *JBL* 74 (1955) 28–32. **Francis, F. O.** "The Form and Function of the Opening and Closing Paragraphs of James and 1 John." *ZNW* 61 (1970) 110–26. **Gelin, A.** *Les Pauvres de Yahvé.* Paris: Gabalda, 1953. **Gordon, R. P.** "καὶ τὸ τέλος κυρίου εἴδετε (Jas. 5.11)." *JTS* 26 (1975) 91–95. **Hadidian, D. Y.** "Palestinian Pictures in the Epistle of James." *ExpTim* 63 (1952) 227–28. **Hengel, M.** *Property and Riches in the Early Church.* Tr. J. Bowden. Philadelphia: Fortress, 1974. **Käsemann, E.** "Paul and Early Catholicism." *New Testament Questions of Today.* Tr. W. F. Bunge. London: SCM, 1969. Chap. xii. **Kilpatrick, G. D.** *Jesus in the Gospels and the Early Church.* Drawbridge Memorial Lecture. London: Christian Evidence Society, 1971. **Meyer, A.** *Das Rätsel des Jakobusbriefes.* BZNW 10. Giessen: Töpelmann, 1930. **Preuschen, E.** "Jac 5,11." *ZNW* 17 (1916) 79. **Rhoads, D. M.** *Israel in Revolution, 6–74 CE.* Philadelphia: Fortress, 1976. **Spitta, F.** "Das Testament Hiobs und das Neues Testament." *Zur Geschichte und Litteratur des Urchristentums,* III.2. Göttingen: Vandenhoeck und Ruprecht, 1907. 139–206. **Strobel, A.** *Untersuchungen zum eschatologischen Verzögerungsproblem.* NovTSup 2. Leiden: Brill, 1961. 255–59.

Translation

5:7 *Be patient then, brothers, until the Lord's coming. See how the farmer waits for the land to produce its choice crop and how patient he is for it until [the land] receives the early and late [rainfall].* [a] 8 *You too are to be patient and confirm your lives, since the Lord's coming is at hand.*

9 *Don't complain one of another, brothers; that leads to condemnation. Remember, the Judge is standing at the door!* 10 *As an example of patience amid adversity,* [b] *brothers, consider the prophets who spoke in the Lord's name.* [c] 11 *As you know, we reckon as blessed those who stand fast.* [d] *You have heard of Job's steadfastness, and you have seen* [e] *the purpose of the Lord [in his case], because the Lord is very compassionate and merciful.*

Notes

[a] The text is problematic. Most editors prefer the shorter reading of P⁷⁴ B vg cop^sa (both Alexandrian and Western text types), which have λάβῃ πρόϊμον καὶ ὄψιμον with the implied subject "the land" or "the fruit" (Ropes, 294; Davids, 183, but not in his translation; cf. Vouga, 135 n.8). The implied object is "the early and late" with ὑετόν, "rain," to be supplied *ad sensum.* ὑετόν is added by A K and the Byzantine authorities including syr to complete the sense. Alternatively ℵ* and some minuscules, with some syr witnesses, add καρπόν from the previous clause, thereby making the subject of λάβῃ the farmer who receives the fruit yielded by the rain showers. These additions (of ὑετόν and καρπόν) probably reflect an editor's ignorance of Palestinian climatic conditions and the OT idiom of Deut 11:14; Jer 5:24; Joel 2:23; Zech 10:1 LXX; cf. Jer 3:3; Hos 6:3. Hence the shorter reading is to be preferred (Metzger, 683; Ropes, 296, who notes the geographical influence on the various editors; Hadidian).

ᵇκακοπαθίας καὶ τῆς μακροθυμίας is best taken as an example of hendiadys (BDF § 442; so Björck, "Quelques cas," 1–4) which may explain why some editors (with ℵ) opt for the more hellenistic term καλοκἀγαθία, "nobility of character" (also found in Ign. *Eph.* 14:1). But the running together of "patience" and "adversity" is a typically Jacobean paradox (1:2–4).

ᶜἐν τῷ ὀνόματι κυρίου is an OT phrase, used of the prophets. A *lectio brevior* (in ℵ) has simply ἐν ὀνόματι, but this is an improbable reading, given the OT phrase.

ᵈReading with ℵ B A τοὺς ὑπομείναντας, "those who have stood firm," in place of a present participle τοὺς ὑπομένοντας in K L and some minuscules. "The meaning differs only by a shade" (Ropes, 298). But does it? See *Comment.*

ᵉReading εἴδετε, implying an acquaintance with the story of Job and read by ℵ B; ἴδετε in A B² L P Ψ is secondary, though Dibelius has questions (247–48). Davids, 188, gives good reasons for supporting εἴδετε, but the τέλος of the Lord which the readers are called to consider (lit., "you saw") is better understood as his beneficent purpose (so RSV; Mitton, 189–90) rather than "the result the Lord produced" (Davids; cf. NIV; Adamson, 193; Vouga who also takes the gen. as subjective, 137). A teleological meaning, however, is part of James' overall hortatory purpose; see 1:4; 3:2. On the other possibilities of meaning for τέλος see *Comment.*

Form / Structure / Setting

At 5:7 a new section is obviously introduced, a fact denoted by the editorial spacing in Nestle-Aland²⁶. Part of the reason behind this conclusion is the apparent lack of continuity between 5:6 and 5:7. There is an evident caesura at this point. But stronger reasons for seeing 5:7 as introducing not only a new section but a final epistolary segment are given by F. O. Francis, "Form and Function," 110–26 (see *Introduction,* pp. xcviii–cii). His chief supports are (i) the main "body" of the letter naturally terminates at 5:6; and (ii) the section 5:7–20 is best regarded as a letter-closing—parallel with some features of other NT and hellenistic letters, even though it lacks the conventional formulae (cf. Doty, *Letters,* 39–42) where three elements are present: (a) an eschatological injunction (5:7, 9); (b) the close of the present age as the background of the letter (5:8, 11, τέλος τοῦ κυρίου, according to one interpretation); and (c) a rehearsal and recapitulation of the themes of the letter. In particular these themes are listed as the call to patience and hope, a further warning against the misuse of the tongue in oath-taking, the emphasis on prayer and faith, and the summons to reclaim the errorist.

Francis maintains further that it is possible for a writer just to stop writing without a fixed formula of "farewell." Yet James does signal the close of his tract by the phrase πρὸ πάντων (lit., "above all," cf. 1 Pet 4:8; 3 John 2) in 5:12, which serves to indicate the imminent end of the letter, coupled with the topic of prayer (5:16–18) and parenesis (5:19–20). The upshot of this argument is that James does bear several marks of an epistolary composition, a designation that opposes the customary critical evaluation of this document as "no letter" (Windisch, 4, laconically: *kein Brief*). On some substantial grounds, then, the case for treating the document as epistolary and, in particular, for taking 5:7–20 as marking the letter's close seems well grounded.

On the other hand, it is difficult to overlook the connecting οὖν in v 7 (which, of course, may be editorial and inserted by the final redactor of the work to bind it together). Vouga, 133 n.2, therefore, makes the good point that 5:1–6 and 5:7–11 stand in parallelism, though he tends to downplay the change of addressee, a feature that separates the two sections. What may be taken as one notable item in joining the sections—in addition to the more obvious way in which, as in apocalyptic piety, the day of God will bring both judgment on the godless and deliverance to the poor who await Yahweh's interposition (Mussner, 200)—is the same negative attitude to active resistance to the church's persecutors. In 5:6 the advocacy of such resistance is noticeably absent, since the righteous leader has paid the price in his submissive martyrdom. Then, at 5:7–11 the theme is reintroduced as a warning not to miss the example he has bequeathed, and to those who were inclined to emulate the Zealots in violent opposition the warning is given, although couched in affirmative tones: "be patient . . . as an example (ὑπόδειγμα) of patience amid adversity."

The features that are familiar to the reader up to this point have been mentioned, chiefly the teaching on the need for ὑπομονή, "steadfastness," and the assurance that the character of God is displayed in his purpose, which those who persevere in their trials come to learn (v 11). A term that is closely linked with ὑπομένειν, "to stand firm," is μακροθυμεῖν, "to be patient," frequently repeated in our section (vv 7, 8, 10). Both Greek roots belong to the LXX vocabulary describing the patient endurance needed by the afflicted people of God in times of persecution. The terms (brought together in Col 1:11; for a discussion of the possible distinction between "patience" and "endurance" see N. Turner, *Christian Words*, 315–19) are both associated with the eschatological desire to await God's vindication of his cause as his people represent it in a hostile world. It may be that James' recourse to this call to patient endurance has its setting in a Zealot (or Zealot-like) impatience that sought to take up a crusade of violence (4:1–3) and so ensure the victory of God's cause by strife and revenge on the rich, as Josephus (*J.W.* 2.264 f.) noted at the time of the first Jewish War (Rhoads, *Israel in Revolution*, 80–82). If so, James counsels an alternative route, building on his earlier denunciation of human anger and strife (1:20; 3:17–18). This call is now the positive side to his earlier negative proscriptions. The thrice repeated ἀδελφοί (vv 7, 9, 10) suggests that James' pastoral role is directed to just such a situation in his community, where there was a resort to force of arms, which in turn bred a bitter spirit (5:9, reverting to 3:14; 4:5) and angry words of mutual recrimination (5:9, recalling 4:11–12). Both symptoms betray the sad fact that fraternal relations between "brothers" have been strained to the breaking point.

The other dimension is that they have forgotten that God is the judge (as in 4:11–12) whose coming (παρουσία) is close at hand—an eschatological motif for conduct which most commentators see here (Dibelius, Mussner, Cantinat, Vouga, Davids). That motif has two parts to it: (i) The coming of the Lord, based on the use of the *terminus technicus* in early Christianity, παρουσία, carries with it the call to "confirm your hearts" (στηρίξειν τὰς καρδίας ὑμῶν, v 8). The eschatological idiom is especially emphasized in 1 Thessalonians and Matthew, leading to the bold suggestion that it arose as theologoumenon in the church at Antioch, whether employed in the direction of eschatology or in the service of Christian ethics (Vouga, 134 n.6). (ii) The second part of the Parousia teaching is on its hortatory side, with a repeated summons to curbing impatience. The horticultural setting is explored as this characteristic of the farmer is praised (the similarity to Mark 4:26–29, on which see C. E. B. Cranfield, "Message of Hope: Mark 4:21–32," *Int* 9 [1955] 158–62, is clear); and then the Old Testament prophets and the worthy Job are introduced to enforce the point of ὑπομονή. The appropriateness in Job's case is seen in the term κακοπαθίας, "hardship," "adversity" (a NT *hapax*, but in LXX at Mal 1:13; 2 Macc 2:26–27; cf. Jonah 4:10). Job's trials and misfortunes are brought to the reader's notice in view of the point of correspondence between him (Job chaps. 1–2) and them (1:2, 12). The way the adversities were faced constitutes the parenetic call, namely the "lesson" to be learned and applied in endurance.

Two interesting deductions are to be drawn from this hortatory reference. (i) The congregation to which James wrote was evidently racked by confusion over the Parousia. Only on this assumption can we account for the strong eschatological tones and the explicit references in these verses. But, as Mussner (203) points out, the type of eschatological puzzlement is not like that in other places of the NT. The issue is not a need to warn against seeking the unknown hour of the Parousia (Mark 13:28–37; 1 Thess 5:1) or against a denial of its imminence or an overconfidence about its nearness (2 Pet 3:3, 4, 9; cf. Luke 19:11; 2 Thess 2:1–4). Rather it is a practical concern to inculcate patience. The postponement of the Parousia is not the problem vexing James' readers, nor the question of why the end does not come soon, to which 2 Peter 3:9 addresses the rationale of the divine forbearance (μακροθυμία). James, on the other hand, makes much of the interval "between the times," specifically employing the horticultural allusion to sowing and reaping and enforcing the need to wait in patient hope for the harvest of divine judgment and redemption to come. There is no way the readers can accelerate the arrival of that day (contrast 2 Pet 3:12). In fact the opposite is the needful reminder: only in God's good time and way will the end come. The Judge is already at the door, but the exact time when the decisive moment (*kairos*) of eschatological deliverance (for the poor) and doom (for the rich, 1:10–11; 4:9–10; 5:1–6) comes is not to be hastened; it can only be awaited. Any other disposition is not only frowned upon and treated as useless (as an impatient farmer who cannot wait for harvest will always be disappointed); it is positively injurious, ἵνα μὴ κριθῆτε, lit., "lest you be judged."

A false hope about the coming of the kingdom and an invalid way the readers were tempted to seize in order to bring it about will lead to a reversal of roles (see v 12 for parallel). Their expected deliverer from the oppressing rich will become their judge. If there is plausibility in seeking a historical setting in the mid-sixties in Palestine, it is a sad confirmation of James' prophetic admonitions that the Zealot movement led to Jerusalem's fate and the sentence on Israel at the hands of the Roman armies. Feuillet, "Le sens" (279), argues that παρουσία in James carries a distinctive (i.e., non-Pauline) sense. It looks ahead to the imminent and historic judgment of God on Israel, seen in the fall of the temple and the city in A.D. 70. But there is no certainty about this conclusion, attractive as it is (it is criticized by Laws, 13 n.1; cf. M. Hengel, *Property and Riches*, 17–18). Yet the variant meaning of "Parousia," different from the sense of Christ's ultimate manifestation to consummate history, is to be noted.

(ii) Another window into the internal conditions of the Jacobean community is opened at 5:9: "Don't complain." The complaining spirit has led to congregational strife, but we are not told the reason for this or given information about the issues that caused the dissension. If Job's example is meant to be taken at face value and corresponded to the readers' needs, it becomes difficult to construe patience in the accepted sense of passive resignation (see Carr, "The Patience of Job"). Job's complaining attitude (e.g., Job 10:1) is so well attested in the canonical book that it is troublesome to see why he is invoked as an example of what is meant to be the antidote to grumbling. We are pressed to seek a specific reason for the readers' complaint, namely, that God had forgotten them and was dealing harshly with their situation in a way that was out of character. Hence James' role is to offer a theodicy, that is, to reassert the divine character as good (v 11: he is πολύσπλαγχνος . . . καὶ οἰκτίρμων), and the actions of God in allowing suffering to come are appealed to as serving a benign purpose (v 11). In Job's case, while he did complain— of his fate, his friends, and of God's apparent neglectful treatment of him— he never renounced his faith (Job 1:21, 22; 2:9–10; 13:15; 16:19; 19:25– 27). And that summons to ὑπομονή (a term frequent in the *Testament of Job*, where Job's wife Sitis is the chief complainant, e.g., chaps 24, 25, 39, and Satan is given a prominent role as tempter: see R. P. Spittler in J. H. Charlesworth, *The Old Testament Pseudepigrapha* 1:829, 834, 836 on the origin of this in Jewish and Christian sectarian teachings) is the main facet of Job's experience on which James fastens in order to drive home the single point that his readers should learn how to see *their* troubles as part of God's design (τέλος). Like the canonical Job they will be brought to vindication (4:10) only if they maintain this faith and fortitude and endure to the end. *T. Job* 27:7 could well be James' motto as well as Job's: "Now then, my children, you also must be patient in everything that happens to you. For patience is better than anything."

Comment

7 Μακροθυμήσατε οὖν, ἀδελφοί, ἕως τῆς παρουσίας τοῦ κυρίου, "Be patient then, brothers, until the Lord's coming." See the discussion above on the question of 5:7 ff. as the closing section of this epistle (*Form/Structure/Setting*). Although there is a sudden change of audience in 5:7, there is no reason to rule out the possibility that the author means for 5:7–11 to complement 5:1–6 (cf. Davids, 181; Mussner, 200–201, who notices how the tender word ἀδελφοί joins together the threatenings of vv 1–6 with the comfort supplied by an appeal to μακροθυμεῖν in vv 7, 10). The οὖν ("therefore") suggests that James is concluding and enforcing his previous thoughts by erecting a bridge to the present section of *applicatio*. In the light of vv 1–6 (especially 5:6) and their theme of the rich versus the poor, James is urging his readers to keep the faith that centers on a divine visitation to rescue the "pious poor" who trust God; it is an expression of Jewish *Armenfrömmigkeit*. The use of "brothers" (5:7, 9) directs his remarks to those of the church (who, in the main, were economically as well as religiously poor), though it was discussed earlier that the entire piece of 5:1–11 was meant for the attention of the church members. Verses 1–6 point out that judgment awaits the rich oppressors of the poor. Vv 7–11, however, inculcate in the poor the proper attitude required until judgment (which is near, 5:3, 5) comes.

Patience is the major theme of vv 7–11, expressed by μακροθυμεῖν / μακροθυμία (5:7 [twice], 8, 10) and ὑπομένειν/ὑπομονή ("stand firm," 5:11 [2x]). Although these words appear as synonyms in Col 1:11, the former group carries the added nuance of expectant waiting, while the latter suggests fortitude (Horst, *TDNT* 4:385–86). The idea of the former is stressed in vv 7–8, set in the context of persecution (Strobel, *Untersuchungen*, 255–57).

Christians are exhorted to be patient until the Lord comes. ἕως ("until") contains the idea both of purpose (goal) and time (Moo, 168). The term παρουσία is a technical term for the coming of Christ (see Matt 24:37, 39; 2 Thess 2:8; Oepke, *TDNT* 5:865–71; Dibelius, 242–43; Laws, 208–9; Mussner, 201). Thus, the title "Lord," used in 5:4 to refer to God, probably is understood here to refer to Jesus (*pace* Kilpatrick, *Jesus*, 2), and the phrase the "coming of the Lord," though connected with the discussion of judgment, refers to Christ's Parousia rather than God's judgment (as Meyer, *Rätsel*, 159, proposed on the basis of his thesis that the original draft of the letter was Old Testament-Jewish; cf. W. Bousset, *Kyrios Christos*, tr. J. E. Steely [Nashville: Abingdon, 1970] 291 n.159). The Christian here is to wait for the time when Jesus will come to set the oppressed free (which, in terms of the overall plan of God for the end of history, includes the judgment of evildoers).

ἰδοὺ ὁ γεωργὸς ἐκδέχεται τὸν τίμιον καρπὸν τῆς γῆς μακροθυμῶν ἐπ᾽ αὐτῷ ἕως λάβῃ πρόϊμον καὶ ὄψιμον, "See how the farmer waits for the land to produce its choice crop and how patient he is for it until [the land] receives the early and late [rainfall]." The call ἰδού ("See") introduces an illustration to explain James' point in the first part of the verse (see *Comment* on 5:4). The example is that of a farmer (ὁ γεωργός, in contrast to the hired laborer mentioned in 5:4 [ὁ ἐργάτης]). After planting his seed, the farmer waits for (ἐκδέχεσθαι) the rain (ὁ ὑετός, v 1; see *Note* a; see also BDF § 241.5) to fall upon his choice crop (τὸν τίμιον καρπόν; it is called "choice"—or perhaps "precious," "valuable" [τίμιος]—because his family needs a good harvest to survive). He has a long wait, corresponding to the time of growth, so he must do so with patience (μακροθυμῶν). He must also depend on the early and late rains (πρόϊμον καὶ ὄψιμον). About three quarters of the annual rainfall takes place in the months December-February, and the rains at the beginning and end of the growing season are the most crucial; the early rain falls in the period from mid-October to mid-November, with the late rainfall occurring mainly in mid-December to mid-January. Rains in the period March-April are especially important for the ripening of spring harvest.

The motif behind these expressions, as in Joel 2:23; Hos 6:3, became invested with a liturgical flavor, especially as the harvest was linked with Passover—set during the month Nisan (Strobel, *Untersuchungen*, 258–59)—and was associated by some rabbis with Israel's deliverance (R. Jose, cited in Str-B, 4:827–28). But James draws no *heilsgeschichtlich* meaning from this allusion, as Mussner notes (202 n.3).

The example of the farmer is fitting as a means of expanding the thought of 5:7a. The farmer must exhibit patience during the period of waiting. This period easily could include hard times and privations and most likely hunger (for him and his family). Yet, no matter how much hunger and shortage plague the farmer's life, he must remain patient and expectant. There is absolutely nothing he can do to speed up the process of rainfall and the subsequent harvest. They will take place, but only in the due processes of nature. Everything has its appointed time (Eccl 3:2).

Likewise, the Christians of James' church must exercise patience, even in the midst of suffering. The Parousia will come (and shortly, it may be) but only in terms set by God's timetable. There is nothing anyone can do to hasten the coming of Jesus (but see 2 Pet 3:12), though James is evidently fearful that some church members will grow impatient and attempt to force the pace. The action that is forbidden may be deduced from earlier references (1:20; 3:15–16; 4:1–10) and identified as a bid to secure redress of wrongs by revolutionary methods. This makes good sense in the light of the probable *Sitz im Leben* of the letter's first draft. James has already had to reprimand his readers for killing others (4:2). That thought, taken with 5:6, supports a strong possibility that some Zealots (or Zealot-like types) might seek to hasten the coming of the kingdom of God by slaying the rich. The advent of the Lord (as with the production of crops) will come in due time. Until then, the Christians (like the farmer) must wait patiently, letting God (whether in terms of world history or as happens in nature) act according to his schedule. There is not much evidence that the delay of the Parousia (often a sore trial to the faith of second- and third-generation Christians, according to Strobel, *Untersuchungen*, 222 n.2) was the chief cause of trouble. Rather, as was observed earlier (p. 188) the way believers were to respond in the interim between "sowing" and "harvest time" was the issue (Mussner, 203). The Jacobean community had its main problem in the need to hold on to the end and await with patient endurance until the final day.

There is more evidence to conclude that James' teaching is a meditation on Psalm 36 [37]:10–11 with its double assurance: (i) in a short time the ungodly will pass away and equally (ii) the poor whose hope is anchored in Yahweh will soon inherit the land and be exalted to peace and security in God's kingdom (37:24). This is parallel with Sir 35:12–20 (cf. Luke 18:7) and may be said to be a recurrent theme in the wisdom literature (see *Introduction*, pp. lxxxvii–xciii). Cf. Ps 36 [37]:34 and *Pss. Sol.* 16.15.

Not all interpreters, however, are convinced that James' example of the farmer is actually an illustration from the everyday lives of his readers. Some think that James has simply plucked an image from the tradition and used it to explain his case (Dibelius, 243–44; Laws, 212). But many others (Mayor, 162; Adamson, 191; Moo, 169; and especially Davids, 183–84 [who produces several reasons for doing so]) conclude that our author has again chosen an everyday happening to elucidate his point. He had done this earlier (chap. 3), and furthermore, since 5:1–6 speaks of an agricultural setting, we concur with the opinion that the farmer is a well-known case study familiar to James' readers.

8 μακροθυμήσατε καὶ ὑμεῖς, στηρίξατε τὰς καρδίας ὑμῶν, ὅτι ἡ παρουσία τοῦ κυρίου ἤγγικεν, "You too are to be patient and confirm your lives, since the Lord's coming is at hand." James repeats the thought expressed in the opening of 5:7: "Be patient" (μακροθυμεῖν). The plural pronoun (ὑμεῖς) replaces "brothers" of 5:7, but the emphasis is the same. Thus, stylistically, the example of the farmer is placed between two commands to be patient until the coming of the Lord.

The idea of the nearness (implied in ἐγγίζειν) of the Lord's return keeps the tension of the endtimes before his audience (contra E. Käsemann, "Paul and Early Catholicism," who wants to see in the later Catholic epistles a fading of the imminence-motif; Mussner, 211 n.2, rightly disagrees) and teaches his readers that their generation could be "the last." James' point (so Davids, 184, and citations there) is not the length of time between the present and the coming of Christ but how one deals with the interim of waiting. The imperative mood calling for patience is followed by the imperative of the parallel verb to "confirm" (στηρίξειν, cf. 1 Thess 3:13; cf. 2 Thess 2:17; see also Heb 13:9).

9 μὴ στενάζετε, ἀδελφοί, κατ' ἀλλήλων ἵνα μὴ κριθῆτε, "Don't complain one of another, brothers; that leads to condemnation." At first glance, the prohibition against groaning (στενάζειν) seems out of place (so Dibelius, 244), but this is not necessarily the only way to interpret the verb. If groaning is understood as complaining against one another (BGD, 766), then it may be that such behavior would be a consequence of difficult circumstances (Mark 7:24; Rom 8:23; 2 Cor 5:2, 4). To complain that life brings its trials may be acceptable for James (but the better attitude is that in 1:1–2), but to complain against (or blame) one another (κατ' ἀλλήλων) is not. It is only natural that afflicted people would express frustrations at the situation described in 5:1–6, but harmony is destroyed when the bitter spirit becomes personal and directed as criticism against fellow believers. This recalls 4:11 and the command to refrain from speaking evil of others. For James, the result of criticizing others is condemnation, as was considered in 4:12. The thought of 5:9 is reminiscent of Jesus' words in Matt 7:1–5 (cf. CD 19.15–26), where those who judge others have the same severity turned against them.

In our present verse condemnation is accentuated by the reference to the approaching judgment. "Remember [ἰδού, rather than γάρ; see BGD, 371] the judge [ὁ κριτής] stands at the door." The use of πρό, like the role of the preposition in ἐπὶ θύραις (Mark 13:29), is not to describe "location" (as in "just outside the door"; contra Cantinat, 237; Moule, *Idiom Book*, 74) so much as to underscore the imminence of judgment (so Davids, 185). The judge is probably Christ (Mussner, 205; cf. Matt 24:33; 1 Cor 3:13; 2 Cor 5:10; Rev 3:10), not God (Laws, 213).

10 ὑπόδειγμα λάβετε, ἀδελφοί, τῆς κακοπαθίας καὶ τῆς μακροθυμίας τοὺς προφήτας οἳ ἐλάλησαν ἐν τῷ ὀνόματι κυρίου, "As an example of patience amid adversity, brothers, consider the prophets who spoke in the Lord's name." The topic of 5:10 makes the point of 5:9 somewhat parenthetical (though it is surely related to 5:8). The thought of vv 10–11 naturally connects with that of vv 7–8, with the common theme an exhortation to patience. The final two verses of this section offer two more examples of patience. While the illustration of the farmer is not necessarily "religious" in character, that of the prophets and Job surely is.

The use of ὑπόδειγμα ("example") can either be positive (Sir 44:16 [Enoch as example]; 2 Macc 6:28, 31; 4 Macc 17:23; John 13:15; *1 Clem.* 5.1; 6.1; 46.1; 63.1; Josephus, *J.W.* 6.103) or negative (Heb 4:11; 2 Pet 2:6), though obviously the former sense is intended here. The brothers are expected to be conversant with this example, namely, the prophets (τοὺς προφήτας is an instance where the accusative is used predicatively; so Moule, *Idiom Book*,

35). The phrase κακοπαθίας [a *hapax legomenon*] καὶ τῆς μακροθυμίας ("patience amid suffering") appears to be a hendiadys (see *Note* b with reference to Björck, "Quelques cas," 3). Moo (171), however, argues that μακροθυμία should be understood as indicating the manner in which the prophets endured hardship ("endurance of suffering"). But this is questionable in the light of James' penchant of combining patience and adversity (1:2–4).

The prophets are depicted by James as speaking in the name of the Lord. Such action should be interpreted to imply that these messengers of Yahweh were subject to suffering because of their service to him. The point made is that despite such suffering (which may well have included martyrdom; Mussner, 205, refers to Jer 2:30b and especially to H. J. Schoeps, "Die jüdischen Prophetenmorde," *Aus frühchristlicher Zeit* [Tübingen: Mohr, 1950] 126–43) the prophets waited patiently and expectantly. James' choice of the prophets does not exclude other martyrs from the thinking of his readers (cf. Heb 11:32–38; also see 1 Macc 2:49–61; Sir 44:16–50:21; *Jubilees*; *Testaments of the Twelve Patriarchs* for illustrations of *Ruhmeskataloge* ["lists of fame"] written in celebration of Israel's worthies. See especially 2 Macc 6:31, as well as 4 Macc 1:10–11, which numbers among the "exploits of excellence" [καλοκά-γαθία] the trait of ὑπομονή). We might have expected a list of those who died for Christ (or Christ himself; see Cantinat, 238) but James' main concerns are to underscore the worthiness of patience and to strengthen his community by showing it that indeed patience is a characteristic common to all those who have walked on this earth and served God (see Hauck, *TDNT* 4:585–88; W. Wichmann, *Die Leidenstheologie* [BWANT 53; Stuttgart, 1930]).

11a ἰδοὺ μακαρίζομεν τοὺς ὑπομείναντας, "As you know, we reckon as blessed those who stand fast." These words summarize the thought of v 10 and pave the way for the remainder of v 11. The use of ἰδού in this letter precedes an important point (see above): those who have stood firm are considered blessed (which of course includes the case of Job). The use of the aorist participle of ὑπομένειν suggests that this attribute of "blessedness" applies only to those of the past as referring to those who stood firm till the end (Adamson, 192). This thought implies that this particular blessing of God is delayed for those still alive. Only those who have endured until the end can be called blessed by others. The prophets, who have died, and Job, who likewise is no longer alive (and other past faithful Christians), are to be called blessed (not "happy" [RSV], which suggests an emotional reaction based on circumstance and not on God's faithfulness). In other words, those who have gone into God's presence are the truly blessed. This is not to say that James' readers are unable to anticipate with joy this future blessedness but that those in the present have yet to enjoy it in its fullness (it may be that some copyists wanted the text to say that those still alive [i.e., those enduring] are to be called blessed [so the reading ὑπομένοντας (present tense) in K L in place of the best authenticated text]).

The idea of blessedness as a reward for steadfastness in the face of persecution is found in the common tradition (H. A. Fischel, "Martyr and Prophet," *JQR* 37 [1946] 256–80, 363–86; Jeremias, *TDNT* 5:711–12; Friedrich, *TDNT* 6:834–35). Jesus' words were that those who are persecuted for his name's sake are blessed (see Matt 5:10–12; 23:29–36; and in particular the sapiential word of Luke 11:49) and those who endure to the end will be saved (Matt 10:22; 24:13; Luke 21:19). In 4 Maccabees the "blessed ones" are those who exhibit ὑπομονή ("endurance") in the face of death (1:10; 7:22; cf. Becker, *NIDNTT* 1:215–18). The teaching of James is clear: those who endure until the end will be rewarded, i.e., by God. The proof he offers is the ὑπόδειγμα of the prophets and that of Job.

11b τὴν ὑπομονὴν Ἰὼβ ἠκούσατε καὶ τὸ τέλος κυρίου εἴδετε, ὅτι πολύσπλαγχνός ἐστιν ὁ κύριος καὶ οἰκτίρμων, "You have heard of Job's steadfastness, and you have seen the purpose of the Lord [in his case], because the Lord is very compassionate and merciful." No doubt the example of the prophets in v 10 was meaningful to James' readers. He assumes that they will have become acquainted with the prophetic figures of the OT through public readings in the synagogue lectionary. But the author now turns to a concrete example of endurance (ὑπομονή; note the relation to the participle of the preceding clause). On the surface, it is not clear why Job is chosen to exemplify patience in suffering. He was anything but an example of a godly person who was patient in the midst of adversity. The character Job in the canonical Scripture was not a silent party to his suffering; rather, he was one who complained bitterly to God because of his dire circumstances (7:11–16; 10:18; 23:2; 30:20–23; cf. Cantinat, 239). It may very well be then that James' knowledge of Job did not come exclusively from the book of the OT with the same name. Instead, James may be referring to Job as described in the apocryphal work *Testament of Job* (Davids, 187). In this latter work it is Job's wife (named as Sitis), not Job, who is the one who complains. Thus, the *Testament of Job* casts the protagonist in a positive light. Yet, the picture of Job in the canonical book may still be claimed as a source of James' example in 5:11. Despite his grumblings, the biblical Job never ceased to believe in God (1:21; see earlier: "Job's refusal to curse God is the vital issue involved in the legend of a pious Job" [Fine, "The Tradition," 30]). Though he complained, "the flame of faith was never extinguished in his heart" (Barclay, 125), and his example could be described as one of steadfast endurance in the time of suffering. This fits in well as a counterpoint to a picture of a grumbling and complaining church (5:9). James is urging his readers (who were a groaning community) to persevere.

The readers of James have heard (ἠκούσατε) of Job's steadfastness and have seen (εἴδετε) the purpose of the Lord. The second verb εἴδετε (which appears to be the correct text; see *Note* e) is to be connected to the story of Job (note how the verbs "to hear" and "to see" recall Job 42:5: "My ears have heard of you, but now my eyes have seen you"; cf. Adamson, 193). Some interpreters understand τέλος to mean "result" or "outcome" (Moo, 172), so that the issue of Job's steadfastness is the blessing restored to him after his sufferings (Job 42:12–17, especially v 12: ὁ δὲ κύριος εὐλόγησεν τὰ ἔσχατα Ἰώβ, which the readers are said to have "seen" in holy Scripture). But this suggests that the favor of blessedness promised to all who endure until the end is actually received before the end comes, which opposes our exegesis of ὑπομείναντας (see above) and the context of 5:7–11, which teaches that endurance must be exhibited until either the Christian dies or the Lord returns. James is not promising that temporary steadfastness in the face of suffering will produce material prosperity as the end of Job's story would suggest.

Also to be considered is the understanding that τὸ τέλος is necessarily referring to the death or the Parousia of Jesus (Gordon, "τὸ τέλος"; Bischoff, "τὸ τέλος"; this view, which goes back to Augustine, thought the phrase referred to the Lord's end-of-life experience [*Herrnende*, Bischoff, 275]: *Verba sunt Domini pendentis in ligno . . . ibi est finis Domini*, cited in Mussner, 206 n.7). On this understanding the verb εἴδετε, "you have seen," could conceivably refer to the readers as eyewitnesses of the crucifixion; but then 1:1 relating to a wider constituency than Jerusalem has to be dismissed, and it is hard to see how the death of Jesus proves the Lord's compassion. There are greater problems if the verb is connected with a Parousia appearance. How can one have seen (εἴδετε, past tense) something that has yet to happen? No doubt the reward of God played an important part in a Christian's standing firm in the faith; that has already been discussed by James in v 7, which refers explicitly to the Parousia (Strobel, *Untersuchungen*, 259, who wants to see a double sense of τέλος: (i) Job's issuance of vindication, and (ii) the eschatological hope that will encourage the reader to endure). What he hopes to accomplish by the example of Job is the edification and encouragement of the church. He does this by providing an uplifting (though realistic) glimpse of what God has to offer in the present, rather than the past (the crucifixion in Jerusalem) or the future (the Parousia), *pace* Gordon, "τὸ τέλος," 94.

τὸ τέλος, then, probably means "purpose" or "design" (so RSV; Mitton, 189–90). The genitive κυρίου is objective, i.e., it is the end which the Lord designed with a parallel in *T. Benj.* 4.1: εἴδετε, οὖν, τέκνα μου, τοῦ ἀγαθοῦ ἀνδρὸς τὸ τέλος, "you saw . . . how a good man was rewarded in the end." Mussner, 207, appeals to Heb 13:6–7 for ἔκβασις with the same meaning as τέλος; and to Wisd Sol 2:17b; 3:19. But this parallel in the *Testament of Benjamin* is challenged by Gordon, "τὸ τέλος," 92, though the objective genitive is defended as giving the only possible sense by Preuschen, "Jac 5,11," 79. There is a reason for suffering and that is to produce Christians who are mature and complete (1:4; 3:2; cf. Rom 5:1–5). If this were to happen, there would be no fighting or name-calling or (even) killing in the church. From the readers' standpoint, they can call Job blessed because he has endured until the end (Adamson, 192). Job's example offers the Christian hope because it becomes apparent from the biblical story that Christians can withstand adversity. By examining Job's life, the readers may appreciate that there was a purpose behind what happened to him (again the sovereignty of God is in view; see 4:15). Job came to understand God's faithful nature (Job 42:5) before his material possessions were restored, and as he persevered, he found his closest communion with God in the midst of adversity.

Most likely Job was not called "blessed" while he was alive (nor would he necessarily have considered himself steadfast), but once his life was over, this description was quite appropriate. While the prophets held out a more expectant attitude (implied in μακροθυμία) than Job, it was his dogged perseverance (ὑπομονή) that carried him through to the end. The Christians of James'

church are to exhibit the prophets' eagerness for the end to come and the
steadfastness of Job so as to ensure that they will be there when it happens
in God's time and way.

The purpose or design of the Lord reflects his compassion (πολύσπλαγχνος,
a *hapax legomenon*; but see *Herm. Man.* 4.3.5; *Sim.* 5.7.4) and his mercy
(οἰκτίρμων). Such attributions to God here reflect OT teaching (Pss 103:8;
111:4; cf. Exod 34:6). Yet there is a problem for faith. How is the Lord
compassionate and merciful if his children continue to suffer? He is loving
and gracious in that he provides the strength to endure to the end, which is
a denouement that consummates in glory and vindication for the faithful.
That is a purpose of the Lord: to create his people as mature and complete
persons of God and to uphold them so that in the teeth of persecution (1:1–
4) they may enjoy the blessedness of the new world (4 Macc 17:17–18). Thus
James closes his exhortation to patience (5:7) with a theodicy that rests on
the assurance of the Lord's goodness (5:11).

Explanation

The two-beat rhythm of biblical faith includes the bringing together of
the related concepts of divine reckoning and divine recompense. These foci
of the ellipse are evident as James carries forward the teaching in 5:7–11.
Up to v 6 the emphasis has been on the Day of the Lord as the day of
retribution that awaits the godless farmers and their selfish and indulgent
pursuits. The farm laborers are the hapless victims whose voices cry to high
heaven (5:4). The tale of these verses is one of unmitigated evil, with serious
miscarriages of justice and mounting crime adding to the dismal picture.

With v 7 James faces an issue that the OT saints have wrestled with ever
since the time of Habakkuk, Jeremiah, the psalmists (e.g., Pss 37, 49, 73),
and Job. Why do the righteous suffer? is a question that in our pericope
becomes the more urgent and practical query. In time of distress and personal
loss, as when wages are withheld and cruel oppressors apparently succeed
in their murderous plots (v 6), what can godly believers do? The honest
answer is that usually they can do very little—except wait and hope for better
days to come. This attitude is not to be construed as stoical fatalism or pious
resignation; rather it is offered as a call to endurance (the key word in vv
5–11).

Endurance (*hypomonē*) in this context is to be understood in the same
way as in 1:2–5, 9, 12, 19; 4:6, 8, 10, where James sets it against the background
of God's sovereign control of events and the need to wait for him to act in
his own time and way. It is a rugged determination not to renounce one's
faith and not to fall out of the race. Moreover it is an activity *demanding
strenuous courage and firm fortitude*, once we are persuaded that our lives are
in God's hands even though outward circumstances seem to overwhelm. Above
all, if Job's example is to be reckoned (v 11) along with the prophets' experience
(v 10), then there is a natural human reaction to be questioning and sometimes
petulant—but never to the point of losing faith or turning away from God.

And there is no point in trying to attach the blame for our present miseries to other people, as evidently was the case in James' community (v 9).

Part of the ability to endure is the long-term prospect with which the eye of faith is gifted. The agrarian illustration of the farmer is chosen to enforce this point (v 7). Perhaps as a deliberate counterpoint to that of the unjust farmers of vv 1–6, the case of the patient tiller of the soil is brought out to stress the need for waiting in hope. Harvest is never produced except by the natural processes of sowing, germination, and slow growth. Only the farmer who respects natural laws, as understood in James' day, will rejoice at harvest home. Any lack of patience on his part will serve only to increase frustration and disappointment, and will lead to disaster. The lesson would not be lost on Palestinian readers who lived near to mother earth; and it would be a pointed rebuke directed at Zealot militarism.

A second factor is eschatological. The buoyancy of faith is sustained by the hope of a Parousia, a term twice repeated (vv 7, 8). How James envisaged the Lord's coming is not spelled out, but it may be safe to conclude that, in the light of the OT promise of a coming Day of Yahweh, the judgment on Israel's foes would imply the deliverance and regathering of Yahweh's people. So with the assurance that the Lord's Parousia is "at hand" (v 8), James' audience may be able to take fresh heart that the present evil regime will not last much longer. If the divine judge is already at the door (v 9), they may safely anticipate that aid is on the way. So there is a renewed summons to hold on—until the end comes, as it did in Job's case (v 11).

The two ideas of patient steadfastness and confident expectation need to be set in equipoise and viewed together. In a sense each stresses a different aspect of the Christian's hope in every age and especially in time of stress and storm. We need the reminder of patient endurance lest we (like some of James' readers) are tempted in premature or precipitate activity to do God's work for him in our way; we require equally an optimistic outlook that waits for God to intervene even when the scene is dark and forbidding. Patience is not quietism, just as expectancy is not fanaticism. Christian eschatology has swung between these polarities; the observant reader of James' counsel will seek to find the truth not in one or other extreme, but in both.

5. Community Issues: Oath-Taking; Reactions to Trouble, Sickness, and Sins (5:12–18)

Bibliography

Althaus, P. "'Bekenne euer dem anderen seine Sünden': zur Geschichte von Jak 5,16 seit Augustin." In *Festgabe für Theodore Zahn.* Leipzig: Werner Scholl, 1928. 165–94. **Berandy, R.** "Le sacrement des malades. Etude historique et théologiques." *NRT* 96 (1974) 600–634. **Bonhoeffer, D.** *Life Together.* Tr. J. W. Doberstein. New York:

Harper, 1954. **Brown, C.** *That You May Believe.* Grand Rapids: Eerdmans, 1985. **Bult-mann, R.** *Der Stil der paulinischen Predigt und die kynisch-stoische Diatribe.* FRLANT 13. Göttingen: Vandenhoeck und Ruprecht, 1910. **Clarke, K. W.** "The Meaning of ἐνεργέω and καταργέω in the New Testament." *JBL* 54 (1935) 93–101. **Condon, K.** "The Sacrament of Healing (Jas. 5:14–15)." *Scripture* 11 (1959) 33–42. **Cooper, R. M.** "Prayer: A Study in Matthew and James." *Encounter* 29 (1968) 268–77. **Coppens, J.** "Jacq v, 13–15 et l'onction des malades." *ETL* 53 (1977) 201–7. **Cothenet, E.** "La maladie et la mort du chrétien dans la liturgie. La guérison comme signe du Royaume et l'onction des malades (Jac 15,13–16)." *Esprit et Vie* 84 (1974) 561–70. **Dautzenberg, G.** "Ist das Schwurverbot Mt 5,33–37; Jk 5,12 ein Beispiel für die Torakritik Jesu?" *BZ* 25 (1981) 47–66. **Francis, F. O.** "The Form and Function of the Opening and Closing Paragraphs of James and 1 John." *ZNW* 61 (1970) 110–26. **Friesehahn, H.** "Zur Geschichte der Überlieferung und Exegese des Textes bei Jak V,14f." *BZ* 24 (1938) 185–90. **Gross, E.** "Noch einmal: Der Essenereid bei Josephus." *TLZ* 82 (1957) 73–74. **Hayden, D. R.** "Calling the Elders to Pray." *BSac* 138 (1981). 258–66. **Heitmüller, W.** *Im Namen Jesu.* Göttingen: Vandenhoeck und Ruprecht, 1903. **Hiebert, D. E.** "The Worldliness of Self-Serving Oaths." *Direction* 6 (1977) 39–43. **Kutsch, E.** "Der Eid der Essener." *TLZ* 81 (1956) 495–98. ———. "Eure Rede aber sei ja ja, nein nein." *EvT* 20 (1960) 206–18. **Lys, D.** "L'onction dans la Bible." *ETR* 29 (1954) 3–54. ———. *L'onction dans la Bible.* Paris: Presses Universitaires, 1954. **McKenzie, J. L.** "The Elders in the Old Testament." *Bib* 40 (1959) 522–40. **Meinertz, M.** "Die Krankensalbung Jak 5,14f." *BZ* 20 (1932) 23–36. **Michel, O.** "Der Schwur der Essener." *TLZ* 81 (1956) 189–90. **Minear, P.** "Yes or No. The Demand for Honesty in the Early Church." *NovT* 13 (1971) 1–13. **Moldenke, H. N.,** and **Moldenke, A. L.** *Plants of the Bible.* 1952. Reprint. New York: Dover, 1986. **Montefiore C. G.,** and **Loewe, H.** *Rabbinic Anthology.* New York: Schocken, 1974 ed. Nos. 1078, 1087, 1088, 1092, 1394. **Patai, R.** "The 'Control of Rain' in Ancient Palestine." *HUCA* 14 (1939) 251–86. **Pickar, C.** "Is Anyone Sick among You?" *CBQ* 7 (1945) 165–74. **Puller, F. W.** *The Anointing of the Sick in Scripture and Tradition.* London: SPCK, 1904. **Reicke, B.** "L'onction des malades d'après S. Jacques." *Maison-Dieu* 113 (1973) 50–56. **Schoeps, H. J.** *Theologie und Geschichte des Judentchristentums.* Tübingen: Mohr, 1949. **Stählin, G.** "Zum Gebrauch von Beteuerungsformeln im NT." *NovT* 5 (1962) 115–43. **Unger, M. F.** "Divine Healing." *BSac* 128 (1971) 234–44. **Wilkinson, J.** "Healing in the Epistle of James." *SJT* 24 (1971) 326–45.

Translation

[12a] *Above all, my brothers, do not swear an oath—either by heaven or by the earth or by any other thing. Let your "Yes" be yes, and your "No" no; otherwise you will come to judgment.*[b]

[13] *Is anyone of you facing adversity? Then pray. Is anyone in good spirits? Then sing a song [to God].* [14] *Is there one of you weak? He should summon the elders of the congregation to pray over him*[c] *and anoint him with oil in the name of the Lord.* [15] *And the request*[d] *based on faith will make the sick one well; and the Lord will raise him up; if he has committed sins, he will be forgiven.* [16] *Confess your sins to one another then, and pray for one another so that you may be healed. The righteous person's prayer is very powerful in its effectiveness.*

[17] *Elijah was a man with a nature like ours; he prayed earnestly that it might not rain, and it did not rain on the land for three and a half years.* [18] *He prayed later, and the heavens gave rain, and the land produced its harvest crop.*

Notes

ᵃSome editors, puzzled over the random position of this verse, treat it as a gloss or an adscript to 3:9–10 (so Rendall, *The Epistle of St. James*, 68 n.1) in view of the idea common to both sets of verses, namely, the use and misuse of the tongue.

ᵇἵνα μὴ ὑπὸ κρίσιν πέσητε, lit., "lest you fall under condemnation," parallel with v 9; εἰς ὑπό-κρισιν in TR is a moralistic emendation.

ᶜTaking ἐπ᾽ αὐτόν with "pray" (which may include the imposition of hands: Ps-Mark 16:18) rather than with the rite of anointing, as Coppens, "L'onction," 204, proposes. See H. Schönweiss and C. Brown, *NIDNTT* 2:875.

ᵈεὐχή has the strict sense of "request," "wish," and should be so rendered, unless we prefer, with Coppens, "L'onction," 203, to note that in the hellenistic period the distinction between εὐχή and προσευχή ("prayer") no longer held good. Cf. Marty, 212. The verb προσεύχεσθαι is found in vv 13, 14, 16, 17, 18 and the appeal to faith recalls 1:5.

At v 16 εὔχεσθε is read by Nestle-Aland²⁶ and supported by Metzger and UBS text with ℵ K P Ψ, over the claim of προσεύχεσθε found in A (B προσεύχεσθαι) and a few minuscules and preferred by Ropes, 309. But a harmonizing tendency in the latter case is suspected.

Form / Structure / Setting

At 5:12 the close of the letter is anticipated (see earlier, p. xcviii). On πρὸ πάντων, lit., "above all," see J. A. Robinson, *St. Paul's Epistle to the Ephesians* (London: J. Clarke, 1904) 278–79. As evidence of an epistolary style, it could carry the meaning "finally," in the sense of "before I forget" (so Mussner, 211), though Laws, 219–20, takes it to imply the thought of "most importantly." The short section on oath-taking is, at first glance, unexpected and is sometimes treated as a stray logion, out of place here and better suited to the section of 3:9–10 (see *Note* a). But the one element that connects the verse with the foregoing is the use of the tongue (to be restrained, as in 3:3–8, when the question is that of binding one's allegiance by invoking God's name as an asseveration of one's truthfulness as in Matt 5:33–37; 2 Cor 1:15–24). Davids, 190, speaks for the majority of commentators here: "James . . . prohibits . . . the use of oaths in everyday discourse to prove integrity." The conclusion drawn is that James is in line with the Old Testament teaching on vows, where the fundamental objection to "false swearing" and oaths is in Lev 19:12; Num 30:3 and amplified by the prophets (Hos 4:2; Jer 5:2; Zech 5:3–4; Mal 3:5) and developed in Israel's wisdom tradition (e.g. Sir 23:9–11: "Do not accustom your mouth to oaths . . . the man who swears many oaths will be filled with iniquity"). But this rejection of oaths may have a more nuanced meaning than this. James is usually thought to embody a more primitive form of the prohibition than those in Matthew or that in Justin, *Apol.* 1.16.5: μὴ ὀμόσητε ὅλως ἔστω δὲ ὑμῶν τὸ ναὶ ναὶ καὶ τὸ οὒ οὔ. τὸ δὲ περισσὸν τούτων ἐκ τοῦ πονηροῦ (cf. Minear, "Yes or No," 7: "each of the three writers was incorporating catechetical materials which were still circulating orally in their several communities"). The historical *Sitz im Leben* of the verse may be traced to the Jerusalem community under James' patronage as he was looked upon as the leader who sought to achieve a *modus vivendi* between his brothers of the messianic faith and the Zealot faction. The chief datum of evidence for this theory is taking of oaths by the revolutionary *sicarii*, according to Josephus (Gross, "Noch einmal," 73–74). This is a more probable suggestion than seeking to relate the Jacobean prohibition of oaths to Essene practice (Josephus, *J.W.* 2.135 [cf. *Ant.* 15.370–72; 1QS 2.1–18; CD 15.8–10], which attributes a pragmatic value to the question: "for they say that he who cannot be believed without [swearing by] God is already condemned"; cf. Michel, "Der Schwur," 189–90; Kutsch, "Der Eid," 495–98). In any case, the objection to oath-taking in this general sense was a commonplace among the rabbis (see Str-B 1.336; Montefiore and Loewe, *Rabbinic Anthology*, nos. 1078, 1087, 1088, 1092, 1394).

On the section 5:13–18, J. Wilkinson, "Healing," 339, rightly comments that the key verse is 16b: "pray for one another," and the entire pericope is dedicated to the issues of pastoral and community prayer (cf. vv 13, 15, 17, 18, all of which contain some allusions to praying; hence rightly Ruckstuhl's heading). In fact it is possible, with Motyer, 186–208, to arrange the verses to cover several topics all to do with prayer; the individual at prayer (v 13); the elders at prayer (vv 14–15); the friends at prayer (v 16); and the prophet who prayed (vv 16–18).

Another way of encompassing this seemingly disparate material is to think of James as addressing the issue of pastoralia but with an eye on some pressing needs in his community. Indeed, with this approach, it is feasible that vv 13–18 are not so detached from v 12 as most scholars believe. Given our hypothesis of anti-Zealot or anti-nationalist polemic in v 12, James now sets in direct antithesis to the activism of those who wished to bring about God's kingdom by violent means the teaching on submission (cf. 4:7–10). Opposed to the assertions that underlie the oath-taking in v 12 is the author's "better way" of acquiescence with the divine will. That will embraces the whole of life, with its extremes of pleasure and pain (v 13), and all its facets are set in a corporate context. Suffering and sinning form the major pastoral themes, and the antidote to both distressing conditions lies in the practice of prayer to God.

Stylistically the imperatives προσευχέσθω, ψαλλέτω, προσκαλεσάσθω describe the three "life situations" (Mussner, 216) confronting the readers. The verbs do not suggest a simple conditional sense, but make a statement (in the form of a question) in order for the author to indicate the conduct appropriate to the three problems. This is a feature of the diatribe style (Bultmann, *Der Stil*, 15; BDF § 494; cf. 1 Cor 7:18, 27).

For the messianic pietist, represented par excellence in the person of James himself (v 16b: "the righteous man" here recalls 5:6, where in both instances it is probable we should see references to the hero of our chapter as viewed in the testamentary encomium of his followers including the letter's editor), prayer is understood as a disposition of trustful submitting to God's good will (see 1:2–9), especially in time of trial. It is set in contrast with a type of requesting that is, for James, little more than an exercise in selfishness and futility (4:1–3). So the appeal is to the Old Testament worthy Elijah who provides the counterpoint to Job (5:11). The prophet was a man of action whose life was cast in tumultuous times of national crisis, false religion, and pagan pressures (1 Kgs 17–19). Yet it is not Elijah's vigorous opposition to Baal religion or to the Ahab-Jezebel coalition that threatened "pure" Yahwism that is picked out; and it is not the prophet's zealous determination to root out the cultic devotees of Melkart after the encounter at Carmel (1 Kgs 18:40) that is praised for emulation. Rather what is lauded is Elijah's role as national intercessor and as a person of prayer who is said to have controlled the natural elements of drought and rainfall. The latter idea goes back to the example of the patient farmer in 5:7. James' text marks an explanatory addition to the Hebrew Bible, which says nothing—except by inference—about Elijah's prayer producing first a drought, then a rainstorm (cf. 1 Kgs 17:1; 18:42–46). James's purpose seems evident. It is to downplay the nationalist and jingoist side of Elijah's career and to build up a case for reliance on God's help alone, expected in his good time from the prophet's recourse to prayer. The latter is seen as a species of faith in Yahweh as Lord of creation and giver of rain and harvest (Ps 65:9–13: note the repetition in vv 9–13 of "*Thou* visitest the earth and waterest it . . . *Thou* crownest the year").

This emphasis, we submit, with its stress on contemporary human needs that are met by God's response, is designed to ward off any false hopes pinned to revolution and strife; and the efficacy of prayer is connected with his readers' willingness to submit to the divine plan and to await God's intervention like the wise farmer.

What, then, of the personalized needs of sickness and distress (v 13), which are promised an apparently immediate deliverance and cure? Here again it is important to keep central the teaching that James evidently sought to promote, namely, the value and efficacy of prayer. Hence the frequent repetition of prayer words: προσευχέσθω (v 13); προσευξάσθωσαν (v 14); ἡ εὐχή (v 15); εὔχεσθε (v 16); δέησις (v 16); προσευχῇ προσηύξατο (v 17); προσηύξατο (v 18).

While that much is clear, as the lexical data show, it is less obvious what kinds of affliction are in view in v 14, and what is the nature of the promised deliverance in the verb σώσει (v 15, lit., "will save"). σώζειν is usually in James employed with the eschatological sense of salvation in the last days: see 1:21; 2:14; 4:12; 5:20. Vouga comments (142) that σώζειν in these four texts has both a soteriological and an eschatological meaning. He continues that with the future tense in v 15 along with ἐγερεῖ ("will raise up") we should suspect a similar setting. There is a built-in ambiguity with these verbs when applied to the context of prayer for healing. Is it a cure of the whole person that is promised (Wilkinson, "Healing," 334–35), or is it the assurance of divine faithfulness that a desire for healing, expressed in faith, will not go unheeded by God, who at the last day will raise the dead? (This typical Jewish conviction is attested in the Eighteen Benedictions, no. 2: "Blessed art thou, O Lord, who makest alive the dead": see R. A. Stewart, *Rabbinic Theology* [Edinburgh: Oliver & Boyd, 1961] 183–86.) The ambiguity is noted by Mussner, 221–23, who on balance takes the future verb as logical, not eschatological. But see C. Pickar, "Is Anyone Sick?" 173, *per contra*. It is noteworthy that the specific medical term for bodily healing (ἰᾶσθαι) belongs to the corporate actions of v 16, and the prayer which yields the result of healing is that made in the assembly in fellowship, with a possible note of intercessory praying as effective in producing the desired result (ὑπὲρ ἀλλήλων ὅπως ἰαθῆτε). This mutually supportive ministry of supplicatory prayer "*for one another*," ὑπὲρ

ἀλλήλων, stands in direct contrast to what James has written critically at
4:11 (don't slander *one another*) and 5:9 (don't grumble against *one another*).
His thought, to that extent, flows in a sequential pattern, catching up earlier themes either by way of development or with a view to correcting
abuses.

This pericope is interesting also for its mention of the rite of anointing
administered by church leaders (πρεσβύτεροι, v 14). The fact that the weak
person should summon these people makes it plain that it is not a case of
the needy one being *in extremis*, and it is difficult to read into this verse any
teaching regarding sacramental action (cf. Coppens, "Jacq v, 13–15," 201–
7) or priestly ministrations at a deathbed (the rite of Extreme Unction). The
anointing is with a promise of life, not as an anticipation of one's preparing
for death (contra Brown, *That You May Believe*, 195). Moreover the "elders"
are not called as faith healers (in the sense of 1 Cor 12:9, 28, 30) but as
church leaders who bring their faith to the scene of distress. The use of
(olive: Moldenke, *Plants*, 158) oil is much disputed, with the options that it
was regarded as prophylactic (in a quasi-magical way) against sin or sickness
or death, or as therapeutic in promoting healing. Olive oil was believed by
the ancients to have medicinal properties for all manner of complaints and
ills. There may also be a symbolic use as signifying the action of God, whose
healing presence is brought to bear on the human situation. See *Comment*,
and *TDNT* 1:230–33 (H. Schlier); *TDNT* 2:467–69 (J. Behm); Reicke, "L'onction," 51–56. On balance, the last-named suggestion, that oil is mentioned
to certify the interest of God in human need and to suggest a mood of
"joy" in the midst of trial and divine purpose in suffering—a common Jacobean
trait (1:2–3, 12; 2:13; 5:11, 13)—is to be preferred. The idea of oil-anointing
as a mark of honor and joy derived from God's electing mercy is well attested
in the Jewish and NT literature (Deut 28:40; Isa 25:6–7 LXX; 61:3; Amos
6:6; Mic 6:15; Pss 23:5; 45:8; 92:11; 133:2; Prov 27:9; Eccl 9:8; Matt 6:17;
26:6–13 par.; Luke 7:36–50). This would fit James' overall tenor admirably:
the elders bring and apply to the afflicted one the outward tangible sign of
God's covenant faithfulness in regard to human distress, and the pledge that,
in adversity as in happiness, God's plan does not miscarry.

The pericope of vv 13–18 is one unit, moving in a succession of ideas
(Vouga, 143). The human conditions of joy and sorrow are occasions for
divine intervention. But God uses one's fellow believers, whether church offi-
cials or the assembled congregation (v 16), and the external means of oil to
minister his grace in both restoration and forgiveness. Prayer that moves
the human exigency to conform to the divine plan is seen to be the appropriate
attitude expressing faith and confidence. Hence the import of the phrase in
v 14b: ἐν τῷ ὀνόματι τοῦ κυρίου, which is not a magical or mechanical talisman
and not an exorcistic form of words; rather it is the phrase that marks out
the sphere of faith in which God's perfect will is acknowledged and trusted
as the best—whatever the outcome.

Elijah's case is brought forward to show how effective prayer—seen in
this positive context (i.e., in antithesis to the doubting of 1:6–7 or the selfish
prayers of 4:1–3)—can be. There is a conscious play on words, framing vv
13–18 into a single, homogeneous literary and ideological unit. κακοπαθεῖ in

v 13 sets the stage: "facing adversity" describes the plight of the readers. Yet this is no isolated case, since Elijah of old was ὁμοιοπαθής, lit., "a man of fellow sufferings," with James' friends. The hostility of religious opponents and the experience of persecution were factors that bound together the prophet of old and the harassed audience of this epistle, especially in its later setting. Hence, if Elijah found recourse in prayer the readers may expect no less. This leads us to conclude, regarding the setting of 5:13–18, that its teaching was evoked by believers under trial, whose sufferings were the occasion of a challenge to faith, and whose weak and sickly condition was not due to the "slings and arrows of outrageous fortune" but to their being attacked as loyal followers of the messianic faith.

Comment

12 Πρὸ πάντων δέ, ἀδελφοί μου, "Above all, my brothers." The appropriateness of this verse in the epistle (see *Note* a) has been queried. The topic of "oaths," at first glance, seems out of place. Yet the words πρὸ πάντων, "above all" (see Moule, *Idiom Book*, 74; 1 Pet 4:8), especially with δέ suggest that what is to follow is somehow connected with what precedes. But what is the writer (or the editor) connecting 5:12 to? Is it to what immediately precedes 5:12 or to a particular topic discussed earlier? Reicke (56) opts for the link to that which immediately precedes and argues that the swearing of oaths is a sign of impatience with the order of things. In the light of the topic of 5:1–11—the rich oppressing the poor and James' encouragement to the latter that they should be patient and await God's deliverance (vv 7–8, 10)—the position taken by Reicke may be correct. Davids (188) hints that judgment (5:9 and 5:12) may be a connective, but he is not convinced. Any attempt to connect the topic of 5:12 with its immediate context is usually regarded as somewhat "artificial" (Moo, 173), and a typical solution (perhaps the best) is to understand James as summarizing the general content of the letter (Vouga, 138). That is, the prohibition against oath-swearing reflects the misuse of the tongue (see *Form / Structure / Setting* where a connection with Zealot oath-taking and James' polemic against such a practice was suggested).

As was noted under *Form / Structure / Setting* above, the phrase "above all" does not imply that oath-swearing is more grievous than other sins mentioned in this epistle, but that what follows is important (Davids, 189) and that James is drawing his work to a close (see Francis, "Form and Function," 125; Vouga, 139; note λοιπόν, "finally," in Paul at 2 Cor 13:11; cf. Phil 3:1; see Martin, *2 Corinthians*, WBC 40 [Waco: Word, 1986] 497–98).

μὴ ὀμνύετε μήτε τὸν οὐρανὸν μήτε τὴν γῆν μήτε ἄλλον τινὰ ὅρκον, "Do not swear an oath—either by heaven or by the earth or by any other thing." The idea of swearing (ὀμνύειν) involves invoking the name of God to ensure the truthfulness of what one says, although paradoxically, "swearing is necessary only in a society where truth is not reverenced" (so Adamson, 194–95).

The OT teaching on the swearing of oaths emphasizes the need to limit such oaths to those which could be fulfilled (Exod 20:7; Num 30:3 and especially Lev 19:12). Sometimes the swearing of oaths was commanded (Exod 22:10–11), and there are examples where God swore oaths himself (Deut

4:31; 7:8; Heb 3:11; 4:3). But the OT also contains warnings against taking oaths too lightly (Jer 5:2; 7:9; Hos 4:2; Zech 5:3–4; Mal 3:5), and in Judaism it came to be accepted that the best policy was, whenever possible, to avoid oaths altogether (Sir 23:9, 11; Philo, *De Decal.* 84–95; *Spec. Leg.* 2.2–38; see Laws, 221–22; Schneider, *TDNT* 4:459–61; see also CD 9.9–10; 15.1–2, 8–10; 16.8–9; 1QS 2.1–18; 5.8–11; Josephus *J.W.* 2.135, 139–43; *Ant.* 15.370–72). Both the Synoptic record (Matt 26:63) and the teaching of Paul (Rom 1:9; Gal 1:20; 2 Cor 1:23; 11:1; 1 Thess 2:5, 10; Phil 1:8) are familiar with the practice of oaths. But Jesus was critical of the misuse of oaths (i.e., implying the misuse of the tongue), and the attempt by some to circumvent the obligation to fulfill an oath (Matt 23:16–22; Mark 7:9–13) is condemned. The teaching of James seems to be an independent variant of the logion of Jesus as recorded in Matt 5:33–37 (note that the terms οὐρανόν, "heaven," γῆν, "earth," and ἄλλον τινὰ ὅρκον, "any other thing," lit., oath [which may include Jerusalem; see Matt 5:35], are in the accusative case and repeat the content of the oath; see Moule, *Idiom Book*, 32).

ἤτω δὲ ὑμῶν τὸ ναὶ ναὶ καὶ τὸ οὒ οὔ, ἵνα μὴ ὑπὸ κρίσιν πέσητε, "Let your 'Yes' be yes, and your 'No' no; otherwise you will come to judgment." A comparison of Matt 5:33–37 and our present verse runs like this:

Matt 5:34–37 (NIV)	*James 5:12* (NIV)
Do not swear at all:	Do not swear—
either by heaven . . .	not by heaven
or by the earth . . .	or by earth
or by Jerusalem. . . .	or by anything else.
And do not swear by your head. . . .	Let your 'Yes' be 'Yes'
Simply let your 'Yes' be 'Yes,'	and your 'No,' 'No,'
and your 'No,' 'No';'	
anything beyond this comes from	or you will be condemned.
the evil one	

Several observations may be made (see Davids, 190; Mussner, 214–15, for details). First, Matthew's version contains more examples and explanations than James', which suggests that it may be an expansion of the more primitive form of the logion found in James, but this is not certain. Second, the prohibitions in Matthew (vv 34, 36) are in the aorist tense while those of James are couched in the present. This suggests that James is attacking a practice already present in his church, while Matthew is urging his readers not to begin oath-swearing; but such a distinction in the tenses is not always observed (Moule, *Idiom Book*, 20–21). Third, Matthew may imply that a substitute oath ("Simply let what you say be" [ἔστω δὲ ὁ λόγος]) is permissible: the double 'yes' or double 'no' is an oath (see Davids, 249–51; Cantinat, 243–44). But the yes-yes and no-no can also mean that whatever one says in public should genuinely reflect what is in the mind (see Davids, 150; Mussner, 215–16). If this is true, then a person does not need an oath to supplement or enforce what has been said. Thus, Matthew, like James, is prohibiting all oaths that are used to support a person's promise. As Mitton (193) writes: "Our mere word should be as utterly trustworthy as a signed document, legally correct and complete."

It is doubtful, however, that official oaths, such as those required in the courtroom, are addressed here (so Windisch, 32–33). Rather, what appears to be the case is the "voluntary" (Moo, 174) oath Christians feel must be given in order to ensure the integrity of their speech. The idea of condemnation (κρίσις) comes into operation when oaths are offered as a means of signaling the truthfulness of human intention. To conclude one's remarks with an oath—which usually involved invoking God's name—placed the speaker under even greater obligation to fulfill declared promises, and this in turn placed the oath-taker in greater danger of condemnation by God, since such speech was "more honest than other speech" (Davids, 190). For James (as for Jesus), believers should deal with one another in truth and honesty.

13 Κακοπαθεῖ τις ἐν ὑμῖν, προσευχέσθω· εὐθυμεῖ τις, ψαλλέτω, "Is anyone of you facing adversity? Then pray. Is anyone in good spirits? Then sing a song [to God]." Vv 13–18 form a paragraph whose topic is clearly that of prayer, both personal and congregational. Prayer is mentioned in every verse (see *Form/Structure/Setting*). By concluding his work with an exhortation to pray, especially for one another (v 16b) in the apostolic circle, James follows a pattern that is common in the NT epistles (Rom 15:30–32; Eph 6:18–20; Phil 4:6f.; Col 4:2–4, 12; 1 Thess 5:16–18, 25; 2 Thess 3:1f.; Philem 22; Heb 13:18f.; Jude 20).

James sets out his thoughts on prayer in the context of suffering. He has come a full turn, since he began his letter with a reference to trials (1:2) and now ends his letter on the same note (this *inclusio* pattern frames the theme of suffering that occupies much of the sections in between the opening and closing of the epistle, in particular 1:12; 2:6–7; 5:1–11). In what are ostensibly difficult times, James is thereby not advocating a stoic or impassive response to adversity, but allowing for a positive response to hardship. It may be that his exhortation is an attempt to defuse a volatile situation, suggesting that to pray is much better than to fight—a message particularly apropos in a context of Zealot-type activity. If this piece of advice is followed, then some (but not necessarily all) suffering that is the lot of the afflicted church could be avoided. Suffering that is inevitable (5:1–6) must be endured with patience (5:7–11).

Some interpreters take v 13a to be a declarative statement followed by an imperative: "Someone among you suffers. Let him pray!" (so Dibelius, 252; Mussner, 217). The consensus, however, is that v 13a is in the interrogative followed by an imperative (see Ropes, 303; JB makes the first part a condition). Yet both constructions have the same "rhetorical force" (Davids, 191). The question-imperative pattern in v 13a finds support in the parallel structure of 1 Cor 7:18, which also includes the interrogative (cf. Cantinat, 245).

The two verbs in this verse span the spectrum of emotions. In the first part of v 13, James refers to those who are suffering. κακοπαθεῖν means "to suffer" some type of misfortune. The parallel NT references (in 2 Tim 2:9; 4:5) suggest nothing of illness, and it seems better not to restrict the adversity mentioned in our present verse to physical maladies. James will deal with physical problems in v 14. Rather, κακοπαθεῖν is used here to show that James' readers are afflicted by hardship, probably as a direct consequence of their faith (cf. Josephus, *Against Apion* 2.203). Moreover, his concern is to highlight the need to bear up under this burden with patience (BGD, 397). The noun form related to κακοπαθεῖν is in v 10, where the prophets are cited as illustrating those who were persevering in the midst of suffering. James is not exhorting his readers to pray (προσευχέσθω, signifying "the natural reaction of a Christian in distress"; Pss 30:2, 8, 10; 50:15; 91:15; cf. *Pss. Sol.* 15:1; J. Herrmann, *TDNT* 2:798) for the removal of trouble as much as he is urging them to seek the strength to endure it (Michaelis, *TDNT* 5:937), but not in a stoical way.

The call in v 13 also speaks to those who are in good spirits (εὐθυμεῖν); they are to "sing a song [to God]" (ψάλλειν). Verse 13b repeats the (quasi-conditional) question-imperative pattern of v 13a. To be in "good spirits" is more than to be outwardly happy, an emotion that is dependent on circumstances (see *Comment* on 5:11). The cheerfulness described here is that of the heart (Moo, 175) and is independent of prevailing conditions. A believer can be in good spirits even if the situation is bad (see, for instance, Acts 16:25; 27:22, 25 for illustrative uses of the verbs; cf. Prov 15:15b [Symm.]; Pss 29:7 [30:6]; 67:18 [68:17] LXX; 2 Macc 11:26), and as an evidence of inner joy one should sing to God. ψάλλειν, appearing almost sixty times in the LXX, can mean either praise by means of a harp or a song sung to God with (Pss 33:2, 3; 98:4–5; 147:7; 149:3) or without (Pss 7:17; 9:2, 11) the accompaniment of an instrument (Ropes, 303). It may also be that James is reminding his readers that they must not forget God in the good times (a lapse exemplified in the merchant traders, 4:13–16). As Davids (192) writes: "Turning to God in need is half the truth; turning to him in praise either in the church or alone when one is cheerful (whatever the situation) is the other half." Praying and singing are also related in the practice of worship in the Pauline churches (1 Cor 14:15; Col 3:16–17; Eph 5:19–20: see Martin, *Worship in the Early Church*, 2d ed. [Grand Rapids: Eerdmans, 1974] 43–48). It may be then that this pericope in 5:13–16 was formed in a context of communal liturgy in the Jacobean congregation.

14 ἀσθενεῖ τις ἐν ὑμῖν, "Is there one of you weak?" James lists a third circumstance that engages prayer. Not all find themselves the victims of external suffering or share the experience of inner cheerfulness. Yet it is a much more common feature of life when people fall ill (BGD, 115; Matt 25:39; John 4:46; 11:1–3, 6; Phil 2:26–27; 2 Tim 4:20). ἀσθενεῖν can include weakness of any kind (2 Cor 12:10; Rom 4:9; 14:2; 1 Cor 8:11–12; 2 *Clem.* 17.2), but Davids (192) is probably right to conclude that the context has physical illness in mind. He points out that ἀσθενεῖν stands in conjunction with κακοπαθεῖν (5:13), that the elders are called to come to the disabled person and pray, that oil is used for anointing and that the terms σῴζειν ("to make whole") and κάμνειν ("to be ill") in 5:15 are all features to show that a physical malady is the topic of discussion (see below).

προσκαλεσάσθω τοὺς πρεσβυτέρους τῆς ἐκκλησίας, καὶ προσευξάσθωσαν ἐπ' αὐτόν, "He should summon the elders of the congregation to pray over him." James exhorts the afflicted person to summon (προσκαλεσάσθω, aorist imperative [suggesting urgency] of προσκαλεῖν, "to call to oneself") help. This suggests that he or she is confined to the sickbed and is too ill to go to the elders. The "elders" (πρεσβύτεροι, plural in our text, which speaks of a delegation of church representatives) stand for those who hold here a specific office in the early church (Mussner, 219: *Amtspersonen* is his designation). The term is never used of a Christian office in the Gospels, where it refers to Jewish elders in the synagogue, but appears as such in Acts (11:30; 14:23; 15:2; 16:4; 20:17; 21:28: the last reference is noteworthy, since it shows a scene where "elders" gather around James, who is the head of a collegium) and the epistles (1 Tim 5:17–19; Titus 1:5; 1 Pet 5:1; 2 John 1; cf. Phil 1:1). It may very well be that the office of elder was taken over from the synagogue (drawn from the "elders of Israel" in Exod 3:16; 24:1, 9; Deut 5:23; 19:12; Ezra 10:14; Matt 26:3: J. L. McKenzie, "The Elders," 522–40) and given a Christian character (Bornkamm, *TDNT* 6:651–83; cf. Mussner, 219). Other terms that appear to be synonymous for elder are "overseer" (Acts 20:28, RSV) and "bishop" (Phil 1:1; 1 Tim 3). From Acts (20:17, 28) it is evident that the elders' duties included "overseeing" or "pastoring" the flock. Since "pastors" are never mentioned together in the NT with "elders," it may be that the latter carried out responsibilities which were similar to those of the present-day pastor or "minister" (Moo, 176). If so, it is quite natural for sick members to entreat the elders to come and minister to them. Also, the term "elder" should not be construed simply to mean a person of senior age (as perhaps in 1 John 2:13, 14 addressed to "fathers"). Though some elders would likely be of mature age, the main qualification was spiritual competence (1 Tim 5:17; Titus 1:5; cf. 1 Pet 5:1–3).

Unlike 5:13—where the individual is commanded to pray for himself in times of distress as a result of external suffering—the author of the letter here urges the individual who is ill to call for the elders of the congregation (ἐκκλησία; a term used of a local assembly, in contrast to the editorial 1:1, which has the universal society in view: the best analogy to the phrase "elders of the congregation" is in 1QSa 1.23–25; 2.16 where the Heb. אבות העדה, *ʾabôt hāʿēdāh* designates the leadership at the Qumran monastery) and pray over him. The prepositional phrase ἐπ᾽ αὐτόν ("over him") should be taken (see *Note* c) with "praying" (προσευξάσθωσαν: the aorist hardly refers to a single invocation; it probably stresses urgency with the invocation, as in Acts 19:13; for parallels see Str-B 2.441) rather than with anointing (ἀλείψαντες, aorist participle of ἀλείφειν; the aorist tense may suggest that the oil was to be placed on the sick person before the praying commenced, but this is not certain, since the time of the aorist participle may well be contemporaneous with the main verb [i.e., attendant circumstance]; see Ropes, 305; Mussner, 220). The idea of praying "over" the individual leaves unclear the possibility that hands were laid on the sick person when the prayer was offered (Ps-Mark 16:18); but we must note that the elders as a group, not the individual who holds that office, are pictured as performing this ministry. There does not appear to be a specific reference to a particular elder who is looked upon as the conduit for divine healing. All this is to say that James is not describing for us the practice of "faith healing," a charism claimed by some in the Corinthian church (1 Cor 12:9, 28, 30).

The anointing of one with oil (ἔλαιον) is to be done in the name of the Lord (ἐν τῷ ὀνόματι τοῦ κυρίου). This request for God to act underscores the confidence that God is the source for any healing that is effected (Bietenhard,

TDNT 5:277–78). The "name of the Lord" also gives this practice its thoroughly Christian character (Adamson, 198), though the precise nuance to be given to the expression ἐν τῷ ὀνόματι τοῦ κυρίου is debated. The options are (i) as one commissioned by the Lord (cf. 1 Cor 5:4); (ii) by calling on the name of the Lord (Heitmüller, *Im Namen Jesu*, 86–87; Bietenhard, *TDNT* 5:277); (iii) by appealing to the power released by that name (so Mussner, 220–21, citing Luke 10:17; Acts 3:6, 16; 4:7, 10; 9:34); though options (ii) and (iii) can be combined. If so, it seems certain that "the Lord" is Jesus, reverting to vv 5f., and it is the power of the heavenly Lord (2:1) that is at work in the ministrations of the elders. On the debate in Jewish circles over Jesus' name as an effective agent of healing, see E. Stauffer, *Jesus and His Story*, tr. D. M. Barton (London: SCM, 1960), 19–20. Despite the obvious features that may be conceptualized, there remains uncertainty as to the purpose of the anointing. The only other mention in the NT of anointing the sick with oil is Mark 6:13—to which may be added the partly relevant Luke 10:34, where "oil and wine" are used to dress the wounds of the traveler (cf. Isa 1:6; Josephus, *Ant.* 17.172; *J.W.* 1.657).

There have been two main possibilities offered for the purpose of anointing the sick with oil. The first is for medicinal or practical purposes. Rituals with oil for healing were common in the ancient world (see literature cited by Davids, 193). Mention has been made of how the good Samaritan poured (ἐπιχεῖν, not ἀλείφειν or χρίειν) oil on the victim's wounds (Luke 10:34). If oil was so effective, it is problematic why it was used so infrequently in the NT. Furthermore, why is it here to be applied only by the elders? It may be thought that others—e.g., relatives, physicians—would have been qualified and eager to place curative oil on the sick person. The suggestion that only the elders should administer the oil invites the possibility that their action was meant to stimulate the faith of the sick person (Mitton, 191; D. R. Hayden, "Calling the Elders to Pray," 265). But this is at best conjecture, and we simply do not have much evidence to elaborate how "healing" was practiced. The paucity of data in the NT is itself a caution against drawing too many conclusions regarding early church practice.

The other explanation of anointing with oil sees it as symbolic. It was discussed earlier (*Form/Structure/Setting*) how the anointing with oil symbolized God's concern for and faithfulness to his people in time of distress. This tangible evidence of his trustworthiness lets the afflicted one know that God's plan will be carried out, whatever the outcome. As we shall see, v 15 shows that the uttering of a prayer for healing does not automatically ensure that the sick will recover. The reason why some people recover and others do not remains a mystery to faith, since the NT contains accounts of both recovery (in the Gospels and Acts) and nonrecovery (1 Cor 11:30; 2 Cor 12:1–10; 2 Tim 4:20) and one illustration (Phil 2:25–30) of recovery without any procedure remotely resembling this Jacobean text.

There are two words, ἀλείφειν and χρίειν, both meaning "to anoint." The latter would have been a better choice to show that the anointing of oil was for symbolic or religious reasons; but the choice of the former does not eliminate this understanding. First, χρίειν is never used in the NT for the physical act of anointing, as the action in James 5:14 requires, but it is always used in a metaphorical sense (Luke 4:18 = Isa 61:1; Acts 4:27; 10:38; 2 Cor

1:21; Heb 1:9 = Ps 45:7). ἀλείφειν thus may have been chosen over χρίειν because of standard usage yet still with the intention of conveying the thought that the anointing of oil was symbolic. Second, in the LXX ἀλείφειν as well as χρίειν can be used to depict the consecration of priests (Exod 40:15; cf. 40:13; see also Josephus, *Ant.* 6.165, 167), which shows that the two verbs could be synonymous in describing a symbolic action in the OT. Thus, it seems possible to conclude that the anointing with oil in 5:14 shows that the sick person has been set aside for special favor (and special use?) by God (Moo, 179–81). As will be seen in v 15, this symbolic understanding of the anointing of the sick person with oil fits in with the rest of this paragraph.

The illustrative value of the action is parallel with the "example" given in the *pedilavium* of John 13:1–15. It has been suggested (by Schoeps, *Theologie und Geschichte*, 348) that the anointing rite in James belonged to a phase of Jewish Christianity, from which it then passed into the practices of the Clementine literature (*Clem. Recogn.* 1.44–45; Hippolytus, *Philos.* 9.15; Epiphanius, *Haer.* 19.1.6). On this setting of second-century Jewish Christian piety see *Introduction*, pp. xlv–xlvii.

15 καὶ ἡ εὐχὴ τῆς πίστεως σώσει τὸν κάμνοντα καὶ ἐγερεῖ αὐτὸν ὁ κύριος, "And the request based on faith will make the sick one well; and the Lord will raise him up." Difficulties in deciding what exactly in the preceding verse is meant by anointing should not cause us to overlook the main point of vv 13–18, which is prayer. It is prayer—not the anointing—which leads to the healing of the sick person. This prayer is described as a fervent wish or request (ἡ εὐχή) offered in faith (τῆς πίστεως). The faith mentioned here is evidently, if not exclusively, that of the elders. The results of this "request based on faith" are that the sick person (i) will be made well (σώσει, lit., "made whole") and (ii) will be raised by the Lord. The verb σώζειν is often used in the NT to refer to the eschatological salvation of believers (see BGD, 798; this idea is close to the meaning of the same verb in 5:20), suggesting to some scholars that James is referring to deliverance from spiritual death. This argument gains support if ἀσθενεῖν (v 14) means "to be spiritually weak" (as in Rom 14:2; 1 Cor 8:11–12), as may be the case with κάμνειν (in v 15: see Heb 12:3). Moreover, ἰᾶσθαι ("to cure") can conceivably be understood as referring to a restoration to spiritual wholeness (cf. Meinertz, "Die Krankensalbung"; Pickar, "Is Anyone Sick?"; Hayden, "Calling the Elders to Pray"). Yet these are exceptional meanings attached to the vocabulary. ἀσθενεῖν and κάμνειν are better understood to refer to cases of physical illness (cf. Wisd Sol 4:16; 15:9; *Sib. Or.* 3.588, where the meaning is "to be seriously"—but not necessarily terminally—"ill"). ἰᾶσθαι most naturally refers to the curing of a person who is sick (see Moo, 184). In addition, σώζειν (Mark 5:23, 28, 34; 10:52; John 11:12) and ἐγείρειν (Mark 1:31; 2:9–12; 9:27; Matt 9:5–7; Acts 3:7; Josephus, *Ant.* 19.294) can be used to describe someone who is healed of a physical malady.

What Mussner (221) calls the "chief problem" in this verse centers on how the future verbs σώσει, ἐγερεῖ, and ἀφεθήσεται are to be taken. Is the sense "logical" or "eschatological," i.e., is the action of God in response to the prayer of faith one that effects recovery in healing at the moment or is the restoration that of the last day when the dead will be raised to new life?

The lexical data are difficult to sort out. σῴζειν does have an eschatological flavor in this letter, as was noted (p. 201). But the elders are called to a situation where the sick person is still alive, not deceased, and, as has been noted, ἐγείρειν normally means recovery from illness rather than being awakened at the resurrection of the dead (Oepke, *TDNT* 2:337). The promise of forgiveness more naturally belongs to this life than to the next; and the triad of verbs refer to events that are all in the same time frame, i.e., referring to God's action now in consequence of the prayer of faith. Yet some doubts remain, not least that the specific medical verb for healing (ἰᾶσθαι) is not found until v 16.

κἂν ἁμαρτίας ᾖ πεποιηκώς, ἀφεθήσεται αὐτῷ, "If he has committed sins, he will be forgiven." Though there is no strict equation of illness and sinfulness (a denial that goes back to the book of Job; cf. John 9:1–3; 11:4) James leaves open the possibility that some sickness is connected with sin (cf. Str-B, 4:525 ff.; *T. Reuben* 1.7). This use of the perfect participle (πεποιηκώς) suggests the power of past sins that affect the present situation of the sufferer. This consequence may be in the form of continuing guilt (so Davids, 195), or it may be an illness that remains despite the prayer for healing. If illness is related to sin, the asking of forgiveness of sin (as confessed both to God and to the injured party) will lead to healing (a promise that was known at Qumran, 1QS 1.23–2.1, and in pietist Judaism, *Pss. Sol.* 9.6: "He will cleanse from sins the confessing soul").

16a   ἐξομολογεῖσθε οὖν ἀλλήλοις τὰς ἁμαρτίας καὶ εὔχεσθε ὑπὲρ ἀλλήλων ὅπως ἰαθῆτε, "Confess your sins to one another then, and pray for one another so that you may be healed." James implies that sometimes sin is a cause of illness, as well as a hindrance to healing, which is the thrust of v 16a. The conjunction οὖν ("therefore") connects the thought of v 16a with that of v 15 (see Bonhoeffer, *Life Together*, 86–89). It suggests that the discussion of physical healing and the forgiveness of sin started in v 15 is continued in our present verse (so Dibelius, 255, against Cantinat, 254, and Mussner, 227). Vouga, 143, maintains that there is a remarkable "flow of ideas" in the entire section, and accounts for the presence of ἰᾶσθαι, "to heal physically," in v 16 as the chief conclusion to which James' thought is moving, namely, the restoration of sound pastoral relations within the body of the community more than the cure of illnesses.

Sin and sickness went hand in hand in the ancient mind (cf. the case of Job. This OT figure has been in view in 5:11, where Job was an example of one who remained faithful to God in the midst of suffering. Job's "friends" understood his suffering to be the result of sin, a charge that Job vigorously rejected). The confession of sin was then evidentially necessary if healing was to occur. The present imperative form, ἐξομολογεῖσθε, suggests that James is requiring that confession become a repeated action. The practice of public confession was important to Judaism and the early church (see Davids, 195; cf. Michel, *TDNT* 5:202–20). (The main sources are Pss 37:5–7, 19 [= 38:4–6, 18; 39:13 [40:12]; 40:5 [41:4]; 50:5–10 [51:3–8]; Prov 20:9; 28:13; *Pss. Sol.* 9.6; 1QS 1.23–2.1; CD 20.28 ff.; Bar 1:15–2:10; Tob 3:1–6, 11–15; 3 Macc 2:2–20; 6:2–15. For rabbinic data see Str-B, 1:113. For the early church cf. *Did.* 4.4; 14.1.)

In this context the elders of v 14 are not mentioned, an omission that leads Mussner (225–26) to argue that v 16 begins a new section in spite of the connective οὖν. The word ἰᾶσθαι ("to heal")—except when it is part of OT quotations (e.g., Isa 53:6; 1 Pet 2:24)—is always used in the NT to refer to the healing of physical illness. This comports with the interpretation of the setting of vv 14–16 above (see also Mitton, 202–6). The present verse suggests a corporate setting for the prayer of healing, which is different from the admonition to enlist only the prayers of the elders in v 14. Davids (195, supported by Moo, 183; and similarly Vouga, 143) believes that "James . . . consciously generalizes, making the specific case of 5:14–15 into a general principle of preventive medicine." By saying that church members other than elders can take part in a ministry of intercessory prayer (which is effective; see 5:16b), the author is showing that the prayer, not the person (i.e., not the elders), is the channel through which God's power to heal is conveyed. This speaks against the view that 5:14 is referring to "healing" as a spiritual χάρισμα. Moreover, though the elders are still responsible for the prayer of intercession on behalf of the ill (5:14), the text here widens to make prayer and confession and so pastoral responsibility the "privilege and responsibility" of all in the congregation. The precise setting of this pastoral reminder will be evident from 5:19–20.

16b Πολὺ ἰσχύει δέησις δικαίου ἐνεργουμένη, "The righteous person's prayer is very powerful in its effectiveness." James undergirds his exhortations to pray with a reference to the effective power of prayer. But he is quick to point out that such power is not limited to a special class of elite "charismatics." There is no select group of Christians (e.g., the elders or the teachers) who have a monopoly in the matter of effectual prayer. James associates the prayer described in v 16b with the righteous person (δίκαιος). This is probably not a reference to Elijah (Spitta, 149) or a specific holy person in Judaism, e.g., in Sir 45:23 (cited in Mussner, 228; cf. Davids, 196). "Righteous person" may be a reference to some community member(s) who exhibit the behavior of exemplars committed to doing God's will (a characterization that would fit the church of Matthew's Gospel: Schrenk, *TDNT* 2:187, 190–91; see *Introduction*, pp. xciii–xcviii) which includes, but is not limited to, confessing sins to one another (Matt 1:19; Heb 12:23; 1 Pet 4:18; 1 John 3:7; Rev 22:11). Another possibility is that "righteous person" is the same as the "righteous one" of 5:6. A link between the two verses makes it feasible that James' own prayer is here being held up to emulation by the editor.

On the other hand, belief in powerful prayers is a conviction common enough in early Judaism. The text uses another word for prayer in v 16b (δέησις), but it appears there is little if any difference in meaning (BGD, 171–72; but see Trench, *Synonyms*, 188–89) from the other two words for prayer in this passage (see προσευχή, in vv 13–14, 17–18; εὐχή in v 15). James describes the prayer of a righteous person as "very powerful in its effectiveness"; πολὺ ἰσχύει ("very powerful") has a practical force, denoting that such a prayer "is able to do much" (BGD 383). The question is whether the prayer is "mighty in what it is able to do [or] . . . in what it is enabled to do" (Adamson, 210). This turns on the decision whether the participle ἐνεργουμένη ("effective") is middle voice ("the prayer is very powerful in its working") or passive ("prayer is very powerful when it is energized by the Spirit").

There has been much debate (but hardly "profitless," so Tasker, 137) over the correct interpretation of the participle. Mayor (177–79) understands it to be passive (as does Ropes, 309). Against him stand Adamson, 199, 205–10; Moo, 187; Moule, *Idiom Book,* 26 (and most modern interpreters), who take ἐνεργουμένη as middle. (Other options are to construe ἐνεργουμένη as an adjective, so rendered as "the energetic prayer" [so Dibelius, 256; Cantinat, 256; Laws, 234]; or as a temporal participle, "when it is effective" [Mussner, 228]). No matter how the choice between passive or middle is resolved, James' meaning is fairly clear: the righteous person can (by interceding) offer effective prayer on behalf of those who are ill as a consequence of sinning. It might be argued that the passive highlights God's role as the supplier of the power behind all healing (Davids, 197). But to take the participle as middle in no way limits God's participation in the healing of the sick and fits the context better. The use of the middle does not diminish God's role in healing; instead it emphasizes the fact that those who are ill because of sin (and have confessed this sin) have immediate access to the channel through which they can receive healing from the divine source.

17–18 Ἠλίας ἄνθρωπος ἦν ὁμοιοπαθὴς ἡμῖν, καὶ προσευχῇ προσηύξατο τοῦ μὴ βρέξαι, καὶ οὐκ ἔβρεξεν ἐπὶ τῆς γῆς ἐνιαυτοὺς τρεῖς καὶ μῆνας ἕξ· καὶ πάλιν προσηύξατο, καὶ ὁ οὐρανὸς ὑετὸν ἔδωκεν καὶ ἡ γῆ ἐβλάστησεν τὸν καρπὸν αὐτῆς, "Elijah was a man with a nature like ours; he prayed earnestly that it might not rain, and it did not rain on the land for three and a half years. ¹⁸He prayed later, and the heavens gave rain, and the land produced its harvest crop." James cites an OT figure (the other three worthies mentioned in the letter are Abraham, Rahab, and Job) in order to illustrate the truth of v 16. The first point James makes about Elijah is that he "was a man with a nature like" the readers of the epistle. The term ὁμοιοπαθής denotes one with the "same limitations" as all human beings (Adamson, 200). The best comparison is with the use of the adjective in Acts 14:15 (its only other occurrence in the NT), where Paul and Barnabas implore the startled citizens of Lystra not to consider them as gods but as people just like themselves. James intends to reinforce the thought of v 16 that any human being who is righteous can offer an effective prayer. This type of prayer is, then, not out of the reach of the people of James' church (Mayor, 179). Included in the idea of "like nature" is the thought of suffering (πάθος; so Reicke, 66, and earlier, p. 203). Thus, James is describing the common bond between his readers and Elijah.

προσευχῇ προσηύξατο, lit., "in prayer he prayed," a construction reflecting the influence of a Semitic idiom (with an imitation of the Hebrew infinitive absolute; BDF § 198.6), may imply nothing more than the simple fact that Elijah prayed (Moule, *Idiom Book,* 177–78). Elijah prayed "intensely" and "earnestly desiring" (see Luke 22:15; Acts 12:5; Col 4:12 for other specimens of urgent praying) that God might answer his prayer. This is not to deduce that all "intense" prayers are answered (see *Comment* on 5:15–16). James is informing his readers that they like Elijah have access to the power of the divine, even if the precise way that prayer "succeeds" must be left open (see *Explanation*).

The situation concerning Elijah is recorded in 1 Kgs 17–18. These chapters do not say explicitly that Elijah prayed that it might not rain, though 18:42 suggests that the prophet did pray for the drought to cease. Except for

1 Kgs 18:42 (and 27:20–22), Elijah is not renowned in the OT for his praying (but see Patai, "The 'Control of Rain,'" especially 257, on Elijah as a rainmaker, blending prayer and "magical" practices. Rabbinic legend gave him the title of the "key of rain"). Later Jewish tradition then pictures him as such a person (4 Ezra 7:39–109; *m. Ta'an.* 2:4; *b. Sanh.* 113a; *j. Sanh.* 10.28b; *j. Ber.* 5.9b; *j. Ta'an.* 1.63d; cf. Jeremias, *TDNT* 2:929–30; Str-B, 4:769; see Mussner, 229), and these traditional tributes may be shared by the present text.

The period of three and a half years for the duration of the drought (cf. Luke 4:25) may be a symbolic figure reflecting the yearly number for a period of judgment (Dan 7:25; 12:7; Rev 11:2; 12:14; cf. Dibelius, 256–57). If so, this is a way of comforting the church in the last days (Reicke, 61). "Three and a half" may be taken equally as a more specific number for the approximate "three years" of 1 Kgs (18:1). Davids (197) believes (with some imagination) that a drought-stricken land reflects what a Christian who is ill might feel, namely, "dry and dead." But the picture continues, and the righteous person offers a prayer on behalf of the sick. The result of this prayer is that the Christian, who was formerly ill, is now refreshed, much like the parched land that is revived by rain. Thus the figure Elijah has been chosen by James to show that a righteous person of the church can call upon the grace of God so that sick members are healed. It may be that the fruit to be brought forth (v 18) is meant by James to suggest that the healed (and forgiven) member can now take a productive place in the congregation again; the thought moves from the individual need (v 14) to corporate conditions that require attention (v 16).

Two features permit a more particular setting based on the use made of the Elijah story. Attention has already been drawn to the political trials in which the prophet found himself and to the way he faced a nationalist upsurge in time of distress. (i) The shift from the individual in need to the congregation in v 16 suggests that in the background lies the social circumstance in which the Jacobean congregation was placed, and that its leader is using traditions about James the Just as the second Elijah to moderate their zeal. (ii) The occurrence of καρπός, "fruit," would recall to the observant reader the discussion of heavenly wisdom in 3:17–18 with its promise that the "fruit of righteousness is sown in peace for those who make peace." So the example of Elijah is used as a counterpoint to stress once again the need for a peaceful solution gained by prayer and submission to the divine will. The model of the farmer (in 5:7) whose patience is rewarded when he awaits the "choice fruit" (τὸν τίμιον καρπόν) of the harvest field in due season makes the same point.

Explanation

The plain teaching of 5:12 is that for a Christian his or her word should be binding. James is thereby reverting to one of his favorite themes, namely, the use of one's words to reflect the character of the individual who uses them. Words have to be taken seriously, not regarded as an excuse to evade responsibility by a "nonbinding" oath or a flippant way of speaking. Both types of duplicitous speaking were condemned by Jesus, according to Matt

5:33–37, and the early church took a similar vein, though calling God as a witness in a mild asseveration of truthfulness is also found, notably in Paul (e.g., 2 Cor 11:31).

There is a possibility, however, that the one-verse pericope is more sharply nuanced than a general condemnation of "oaths"; and the earlier *Comment* section has looked at the background in nonconformist Judaism, particularly among the Zealots, which adopted a practice of oath-taking as a solemn pledge of patriotic fervor. If this is the setting, James is opposed to it, for reasons already described throughout the irenic letter. Some examples of what such "oaths" could mean are given in Acts 23:12, 21.

The scene abruptly changes at 5:13, and the reader enters a world of congregational relationships which embrace the entire spectrum of life's experiences, extending from gladness to sadness. The mood oscillates throughout this brief section and offers a tantalizing yet puzzling glimpse of how the early Judeo-Christian believers reacted to life's circumstances. The fact that these verses with their detailed prescriptions and procedures stand out uniquely in the New Testament should give us pause before rushing to the conclusion that here are matters that are normative and essential whenever Christians face the harsh realities of trouble, sickness, sins, and natural disasters. The exegetical results we have surveyed in the *Comment* section need not be rehearsed. But they leave us with the more difficult problems of "saying what the text means" in a modern context. Four considerations should be given due weight before a relevant "application" or *Nachdenken* is reached.

First, if the setting is found in the life of Jewish Christianity, we are looking at the scenario that belonged to the formative stage of the Christian movement and one from which it developed in response to the processes of growth and expansion into a world faith. A comparable instance would be the use of the Apostolic Decree of Acts 15, which laid down "rules" for promoting table fellowship between Jews and Gentiles in the nascent communities. It may be argued, from the Jewish Christian side sponsored by James, that such restrictions, listed in Acts 15:19–20; 21:25, were needful, lest Jewish sensitivities should be damaged. The rules promoted goodwill until the day when a true *koinonia* between both wings of the church could be established on a lasting and theologically valid base. Paul moved to that position more rapidly than other preachers and leaders in his day; hence the debates that run through his epistles (Galatians, 2 Corinthians, Philippians: see Martin, "Setting of 2 Corinthians," in *2 Corinthians,* WBC 40 [Waco: Word, 1986], lii–lxi) and which caused temporary hostility to his mission as a world-embracing manifesto. The future, however, clearly lay with Paul if the church was to fulfill its role as a truly "catholic" movement with a task to reach out to all nations and proclaim Jesus Christ as universal Lord. The Apostolic Decree could have no place in such a widened vision, since, for Paul, it looked back to Mosaic-Levitical regulations and taboos that the advent of a new eschatological age in the coming of Israel's messiah and the world's ruler had antiquated. The "husk"—needful at one stage—had to drop away in order to allow the "kernel" to be seen on its own and for what it was.

This illustration may be useful to account for the way that the procedures outlined in this section of 5:13–18 found no permanent and mandatory place in the life of the church, though the verses may be said to have limited value within the canon as throwing light on what life in a Judeo-Christian community was like (see Schoeps, *Theologie,* referred to earlier). In a different culture and at a time when medical and clinical practice was different from what we know today, the principles of prayer to God for healing and recovery are illustrated and may still hold a place for the faithful Christian. At the same time the manipulative or therapeutic uses of oil—if that is how we are to understand v 14—may be said to belong to the outer "shell," along with the ministry of "elders" who bring the goodwill of the church's fellowship, while the power of corporate intercession is still a valuable aid to healing, as most Christian groups will readily acknowledge.

Second, there is a hermeneutical key to the entire passage in noting that it is prefaced by the verb in v 13 rendered: "to face adversity." It could be that this situation dominates the entire section, with the result that the physical afflictions that incapacitate the sick person and bring the elders onto the scene are the direct consequence of that person's loyalty to the messianic faith. If the entire letter addresses a Judeo-messianic community under trial, here is one special case of what that trial has brought in its wake. The illustration the author cites is, then, not to do with illness in general or sufferings encountered in the rough and tumble of life, but with the specific trials that belong to a persecuted group. In that company the person overtaken in distress is given encouragement to enlist the aid of church leaders who will visit him as a token of both the congregation's continuing concern for him in his need and God's faithfulness in not abandoning him when his faith is at low ebb. Perhaps too the "sins" that need to be confessed and remitted are those lapses from faithful endurance that James has written to warn about throughout the course of this hortatory tract.

The force of these observations is to see the passage in a distinctly contextual setting, and to extract what may be taken as underlying principles without becoming enmeshed in trying to work out how the details of the text are to be carried over into our modern understanding and church pastoralia.

Third, by common consent the chief emphasis is on prayer, as was noted. The passage has much to say about prayer's opportunity and efficacy. Believers will pray in time of need, just as they will raise the note of praise to God when life goes well with them (v 13b). At first glance, James has such an unbounded confidence in the power of prayer that nothing seems impossible— and nothing is denied. The request for physical recovery and reinstatement in v 15 looks to be granted in such an unequivocal way that the results are automatic and inevitable. But this cannot be so, for a number of reasons. James has earlier noted that some prayers do fail (4:1–3) just as some prayers succeed (1:5–6). Much depends on the motive of the person who prays. Then, the verbs "to be made well," "to be raised up" are far from clear, though it may be safest to take them in their natural meaning of a return to wholeness. Yet believers are still mortal men and women, and no person can be so self-deluded as to imagine that v 15 guarantees immunity from a final illness that leads to the terminus of one's earthly pilgrimage, which comes to all and to some sooner than they desire. All prayer is bounded by the providence and sovereign favor of God, who knows believers' truest needs and may not grant their natural requests in just the way they would choose. The same paradox runs through the recorded teaching of Jesus. He encouraged his disciples to pray with unlimited expectation (Mark 11:22–24; cf. John 16:23). Yet he himself prayed always within the ambit of God's will, which cannot be infallibly known in advance (Mark 14:34–42). Always Christian prayer requires our submission to the Father's wisdom and knowledge, and even when our praying is at its most persistent and urgent, the fact remains that God gives only what is for his children's ultimate good (Luke 11:5–13; 2 Cor 12:8–10). James' teaching then has to be set in this wider frame; only disappointment and frustration will come if the modern interpreter fails to heed that caution.

Finally, the place of corporate confession plays a prominent part in this section, and may well be regarded as a Jacobean distinctive the modern church needs to re-hear. No one has perceived this facet better than Dietrich Bonhoeffer in his spiritual classic *Life Together,* chap. 5.

Our text invites us to consider the gaining of spiritual wholeness (which is not to be confused with the curing of disease or illness; these may remain, while healing is granted, as in 2 Cor 12:1–10). It also encourages us to share this ministry with fellow Christians in mutual confession and mutual concern for another's pardon. Obviously there are dangers and pitfalls when we tread on this ground. There is no warrant in the text for "auricular confession to a priest," as popular and polemic Protestantism has dubbed the practice, just as the use of oil in v 14 is far removed from the later sacrament of Extreme Unction, adumbrated by Bede and first stated by Peter Lombard in the twelfth century as a sacramental rite of passage for the dying (see Puller, *Anointing*). Two hazards to do with corporate confession are to be watched for and avoided: they are overmorbidity and introspection on the one side, and exhibitionism and an overzealous interest in another person's spiritual health on the other.

Yet we need often to share a burden, and to respond to the wise counsel of v 16. Observing these precautions and gladly accepting the sound advice of James as his mentor, Bonhoeffer writes (ibid., 92), with due respect for those who feel no need to enter into this practice and yet with a pastoral sensitivity for those who would genuinely benefit from adopting what the text holds out:

Does all this mean that confession to a brother is a divine law? No, confession is not a law, it is an offer of divine help for the sinner. It is possible that a person may by God's grace break through to certainty, new life, the Cross, and fellowship without benefit of confession to a brother. It is possible that a person may never know what it is to doubt his own forgiveness and despair of his own confession of sin, that he may be given everything in his own private confession to God. We have spoken here for those who cannot make this assertion. Luther himself was one of those for whom the Christian life was unthinkable without mutual, brotherly confession. In the *Large Catechism* he said: 'Therefore when I admonish you to confession I am admonishing you to be a Christian'. Those who, despite all their seeking and trying, cannot find the great joy of fellowship, the Cross, the new life, and certainty should be shown the blessing that God offers us in mutual confession. Confession is within the liberty of the Christian. Who can refuse, without suffering loss, a help that God has deemed it necessary to offer?

6. Final Words and Fraternal Admonitions (5:19–20)

Bibliography

Bonnard, P. "Matthieu éducateur du peuple chrétien." In *Mélanges biblique en hommage au B. Rigaux,* ed. A. Descamps and A. de Halle. Gembloux: Duculot, 1970. 1–7. **Gnilka, J.** "Die Kirche des Matthäus und die Gemeinde von Qumran." *BZ* n.f. 7 (1963) 43–63. **Nötscher, F.** "'Wahrheit' als theologischer Begriff in den Qumran-Texten." *Vom Alten zum Neuen Testament.* BBB 17. Köln-Bonn: Hanstein, 1962. 112–25. **Thyen, H.** *Studien zur Sündenvergebung.* FRLANT 96. Göttingen: Vandenhoeck und Ruprecht, 1970. 236–43.

Translation

[19] *My brothers, when anyone of your number* [a] *has strayed from the truth,* [b] *and one [of you] turns him back,* [20] *be assured* [c] *that whoever turns back a sinner from the error of his way will rescue him from death* [d] *and will cover many sins.* [e]

Notes

[a] ἐν ὑμῖν, lit., "among you," as in 5:13–14 could be Semitic, but cf. Moulton-Howard-Turner, *Grammar* 3:210, for classical parallels.

[b] There are additions to ἀπὸ τῆς ἀληθείας (read by TR and the major codices): ἀπὸ τῆς ὁδοῦ τῆς ἀληθείας (in ℵ 31 81 syrP boh), based on v 20's text ἐκ πλάνης τῆς ὁδοῦ αὐτοῦ. P[74] has (ἀπὸ τῆς) ὁδοῦ in place of ἀληθείας, which again is symmetrical with v 20 (Mussner, 231 n.3).

[c] γινώσκετε is read by B 69 1505 1518 2495 syrʰ etc. (Metzger, *Textual Commentary,* 685). It is probably a scribal error for γινωσκέτω in ℵ A K P vg and intended to produce an imperative verb that is in agreement with the earlier plural imperatives. Or else it is intended to avoid the ambiguity as to the identity of the subject of the verb, the one who converts or the one who is converted (Metzger, *Textual Commentary,* 686).

[d] αὐτοῦ ἐκ θανάτου (attested by ℵ A 33 vg) is to be championed as the reading best calculated to explain the others. As Metzger (ibid., 686) remarks, there is the ambiguity of αὐτοῦ with ψυχήν, "his soul," which poses the question, whose soul? the converter's or that of the one who is converted? Scribes either (1) transferred αὐτοῦ to follow ἐκ θανάτου, i.e., "from death itself" (p[74] B 614 1108 1611 1852 2138 itᶠᶠ) or (2) omitted αὐτοῦ but retained ἐκ θανάτου (K L Ψ and most minuscules). Note that Wikgren in Metzger's book prefers ἐκ θανάτου αὐτοῦ.

[e] Later witnesses add ἀμήν and 330 supplies a doxology, ὅτι αὐτῷ ἡ δόξα εἰς τοὺς αἰῶνας ἀμήν.

Form/Structure/Setting

The preceding reference to sin and pardon (5:15–16) has evidently prompted a reversion to these themes at the letter's close. The parenetic appeal is to the danger of the sin of apostasy ("straying from the truth") and the need to recover the errant fellow member. The hortatory spirit is not evangelistic but is directed to the life of the community from which a "brother" is tempted to wander (Mussner, 230 n.4).

The short conclusion gives the appearance of being an isolated unit, devoted to the *topos* of pastoral care. The idioms are OT-Jewish (with terms like "stray," "truth," "error"; cf. the Dead Sea Scrolls evidence in Nötscher, "Wahrheit"), though it may be observed that James speaks of "the error of his way" rather than the way of error, as in Jewish (Wisd Sol 12:24) and Christian Two Ways teaching (in Matt 7:13–14; 21:32; *Barnabas*, *Did.* chaps. 1–4). Nor should it be supposed that doctrinal error leading to heresy is chiefly envisaged. The stress, as throughout the letter, is on practical faith, on orthopraxis more than orthodoxy, as 3:13–18 illustrate.

The *pastoralia*, however, does resemble the ethos and directives of the Rule of the Community (1QS) at Qumran, and even more the situation in Matt 18:15–17 with its individualizing tones (cf. Bonnard, "Matthieu éducateur du peuple chrétien," 1–7) and its stress on the sin of abandoning the fellowship and the steps required to readmit the sinner to community life. We cannot locate the setting of 5:19–20 with any great precision, but if we imagine with James or the redactor a tightly knit and persecuted community from which the temptation to defect was ever-present, it is easy to see how the pastor would want to encourage his people to have regard to the wayward member and to make an effort actively to restore such a person.

Comment

19 Ἀδελφοί μου, ἐάν τις ἐν ὑμῖν πλανηθῇ ἀπὸ τῆς ἀληθείας καὶ ἐπιστρέψῃ τις αὐτόν, "My brothers, when anyone of your number has strayed from the truth and one [of you] turns him back." Vv 19–20 form the closing section of the epistle. Absent from these verses are the usual greetings and benediction, so often found in the endings of Pauline letters. Rather, James concludes his letter (which reads at times like a sermon) with an exhortation to refrain from disobedience. Such an ending is similar to 1 John: "Little children, keep yourself from idols" (5:21). ἀδελφοί μου, "my brothers," is used for the last time by our author. This address may be James' way of signaling that he is finishing his letter (see "little children" at the conclusion of 1 John 5:21). Davids (198) takes "my brothers" to indicate that these verses were originally a separate unit, but such a position does not imply that vv 19–20 are unrelated to what precedes them. The idea of confession in vv 19–20 is an extension of the themes of confession and forgiveness of vv 13–18. Furthermore (as Davids goes on), the intent of James here to turn his readers from error sums up the overall purpose of this letter—indeed the term "wandering brother" recalls many serious problems addressed by this epistle (e.g., misuse of the tongue, jealousy, lack of concern for the poor, worldliness, quarreling; see Adamson, 202). The thrust of the entire epistle has been to prevent any Christian from wandering from the truth; if there is a lapse, he should be brought back. The use of ἐν ὑμῖν ("among you"; see *Note* a) indicates that v 19 is directed at a community member and not at those outside the church who are the object of evangelization (cf. 5:15–16).

The person who wanders (πλανᾶν) is not one who has accidentally or unconsciously departed from the truth (Michaelis, *TDNT* 5:49–53). Rather the term as used implies that the person is guilty of apostasy (i.e., rejection of the revealed will of God; so Davids, 198). Behind the term are the ideas of idolatry (see Isa 9:5; Jer 23:17; Ezek 33:19; Prov 14:8; Wisd Sol 5:6; 12:24; Sir 11:16) and ethical dualism (*T. Jud.* 14.1, 8; 19.4; 23.1; *T. Gad* 3.1; *T. Levi* 3.3; 11.1; cf. 1QS 3.1; 5.4; CD 3.1; 4.14; 5.20). It can be said that actions leading to apostasy are thought of as under Satanic influence (see Braun, *TDNT* 6:233–53). This attribution is borne out in much of the NT literature (see Matt 12:22–37; 24:4–5, 11; Mark 12:24, 27; 13:5–6; Rom 1:27; Eph 4:14; 2 Thess 2:11; 2 Tim 3:13; Titus 3:3; 1 Pet 2:25; 2 Pet 2:15, 18; 1 John 2:26; 4:6; Rev 2:20). James has already given attention to the warning that certain misbehavior is the work of the devil (3:15; 4:7; cf. 2:19). Thus, a person who deliberately forsakes the "way of righteousness" is under the control of the devil and in need of a radical conversion. Otherwise, this person faces the risk of condemnation by God.

The person in question is accused of wandering from the truth (ἀλήθεια). The truth mentioned here may include some type of aberration (2:19), but as Moo, 189, aptly puts it: "truth is something that is to be 'done' as well as believed" (see also Davids, 199, and references in Jewish writings that stress how practical a concept "truth" is; e.g., Pss 25:5; 26:3; 86:11; similarly 1 Kgs 2:4; 2 Kgs 20:3; Tob 3:5; 1QS 1.12, 26; 3.19; 4.17). This is consistent with James' teaching that correct doctrine must be accompanied by corresponding behavior (1:18; 2:14–26; 3:13–18). The person guilty of straying from the truth could easily be characterized as one who emphasizes orthodoxy (as in 2:19) more than orthopraxis. Failure to exhibit a practical faith should (in James' mind) lead those in the community to seek to ensure a recovery (ἐπιστρέφειν) of the apostate. A radical conversion can describe the initial turning to God at the time of salvation (Acts 14:15; 15:19; 26:18; 1 Thess 1:9), but (as is here) it can also refer to a "turning back" to God from whom one has strayed (Mark 4:12; Luke 1:16; 22:32). James has not left the straying person to care for himself but has placed the burden of "reclamation" upon those of the church who are still in the fold (cf. Matt 18:15–20 as part of a *correctio fraterna* in Matthew's church; cf. J. Gnilka, "Die Kirche," 53–55).

20 γινωσκέτω ὅτι ὁ ἐπιστρέψας ἁμαρτωλὸν ἐκ πλάνης ὁδοῦ αὐτοῦ σώσει ψυχὴν αὐτοῦ ἐκ θανάτου καὶ καλύψει πλῆθος ἁμαρτιῶν, "Be assured that whoever turns back a sinner from the error of his way will rescue him from death and will cover many sins." The person who turns back (ὁ ἐπιστρέψας, aorist participle of ἐπιστρέφειν, the same verb as in v 19) a "sinner from the error of his way" (the idea is evidently derived from Ezek 33:11; Mussner, 232, points to Yahweh's action in Ezek 34:11–16 as concerned to win back the erring nation; ὁδός is used here in an ethical sense as in Ps 1:6 and Proverbs [BGD, 554]; note that the noun appears in the text without the article, which reflects some Semitic coloring, BDF § 259.3) should know (γινωσκέτω; see *Note* c) that a soul (ψυχή used here in the theological sense of the "eternal soul" as in 1:21; Moule, *Idiom Book*, 185) has been saved from death (see *Note* d). The connotation of death here is that of eternal consequence rather than only a physical demise (Deut 30:19; Job 8:13; Pss 1:6; 2:12; Prov 2:18; 12:28; 14:12; 15:10; 4 Ezra 7:48; 2 *Apoc. Bar.* 85.13; and especially in this letter, 1:15; cf. Volz, *Die Eschatologie der jüdischen Gemeinde*, 306; Michaelis, *TDNT* 5:48–65). The reference to "the covering of a multitude of sins" (RSV), which parallels the saving of the person from death (see *Note* d), recalls Prov 10:12 (see also 1 Pet 4:8; 1 *Clem.* 49.5; 2 *Clem.* 16.4). The phrase "covering of sins" implies forgiveness (Pss 32:1; 85:2; Dan 4:24; Rom 4:7) and the concept of a plurality ("many") of sins suggests the "extent of the forgiveness" (Davids,

200; cf. 2:13b, which remarks on the wideness of God's mercy). The language used in this verse, with terms such as "turn back," "sinner," "sins," and "save," recalls *T. Abr.* 116.32 ff. (noted by Mussner, 233 n.3, who further suggests that "to save oneself from death" derives from baptismal speech in early Christianity).

An exegetical question is: who is saved from eternal death and whose sins are covered? There is disagreement because the Greek text is ambiguous. Jewish sources are quoted to the effect that the one who turns a sinner to repentance is deserving of forgiveness himself (Dibelius, 259–60). Thus, the person who is the reclaimer (of the reclaimed) is pictured as saving his own soul (Cantinat, 262; see Adamson, 202–4). But while there may be a reward in mind for those who heed James' command (see below), it is not likely that the forgiveness of sin and the resulting salvation are meant to be made dependent on the action of the one who turns the sinner back to God. The one who reclaims the lost is assumed to have *already* experienced forgiveness of sin and received the assurance of eternal life. Even less likely is the position of many commentators that while the soul saved is that of the sinner, the sins covered are those of the one who turned the sinner back to God (so Mussner, 233, appealing to Ezek 3:20–21; Laws, 240–41; Ropes, 315–16). This appears to place an undue burden on the readers of James to have to sort out the promises made to two different persons. It is more than likely that the "soul saved" and the "sins covered" are the two phrases referring to the sinner who was turned back to God (Davids, 201; Moo, 190). But it is wise to note that the accepted interpretation does not rule out two important points, namely, that the Christian who is walking the way of righteousness is responsible for the "wanderer" (Davids) and that there is some type of blessing for the one who rescues the brother or sister from error. Rather than allow the faithful Christian to relish the idea that those in error are to be left to themselves, the writer exhorts the one who is obedient to act wisely and reclaim this errant person (see 3:16–17). Although this should be done without thought of a specific recompense (cf. Ezek 3:21; 1 Tim 4:16) James is hinting that the one who reaches out to the deviant neighbor will receive a blessing, possibly in bringing about a strengthened community reflecting the law of love (2:8) and peace (3:18).

Thus, James abruptly concludes his "sermon in epistolary form" by reminding his readers of his "apostolic goal" (Davids, 201), namely, that all should seek to walk with God in wisdom. The final contrast is one that has pervaded the tract: wisdom versus folly. The "wise" person will already be practicing obedience and will be motivated to act so as to ensure that the "foolish" person will turn back to the right way (Prov 2:20; 4:5; 5:22–23; 7:24–25; 8:4–5). Sin, which is attacked so directly in James' letter, is both a personal and a community problem. His desire is that all his readers deal with its threat to "eschatological perfection" (1:4), both on an individual level and in the lives of others.

Explanation

Community relations that were in prominent view in the preceding section (5:15–16) are brought once more into focus. For the final time the author makes a hortatory appeal to his addressees; this he does by his favorite device, namely, by the appellation "my brothers." The fraternal regard has been seen often throughout the document, and it denotes the essentially pastoral relationship the writer sustains to the readers and hearers who are always in his sights.

At the same time the tractate is more than a letter written to a group of friends. There is a universal appeal, at least in the final redactor's intention. The inclusion of a wider constituency is clear from the wording of 1:1, which may conceivably be a sign that, in its published form, this document represents an authoritative and encyclical letter to Jewish Christians scattered throughout the regions of Syro-Palestine. This broader scope suggests an assortment of congregations to which James' appeal, in the hands of his faithful disciples, was sent. Their experience of trial and attack makes this document one of admonitory encouragement (*Mahnrede*) delivered to believers in time of testing.

These two putative factors of authority and audience—for which there is some evidence in the text—are the key to the closing verses. On the one hand, if the numbers of Jewish Christians had grown in both size and geographical distribution, it is feasible that the care of individuals had become of lesser concern, so that a single member who defaulted would hardly be noticed. On the other side, every time of persecution is an occasion when the weak members and the insecure adherents become tempted to fall away and to choose an easier life. The book of James, it seems, has both realities in its purview as the testamentary document that goes under the leader's name reaches its ending.

Nonetheless it is an abrupt way to close a part of the NT often called "epistolary." Whatever its original format, whether as a collection of "sayings of James the Just" or some specimen homilies that he gave in his capacity as titular head of the Jerusalem *Urgemeinde* or "mother church," the document does carry signs of being dressed up in a letter form. It is natural, therefore, that the editor who appended 1:1 to give the writing authority and wide appeal to the Diaspora would place a final exhortation at the end to drive home the main contentions the letter has emphasized throughout. Warnings about laxity and indifference to moral imperatives and a pastoral solicitude are the dominant notes on which the testamentary legacy of James ends. If there is no prayer for God's grace and peace and no assurance of divine mercy, these themes are implicit, and they have been sounded earlier (1:25; 2:13; 4:6, 10; 5:11). As it is, the letter evidently sought to reinforce an appeal with all moral urgency and earnestness; and a closing section like vv 19–20 matches exactly the rugged and forceful style hitherto displayed.

Index of Ancient Authors

Greek and Roman Writers

Old Testament Apocrypha and Pseudepigrapha; Other Jewish Writings

Other Christian Literature

Index of Modern Authors

Index of Principal Topics

Index of Biblical Texts

A. The Old Testament

B. The New Testament